The State of the World's Mountains

A global report

"This Global Mountain Status Report is a vital first step in gaining a higher priority for the condition of our mountains worldwide. It has my strongest support; it should be repeated periodically."

David Brower
Leading US environmentalist and founder of Friends of the Earth

"The mountains of the world are the most neglected and most threatened of all ecosystems. This book documents the dangers in commendable detail and opens the way for the next and essential step—doing something."

Prince Sadruddin Aga Khan
President
Alp Action

"Fragile mountain ecosystems provide a livelihood for the many people who live in them and environmental services for far greater numbers. Measures to protect them for present and future generations are needed urgently and I commend the efforts of Peter Stone, Ruedi Hoegger and their Mountain Agenda colleagues to draw attention to this important issue."

Maurice F. Strong
Secretary-General
United Nations Conference on Environment and Development

"The relevance of highland areas to human prosperity is beyond dispute. The State of the World's Mountains provides an important background of factual evidence on which a programme of action to control development in those regions should be based."

Lord Hunt of Llanfair Waterdine
Leader of the first expedition to climb Mount Everest

The Swiss Alps above the Grimselpass typify mountains for many Westerners

The State of the World's Mountains

A global report

Edited by

Peter B. Stone

on behalf of Mountain Agenda

Zed Books Ltd

London and New Jersey

The State of the World's Mountains was first published
by Zed Books Ltd., 57 Caledonian Road, London Nl 9BU, UK
and 165 First Avenue, Atlantic Highlands, New Jersey O7716, USA
in 1992

Design and typesetting by Magheross Graphics
Cover design by Keith Pointing

Printed and bound in the United Kingdom at The Bath Press, Avon

A catalogue record for this book is available from the British Library
US CIP is available from the Library of Congress

ISBN: 1 85649 115 3 hb
1 85649 116 1 pb

Contents

Acknowledgements

This book *The State of the World's Mountains—a global report* was produced by a group of people (collectively known as Mountain Agenda) each of whom provided one or more of a number of crucial elements. These ranged from conception and guidelines, to writing, rewriting, editing, proof reading and laying out. Their aim was to have this basic testimony finished in time to back up a much shorter, heavily illustrated document–*The Appeal*–for the Earth Summit at Rio. The aim of both publications was to appeal to governments to put mountains on the world's environment agenda, both at Rio and in the years to come. The international cooperative process by which this book was prepared took a year.

The main working group was:

Authors: Y. Badenkov (Mountains of the Former Soviet Union); W. Baetzing with P. Messerli (Alps); J. Bandyopadhyay (Himalaya); R. Barry (Climate and Mountains); L. Hamilton (Mountain Protected Areas); H. Hurni (Mountains of Africa); J. Ives (Preface, Andes, and Mountains North and South); J. Underwood, D. Schnelling (Appalachians).

Co-ordination: R. Hoegger and B. Messerli.

Editing: P. Stone.

Biographical details of the authors and their collaborators are given at the end of the book with more on Mountain Agenda and its activity.

A draft resolution for the Rio Conference was prepared and circulated and many of those contacted replied with ideas and suggestions. This resolution was, however, overtaken by UNCED's decision to proceed with Agenda 21, which is a consolidated environmental action programme for the coming years. One of Mountain Agenda's members prepared a submission to this under contract to UNCED. Many helped in these various activities and should have all received letters of thanks for their interest and encouragement. Given our limited time and resources we can do no more than list them below and use this as a way of expressing our gratitude for their support. Their reactions went a long way to defining the concern felt by those interested in our mountain environments and the people who live there.

Mountain Agenda warmly thanks the following for their interest, encouragement and, in some cases, written contributions. And it asks to be forgiven by those whose names have been overlooked or just not transmitted through the nascent network:-

P. Rider, A. Dejene, G. Matthews, W. Burhenne, F. di Castri, J. Hunt, L.N. Camacho, R. Chorley, W. Leu, N. Polunin, R. Gardner, S. Edmond, R. Schaad, E. Douglas, I. Hattingh, Z. Roberto, D. Rambaud, L. Chicken, C. Bonnington, J. Wheeler, R. A. Hume, W. Sonelski, H. Norberg-Hodge, A. Blackshaw, L. Gardner, C. Ripa di Meana, P. Nogeira-Neto, M. De Botero, E.U. Botero, C.D. Thalman, V. Sanchez, O. Chave, E. Penalosa, B. Manuel Rodriguez, N. Caldwell, C. Haslam, W. Lindner, R. West, A. Crosby, J. Tinker, S. Prakash, N. Desai, L. Hopkins, V. Rajan, Ma Shijun, M. Brusasco-Mackenzie, B. Comont, C. Eckhardt, G. Hyvernat, C. Joanny, F. Labande, J. Manesse, D. Scheppler, L. Vigouroux, P. Viguie, J. Kishlar, M. Price, Fosco Maraini, J.J. Stone, B. Reynolds, M. Smith, R.F. Morgan, D. Shreeve, D. Pitt, E. Drummond, M.F. Strong, M. Matte Baker, J. Garcia Burgues, J. McNeely, F. Bonnet, K. Collins.

The interest and encouragement shown by the publishers Zed Books is also gratefully acknowledged.

Although a proportion of the cost of our activity was borne by the individuals and institutions participating, it was always evident that the cost of meetings, communications, printing and postage would be substantial. Fortunately the government of Switzerland supported Mountain Agenda to the extent of US $200,000 and the government of Germany to US $100,000 and this is the occasion to express most grateful thanks for their generosity. Without this support the whole effort would have been impossible.

Preface

The last twenty years have witnessed growing concern about the future of the world's mountains. It is worth examining this statement because, to many millions of people, mountain regions may well have the appearance of being remote, durable, and barely affected by the environmental ills that beset the more densely populated areas of our global living space, that is, those areas that are more easily accessible to modern machinery and transportation systems simply because they are not mountains.

One widely held view is that these vast, rugged, and more distant landscapes that, at least to the popular eye, support very sparse populations can hardly rank very high on any environmental endangered list. Another view is in complete contrast. Thus we are told that the over-development of tourist and winter ski infrastructure in the Alps, for example, is destroying that most beautiful and acculturated of all mountain ranges; that the very success of superbly engineered mountain highways is drawing in so many automobiles that the ensuing air pollution is killing off the mountain forests, which is leading to acceleration of avalanche, rockfall and landslide activity, and flooding in the valleys and adjacent lowlands. From this example of western affluence and over-development, we can go to the other extreme, of rapid population growth, poverty and underdevelopment. The Himalayas will suffice for this. Now the popular picture is one of rapid population increase amongst subsistence farming communities dependent upon the forest for their fuelwood. In this context we are presented with the dire prediction, for instance, that Nepal will lose all its accessible forest cover by the end of the century. This loss of forest from steep slopes, assaulted by heavy monsoonal rains, is supposedly being accompanied by accelerated soil erosion, gullying and landsliding, which devastate the plains to the south through siltation and catastrophic flooding and reduced river levels during the dry season.

Which viewpoint should we accept: the complacent view that mountains, as recalled from our childhood folklore, are wild and remote, and therefore, little touched by the mainstreams of rampant "progress", or the melodrama of doom and destruction, indeed, of supercrisis spreading from the mountains to the plains? To answer this quite critical question requires a heightened perception of what mountains are and of how humans have utilized their resources over long periods of time, together with an assessment of future trends. This is no easy task, simply because of the enormous complexity of mountain landscapes, their climates, vegetation, wildlife and history of human occupation. And while many readers may conclude that a lot is known about mountains, relatively speaking they are little known. Their complexity is frequently ignored and this has led to many sweeping generalizations. These in turn have become the basis for the formulation of development policy. Thus a man-made layer of uncertainty has been superimposed on the already bewildering variety of mountain problems. This very uncertainty, together with the seeming determination to impose a grand solution—development—based upon unproven assumptions—the latter-day myths, or sacred cows, of both decision maker and conservationist—has become a large part of the problem.

Mountains have received little persistent, unified attention. Even following the 1972 Stockholm Conference on the Human Environment, many false starts and inadequately funded endeavours have done more to confuse than to set forth in unambiguous prose the actual environmental status of the world's mountains. Foreign aid and development projects have tended to concentrate on the commercial, or cash crop potential of the lowlands, relegating the mountains to unimportant flatland adjuncts. There has been no established consistency for assessment of the environmental status of the world's mountains, despite the fact that mountains and uplands comprise about a fifth of the world's terrestrial surface. Furthermore, they provide the direct life-support base for about a tenth of humankind and indirectly affect the lives of more than half.

The mountain world is vast by any standard: we are dealing with maximum global diversity—from sea level to almost 9 000 metres, from tropical rainforest to permanent ice and snow, and from climates with over 12 metres of annual precipitation to extreme high-altitude deserts. And this is only the physical aspect of mountain diversity. Culturally, we must consider a range from the sophistication of a revolving restaurant with helicopter pad and gondola on an alpine peak, or a network of tunnels, generators, dams and reservoirs on the Grimsel Pass with hydroelectric production controlled by computer many kilometres away, to a recent episode of emergence from the Stone Age in New Guinea, or opium poppy production below the Kyber Pass.

This enormous array of cultural and physical diversity is further complicated by the fact that mountains often form the frontiers between independent, even unfriendly states, they occur on all continents and extend from the equator as far poleward as land persists. They are also marginal in terms of the low political effectiveness of their frequently ethnic minority inhabitants and their economic relationship to world market trends. This fragmentation, and their usual treatment as two-dimensional adjuncts to the more densely populated lowlands that ignores their essential three-dimensional form—whereby altitudinal variation is overwhelmingly more important than horizontal variation—accounts for their neglect on the world's environmental and developmental scene.

The announcement of the planning for the United Nations Conference on Environment and Development (UNCED 1992) provided a first major opportunity to bring the mountain problematique to the highest level of attention. With this in mind, a small group of individuals assembled in the Bernese hamlets of Appenberg and Aeschi in December 1990 and April 1991 respectively. We already had official linkages with the United Nations University, the International Centre for Integrated Mountain Development, the East-West Centre and the International Mountain Society. These meetings produced the *Appenberg Initiative* and set in motion *Mountain Agenda-UNCED 1992*. The "founding members", while few in number, had worked together for almost twenty years and, through their institutional and professional links, were already representative of a much larger group of committed mountain specialists. Thus the essential objective of rendering *Mountain Agenda-UNCED 1992* fully international was easily achieved.

The broad goals of the initiative were readily agreed upon:

(1) to make an authoritative statement on the environmental status and developmental potential of the world's mountains;

(2) widely to disseminate this statement in several forms;

(3) to publicize the urgent need for priority ranking of the mountain problematique for twenty-first century action; and

(4) to provide some guidelines for a practical response to the problems and challenges of the mountains for consideration by world leaders at UNCED in Rio de Janeiro in June 1992.

The report produced herein is one of the major products of *Mountain Agenda-UNCED 1992*. It has been prepared with the full realization that the very fragmentation, vast scale and complexity of the mountain milieu would prohibit an exhaustive, closely analysed treatment in the short time available. Indeed, as the collection of information and writing of numerous sections proceeded—and this was attempted through the recently established World Mountain Network—the inadequacy of our work as a first articulation of the status of the world's mountains became increasingly apparent. The extensive effort to make this fully international (the list of collaborators demonstrates that we have drawn from all five continents, excluding Antarctica) itself cost valuable time. All we have managed to do is to take a first step. Readers will quickly perceive many shortcomings and omissions, even errors, from an academic or rigorous scientific point of view. This in itself lends weight to our recommendation, as one response to the UNCED challenge, that a much fuller and more exacting second edition be produced in four years' time—and that this be followed by subsequent four-year updates. To this end we would welcome criticisms, suggestions for change in format, additions and corrections. Our objective here is progressively to enlarge the World Mountain Network so that the mountain problematique becomes more completely understood. It is also hoped that this will lead to the effective elaboration of possible solutions that will influence mountain environmental and development policy formulation and its application.

Some of us were tempted to draw back from publication and to content ourselves with using the extra four months so gained to produce a more complete and more accurate report for limited circulation at Rio. This course would have failed to recognize that, for this first edition of a world mountain status report, the political goals outweigh the scientific—the latter need attention *after* Rio, and UNCED should provide the path to the resources essential for that much larger task. In the process, the inner coherence of the specific sections, together with their comprehensive nature and chapter by chapter comparability will all be improved. The unevenness and incompleteness of this first edition is justification enough for this post-Rio task. At the very least, the report should emphasize not only the pressing importance of the world's mountains but raise the question that they have been omitted from the world's environment and development councils for so long.

Can we now attempt to answer the questions posed at the beginning of this Preface? Is complacency, because of the supposed indestructibility of the mountains of the world, warranted, or do we give up in despair because mountain topsoil will all be washed into the oceans shortly after the turn of the century and mountain desertification will prevail? Obviously, there is no one problem and therefore no one answer. Neither complacency nor despair is in order. The answer lies somewhere between the two extremes of childhood folklore and conservationist alarm. Our overarching concern must lie with the uncertainty. While we can make many informed guesses, we simply cannot make stringent predictions. Even the informed guesses, based upon a great deal of accumulated mountain research and acquired experience and wisdom, do not reach the decision makers with sufficient force or regularity. Dams continue to be built in ridiculously unsafe places and reservoirs are rapidly silted, generators destroyed, or the entire infrastructure swept away; mountain roads are engineered without adequate knowledge of slope stability, let alone consideration of indirect effects; and the numerous indirect costs, especially cultural and environmental ones, are ignored. Yet bilateral and international millions continue to be put into major projects that do not have the benefit of critical and holistic evaluation. One aspect of sustainable development should be to ensure compromises such that large-scale infrastructures on mountains are placed in the safest possible localities, least impair the local environment and achieve maximum benefits for the investors and the mountain people alike.

Despair is not called for; mountain environments and mountain peoples are far more resilient than is often credited. The word *fragile* can be overused and counter-productive. Mountain forests do grow back on their own and mountain farmers, without government or international aid, do plant trees and tend them. Perhaps one of the most important needs is to recognize that mountain people have much they can do for themselves and much to offer world society at large. After all, the mountain peoples of the world have already provided us with the potato, coffee, maize, teff and many domesticated animals; and there are numerous indigenous food crops that are untapped—quinoa, amaranth, literally hundreds of species and varieties of tubers and chenopods, to mention only a few. And there is the great range of developed and undeveloped medicinal plants, including opium and coca, whether used for good or ill.

Mountain people are also of two genders, and if the role of the subsistence woman farmer, or pastoralist, or person in general, is not recognized and understood, any development effort will likely be confounded. This involves recognizing the humanity of the mountain farmer and the need to support and strengthen existing local institutions. It is reasonable to conclude that the future for some mountain areas is bleak, for others it is rather more secure. We need greatly to improve our ability to predict, distinguish and differentiate. Regardless, the mountains have had major impacts on the human mind since our ancestors first looked up to them and gloried in their splendour; placed their gods and goddesses amongst them; accepted their challenges. They continue to inspire a large sector of society, and this inspiration is greatly needed today. Perhaps the so-called "New World Order" will become a reality as the Cold War and superpower competition fades from memory. Then perhaps the mountain problems, alongside other pressing problems of the next century, can be wisely and effectively addressed. This will never come about, however, until the *mountain issue* is clearly identified and until mountain people, scholars, practitioners and decision makers are working together on a fully international scale. The Earth Summit (UNCED) in Rio de Janeiro should prove the best occasion to attract the attention of world leaders and provide our mountains with their proper place on the twenty-first century agenda.

One major task is simply to increase awareness of the mountain issue. It is hoped that this report will at least assist in this context and will serve to reinforce its readers' appreciation of our wondrous mountain heritage, a heritage that includes both spectacular habitat and some of the richest remnants of indigenous cultures and traditions. The wisdom of the *puranas,* the ancient legends of India, tell us:

As the dew is dried up by the morning sun,
So are the sins of humankind by the sight of the Himalayas

We can just as well select Navajo Mountain, or Denali, Fujiyama or Kilimanjaro, Illimani or Mauna Loa. These sources of awe and inspiration, vital for the mental health of humankind, will be increasingly endangered unless the twenty-first century can set a *Mountain Agenda* to strive for a better balance between mountain environment, development of resources and the well-being of mountain peoples.

Foreword

by the

President of the Swiss Confederation

This global report on the state of world's mountains responds to a long-felt need and provides one of several tools required for a better understanding of the world's key ecological issues and natural resource problems.

Mountains and upland areas cover some 20 per cent of the surface of the earth. Approximately 10 per cent of the global population live there, but perhaps half of humanity depends in some way on mountain resources, such as water, energy, minerals, forests or recreation areas.

In Switzerland, the importance of mountains is even greater. About two thirds of our country is mountainous and both the history and the culture of our various population groups have to a great extent been shaped by this particular topography, its difficulties but also its advantages. Steep slopes, fragile soil and vegetation cover, as well as peripheral social and economic conditions make upland areas especially vulnerable to environmental degradation. In Switzerland, we have learnt and continue to learn this important lesson which is probably true for all mountain systems. But the reverse must also be considered: poverty, lack of economic opportunities and inappropriate patterns of development are often major causes of degradation of the mountain environment.

Historically, the Swiss people have experienced both the negative and the positive aspects of life in the mountains. On the one hand, there are the fragile mountain ecosystems with many natural hazards and man-made disasters and the potentially negative rapid economic changes. On the other hand, there are the mountain people who may creatively adapt economic changes towards sustainable development in the mountain regions.

Based on this experience, Switzerland has, during recent decades, cooperated with a number of Asian, African and Latin American countries in their efforts to promote sustainable development in the mountain areas. In the course of this cooperation, we have learned to look upon the mountains and their specific problems with growing hope despite all the difficulties. We know that environmentally sound development is possible in the highlands as well as in the plains. Fortunately, the complex interlinkages between environment and development are not necessarily contradictory and can be complementary. For instance, a well-developed mountain agricultural system is probably the prerequisite for the preservation of the mountain environment and of the rich cultural heritage of the mountain people. This will strengthen their cultural identity as well as their economic development capacity.

The main purpose of this first global report on the state of the world's mountains is to attract attention to the serious problems that threaten the mountainous areas of the globe and to encourage scientists, development workers and decision-makers to strive for sustainable development practices in the highlands. Such changes are possible and the goal of more sustainable mountain development can be achieved–provided we take up the challenge before us.

May this report contribute to a growing awareness of the dangers as well as the opportunities facing the mountains and may such awareness bear fruit at the UNCED and beyond.

René Felber
President of the Swiss Confederation

Foreword

by the

Rector of the United Nations University

This Global Report on the State of the World's Mountains has been prepared for the United Nations Conference on Environment and Development (UNCED) and it is aimed at creating a wider awareness not only of the significance of the mountain areas to the global environment but also of the threats posed to the mountains and highlands by human activities. It is hoped that this work will help to bring about international approval of a plan for immediate action to promote sustainable development in the mountain regions of the world.

The present report is the result of an enormous collaborative effort by many scholars who have been working for many years on mountain issues. They were brought together within the institutional frameworks of the United Nations University (UNU), the International Centre for Integrated Mountain Development (ICIMOD) and the International Mountain Society (IMS). One of the most important bases on which this collaboration was founded is the UNU-IMS research and training programme on Mountain Ecology and Sustainable Development. This programme, which was originally commenced in 1978, involves research and dissemination of findings within the relatively neglected field of ecologically sustainable development in the mountainous regions of the world, stressing an interdisciplinary, systematic approach with the goal of reconciling the frequently conflicting objectives of conservation and development.

Research has been conducted in a wide variety of geographic regions with particular emphasis on the highland areas in the developing parts of the world, including the Himalayas, the Hengduan Mountains of China and the highlands of northwest Thailand in Asia, Mount Kenya, the Ethiopian highlands and the Atlas Mountains in Africa and the Andes in South America. A new research programme will concentrate on the Asian high mountain range stretching from the Pamirs in the west to the Yunnan mountains of southern China in the east. The objective of the research is to develop a database for the natural and human resources and to devise alternative scenarios for sustainable regional development in the regions studied.

A series of regional mountain workshops has already been organized, including the conference on "Transformation of Mountain Environments: Regional Development and Sustainability; Consequences of Global Change" held in Armenia, USSR, in 1989, the conference on "African Mountains and Highlands: Dynamics of Resource Use Systems and its Consequences for Sustainable Development" in Morocco, in 1990, and the conference on the theme "Mountain Geoecology of the Southern Andes: Resource Management and Sustainable Development" in Chile, in 1991. More regional workshops are planned in the future focusing on different regions.

Training and institution-building are emphasized in the mountain ecology programme. The programme has been instrumental in establishing and supporting regional mountain associations, such as the African Mountain Association and the Latin American Mountain Association. Similarly, through publications and networking with scientific bodies around the world, UNU, together with IMS, has helped to advance current thinking about sustainable development in mountain areas. On a regional level, ICIMOD has been concentrating its efforts–since 1984–on information exchange and research concerning integrated mountain development in the Hindu Kush-Himalayas (Afghanistan, Bangladesh, Bhutan, China, India, Myanmar, Nepal and Pakistan).

Consequently, I dare claim that this present global report is the result of an accumulated experience and history of solid research into the problems and development prospects of the mountainous areas of the world involving many of the best scientists in the field. I would like to express my gratitude to all of them. I would also like to acknowledge the support UNU, ICIMOD and IMS have received from the Swiss Development Cooperation for their manifold efforts. I hope that the report will provide a significant input to UNCED and to the conservation and sustainable development of the often ecologically as well as socio-economically vulnerable mountain regions.

Professor Heitor Gurgulino de Souza
Rector
The United Nations University

1

Overview and Appeal:

sustainable development in mountain areas

Nepal Middle Mountains— terracing helps maintain slope stability in many mountain areas

An urgent and practical possibility

The first steps in approaching sustainable development in the mountains involve making a comprehensive audit of what is going wrong and where, which is why this Global Report looks at specific mountain areas and describes present and future environmental and developmental problems on the ground, and in detail.

Most people interested in mountains are already aware that often the same problems turn up irrespective of where the mountains are on the globe. Therefore common themes recur although not every theme will be found exemplified in every range. A theme such as forestry will not occur in Baffin Land, but several other subjects that feature in the Himalaya or the Alps will turn up there, such as, for instance, pollution, tourism and climate change.

This overview chapter will therefore set out the major themes so as to help the reader navigate through the great diversity that characterizes mountain areas from the equator to the poles.

It will make no attempt to summarize the detailed environmental auditors' accounts which follow because it is those details which testify to the gravity of the problems facing us. It will, however, set out the gist of what the authors of the report collectively consider the world should do about the whole problematique. It will also explain why action is a matter of urgency.

In the following pages, very condensed answers are given to three key questions:

1) What is the role of the mountains in the global environment and development?

2) What are the present threats to the highlands of the world?

3) What needs to be done for the world's mountains and their inhabitants?

The world is vast and using numbers to convey an general impression of the particular global problem area which this global report addresses will only contribute to a feeling that it is all too big for us to cope with. A way to reduce the scale is to regard the world as a village following the now familiar metaphor of the "global village". This has the merit of not only reducing the apparent size of the task but, also, of suggesting to us that most of the remedies will have to be applied by villagers themselves.

❑ Suppose the metaphorical village comprises 1 000 units of land, say hectares. This land consists of arable and non-arable, forest, pasture, wasteland and homestead. Of this, one fifth, or 200 hectares, lies at over 1 000 metres above sea level and is mostly rugged and steep.

❑ Only about one in ten of the people live in the mountainous wards of the village, but five times as many, i.e. half of the village population, depend in some way on this upper land. They call it their weather corner, for it is there that most of the clouds seem to gather and where much of the rain and snow seems to fall. From there, the major village streams flow down and there is a small hydroelectric plant. Most of the community's timber and fuelwood is brought down from the upper wards. On festival days, many families go there to visit religious sites.

❑ In many ways, the customs and the experiences of those 100 villagers living uphill are different from what the other 900 inhabitants are used to. The highlanders even differ from each other in many respects, depending on the altitude of their homesteads and whether they face South or North. Their agricultural and festival calendars, too, are not identical with those in the lower parts of the village. But the inhabitants of the upper wards do admirably well in constantly adapting their agriculture, horticulture, forestry and animal husbandry to the specific conditions of their environment. They also have great experience in managing pastures and forests for the good of the community as a whole.

❑ To complete the picture, it has to be mentioned that the variety of wild animals and plants found on the village uplands is much bigger today than in the lower areas. This used to be different a century ago, i.e. before the lowlands were "human altered" so thoroughly. Nowadays whenever an illness spreads in the village, people will ask the uplanders for various medicines they produce from their plants. During the summer season, the cattle of the lower village move up to the upland grazing areas, where better fodder is available and where the climate is healthier than below.

The upper wards of our metaphorical village are indeed pillars of the economy and culture of the community. And what can be shown at the village level is equally true at a global scale.

It may not be self-evident but mountains are the backbone of civilizations.

The simple truth can be summarized in four specific points.

1 *Mountains are water towers for human consumption, for the expansion of land use and for rising energy needs.*
According to statistics compiled by United Nations institutions, South and East Asia will soon contain more than half of the world's population. The economy of this area depends upon the major rivers flowing south and east from the Himalaya-Karakoram-Pamir-Tibet high mountain region. Snow accumulation in this area is extremely important in feeding the streams and rivers. Forests play a key role in that they delay the melting of snow and prolong the period when water is available. Forests also maintain the infiltration capacity at the highest possible level. Thus climate change and change in vegetation cover might tremendously affect the water tower role of the mountains.

Similar problems can be observed in the Andes. The hydrological regime of the upper Amazon, for instance, will be influenced by progressive deforestation on the mountain slopes. The potential danger of higher flood levels among the entire length of the Amazon is considerable. But also the tropical mountains of Africa (e.g. Mt. Kenya) are most important for a large surrounding area. Rivers flowing from the mountains are the life-lines of whole civilizations.

2 *Mountains are weather makers for large parts of the world.*
Mountains influence and determine the climatology and the circulation pattern from the local to the continental scale. Think of, for example, the influence of the Rocky mountains on the climate of North America, the Andes on South America. Northern India would be an arid land without the Himalaya. Do we understand the influence of the Alps on the atmospheric circulation of Middle Europe? How far north would the border of the Sahara be without the North African Mountains?

On the other hand, it must be assumed that changes in the snow and vegetation cover will also affect local economic and ecological conditions which might result in disturbances of much broader ecosystems. Such disturbances might in turn have consequences for the surrounding more densely populated lowlands.

3 *Biological diversity in the mountains is one of mankind's most valuable natural resources.*
While the absolute number of species in mountain environments may be smaller than in the lowlands, the montane tropical rainforest, cloud forest and the mountain wild land in general are refuges for a great wealth of endemic and endangered species and communities. The small area of Mount Kinabalu in Sabah, Malaysia, for instance, is estimated to have some 4 000 to 4 500 species, more than one quarter of all plant species in the USA. Much scientific and popular concern is focussed on 14 "hotspot" areas in the tropics. Seven of these are either mountains or have at least half of their area in the mountains. Among them are the uplands of Madagascar, the lower Andean slopes of western Amazonia, the eastern Himalayas, the uplands of the Philippines, the Eastern Arc montane forests of Tanzania, India's Western Ghats and the montane forests of Sri Lanka.

From the storehouse of mountains we have taken some of our most important current food staples. Potatoes came to us from the Andes, coffee originally from the Ethiopian highlands. The Sierra Manantlan in Mexico contains the only known stand of the most primitive wild relative of corn or maize. High up in the Caucasus, there is a reserve for the wild relatives of wheat and of fruit trees. We have a tremendous responsibility for the preservation of these mountain treasures, because they will be key elements in the development of future agricultural production patterns, chemical research and medical progress.

4 *Mountains are privileged places for spiritual and physical recreation.*
As great symbols in almost all cultures and religions of the world, mountains have inspired and attracted countless numbers of pilgrims throughout history. They are a core element in the spiritual landscape of hundreds of millions of people. Mountain myths and legends constitute an invaluable part of the human oral and literary heritage.

Something of this significance can even be discerned in modern tourism, which is a quest for both spiritual and physical recreation at the same time. But, in addition, tourism has become a major source of income for many mountain inhabitants. By some measures, tourism is now the world's largest industry and obviously mountains play an important role in it.

In the uplands of industrialized nations, tourism became important even during the early decades of our century. It then boomed after the Second World War, a result of the combination of many factors, including increases in the population of urban centres, rising incomes, more vacation time and more mobility. New perceptions of mountain environments played their role as well as the vast improvements in transportation systems. Low-cost international air transport was a decisive factor in the expansion of tourism in the mountains of many developing nations. Today, tourism constitutes an indispensable pillar of the economies of many mountainous countries in all parts of the world. Its continuance will depend to a considerable extent on the maintenance of an attractive environment and well-balanced economic development in these mountain regions.

The present threats to the mountains are complex combinations of natural and human forces

Returning to our metaphor of the village with its upper and lower wards, the picture should now be completed in the following way:

❑ On average, the families living up the hill are poorer than those on the level lands down below. Their production conditions and their access to central services are more limited. Often –especially during bad weather–their children do not show up at the school which is near the centre. The people from the upper wards pay higher prices for goods transported from the road or railway below. At the same time, they find it more difficult to market their own produce. They do not have very frequent contacts with their fellow villagers, and they are not well informed about what is going on among the majority of the village's inhabitants.

❑ Notwithstanding their many achievements and cultural diversity, the upland people are usually not represented in the village council. Major decisions affecting the overall economy and other aspects of village life are taken without their participation. And some lowlanders patronize them and look down their noses at them as hillbillies.

❑ One reason for this is that many inhabitants of the lower wards are not well informed about the role and life situation of the families higher up. They take it for granted that fields and forests and footpaths in the mountains are maintained. In the eyes of the majority, the upper village and its surroundings are to serve as a quarry, to provide timber, to generate electricity and to be used as recreation ground. No thought is given to the potential consequences of this limited view.

❑ It is only when floods or avalanches and landslides threaten the homesteads below, or when families from the upper wards move down in search of better economic opportunities, that the majority in the village centre starts to think and ask questions. All too often, however, the current answers are extremely simple. They normally put the blame for any problems in the mountains on the people who live there. Have not the uplanders mis-managed their own environment and created all the problems the rest of community now has to suffer?

Again, the parallel between the metaphorical village and a good deal of our global community is obvious.

We have difficulties in fully understanding the complex nature of the various problems affecting the world's mountains today.

Some of these problems may be summarized as follows:

1 *The growing contradiction between marginalization and integration*

By virtue of their three-dimensional morphology, mountains have always been barriers to easy human movement, be it between the mountains and the plains, or between two flat plains separated by mountains. The growth of mechanical transportation technologies and shipping led to the concentration of human economic activities away from the mountains, in the flat plains on the banks of major rivers of the world. In this way, the modern industrial centres grew in the plains, while in contrast, the mountains changed rather slowly and remained largely excluded from the dominant global economic processes. This exclusion of the mountains can be described as marginality, caused by their inaccessibility to the transportation systems developed in the plains.

This situation in the mountains has undergone rapid changes in the more recent past, especially since the widespread extension of mechanically powered transportation systems and the use of modern road and bridge-building technologies. The uses of the new transportation facilities were, however, predominantly determined by the interests of the plains. In this way, while the original, spatial marginality of the mountains became less marked, new kinds of marginality emerged.

As a result of easier access and transportation, the political authority of the central state over the remote mountain areas (which had so far enjoyed relative autonomy) was consolidated. At the same time, mountains were integrated into the economy of the plains. The driving economic forces now had better knowledge about and better access to the rich natural resources of the highlands, such as hydro-power, minerals or timber.

The roads were forerunners of the extraction of minerals in the Andes, to forest exploitation in the Himalaya, or to water power development in the Alps or commercial farming in the African mountains. When the plains needed cheap human resources from the mountains, the new transportation systems quickly made them available. In some cases central state authorities from the plains even forced cheap labour from the mountains to work in the mills. The relationship between the two was characterized by unequal terms of trade and by the enhanced dependence of the mountains on the market in the plains. This new socio-economic marginalization of the mountains areas is the result of their unequal economic integration into the larger economy of the plains.

Thus, there is a growing contradiction between marginalization and integration of mountain areas, one process fatally reinforcing the other. Sustainability of any form cannot be achieved under such circumstances. What is needed is a much deeper understanding of both the mountains' potentials and weaknesses. New concepts of sustainable development must be evolved–with the interest of the mountain communities and their environment as the prime perspective.

2 *Threats and hopes from agriculture and forestry*

The popularly conceived picture of a mountain scalped of its forest is in many places a valid one. But the situation of mountain forests world wide is a complex one, and simple categorization and simple solutions are not warranted.

In many, though not all, parts of the world, the lowlands have been the locale for the earliest intensive settlement, forest utilization and agricultural development. As populations increased, the frontier of logging, grazing and land-clearing moved to the uplands and steeper slopes, and finally into the mountain forests at increasingly high altitudes. As economies have matured and population increase rates have slowed (mainly in temperate zone countries), this massive tide of upland forest conversion has slowed, halted and even reversed in a few instances (e.g. Switzerland). But for the most part, in the tropical developing countries, this frontier of forest destruction is still inexorably moving up the mountains.

It is driven by rapid population increase, uncertain land tenure, inequity in distribution of resources (land reform is needed) and lack of strong and stable institutions on the frontier.

Logging in mountain forests has a greater potential for damage both on-site and off-site than in gentler topography. On steep slopes, where there are many unstable soils, the roads and skidding tracks needed to remove the wood often initiate large mass soil movements. The productivity of the site is thereby reduced and the soil eventually moves downslope into steams and rivers.

Reasonably safe logging techniques for mountains have been developed, but are not applied, so that much mountain logging and road construction in developing countries is still having disastrous impacts.

Logging, fuelwood and leaf fodder collection, slash-and-burn subsistence agriculture, land-clearing for commercial agriculture, clearing or drowning land for reservoirs, bulldozing for new mountain roads, felling for transmission lines or pipelines, harvesting forest game, livestock grazing and burning for many of the foregoing, are negatively impacting the remaining mountain forests in almost all of the countries of the world.

However, the urgent need for better environmental care in the mountains does not necessarily contradict economic and social development. Fortunately, the complex interlinkages between development and environment work not only in the negative sense–as described–but can operate very positively too. The outstanding example for this is mountain agriculture. Detailed measurements in many mountain areas have shown that water run-off from slopes and flooding in the valley bottoms largely depends on the management of land resources. It is, of course, true that dense forests reduce runoff as compared to open pasture or brushland. But–and this is the crucial point–well-kept terraces will serve the mountain hydrology at least as well as forests, sometimes even better! This means that a well-developed mountain agriculture system is the best prerequisite for a sound mountain environment. Some of the present dangers can be converted into realistic hopes.

3 *New economic opportunities with harmful side effects*

Some of the more obvious and important ones are; mining with its pollution and erosion effects, transport systems with the same, and large-scale construction activities.

Tourism was presented above as a growing need for millions of people, but also as an indispensable economic opportunity for many mountain areas in all parts of the world. But tourism is also–and at the same time–an enormous threat to mountain communities and the mountain environment.

Whatever the reasons behind tourism's arrival, its social and environmental effects are often substantial, especially because the change from an economy depending mainly on subsistence activities to one dominated by tourism frequently occurs within a few years. Associated with this economic change, populations increase as

Obergurgl, Austrian Tyrol, centre for Austria's MAB–6 research on "the Obergurgl Model". The modern ski resort has swamped the traditional village, demonstrating the potential hazards of mountain development

emigration decreases and immigration begins. Paid employment, often for activities that traditionally were either not recompensed in cash or not practised at all, is one attraction for immigrants.

Yet of course many immigrants do not share indigenous traditions and values. The needs and expectations of tourists generally differ even more from those of indigenous people. Significant cultural differences, especially those relating to accommodation, sanitation and the preparation of food, can hinder tourism. The lessening of such differences can be a major cause of cultural and environmental change, which may or may not benefit local people.

The rapid transition to a cash economy, fuelled by the comparatively massive amounts of money that many tourists spend, affects patterns of work, food production and preparation and clothing. Yet much of the money associated with the development of tourism in mountain regions does not stay at these destinations. Local people not only have to pay off the loans incurred in developing the facilities required for tourism, they also spend increasing amounts on costly imported food and goods, and even on souvenirs to sell to tourists. Equally, many facilities are built by foreign entrepreneurs who invest their profits elsewhere; and much of the total amount of money spent by tourists is used to buy airline tickets and the services of tour companies based in the home countries.

The negative effects of all processes mentioned above are heavily aggravated by the fact that air pollution produced far away in the plains has become a major threat to the mountain environment. As a result, forest dieback is being observed today in many mountain areas of the world, especially in the industrialized countries. Various airborne chemicals, including sulphur and nitrogen oxides and ozone, deriving from industrial processes and from vehicles, are implicated in this process. The consequences are frightening, affecting the stability of watersheds, water quality and the future of timber industry.

4 *The impact of climate change*

Global warming will have a pronounced effect on mountain ecosystems due to the altitudinal zonation which occurs in relatively short horizontal distances. Changes in the water balance (glaciers, snow cover, rainfall, etc.) and in the vegetation cover will influence not only the life-supporting systems for many animals and the inhabitants, but also the densely populated plains. Here, energy and water suppliers, irrigation systems and shipping opportunities will all be affected.

Mountain ecosystems will have to be considered in future as most sensitive indicators of the slightest changes, as can be seen from changes in the past. Thus, mountain ecosystems and ecotone will not only be primary sufferers of climate change, but also–for this very reason–privileged observation spots for monitoring global and regional changes. It is one of the weakest parts of the global ecology, namely the mountains, that will react in the most sensitive way to what is threatening humanity as a whole.

Thus our brief glance at the mountains reveals them to be a microcosm of the dangers threatening the world as a whole. In the mountains disaster will come more quickly and with fewer buffering mechanisms than elsewhere. Man's dependence on nature and its changing aspects are more direct and acute in the highlands than in the lowlands.

Towards sustainable mountain development: three urgent but possible steps

Again, the comparison of the world's mountain problematique to the highland-lowland interactions within our imaginary village may shed some light on the urgency, but also on the potentials of the present situation.

❑ The first initiative to change the situation which threatens the aforementioned village is to be undertaken by the people of the upper wards. Realizing the dangers of growing deforestation and declining crop yields, they start trying out new community-based management systems for their pastures and forests. Some raise their voices against reckless tree-felling and careless methods of road construction. Still others join hands in forming a cooperative for the marketing of their agricultural produce. They specifically take advantage of their different agricultural calendar while serving the whole village market. Slowly, awareness of their strength and comparative advantages grows. Later, through many discussions and against much resistance, the village council realizes that the best way to prevent further ecological and economic hazards is to support the people of the upper wards. Their role as the stewards of the village hinterland and resource base is slowly being recognized. Investment in the uplands will also serve the community as a whole. The significance of that upland minority is far bigger than the abstract figure of 10 per cent would suggest.

❑ The breakthrough to new relationships between the higher and the lower wards becomes apparent when village council meetings are occasionally held in one of the upper wards. There, lively debates develop between the representatives of the different wards with their different background and training. Merging all this know-how brings about new ideas for the promotion of the sustainable development of the village area. Contacts are taken up with neighbouring villages which face many of the challenges described. Of course, competition, short-sightedness and selfish interests will not disappear from the scene, but the road is more open for progress in the social, the economic and the ecological fields.

We, the authors of *The state of the world's mountains—a global report*, are obviously aware of the fact that in our real world things will not develop as smoothly as in our metaphor. But at the same time, we are convinced that sustainable mountain development can be brought about. The steps leading to it are not fundamentally different from what the metaphor describes, although more complicated and probably much longer. Three steps seem to be paramount during the next few years:

1 *Be aware of, study and support the many courageous efforts of the mountain inhabitants themselves to reverse the present trends*

There is a growing number of convincing, well-documented examples for almost any mountain area, which prove that the local communities are capable of taking up the present challenges and of responding to them with new patterns of management and behaviour. Many such examples can be found in the hills of Nepal, where changes in tree cover were examined on various classes of land. Comparisons were made using aerial photographs taken in 1972 and in 1989. The results indicated that the percentage of tree crown cover on the major agricultural landuse category (upland terraces) and the common land showed a significant increase. Thus, there are strong indications that the overall landscape is undergoing a steady afforestation process at the hands of the farmers. This process is completely different from fears and actual trends noticed three decades ago. It is the mountain people who have wrought this fundamental change.

To study, understand and support these complex forces at work is the primary and most important step towards a better future for the mountains.

2 *Create more awareness on a worldwide scale concerning the formidable dangers looming over the mountains and build up a relevant, effective mountain constituency on all continents.*

It is remarkable that the world's great biomes, perceived to be under threat from modern technology, rapid population growth and natural or man-induced climate changes, have almost all attracted the formation of powerful constituencies dedicated to their protection. Some examples are the oceans, the arid lands, the tropical rainforests, the Antarctic. The reasons for lack of mountain advocacy are probably numerous, complex and not fully explicable. One influence, perhaps, is the total geographical and political fragmentation of mountains; they occur on every continent and from the equator polewards as far as land persists. They are frequently intersected by national frontiers, and their inhabitants are often poor peasants and minority ethnic groups, themselves severed by numerous languages and religions, but also by subordination to a distant central power, both political and economic in character. These are, together with the sensitive environment, the limited production and the difficult accessibility the reasons for their marginality.

But the global ecology does not recognize any economic, political, administrative or cultural marginality. The retaliation of nature will be global in character although, of course, the mountain people will be hit hardest. If international and national organizations, institutions and governments continue to neglect the mountain areas, or treat them as mere two-dimensional adjuncts to other world biomes, no balanced approach to the world environment and global development will emerge. We need the mountains. And the mountains need us!

A deeper awareness on the part of the global community of the threats to the mountains should permit the beginning of a regular global audit of the conditions of the mountain environment to provide a sound basis for action. Regular reviews of the situation among all governments and institutions concerned should follow. This would also permit better cooperation between the various countries directed towards more sustainable developments in the mountains.

This book may be considered as a modest starting point in such a long-term process.

3 *Build up an effective cooperative network of national, regional and international institutions dealing with the issues of sustainable mountain development.*

Such a network should be based on the principle of an open, permanent dialogue between the concerned countries, especially between South and North, but also between researchers and decision makers, between mountain people and administrators. It is by bringing together the different types of experience and know-how that new approaches to sustainable mountain development must be evolved.

Practically, this will necessitate:

❑ Strengthening those national and regional institutions which concentrate their efforts on mountain environment and sustainable mountain development. The eight countries of the Himalayan region have already joined forces in creating ICIMOD, the International Centre for Integrated Mountain Development. Similar efforts should be encouraged and supported in other parts of the world, especially in Africa, Latin America, the Western Pacific Rim and the mountains of the former Soviet Union.

❑ Creating suitable mechanisms for stimulating cooperation and information exchange between national and regional institutions, with a view to promoting mutual learning processes and effective action towards sustainable mountain development.

❑ Encouraging scientific institutions and governments of industrialized countries to extend their cooperation to the institutions promoting sustainable development in the mountains of the world. Without their support and funding, progress towards such development will not be sufficient.

The purpose of this report is to demonstrate the urgency of these three steps, but also to testify to the realistic perspective that has presided over their formulation. As authors, we are convinced that, by taking these steps, the global community will not only greatly contribute to a more sustainable development in the world's mountains, but at the same time avoid enormous amounts of unfruitful, unenlightened investment in erroneous mountain development concepts. At the present moment, learning from each other, dialoguing across traditional frontiers and cooperating from continent to continent is more important for the future of mountains and mountain people than intensifying conventional planning and investment.

This is the core idea of *Mountain Agenda–UNCED 1992*. Let us take it up, step by step.

2

African Mountain and Highland Environments:

suitability and susceptibility

Figure 2.1: The mountains and highlands of Africa

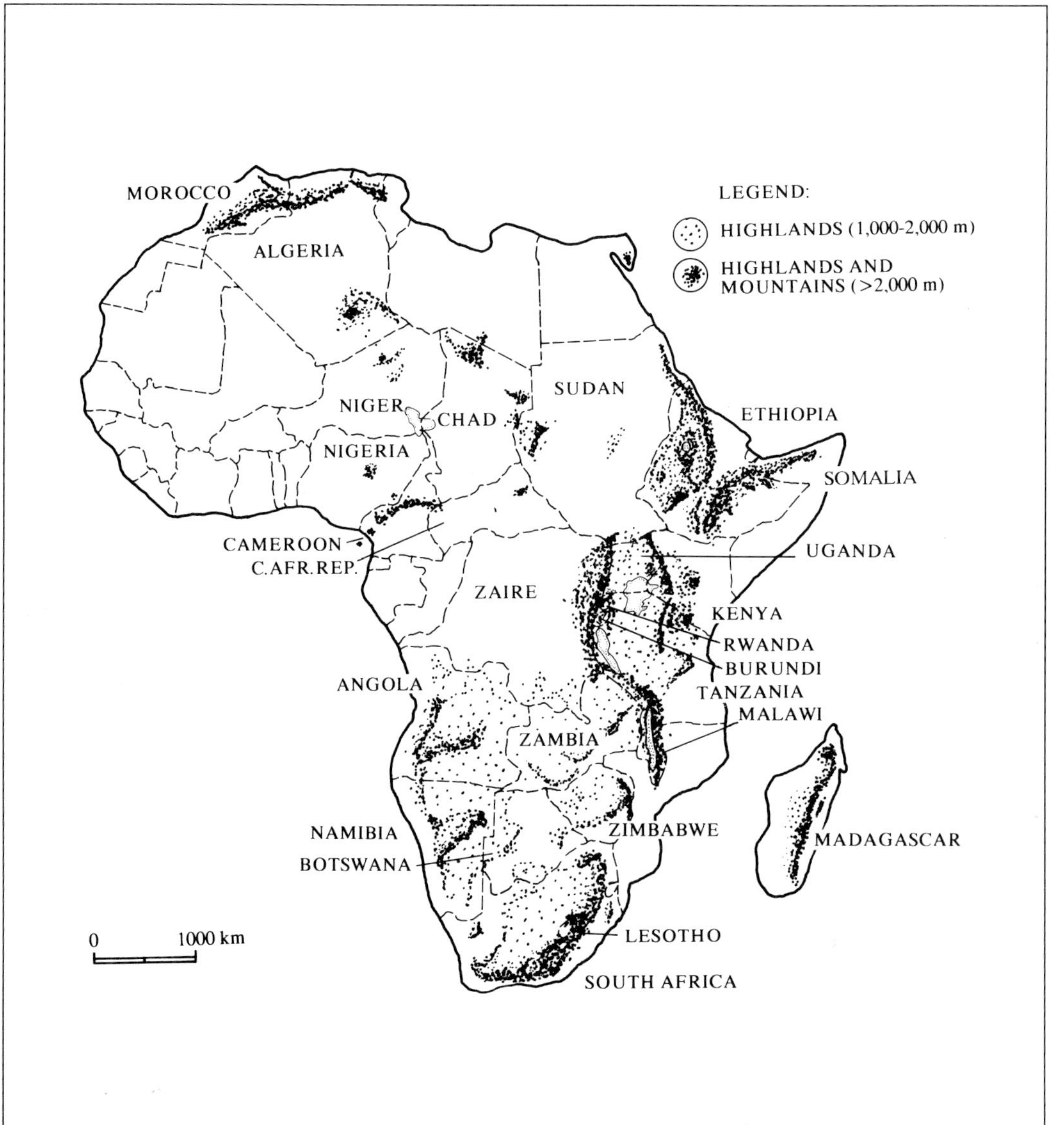

African mountains and highlands: a synthesis

Suitability for agricultural use

Africa, with its land mass of 30 million km^2, covers about 20 per cent of the Earth's land surface and houses nearly 500 million people. About 50 per cent of the countries in Africa contain mountains or have steep land problems, and about 10 per cent (3 million km^2) of Africa's surface area is highlands, mountains or steep sloping areas. The number of people affected by mountain problems, however, is about 20 per cent of Africa's population, or approximately 100 million people, while a further 30 per cent, or 150 million people, depend on water resources originating in mountain systems. Twenty-five out of 48 African countries in the general map presented in Figure 2.1 have specific mountain problems. Several regions can be delimited, namely the large and complex East African mountain systems, the northwestern Atlas mountain region, the isolated West African mountain peaks, the dispersed southern African mountains, and the mountains and highlands of Madagascar. The succeeding sections of this chapter provide surveys of countries with mountain problems and examine prospects for the future in virtually all of the above mountain regions of Africa.

Mountains are generally perceived as areas where the conditions of human life are difficult. Nevertheless, African mountains and highlands have been very attractive for human land use. They stand out as areas with favourable climatic and ecological conditions by contrast with the surrounding lowlands, which are generally much drier. These factors are a key to understanding the attraction of Africa's mountains and highlands. As a consequence of this attraction, the average population density in all African mountains together is more than double the density of the lowlands, i.e. above 33 persons per km^2 as compared to less than 15 persons per km^2. These average figures are misleading, however, since some mountain regions have densities of up to 500 persons per km^2.

Except for Egypt, African agricultural development throughout human history has taken place in areas of higher rainfall—mountainous or highland areas on the continent—and spread to surrounding lowland and irrigable areas at a later stage. Moreover, mountains were selected as a refuge and as places offering security, since they are also relatively less infected by tropical human and animal diseases than the more humid and hotter lowland areas surrounding them. For example, 80 per cent of Ethiopia's 50 million people live in areas above 1 500 m, where rainfall, soils and conditions for human life are much better than in the semi-arid and arid lowlands which make up nearly 60 per cent of the country's 1.2 million km^2.

Subsistence agriculture and weak economies

African mountains host a variety of ethnic groups consisting of peoples who originated in different parts of the continent or immigrated from outside. Consequently, the cultural heritage of the mountains is extremely rich and merits strong

Mountain people generally make best use of the ecological suitability and susceptibility of mountain resources for agricultural use–Mandara Mountains Cameroon, March 1978

preservation efforts. In most African mountains traditional agriculture is dominant. Population pressure has put many of these agricultural systems increasingly at extreme risk, with the result that cultures and the natural environment are both being degraded at an alarming rate.

Depending on the economic status of each African country, mountain people may have opportunities for off-farm employment. In the northwestern mountain regions of Morocco, Algeria and Tunisia, economic development of the lowlands has shifted the centre of importance from the Atlas mountain ranges towards the coastal regions, resulting in emigration and abandonment of settlements and farming areas. In West Africa, the mountains consist of relatively isolated areas whose inhabitants are seeking employment in the rapidly growing cities. The mountains and highland systems of East Africa cover much of the land surface of the countries in that region, including the cities, where off-farm employment draws people from rural mountain areas. The mountains of southern Africa are strongly influenced by economic activities in South Africa, which attract the male labour force in particular. Finally, the mountains and highlands of Madagascar have undergone hardly any economic development due to the isolated position of the island.

Susceptibility to irreversible exploitation

Since more than 70 per cent of the African workforce is engaged in agriculture, problems of degradation and their negative effects on agricultural production affect African people more seriously than people in other mountain systems of the world. Where there is little or no economic development, people in African mountains are highly dependent on local ecological conditions and extremely vulnerable to negative trends affecting these conditions.

In almost all mountain systems on the African continent degradation of natural resources such as vegetation, wildlife, water and soil, particularly in former forest ecosystems with great biodiversity, has been constant over the last few centuries. The rate of degradation has been extremely alarming during the second half of the 20th century in particular. Many factors have been responsible but chief among them is a very rapid population increase, which has put increased stress on natural resources through rapid expansion and intensification of agricultural land use in most African mountains. These factors, coupled with difficult conditions of relief and edaphic variability, are partly responsible for the susceptibility of mountains to human-induced environmental problems.

Deforestation by agricultural land users and commercial forest mining companies is widespread in African mountains, since the process of deforestation was initiated much earlier here than in the tropical rainforest areas of the lowlands of Africa. As a consequence of vegetational changes over the last 2 000 years, runoff has increased and evaporation has decreased on the land surface. These processes have been occurring at an accelerated rate in the second half of the 20th century.

Due to long-term land use, soil erosion and soil degradation are extreme in many mountain systems in Africa. This induces changes in the water regime such as floods and lack of water during the dry seasons. Many of these processes are irreversible within one lifetime. Decades or even centuries will be needed for adequate regeneration –if the land is protected from human use. The water-retention capacities of the soil are decreasing on degrading agricultural land, thus increasing the susceptibility of agricultural production to drought.

National parks and biosphere reserves are particularly threatened in all African mountains. At present, they do not cover sufficient areas to guarantee biodiversity, especially since the different mountain complexes were naturally formed islands with site-specific ecological developments even before human intervention took place.

The degradation of vegetation on communally owned land used to the maximum extent is of particular importance. This process is much faster in such areas than on individually owned land. Many African governments which did not clearly define land titling realize that institutional and genuine legal changes are badly needed to solve the problem of land ownership, and hence degradation.

However, there are some exceptions to this general picture, particularly in those areas where the surrounding lowlands have undergone rapid economic growth, thereby attracting people from mountains to move there and to abandon traditional agricultural systems. The potential for technological improvement in African mountain agriculture will remain small, however, as long as economic development in African countries does not advance more rapidly. These problems have in fact emerged as crucial questions of survival, threatening millions of Africa's inhabitants, as exemplified in the section on Ethiopia's mountains.

Commitment to mountain development

Security of land ownership and managed access to communally owned land will be important issues in African mountain development. A major reorganization will be needed, involving strengthened institutions at all levels of society, from local to national. This is a highly complex matter which affects the basic socio-cultural framework of communities and calls for great sensitivity and innovative thinking. In this context the role of women in African mountain agriculture must be reassessed and used as a new basis for development. Women are primarily responsible for subsistence production in most African countries—hence their importance.

Without external assistance on a much greater scale, sustainable development may not be achievable in many instances. Therefore, strategies to improve ecology and human life in African mountains cannot be developed only among mountain people and in the mountains themselves. They must also be supported by economic and financial aid from the surrounding areas and from economic systems outside the African continent.

Nevertheless, in the recent past, the potential of mountain inhabitants on one hand and the regenerative power of their environment on the other hand have provided signs of hope for developing African mountains into stable and sustainable ecological, social, cultural and economic systems.

Climate change: hazard or opportunity?

In Africa the multiple effects of mountain environmental change on the local and regional climate during this century have already been considerable, as deforestation has increased in the surrounding lowlands and on the mountains themselves. As a consequence, despite the lack of significant statistical evidence, it is assumed that the variability of rainfall is increasing, while total rainfall in semi-arid to sub-humid areas is decreasing.

The effect of global temperature change on African mountains may be relatively small unless changes exceed 5°C. Altitudinal belts will probably move upwards, but will affect a much smaller area than what must be expected in the case of lateral shifts of ecological zones in the surrounding lowlands. Rainfall patterns may change considerably, and predictions indicate better rainfall conditions for much of Africa's semi-arid zones, including the highlands, if global warming increases.

The need for solidarity

In many African mountain systems assistance in the form of food aid has been increasingly necessary during periods of food shortage. One way to prevent such a necessity is to consider integrated development programmes such as small industries in marginal areas in order to relieve pressure on the land and enable those who really want to farm to acquire adequate land for survival. People migrating to other less affected areas might be encouraged and should be strongly assisted to become well-established in their new environments.

Without multiple efforts from within Africa and from outside the continent, however, it will be very difficult for affected countries to master mountain problems on their own. Apart from obvious research needs, it will be indispensable to support institutional development and to offer assistance for training and education at all levels. African mountains and their inhabitants will need heavy internal and external support on much larger scales than at present in order to achieve sustainable development in the medium term.

Reversing Africa's decline is a task which primarily concerns its mountains and needs the active participation of humankind on a global scale if the poorhouse of the world is not to remain in its present miserable state. Unfortunately, it is not infrequently that the major powers of the world and the UN take measures to punish or oust a government which they do not like. This can be extremely destructive to poor people in rural areas and to the environment. Decision makers, therefore, should look carefully at all the consequences of their actions before they decide on political punishments of unpopular regimes. ■

Survival in the highlands and mountains of Ethiopia

Africa's largest mountain complex

The surface area of Ethiopia is 1 223 million km², of which 43 per cent is highlands above 1 500 m. The altitudinal belts ranging from 1 500 to 4 543 m are defined as mountains and highlands. These offer much more favourable climatic and ecological conditions for agriculture than the surrounding lowlands. As a result, 88 per cent of Ethiopia's population of 50 million (1990), 60 per cent of its livestock, and 90 per cent of its agriculturally suitable land are concentrated in the country's highland areas (UNDP/FAO/LUPRD, 1984).

Some 44 million people and 18 million tropical livestock units (about 70 million head) live in the Ethiopian highlands and mountains, reflecting the relative importance of this mountain system. For example, the above numbers exceed the total populations of all other countries in the Sahel belt together. Favourable natural resources attracted early human settlers to this the largest mountain complex in Africa, so that, gradually, most agriculturally suitable lands were occupied, including marginal lands on slopes which are highly susceptible to soil erosion and other land degradation processes.

Attractive land use conditions in the highlands

Ethiopia benefits from the diversity of natural resources in its mountains. A variety of temperature as well as rainfall conditions permits the cultivation of temperate as well as subtropical and tropical crops. Historically, a variety of rural economies has developed, including highland animal rearing, various types of mixed farming systems with different crop and livestock associations, and several types of pastoralism (IUCN, 1990).

In the Ethiopian highlands and mountains, about 80 000 km², or 15 per cent of the highland part of the country, is cultivated land, about 380 000 km² (70 per cent) is grassland used as grazing and browsing land, about 55 000 km² (10 per cent) is non-usable or degraded badlands.

Table 2.1: Estimated current rates of soil loss in the Ethiopian highlands and mountains. Source: Hurni, 1990, adapted for highlands only, the country total being around 1 500 million tons per year

Land Cover	Area (per cent of high-lands)	Estimated Soil loss (t/ha/yr)	Total soil loss (million t/yr)	(per cent)
Annual crops	15	42	342	33
Fallow land	15	42	342	33
Grazing	55	5	149	14
Forests	5	1	3	-
Badlands	5	70	190	18
Unproductive	5	5	14	2
Total	100 (543,000 km^2)		1040	100

Only about 28 000 km^2 (5 per cent) is forests, which have declined from about 430 000 km^2 (80 per cent) several millennia ago to their present low level. This is due to man's impact on natural forest ecologies, which has changed the highlands into a man-made agricultural landscape. Most of the remaining forests are located in the southwest and western parts of the highlands, while the northern and eastern parts are almost completely deprived of forest land.

A vulnerable mountain economy

Ethiopia's mountain inhabitants practise subsistence agriculture in a combination of crop cultivation and livestock rearing. Cattle, in particular oxen, are used in the farming system as ox-plough draught animals. About 80 per cent of the production is for home consumption, while only 20 per cent goes into the national economy. Eighty-four per cent of Ethiopia's population of 50 million are mountain farmers in the highlands.

Ploughing steep slopes with a pair of oxen is a traditional farming system with low external input but with high risks of soil erosion and degradation if practised over long periods on steep slopes. Barley cultivation is possible at altitudes up to 3 700 m, as shown in this picture from the Simen Mountains

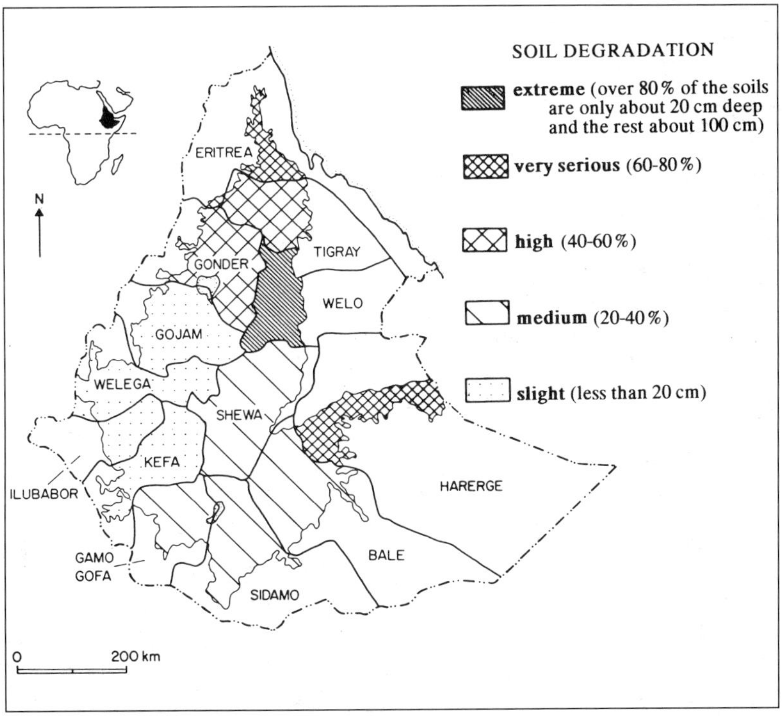

Figure 2.2: The effect of historical and present-day soil erosion on the status of soils in Ethiopia. Source: Hurni, 1990, generalized from Barber (1984) based on Henricksen et al. (1983)

Another 3 million people live in towns also situated in the highlands, while only 5 million people live below 1 500 m. Owing to low economic activity and rugged relief conditions, Ethiopia has a very limited transport network and hence a very low transport capacity. Due to the low level of exchange of goods, these factors contribute to the high vulnerability of the rural population to famine situations.

Catastrophic land degradation

Land degradation in the Ethiopian highlands and mountains concerns processes of deforestation, soil erosion and biological soil deterioration, and overgrazing on most types of agricultural land. Extreme deforestation rates on agricultural land have reduced the biodiversity of natural vegetation and wildlife to a low level, although the diversity of mountain situations still permits its preservation in small patches distributed all over the highlands. Soils which were originally extremely fertile and deep throughout the highlands have declined as a result of cultivation and grazing over thousands of years. Soil erosion on agricultural land, caused by rainfall and runoff, is a process as old as the history of agriculture in the highlands.

Soil erosion is particularly severe in the northern part of the country, where in some cases soil has been completely removed from slopes and has accumulated in valley bottoms (see Figure 2.2). Shallow soils with less fertility and vegetative cover are more susceptible to erosion, since their water retention and holding capacity decrease with decreasing soil depth. Consequently, less production is obtained from such soils; this in turn accelerates degradation. This vicious circle has resulted in degraded soils and vegetation over much of the highlands, with runoff rates of up to 80 per cent of the rainfall, while well-covered soils would retain more than 90 per cent of the rainfall.

Current soil loss rates are highest on cultivated and fallow land (country average: 42 t/ha/year; see Table 2.1), where more than half of all field losses occur. Other types of land use produce only half as much total soil loss, although their areal extent is up to 4 times larger. Such soil loss averages for cropland will totally remove the soil on present cropland in the Ethiopian mountains

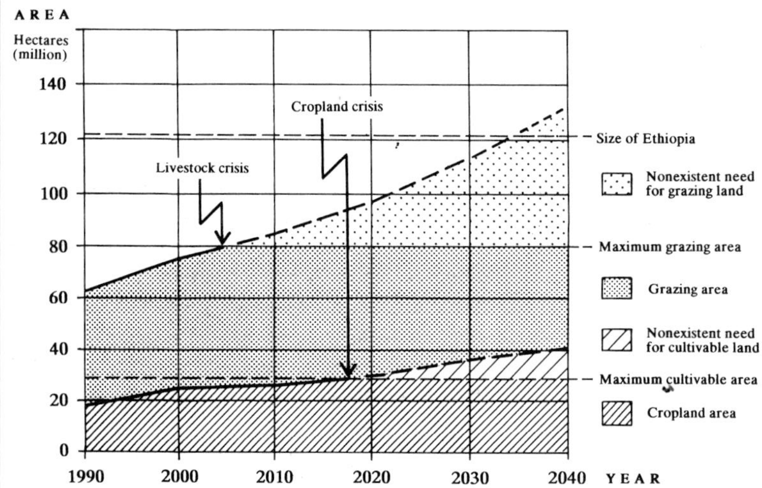

Figure 2.3: Trends in land-resource utilization in present-day levels of development in Ethiopia extrapolated for the next 50 years
Source: Hurni, 1988

Fuelwood scarcity in an originally forested area can put an enormous strain on women, who are primarily responsible for supplying home energy–Merhabete, central Ethiopia, 2 100 m

within 100-150 years. The resulting annual production loss due to soil loss is estimated at 1-2 per cent. Biological soil deterioration may add a further 1 per cent loss to annual production because dung and crop residues are being burned instead of brought back to the field.

Overgrazing on almost all grazing land is another severe problem which seriously affects agricultural production in the ox-plough system.

All these ecological factors lead to severe constraints and increase famine vulnerability at alarming rates. Ethiopia is facing severe mountain problems as the result of degradation coupled with the current rate of population increase of around 3 per cent per year. These problems not only affect the country itself but also increase the demand for international assistance in the form of emergency and rehabilitation projects. Land resource scenarios indicate that if present trends continue, Ethiopia will have an overall crisis involving livestock grazing land in less than 15 years, and an arable land crisis in about 25 years (see Figure 2.3). In some regions, however, both crises are already present virtually every year.

Cumulative mountain problems

History indicates that Ethiopian mountain systems are particularly vulnerable to repeated famines. It is in this light that Ethiopian mountain problems must be visualized. In the natural subsystem, climate (variability of rainfall), pests, and animal and crop diseases are major forces. Since these all have short-term impacts, they must be considered seriously when designing a famine prevention strategy.

Some present trends involving individual factors in the natural subsystem contradict each other, however. While the climatic trend is towards more frequent drought and greater variability, especially in the north of Ethiopia, the impacts of animal and plant pests and diseases are currently decreasing due to the recent availability of chemical treatments.

The land use subsystem is characterized by threatening ecological processes, decreasing crop reserves, few innovations and, most importantly, by an economy based on subsistence agriculture. Land users in marginal areas–on steep slopes or eroded soils, for example–subsist at a low level of production, which barely guarantees their survival, and are in constant threat of hunger. Necessary changes and trends which should be introduced in the land use subsystem, however, would all have medium- to long-term effects. Furthermore, they may be positive or negative, depending on development impacts.

It is important to note that the human subsystem also contributes to specific mountain problems. Social organization of individuals into communities is a rather recent phenomenon, and political stability has not been attained on a country-wide basis. The great isolation of farming families with little accessibility to roads, very low market integration, highly fragmented land, a low level of mechanization in agricultural production and recent population density combined with heavy population growth all contribute to an ever-increasing vulnerability to famine. These forces, which also have medium- to long-term effects, may increase vulnerability.

A further important factor hindering positive developments in the Ethiopian mountains is the relatively low level of knowledge about mountain systems and about the farming population. There is also very little information on the actual effects of degradation on production and on positive experiences with rehabilitation techniques and approaches.

In addition, one should not forget that Ethiopian mountain problems are still further influenced by external impacts, which may increase famine vulnerability to an even greater degree. Population growth rates resulting from medical and hygienic developments outside the country, terms of trade and food aid without development support all increase famine vulnerability for millions of mountain inhabitants. Unless these international impacts are recognized and better coordinated, Ethiopia will have little chance to improve its situation.

Do promising mountain options exist?

Despite the negative picture outlined above, Ethiopia's mountain system provides inviting opportunities for development. On a regional basis, the mountains receive much more rainfall than would be expected at this latitude. Mountains can be utilized and have been utilized for millennia as water towers for irrigation in the lowlands. The Nile Basin is fed by rivers from the Ethiopian mountain system in summer. Energy and irrigation, nevertheless, can also be developed in the highlands to a much greater extent. Soil

conservation and reafforestation activities contribute to regional development. In addition to this, projects to preserve the biodiversity of cultivated plants, natural vegetation and animal life can be enhanced.

The multitude of agricultural products invites a much greater degree of local exchange. Market integration and transport development offer many positive options. Specific agricultural products can be exchanged on a regional basis. Export to the Arab countries as well as to other neighbouring African countries represents a clear opportunity for more exchange of goods.

Nevertheless, without a considerable re-orientation of land use and improved political organization, these things will hardly be manageable. International support will be needed over many decades and to a much greater degree than at present.

Prerequisites for sustainable development

Cultural and ethnic diversity and problems of degradation and productivity decline have produced political instability in the mountain system of Ethiopia. A number of policy recommendations are needed concerning policies on population growth–including family planning in its broadest sense–food security, agricultural and livestock development, rehabilitation and conservation strategies, economic strategies favouring market development, and regionalization and federalization of the Ethiopian highlands based on smaller units. Furthermore, a better appreciation and knowledge of the situation and the environment of peasants in rural Ethiopia will be an indispensable basis for rational planning and strategic thinking.

Ethiopian mountains and highlands are a marginal area, but they are of paramount global interest owing to (1) the biodiversity of both their cultivated plants and natural life, (2) cultural diversity involving over 70 ethnic groups, (3) their function as water towers for irrigation and (4) their role in supplying energy on a truly regional scale. To achieve better, sustainable use of these resources, local competence supported by external assistance in the form of political, technical and financial support must be mobilized on an extremely large scale.■

"Reproductive" activities such as soil conservation call for subsidies from outside the farming system. Furthermore, they can only be based on communities willing to maintain such improvements

Scientific knowledge of runoff and sediment yield for catchments in mountain ecosystems used by man provides an excellent indicator of natural processes and human-induced acceleration–Andit Tid, Ethiopia

The changing use of mountain resources in Morocco

Outstanding geo-ecological richness

A first range of the Atlas mountains of northwestern Africa (Figure 2.4) was formed in Pre-Cambrian times. The southernmost mountain system of the Anti-Atlas thus consists of crystalline basement and Paleozoic sediments. The second range, called High Atlas, consists of Mesozoic sediments and was uplifted in the Cretaceous period of the late Mesozoic era. Finally, the northernmost Rif Mountains were formed in the Tertiary period and consist mainly of clay schists. In addition, some volcanic eruptions formed basalt layers in the central part of the High Atlas. The highest peak in Morocco is Jebel Toukal, rising to an altitude of 4 165 m in the High Atlas.

While the Rif Mountains have a Mediterranean climate with relatively high rainfall (over 1 000 mm per year), the Middle and High Atlas mountains also have considerable rainfall of around 1 000 mm per year. Generally, rainfall increases with altitude, thus providing favourable conditions for plant and animal life at higher elevations. Along the southeastern slopes of the mountain range, towards the Sahara Desert, aridity becomes predominant and rainfall drops sharply to less than 200 mm per year. The temporal variability of rainfall increases with decreasing amounts, thus giving mountains in Morocco a more secure rainfall pattern than the surrounding lowlands. Since the rainy season is in winter, it coincides with relatively low temperatures. Although snowfall above 2 000 m is regular for about three months per year, there is no actual glaciation in the Atlas mountain range. Frost occurs frequently above 1 500 m. The tree line is at about 2 900 m.

Figure 2.4: *Location of the Moroccan mountains and surrounding lowlands*

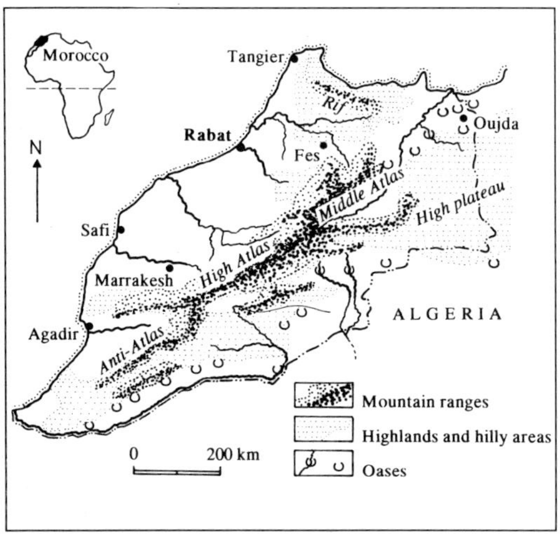

While the surrounding lowlands have desert vegetation or specific types of oasis vegetation, the mountains were once covered by oaks, cedars and juniper trees. Degradation of tree vegetation, however, has been extensive in many parts of the Atlas mountains over thousands of years. As a result, few forests exist at present. Afforestation activities have taken place in this century to renew the forests in some parts of the mountains.

Water is the main limiting factor in agriculture and human life generally; this stresses the relative importance of mountain systems as water towers. Rainfall in the mountains generally is double what it is in the surrounding lowlands. Major rivers draining from the High Atlas towards the Atlantic are important sources for water storage and irrigation systems on the northwestern pediment of the mountain range. The southeastern side of the Atlas has additional rivers which dry out quickly when merging into the Sahara. However, important oases are scattered along these groundwater carriers. While rainfed agriculture is possible in the mountains, the northwestern lowlands normally need additional irrigation for agriculture, and the southeastern lowlands are fully dependent on irrigation. The hazards of water quality and salinity are major constraints on irrigation. High evaporation further aggravates this problem.

Culturally adapted 'traditional' use of mountains

The Atlas region has undergone a remarkable change in the 20th century, from a traditional land use system adapted to natural conditions, to a system of modern technology and agriculture. Traditional use of the area was based on the mountain ranges, with their altitudinal zonation and ecological differentiation, and the climatic patterns around them (Winiger, 1988).

Land use practices in the mountains and adjacent lowlands are characterized in the cross-

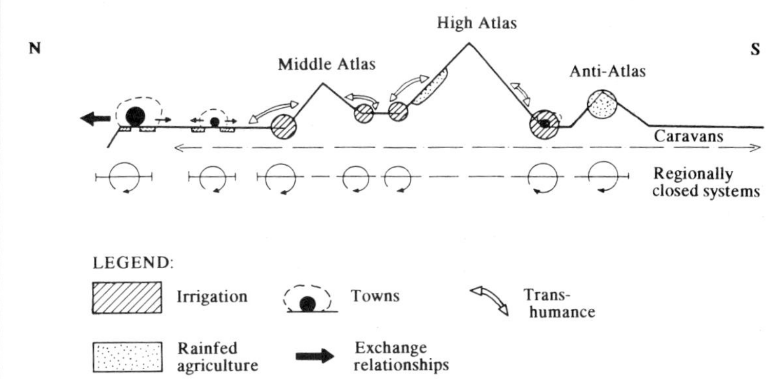

Figure 2.5: *Spatial distribution of land use and resources in Morocco in pre-colonial times (*Winiger, 1988*). Note that resource areas function simultaneously as living areas*

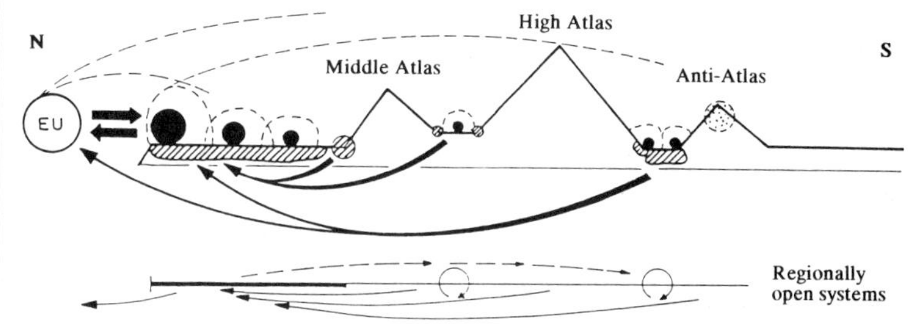

Figure 2.6: *Present-day spatial distribution of land use and resources in Morocco (*Winiger, 1988*). Note: resources like water and workforce are dislocated over great distances; external means are reinvested; large-scale relationships exist*

sectional diagram in Figure 2.5. Important sea ports were located along the coast for the exchange of goods. In the lowland plains, between the coast and the mountains, there were grazing grounds for the livestock of migrating nomadic people, used particularly during the winter rains. The mountains traditionally served as large-scale grazing grounds for herds during the rather dry summer months. The Anti-Atlas and some slopes of the High Atlas were used for rainfed agriculture.

The mountains functioned as catchments of rainfall and snow, thus feeding water to the groundwater tables and rivers. Groundwater and rivers supplied intermediate valleys, which were used for intensively developed irrigation systems (Abdellatif Bencherifa, 1990). Along the southern foot of the Atlas range, specific locations were developed for irrigation whenever groundwater or surface water was available for the development of such structures.

In sum, traditional land use systems were characterized by a strong pattern of transhumance, which resulted from grazing livestock moving between the plains and the mountains according to the growing seasons. Towns developed either along the coast or in important locations at the foot of the mountains. The exchange of goods was limited to the ports, while most land use systems were subsistence systems. Resource areas simultaneously served as areas of habitation. These systems were regionally closed, interacting with each other only for the exchange of essential goods, such as salt, and products such as tea, coffee, etc. The population adapted to the respective carrying capacities in different ecological situations. Forceful and hence cruel control mechanisms, such as periodic famines or emigration when carrying capacities were exceeded, guaranteed demographic stability. Trade was conducted on a transcontinental basis and with neighbouring tribes using caravans and ships.

This traditional use of the Atlas mountain ranges changed with colonial occupation, when the resources for increased agricultural production were developed and integration into the supra-regional marketing system was enforced, thus making the mountains a peripheral region.

Disrupted 'modern' use of mountains

The colonial period brought a complete change in resource utilization and subsistence land use (Winiger, 1988). The plains and coastal towns became focal areas for development, thus forming the "Maroc util", while the mountain ranges and intermontane valleys were considered "Maroc inutil", and served as delivery systems for resources such as water, people, and, to some degree, livestock. Rainfed agriculture significantly diminished in the mountains, irrigated terraces were increasingly used for specialized crops such as apples, etc., with financial inputs from outside. Lowland plains to the west were increasingly developed into irrigable areas; swampy areas were drained and reused for agriculture, and grazing was increasingly prohibited there. This process of emigration is described in Figure 2.6. It resulted in a gradual replacement of the traditional nomadic systems based on transhumance. Most of the population is now being integrated into the system of modern agriculture and development, while the rest is being marginalized.

In the post-colonial period, Morocco continued development processes already initiated, thus intensifying production in the plains and exchanging goods throughout a wider area including Europe. Today, most of the resource potential of the country is concentrated in the plains: investment as well as labour, industrial as well as agricultural production, and the dominant aspects of cultural life.

The Atlas Mountains, on the other hand, are still important as resource areas for water, energy and labour (see Abdellatif Bencherifa, 1990). Also, the southern oases are formally maintained as cultural areas. Functionally and structurally, however, they are increasingly dependent on external investments in the form of reinvestment of money from emigrants and government subsidies. Some state intervention is directed towards the preservation of land use systems in the oases. Efforts to preserve subsistence agricultural systems in the mountains, however, seem to be much more difficult.

Squeezed between Europe and the Sahara: challenges for the future

The gradual destruction of resources in the Atlas Mountains is leading to an impoverishment of traditional systems on a scale which may produce negative feedback mechanisms for the development process in the countries of the area. The Morocco of tomorrow will have to deal with major challenges concerning its mountains, such as preservation of the mountains as water towers, reduction of sedimentation in rivers, dealing with salinity problems in irrigated areas, and socio-cultural degradation occurring everywhere.

Ecological balance in the mountains is being disrupted by changing use and increasing neglect. Restitution, however, must be founded on the cultural renewal of human life in the mountains. This calls for increased efforts by governments to provide incentives and subsidies to mountain people who will only be able to take care of their own resources and seek a new identity and responsibility if supported from outside.

Like most African mountains, the Atlas system is particularly susceptible to human impacts, whether through intensification or emigration. In the latter case, the result is cultural and ecological degradation owing to the attracting forces of the surrounding areas. A crucial question for the Atlas will be the economic potential of the country, and the need for concerted policies not only to develop areas of concentration around the mountain systems but also to preserve human as well as animal and plant life in originally balanced mountain systems which evolved traditionally and have existed since time immemorial.

Economic relations and eventual integration with Europe, on the one hand, and the ecologically sensitive neighbourhood of the Sahara Desert, on the other hand, are the two main factors which will have to be carefully observed as key processes which will influence most future trends in the region.■

Mountain and highland preservation for development in Kenya

Natural resources of the highlands

Mountains and highlands, that is areas above 1 500 m, cover 15.2 per cent or 88 500 km^2 of Kenya's total surface area of 582 600 km^2. They are situated in the southwestern part of the country (see Figure 2.1). The central Rift divides the mainly volcanic highlands into two major parts: one sloping west from the Rift Valley towards Lake Victoria, and the other sloping east towards the Tana river basin. These highlands, which are characterized by undulating relief and plateaus, are overtopped by huge volcanic massifs. The most important of these tropical mountains are the Nyandarua Range (3 999 m) and Mt. Kenya (5 199 m) east of the central Rift, and Mt. Elgon (4 121 m) on the Kenya-Uganda border.

Though highlands and mountains cover only about one-seventh of Kenya, they are of major importance in terms of natural resources, as shown by the distribution of the agro-climatic potential (Table 2.2).

While 92.4 per cent of the lowlands (below 1 500 m) is arid to semi-arid, 72.7 per cent of the highlands (above 1 500 m) is humid to semi-humid. In other words, the highlands and mountains of Kenya constitute 75.6 per cent of all high-potential agricultural areas, and 52.9 per cent of all medium-potential areas in the republic. The remaining high- and medium-potential areas are found mainly around Lake Victoria and partly in the coastal belt.

Besides being the core of the republic in terms of agricultural potential, the highlands are also important with regard to other natural resources: only 3.4 per cent of the surface of Kenya is still covered by forests, but most of these are found in the highlands, where they cover around 17 per cent of the surface area. Furthermore, the highlands are the water tower of Kenya: they feed the main rivers, which are also vital to the surrounding drier lowlands. During the dry seasons these rivers are fed mainly by the forest belts and the afro-alpine zone of the high tropical mountains.

The outstanding importance of the highlands and mountains of Kenya in terms of natural resources is reflected in the distribution of the population. In 1990, around 60 per cent of Kenya's 24.4 million inhabitants (GOK, 1989) lived in the highlands.

Historical development of land-use systems

In the past 100 years the highlands of Kenya have experienced several important transitions which have left traces up to the present day. Up to the end of the 19th century the central Rift and large parts of the drier highlands north and south of it were used by pastoralists. The parts east and west of the central Rift were inhabited by peasants who practised mixed crop and livestock farming.

In colonial times the land use system was completely transformed: the colonial government established the so-called "white highlands", which covered large parts of the Kenyan highlands and which were subsequently occupied by white settlers. During this process the pastoralists were displaced to the drier lowlands and the peasants were enclosed in "African reserves". The white settlers developed an export-oriented agriculture that included the production of beef, wheat, coffee

***Table 2.2:** Altitudinal belts and agro-climatic zones in Kenya (as per cent of total surface of Kenya)*
Source: Braun et al., 1982. Own calculations.

Altitudinal belts	Agro-climatic zones			
	High-potential (humid /sub-humid)	Mid potential (sub-humid)	Low-potential (semi-arid /arid)	Afro-alpine zone
0- 900 m	0.03	1.22	67.16	
900-1 500 m	2.04	3.18	11.17	
1 500-2 150 m	3.26	3.74	3.88	
2 150-3 050 m	2.83	1.20		
> 3 050 m				0.27
Total	8.17	9.34	82.22	0.27

and tea, and, later, horticultural products. African peasants were prevented from participating in this development. After 1945 the situation worsened in the "African reserves" due to high population growth and further resettlements by the colonial government.

Following independence, large parts of the former "white highlands" were transferred to Africans through government settlement schemes and private land-buying companies, resulting in the subdivision of formerly large-scale farms and the encroachment of indigenous capital into the highly profitable agricultural export sector (Ochieng, 1985). This development spread small-scale farmers with their mixed farming (livestock, staple food and cash crops such as tea or coffee) over large parts of the Kenyan highlands. They subsequently emerged as the backbone of the agriculturally based economy of Kenya.

The complexity of development trends

Kenya is experiencing very rapid population growth, with an annual growth rate of around 3.7 per cent. This led to an increase of population density on arable land in rural areas from 125 persons/km^2 in 1979 to 193 persons/km^2 in 1990 (GOK, 1989). In conjunction with the tendency of the real value of farm products to decrease, population pressure in the small-scale farming areas of the highlands provokes and accelerates the processes described below.

First, land use in the high- to medium-potential areas of the highlands is intensified in terms of production and space, affecting the remaining natural vegetation cover. Since the production base tends to decrease for some smallholders, cash crop production diminishes relatively in favour of subsistence production, resulting in an economic marginalization which might hinder conservation inputs.

Second, population pressure in the highlands is responsible for an increase in migration from rural to urban areas. While the rural population increased by 52 per cent between 1979 and 1990, the urban population doubled during the same time. These migrants can hardly be absorbed into the urban economy, since only about 30 000 formal jobs are added annually, while 400 000 persons enter the job market annually from school alone. Therefore, many migrants are still partly dependent on the (subsistence) production of family farms in rural areas without being available as part of the labour force for this production. The need for increased farm production combined with labour constraints may further

Large-scale farm and newly subdivided small-scale farming areas on the slopes of Mt. Kenya

hinder conservation inputs, even though traditional farming systems are well adapted to the ecological conditions of high- to medium-potential areas.

Third, heavy population pressure seeks a further outlet through the extension of small-scale farming to areas of lower potential which border the high-potential core of the highlands. The resulting pace of smallholder migration to newly subdivided semi-arid areas is similar to the pace of urbanization. The Mt. Kenya region serves as an example: the population of high- to medium-potential areas south and east of Mt. Kenya increased by 43 per cent from 1979 to 1988, while the population of the semi-arid areas northwest of Mt. Kenya increased by more than 70 per cent due to migration during the same period. The resulting hazardous pressure on natural resources in the newly settled semi-arid areas is due not only to the rapid increase in almost purely subsistence-oriented small-scale farms, but also to the difficulty these farming systems have in adapting to the newly exploited environment.

The hazards of ecological degradation

Intensification, urbanization and extension of agriculture to areas of lower potential represent hazards in terms of further ecological degradation. Even though traditional farming systems in high- and medium-potential areas are ecologically well adapted, soil erosion seems to be a growing problem due to intensification of agriculture on steeper slopes and along river courses. Besides soil losses on productive land, erosion also causes increasing sediment loads in rivers. This affects economically important hydroelectric plants and is responsible for the high costs of rehabilitating dams. Sediment loads are further transported to the coast, where they affect the shore and the quality of the water behind the reef, hence endangering features important to tourism, which is of crucial economic importance.

Pressure on the land and the increasing demand for wood and fuelwood (30.3 million tons of oil equivalent in 1990) are endangering the remaining forests. It is estimated that forest areas are being depleted by 1 per cent annually in spite of the government's strong conservation efforts (GOK, 1989). In the last 100 years there has been a decrease in highland forest areas at altitudes between 1 500 and 2 500 m of almost 80 per cent, while mountain forests above 2 500 m have decreased by 20 per cent (Kohler 1976). When the crucial function of the remaining forests relative to

Well-adapted small-scale farms in a high-potential area near Meru on the eastern side of Mt. Kenya

river water balances is considered, it becomes clear that any further depletion may also have a negative effect on the drier lowlands of Kenya.

The extension of small-scale farming to semi-arid areas not only aggravates the problems of soil erosion and forest depletion but also leads to an over-exploitation of river water. Since water is perceived as the main limiting factor in farming, and since peasants are having difficulty adapting their farming system to semi-arid conditions, the pressure on these easily accessible water sources is rapidly increasing.

Over-exploitation of the perennial rivers, which all originate in the high mountains, causes severe problems in the drier lowlands, where pastoral systems and game reserves and national parks important to tourism depend on these water resources. For example, the base flow of the Ewaso N'giro River, which flows north from Mt. Kenya into the drier lowlands, has been diminished by 50 per cent in the dry season during the last 30 years owing to the immigration of small-scale farmers to the semi-arid plateau northwest of Mt. Kenya. These farmers use the water upstream for irrigation and home consumption.

Effects on the high mountains

The trends described above also create pressure on the high tropical mountains, whose forest belts can serve as suitable agricultural land. For example, 41 000 ha of gazetted forests were excised for conversion to settlement around the flanks of Mt. Kenya, the Nyandarua Range and the Mau Escarpment between 1970 and 1977 (Muiruri, 1977). It also seems that mountain forests are increasingly being exploited to obtain wood.

Despite this potentially heavy pressure, the government's strong conservation policy has hindered major transformation and degradation in the high tropical mountains. The forest belts are still intact for the most part, and the afro-alpine zone is hardly affected by human activities. This success in conserving the high tropical mountains allows them to retain their crucial functions as water towers, as reserves with great biodiversity, as suppliers of wood and forest products, as an important tourist attraction, and as sensitive natural indicators of global climatic change.

Traces of climatic change in the form of fossil lateral moraines manifested along the upper timber line of Mt. Kenya (view from the top)

The vital role of mountain resources

The high agro-climatic potential of the highlands and mountains is the backbone of the Kenyan economy and gives these areas a leading role in the development of Kenya. On the other hand, heavy population growth and pressure on the land are hazards which threaten ecological degradation as well as marginalization for parts of the population. This will also affect areas outside the core of the highlands.

Aside from land and population policies, efforts in conservation (soil, water, forests), development of adaptable farming systems (for semi-arid areas) and non-farm employment must counter the hazards mentioned here if the highlands and mountains of Kenya are to be maintained as areas of crucial importance. The extensive efforts of the government of Kenya in all these areas deserve and require outside assistance. ■

Mountains as vital factors in regional development in southern Africa

Climate, water, and soil: rich mountain resources

The mountain regions of southern Africa are found in all four provinces of the Republic of South Africa (Transvaal, Orange Free State, Natal and Cape) and in Lesotho, Namibia and Angola (Figure 2.7).

Although the mountains of the escarpment cover only a small proportion of South Africa, they provide resources that are absolutely vital to the economy of the whole country. Almost the whole of Lesotho is dominated by high mountains. In Namibia and Angola the resources provided by the mountains are less dominant but still significant.

The mountains of southern Africa have highly differing climatic characteristics. The interior plateau and the western and southwestern coastal areas of South Africa are arid to semi-arid. At least 65 per cent of the country has a mean annual rainfall of less than 500 mm, which is considered the minimum for successful rain-fed cropping, while 21 per cent of the country receives less than 200 mm. Severe droughts, which may last several years, are often followed by torrential rains. In contrast, the mountains of the eastern escarpment and the windward ranges of the Cape Folded Belt receive well in excess of 1 000 mm of rain annually, with some areas receiving as much as 3 000 mm. More than 40 per cent of the total mean annual rainfall of southern Africa falls in the Drakensberg/Maluti region (Bainbridge et al., 1991).

Rainfall in the mountains of the western escarpment (Region F in Figure 2.7) of South Africa is low, becoming progressively lower towards the north. The northwestern corner is a

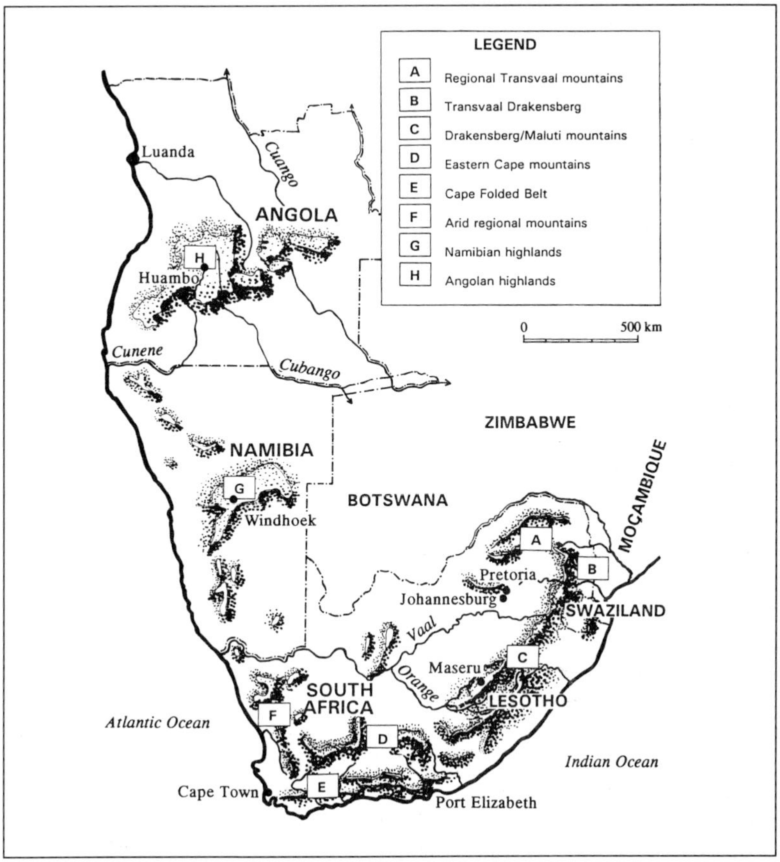

Figure 2.7: Overview of the mountains and highlands of South Africa, Lesotho, Namibia and Angola

mountain desert. The main reason for this is the presence of the cold Benguela current, which yields very little moist air. Another factor precluding orographic rain effects in this region is the reigning winds, which are predominantly parallel to the coast and the escarpment.

The cold Benguela current and wind blowing parallel to the coast and the escarpment are also responsible for the absence of orographic rain effects in the mountains of Namibia. Rainfall in the mountains is low and they yield very little water to this predominantly arid country. In contrast to South Africa and Namibia, the average rainfall in Angola is high. More than 80 per cent of the country receives a mean annual rainfall in excess of 800 mm. With the exception of the southwestern tip, the central highlands have a mean annual rainfall of more than 1 000 mm. Because of their milder climates, living conditions in the mountains and highlands of Namibia and Angola are more pleasant than those in the surrounding areas.

The diverse rainfall patterns in the mountain systems described above influence the hydrological patterns of major rivers. In general, mountain catchment areas comprising crests or watersheds, plateaus, slopes, foothills and connecting valleys (Jordaan, 1987) receive heavy rainfall and are the most important sources of rivers in South Africa. Although mountain catchment areas occupy only 8 per cent of the surface area, they produce 49 per cent of the mean annual runoff (Department of Water Affairs, 1986).

The Drakensberg escarpment is the most important watershed on the subcontinent, yielding 25 per cent of South Africa's total stream flow (Department of Environment Affairs, 1986). The head streams which originate on the western side of the escarpment flow across the gradual slopes of the eroded plateau of Lesotho to feed the tributaries of the Orange River. This river carries one third of South Africa's usable water. Water flowing east towards the Indian Ocean forms strong perennial rivers which are relatively short and flow rapidly due to the steep slopes of the whole eastern region (Liebenberg, 1976).

Due to the influence of differences in climate and geology, soil patterns in the mountains of South Africa and Lesotho vary markedly between regions. In the Transvaal Drakensberg region (Region B in Figure 2.7), where rainfall is high, the dominant soils (MacVicar, 1973) are freely drained, non-humic red and yellow Latosols (highly weathered soils) with varying amounts of rock, and Lithosols (shallow, stony soils). Deep, high-potential red and yellow soils are more common on the foothills and pediment slopes of these mountains.

In the Drakensberg/Maluti region (C) the highest parts consist mainly of rock cliffs and the soils are described as rock/Lithosol complexes (MacVicar, 1973). The alpine part of this region is covered by black, well-structured, base-rich, medium-textured to clayey soils that are fairly shallow (Bainbridge et al, 1991). The soils on the foothills and pediment slopes on the South African side are predominantly freely drained, non-humic red and yellow Latosols with varying amounts of rock, and Lithosols.

The mountains of the Cape Folded Belt and the semi-arid to arid mountains (Regions D and F) are dominated by rock and very shallow Lithosols (MacVicar, 1973; Ellis, 1988). The soils in the small valleys of Region D consist mainly of duplex soils (highly erodible soils with very low agricultural potential). In the western and eastern parts of Region E, where rainfall is higher, soils in the relatively wide intermontane valleys and basins are well-developed but often gravelly or sandy; hydromorphic soils are also found. In the dry central part of the region soils are mainly shallow eutrophic (unleached) to calcareous sandy soils overlying duripans (harpans)(Ellis, 1988).

Soils in the Namibian highlands consist of rock/shallow Lithosol complexes, with sandy soils of varying depth in the valleys. In the highlands of Angola, highly weathered well-drained to somewhat poorly drained Latosols dominate (Erasmus, 1991). Shallow, stony Lithosols are also common, and in valley bottoms alluvial soils and duplex soils are found.

Flora, fauna and cultural values: exclusive mountain life

The physical complexity of the mountain areas in South Africa is the main reason for the great diversity of mountain flora (Department of Environment Affairs, 1986). Acocks (1988) believes that high forest was the climax vegetation of the entire

Transvaal Drakensberg area (Region B in Figure 2.7). Most of it has, however, been replaced by pure sour grassland.

The vegetation of the alpine zone in Region C is short, dense grassland, varying from sweet to mixed (Acocks, 1988). Such sweet to mixed grasslands have much better grazing potential, especially during winter, than sour grassland. The vegetation of this alpine zone is not found elsewhere in Africa. Current research shows that 95 plant species are endemic to the Drakensberg/ Maluti region (Granger, 1991). Thirty species are listed as endangered (Department of Environment Affairs, 1986) while many more species which are endangered elsewhere in South Africa are found here (Granger, 1991).

The wetland systems of this area are extremely important to the hydrological cycle: they maintain river flows during the winter and reduce flood peaks during the high rainfall period (Bainbridge et al., 1991). The drier central to north-eastern parts of the Cape Folded Belt (Region E) and adjacent areas have a semi-succulent to succulent scrub type of vegetation which is ecologically extremely sensitive.

In the highland/scarp areas of Namibia, the vegetation on the slopes and crests of mountains in the arid south consists of scrub, including succulents and euphorbias, with grass and acacias (thorn trees) on the sandy soils in the valleys. As the rainfall increases in the north-central areas, this changes to acacia savanna.

The vegetation in the Angolan highlands and escarpment consists of hardwood forests and forest/grassland combinations due to the high rainfall and deep soils.

Mountain conservation areas provide protection to an extensive list of animal species. In eastern Lesotho, 248 species of vertebrates are found, including 31 species listed as endangered in the South African Red Data Books (Bourquin and Tlale, 1989). Up-to-date research has shown that 206 ecologically significant birds, of which 32 are endemic to southern Africa, occur in the Drakensberg Mountains (Little and Bainbridge, 1988). About 90 mammal species and 250 species of birds have been recorded in the Cape Folded Belt area (McMahon and Fraser, 1988). A reduction of wildlife species and their numbers has occurred in the recent past as a result of habitat changes caused by human use (Bainbridge et al., 1991).

Finally, one cultural resource which constitutes a rich heritage deserves major attention. Thousands of overhanging caves and rock shelters throughout the mountains of southern Africa contain Bushman (San) rock paintings. This is considered a heritage of international importance, both as a cultural treasure and as a source of archaeological information (Department of Environment Affairs, 1986). These paintings are concentrated in the Drakensberg/Maluti region, the southwestern Cape Folded Belt, and the Brandberg in Namibia. Many rock engravings are found in northern Namibia and in the Angolan highlands. Vandalism is causing irreparable damage to this heritage and warrants serious international concern. The preservation of these paintings and engravings is of particular importance since the Bushmen have been driven from all the mountains in the region. A small number of surviving Bushmen are presently living in semi-desert plains, where they have no opportunity to practise their art.

The potentials of land use and mountain economy

Land use in the South African mountains is diverse, whereas land use in the mountains and highlands of Namibia and Angola is less varied.

In the mountain areas of South Africa as a whole, at least 80 per cent of the population is involved in agriculture and related enterprises. Approximately the same proportion of the land area is utilized for agriculture. Population density is relatively low, with the exception of a few tribal areas.

In South Africa agriculture in the mountains consists almost exclusively of extensive livestock farming practised mainly by white commercial farmers. In high rainfall areas (Regions B, C and the eastern part of D in Figure 5.1) the low average temperature, shallow soils, steep slopes and rocky terrain do not favour cropping. In the drier north-eastern zone of the Cape Folded Belt, where semi-arid scrub vegetation is found (the north-eastern part of Region E and parts of Region D), angora goats for mohair production constitute the main type of livestock. Extensive sheep farming is practised in the western regions. The southern and western Cape Folded Belt mountains are virtually devoid of livestock. In the past the majority of farmers kept small herds of cattle and goats for their own consumption. A combination of deep colluvial soils on the pediments, favourable microclimates, and water from the mountains creates favourable conditions for successful farming on the foothills, pediment slopes, basins and intermontane valleys in high rainfall areas of the mountains of South Africa. Intensive high-income agriculture is practised on large commercial farms, including many company-owned estates, which may derive irrigation water from these mountains.

All the land in the mountains of Lesotho is considered unsuitable for cropping according to the USDA land capability classification system (Bainbridge et al., 1991). Nevertheless, crop farming is the most important agricultural activity and 15 per cent of the surface area is cultivated (Makhanya, 1979). At present this generates little income and fails to provide the population with its subsistence requirements. The remaining land is managed under a system of extensive communal grazing (Bainbridge et al., 1991).

In the highlands of Namibia extensive livestock farming, mainly with cattle, is virtually the only economic activity practised by commercial farmers on large units. The highland areas are of crucial importance during droughts because they provide the only means of sustenance to livestock (Sartorius von Bach, 1991; Schoeman, 1991; personal observation by one of the authors). The northernmost highlands are occupied by nomadic tribal livestock farmers.

The Angolan highlands have tremendous agricultural potential which has not been exploited since independence, when all commercial European farmers fled the country. The subsequent bush war over the last 16 years has caused further severe damage. At present 75 per cent of the population is involved in subsistence farming.

Nature conservation, tourism and recreation are important activities in all the mountain areas of South Africa, especially along the eastern escarpment and in the southwestern Cape Folded Belt. The beauty of the mountain peaks, indigenous forests and flowers, waterfalls and numerous special features contribute to this.

Two conservation areas in drier parts of South Africa warrant special mention. The first is the Mountain Zebra National Park, which was established to save the mountain zebra from extinction. The second is the Richtersveld Mountain Desert Park, which has recently been proclaimed. A unique feature is the combination of a conservation area and its use by nomadic Nama herdsmen presently living in the area.

The alpine zone of Lesotho has tremendous tourist potential, which is presently unexploited (Bainbridge et al., 1991). The Waterberg Nature Reserve is the only conservation area in the Namibian highlands. No information is available on nature conservation, tourism and recreation in the Angolan highlands, but it is believed that the bush war has rendered it non-existent.

Plantations of exotic trees, mainly *Pinus* and *Eucalyptus* species, cover about 1 million ha, 1 per cent of South Africa's surface.

Although economic activities in the mountains of South Africa are important, they are dwarfed by the impact of the mountains on economic activities outside the mountain regions. All the major mining, industrial and urban centres and irrigation schemes are largely or totally dependent on water from the mountains.

The Drakensberg/Maluti area (Region C in Figure 2.7) plays a key role in water supply. It supplies most of the water for the Johannesburg-Pretoria industrial area and the surrounding gold mines–the economic heartland of South Africa (see Figure 2.7). It also supplies the water for all the central irrigation areas around the Orange River. It is often necessary to transfer water from areas with abundant water to areas experiencing water shortages. Numerous dams and pipelines have been constructed for this purpose. Water transfer schemes across the main watersheds are also in progress (Department of Water Affairs, 1986). The Orange River has become the main source of water for irrigation in the Fish and Sundays rivers and a major source for the Port Elizabeth industrial area.

Erosion and degeneration of vegetation

In the absence of human impacts, mountain areas with high rainfall are inherently among the most erosion-resistant areas in South Africa. High rainfall promotes a dense grass sward and more advanced soil formation, resulting in more stable soils. The mountain areas of Lesotho are also inherently much more stable than the lowlands. Although the high-rainfall mountain regions are relatively robust environments, they deteriorate rapidly when subjected to unsympathetic land use practices (Bainbridge et al., 1991).

For example, changes in land use in the past century, caused by great increases in population, poverty, and inappropriate agricultural practices, have accelerated the process of soil erosion in most parts of South Africa. The environment was rendered unstable, and steep slopes and highly erosive rain have aggravated the serious erosion problem. During prolonged droughts the vegetative cover is destroyed and subsequent torrential rains strip away the bare soil. The same combination of factors has made Lesotho one of the most severely eroded countries in Africa (Makhanya, 1979). Because the natural recovery rate of soils in mountain areas is very slow, this damage is largely irreparable (Department of Environment Affairs, 1986).

Recent observations in Lesotho have indicated that several rivers that ran clear in the 1970s now show signs of increased suspended sediment loads. This indicates that most of the degradation in upstream catchment areas and wetlands has occurred in the past 10 to 15 years. In drier mountain areas, overstocking of sheep by commercial farmers has led to almost complete removal of the soil cover (Acocks, 1988). Sheep are short grazers and are much more destructive than an equivalent amount of cattle or goats.

Soil erosion in the Namibian highlands has not become a serious problem because farming on large units is extensive. According to the World Map of Human-induced Soil Degradation (Oldeman et al., 1990), the Angolan highlands are one of the most severely eroded areas in Africa.

The most serious effect of continuous accelerated erosion in the mountains is the impact on the hydrology of the region. Increased runoff and lower infiltration lead to a less stable water supply. Normal seasons become seasons of drought, water is restricted in towns and industries, and irrigation becomes a severe problem. Flash floods are more frequent and more intense. Soil erosion is aggravated by this increased flow. Sediment loads increase, leading to silting up of dams and reduction in their storage capacity (Department of Water Affairs, 1986). Silting up of ecologically or economically important estuaries is another detrimental result of increased sediment loads.

Besides soil erosion, reduction in basal cover and species degeneration are serious problems which have led to sharp reductions in the grazing capacities of the rangelands in the drier mountains and tribal areas of South Africa. Overstocking, incorrect livestock ratios and injudicious use of fire have been the main causes of these problems (Trollope and Coetzee, 1978).

Grassland has been invaded by arid bush vegetation where overgrazing by cattle and sheep has occurred. This is especially the case where goats have been eliminated from the livestock programme. Because goats are browsers, they keep bush encroachment in check. In their wild state the grasslands were maintained because the wild ungulates roaming these areas included a high proportion of browsers. Incorrect use of fire as a management tool has made a large contribution to rangeland and macchia degradation in the mountains of South Africa (Jordaan, 1987). Controlled burning is, however, essential for the maintenance of high-quality grasslands and healthy macchia vegetation (Granger, 1991; Jordaan, 1987).

The variety of invasive alien plant species is another important aspect of degradation in most mountain areas in South Africa, especially in regions with high rainfall. These plants are mostly exotic species introduced for use in timber plantations or as ornaments in domestic gardens. Maintenance of natural vegetation is considered the best way of ensuring a continued supply of high-quality water from the mountain catchments. The stream flow of water catchments is significantly reduced when the natural flora are replaced by invasive alien vegetation (Department of Environment Affairs, 1986). It has been estimated that water yield could be reduced by as much as 50 per cent if government funding for the eradication of alien species decreases in the future (Van Wilgen, 1991).

Afforestation, although beneficial in arresting soil degradation, has a major negative impact on runoff from mountain catchments. Hydrological surveys have shown that where plantations cover between 58 per cent and 100 per cent of a catchment area, the mean annual runoff is reduced by between 65 per cent and 90 per cent (Department of Water Affairs, 1986). This has serious implications for water supplies to towns, cities and industries.

Cultural, economic and political aspects of development

Traditional systems of land tenure and cultural and religious attitudes toward livestock contribute to land deterioration in tribal areas of South Africa as well as in the other three countries. These established systems are not easy to change, although this will be necessary in some cases. The tribal areas of South Africa generally have much higher agricultural potential than most of the rest of the country. In many cases, however, production is far below the subsistence level.

The resources of Lesotho are insufficient to provide a subsistence level of agriculture for the inhabitants of the mountains. The remainder of the country does not have the means to absorb a significant number of people from the highlands in order to make subsistence possible for a smaller mountain population. Hence, survival of communities and stabilization of the environment in Lesotho and the tribal areas of South Africa are dependent upon a healthy South African economy. Since international boycotts and disinvestment have caused a great deal of unemployment in South Africa, the struggle for survival of the rural population has put additional pressures on the environment.

In Namibia, the new government will have to be very realistic in its land re-allocation policies in arid to semi-arid mountain areas if it hopes to avert disastrous consequences. In Angola, the civil war has largely destroyed agriculture and massive international assistance will be required to rebuild the country (Erasmus, 1991).■

The threatened biodiversity of the mountains of Madagascar

A would-be attractive mountain system

The island of Madagascar can be considered a separate continent in virtually every respect. Separated from the African continent at least 60 million years ago during the Mesozoic period, it has developed its own flora and specific fauna, which today form a multiple set of ecosystems with immense biodiversity in the mountains. Madagascar is also culturally separate from the rest of Africa. The first human settlers probably arrived around 1000 AD from Southeast Asia. Ethnic intermixing took place with many peoples along the shores of India, Arabia and Africa. Madagascar has a total area of 580 000 km^2. Its highlands and mountains, where most agricultural development has taken place, occupy about 30 per cent of the island. Today, agriculture provides a livelihood for about 60 per cent of Madagascar's population of 12 million. As a consequence of the overuse of mountain resources, environmental problems threaten not only the island's biodiversity but also the long-term survival of its human population.

Geologically, Madagascar is composed of Pre-Cambriam rocks, Cretaceous sediments, and Tertiary volcanic eruptions which formed the high mountains on the top of the highlands. Except for recent volcanic soils, the fertility of highland soils is relatively low due to the extreme age of the surface relief. Figure 2.8 is a cross-sectional view of altitudinal features of the island as they extend more or less similarly from north to south. To the east, an area of hilly terrain and escarpment up to about 900 m is partly covered by dense tropical forest due to the extreme relief, heavy rainfall, and high temperatures. Deforestation, a consequence of shifting cultivation, is encroaching on the region at an accelerating rate. A further escarpment, less forested due to human land use practices, rises to the central highlands, which are practically devoid of natural forests and situated at an altitude of about 1 600 m, with peaks as high as 2 880 m. To the west, there is a gradual descent and a drier climate extending to the west coast, with intermediate hilly terrain that currently consists of regularly burned grassland and patches of natural

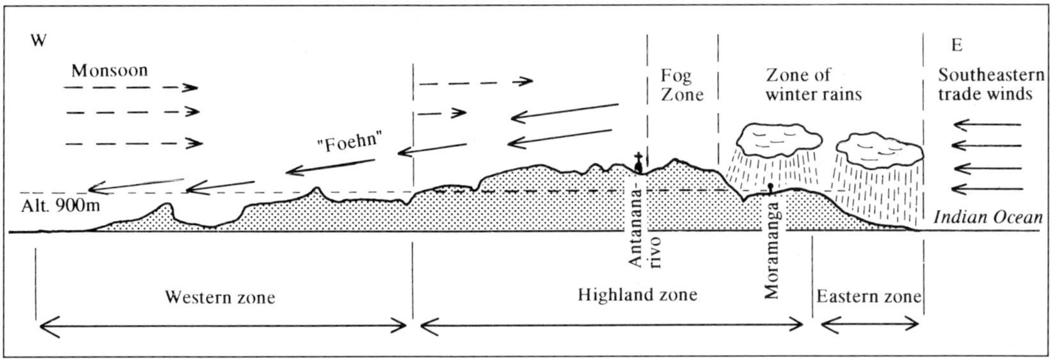

Figure 2.8: *Cross-section of Madagascar at 19° South latitude, indicating climatic and relief zones*

Table 2.3: *Land cover distribution in Madagascar.* Source: RDM, 1988, with some adjustments and personal estimations

Land cover type	All of Madagascar (area in km²)	All of Madagascar (area in per cent)	Highlands alone (in km²)
Cultivated land	52 000	9	40 000
Pasture land	336 000	58	100 000
Forest	122 000	21	10 000
Rivers and lakes	12 000	2	5 000
Rocky areas	29 000	5	15 000
Infrastructure (roads, towns, villages)	29 000	5	10 000
Total	580 000	100	180 000

forests along the coastal areas. The western part of the island contains large watersheds whose alluvial plains can potentially be used for crop cultivation.

The central highlands are characterized by the predominance of steep slopes and intermediate swampy areas that were developed into irrigation systems for rice cultivation centuries ago. This is where the cultural centre of Madagascar and its capital, Antananarivo, emerged. Rather low temperatures give the highlands a favourable climate with a rainy season from November to March and about 1 500 mm of rainfall annually. Despite the modern industrialization which accompanied French colonization in the 20th century, subsistence agricultural practices still dominate, and no agricultural products are produced for export. Due to overpopulation in the highlands, much of the workforce is migrating towards the coast, while primary products and industrial goods are being imported from coastal areas.

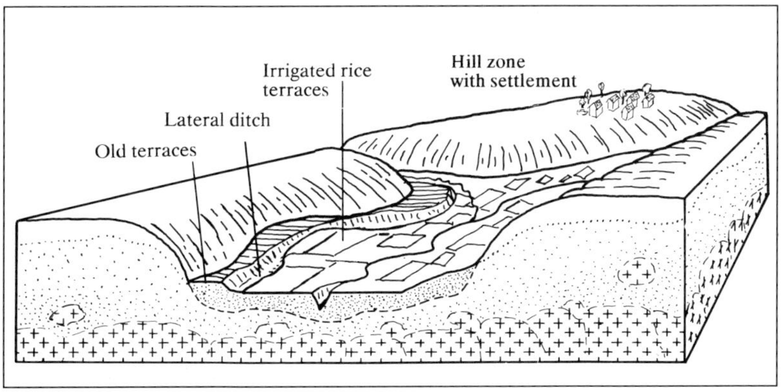

Figure 2.9: *Diagram of a typical rice-producing environment in Madagascar's central highlands*

Primary tropical forests are threatened and replaced by secondary and degraded vegetation systems wherever shifting cultivation is intensified and extended–near Beforona, Madagascar, at 700 m June 1987

Specific land-use problems in the island's highlands

A distribution of land use in Madagascar is given in Table 2.3. The proportions in the highlands and mountains are estimated in order to give an idea of the land cover distribution there.

Cultivation in the highlands is predominantly on valley floors, where irrigated rice terraces cover much of the surface. Problems relating to soil fertility, rice varieties and water management prevent agricultural production from being sufficient to feed the growing population. Rainfed terraces and cultivated slopes are utilized to produce manioc, sweet potatoes, maize and peanuts. Even very steep slopes are used in this way and it is estimated that today almost 50 per cent of the agricultural production is on slopes. Figure 2.9 illustrates such a situation, where the hilltops are little used except for grazing livestock. The production of horticultural crops in gardens is an additional option favoured by the temperate climate of the highlands.

Forest cover in the highlands is very small. For example, in the province of Antananarivo, it is only about 3 per cent of the surface area. Although dense forests mixed with types of secondary forest can be found on steep escarpments along the eastern coast, shifting cultivation, the extension of agriculture and the growing need for fuelwood are continuously diminishing these last reserves of Madagascar's biodiversity. Although reafforestation is badly needed, projects initiated during the colonial period have shown little success. Major problems faced by local land users are a lack of seedlings, bush fires that destroy newly planted trees, security of land ownership, and lack of training. About 10 per cent of the total area in the highlands could be more intensively used for agriculture if major constraints due to relief, questions of soil fertility, and accessibility could be overcome.

The highlands are particularly susceptible to bush fires. The hills are burned annually or biannually to aid the growth of new grasses at the onset of the rainy season, to clear hills for agricultural cultivation, and to clear watersheds for increased runoff into irrigated areas. There are also wild fires and fires set to demonstrate opposition to political leaders and the government. Preserving the biodiversity of natural ecosystems distributed throughout the steep escarpment zones will require an immense development effort to halt degradation.

Degradation of the economy and natural resources

Despite Madagascar's large surface area, there is considerable pressure on cultivated land to feed its 12 million inhabitants. Production on potentially fertile land must be increased and pressure on marginal lands reduced. As long as subsistence agriculture dominates, there will be virtually no crop designed for export and the potential for developing livestock will be limited. Land inheritance traditions make cultivated plots more fragmented and provoke emigration to coastal areas. Structural adjustment programmes since the mid-1980s have led to continuing impoverishment among the rural poor, and, together with other factors, caused political turmoil in 1991.

Physical, chemical, biological and hydrological degradation can be observed on most agricultural lands in the highlands. These forms of degradation continuously reduce agricultural production, make restitution more difficult, and force farmers to emigrate in order to find new virgin land and places to cultivate irrigated rice. For example, physical degradation involves soil erosion and accumulation. The landscape appears red almost everywhere when flying over Madagascar. Rivers are full of sediment, testifying to the immense loss of soil.

Observations on test plots have shown that soil loss on 90 per cent of the highlands is rather low, between 0 and 3 t/ha/yr. Erosion is observed, especially after bush fires, but stability is rapidly restored when vegetation recovers. Cultivated land is more sensitive to erosion; losses of 20-50 t/ha/yr and even as high as 150 t/ha have been observed. Table 2.4 gives an overview of soil loss estimates made for the highlands. The threatening Lavaka, i.e. large-scale gullies, account for only a small portion of the total soil loss in Madagascar.

Chemical and biological degradation are equally serious, particularly on burned pastures and cultivated land. Great amounts of nitrogen, phosphate, potassium and calcium are lost annually from burned pasture land (200 000 km^2). Immense amounts of fertilizer would be needed to restore these losses and to improve forage crops, although livestock does not play the economic role it once did. Actual fertilizer inputs are at present much lower than the amounts that would be required to replace the losses.

Biological degradation, often not recognized, threatens the destruction of entire species which are almost all endemic to Madagascar. These include forest and pasture species as well as wild animals. Constraints in forestry include having to bring firewood to the capital from more than 140 km away. There is also hydrological degradation, with concentrated runoff from degraded slopes which leads to flooding, while very little water is received downstream during the dry season. According to test plot measurements, runoff could be reduced by a factor of six through changes in land use involving dense vegetation cover.

Elements of a development strategy

Because of serious degradation in the highlands, development at the present low level of technology has reached the limits of the region's capacity. Further activity must include development in the coastal regions as a complement to strategic planning in the highlands. This planning must include increased production of perennial crops as an alternative to annual crops, a strengthening of local institutions and organizations, institutional support of local organizations, an integration of markets, and a development process which is adapted to the potentials of the different mountain ecosystems in Madagascar.

Water management, soil fertility and rice varieties must be improved to intensify production on irrigated rice terraces. Perennial cropping on large grassland areas could include the planting of trees that produce commercial and industrial products. Local cooperation among farmers has shown that production can be increased while natural resources are stabilized and conserved. Compost is a means of increasing agricultural production and has been promoted by non-governmental organizations, whose work must be given more support in the future. Transport networks

Table 2.4: *Annual soil loss in different land use practices in the Malagasy highlands, from test plots.* Source: Rakotomanana (various reports)

Land use type	Surface area (in km^2)	Mean soil loss (in t/km^2)	Total soil loss (million tons)
Non-cultivated land	210 000	100	21
Cultivated land	20 000	3 000	60
Lavaka	100	20 000	2

Sustainable use of land and soil resources is impossible as long as immense gullies, called Lavakas, threaten rice fields with sedimentation problems–March 1988 near Ambatofozy, Madagascar

and marketing systems must be improved throughout the country to guarantee a steady flow of goods between the coastal regions and mountain and highland areas.

Through conservation and development it should be possible to secure agricultural production for the medium term without further degrading and threatening biodiversity. Specific production systems should concentrate on horticulture, tree planting and upbringing, agroforestry technology, livestock and milk production, commercial forestry, and small-scale animal husbandry. In conservation, three levels of interaction have to be considered. First, conservation structures must be developed and propagated at the farm level for use by farmers. Second, at the watershed level, water sources and their significance for water conservation must be identified, development zones established, and all conservation needs met. Third, at the level involving large river basins, the immense threat of bush and grass fires will have to be controlled.

In general, communities must be given more responsibility as well as training in order to implement programmes such as protection work in agroforestry, etc. Certain areas with natural ecosystems will have to be safeguarded to guarantee that the country's biological diversity will be protected.

Prerequisites for sustainable development

Since it is man who promotes development, man must be the primary focus of development efforts. A family planning programme must be implemented to reduce pressure on the land. If population doubles within the next 25 years, all cultivable land in Madagascar will be in use before the year 2015. Simultaneously, a programme of support for people emigrating from the central highlands will be indispensable.

Land ownership and allocation are important problems in the mountains and highlands of Madagascar. With few plots now allocated to farmers and most held by the government, the population will not feel responsible for improving the land on their own. Legislation on land management must be adopted and power must be shifted to communities to enable them to manage their land. Institutional support is equally important. This concerns research, extension, education, and communal development. Inter-regional exchanges of knowledge and goods will be necessary in all directions.

Considering the low economic status of Madagascar and its development problems, international cooperation will be indispensable in finding appropriate solutions. International support should be directed at the real needs of a region, and include knowledge of how to implement land use systems compatible with the land. Sustainable development can only be achieved if applied research and cooperation are secured at every level.■

The attraction of mountains as a cause of environmental problems in Uganda

The uniqueness and importance of mountains

Mountains and highlands in Uganda have been defined as land at altitudes of 1 500 m and above (Bagoora, 1988). This land comprises about 11 per cent, or 21 000 km^2, of the total area of Uganda, and can be divided into southwestern, western, eastern and northeastern mountains and highlands (Figure 2.10). Geomorphologically, these mountains and highlands resulted from tectonic and volcanic activities which occurred in association with the formation of the East African Rift Valley. Although relatively small in proportion, this area is unique and important for the following reasons:

❑ Mountains and highlands in the eastern half of the African continent, between 10°S and 17°N, form the roof of the continent. Numerous streams and rivers, some of which are glacier-fed, flow from these mountains and highlands and are the principal sources of water for people both in the mountains and in the surrounding plateaus and plains. For example, the White Nile derives its water from a wide catchment, extending as far south as the Central African mountains and highlands in the southwestern part of Uganda. Mount Ruwenzori in the west is an important watershed of the Nile.

❑ The mountains and highlands of Uganda have a significant spiritual status. From time immemorial they have been perceived by societies in Uganda as the home of their gods. The highest peak, Mt. Elgon, in the eastern part of the country, is known locally as Masaba, an ancestor of the Gisu people.

Figure 2.10: Ugandan mountains and highlands

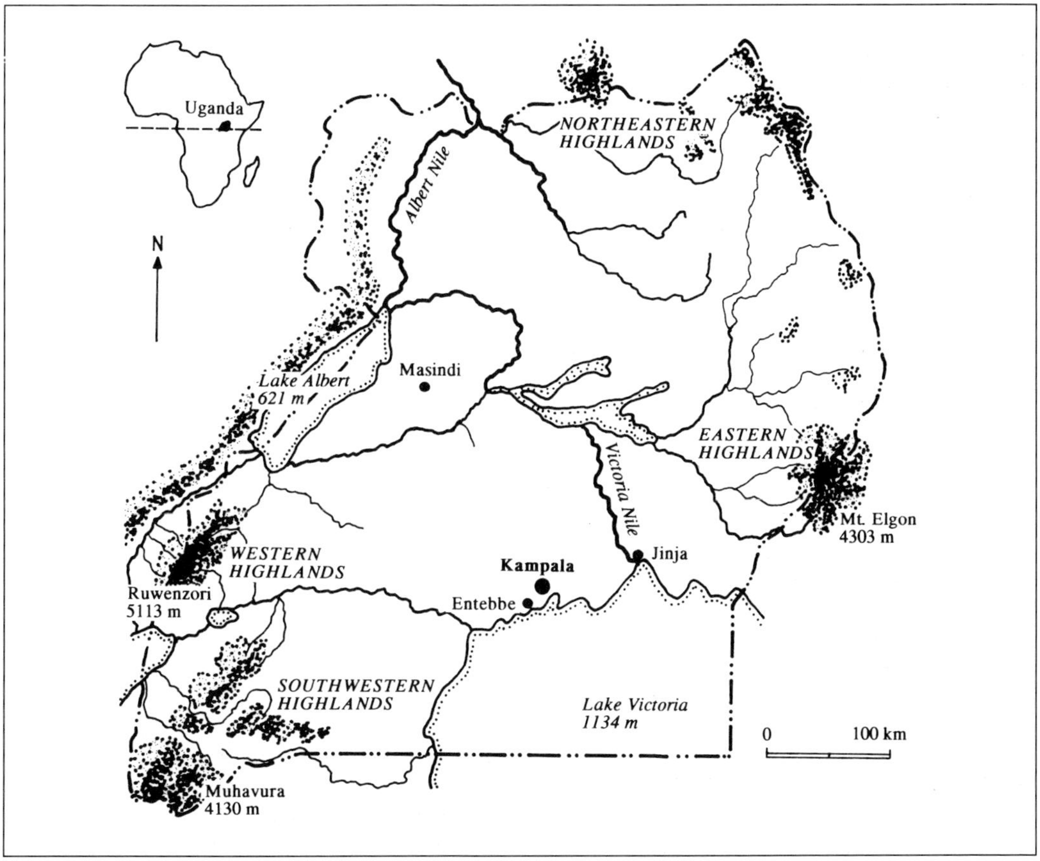

❑ The mountains and highlands are themselves a unique environment. They are located near the equator, yet because of altitudinal effects they are generally cool and have reliable rainfall, which is necessary for the agricultural economy of the area. Mt. Ruwenzori, towering to an altitude of 5 109 m, is capped by glaciers and ice fields which cover a total area of about 5 km^2.

❑ For physical, historical and cultural reasons, some of the most densely populated areas in the country are found in the highlands. All in all, these areas contain about 34.4 per cent of the population, a significant proportion of Uganda's total population of about 16 million people.

❑ Mountains and highlands are naturally fragile and therefore require proper management if there is to be sustainable use of their important natural and cultural resources.

The attraction of mountains

The mountains and highlands of Uganda are occupied by different ethnic groups of Bantu stock. They have lived in this environment for many centuries, having migrated during the general Bantu migration from West and Central Africa over a long period between AD 1200 and 1800.

High population density despite the difficult terrain is a typical feature of Ugandan mountains and highlands. Why is this so? There are a number of possible reasons. First, as a result of many inter-tribal wars over settlement of land in the more favourable environment on the plains and plateaus, the weaker tribes took refuge in the highlands and the mountains. Others simply stayed in the mountains and highlands to avoid prevailing troubles in the surrounding lowlands. Second, the continued occupation of this highland environment can be explained in terms of pleasant climate and fertile soils, which is true in the case of the southwestern and eastern mountains and highlands. Owing to the influence of altitude, the climate is generally cooler, making the area less prone to the diseases common in the surrounding tropical lowlands. The soils in these highlands are either of volcanic origin or associated with volcanism. They are of medium and high productivity and are therefore capable of supporting a rich peasant agriculture.

Land use and the economy

The main forms of traditional land use are mixed farming and grazing; forest and game reserves were added at a later stage of development. Table 2.5 shows the proportion of land used for each of these purposes. Land use is intensive in the mountains and highlands, and as population pressure increases, land shortage becomes a major problem. This causes occasional migration to the lowlands, although migration does not reduce population density in the highlands. The customary sharing of land among individual members of families over generations has produced one of the word's most fragmented systems of land use. In general, marginal land is used for grazing, while crops are grown on more gentle land.

Forest and game reserves, the result of the government's policy of protecting the upper slopes of mountains and highlands, constitute another form of land use. The aims are to protect water catchments, preserve wildlife, and avoid potential environmental catastrophes. Of particular importance is the preservation of biological diversity and of endangered species. The reserves contain a variety of mountain and highland species of flora and fauna, and are consequently extremely important for scientific research, especially in tropical medicinal plants. Flora and fauna elsewhere in Uganda show less diversity and greater degradation.

In addition, the reserves represent great potential for wildlife. The most important reserves are the Bwindi ("Impenetrable") Forest Reserve and gorilla game reserves in the southwest. Of the total world gorilla population of approximately 600, it is estimated that 400-500 live in this natural environment in Central Africa. A large proportion of these rare animals live on the Uganda side of the border. But, as in the southwestern part of the country, the present status of wildlife is not known because no detailed surveys have been made to date.

The economy of the mountains and highlands of Uganda is basically mixed peasant farming. The farming systems in this environment are primarily influenced by altitude and relief. The growing of annual food crops is the main activity in the southwestern, western and eastern areas. The main annual crops are sorghum, maize,

Table 2.5: Land cover and land use distribution in the Ugandan mountains.
Source: UNEP, 1988; MIAF, 1989

Area of Uganda:	240 000 km ^{2}	(100 per cent)
Mountains and highlands:	21 000 km ^{2}	(9 per cent)
Land use types in the highlands:		
All highlands	21 000 km ^{2}	(100 per cent)
Crops:	7 500 km ^{2}	(36 per cent)
Grazing:	10 000 km ^{2}	(48 per cent)
Forest/reserves:	3 500 km ^{2}	(17 per cent)

potatoes and vegetables, with green banana as a perennial crop. Domestic animals found here range from poultry to cattle. In the northeastern mountains, cattle keeping has traditionally been dominant. Animal keeping represents different values to different societies in the mountains and highlands. Smaller animals are kept mainly to provide animal protein in the diet, while cattle are primarily of cultural value.

Often there is a surplus of farm products which are sold to purchase basic necessities such as soap, salt and clothing. Keeping animals requires more land than cultivating crops. Consequently, as population pressure on land increases, there is a tendency for animal keeping to give way to crop cultivation. The number of animals, especially cattle, is gradually declining.

Wildlife, if well utilized, can provide an additional source of government income. For example, the rare animal species in the southwest (Bwindi and Mgahinga game reserves) are a great tourist attraction, although plans to take advantage of this have not yet been put into effect. In Rwanda, which shares the Mgahinga mountain reserves, plans have already been implemented and it is reported that tourists are charged US$170 per person for one hour to see the gorillas. This brings in about US $6-8 million a year (*New Vision,* 13 August 1990). The same potential is being exploited by Zaire. Forest reserves provide additional income from timber and fuelwood harvesting, but this is only sustainable under proper governmental supervision.

Environmental problems

The main environmental problem is accelerated soil erosion. Since the environment itself is very fragile, the continual increase of population pressure on the land, among other factors, has led to a number of adverse effects. Overcultivation is not only reducing the soil's productivity but also destroying its structure, making it more prone to erosion (Bagoora, 1988).

Declining productivity has increased the demand for arable land, especially in view of the growing population. Since all the good land has been used up, additional land can only be obtained by encroaching on more fragile steep slopes, including the forest and game reserves. This has provoked a more pronounced erosion process. The soils in the mountains and highlands are rapidly degrading, while population pressure on the land is increasing just as rapidly.

Figure 2.11 shows the population increase in the recent past and trends projected for the near future. The extremely high rates resemble urban situations. Such population pressure certainly cannot be contained in this fragile environment. Although other dynamic demographic factors may operate to modify these projections, high densities must be expected in the future. If the expected pressure on land continues, it will only be contained by the active incorporation of efficient land husbandry and conservation practices in farming systems, supplemented by the adoption of alternative economic activities and family planning policies.

Currently, additional land is being acquired through the reclamation of swamps, particularly in the southwestern highlands. While it is true that soils in these swamps are sometimes fertile, this practice provides only a temporary solution because the amount of swampland is very small. Unfortunately, reclamation appears to be producing other forms of environmental degradation, undermining the micro-climatic and hydrological potential of the highlands and wetland biodiversity in particular (Bagoora, 1989).

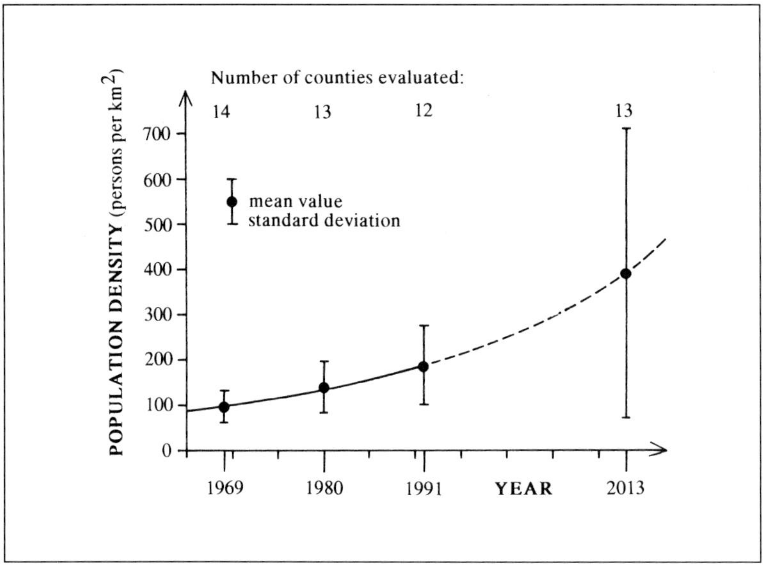

Figure 2.11: Trends in population density for selected mountain counties in Uganda, extrapolated to 2013. Sources: Langlands, 1974; MPED, 1982; MPED, 1991; with the author's projections for the year 2013

Forests and game reserves are under tremendous pressure of encroachment as the shortage of land becomes more acute in the surrounding areas. Such encroachment on the forests and game reserves and their subsequent diminution would certainly be disastrous.

Potentials

The natural resources in the mountains and highlands represent an immense potential, provided that sustainable use is achieved. To accomplish this, deeply rooted problems, as well as people's ideas, indigenous knowledge, and spontaneous responses must all be understood, respected, and dealt with.

Examples of sustainable techniques adopted so far include land husbandry, emphasis on green manure application, improved tilling methods, and the implementation of soil and water conservation structures such as bunding and terracing with biological or mechanical techniques. Agroforestry practices and the creation of community forests and woodlots both provide strong support for these endeavours. Most important, a policy of sustainable use of resources in the highlands will have to begin by addressing the question of poverty. As long as people have a precarious daily existence, struggling to survive on the basis of low productivity on increasingly marginal and low acreage farms, they will not see conservation programmes as a priority. This may partly explain the decline of conservation practices in the highland areas of Uganda. Poverty is one direct cause of degradation, while negligence and declining interest in conservation are merely symptoms.

Exploitation of natural resources will have to be guided by public policy. There is a need to strike a rational balance between land use for farming and other profitable activities which use local resources like tin and gold. Furthermore, we recommend an exploration of truly alternative activities, such as the creation of small-scale industries in degraded areas, as an additional vital prescription. Mountain and highland industries might include agro-based or small-scale cottage industries using forestry and swamp products, or industries aimed at supplementing the productive potential of agriculture and food processing. ■

References

ABDELLATIF BENCHERIFA. 1990. Demography and cultural ecology of the Atlas mountains of Morocco: Some new hypotheses. Messerli, B. and Hurni, H. (eds). *African Mountains and Highlands: Problems and Perspectives.* Marceline, Missouri (USA): African Mountains Association. 369-377.

ACOCKS, J.P.H. 1988. Veld types of South Africa (3rd edn.). *Memoirs of the Botanical Survey of South Africa No. 57.* Pretoria: Botanical Research Institute.

BAGOORA, F.D.K. 1988. Soil erosion and mass wasting risk in the highland area of Uganda. *Mountain Research and Development,* Vol. 8 No. 2/3. 173-182.

BAGOORA, F.D.K. 1989. A preliminary investigation into the consequences of inadequate conservation policies on the steep slopes of the Rukiga Highlands, southwestern Uganda. In Thomas, D.B. et al (eds). *Soil and Water Conservation in Kenya.* Dept. of Agricultural Engineering, University of Nairobi, and SIDA. 496-508.

BAINBRIDGE, W.R., Motsamai, B., and Weaver, L.C. (eds). 1991. *Report of the Drakensberg/Maluti Conservation Programme.* Natal Parks Board, Pietermaritzburg. 55 pp.

BARBER, R., 1984. An assessment of the dominant soil degradation processes in the Ethiopian highlands. *Ethiopian Highlands Reclamation Study.* Addis Ababa and FAO. 53 pp. and 12 maps.

BOURQUIN, O., and TLALE, S. 1989. *The Drakensberg/Maluti Mountain Catchment Conservation Programme: Faunal Assessment Project.* Natal Parks Board, Pietermaritzburg. 69 pp.

BRAUN, H.M.H, SOMBROEK, W.G., and VAN DER POUW, B.J.A. 1982. *Exploratory Soil Map and Agro-climatic Zone Map of Kenya.* Nairobi.

Department of Environment Affairs. 1986. *Drakensberg State Forests.* Pietermaritzburg: Department of Environment Affairs. 112 pp.

Department of Water Affairs. 1986. *Management of the Water Resources of the Republic of South Africa.* Pretoria: Department of Water Affairs. 420 pp.

ELLIS, F. 1988. *Gronde van die Karoo. ("Soils of the Karoo").* Ph.D. thesis, Univ. Stellenbosch.

ERASMUS, J.F. 1991. Personal communication. Dept. of Soil Science, Potchefstroom University for CHE.

GRANGER, J.E. 1991. *Interim Report on the Findings of a Plant Ecological Survey of the Cathkin Key Area, Northern Sector of the Drakensberg.* University of Natal, Pietermaritzburg.

GOK. 1989. Government of Kenya: *National Development Plan for the Period 1989 to 1993.* Nairobi.

HENRICKSEN, B., SULTAN TILIMO, ROSS, S., WIJNTJE-BRUGGEMAN, H.Y., and FITSSUM FITWE. 1983. *Provisional Soil Depth Map of Ethiopia.* Land Use Planning and Regulatory Department, Ministry of Agriculture, Addis Ababa.

HURNI, H. 1988. Ecological issues in the creation of famines in Ethiopia. *National Conference on a Disaster Prevention and Preparedness Strategy for Ethiopia,* Addis Ababa.

HURNI, H. 1990. Degradation and conservation of the soil resources in the Ethiopian highlands. Messerli, B. and Hurni, H. (eds). *African Mountains and Highlands: Problems and Perspectives.* Marceline, Missouri (USA): African Mountains Association. 51-64.

IUCN 1990. *Ethiopia, National Conservation Strategy. Phase I Report.* 164 pp.

JORDAAN, J.V. 1987. Multiple-use in Fynbos Mountain Catchment Areas. *Directorate of Conservation Forestry,* Pretoria. 59 pp.

KOHLER, T. 1976. *Wald und Waldnutzung in Kenya.* Institute of Geography, University of Berne, Berne, Switzerland.

LANGLANDS, B.W., 1974. Uganda in maps. Parts 2-3, the Environment. *Preliminary Non-Edition Occasional Paper,* Department of Geography, Makerere University, Kampala.

LIEBENBERG, D. 1976. *Mountain Areas of South Africa. Mountain Environments: Conference proceedings 2nd Council for the Habitat,* Johannesburg. 12-35.

LITTLE, R.M., and BAINBRIDGE, W.R., 1988. Avifaunal conservation in the State Forests of the Natal Drakensberg. *Proc. VI Pan-Afr. Orn. Cong.* 263-280.

MCMAHON, L., and FRASER, M. 1988. *A Fynbos Year.* Cape Town: David Philip. 162 pp.

MACVICAR, C.N. 1973. *Generalized Soil Map of South Africa.* Pretoria: SIRI.

MAKHANYA, E.M. 1979. *The Use of Land Resources for Agriculture in Lesotho.* National University of Lesotho. 208 pp.

MIAF. 1989. *Agricultural Sector Survey 1986-1987.* Ministry of Industry and Fisheries, Planning Department, Government of Uganda. EEC/WFP Development Committee, 2nd edn., July 1989.

MPED, 1982. Ministry of Planning and Economic Development: *Report on the 1980 Population Census, Volume 1. The Provisional Results by Administrative Areas.* Census Office, Kampala.

MPED, 1991. Ministry of Planning and Economic Development: *Provisional Results of the 1991 Population and Housing Census.* Statistics Department, Kampala.

MUIRURI, W. 1977. *The Aberdare Ecosystem: Its Bio-economic Functions, Interactions and Problems of Management.* Ph.D. thesis, University of Nairobi, Nairobi.

Ochieng', W.R. 1985. *A History of Kenya.* London and Basingstoke: Macmillan.

OJANY, F.F., et al. (ed). 1990. Mount Kenya area: Differentiation and dynamics of a tropical mountain ecosystem. *African Studies Series A8.* Berne: Geographica Bernensia.

OLDEMAN, L.R., VAN BAREN, H., and SOMBROEK, W.G. 1990. *World Map of Human-induced Soil Degradation.* Wageningen: ISRIC.

RAKOTOMANANA, J.-L. 1975. *La Conservation des sols à Madagascar.* Antananarivo: FOFIFA-Département de Recherches Forestières et Piscicoles, B.P. 904. 9 pp.

RAKOTOMANANA, J.-L. 1987. *Climat, érosion et techniques culturales sur les hauts-plateaux de Madagascar.* Antananarivo: FOFIFA-Département de Recherches Forestières et Piscicoles, B.P. 904. 18 pp.

RDM. 1988. Republique Démocratique de Madagascar, Plan d'action environnemental. Vol. 1, Document de synthèse générale et propositions d'orientations. Version préliminaire.

SARTORIUS VON BACH, H.J. 1991. Personal communication. Dept. of Agricultural Economics, University of Pretoria.

SCHOEMAN, S.J. 1991. Personal communication. Dept. of Animal Science, University of Pretoria.

The New Vision, 13 August, 1990.

TROLLOPE, W.S.W., and COETZEE, P.G.F. 1978. Vegetation and veld management. Chapter 5 in *The Agricultural Potential of the Ciskei–Amended Report* (Ed. M.C.Laker). University of Fort Hare, Alice.

UNDP/FAO/LUPRD. 1984. *Land Use, Production Regions and Farming Systems Inventory.* Technical Report 3. Rome and Addis Ababa.

UNEP. 1988. Strategic Resources Planning in Uganda, Natural Resources and Environment in Uganda, *Strategies for Environmental Management,* including Vol. III: *Forests.*

Van WILGEN, B.W. 1991. Water catchment areas in the fynbos: what of the future? *Veld and Flora Vol. 77 (2).* 34-35.

WASWC. 1990. World Association of Soil and Water Conservation: *A Report on the Sixth Conference of the International Soil Conservation Organization in Africa.* WASWC Newsletter, Vol. 6, No. 1, pp. 2-4.

WINIGER, M. 1988. *Marokko. Feldstudienlager 1988.* Geographisches Institut der Universität Bern, 435 pp.

3

The Alps:

an ecosystem in transformation

The Alps seen from the Jura to the north. The name "Alps" refers to the high mountains, the hill regions and the intermontane valleys

Introduction

What are the Alps?

The Alps are the highest and most extensive mountain system in Europe. They comprise a total area of 240 000 km², extend to a length of 1 000 km, and are between 130 and 250 km wide. Many summits rise above 4 000 m (the highest of which is Mont Blanc at 4 807 m), while most mountain groups in the Alps exceed 3 000 m and have snow- and ice-capped peaks. Only in the eastern part of the eastern Alps (somewhat east of the line connecting Linz and Klagenfurt) is their elevation less pronounced, giving them the character of mountains of moderate height.

Typical of folded mountains of the Tertiary period, the Alps are composed of greatly extended parallel mountain chains. In the western part of the western Alps, between the Mediterranean and Lake Geneva, these chains are curved, while in the rest of the Alps they are almost straight, running from east to west. They include very large intermontane valleys and basins in numerous places (the largest of which is the Klagenfurt Basin in Austria), which are nonetheless considered part of the Alps for natural and cultural reasons. When we speak of "the Alps", we basically mean not only high mountains per se but the entire mountain region, including deep valley floors and hill regions.

It is not difficult to distinguish the Alps, since they rise steeply above the surrounding lowlands practically everywhere. Only where they merge with the Apennines and the Dinaric Alps is there any difficulty in making a distinction. In earlier times, the borders of the Alps were determined according to geological and geomorphological features. But a new criterion has been adopted since the Second World War. In all Alpine countries so-called mountain regions have been designated by law in conjunction with specific mountain policies. These regions are distinguished on the basis of natural (for the most part topographical) and socio-economic criteria. The result is a new socio-economic definition of the Alpine area which is becoming increasingly important. This chapter is based on this new definition of the Alps.

What do mountains mean to people?

The Alps are among the earliest-settled regions of Europe and have never played a solitary "backwoods" role. But the image of the Alps in the mind of the European public has always been and continues to be formed by European cities. The viewpoint of those who live in the mountains contributes almost nothing to this image.

Figure 3.1: *The Alps, showing mountain groups*
Source: Bätzing 1984

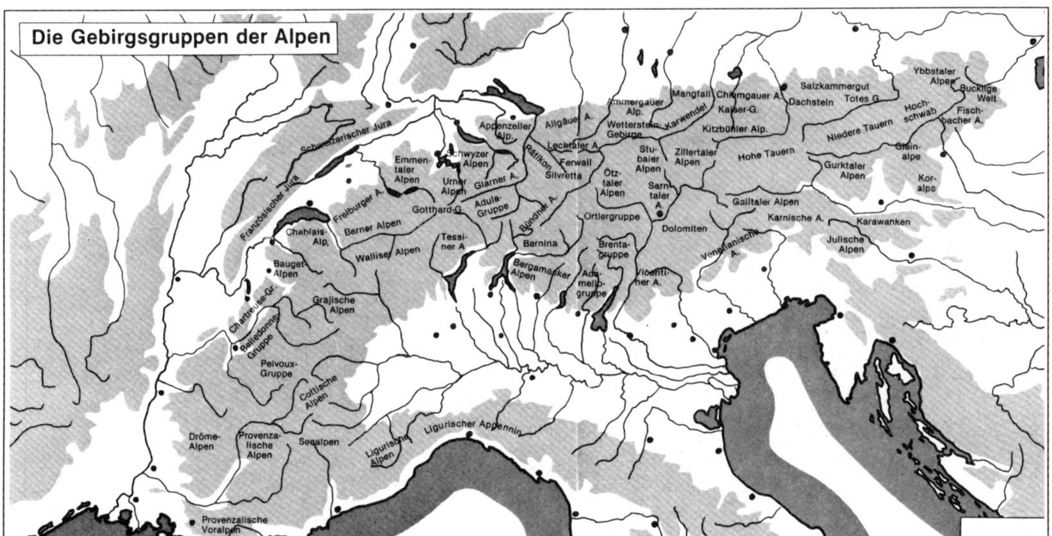

Three different images of the Alps have predominated throughout European history:

a) The Alps as "montes horribiles"

This image of mountains as frightening was shaped by the first highly advanced European cultures, the Greeks and Romans, and established in Roman literature around the time of the birth of Christ. It continued to influence the European view of the Alps until well into the 18th century. Scholars, traders, pilgrims and travellers who traversed the Alps quoted portions of Roman writings on the mountains verbatim.

The Alps were long seen as a hazard to travellers

This image characterized the Alps as a region hostile to man and a source of fear and terror. Should one be forced to cross them, the mountains were to be abandoned as quickly as possible thereafter. That such a hostile region was actually inhabited by human beings was perceived only peripherally; this fact remained inexplicable and was of no interest. The Alps formed the northern border of Mediterranean Europe; behind them began the unknown regions of "barbarian" Europe in which there was little interest. For central and northern Europe, on the other hand, the Alps represented the final barrier to be surmounted before reaching the "promised land" which was the "cradle of European civilization". Thus the motivation to make the dangerous crossing over the Alps was greater in the north than in the south.

b) The Alps as an idyllic world

This was a completely new image which arose during the age of European industrialization and was first developed by poets, writers and painters (the most important of whom was Jean-Jacques Rousseau) before it was widely popularized. Its origins were already apparent in the 16th and 17th centuries, but it only became widespread around 1780. This occurred first in England, the birthplace of industrialism. This view of the Alps

Summer tourism's simple pleasures: hot sun, a high walk, a famous view and a cold drink. Nevertheless, winter tourism's more mechanized pleasures earn twice as much

enjoyed its first great vogue during the age of Romanticism and achieved a second peak of popularity during the so-called Belle Epoque (1880-1914), when Alpine tourism was first beginning to flourish. This image has continued to influence the European perception of the Alps virtually to the present day and provided a spiritual background for mass tourism in the Alps after 1950.

Implicit in this image is a view of the Alps as a paradise which existed prior to the Fall of man–a world in which there was still complete harmony between man and nature and in which man partook of nature without destroying or exploiting it. It portrayed Alpine residents as "noble savages": ideal, virtuous human beings living in free, pristine democratic conditions. Somewhat later, non-European cultures (North American Indians and South Sea islanders) were also described in terms of this image.

Although the idyllic image owes something to certain traditions in Graeco-Roman culture, European industrialization was fundamental in shaping it. For while nature was being carelessly exploited and destroyed by industrial processes of production on the one hand, there arose on the other hand a need to idealize nature and derive aesthetic enjoyment from the beauty of the natural landscape.

c) *The Alps as a region of natural disasters and major environmental destruction*

This is the most recent image of the Alps. It has been developing gradually since the end of the 1970s, when it was first recognized in Europe that Alpine environmental problems were continuing to grow in scale. This new image has been primarily shaped by journalists in the mass media (newspapers, magazines and television) who tend to make sweeping judgements in their indictments of environmental destruction. The picture of the Alps as a "disaster region" therefore becomes more extreme the further away one is from the mountains.

Ecological problems relating to ski slopes, the impacts of mass tourism (oversettlement, air pollution), traffic and forest decline form the basis of this image. The main focus is characteristically on the problems of overdeveloped Alpine regions while the problems of remote, economically weak regions in the Alps are not recognized at all. In this perspective the Alps are seen as a unique, disaster-prone region in which there is such a marked increase in avalanches, floods, mud flows and landslides resulting from human destruction of the environment that the survival of every individual is threatened.

These three images of the Alps were developed in European urban centres. Although partially accurate, they also contain clichés or present a distorted picture which does not correspond to reality. The Alps are a region of striking diversity and great internal variety. Nature and culture, indigenous economic structure and the influence of outside capital, environmental protection and environmental destruction, and local tradition and the infiltration of post-modern values all interact and penetrate in so many ways that simple, all-inclusive statements are inadequate to describe the situation. ■

Romantic 18th century view of Alpine life

Figure 3.2: *Relief map of the Alps. The diversity of massifs throughout the Alps can be seen clearly here. The map stops at the points where the Alps merge with the Apennines at the Colle di Cadibona and with the Dinaric Alps south of Ljubljana, since these regions are not considered part of the Alps. Actual Alpine relief does not have boundaries as clear as those suggested by this map.*
Source: Veyret, 1967

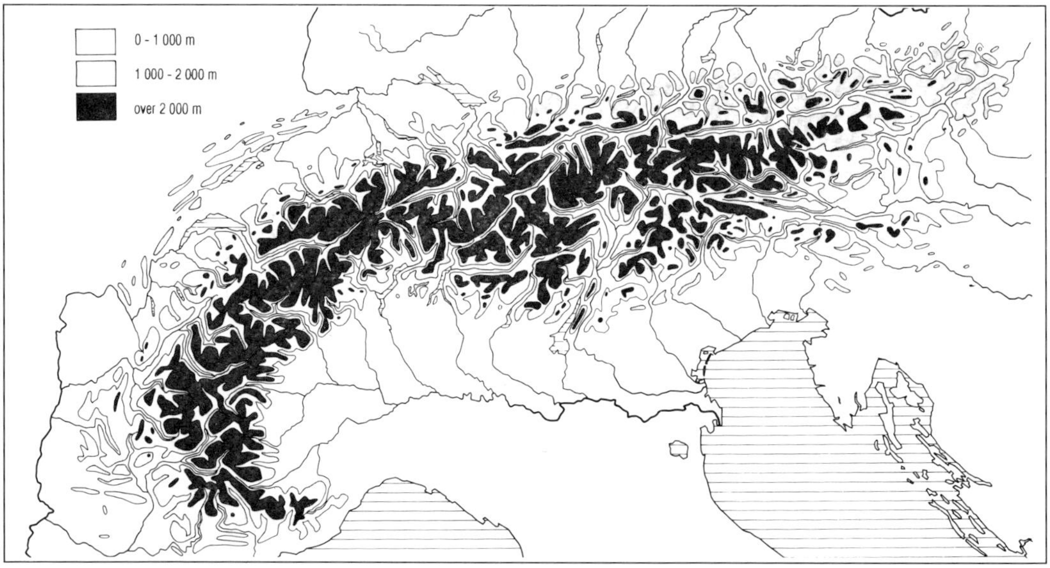

Mountain ecology and environment

Alpine ecology has been shaped by two different forces. One is parent rock and the weathering and landscape forms associated with it. The other is climate (precipitation and temperature). The flora and plant associations of the Alps are influenced by the specific interplay between these two forces.

Geology and geomorphology

Alpine geology can be sketched in terms of the following typical features:

1) The highest, most centrally located portion of the Alps (the major range or crest) consists of extremely hard rock (crystalline rock, gneiss and granite) which weathers slowly and produces steep formations, although vertical walls are rare. (Land use is difficult owing to slow soil formation and great elevation.)

2) To the north and to the south (and in the western part of the western Alps, to the west and east) there are areas of relatively soft rock (sedimentary rock such as calcareous schist) which weathers rather quickly and produces smooth formations. These areas have already been greatly worn down. The major intermontane longitudinal valleys are located here and rivers such as the Rhone, the Rhine, the Inn and the Salzach have made deep incisions, so the average height of the summits is relatively low. (Land use conditions are very favourable.)

3) Further out towards the exterior we find northern and southern Alpine limestone everywhere except within the interior arc of the Alps between the Lago Maggiore and the Ligurian Apennines. This limestone weathers slowly and water frequently drains underground. Large vertical rock walls and extended arid high plateaus are typical of this region. (Land use conditions are hostile.)

4) The entire exterior zone of the Alps is composed of soft sedimentary "flysch" which weathers quickly and produces soft formations. This zone is rather narrow, however. (Land use conditions are very favourable.)

There are many exceptions which modify this geological and geomorphological pattern, including formations in the western Alps which are substantially more complicated than those in the eastern Alps. Alpine geology is characterized by a marked confinement of formations within small areas, the result of highly complicated processes of folding and overthrust.

Alpine relief was heavily altered by the four major Ice Ages. Valleys became deeper and wider, many low and accessible mountain passes were created, numerous terraces (erosional surfaces)

Figure 3.3: National and regional administrative structures in the Alps

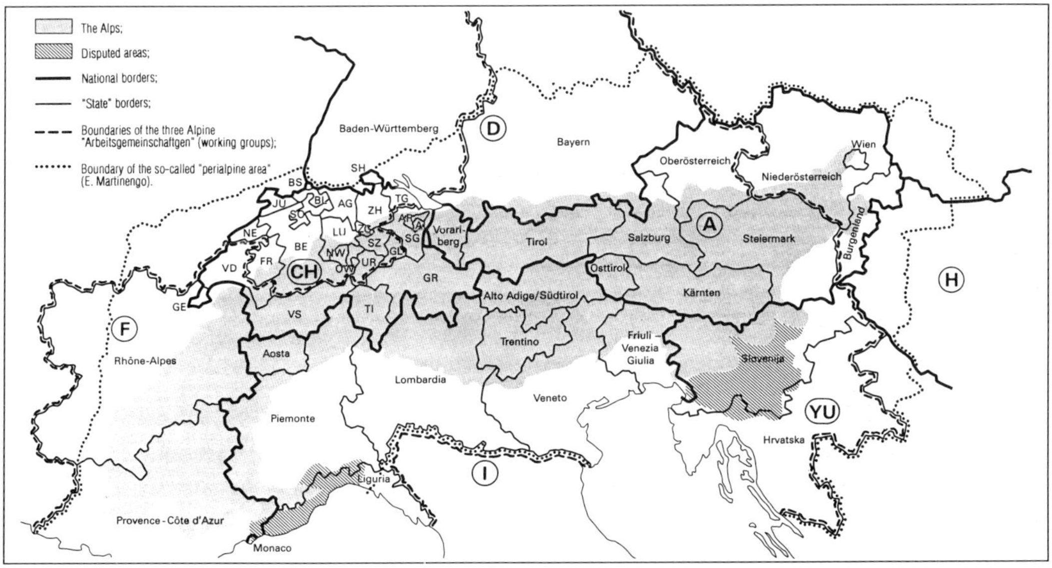

Numerous high sunny plateaus and terraces resulted from the major Ice Ages and provided hospitable locations for agriculture when warmer conditions arrived

The highest peaks are found where the rock is most resistent to weathering. This is the Weisshorn at 4 505 m in the Pennine Alps where the rock is mostly granite or highly metamorphosed types such as gneiss

were created on valley sides, and Ice Age glaciers deposited morainal material in many places, which greatly improved the process of soil formation. As a result of the Ice Ages, the conditions of land use and settlement in the Alps were made much more hospitable.

Climate

Because of their size and their location in a double border area between the temperate latitudes and the Mediterranean subtropics, and between oceanic and continental Europe, the Alps exhibit a great

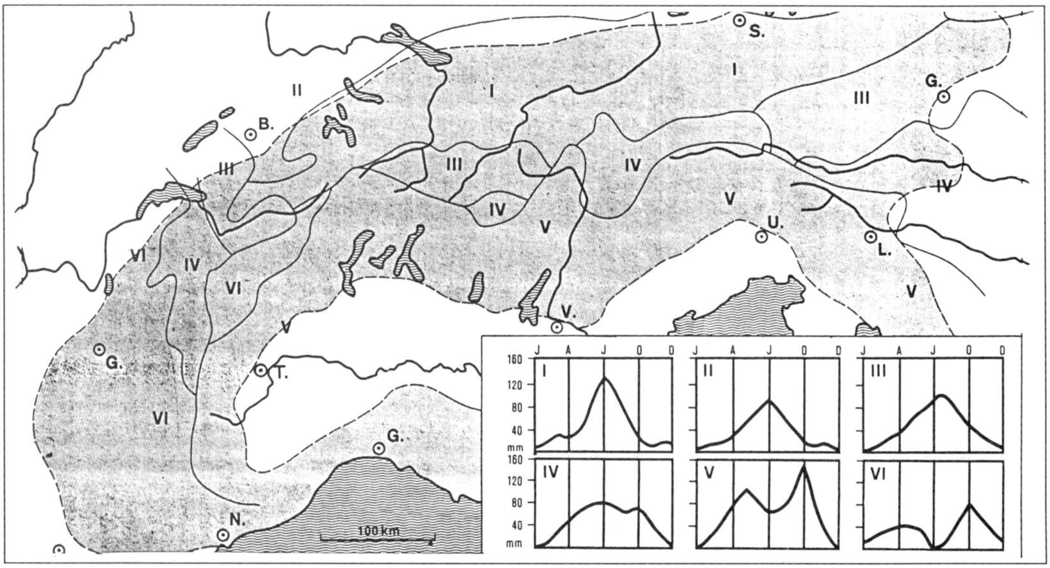

Figure 3.4 : *Monthly variations of rainfall throughout the year can be grouped. They testify to the popular perception of a Mediterranean climatic influence in the south with dry summers, with rainier summers to the north.* Source: Glanert, 1975

range of climatic conditions. Virtually every Alpine valley has a different local climate. There are no clear boundaries, only broad, gradual transitions. This makes it convenient to describe the variety of Alpine climates in terms of "geographischer Formenwandel" (geographic change), a concept developed by Hermann Lautensach (1952):

Hypsometric change As elevation increases, the average temperature drops, the annual growing season becomes shorter, and there is greater precipitation. Precipitation increasingly takes the form of snow at higher and higher altitudes. At the same time, sunlight is more intense and small-scale differences in temperature between sunny and shaded areas become greater because the atmosphere becomes thinner. This is the most basic form of change which has an influence everywhere in the Alps and is responsible for less and less hospitable conditions for vegetation and land use at higher and higher altitudes above sea level. There is just one exception to this pattern. Since the valley floors in intermontane basins and longitudinal valleys are in the shade of neighbouring mountains for most of the day, the boundary layer seldom warms up; instead, it remains cool, producing a pool of cold air and temperature inversion. The valley floors are thus climatically disadvantaged even though they are at very low altitudes.

Peripheral-central change: The Alps are a high mountain system in the path of prevailing westerly winds. They force advancing moist air masses from the Atlantic to rise and produce rain. As a result, the exterior zones of the Alps have heavy rainfall. A combination of reduced sunshine and heavy precipitation means that the upper limit for vegetation is at a low elevation. The climate of the inner Alps, however, is completely different. Clouds have already dissolved and discharged rain so there is a great deal of sun with very little precipitation. Whereas oceanic influences (temperate and humid) prevail in the climate of exterior Alpine zones, a distinctly continental climate (dry with great variations in temperature between summer and winter, day and night, and sunny and shaded areas) is found in the inner Alps. The major longitudinal valleys of this region, known as the "intermontane dry zones", are thus much more desirable climatically than the exterior zones.

Planetary change: Climatic differences between warm southern regions and cold northern regions are also noticeable in the Alps. The southern Alps are subject to Mediterranean climatic influences (high temperatures, dry summers and precipitation in winter), while the northern Alps have a central European climate (low temperatures, precipitation

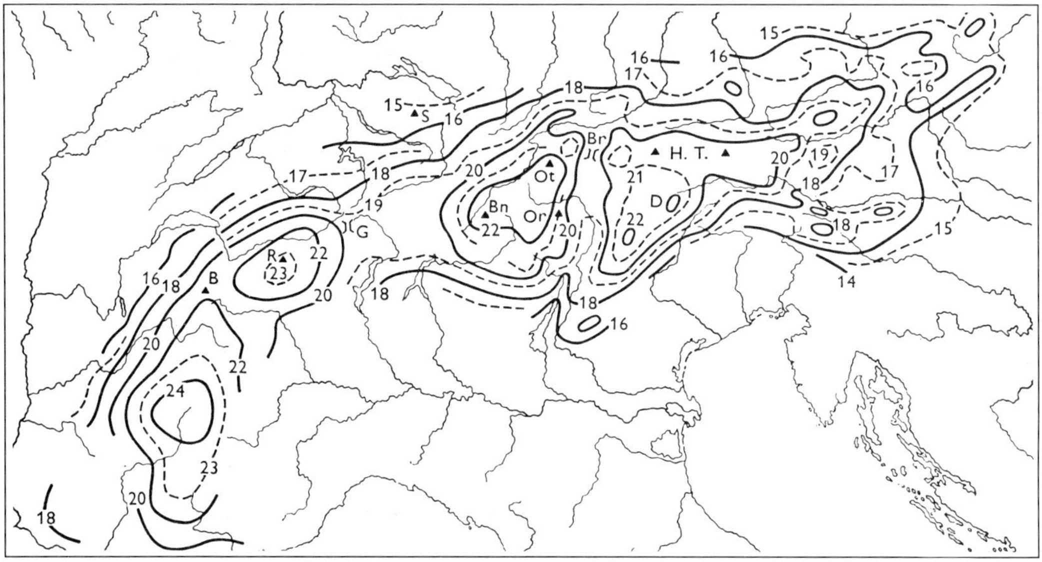

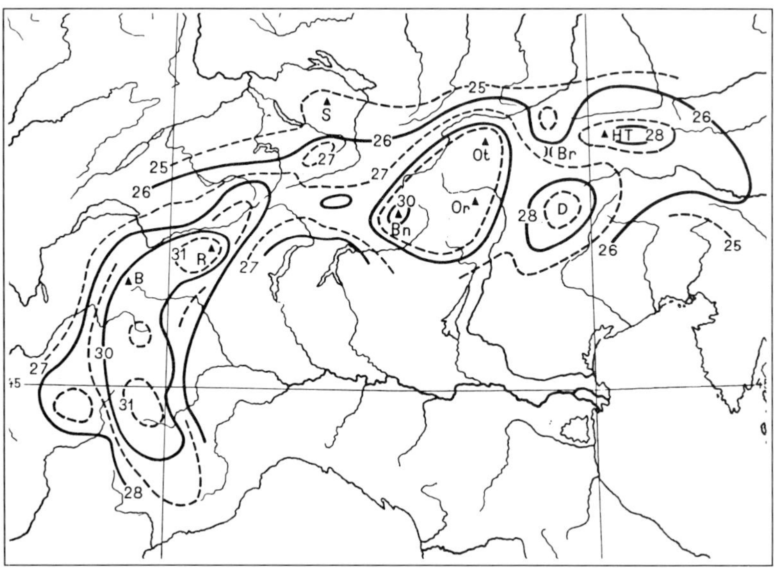

***Figures 3.5 and 3.6:** The tree line (above) and the snow line throughout the Alps. The higher the tree line and the snow line, the more favourable the climatic conditions for vegetation and human settlement. 24=2 400 m; 30 = 3 000 m. Particularly noticeable are the disadvantages in Alpine border areas, particularly the northern zone, and the advantages in the large massifs located primarily in the western Alps.*
Source: Danielli, 1963

throughout the year and no dry periods). This produces distinct climatic differences on northern and southern Alpine slopes. It is colder in the northern Alps than in the southern Alps and precipitation is distributed throughout the entire year, with a bare maximum coming at the height of summer. In the south, it is noticeably warmer than in the north, even in the Alps themselves. Precipitation comes primarily in spring and autumn and usually tends to be extremely heavy. This change also occurs on a small scale throughout the Alps. Slopes exposed to the south in Alpine valleys receive substantially more sun and warmth than slopes exposed to the north in the same valleys and thus have a climatic advantage.

Change from west to east: Since the Alps extend for over 800 km from west to east, they are subject to climatic changes in Europe ranging gradually

Alpine flowering plants have long been a source of garden stock and new varieties for the nurseryman

from the moist oceanic climate in the west to the dry continental climate in the east. Because of the influence of the Mediterranean Sea, a continental climate first prevails in the eastern part of the eastern Alps, somewhat east of a line between Linz and Ljubljana. Since altitudes in this region are not great and the Alps take on the character of mountains of moderate height, climatic disadvantages (aridity and great variations in temperature with extremely low temperatures in winter) are not extreme. Change from west to east is the mildest form of change in the Alps.

These four forms of change can be summarized in terms of typical patterns. In accordance with the general rule that climatic conditions for vegetation and land use become worse as altitude increases, the intermontane dry zones have by far the most favourable conditions despite their greater altitudes, while valleys on the southern side of the Alps offer better conditions than valleys on the northern side at the same altitude, just as slopes exposed to the south have a distinct advantage over slopes exposed to the north at the same altitude. But these climatic regularities are altered by the irregular shape of the Alps. Summits are higher in the western Alps than in the eastern Alps because rock formations there are more compact. Since intermontane dry zones can only form where mountain chains are very high, they are found primarily in the western Alps, which are thus climatically preferable to the eastern Alps.

Alpine vegetation

Vegetation in the Alps is a product of the interplay between geology, geomorphology and climate. It can be roughly categorized as follows for each region of the Alps.

The intermontane dry zones, with very little precipitation and very distinct continental climatic conditions, have very high upper limits of vegetation (the tree line is between 2 200 and 2 400 m).

The southern zone, with Mediterranean influences including high temperatures, a great deal of precipitation in spring and autumn, and dry summers, has high upper limits of vegetation (the tree line is between 1 800 and 2 200 m).

The northern zone, with the central European climatic influences of low temperatures and high amounts of precipitation throughout the year, has low upper limits of vegetation (the tree line is between 1 600 and 2 000 m).

The eastern part of the eastern Alps, where the continental climate is responsible for little precipitation, great variations in temperature and very cold winters, has very low upper limits of vegetation (the tree line is between 1 500 and 1 900 m).

In relation to the rest of Europe, the Alps are neither a favourable nor an unfavourable region. The intermontane dry zones and the Mediterranean southern zone are among Europe's favourable regions and to some extent have climatic and geographic conditions more beneficial to vegetation than the neighbouring lowlands. But the northern zone, with its central European climate, and the continental eastern part of the eastern Alps are unfavourable regions by European standards.

Basic features of Alpine ecosystems

a) The interaction between highly complex geology and the four forms of climatic change discussed above has resulted in small-scale ecological differentiation. Every valley in the Alps exhibits fundamentally different natural conditions and can be compared with neighbouring valleys only in very limited ways. This means that all general statements about Alpine ecosystems are questionable because there will always be exceptions. The practical significance of scientific pronouncements is thereby limited, since it is almost impossible completely to comprehend the diversity of the Alpine environment.

b) Owing to sharp relief, heavy precipitation, low temperatures and short growing periods, all natural processes in the Alps are different from natural processes in lowland areas. Avalanches, mud flows, floods, erosion, landslides, etc., are natural processes in the Alpine environment whose highly abrupt character is often evident. It is characteristic of such processes that nothing at all happens for extended periods (while masses of snow accumulate or streams are blocked by fallen trees or glacial ice); then, a sudden eruption will occur in the form of a highly destructive event. The abruptness of these natural events represents a constant threat to land use in the Alps. This threat can be neither accurately assessed nor completely overcome because of the complex factors at work.■

The traditional mix of meadow and forest areas has supported Alpine populations for millennia, and more recently has become the setting for tourist development

The potential of natural resources

Any view of natural resources in the Alps must take account of man. Alpine resources are shaped by man's use of them and his interest in them. Human use of Alpine resources is based on two assumptions. One is that such use is convenient (easy access from the outside as well as from within the Alps): the changes in Alpine relief affected by the Ice Ages play an important role here. The second assumption is that the abruptness of natural processes does not produce destructive effects. This in turn is based on the assumption of experience and a certain ability to deal with nature. Provided that these conditions exist, Alpine natural resources may be described as follows.

Wildlife: In Paleolithic times, wildlife was the most important natural resource in the Alps because many animals were hunted. The variety of Alpine animal species and breeds in existence today still represents an important Alpine natural resource. Many such species which have died out elsewhere in Europe have continued to survive in this environment.

Forests: Even though forests have been substantially reduced as the result of human intervention, they remain a very important resource in the Alps. They are a major source of wood (for dwellings, fences, tools, firewood and charcoal) and other forest products such as berries, mushrooms and truffles. Finally, but by no means of negligible importance, some forest ecosystems are also used as grazing ground. Forests were very important to both Alpine and non-Alpine populations when societies were based on farming. Their economic importance declined with the coming of industrialization because it became too costly to make use of them. However, in the latter part of the 20th century, forests have become newly important as sources of renewable energy. Their functions in providing protection (given the increasingly intensive use of valley floors) and serving as recreational areas are also increasing in importance.

Pastures: Alpine pastures above the tree line are one of the most important natural resources in the Alps. They were used very early in human history and are still of importance today. Even though their yield is not great in quantitative terms because of short growing periods, these areas are nonetheless of great value (as a source of easily digestible fodder which helps keep livestock healthy and raises their resistance to diseases).

Mineral resources: Geological processes in the Alps produced great intermixing of rock. There are no major mineral deposits, but there are many small deposits of limited economic significance. Only three minerals produced in the Alps, copper, gold and salt, were of significance in Europe for any length of time. Copper was mined primarily during the Bronze Age (1800 BC to 800 BC) since Europe had very few copper deposits. Accordingly, deposits of copper in the Alps were very important despite their small size and disadvantageous locations (frequently at altitudes between 2 000 and 3 000 m). When bronze was replaced by iron, there was a great decline in the importance of Alpine copper. Gold, found mainly in the Hohe Tauern (Salzburg and the eastern Alps), was mined in great quantities in pre-Roman and Roman times and played an important role in the Roman Empire. Gold mining flourished once again during the Middle Ages, when it contributed significantly to the economic strength and power of the archbishopric of Salzburg. In the 18th century, however, gold veins were slowly exhausted and mining ceased. Salt was similarly mined only in a few places in the Alps (chiefly around Salzburg and the Lower Inn Valley) in salt pits which produced valuable yields that increased the wealth of the areas involved. Today, however, its significance has virtually disappeared.

Iron working in the valleys of the Brescian Alps was of minor significance in Europe. Iron ore in this region was mined and smelted on the spot as early as 800 BC, as depicted in numerous rock paintings in the Val Camonica. The use of iron continued and contributed to the prosperity of the city of Brescia in the Middle Ages and in modern times (Brescian steel). Iron and steel are still produced here today, although not from local mineral resources. Aside from playing a role in the wider European sense, Alpine mineral resources have been used throughout history on the local level, where they contributed to the strength of local economies. But all production had been abandoned by the 20th century; either mineral production in these areas was no longer worthwhile owing to competition, or else mineral deposits had been exhausted. Because of disadvantageous locations and the small size of the deposits, it no longer appears feasible to attempt renewed use of these resources.

Biological diversity: Very small-scale ecosystems in the Alps have produced a particularly rich biological diversity. This diversity was made even richer because glaciers did not completely cover the Alps during the Ice Ages. Many plant species which have died out in other parts of Europe since the Ice Ages survived as "endemic species" in ice-free Alpine areas. The southern part of the southwestern Alps between Avignon and Turin and the southern part of the eastern Alps between Lake Comer (Comer See) and Maribor (Marburg an der Drau) have a particularly rich diversity of species; glaciation was minimal in both these areas. There was already a much greater diversity of species in the Alps than in the rest of Europe prior to human settlement; in our own time, this is all the more so. Intensive land use throughout almost all of Europe has led to the extinction of innumerable plant species. The Alps have meanwhile become their last native habitat, even though they are not "Alpine" in the true sense of the word. Accordingly, the Alps today have become an important refuge area for a variety of European species without which the biological universe in Europe would be considerably poorer. This constitutes an especially significant resource for the future in Europe.

Also worthy of mention in this connection are agriculturally developed resources, such as numerous traditional grains and domestic animal breeds distinguished by their optimal suitability to Alpine conditions. They are the result of processes which took hundreds and thousands of years. They are indispensable for sustainable agriculture and cross-breeding with highly developed stocks in Europe (to improve both sturdiness and resistance). Their disappearance would represent a major loss. Currently, however, the problem is that these agricultural resources have almost disappeared as a result of minimal yields and in some cases no longer exist in purebred forms. In recent years, however, significant attempts have been made to renew these resources; these attempts have met with initial success. Such approaches to the problem will be increasingly important in the future.

Hot springs: As a result of Alpine geological structure, there are many thermal sources and therapeutic hot springs in the Alps. In use since Roman times, they experienced a new peak of activity in the Middle Ages when many "Bauernbäder" (farmers' spas) existed throughout the Alps. With the beginning of proper tourism, use of these sources was limited to relatively few well-developed centres and the many farmers' spas disappeared. At a time when concerns about health are growing rapidly, hot springs and spas in the Alps are an important resource because they represent an ideal form of preventive health care. They are all the more valuable since they are not frequently found in Europe.

Water: Because of their great elevation and the heavy amounts of precipitation they receive (extensive snow-covered surfaces where precipitation takes the form of snow throughout the year), the Alps function as an enormous European water reservoir. Their numerous glaciers store water over periods of many years which is discharged only much later. The presence of glaciers and snow ensures that outflow of winter precipitation occurs in summer. Although the Alps are not especially important as a water reservoir for central Europe (where there is year-round precipitation), they are of great importance to Mediterranean areas where summers are dry. Artificial irrigation had probably already been developed and practised in prehistoric times in the intermontane dry zones. In the Mediterranean southern zone and the neighbouring lowlands, the Alps have been an important reservoir for drinking water and irrigation since the Middle Ages. With the development of modern, intensive cultivation in the Po Valley and southern France, where the need for irrigation continues to grow, the Alps have become more important as a vast water reservoir. In light of the water pollution in major urban areas, they also have an important role to play in supplying urban populations with drinking water (Vienna, Turin and other cities obtain drinking water directly from the Alps conducted over great distances). With the development of hydroelectric power in 1880, the Alps gained additional importance as a source of energy produced from water power. Their significance in this regard increased enormously once again when long-distance transport using electrical power was introduced (starting in 1920). The potential value of water power in the Alps became apparent in yet another way in the 1980s when mass-produced electricity from

Alpine water resources could be exploited still further. The Grimsel 1920s hydroelectric reservoir could be increased threefold to serve as a pumped-storage facility to store base-load nuclear power station output

atomic power plants was used to pump water into Alpine reservoirs. This water was in turn converted into peak current in winter at times when demand was heaviest, making the Alps even more important as an immense high-altitude reservoir supplying power to Europe.

Wind: Wind is a resource which has not been used in the Alps at all up to now. There are, however, many sites where the use of wind energy is likely to be highly worthwhile in view of the conditions of wind currents. Wind is likely to become a more valuable resource in the future.

Solar energy: Although the intermontane dry zones offer ideal conditions for its use, solar energy is another resource which has remained virtually unused in the Alps. Initial pilot projects are already in existence, however, and the importance of solar energy is likely to increase in the future.

In sum, it can be said that the ways in which the Alps function as a European water reservoir and as a repository of biological diversity (forests, meadows, varieties of plant and animal species, including domestic animals and plants) constitute the most important Alpine resources. Solar energy and wind energy, unused as yet, will become important in the future but will not come close to matching the significance of water and biological diversity as resources.

Constraints and dangers

Constraints and limitations on land use in the Alps may be summarized as follows.

The greatest constraint is height above sea level. As it increases, the annual growing season becomes shorter and biological processes slow down, including the regenerative capacity of ecosystems. A second constraint is the frequently poor and slow formation of soil due to very slow weathering of parent rock, so that growth of vegetation is often very modest. A third constraint is the interdependence of precipitation and warm temperatures (sunshine). This often gives rise to situations in which there is too little precipitation and too much sun or vice versa. Both limit development of vegetation. Truly optimal conditions for vegetation in the Alps are usually confined to small areas and are more often the exception than the rule. Most areas have certain natural limitations. Because the Alps are so ecologically sensitive, every favourable geological, geomorphological, climatic and hydrological factor is linked with a specific hazard.

- Where soil is deep, there is a potential danger of degradation and erosion from relief and precipitation.
- Where rock weathers particularly rapidly and easily, there is usually a great danger of landslides, rockslides, and mud flows.
- Glacial periods have made it easier to use land in the Alps, but, in many cases, they have at the same time created great hazards: landslides on extremely steep valley sides, erosion of morainal material, development of particularly easily erodible limnicolous sediments through temporary damming of lakes, etc.
- The favourable climate in the intermontane dry zones is inseparably linked to summer dryness and summer nocturnal frost.
- The favourable climate in the Mediterranean southern zone of the Alps is inseparably linked with disastrously heavy precipitation in spring and autumn.

❑ The flat, deep and wide valley floors in intermontane longitudinal valleys are constantly subjected to the formation of pools of cold air (temperature inversion) and threatened by floods.

Since every favourable environmental situation is linked with a specific hazard, there is an especially great danger that expanded land use and urbanization will provoke natural catastrophes. Above all, man must be careful to use nature in ways that are both environmentally compatible and sustainable.

Climate change

Small-scale climate changes, or "fluctuations" in climate, are typical of the Alps and can be most clearly seen in the behaviour of glaciers, which advance during periods when summers are moist and cool, and recede during warm, dry summers. Particularly warm periods occurred in Roman times and in the high Middle Ages, while cold periods occurred in the early Middle Ages and between 1600 and 1850 (the so-called "Little Ice Age"). Glaciers have been continually receding since 1850 (the final phase of a major glacial advance); at present they have melted down as seldom before in the last 2 000 years. This means that we have had favourable climatic conditions in the Alps for about 100 years (i.e. relatively warm and dry), while at the same time the threat of natural disasters has been somewhat reduced.

By chance, the Alps are thus in a relatively favourable and stable phase just at the time that modern large-scale development is taking place and the Alpine environment is being used intensively for modern tourism, hydroelectric power production and transit traffic. This is probably the reason why so much environmental destruction in the 20th century has not led to an increase in natural disasters. The greatest danger in the future is that the general climatic situation will worsen somewhat, once again becoming more moist and colder. In this case there would be a greater danger of natural disasters, particularly floods, mud flows and erosion. All current safety measures are based on the greatest amounts of water discharge measured to date. But since measurements with instruments have only been made with regularity for the past 100 years, all roads, bridges, dams, construction alongside streams, fortifications, etc. have been geared to the "good climate" conditions of the last 100 years. Safety measures will be insufficient if the climatic situation changes. In the light of experience with the most recent major catastrophes in the Alps resulting from extreme precipitation in the summer of 1987, it must be assumed that the suitability of the entire Alpine environment for human habitation could become questionable if climatic changes occur.

In addition, there is the question of what effect global warming would have on the Alps. It is still very difficult to distinguish between natural climatic fluctuations and warming that results from human intervention. However, the three warm winters between 1987/88 and 1989/90, when there was little snow, and the distinct increase in sultry days on the north side of the Alps appear to offer evidence of anthropogenic climate change.

But the main question is still what effect warming would have in the Alps. Would the boundary dividing the Mediterranean and central European climates (which runs through the middle of the Alps) remain fixed, with both climatic zones showing a distinct rise in temperature (rather unlikely); or, would warming have the effect of enlarging the Mediterranean subtropical zone, extending it northwards? In the first case, Alpine ecosystems would "merely" have to cope with higher temperatures. The composition of vegetation would change in all ecosystems and the ecosystems themselves would be unstable and susceptible to natural disasters during this transition period. Moreover, masses of debris currently lodged in areas of permafrost and stabilized by ice would thaw and begin to move. In the second case, however, the effects would be incomparably more dramatic, because the intermontane dry zones and major parts of the north side of the Alps would be subject to the influence of the Mediterranean climate. In addition to the consequences resulting from higher temperatures, there would be consequences resulting from a completely different precipitation regime. Severe, heavy precipitation would fall in spring and autumn in regions of the Alps which are not prepared for it (ecosystems in the present Mediterranean zone have adjusted to such precipitation over thousands of years) and cause innumerable mud flows, erosion events and floods.

These changes and the natural disasters they would bring are likely to have such force that any technology currently at our disposal would probably have little influence on them. There would then be fundamental questions about land use in the Alps. ■

The Alpine people

The history of Alpine land use, settlement and economic conditions shows that the Alps have been closely linked with European development at all times throughout human history. By contrast with the mountains of Scandinavia, for example, "backwoods" or remote conditions have never developed in the Alps.

There is evidence of human life in Europe as early as 1 million years BC. The first settlers probably crossed the Mediterranean Sea to reach Europe, since our earliest evidence comes from the Riviera. This is an area bordering the Alps, where, at that time, in the middle of the third Ice Age, conditions were probably satisfactory for human life (gathering of fruit and mussels, hunting and fishing–the cultures of hunters and gatherers).

There is little evidence of these cultures of hunters and gatherers in the Alps because the fourth Ice Age (from about 35 000 to 8 000 BC) erased almost all traces of them. But in view of the relatively favourable conditions for vegetation and animal life in the intermontane dry zones and the Mediterranean southern zone of the Alps, we are justified in assuming that hunters and gatherers lived here during warm interglacial periods.

The next great step forward–the development of farming and animal husbandry which led to the rise of settled agricultural societies–occurred in the Near East around 10 000 BC. These developments reached the Riviera (the border of the Alps) about 5 500 BC via the Mediterranean Sea and the eastern boundary of the Alps by way of the Balkans approximately 1 000 years later. Because the new agricultural societies displaced the cultures of hunters and gatherers, we must assume that some groups of hunters and gatherers found a temporary new home in the Alps. There is only circumstantial evidence for this assumption, however. Agricultural societies spread rapidly throughout Europe from the Riviera and the hills bordering the Rhone Valley (foothills and border of the Alps). They were characterized by the equal importance they assigned to farming and animal husbandry. While farming could be practised easily in areas with a Mediterranean climate (high temperatures and long dry periods in summer), dry summers brought considerable problems for animal husbandry because pastures withered. By contrast, Alpine pastures in the neighbouring mountains offered ideal grazing at this time of year because they had recently become free of snow and were located where sufficient water was also at hand. Many wild animals took advantage of these complementary natural conditions, changing from one type of grazing to another over extended areas between the Alps and the Mediterranean lowlands. Prehistoric farmers, learning from this, developed

Valle Stura in south Piedmont is the site of one of the earliest settlements in the Alps (3800 BC) in caves on the left of the valley floor

what has come to be known as "transhumance": animals (chiefly sheep) graze in the lowlands near the Mediterranean Sea in winter, in the hills in spring and autumn, and on Alpine pastures in summer. This practice makes seasonal use of the vertical structure of the Alps.

There are numerous indications that this form of agriculture began around 4000 BC It existed only in Alpine regions bordering Mediterranean areas, however. The entire northern side of the Alps and the eastern part of the eastern Alps were not involved. This form of land use was not exceptional; it existed in all Mediterranean mountain regions and in many mountain regions in the Near East.

At about the same time or a little later, a second, different type of land use developed in the Alps. Farming cultures established themselves permanently in the mountains, settlements were founded, and cultivation and animal husbandry were practised. For a long transitional period, these settlements could be inhabited only in summer. In winter people lived in areas bordering the mountains. Only when settlement became sufficiently dense were the Alps inhabited throughout the year. The earliest evidence of this new economic development dates from about 4 000 BC , but it very likely took 1 000-2 000 years before man could inhabit the Alps for the entire year. In contrast to transhumance, this way of Alpine life involved complete self-sufficiency in food production. Based on the economy developed in the Neolithic age in the Near East, which influenced Europe, this way of life put farming and animal husbandry on an equal basis in order to achieve self-sufficiency. Since farming requires a great deal of warmth and sun, it can be practised in the Alps only at low altitudes and where it is relatively warm, i.e. in the intermontane dry zones and the Mediterranean southern zone. The north side of the Alps and the eastern part of the eastern Alps are too cold or too humid.

The earliest subsistence economies of this type were located in the major valleys in intermontane dry zones and in the Mediterranean southern zone at low altitudes, usually below 1 000 m. The best areas at low altitudes were reserved for farming, while animal husbandry was practised at Alpine and sub-Alpine elevations, giving rise rather early on to so-called "Almwirtschaft" (Alpine farming). This system is characterized by close ties between economic activities in valleys and in Alpine pastures, which are closely intertwined in terms of operations, economic structure and law.

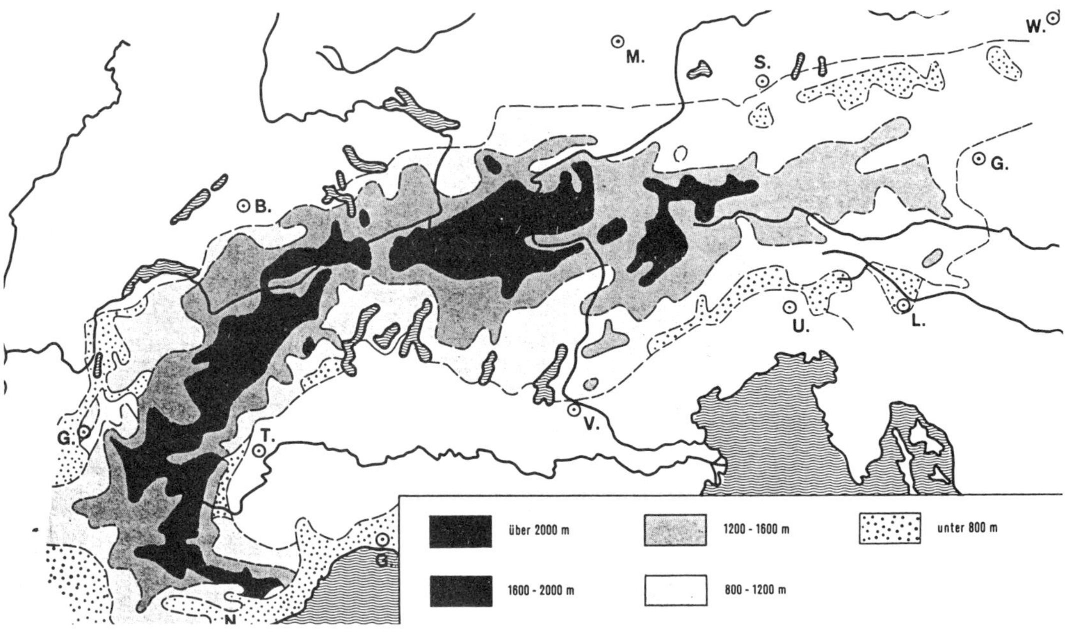

This model of Alpine subsistence economy (known as "Acker-Alp-Betrieb" or Alpine field farming) is found in all mountain areas of the world wherever there are settled farming societies influenced by Near Eastern patterns of development, i.e. in the entire "alpine" arc from the Pyrenees in the west to the Himalaya in Asia. The only type of land use found in this mountainous arc that is not known in the Alps is mountain nomadism, in which nomadic tribes change pastures over extensive areas from winter pastures in the lowlands to summer pastures in the mountains (in transhumance the entire family does not migrate, only the shepherds; the rest of the population stays in its native villages and practises cultivation). The reason for this is that there is no unsettled land in the lowlands near the Alps.

Thus the Alps were fully involved in the general economic and social development of the Near East and Europe, starting at the dawn of history prior to the rise of the first major European cultures. Similarly, the next major advances–the discovery and processing of copper, bronze and iron–arrived rather quickly in Europe and the Alps from the Near East (copper mining and bronze workmanship from 1800 BC; iron mining and smelting from 800 BC). This intensified agricultural land use in the Alps since the many miners and metalworkers had to be supplied with food from the immediate surroundings.

By the time the Alps first received attention from a major culture–the first written reports of them date from Roman writers around 200 BC–they were already rather heavily settled and intensively used. Local economic development had resulted in many specialities (Alpine farming, cheese production, special types of grain and breeds of sheep and cattle, etc.) which have remained "typically Alpine" to the present day. At that time, however, not every part of the Alps was used. Only the intermontane dry zones and the southern zone were affected. Extensive areas on the north side of the Alps and in the eastern part of the eastern Alps had no human inhabitants since strongly Mediterranean cultural patterns were not suitable here.

The incorporation of the Alps into the Roman Empire (0-500 AD) brought a great increase in population and new economic activity, although these affected only the areas previously mentioned. With the fall of the Roman Empire and the invasion of numerous "barbaric" tribes (the Saracens, among others) who also laid waste to the

Figure 3.7: *Upper limits of permanent settlements in the Alps. This map shows the advantages of intermontane zones as opposed to areas bordering the Alps, and the advantages of the western Alps*
After E. Deichmann, 1936

Alpine meadow farming —a system combining animal husbandry with hay meadows to provide winter fodder—permitted a new wave of settlement from 500 AD onwards. The landscape shows isolated farm buildings on slopes

Alps, there was a marked decline in population and many fields and pastures were left fallow, growing wild and turning to forests.

Around 500 AD, a new development took place in the Alps. Germanic tribes–the Alemannen in the West and the Bavarians in the East– advanced from the North to the edge of the Alps. This process was intensified by the addition of Slavic tribes (Slovenes) who reached the Alps from the Southeast. The previous inhabitants of the Alps had been strongly subject to Mediterranean cultural influences. Wheat, olives and wine were the most important foods and the products of animal husbandry, while undeniably important, were of somewhat secondary significance. These tribes introduced another culture and with it another diet. Like the entire area from the Atlantic to the Indus, they too had been influenced by the Neolithic economy of the Near East (with an approximately equal emphasis on farming and animal husbandry). But farming played a less important role in their culture than it did in Mediterranean areas, while animal husbandry was much more important. In their environment of immense forests in central, northern and eastern Europe with relatively low temperatures, farming was of secondary importance to animal husbandry, which was based on forest grazing. Roman writers had already described this with great amazement. As these tribes advanced into the Alps at the end of the major European folk migrations from the North, they settled scarcely used areas because farming, which was difficult and produced small yields here, was of so little importance to them. But the humid regions here offered optimal conditions for animal husbandry, which was central to their diet (many dairy products and meat, little grain production).

Thus parts of the Alps which had previously escaped human intervention were now settled. Because the most favourable areas at low altitudes were reserved for meadows (production of fodder for animals in winter) and fields occupied only small areas by comparison, this economic system is known as "Wiesen-Alp-Betrieb" (Alpine meadow farming).

Among non-Alpine areas, this economic system was also found in the mountains of Scandinavia. But it is limited to Europe and is unknown in Mediterranean and Near Eastern mountains.

Between 1000 and 1350 AD all of Europe experienced great prosperity, which was characterized by heavy population growth, the expansion of agriculture and of cities, and cultural advance. The Alps shared fully in this Europe-wide development. Heavy population growth, extensive clearing of forests, and a substantial increase in the amount of cultivable land (in the western Alps from 1000 AD and in the eastern Alps from 1100 AD to the end of 1349, when bubonic plague broke out) occurred at this time. Alpine culture flourished along with the rest of Europe and was characterized by numerous technological, economic, social and cultural innovations. The economic, social and cultural systems that developed to a high level at this time continued to have an influence in the Alps into the 19th and 20th centuries.

During this flourishing medieval period, two important innovations were introduced. They affected only small areas because the Alps were already rather densely settled. These were the "Schwaighof" (dairy farm) and the Walser economy. "Schwaighöfe" are farms that specialize purely in animal husbandry (meat, butter and cheese production) and can accordingly exist at very high altitudes. Locations at the lower edges of Alpine pastures can thus be used for annual or permanent settlement, thereby intensifying land use. But because farmers here needed grain to survive, they traded cheese for grain. There was no market in which to conduct this exchange, which certainly would have been too complicated at that time. It was organized instead by a feudal lord who had a strong interest in more intensive land use because it meant an increase in his income. These "Schwaighöfe" were located primarily in the western part of the eastern Alps (the Tyrol and also Salzburg and Kärnten).

The Walser were farmers from the German-speaking upper part of the Canton of Wallis (Switzerland) who settled at the highest altitudes in the central Alps (between Lake Geneva and Lake Constance) during the high Middle Ages. This was possible because they too specialized only in animal husbandry and were thus not bound to farming. They also owe their settlements to the interests of local feudal lords who wanted more

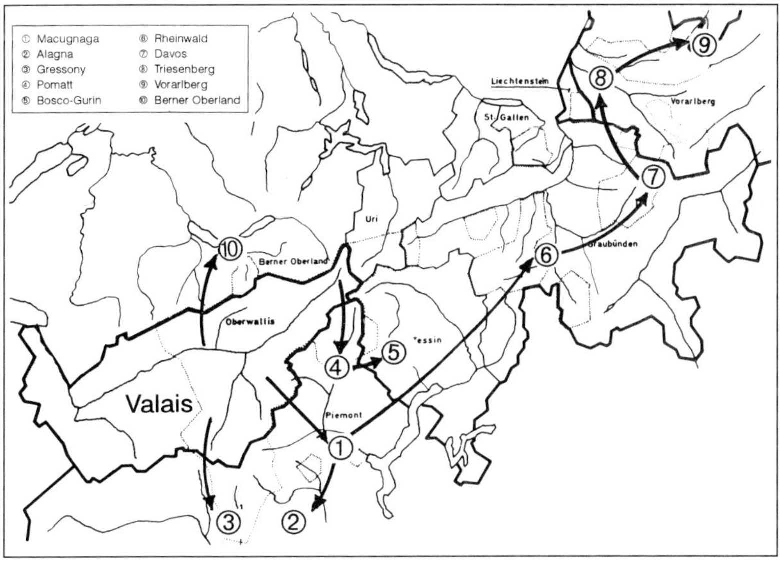

Figure 3.8: *Walser settlements. Settlements were found in the central Alps between the area around Monte Rosa in the west (Piemonte) and Walsertal in the east (Voralberg). The Walser sometimes settled in very high valleys which had previously been extensively used only as Alpine pastures.* Source: *Wir Walser* 16 Jg. (2) 1978

intensive land use; Walser settlements were frequently found in areas which had previously been used only extensively as Alpine pastures. The Walser earned additional income by doing military service in wartime, driving pack animals in transit traffic and dealing in cattle, which all brought money to buy the grain they needed.

The development and spread of the "Schwaighöfe" and the Walser settlements meant land use was at a maximum in the Alps by around 1350 AD. More intensive use for agricultural purposes was no longer possible. The Alps as of 1350 AD were little different from the picture they presented in the 19th century.

The economic systems described here–transhumance, Alpine meadow farming, Alpine field farming, the "Schwaighof" and the Walser economy–each use different Alpine environments and regions. There is relatively little crowding out or overlap of one system with another. All these economic and social systems, though they developed at different periods in history, coexisted in the Alps into the 20th century. There is a cultural diversity which corresponds to this economic diversity. The Alps are an environment in which three major European cultures and languages–Romance, Germanic and Slavic– meet and intersect. Alpine Romance culture is composed of the Occitanian (southern French Alps, southern Piemonte Alps), the Franco-Provencal (northern French Alps, western Swiss Alps) and the Rhaeto-Romanic (eastern Swiss Alps, Dolomites, eastern Italian Alps). Germanic culture stems from the Alemannen (German-speaking Switzerland, Liechtenstein, Vorarlberg, Allgäu) and the Bavarians (Austrian Alps, southern Tyrol, German language groups in the Italian eastern Alps, Bavaria). Slavic cultures consist of the Slovenes (primarily in Slovenia/Yugoslavia but also including minorities in southern Austria and the Italian eastern Alps). In some cases there is small-scale linkage between these three major linguistic and cultural groups and their six smaller subdivisions, and there are many areas in which they intermix.

Therefore, it is impossible to summarize Alpine culture easily in terms of ethnic or linguistic groups. It is no coincidence that the concept of the European nation state could not be applied in the Alps. All attempts to establish national borders hindered and destroyed mature economic and cultural relations. Nor is it surprising that Switzerland, the "most Alpine" European country, is not a nation state in the European sense; Switzerland contains four different languages and cultures. Developments which produced the strengthening of absolutist states and led to the large nation states of the 19th century in modern Europe were not suited to the Alps. It is thus no accident that this process put the Alps at a basic disadvantage. As a result of the formation of nation states, the Alps have been distributed over seven different countries whose borders were imprecisely defined for a long time and have been adjusted anew in the 20th century. As a result, the Alps become border regions in every country and are consequently treated as a borderline or peripheral area. Even though they form a large, continuous region in the middle of Europe, this central location has not prevented them from being completely divided up and made marginal by the formation of nation states. ■

Land use and sustainable development

Every type of land use in the Alps changes the ecosystem in which it takes place in some definite way. If Alpine meadows are regularly grazed, for example, there is a distinct change in the composition of vegetation. On surfaces which are not grazed (left in a natural state) the ratio of grass to other plants is 2:1; on surfaces where grazing takes place this ratio is exactly reversed. Man has not only used the ecosystems he found and changed them by using them. He has also intervened directly by clearing forests, draining areas that were already too arid and reclaiming areas that were too moist. This has resulted in the creation of completely new ecosystems which did not previously exist in the Alps. Fundamentally, three major types of change in Alpine ecosystems can be identified: 1) Alpine pastures have been enlarged through the clearing of forests; 2) Cultivable land has been opened up on the lower slopes; and 3) Flood plains have been claimed for agricultural use.

Alpine pasture enlargement begins virtually unintentionally when animals take refuge in forests from heat or storms and graze on young sprouts. This weakens a forest's ability to regenerate. In addition, the construction of buildings and fences,

Figure 3.9: *Cultural and linguistic groups in the Alps.*
Source: Bätzing 1984

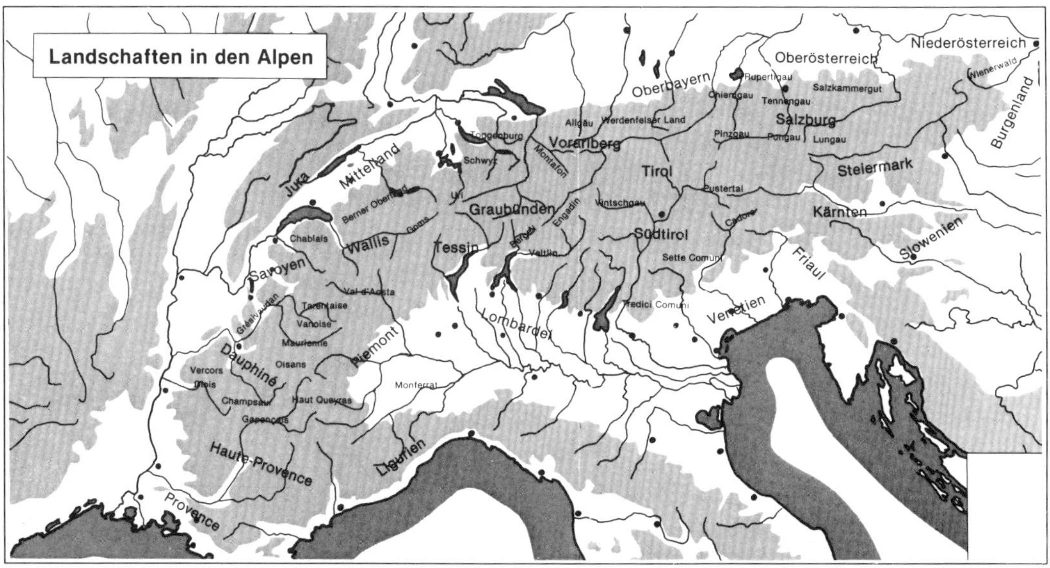

the production of heat and the making of cheese all require great amounts of wood on a regular basis. This wood is supplied by nearby forests; the upper limit of the forest on the lower edge of the pasture is thereby continually pushed downward. This effect, unintended at first, did have the advantage of enlarging the grazing area, however. Pastures were thus made more productive. Forests were probably purposely cleared to enlarge grazing areas in prehistoric times. We do have precise reports from the Middle Ages documenting many instances where extensive clearing of forests took place. This resulted in a noticeable enlarging of Alpine pastures, which are relatively small in their natural condition. They were enlarged to three or four times their size (more often in the western Alps than the eastern Alps). Today, the best and most fertile Alpine pastures are found on surfaces that were previously cleared. Such pastures are important because they are a natural resource and because purposeful human intervention has enlarged and enhanced them.

Cultivable land on lower slopes: From the time he first practised agriculture in the Alps, man has had to clear forests in order to survive, since all potentially cultivable land was originally forest land. Since flat valley floors were greatly threatened by floods and often at a climatic disadvantage (temperature inversion resulting from cold air pools), the first fields were cleared areas on the alluvial cones of tributary streams. These were on sites where the tributary streams opened into the main valley and deposited large amounts of gravel in the form of cones. Such sites were protected from floodwaters and were exceptionally fertile, although they were inseparably linked with the disadvantage of flooding from the tributary stream. Settlements in these areas are among the oldest in the Alps and have remained intact to this day. Somewhat later, the flatter portions of slopes facing south in the vicinity of the valley floor were also cleared and converted into cultivable land. Shaded slopes (facing north) were usually not cleared since they promised little yield; their forests were used for economic purposes. In time, cleared and cultivated areas near valleys became larger and larger. There was a threat that the process of clearing Alpine pastures downwards from above would encounter the process of clearing valley floors upwards from below. At this point farmers noticed that the uninterrupted clearing of mountain slopes was accompanied by uncontrollable avalanche problems. Thus a so-called "Bannwald" (protective forest) was purposely left between the two cleared areas. Early references to these protective forests were made in some of the oldest documents of the Middle Ages, and their preservation was considered absolutely necessary to prevent natural disasters.

Flood plain reclamation on valley floors for agricultural use represents the most recent type of change in the Alps. Valley floors, which are used so intensively today and appear to offer a very hospitable form of land use, have been a source of great difficulty throughout human history because the problem of large amounts of water here could not be overcome by simple technology. Consequently, many flood plains, often extensive in area, were either totally unused for a very long time or used only very extensively as grazing areas in times when the water receded. Only in the 19th and 20th centuries did improvement take place on a large scale. Rivers were straightened and deepened, and land which had previously been very moist was claimed for use, divided into plots, and used as pasture land. Despite this, there were no homes or settlements in these areas until about 1960. Only barns could be found; the inhabitants knew all too well that the threat of floods was constant.

All altitudinal belts were affected by these changes in Alpine ecosystems. Even the most remote grass plots above rockslides were used, with the result that their vegetation was altered too. Basically, *all* Alpine ecosystems, with the exception of rocky areas and glaciers hostile to vegetation, were altered by traditional land use.

These changes are linked to severe ecological problems. Since forests are the best possible protection against erosion, avalanche and floods, large-scale clearing of forests has resulted in greater runoff on fields, meadows and pastures and a marked increase in avalanches and erosion. Land under cultivation is therefore less stable than land in its natural state. This is related to the increase in natural disasters and threats arising

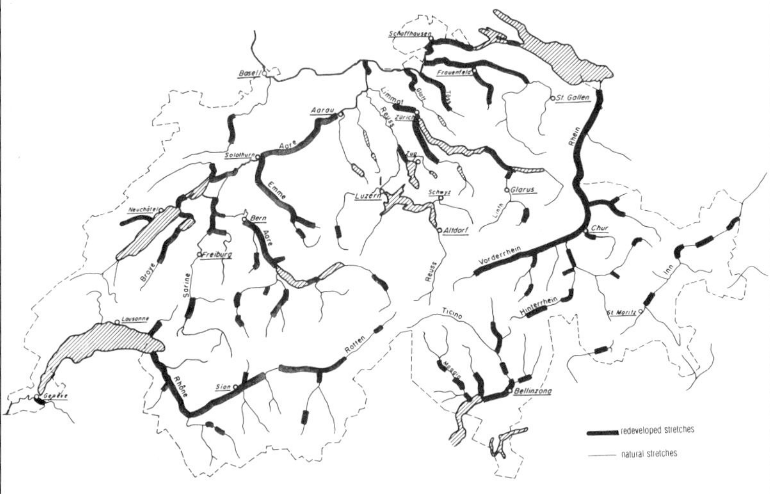

Figure 3.10: Swiss rivers showing the portions redeveloped by man in the 19th century
Source: Götz, 1987

from natural processes. If man does not want to surrender the chance to live in the Alps, he will have to engage in sustainable economic activity. This activity must be aimed not only at producing food but also at stabilizing the ecology on cultivated land. The following four points summarize our knowledge of this problem based on experience in the Alps over thousands of years:

1) Man must take account of different ecosystems as he uses the land and make adjustments accordingly. Any monostructural, large-scale land use practice will automatically produce environmental damage, given the environmental differences that occur within small areas. Attention must be given to existing natural variations, and land use patterns must be developed on a correspondingly small scale.

2) Specific land use practices must be chosen not only to produce food but also to ensure ecological stability at the same time. The threat of erosion is severe on cultivated land because there is no protective vegetation cover between harvesting and the time newly planted seeds begin to sprout. Therefore, fields must be terraced to reduce the gradient of slopes and hence the threat of erosion. On meadows, proper intervals between cutting are important. If they are cut too frequently, regeneration of the vegetation will be poor; if they are not cut often enough, bush and shrubs will grow, making the meadow unproductive. Just as important is the correct cutting time. If meadows are cut too early, vegetation will not regenerate well, but if they are cut too late, the hay will lose its nutritive value. On grazing land, the proper number of animals is an important factor. Alpine pastures can be overgrazed and their vegetation cover destroyed by too many animals, while if there are too few animals, grazing will be selective, the best plants will soon disappear, and the pasture will turn to weed. The same holds true for the beginning and end of the grazing period. In sum, this means that the environmental suitability of a particular land use practice–the "proper" type of cultivation–plays a key role in sustainability. Farmers throughout the Alps were thoroughly aware of this, and such "proper" uses were set down in many detailed regulations, the application of which was enforced by communal ordinances, etc.

3) Not every slope in the Alps can be cleared and used intensively if we wish to avoid inducing natural disasters. Depending on specific local conditions, slopes whose gradients were above a certain limit (with steepness always considered in relation to exposure and altitude) remained untouched and protected. This meant recognizing certain limits on land use. Yet this is not a matter of absolute but of relative limits, as the history of land use in the Alps has shown. As various new developments

Rich Alpine meadow flora is a resource with multiple uses: as food for cattle and sheep, a source of alpine liqueurs and thus a double pleasure to the summer walker

(transhumance, Alpine field farming, Alpine meadow farming, the "Schwaighof" and Walser economies) came about, limits on use which had previously seemed insurmountable were removed in every case and available space in the Alps was expanded. But in each case new limits on use were also established and respected.

4) Even if these three land-use strategies are observed, cultivated land in the Alps will not have the ecological stability man needs in order to live in relative security. A great deal of maintenance and repair work will also be necessary to give cultivated land additional stability. This includes transporting eroded soil uphill, improving eroded areas, and clearing away debris from avalanches on Alpine pastures in spring. Such work should also be aimed at reducing and neutralizing the "erratic" dynamics of nature somewhat by clearing stream beds to prevent obstruction (blockage and damming caused by trees, rocks, etc. with consequent floods), building levees to prevent flooding, etc. This maintenance and repair work has always required a great deal of labour in the past, but there was never a shortage of manpower.

As long as these four principles of land use were observed, it was possible to maintain the same degree of ecological stability on cultivated land in the Alps as on land untouched by man. In some cases, where the natural environment was particularly unstable, it was even possible to reduce this instability somewhat by using the land.

In principle, it can be said that the actual question of how land should be used in the right manner has always been open to controversy. On the whole, however, sustainable use has prevailed and has been maintained for centuries.

This sustainability was also the cause of two further important changes. Vegetation in the Alpine environment is for the most part composed of different forest societies, some of which do not have a very wide variety of species. By clearing and opening up forests and introducing new plants (agricultural vegetation and plants from the Near East), man markedly increased the diversity of plant species. At the same time, he changed the landscape by dividing it into smaller areas and making it more diversified. While a forest levels the differences on a slope and blends into the landscape, land use adapted to these ecological differences on a small scale brings out the differences and emphasizes them. This caused a fundamental change in the Alpine landscape. While it had been rather stark and somewhat monotonous in its natural state, human intervention changed this by making it considerably more diversified and dividing it up into smaller ecosystems. This was an important precondition for the later development of tourism which is often overlooked.

A certain amount of social control and cultural identity is necessary to put these four principles of sustainable activity into practice and ensure their continuance. Even in the Middle Ages short-term overuse of Alpine pastures using "Lehnvieh" (livestock owned by people living in the lowlands which was grazed on Alpine meadows in exchange for payment) would have been very profitable for an individual farmer or a commune since demand at the time was very high. But short-term gain had to be balanced against the long-term disadvantage of degradation of the vegetation cover. As early as the Middle Ages it was clearly decided that short-term gain at the cost of long-term damage was not acceptable. This meant that selfish individual interests had to be restrained in the interest of the entire community and future generations. Community interests came first because Alpine farmers, like all other European farmers until well into the 19th century, did not think and act as individuals but regarded themselves as one link in a chain of the many who had come before them and who would succeed them. In addition, farmers throughout the Alps are known for their aversion to innovation and risk. Because reaction in the form of natural disasters is swift when one makes a mistake in dealing with nature in the Alpine environment, the willingness to experiment is not very great as a rule. Furthermore, two social and cultural systems guaranteed and exercised control over sustainable agriculture, the "Gemeinde" (commune) and the "Hof" (farmstead) systems.

The "commune system" is the older form, found in those regions of the Alps that were already heavily settled in Roman times. Here, where Alpine field farming was practised, there was equal inheritance (with each child receiving patrimony in equal portions) and dispersion of property, with each family farming numerous small plots distributed at different altitudes. The communal statutes were a characteristic feature of such communes. Most of these statutes were fashioned in the Middle Ages (modelled on the "communal" origins of northern Italian cities) and contained specific expressions of limits on land use as well as land use regulations. Strict enforcement of these statutes was exercised by the village community and many villages had an official field warden who enforced statues with police authority. The individual was thus limited in the use of his own property and could not use it merely as he pleased. This system also existed in a similar form throughout Europe but only in areas of early settlement, i.e. those parts of Europe which had already been heavily settled and used in Roman times.

The "farmstead system" is the more recent system. It was found in those regions of the Alps that were settled late by Germans and Slavs. Here there were usually no actual villages but dispersed settlement in which individual farmhouses stood alone. Only where there was a church could three or four adjoining farms be found. Alpine meadow farming was practised in this system and the law of entail prevailed, meaning that only one son could inherit the entire farmstead while his siblings received nothing. All property usually adjoined the farm so that each was fully independent of others in terms of space. In some cases there were as many as 20-30 domestic servants on large farmsteads, while in other cases the farms were small and had only a few domestic servants. But common to all was a highly independent lifestyle and little contact with other farms. Control over sustainable use rested solely with a farmer or married couple engaged in farming; these individuals possessed a great deal of personal freedom of action. The future heir was prepared from early childhood to fulfil the responsibilities of this task in accordance with the motto, "Übergib den Hof so an deinen Sohn, wie du ihn von deinem Vater übernommen hast" (Leave the farm to your son as you received it from your father). In other words, take no short-term gain for yourself at the expense of future generations. The novels of Jeremias Gotthelf, a pastor from the Emmental (Emme River Valley, Switzerland), illustrate very clearly what a struggle it was to teach a sense of ecological responsibility and how difficult this was to achieve in actual practice (see, above all, *Uli der Knecht* and *Uli der Pächter*, 1840).

But to make such environmentally responsible behaviour possible in practice, a certain political framework was necessary. Only where farmers had a certain freedom to manage their own affairs could they act in an environmentally responsible way. If they were directly subject to a superior only interested in obtaining the greatest yield from "his" land in the short term, then they had very little such freedom. Very different political structures developed between the Middle Ages and the 19th century in the Alps. But despite pronounced differences, one thing became quite common: farmers in many cases were able to fight for and obtain conditions which made environmentally responsible land use possible. They were sometimes supported in this by minor feudal lords (the counts of Tyrol, for example) who had realized that short-term exploitation of their land would undermine their own sovereign authority as well as their power.

Since the Alps are situated in the centre of Europe and control of Alpine passes during the Middle Ages and afterwards was extremely important for reasons of military strategy, autonomous political organization was almost impossible. Instead, political development was increasingly subject to and shaped by external forces. As early as the Middle Ages, associations similar to alliances between small states (Alpine regions with a certain amount of political autonomy) developed in many regions of the Alps, usually to unite different Alpine valleys in the vicinity of an important mountain pass. These "states" generally enjoyed complete equality on the basis of federalism, while environmentally sound behaviour within each one was taken for granted in most cases. If the great European powers had not intervened in the Alps in order to control mountain passes, a large confederation with many entire Alpine valleys probably would have come into existence. Switzerland represents the only case in which a small part of the Alps remained exempt from the developments which led to large European nation states. The political structure of Switzerland dates from the time of one of these state-like alliances on the Gotthard pass ("Urkantone" or original cantons) which allied with cities beneath the Alps (Zurich, Berne) since they had a mutual interest in increasing their strength. This political form has survived to the present day. The development of the Tyrol in the eastern Alps followed a similar course for a long time until the Habsburg Empire became too powerful for it. In the western Alps, the Federation of Briancon existed from the Middle Ages to 1715 as an almost completely independent state until it was absorbed by France.

Although autonomous Alpine development that would have ensured sustainable agriculture in the Alps was prevented at the highest political level, farming societies frequently fought for and gained thc political freedom and autonomy at lower levels that were necessary to guarantee such sustainability.

Of course, this does not mean that there was no human involvement in environmental destruction in earlier times. The most damaging interventions occurred as the result of mining, smelting and salt pit operations, whose enormous need for wood led to complete deforestation in many places. Overuse of the land for agricultural purposes also regularly produced environmental destruction. Yet despite this, we know today that sustainable use of resources in the Alps usually prevailed over short-term exploitation and overuse throughout the course of history. For this reason, the Alps in their traditional form–as a primarily agricultural landscape–are particularly valuable and worthy of protection in the 20th century. This assessment does not reflect the judgement of tourists. It is based on established facts in biology, plant sociology and landscape ecology. ■

The industrial age– breakdown of the traditional Alpine world

Modern industrial society began to develop at the end of the 18th century and spread throughout Europe in the 19th century. It was characterized by economic production in which manual labour was separated from intellectual tasks and further divided up into very small steps. Machines and tools were used on a large scale to replace human labour, and external sources of energy were employed to run machines. This resulted in such a revolutionary reduction in the costs of production that all preindustrial production methods met with ruin because they were too costly. For this new economic form to triumph, the dismantling of customs barriers (one of the guiding political principles of liberalism) was necessary at the political level. A radical reduction in transportation costs was also necessary and was accomplished with the invention of the railway and the steamship and, later, the automobile and the truck.

The social changes which accompanied industrialization were so great that they can only be compared in human history with the transition from the Paleolithic Age (cultures of hunters and gatherers) to the Neolithic Age (agricultural societies).

Industrialization was the main cause of the total breakdown of traditional economic and social structures in the Alps in the 19th and 20th centuries. This has involved breakdowns of traditional Alpine agriculture, forest use, local industries (mining, smelting, salt pits) and handicrafts, and traditional cultural identity, values and attitudes. Only relicts of this traditional world remain today. On a worldwide scale, this revolutionary change can be compared with the subjugation of the countries of the Third World, the only difference being that it occurred in central Europe.

Changes began to take place around 1850 with the first railway line through the Alps. Alpine agriculture was now exposed to competition from substantially more productive areas of Europe where growing conditions were more favourable. In the wake of major agricultural crises in all European countries (owing to the import of cheap grain from new colonies), large-scale collapse began in the Alps between 1870 and 1880, when Alpine inhabitants ceased farming and migrated to large cities. This breakdown proceeded much more rapidly in regions

Figure 3.11: Regions of high population density and distribution of population density in the Alps

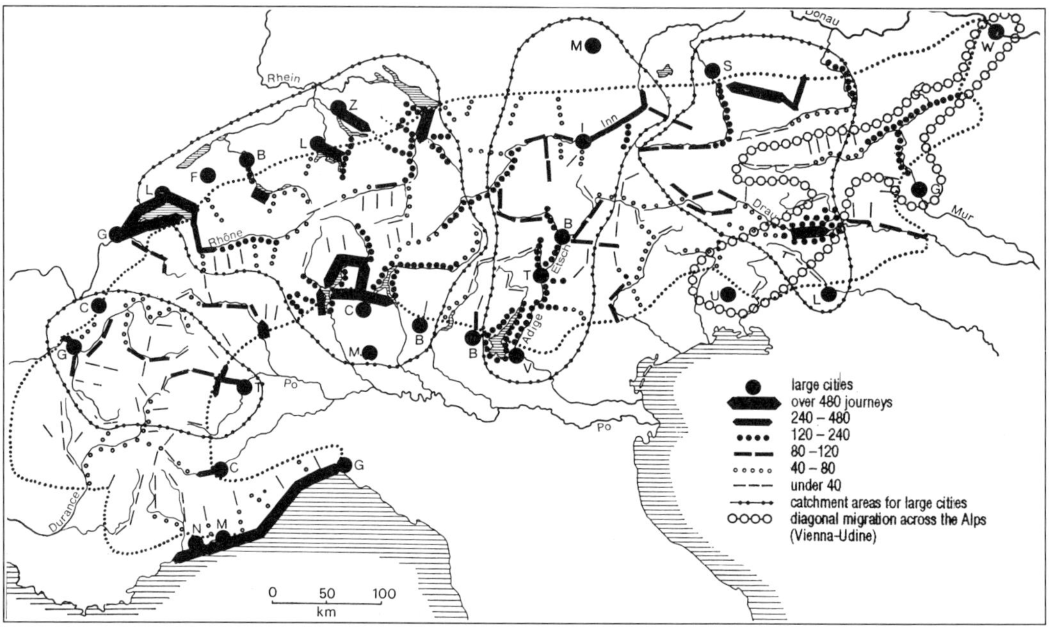

practising Alpine field farming (very small farms, grain production under extremely difficult conditions and hence low yields, innovation severely restricted by the "commune system") than it did in regions practising Alpine meadow farming (relatively large farms, animal husbandry still competitive to an extent within western Europe, capable of innovation on the basis of the "farmstead system"). Migration at this time from the French and Italian Alps was much greater than from the Swiss and Austrian Alps.

Along with agriculture, local handicrafts and industries also failed. Between 1850 and 1955 there were only three countermovements: tourism, industry and transportation.

Tourism in the Alps is closely connected with new perceptions of the environment in the industrial age (exploitation of nature through processes of production accompanied by a simultaneous idealization of nature, including an aesthetic integration of nature and leisure-time activities). Alpine tourism began around 1780, although it remained highly exclusive for a long time, drawing very few people to the Alps. Only between 1880 and 1914, the so-called Belle Epoque, did a quantitative increase in activity occur; many large hotels and mountain railways were built during this period. But the development of tourism continued to be limited, with only a few communes (primarily in Switzerland) profiting from it.

Starting around 1880 (with the invention of hydroelectric power) industry came to the Alps on a large scale wherever water power could be easily used (the Swiss canton of Wallis, Sillon Alpin in the northern French Alps). The communes affected experienced great increases in economic development and population, although once again very few communes were involved.

Transit traffic through the Alps, which existed only in the form of railway transportation until 1955, meant that communes along major railway lines enjoyed advantageous locations and prosperity which often led to further positive development.

Given the widespread breakdown in agriculture, mining and handicrafts throughout the Alps, the prosperity brought by tourism, industry and transport was only of secondary importance and affected only small areas. Crisis overtook the Alps, and the entire region became an economically weak area with a high rate of emigration.

Tourism infrastructure puts its mark on an Alpine slope. Gastein (Austria) shows the straight lines of a ski lift and the curved tracks of the pistes

Beginning around 1955, the industrialized countries of Europe entered a new phase characterized by the transition to a service economy. The basic features of industrial society were maintained (division of labour, manpower replaced by machines and computers, greater use of outside sources of energy). But such great change occurred that this period must be designated as a new phase of the industrial age.

The service sector is now becoming more and more important as a part of the overall economy for several reasons, while improvements in efficiency in agriculture and industry have continued, with an accompanying decline in jobs. A constant increase in the division of labour means there is a greater need for administration, coordination and regulation. More and more jobs which were formerly done in families or by women (caring for and raising children, caring for the elderly, housekeeping) are becoming paid positions. And great increases in income with a simultaneous shortening of working hours are giving rise to an independent sector based on leisure-time pursuits and cultural interests. The importance of this sector continues to grow.

All of this is helping to restore the importance of the Alps within Europe. Starting about 1955, mass tourism became a part of life in Europe, with summer tourism beginning around 1955 and winter tourism around 1965. Large areas of the Alps are being newly enhanced as resort locations. Although widespread, the phenomenon of mass tourism is not prevalent throughout the Alps; it has affected only about 50-60 per cent of their total area. In the 1980s there was a second development. Increasing numbers of people in Europe began to flee heavily polluted urban areas and seek places to live and work where they would have healthy and pleasant surroundings. New jobs (usually in the service sector or state-of-the-art industrial operations) are being created at the edge of the Alps and to some extent in the mountains themselves. Those who hold these jobs live in or near Alpine farming villages, which are being completely restructured and are assuming a new character. The Alps are being enhanced by this latter development thanks to their central location within Europe and their healthy environment.

The relation of the Alps to Europe is once again being fundamentally altered. No longer are they a culturally and economically weak region. They are a developing European resort area and a newly discovered economic region with a high-quality environment. ■

The use of Alpine resources in the age of the service economy

Alpine agriculture

The process of breakdown in Alpine agriculture which had started in the second half of the 19th century continued after the Second World War. There is an important parallel to European economic conditions in this process. At times when the European economy flourishes, jobs are plentiful, and manpower is needed, there is a sharp decline in Alpine agriculture, as many former farmers migrate to cities. In times of recession and unemployment, there is a much less marked decline in Alpine agriculture, but at the same time farming shows no increase in economic stability because it is not in a position to be competitive in the European marketplace. This was perhaps best illustrated in the first half of the 1960s. Great economic growth in Europe (the "economic miracle") coincided with a sharp decline in Alpine farming, during which time many unfavourable and poorly accessible cultivated areas were abandoned. The results of this period of decline are clearly noticeable on the landscape today. In the 1950s the first governmental measures to aid agriculture were instituted in an attempt to halt the process of breakdown and these measures have been considerably expanded and strengthened since the 1970s. But despite heavy subsidies in some cases, it has not been possible to stop this process, only to delay it. Currently, the status of agriculture in the Alps varies greatly from region to region.

The intermontane dry zones and the southern zone with traditional Alpine field farming are almost at the point of final breakdown; in many Alpine valleys impending breakdown can no longer be halted. In the eastern part of the eastern Alps, massive reafforestation has been carried out in the 19th and 20th centuries, forcing farmers who lived there to migrate on a large scale. In the northern part of the Alps, with traditional Alpine meadow farming, the situation is relatively good by comparison. This is the area which has profited directly from government subsidies and where many operating farms can be found. But farmers here are usually older and it is often unclear whether anyone will succeed them. Or they are part-time farmers who earn their living in tourism, industry and the service sector. If these conditions persist, farming here will have no future either, although final breakdown is still 10-15 years away, so there is still time to take countermeasures.

It is characteristic of Alpine agriculture today that traditional forms of sustainable use can no longer be carried out because they are too costly (manual labour has become too expensive). Above all, the maintenance and repair work that was so important was suspended 30 years ago. In the meantime, Alpine agriculture has been abandoned in all unfavourable and poorly accessible areas because the expenses associated with it there are greater than the yields. At the same time, favourable areas on valley floors whose soil has since been enriched, areas on lower slopes, and well-situated Alpine pastures are all used more intensively today than in earlier times.

There are considerable ecological problems associated with both of the above situations. Abandoning steep Alpine pastures increases the danger of avalanches and erosion, while species diversity disappears because wild brush or forests begin to grow. Yet this is a very slow process; new forests arise spontaneously mainly where they are not needed as a protection against avalanches. During these stages of plant succession (stages of vegetation in the transition from cultivable land to climax vegetation in accordance with the particular location) ecosystems are unstable and there is a greater danger of natural disasters. This transitional period lasts for approximately 200-300 years depending on the site; in high and arid locations, however, it lasts for many hundreds of years.

Today farmers in intensively cultivated areas are forced to produce the greatest quantities possible for economic reasons. Land use everywhere is exceeding the limits of what has historically constituted sustainable agriculture. On meadows used for fodder this occurs primarily in the form of large-scale application of artificial fertilizers and manure and also in the change from traditional cutting twice a year to silage cutting every three or four weeks. The production of hay is thereby greatly increased but at the expense of both species diversity and ecological stability on these traditional meadows. In many places today great changes in contour are also being made, using bulldozers to level hills and other uneven relief so machinery can be employed on the land. Soil which has developed over a long time is thereby being destroyed and so is the traditional small-scale nature of agriculture. This involves severe disturbances to ecological stability as well as substantially less biological diversity in the vegetation, introducing monotony on landscapes which were once richly diversified within small areas.

On pasture land today, and on Alpine pastures above all, animals often graze unsupervised, with the result that grazing is concentrated in areas that are level, very favourable, and easy to reach, while the remaining areas are hardly used at all. There is severe overgrazing in the good areas, with the corresponding ecological problems, while pronounced underuse and its corresponding ecological problems (increase in avalanches and threat of erosion on steep surfaces, wild growth, less species diversity, less valuable fodder) are apparent in the remaining areas.

Alpine agriculture today can thus hardly be called sustainable. For all practical purposes, only elderly farmers who do not yet think in modern economic terms practise sustainable agriculture. Soon, however, such farmers will no longer exist.

Nonetheless, agricultural practices are exhibiting several encouraging and positive trends. Young people are rediscovering the virtues of traditional agriculture and its sustainable forms of land use. They are founding new agricultural associations, and traditional strains of sheep and cattle are increasingly being bred once again. Traditional grains are also being cultivated anew and alternative agricultural products such as herbs and curative plants are being developed. But all these initiatives, important as they are, will only be able to reinvigorate Alpine agriculture if new economic and political conditions are created throughout the Alps which make agriculture economically feasible. A very important precondition in this regard will be a new agricultural policy in the European Community.

Forestry

Throughout human history forests have always been one of man's most important resources. But industrialization has completely devalued forests as an economic resource. The need for wood has dropped sharply in Europe because it was first replaced as a source of energy by coal and later by oil and natural gas. The prices of energy from these sources are so low that domestic timber cannot compete with them. In addition, harvesting timber in the Alps is very costly and trees there grow relatively slowly due to the elevation. Wood imported from the Third World or cut very inexpensively in Scandinavia (huge tracts of forest land which can be cut cheaply and in which timber harvesting is almost completely automated) is cheaper than any other source of supply. This situation brought about a gradual breakdown in the market for Alpine timber following the Second World War. Since the 1970s prices have been so low that many Alpine forests are no longer used.

Alpine forests have now often grown too old as a result of disuse. This superannuation is leading to ecological instability in forests once used for commercial purposes. There is also a danger of large-scale deterioration in the near future, as extensive forest stands of the same age continue to grow old. It will be necessary to institute measures which aim at the gradual conversion of these former commercial forests into forests where natural regeneration takes place.

Air pollution is another danger which threatens forests. There are two sources of such pollution. One is general, European-wide pollution emitted in industrial and urban areas which reaches primarily the northern zone of the Alps, where it causes damage to forests. A second source is the severe local pollution caused by transit traffic through the Alps, heavy traffic in the inner Alps (including tourist traffic) and home heating emissions from numerous areas where large-scale settlement has developed. This type of pollution is especially heavy in cities in the inner Alps, in major tourist centres, and along major transport routes. Some settlements have already had to be evacuated in these areas owing to pollution which has weakened forests so much that they no longer provide protection against avalanches.

Superannuation of forests in the eastern Alps has been intensified by hunting. In this region the hunting of red deer and chamois is a privilege of the rich and of highly placed politicians who do not like to wait long while stalking their prey. Accordingly, wildlife here is very dense. In winter these animals browse young trees and severely diminish forest regeneration.

All these factors intensify one another. As a result, forests are now becoming ecologically unstable and gradually less effective in providing protection–an extremely important function. Their role as a valuable commercial resource is disappearing. The problem is especially acute in valleys, where the protective role of forests is particularly

Figure 3.12: *Industrial regions of the Alps: all are situated along major rivers which provided water, power and communications*

Widespread death of trees in Alpine forest is generally agreed to be due to air pollution but the mechanisms are still disputed. There is no dispute about the associated rise in avalanche threat

important. This is true above all in those valleys where transit and tourist traffic are heavy. It is here that the threat of ecological problems is greatest.

Yet encouraging and important new approaches can also be seen in the areas of forestry and forest use. Examples include afforestation and new uses of wood as an energy source in "Schnitzelfeuerungsanlagen" (installations fired by wood scraps). These new approaches will only have an effect, however, if European energy policies are changed. As long as non-renewable sources such as coal, oil and natural gas are so inexpensive, wood from regenerated European forests will remain a non-competitive resource.

Industry in the Alps

Major industrial establishments in the Alps from the period prior to the First World War suffered a crisis after the Second World War because their advantageous locations (based on energy from hydroelectric power) no longer played any role and their remote sites in the mountains had meanwhile become a major competitive disadvantage. Many jobs are currently being eliminated at such locations and the future does not look at all encouraging. During prosperous times in the 1960s, a great number of industrial branch operations were located in the Alps because inexpensive manpower had become scarce in major urban areas. But many of these operations closed down with the onset of recession after 1975.

Although the outlook for industry in the Alps may not be good at present, many industrial jobs exist nonetheless, probably considerably more than one might think at first glance. Forty per cent of all jobs in the Austrian Alps are said to be industrial jobs, but jobs in the construction industry which are primarily dependent on tourism (especially the building of condominiums and vacation homes) must be subtracted from this estimate. Yet even accounting for this, it is likely that 20-25 per cent of all jobs are in industry. From an ecological point of view, industrial operations are major polluters (sources of air and water pollution) and do damage to entire Alpine regions. Economically, industrial jobs are very important, however, in order to avoid development of infrastructure devoted only to tourism and to prevent the Alps from becoming totally dependent on trends in the tourist industry. There is also a cultural dimension. It is very important that well-trained, innovative individuals stay in mountain regions and do not have to emigrate due to a lack of skilled jobs. Maintaining industrial jobs in the Alps while at the same time ensuring their ecological soundness will be a major task for the future.

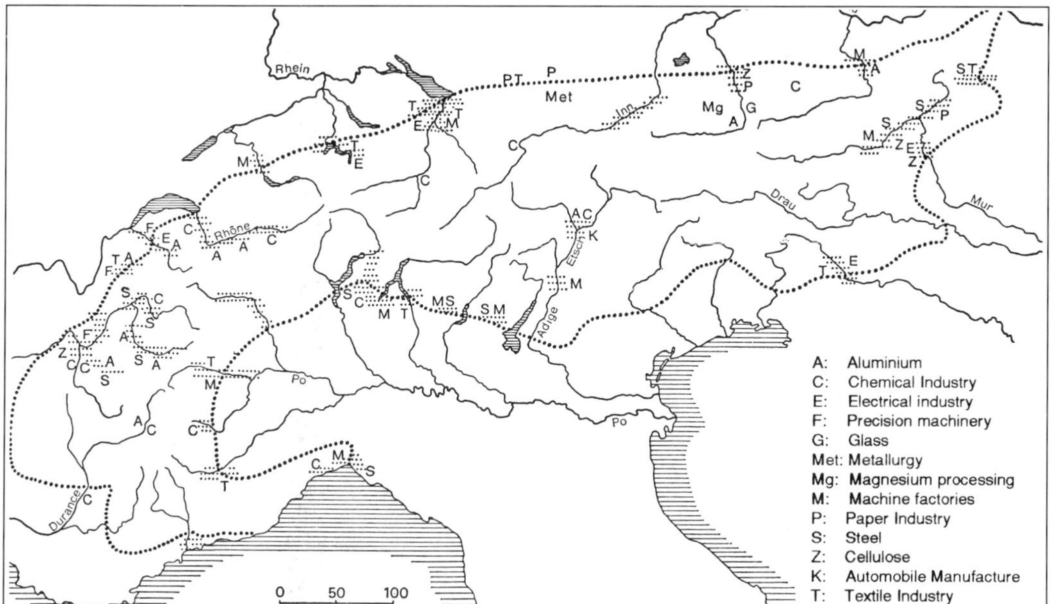

Currently there is sharp debate in the Alps over the question of whether new technology (EDP and computer-related jobs) could enhance the region as the site of information processing operations and other services. Here there is a distinct cultural gap between the "Mediterranean" and the "Germanic" areas of the Alps. In France, Italy and French-speaking Switzerland, there is great enthusiasm about these new options and some feeling that the future of the Alps lies in locating such new operations there. In Germany, Austria, and German-speaking Switzerland, by contrast, this development is viewed with great scepticism. Here it is assumed that nothing like this is likely to materialize in the Alps because very few skilled jobs will be relocated in the mountains. For cultural and social reasons, skilled jobs are likely to remain within commuting distance of major urban areas.

The present challenge is to use new technology to maintain at least those industrial sites and jobs that currently exist.

Tourism

Tourism is presently the strongest economic force in the Alps. Without it, many people would have had to abandon the mountains in the 20th century. Until about 1955 there was only a very modest infrastructure devoted to tourism. Between 1955 and 1965 the first period of expansion and boom in the tourist industry occurred, and between 1965–when mass tourism in winter began–and 1980, an even greater second period of boom and expansion took place. Between 1980 and 1990 there was some evidence of high-level stagnation and saturation, which led to greatly intensified and often ruinous, competition.

At present, lodging capacity is approximately 5 million beds; about 100 million people (40 million vacationers and 60 million weekend excursionists) visit the Alps annually. Roughly 25 per cent of annual worldwide turnover in the tourist industry is generated in the Alps.

There are considerable differences from country to country, however. An awareness of these differences is necessary to understand the problems of tourism as they currently exist.

❑ In *France* there are many huge winter sports centres which have been conceived, planned and financed in Paris. They are completely independent of the local economy and culture of the French Alps and represent economic, social and cultural influences foreign to the area. The tourist industry in France is further distributed among many small and very small tourist communes which are now barely able to remain competitive.

❑ In *Italy* a number of large tourist centres have been built with outside financing. In addition, there are many medium-sized and smaller ski areas developed for speculative purposes by real estate companies in order to sell condominiums. These often exhibit chaotic planning, are poorly built, and represent a waste of resources. Many small tourist resorts also still exist today, although the conditions of their existence are becoming increasingly difficult.

❑ In *Switzerland* the infrastructure of the Belle Epoque (large old hotels, rack railways) still exists and is currently enjoying new esteem (based on nostalgia). Many resort areas developed at this time have now become large tourist centres (Davos, Zermatt). In addition, tourism based on second homes and vacation homes is very widespread and has provided a great deal of work in the construction industry. A cutback in new construction, although desirable on ecological, cultural and social grounds, would be linked with the disadvantage of loss of skilled jobs in the construction industry.

❑ In *Austria* tourism has been purposely decentralized under governmental supervision. There is an extensive network of bed and breakfast establishments, small pensions, and small hotels owned by native inhabitants. Nonetheless, it is precisely these small local operations that are today barely able to compete with big hotel chains and international operators.

❑ In *Bavaria* land use in the Alps is especially dense because the area is used both by tourists for holidays and by people in Munich for recreation. Accordingly, the volume of tourism here is especially heavy.

❑ In *Slovenia* development of tourism has been minimal because the previous socialist Republic of Slovenia promoted industrialization in the Slovenian Alps on a systematic basis and prohibited tourism. Recently, there have been new developments very detrimental to making tourism attractive in Slovenia: the many industrial operations here have produced major air and water pollution in the Alps, which will make it difficult to develop the area for tourism.

Present-day problems relating to tourism in the Alps can be summarized as follows:

1) Small-scale local operations–small pensions and hotels owned by native inhabitants and small tourist resorts–have less and less chance of succeeding in the tourist industry owing to stiff competition. Major operators such as international hotel chains and large tourist centres, which book more than 1 million overnight stays annually, are continuing to gain a greater share of the market. Native inhabitants are being forced from this very important sector of the economy while the domination of well-capitalized, externally based operations grows stronger.

2) In the last 100 years, tourist centres have often trebled and quadrupled their populations. Many new residents drawn to these areas have increasingly been taking over positions of responsibility in the commune, while local residents are starting to become alienated from their native habitat.

3) Land has been used intensively for infrastructure to support tourism and transport. This has combined with population increase to cause such a sharp rise in property values in tourist centres that counterproductive effects have been produced (prices are now similar to those in major European urban areas). Only major commercial enterprises can pay the high prices for land in these areas. Small hotels and pensions are facing ruin as a result. Above all, building sites and rental apartments are becoming unaffordable for local residents. Many natives have already been forced to leave. This process is bound to bring considerable social tension in the future.

4) Environmental damage in the form of soil, water and air pollution, and excessive noise are present in major tourist centres. This has been caused by intensive development and the traffic brought by tourists and those who supply the tourist industry. Pollution and noise now exist on a scale comparable to that in major European metropolitan areas. Additional environmental damage is caused by ski pistes, innumerable hikers in sensitive highland areas, restaurants located on mountain summits, etc. Even though there have been noticeable improvements and ecological restoration was undertaken precisely in these areas during the 1980s, mass tourism on the whole poses a major environmental threat to Alpine ecosystems in sensitive highland areas.

5) Native inhabitants in tourist centres are being confronted with the values of post-industrial society and find themselves becoming the "servants" of their visitors. Modern values appear to be exemplary and traditional values seem outmoded and outdated. The conflict between these two worlds is so great that it is almost impossible to deal with in personal terms. Because the subject is not discussed publicly and no connections exist between these two worlds, there is an attempt to solve existing problems on an individual level. Alcoholism (since alcohol is a socially acceptable drug), misuse of tablets, and drug use (primarily among the young) are found frequently. These developments constitute a problem more surrounded by taboo than any other subject in the Alps and whose very mention excites strong reactions. Cultural and social tensions and conflicts threaten to break out. This could severely disrupt the further development of tourism.

Despite the stagnation of the 1980s, there seem to be no economic difficulties with regard to the further development of tourism in the Alps (continued growth appears to be proceeding without problems in the 1990s). On the other hand, major ecological, social and cultural problems have arisen which have the potential to grow quickly and produce counterproductive results. A few regions (e.g. the Tyrol) have recognized these problems and have declared their intention to halt their further development. These regions are currently emphasizing the ecological soundness of tourist installations and the solution of social and cultural conflicts. But these are only isolated undertakings which point in the right direction; they must be applied in all regions where tourism exists.

Non-tourist services

Non-tourist services are defined to include all forms of government administration down to the communal level, social services, training programmes, health and educational services, commerce, banking and insurance, and cultural affairs. Historically, these services have always played a certain role in Alpine cities. But since the Second World War this sector of the economy has become generally much more important. It experienced a certain boom in the 1980s which is likely to continue in the future.

The reason for this growth is the presence of many people with great purchasing power in Alpine tourist centres. Major tourist centres have thus become important locations for banks, insurance companies, real estate agencies, holding companies, and other services (the so-called tourist-related non-tourist services). Moreover, services which are not dependent on a specific location, such as advertising, design, information processing, etc., are increasingly being moved to the Alps or their immediate vicinity because the environment is considerably more attractive and healthier there than in major urban areas. This development is already quite advanced in France, in the Geneva-Annecy-Chambéry-Grenoble metropolitan belt. Here, in large valley channels easily accessible by car, many new businesses have appeared. Their employees live in what were once mountain villages, where there has been a sharp drop in population in the last 100 years. The French refer to this as "rurbanization", the urbanization of rural areas without the introduction of city structures. There has been little study of this phenomenon in other countries to date. But it can be assumed that it already plays a considerable role in all large cities in the Alps or bordering them. Its significance is likely to increase substantially in the future because of the central European location of the Alps and the attractive environment they offer.

Water resources management

Production of hydroelectric power in the Alps now takes place on such a scale that there is no longer a single major river which flows for its entire course in a natural condition, and there are fewer than ten major Alpine rivers whose courses are uninterrupted for more than 15 km.

The use of water resources can be subdivided into four different categories:

1) drinking water (obtained in the Alps and piped into large cities);

2) water for irrigation (the largest reservoir in the Alps, the Lac de Serre-Poncon in the southern Alps of France, is devoted primarily to this purpose);

3) production of electricity in run-of-river power stations and

4) storage of electricity.

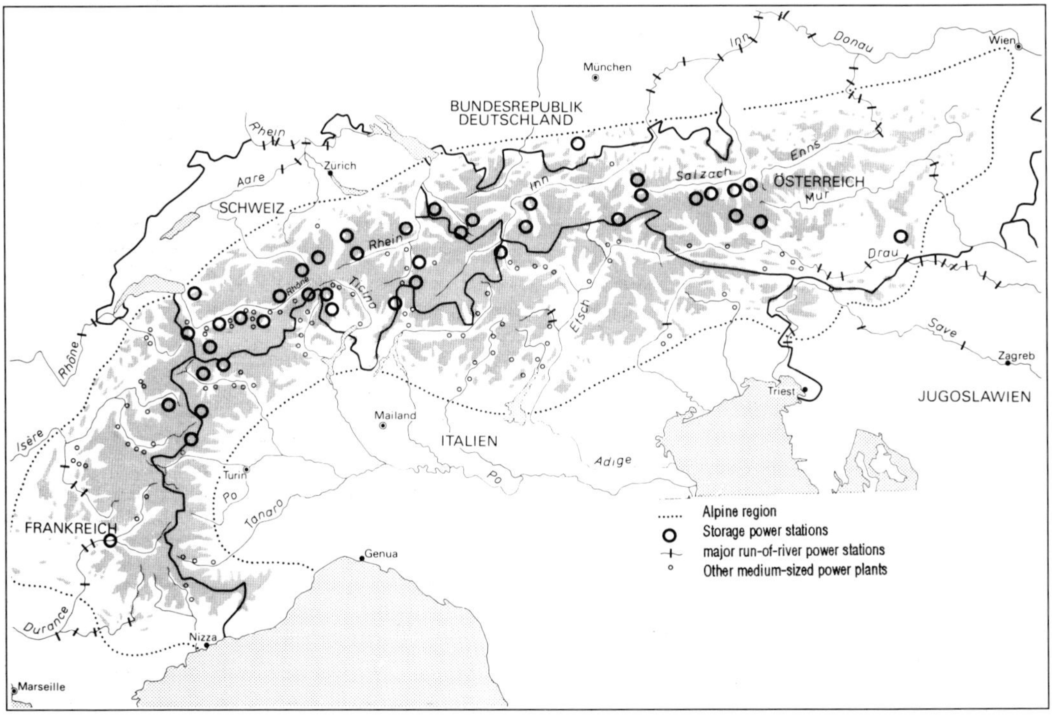

Power storage stations represent the greatest intervention in the environment because natural lakes at high altitudes in the vicinity of Alpine pastures have been artificially enlarged and flat valley floors have been converted into lakes. The watcr is usually used to produce electricity in winter, so stream flow patterns are completely altered. In earlier times rivers and streams conducted the most water in summer and the least in winter, today this situation is often reversed. The result is extensive change in all river ecosystems. An even greater environmental impact has been caused by the diversion of many streams since 1955. In order to expand the production of water power in high-altitude stations, tunnels were built for large-scale diversion of streams over extensive areas. The streams were then conducted into reservoirs. The water budget in many Alpine regions has been completely altered as a result. Many streams have dried up today or have very little water left, while a disproportionate share of water flows under large power stations.

In the second half of the 1980s new plans were developed to expand the production of hydroelectric power. Since there was already an adequate supply of mass-produced energy in Europe (chiefly from atomic power plants), it became economically feasible to use this energy to pump water upwards into high-altitude reservoirs. This way, hydroelectric power could be produced and sold later at times of peak demand (winter) as "peak current" (costing four times as much as less expensively produced energy). This does not constitute "energy production" but "energy enrichment", an economic transaction which produces no new electrical energy. New and extraordinarily large water reservoirs for this purpose are planned for the Alps with total volumes approximately four times as large as those now in existence. Because these plans are linked with major environmental impacts, they are being vigorously opposed by environmentalists. The idea is to make the Alps into an immense water reservoir which will supply Europe. Many Alpine valleys which are currently not used for tourism are also destined to be converted into reservoirs.

Fundamentally, man's use of water resources constitutes a severe, large-scale intervention in Alpine ecosystems. To date, virtually no major Alpine stream or river has remained untouched. This

Figure 3.13: *Hydroelectric power stations in the Alps in 1980*

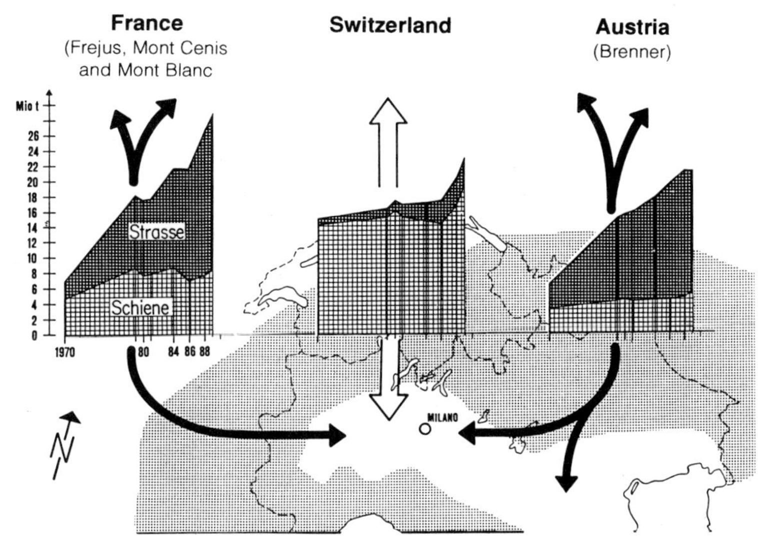

	1970 (million tons)	1979/80 (million tons)	1984 (million tons)	1989 (million tons)
Road	6.1	18.25	28.80	40.60
Rail	22.1	29.02	27 63	32.28

Figure 3.14: *Transalpine commercial transport by road and rail 1970-89*

has completely altered Alpine hydrological conditions in two ways. There have been extensive changes in regional stream flow patterns as the result of widespread diversion of water into large reservoirs, and there has been a shift in the main discharge of water from summer to winter.

It is clear that European interests outside the Alps have determined that water resources must be used and also how they are used, while taking relatively little account of the interests of Alpine inhabitants. "Colonization of the Alps by European cities" is an expression applicable in the case of water resources, and is heard primarily in Italy. Provisions for financial compensation for Alpine residents vary greatly throughout the Alps. In countries with centralized political systems like France and Italy, there is hardly any compensation. In Germany and Austria, it is substantially greater, and it is highest of all in Switzerland. But even here there is the question of whether any payment can compensate local inhabitants for loss of the power to determine the availability and the use of one of their most important resources.

Transit traffic in the Alps

In the case of transit traffic, no specific Alpine "resource" is actually being used. European transit traffic passes through the Alps because they stretch across the middle of the continent, separating the very important economic area of northern Italy from the rest of Europe and blocking access to the Balkans. For a long time transit traffic was completely confined to railways; since 1900, there have been seven major rail lines through the Alps. Since 1955, however, the volume of traffic on roads has been steadily increasing. While virtually no expansion or improvement of railways has taken place in the 20th century, a completely new road network with motorways, highways and many tunnels has been constructed since 1955.

This has brought fundamental changes in the valleys used by transit traffic, which are usually narrow. Traffic has steadily taken up more space in the most desirable valley locations, forcing agriculture out of these areas and contributing to an increase in the price of land, to the disadvantage of local residents. Air pollution and ceaseless noise have made life less attractive and caused environmental deterioration. Forest decline in these valleys is especially severe, and the danger of avalanches and erosion is increasing. Many people are under such stress that they no longer feel at home in their native habitat. Moreover, areas on both sides of major motorways have become desirable sites for commercial operations and services, so these valleys are becoming more heavily settled. The natives are increasingly being forced to leave. There is now an almost unbroken line of settlement on both sides of the Brenner Pass from Kufstein (in the northern Alps) to Innsbruck and from Veron (in the southern Alps) to Bozen. A similar development can be seen on both sides of the Gotthard Pass. The Alps are becoming urbanized along major transport routes and losing their typically Alpine character.

The problem is not confined only to major valleys used by transit traffic, however. It is also present in valleys heavily used for tourism, although in less pronounced form. Tourist traffic also causes severe pollution in valley ecosystems, takes up a great deal of space, and makes central locations in tourist communes much less attractive. Some places such as Serfaus in the Tyrol (not cities by any means, but rural tourist centres) have begun to construct subway systems to combat the problem of traffic. But this is too costly an approach to constitute a real solution. Extensive improvements must be made in public transportation systems between major European cities and tourist centres in the Alps to deal with this problem. Since almost all Alpine tourist centres have rail connections, this appears to be a feasible approach.

Major new construction is now being planned. Three new railway tunnels (Lötschberg, Gotthard and Brenner) will considerably increase railway transport capacity. But this will not be enough if traffic in Europe continues to increase at the rate it has in the last two decades. The new European single market is also likely to account for additional growth in the volume of traffic by 1993. The problems of Alpine transit traffic will be finally solved only when there is a new traffic policy for all of Europe which starts with ecological considerations and aims at reducing growth in the volume of traffic. ■

Economically weak Alpine regions

The primary problem in the Alps, as usually perceived in the public mind, is overuse of the land. Mass tourism, transit traffic and use of water resources are at the centre of this perception. What is overlooked is that these problems are typical of some Alpine regions only, and not of the Alps generally. So-called "economically weak regions", in which the traditional economy and way of life are breaking down and not being replaced by new developments, constitute approximately 40 per cent of the total area in the Alps. These regions are located primarily in the southern French Alps, the western and eastern Italian Alps, the southern Swiss Alps (the Canton of Tessin and parts of the Canton of Graubünden), the eastern part of the eastern Austrian Alps (eastern Tyrol and large parts of upper Austria, Steiermark and Kärnten) and the western Slovenian Alps. The existence of such regions in central Europe clearly shows that modern European development has not included every area of the continent and that there are great disparities between active (developed) regions (with solid economic growth and a good population base) and passive (stagnant) regions (with declining economies and populations). These disparities, which in some cases exist on a very small scale, correspond to large-scale disparities between industrialized and developing countries.

Economically weak regions are characterized by a 60, 70 or 80 per cent drop in population over the past 100 years, a gradual decline in traditional agriculture, and no new jobs in tourism, industry or non-tourist-related services. Two factors are responsible for this. There is very little direct pressure from European urban areas to use land here; not every Alpine valley is destined to be used for tourism. The Alps are so extensive and the competition so intense that many valleys have no chance for this type of development. But another force is also at work: the native inhabitants refuse to accept innovation and new developments. In the confrontation between the modern world and the world of tradition, they attempt to preserve their traditional ways by insulating themselves

Figure 3.15: Italian Alpine communities (comunità montane) with population level 1981-85

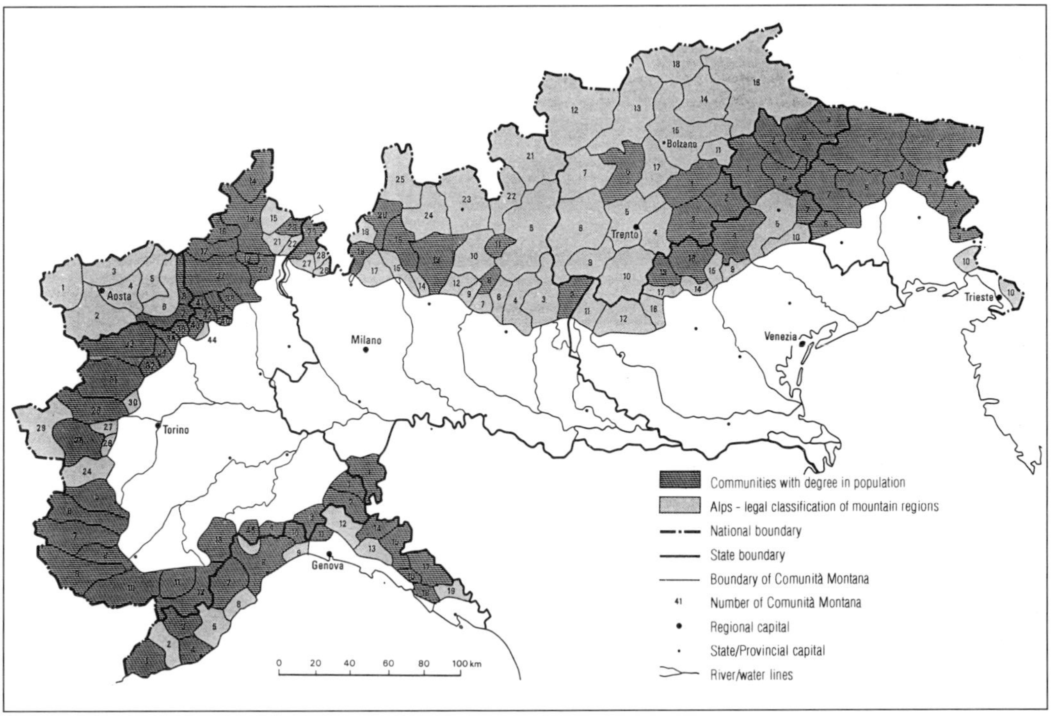

from the modern world as completely as they can, and insist on living the life to which they are accustomed. Anthropologists call this attitude "kulturelle Erstarrung" (cultural rigidity).

At first it appears that this rigidity has very positive effects. Traditional Alpine agriculture continues, along with its sustainable practices that protect the environment. But problems begin to develop unnoticed, precisely because no changes are introduced, not even worthwhile and environmentally compatible changes. Thus the conflict between traditional and modern agriculture grows over years and decades until finally there are only a few old men who farm as they always did but take care not to allow new forms of agriculture to develop. Innovation is rare. Given the "commune system" that is usually in force in these areas, innovations can only be introduced if a majority of the commune's inhabitants vote for them. Since the majority of the farmers who remain there oppose anything new, young people willing to try new ways leave these regions. In time, a social structure develops which intensifies the climate of rigidity. It is this development that currently prohibits sensible and sustainable use of valuable agricultural resources. It will only be possible to restore sustainability when this traditional way of life breaks down completely and when traditional land use is abandoned because of death, old age or illness. Then there will be freedom to adopt new forms of agricultural land use, but only during a limited period of transition. There can only be a new beginning here as long as fields, meadows and pastures do not grow wild, roads and footpaths do not disintegrate, and houses do not deteriorate or become part of the infrastructure of tourism. In another 10-15 years at the most a new start will no longer be possible because the costs of restoring cultivable land and infrastructure will be too high. The question is whether natives of the area interested in innovation and others from outside who are also willing to introduce innovations can exploit the chance for a new start, or whether the chance will be lost, since state and communal conditions also make innovation more difficult rather than helping to promote it. This would mean losing a chance to restore and use valuable agricultural and forest resources.

A new development took place in economically weak Alpine regions in the 1980s. Small vacation homes were built everywhere, often by former property owners who had migrated from these regions to the city a generation earlier. This building boom can be explained by general social conditions in Europe. It is gradually becoming "normal" in modern consumer culture for many employees or skilled workers to have their own vacation home. In view of increasing environmental problems in major metropolitan areas, the desire to flee the cities for a pure environment during increasingly long holiday periods continues to grow.

At present, this new development is concerned solely with dwelling space and has few secondary effects. Only the local building trades have profited from it, but in modest ways, since much of the labour was done by the owners themselves. In addition, food consumed here is usually brought from home rather than being purchased locally.

It is questionable whether this development will bring improvement to these Alpine regions. Although it is rather modest in scale at present, if this form of land use increases, population in these regions will begin to grow. All current surveys and projections are based on the assumption that leisure time will be an even more important factor in Europe in the coming decades. This indicates that a further boom in the building of private vacation homes in economically weak Alpine regions is probable. But there is also a danger that this development will be one-sided. Only homes are being renovated and newly built, while agriculture is breaking down completely and practically no jobs are being created in the tourist sector. On the other hand, there is also an opportunity to use the building boom to improve agriculture and local businesses and services on a systematic basis. This, however, will require careful planning at the communal and regional levels.

Loss of cultural identity

Analyses of tradition in the Alps have shown how important cultural identity is as a factor in sustainable use of the environment. Traditional Alpine culture, with its emphasis on thinking beyond the present generation to consider the next, is breaking down as it confronts modern industrial society. It is characteristic of this process that these two worlds exist in close proximity as complete strangers with nothing in common. Either the modern world dominates, as in tourist communes, and traditional Alpine cultural values seem old-fashioned and are pushed aside (repression), or the world of tradition insulates itself from modern society and becomes more set in its traditional ways (rigidity). In both cases there are no conscious connections between the traditional and the modern in which central components of traditional and modern culture are bound together in new ways.

This is the cultural reason why sustainable use of the environment is so difficult in the Alps today. Where the values of modern society dominate, *all* traditional values are excluded, including those relating to sustainable use of nature and the knowledge that nature can never be completely dominated by technology. Instead, all modern values are embraced, including attitudes in which nature is regarded merely as a raw material, and environmental problems simply as technical difficulties which can be solved by large-scale use of technology if necessary. And where the traditional world dominates, existing sustainable land use practices are undermined because traditional forms of agriculture (very small operations, many small plots, no quality production) are no longer competitive. They appear to be completely unable to survive and their total breakdown becomes merely a question of time. Rarely, if ever, is there a chance in either situation to combine the positive values of the past (above all knowledge of sustainable use of the environment) with the positive features of the present (greater freedom of competition) in such a way that the result would be a viable new culture with a satisfactory quality of life.

In the second half of the 1980s, organizations representing cultural, tourist and agricultural interests were formed in opposition to current trends. These organizations deliberately advocate sustainable development and a strengthening of cultural identity. The Austrian Hans Haid has spoken of "the greatest protest movement in the Alps since the Peasants' War". There is a hope that these initial steps will result in a major attempt to build a new cultural self-awareness committed to sustainable use of the environment.

Environmental problems in the Alps

Our studies of pre-industrial society have shown that human life and economic activity in the Alps were based on farming. Natural resources were not *directly* available for use, however; man first had to make the landscape cultivable in order to live in the Alps and use Alpine resources. But since cultivable land is not inherently ecologically stable, man must give it the stability necessary to prevent natural disasters from making life impossible. It became apparent that the correct manner of using natural resources–the proper mean between overuse and underuse–is very decisive in determining whether cultivated land remains stable or not.

For these reasons "environmental destruction" in the Alps today results not only from overuse of available resources, as is often assumed, but also from underuse, when land which was once cultivated is allowed to lie fallow.

This is linked to the problem of restricting nature protection and environmental protection to nature reserves, which is an insufficient measure. In the first place, national parks and nature reserves today are not natural landscapes; their ecology has been greatly influenced by man. Making them protected areas and limiting or completely forbidding their use does not always seem sensible from an ecological point of view. Second, protected areas in the Alps are small and do not represent the diversity of Alpine ecosystems. Concentrating environmental protection in these small areas would cause other unprotected areas to be heavily overused and destroyed more quickly. Environmental protection would thus be counterproductive because many valuable ecosystems and biotopes are in unprotected areas. Environmental protection in the Alps must be formulated and implemented with regard to all ecosystems if it is to be effective. Third, the creation of national parks –one each in Germany, Switzerland and Yugoslavia, two in Italy, and three in France–is a political process which must take account of many different interests. Environmental protection is often not a decisive factor. Many protected areas at the regional level today were created mainly for purposes relating to tourism, which helps promote economic weakness in these regions. For all these reasons it would be unfortunate if environmental protection were to be restricted to or concentrated in existing protected areas. Therefore, the international initiative launched by environmentalists to create another national park in the Mont Blanc region should be rejected. The danger is too great that it will become a politically inspired project primarily of benefit to voters living in urban areas.

The problems of underuse are associated with wild growth and forest growth in places that are no longer used or used only very extensively. Underuse is usually linked to a decline in the variety of species and more frequent occurrence of avalanches and erosion on steep surfaces, thus increasing the danger of natural disasters. These developments can be found in many areas in economically weak Alpine regions. But they also occur in tourist centres because here only selected areas are devoted to very intensive modern forms of use. The remaining areas are virtually unused and deteriorate.

By contrast, the problems of overuse are found primarily in favourable and centrally located areas or parts of larger regions, i.e. on wide valley floors and lower mountain slopes. Farming and tourism, as well as the general pressure of settlement and the oversettlement of entire valley floors, are all causes of overuse. Water resources management, industry and transit traffic also contribute to overuse of resources.

The problem of air pollution in Europe is being superimposed on both these developments. This further weakens the ability of Alpine ecosystems to regenerate.

The consequences of these problems are a decline in the diversity of traditional plant societies (species loss), a disappearance of typical small-scale landscapes, a diminished ability of various ecosystems to regenerate, and less ecological stability. These developments are accompanied by the fundamental danger of more frequent natural disasters. Yet given the enormous complexity of the natural and social factors involved, it is fundamentally impossible to calculate precisely the increase in danger and predict the next major catastrophe. The "catastrophic summer" of 1987 with its many floods, mud flows, and a major landslide in Veltlin made it clear, however, that all the technology we can employ to prevent natural disasters is only of minor importance and that technology will not become the master of nature in the Alps. Sustainable use of nature and measures to prevent disasters are of the utmost importance. ■

Figure 3.16: *Regions threatened by erosion in the Bavarian Alps. This map clearly shows that large areas in the Alps must be considered ecologically endangered, threatening all transit roads and tourist centres*
Source: *Beilage zur Beantwortung der Interpellation Gefährdung von Mensch und Umwelt in Alpenraum* (Landtagsdruckesache 11/3444)

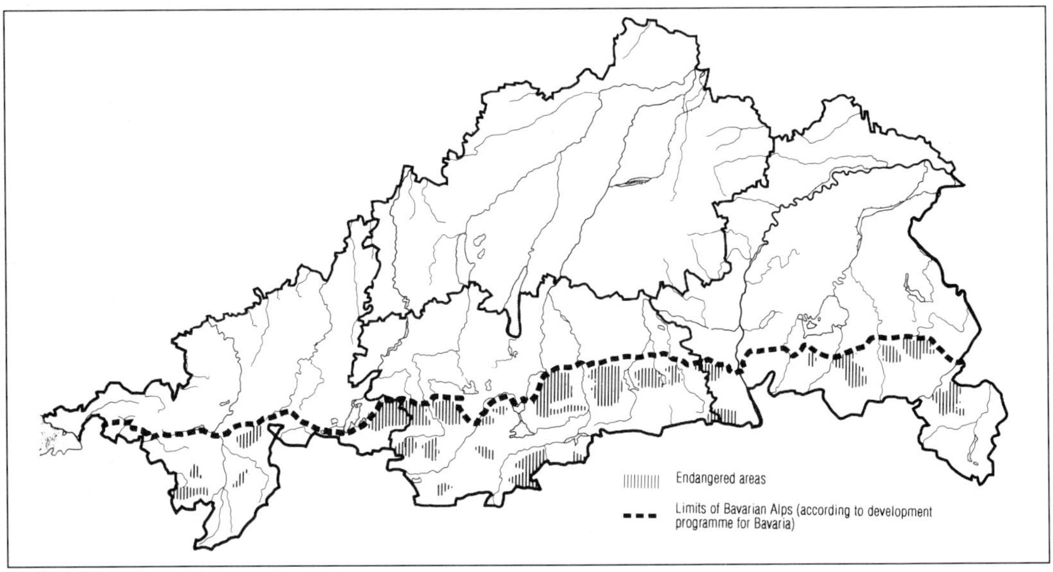

Ensuring a viable economic future and satisfactory quality of life in the Alps

The starting point: enhancement of Alpine resources

The Alps are the world's best known and most precisely scientifically studied mountain system. Recently, very specific suggestions and projects have been formulated for new, alternative and positive types of development in the Alps. Many encouraging initial steps have been taken in virtually every Alpine area: agriculture, forestry, energy use, industry, tourism, transport and environmental protection. Initiated by independent groups, government representatives and scientists, these steps cannot be presented in detail here. They all aim in approximately the same direction, however, and will be characterized in what follows.

Human intervention has completely transformed the ecology of the Alps. They are neither a natural nor a near-natural landscape, but an anthropogenically shaped cultural landscape. This cultural landscape is the foundation of all human life and economic activity there. If the Alps are to have a viable future, the first and foremost task must be responsible management of this landscape, including a commitment to its ecological stability, which will first have to be purposely and laboriously restored in the case of each ecosystem.

The easiest and most effective way to achieve this is through farming and forestry practices adapted to environmental conditions on a small scale. Renewal of ecological stability must be just as important as the tasks of production (sustainable use). Modern forms of land use–tourism, water resources management, industry, labour, transport–must be conducted in such a way that they do not overstrain and destroy ecological stability. On the contrary, their managers must feel responsible for ecological stability and cooperate closely with the farming and forestry sectors to help maintain it. Sustainable use of the Alpine environment can be most sensibly carried out in this way. Theoretically, of course, farming and forestry could be completely given up (they are in any case no longer competitive in today's economic climate), and the job of maintaining the ecological stability of the cultural landscape left to modern-day land users alone. There are three arguments against this on principle, however.

a) Agriculture and forestry can make use of the vast and valuable natural resources in the Alps. Failure to use the Alps for these purposes would be a waste, even though there are economic difficulties at present. Moreover, only if the Alps are used for agriculture and forestry can the great variety of vegetation and the small-scale, highly diverse character of Alpine ecosystems be maintained.

b) Giving up agriculture and forestry in the Alps would represent a complete break with tradition and base all economic activity on a new foundation lacking in tradition. Extremely valuable knowledge of how to deal with nature, gained through experience in farming and very seldom put down in writing, would be lost. There would also be a very great danger that the significance of ecological stability in the cultural landscape would not be recognized by those engaged in modern forms of land use.

c) The disappearance of agriculture and forestry in the Alps would mean the loss of one aspect of European diversity. By contrast with the USA, for example, Europe is characterized by many different economic and social systems which have existed in close proximity within very small areas. Their mutual assimilation, which has been progressing in the 20th century and will be hastened by the creation of the European Community single market in 1992, raises doubts about a central feature of European identity.

There is a pragmatic argument too. Renewal of ecological stability included as a part of agricultural and forestry practices is likely to be accomplished less expensively in all probability (it does not represent a cost; it brings gains owing to its close connection with the production of food and raw materials) than renewal carried out by the tourist, transport and industrial sectors merely as maintenance work (where it represents purely extra costs).

This is why considerable details have been given in this report about traditional agricultural systems in the Alps: they are of particular importance for the future. Traditional forms of agricultural land use are by no means outmoded today. On the contrary, they are especially important because they contain empirical ecological knowledge about sustainable use of nature. This

Traditional farming methods are still to be found in some of the remoter parts of the Alps

knowledge is essential if modern land use is to be made sustainable. This does not mean, however, that traditional forms of land use should be continued unchanged today (which is virtually impossible). But we must be very well aware of them in order to know which features and which parts must be retained and which can be altered. Knowledge based on the experience of earlier generations in the Alps is indispensable today in shaping the ecological components of land use in an industrial and service economy.

Against this background, agriculture and forestry are confronted with the following tasks.

Alpine farming cannot be concerned only with the production of food. It has instead a fourfold task. It must produce food, maintain the ecological stability of the cultural landscape, and maintain biological diversity through small-scale cultivation precisely adapted to different locations. It must also maintain a diverse and varied landscape that can provide a base for tourism and cultural identity. Production in the Alps cannot be concerned with large quantities. It must first of all be devoted to high-quality products typical of their respective regions and thus capable of commanding better prices. Second, Alpine agriculture must maintain and continue development of the traditional diversity of domestic animals and grains precisely because they are usually very well adapted to the environment, facilitate sustainable agriculture, and also constitute a valuable genetic resource which we cannot afford to lose. If these tasks are to be accomplished, however, new economic, social and political arrangements will be required at the national and international levels.

Forestry also has several distinct functions. Since forests often play an important protective role, their ecological stability must be maintained along with the production of wood as a raw material and a regenerating natural resource. Attention must also be given to maintaining and increasing the diversity of species in forests (reducing the spruce monoculture of the 19th and 20th centuries) and to preserving forests as valuable recreation areas. New conditions will also be necessary to accomplish these tasks.

In the case of modern land uses–tourism, water resources management, transport and industry–the most important thing is that they be environmentally compatible. They must not threaten ecological stability. In the 1980s, important progress was made in this area with regard to tourism. But the aim must be to subject all modern forms of land use to environmental impact analysis (EIA). Second, these modern developments must not become the rivals of agriculture and forestry (e.g. with regard to high land prices) or drive them away. Instead, they must support these traditional sectors (through economic links such as direct sale of agricultural products to tourists) and strengthen them (by providing additional sources of income). But this, too, will only succeed when new, appropriate conditions are created. Initial steps in this direction have already begun, however.

A policy framework for sustainable development

To restore Alpine resources in conjunction with sustainable use of nature as outlined in this report, new political and economic frameworks will be necessary. These frameworks must be created on four different political levels which are, or must be, directly linked.

1) The communal level: this is the lowest political level. Currently, existing conflicts are most apparent here and the task will be to develop a common concept of natural resource use which applies to all users. This is necessary to prevent many individual interventions from multiplying and producing ecological disasters. Various communes in the Swiss and Austrian Alps have developed "Gemeindeleitbilder" (communal master plans). These represent an attempt by the commune to achieve integrated development planning. These communes also hope to reduce conflicts and competition between different areas of economic activity and between the economy, the environment and the culture on a broader level. Such development plans usually set limits on the amount of infrastructure devoted to tourism. This represents a deliberate, self-imposed limit on growth in the interest of positive future development. There is an urgent need to devise such approaches for all communes in the Alps, and they must prescribe limits on specific land use practices. This should be an institutionalized movement in the form of a citizens' initiative involving all the citizens of the commune.

2) In the 1970s a number of Alpine countries created what are known as "regions", usually associations of 10-15 communes. These regions have been given important planning functions because Alpine communes are often too small to do their own planning and because a valley with many communes often constitutes a single tourist area, thus making common action necessary at a higher level. In some cases they have developed quite important and forward-looking "integrated regional plans" which consciously take into account the changing interrelations among agriculture, forestry and tourism and their interaction with the environment and the culture. These plans have sometimes been impaired by the lack of financial and political options at this level. There must therefore be a purposeful attempt to increase the power to act at this level. These associations also have the task of trying to resolve the many conflicts and forms of egotism that occur in individual communes (parochialism) at the regional level, thereby slowing counterproductive developments.

3) At the state level, there has been international cooperation since the 1970s in the form of what are known as "alpine Arbeitsgemeinschaften" (working groups concerned with the Alps). These are known as "Arge Alp" (central Alps), "Arge Alp-Adria" (eastern Alps), and COTRAO (western Alps). Today these groups are represented almost everywhere in the Alps. At this level, important national decisions are put into practice and countries with federal systems have considerable freedom of action here, making it a particularly significant level in political terms. These three working groups have also formulated models for future development in their respective regions of the Alps. The commitment to cooperative integrated planning evident here is a step in the right direction. It is the task of these groups to function as a control centre operating between the international and national levels above them and the regional and local levels below them, and to consider the interests and needs of the Alps in the light of European-wide interests. Efforts are presently still in the initial stages because, at this level, there is a fundamental lack of political power to control and change international trends in development from within the Alps.

4) Since 1989 the environment ministers of all seven Alpine countries have been negotiating an Alpine Convention. The convention itself aims to create a central political framework to deal with the most important problem areas (agriculture, tourism, transport, environmental protection) and make compliance mandatory in order to prevent uneven competition among Alpine countries. The environment ministers are taking sustainable

development as their fundamental starting point, even though details on what this means and how it should be interpreted are not yet clear. Cooperation of this sort partly eliminates division along national lines and marks the start of a new era in which the Alps will be regarded as a large, uniform geographical area within Europe. This creates preconditions which should make it possible to advocate sustainable development in the Alps with a much better chance to prevail over the interests of the European metropolis.

Sustainable development in the Alps will only be possible if appropriate frameworks are created at all four of these political levels. There is such great interconnection between present-day problems that conditions for sustainable development cannot be guaranteed at any one political level. This makes it clear that sustainable development can only be meaningfully formulated if it is designed in the most decentralized manner possible. However, in Europe, corresponding national and international frameworks will be essential.

The four political levels in the Alps reflect Europe in microcosm. Ecological problems in the Alps are not specific to the region nor are they extraordinary. It is rather that fundamental European environmental problems are distinctly pronounced in the Alps. Whereas these problems can frequently be concealed by their extensive distribution throughout Europe, in the Alps it is unmistakably clear that misuse of nature leads to damage and disaster which directly threaten man's existence. The political approach to ensuring sustainable development, based on common frameworks throughout the Alps which are strongly decentralized, could also apply to all of Europe. Development can only be made sustainable throughout Europe if no European-wide central levelling structures dominate. Such structures do not take account of Europe's many environmental and cultural differences; therefore, sustainability cannot be achieved within a central, European-wide framework alone. Instead, it is important that regions with common environmental and economic problems determine regional frameworks. Europe, like the Alps, must be divided into regions, each of which sets its respective special conditions for achieving sustainability. Economic policy and development can be formulated in sustainable fashion only if spatial division of labour and European-wide interconnections are consciously devised at the regional level. Only a "Europe of regions" can engage in sustainable economic activity.

From an Alpine point of view, the Alpine Convention, coupled with a deliberate regionalization of economic development, could serve as a model for other mountain regions of the world. This should not be understood as European dominance, but rather as a way of supporting and strengthening decentralized, independent initiatives which already exist in many high mountain areas.

Further research

All past research on the Alps has been heavily nationalistic in focus because the Alps are located within the borders of seven different European countries. International research efforts have been rare. As a result, no common and comparable meaningful data are currently available on the entire Alpine situation, a seemingly absurd state of affairs. Such data must first be laboriously compiled. Likewise, research must be conducted throughout the Alps and be international and interdisciplinary in character. These conditions are essential to aid and support the aims of the Alpine Convention. The greatest challenges facing scientists at present are the creation of a joint research centre (with a decentralized structure in each country) and agreement on aims and methods in research. ■

References

Since many studies of the Alps have been published, it is not necessary to provide a detailed bibliography here. Listed instead are three publications which contain bibliographies of important works and present general overviews.

1. BÄTZING, WERNER, AND MESSERLI, PAUL, eds. *Die Alpen im Europa der neunziger Jahre - ein ökologisch gefährdeter Raum im Zentrum Europas zwischen Eigenständigkeit und Abhängigkeit* (The Alps in the 1990s: an ecologically endangered region in central Europe between autonomy and dependence). Geographisches Institut der Universität Bern, Bern. 1991. (Published in the Geographica Bernensia series as *Geographica Bernensia* P 22).

This work contains articles on the Alps from all seven Alpine countries, written from the respective national points of view. The main topics covered are present-day problems, national policy on mountain regions and land use planning, and perspectives on future development. There is a bibliography of the most important publications between 1975 and 1980 covering the Alps as a whole. There is also a comprehensive bibliography on the Alps (approximately 600 titles) for the years between 1980 and 1990, covering environmental, economic and cultural problems, as well as policy on mountain regions, land use planning, and development policy. It is arranged by country.

2. BÄTZING, WERNER. *Die Alpen - Entstehung und Gefährdung einer europäischen Kulturlandschaft* (The Alps: development and endangerment of a European cultural landscape). C.H. Beck Verlag. München. 1991.

This work gives a survey of all current problems in the Alps (with a relevant bibliography). There is an overview of the situation in each Alpine country (with a bibliography of the most important works). Important proposals for new, alternative forms of development in the Alps are presented (with a bibliography). A comprehensive bibliography covering environmental, economic, cultural and historical topics is included (approximately 600 titles).

3. MESSERLI, PAUL. *Mensch und Natur im alpinen Lebensraum - Risiken, Chancen, Perspektiven zentrale Erkenntnisse aus dem schweizerischen MAB-Programmem* (Man and Nature in the Alpine Environment: risks, opportunities, and perspectives. Main Results from the Swiss MAB Programme). Verlag P. Haupt. Bern/Stuttgart. 1989.

This work contains a summary of the Man and Biosphere Programme (UNESCO) in Switzerland. This is the most comprehensive research programme in the Alps to date, and is concerned with the problem of man and the environment in high mountain regions. An appendix is included with a bibliography of the Swiss MAB Programme (pp. 349-368).

4

The Himalaya:
prospects for and constraints on sustainable development

Ama Dablam and the rapidly expanding lake on the Imja Glacier. Drainage of the lake could devastate trails, campsites and bridges along the tourist route to the Everest base camp

Introduction

The Himalaya, the most populous and most fragile of the world's mountains is also the most significant crustal feature of Asia. Lauded with superlatives, this mountain range boasts the highest point on the surface of the Earth in Mt. Everest and the world's second wettest location in Cherrapunji. It is the habitat of an extraordinary mix of people with diverse languages, cultures or racial origins. This high mountain chain, viewed with divine respect throughout the Asian region, consists mainly of an arc, convex to the south, more than 2 500 km in length and flanked by the Hengduan on its eastern end and Karakoram and the Hindu Kush on its northwestern extremity (Fig 4.1).

The general definition of the Himalaya, which, in the original Sanskrit means "the Land of Snow and Ice", includes the larger high mountain region encompassing all the above four chains of which the Himalayan arc is the most imposing and longest. In the Hindu mythological texts the snow-clad peaks of the Himalaya were described as the abode of the gods, probably due to their environmental purity and absence of human settlements. In the last few decades degradation of the environment and the poverty of the Himalayan people have been the object of much discussion and development effort. While the solution to the problem of poverty requires the accelerated use of natural resources, the ecological fragility of the region and the need for conservation pose serious restrictions. This apparently insoluble dichotomy has become well-known in academic literature as the "Himalayan Dilemma". This chapter is an attempt to understand the dilemma and to present a report on aspects special to the development-conservation relation. Some steps for future possibilities of sustainable development in the Himalayan region will be suggested on this basis.

The Asian upland identified as the Himalayan region covers an approximate area of 3.4 million km^2 and is spread between latitude 20-38 degrees N and longitude 63-104 degrees E. The area is drained mainly by the three major rivers Ganga (Ganges), Indus and Yarlungtsangpo -Brahmaputra, and partly by rivers like the Jinsha, Mekong, Salween, Irrawadi, Karnaphuli, Amu Darya etc. (Fig 4.2). The Himalayan region thus defined is spread over eight Asian countries, namely Afghanistan, Bangladesh, Bhutan, China, India, Myanmar, Nepal and Pakistan and is the habitat of about 116 million people. The Himalaya

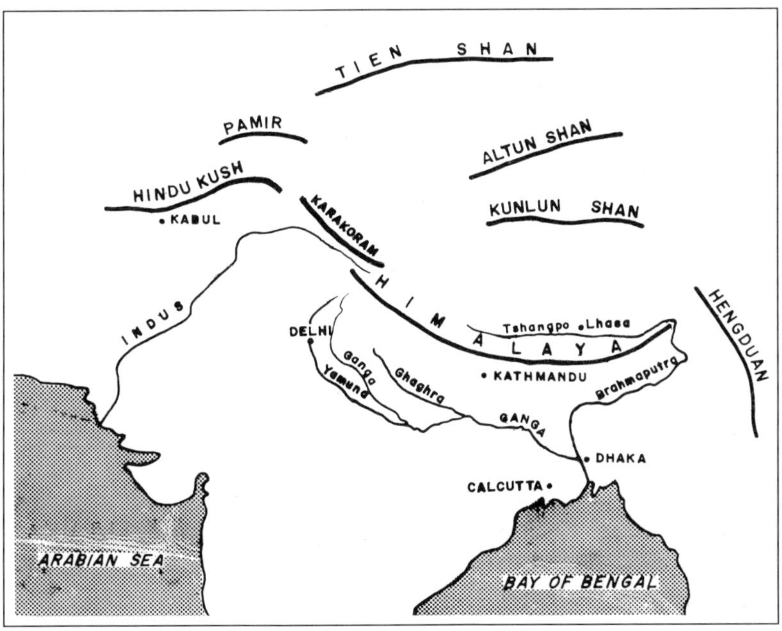

Figure 4.1: The location of the various mountain ranges in and around the Himalayan region

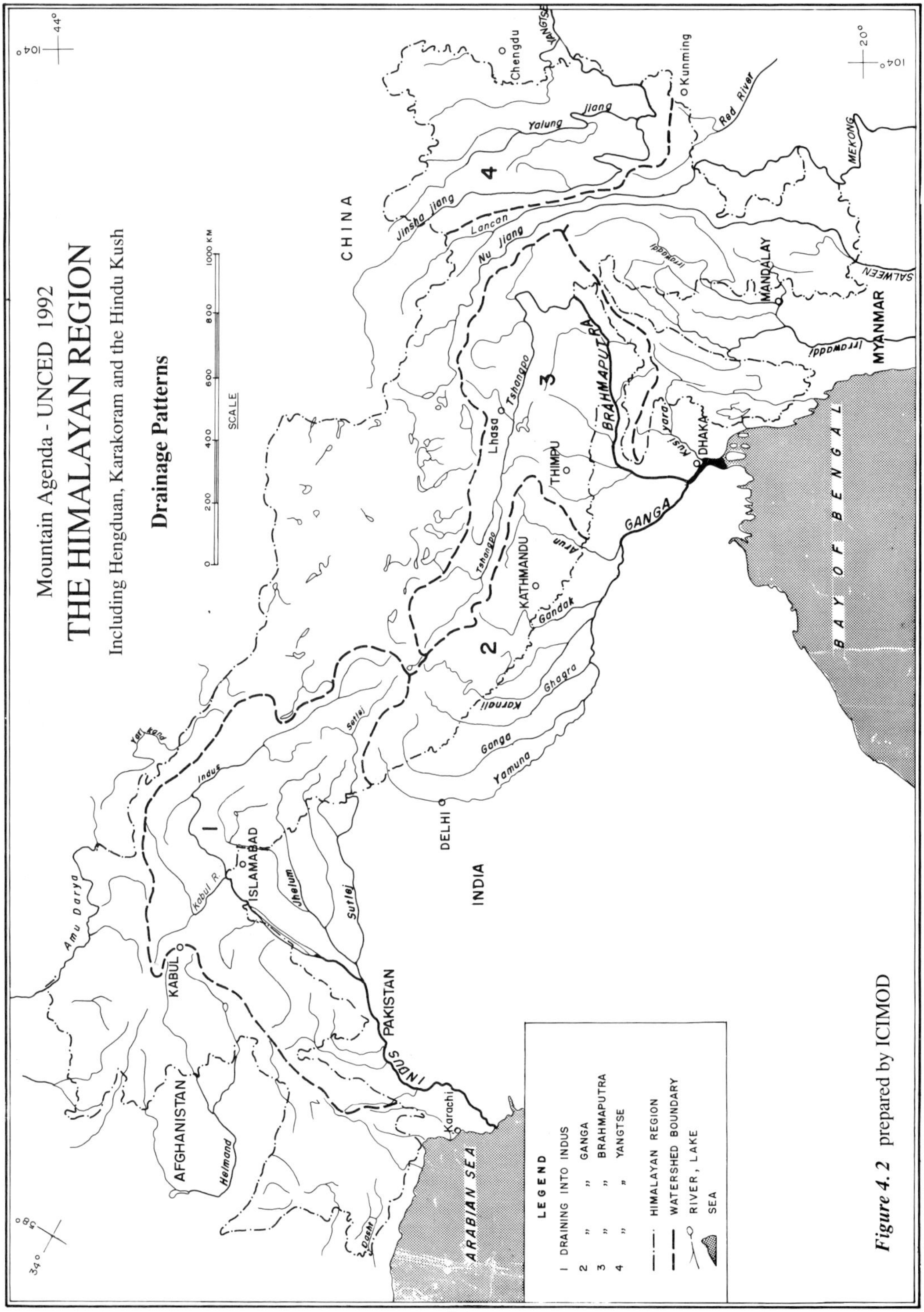

Figure 4.2 prepared by ICIMOD

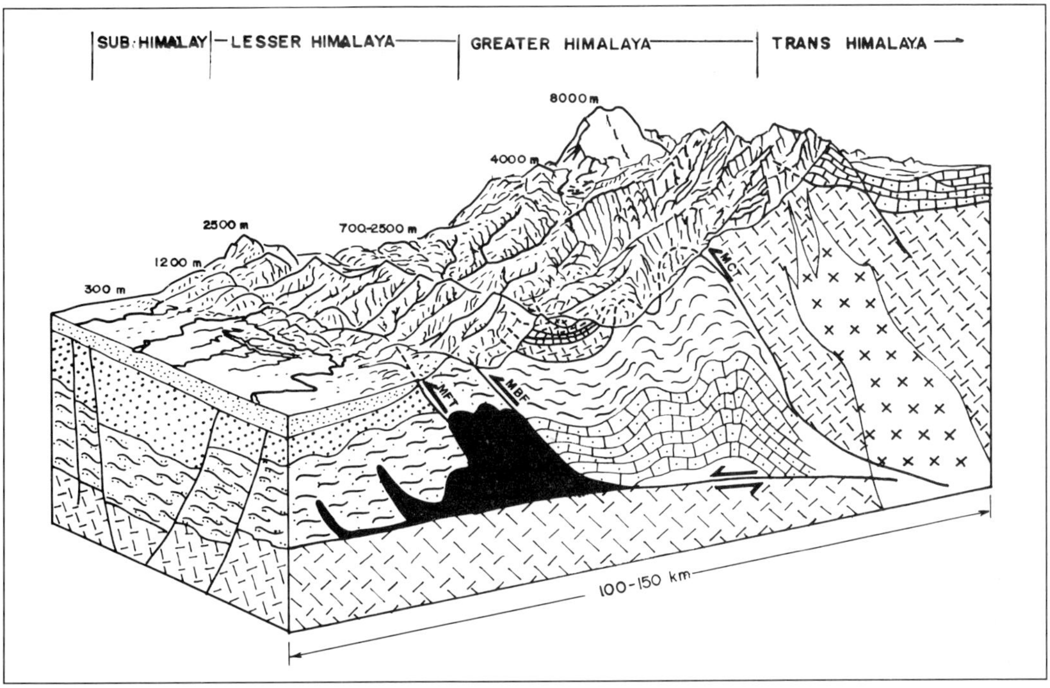

Figure 4.3: *Transectional view of the Himalaya showing the three important thrusts and the latitudinal belts.* Source: Daniel Vuichard, Inst.Mineralogy, University of Berne. Topography modified after W J H Ramsey

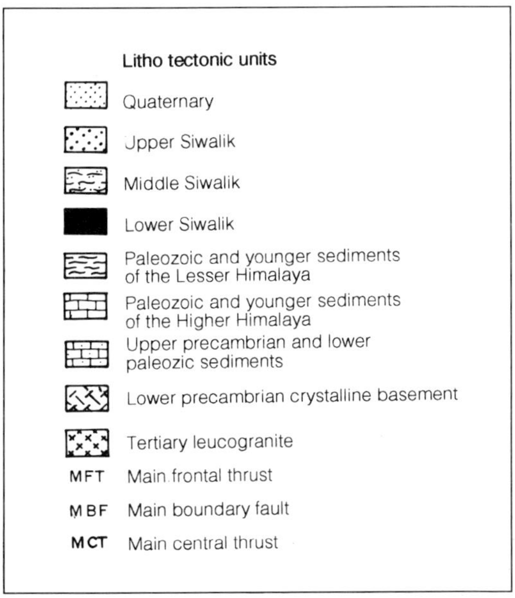

and the neighbouring plains receiving the waters of these major rivers are also the homes of some of the world's greatest civilizations which have always regarded the highest physical feature on the planet with divine respect. Today the root of this respect probably lies the fact that the water resources of the Himalaya are vital for the survival of people now numbering half a billion who live in the crowded plains below.

Another important reason for this respectful attitude to the Himalaya is probably rooted in the fact that the rich biodiversity of the vegetation cover of the Himalaya has served as a resource base for a great variety of important medicinal plants. On these were based a number of world-famous medical systems such as the Ayurveda in the Hindu tradition or Tibetan medicine in the Buddhist tradition or the Yunani medicine adopted in the Islamic tradition. The growth of this knowledge of the Himalaya was accelerated by the constant movement of traders and pastoral peoples across the high passes, thus connecting the various geophysical regions economically, culturally and socially, from the foothills in the south to the Tibetan plateau in the North, from the flat plains in southwestern China to the highlands of Afghanistan. Settlements like Leh (India) and Kathmandu (Nepal) emerged not only as very important meeting points along the various trade-routes, but also as a meeting ground for diverse peoples and cultures.

The close and complex interrelationship between the Himalayan ecosystem and the economy of its human societies needs to be seen against the background of the equally complex natural ecological processes so characteristic of the mountains in general and the Himalaya in particular. The ecology of the Himalaya is delicate and has very limited capacity to accommodate to change. At the same time it does also make feasible a number of economic activities based on its specific environmental advantages. Clearer understanding of the main features of the ecology of the Himalaya is necessary to identify these possibilities as well as to understand the concomitant sensitivities.

There is a tendency among ecologists to start with the vegetation, the green cover in describing the Himalayan ecosystem. A more scientific point of departure will be the underlying geology. While the orogeny of the Himalaya will be discussed in the next section, it is important here to introduce the four latitudinal belts into which the Himalaya can be divided on the basis of geology. The various economic activities and settlement patterns in the Himalaya are very much influenced by this substantial division. This classification shows up most clearly in the main Himalayan arc between the Namche Barwa peak (7 755m) in the east and Nanga Parbat (8 125m) in the west. These gross geological belts are

1) the Sub-Himalaya,
2) the Lesser Himalaya,
3) the Great Himalaya and
4) Tethyan or Trans-Himalaya.

These belts reflect the tectonic movements which gave rise to the Himalaya. The tectonic process is one in which the Indian plate was thrust beneath the Eurasian or Tibetan plate over a period of several million years. Thus the zone is characterized by the geological processes of faulting, folding and thrusting which still continue. There are three major thrusts which run almost parallel to the Himalayan range and are at the root of much of the geological instability of this mountain region. They are

1) the Main Frontal Thrust (MFT)
2) the Main Boundary Thrust (MBT)
3) the Main Central Thrust (MCT).

A sectional view of the four belts and the location of the thrusts is shown in Figure 4.3.

The Sub-Himalaya forms the outermost part of the Himalaya bordering the Indo-Gangetic alluvial plains to the south. The MFT can be taken as the southern boundary of this belt which is the youngest of the four belts. It is characterized by broad open folds. North of the Sub-Himalaya lies the Lesser Himalaya, separated by the Main Boundary Thrust. This belt is the main habitat of the Himalayan people and is of prime significance in the understanding of the prospects and constraints for sustainable development at the micro level. The Great Himalayan belt, which lies further to the north, is separated from the Lesser Himalaya by the Main Central Thrust and constitutes the "central crystallites". This part of the Himalaya is quite inaccessible and includes the crest-line with peaks frequently exceeding altitudes of 7 000m. The region to the north of the main Himalayan ridge is known as Tethyan Himalaya or more commonly the Tibetan plateau and is characterized by intense folding and minor thrusting. The plateau slopes down northwards to the Yarlungtsangpo valley and again attains considerable heights further north near the Gangdise mountains. The Tibetan plateau north of Gangdise extends up to the Kunlun mountains which form the border between the Tibet and Sinkiang provinces of China. The population living in this part of the Himalaya, also known as the Trans-Himalaya, is quite sparse. Most of the population of the Himalayan region is concentrated in the Ganga and Indus valleys along the southern aspect of the main Himalayan arc and the northeastern parts of the region in the western Sichuan and Yunnan provinces of China, adjoining the thickly populated flatlands of the Yangtse basin.

The other aspect of the geographical role played by the Himalaya is that with the passage of time, it became an arena of conflict between empires, kingdoms, chiefdoms and even between religions. Largely due to their remoteness and relative inaccessibility, the mountainous areas of the

Highway construction below Darjeeling 1968. Such projects can lead to massive maintenance costs and risk massive slope instability

Himalayan region became unified into larger kingdoms much later than the analogous areas in the surrounding plains. The Himalaya was, however, strongly influenced by wars and invasions in the plains and by the growth and decay of kingdoms and empires. The Himalaya was influenced profoundly in its southern and western parts by the waves of invasion by Greeks, Syrians, Kushan, Mongols, etc. into the Hindu Kush area while the changing relations of the rulers of Tibet with those in Nepal, Mongolia and China influenced military and demographic movements in the south, north and the east.

Thus despite its inaccessibility, major historical events from the Atlantic to the Pacific influenced the Himalayan region. The consolidation of Buddhism in Tibet, the extension of Islamic rule into western parts and the migratory push from the Hindu-dominated plains to the south resulted in serious conflicts between these important religions. The consolidation of Tibet in the seventh century and the emergence of its strong army brought conflicts to the core of the Himalaya. Later the consolidation of Nepal on the southern flanks of the Himalaya in the 18th century and its emergence as a strong military power led to the occurrence of the Gorkha War (Tibet) of 1788. This tendency to conflict is a historical characteristic and is still seen in the region in the form of disputes over border areas involving large parts of the main Himalayan ridge, from Gilgit in the west to Arunachal Pradesh in the east.

Thus the Himalayan region is characterized not only by ecological fragility but also by a deep and historical geopolitical sensitivity. In expounding the prospects and constraints of sustainable development in this region it will be important to keep in mind both of these two factors. These aspects of the Himalaya become especially important when making ecosystem-based natural resource management strategies, especially in respect of water in the many international rivers originating in the Himalaya.

It is against the background of the ecological fragility and geopolitical sensitivity of the Himalaya that the evolving relationship of environment and development must be seen. An historical perspective of natural resource use and economic activities in the Himalaya will help understanding.

In this respect the victory of the British in the Gorkha War (British) of 1814 can be taken as a landmark. After this event the nature of socio-economic transformations over large parts of the southern flanks of the Himalaya took a new turn. This new direction was followed up in the early 1950s when the newly independent nations of Asia which shared common boundaries in the Himalayan region quickly improved accessibility to these remote mountain areas, most probably for military reasons.

Accessibility in general in Tibet, western Sichuan and Yunnan started to improve in the late 1950s but progressed very quickly. Road building quickly brought in, perhaps more as a by-product than as a primarily intended result, significant changes in the economic conditions of the Himalaya. No more need armies manoeuvre on horseback and no more do traders have to depend on yaks, mules or camels wherever roads have been built. Notwithstanding the debate on the desirability or otherwise of the roads, larger and larger parts of the Himalaya are becoming more and more accessible, giving rise to fast-changing patterns of socio-economic development and exploitation of natural resources.

Economic development in the Himalayan region in the last few decades mainly consists in the felling of forests, the increased export of medicinal plants, the construction of water resource works, exploration and mining of minerals, enhanced tourism, the introduction of commercial farming together with limited urban industrial growth in the foothills. To this could be added the outward migration of the male population in search of work in the plains. Small urban areas have sprung up in the wake of the increasing trade and human movements between the highlands and the surrounding plains. This process is very conspicuous in the whole length of the Himalayan arc from Kashmir to Kunming as well as in the eastern parts of the Hengduan mountains. The enhanced accessibility generated by the newly constructed roads thus not only integrated politically many parts of the Himalaya with the various nation states but also integrated them economically with the economy and market in the surrounding plains.

Significant among the newly constructed roads are the Karakoram highway, the Chengdu Lhasa Kashgar highway, the highways connecting the Nepalese capital Kathmandu with the Indian plains and the Tibetan plateau, the Sringar Leh road and the highway connecting Kabul with Sher Khan Bandar on the Afghan border with the former Soviet Union through the Hindu Kush.

The accessibility introduced by the new roads and by certain new air-routes has had another impact. With more people visiting the mountains, news and information about the Himalaya became more easily available and the region suddenly became a reality in the global mind. On the other hand quicker communications made the mountain people more aware of the easier life in the plains with its broader horizons. The integration of the Himalayan areas with the relatively richer peripheries and more powerful political centres raised the economic aspirations of the mountain people as well as their dependence on the state. Enhanced accessibility also increased the information of the state and the market about the resource potential of the mountains. Forests, minerals, hydro-power, biodiversity, climatic advantage etc. in the Himalayan region which were so far utilized only at the local levels began to be exploited on an unprecedented scale once integration with the economy in the plains had occurred. The availability of food supplies from the plains during periods of acute scarcity and the expansion of health-care services made possible by better transportation reduced death rates and thus led to quicker population growth.

In short, the enhanced accessibility brought about an accelerated economic transformation and population growth in a way which had little regard or concern for the ecological fragility of the Himalayan region. Forests became denuded, roads and mines created enormous land instabilities, the intensification of agriculture led to soil degradation and erosion, pastures were damaged by over-exploitation while the natural courses of rivers were dammed and all these factors together created a massive sedimentation problem. Tourist concentrations created pollution even in the "abode of the gods". Much of the blame for environmental degradation in the Himalaya was directed at the growing local population, whose indigenous modes of natural resource management were, however, made increasingly redundant by the pace of socio-economic and cultural transformation and state intervention. It was also during the 1970s that some environmentalists began to link the devastating floods in Bangladesh with environmental degradation in the Himalayan catchments. In this way improvement in the quality of life of the people and environmental regeneration became the two focal points for development concern in the Himalaya.

The development interventions were dominated by the ideas of people from the plains. As a result, development in the Himalayan region, which was characterized by poverty on one hand and ecological fragility, hazard proneness, cultural diversity and inaccessibility etc. on the other, started to manifest itself as a dilemma. In the absence of a comprehensive understanding not only at the physical ecosystemic level but also of local knowledge and organizational strength among the mountain peoples, the deeper interdependence of development and environment came to be mistaken as a basic dichotomy.

Economic transformations motivated by the market or by economic development programmes prescribed by the state with narrow disciplinary bias have led to development-induced ecological instabilities. The close and delicate ecosystemic linkage in fragile mountains like the Himalaya has long demanded a deep cross-disciplinary grasp of its processes. There has been belated and slow growth in such knowledge. This growing stress on an ecosystemic approach and the emerging concept of mountain characteristics have together provided an approach to reversing this environmental degradation. and so reducing the dilemma. Within the limited scope of this report it is not possible to describe these characteristics in detail. However, in the presentation of the status of the environment and development relationship in the Himalaya, the perspective generated by these characteristics will be kept in mind. In the following sections an approach to sustainable development of the Himalayan region will be attempted. To this end, at first a general geo-climatic description of the Himalayan region together with an account of its natural resources will be given. This will be followed by an indicative description of the serious constraints the Himalayan region imposes on economic activities and the use of natural resources. Against the background of this resource potential and environmental constraint, the gradual growth of the utilization of the various types of natural resources will be examined. In particular, the relationship of the natural environment with developmental interventions, either by state mechanisms or by market forces, will be viewed in an historical perspective. Having identified the main areas of environment-development conflicts in the last section, their complementary and mutually dependent aspects will be highlighted as the starting point for an approach to sustainable development. In this process the role of the dual base, the indigenous-folk and exogenous-scientific knowledge, will be clearly identified. New organizational measures for local, national and regional levels will be suggested. ■

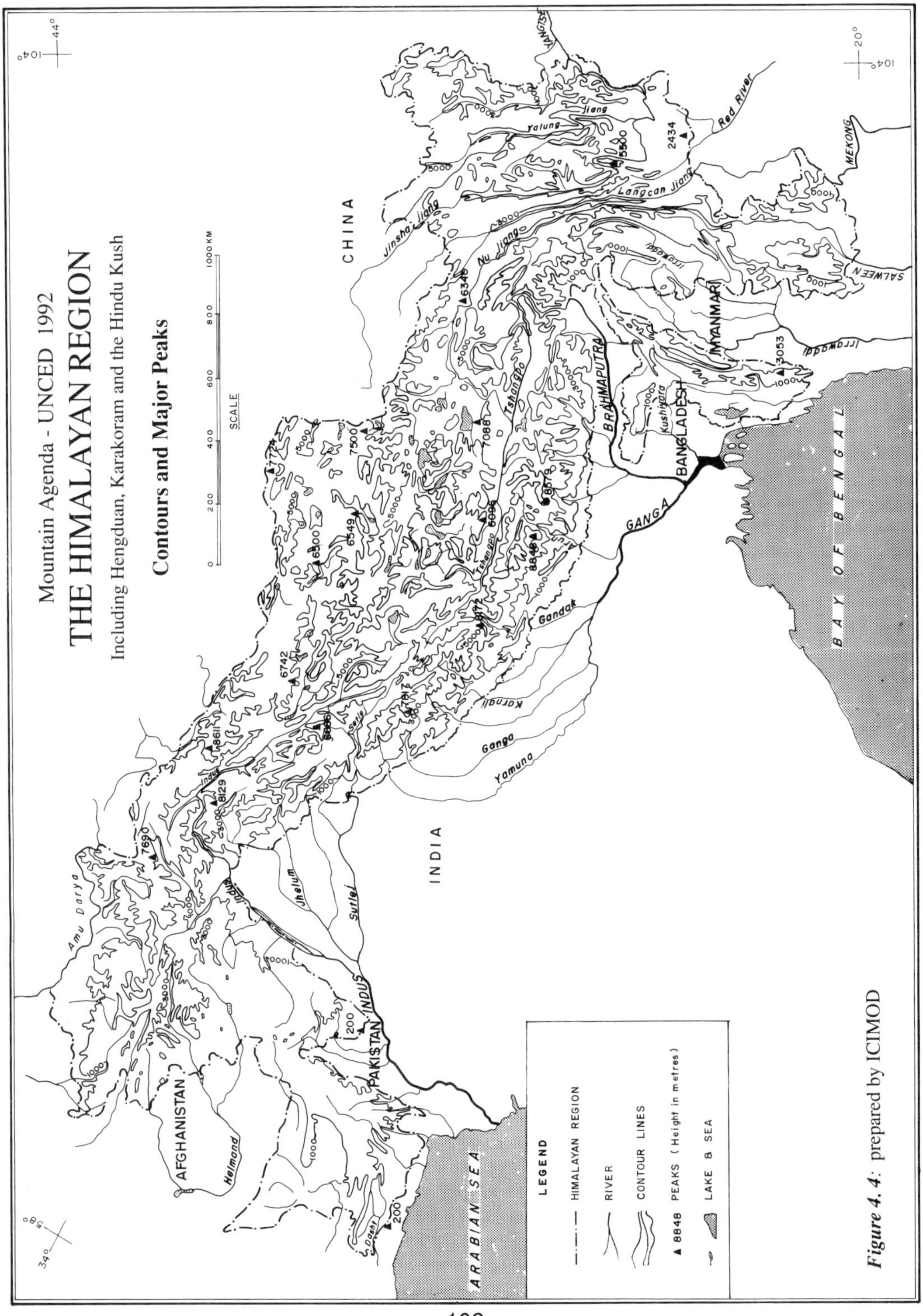

Figure 4. 4: prepared by ICIMOD

Mountain building, climatic influences and natural resources

The geological story

In the global context, the Himalayan arc is a part of the orogenic belt that starts in Indonesia and passes through Southeast Asia, South Asia, Central Asia, Central and West Europe finally ending up in Spain. Mountain ranges like the Alps, Carpathians, Sulaiman, Himalaya, Arakans etc. are part of a physically continuous belt that originated, broadly synchronously, during the Cenozoic period. The Himalaya is characterized by complexly deformed zones of strike slip movement and its age is estimated at about 30 million years. This compares to the age of the Earth at 4 500 million years and the peninsular shield of the Indian sub-continent at 600 million years. Although the grandeur of the Himalaya, youngest and loftiest of all mountain ranges, conveys an impression of immutability, it actually has an inbuilt fragility and is susceptible to rapid structural collapse. This is due to the geotectonic processes which have been and are, still, building it.

The formation of the Himalaya is nowadays explained by the theory of plate tectonics. With limitations of space, it is difficult to explain in detail the crustal processes involved. In brief, the Himalaya is the result of the collision between the Indian plate and the Eurasian plate which were originally separated by an ocean, now named the Tethys. As a result of northward movement of the Indian plate it has been drawn downwards and thrust below the Eurasian plate. This long process led to the marine sediments being compressed, crumpled and then squeezed up into a mountain chain which which we now know as the Himalaya. The shortening of the original extent of the sediments caused by the collision of these plates was so great that, if all the folds of the Himalaya now crammed into a horizontal space of 150 km, were to be stretched out flat, they would stretch for 650 km. The uplift is still continuing and is manifested in the form of regular earthquakes of varying magnitudes in all parts of the mountain range. The most recent and notable one occurred in the early hours of 20 October 1991 in the Garhwal region of the Indian Himalaya. As a result of this long process of building, the Himalaya, the tallest physical feature on the Earth and still growing, has a crest-line of numerous peaks of more than 7 000m above sea level. It has large areas above 5 000m which are mainly under permafrost (Figure 4.4).

Himalaya—the climate maker of Asia

The Himalayan region is dominated by the Asian monsoonic system for which the great heights of the mountain chain make a very important climatic barrier. Without the existence of the high ranges, the climatic pattern of Asia, extending up to the northern border of China, would have been very different. The moisture-bearing summer monsoon air mass which first touches the Himalaya at its eastern end, through the tip of the Bay of Bengal, is limited in its altitude to a maximum of about 5 000m and cannot cross the Himalayan range. Only a small part can do so through the Yarlungtsangpo valley, where the river enters the plains of Assam. This entry of the monsoon into the land north of the Himalayan crest-line is then impeded only by the ridges of the Hengduan mountains and so creates reasonably water-rich areas in parts of eastern Tibet.

The greater length of the Himalaya receives the monsoon as a result of the deflection of the main monsoonic flow arriving in the Assam region in early June. The deflected air mass, caused to move westward along the length of the mountain arc, exhausts its moisture by the end of July and precipitation from this branch of the summer monsoon becomes almost insignificant after it crosses the state of Himachal Pradesh in India. The summer monsoon normally lasts from mid-June to mid-September. The Himalaya acts as a similar barrier in the winter when by virtue of its height and extent it prevents the spread of the current of extremely cold air from Central Asia, giving the plains to the south a much warmer winter than the regions to the north. In this way, while much of eastern Himalaya and Hengduan receive almost all their annual precipitation from June to September, the western Himalaya, the Hindu Kush and the Karakoram receive most precipitation as snow during the winter months of January to March. The variation of annual precipitation and climatic conditions along and across the Himalaya thus provide an almost unparalleled assortment of micro and regional climatic conditions.

The Himalayan region is characterized by a sharp divide in rainfall. The Himalayan ridge with a southern aspect receives far more precipitation

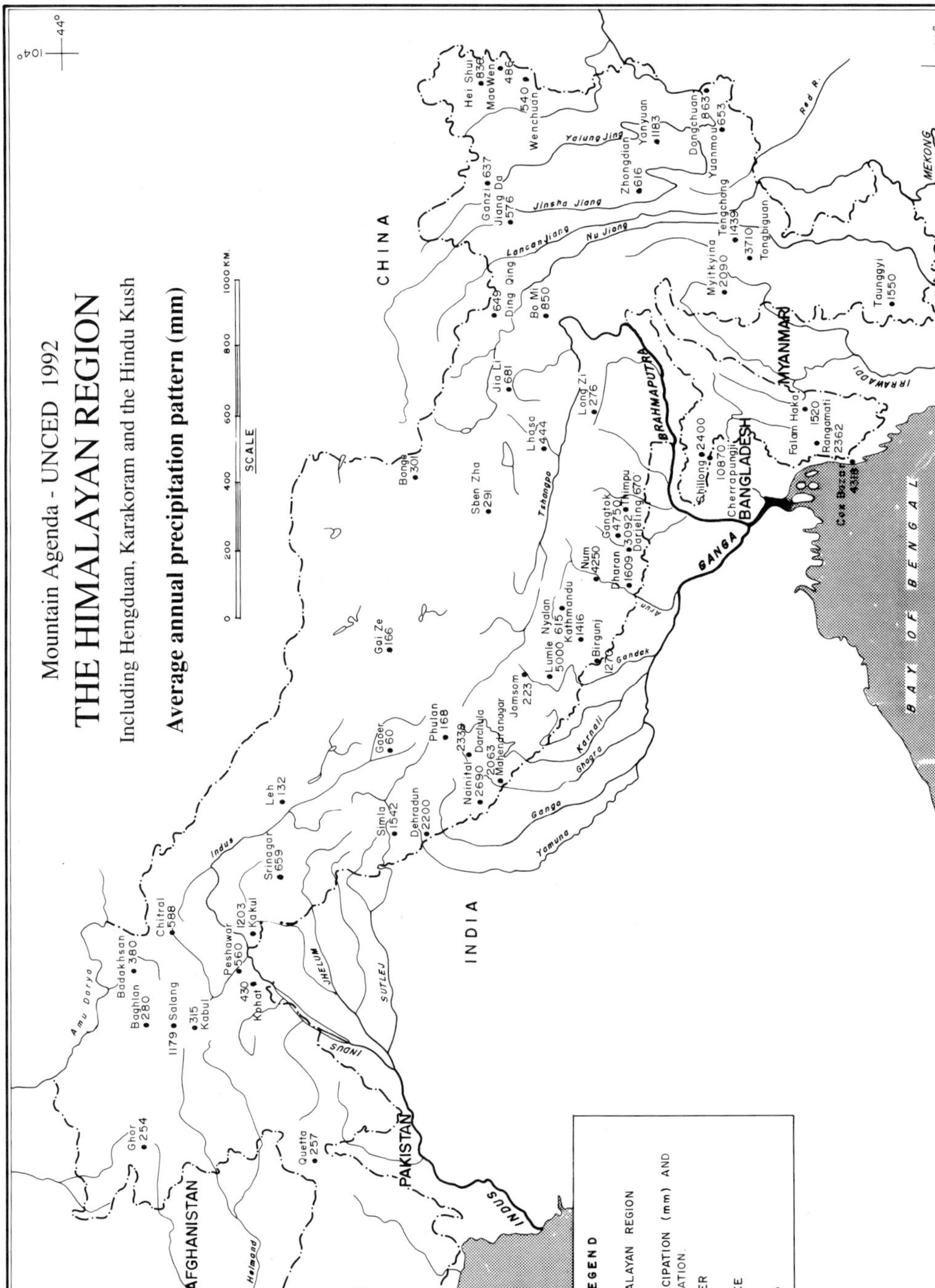

Figure 4.5: prepared by ICIMOD

than the northern flanks and the Tibetan plateau. In the eastern end, the Hengduan mountains receive summer monsoon precipitation directly from the southwest monsoon as well as from the branch of the monsoon that enters the eastern parts of Tibet through the Brahmaputra Valley.

Within a horizontal distance of about 200 km, from the foothills to the Tibetan plateau, the climate changes from wet sub-tropical to dry desert giving rise to conditions favourable to the existence of rich bio-diversity. The mean annual precipitation of some stations in the Himalayan region is shown in Figure 4.5 which gives the quantitative picture of this diversity.

Natural resources

The natural resources of the Himalayan region may be divided in three categories, viz: non-renewable, renewable and specific advantages. The third category provides an important set of mountain advantages which can form the basis of economic activities of substantial magnitude. Elements in that category can also play a greater role in human lives than can be easily quantified within the limits of modern economics. The solitude and tranquillity of the Himalaya, for example, is the reason that great saints and thinkers throughout history have chosen mountain sanctuaries for their religious, intellectual and spiritual pursuits.

Non-renewable resources in the Himalaya include the rocks, minerals and hydrocarbons.

The renewable resources include forests, pastures, bio-diversity, water.

The specific mountain advantages include the scenic beauty, hilly landscapes, tranquillity, temperate climate and wide open spaces.

There has been no extensive detailed exploration for non-renewable or mineral resources in the Himalayan region. Inaccessibility is itself a major obstacle and the feasibility of transporting the minerals economically is equally doubtful. The stratigraphy of most parts of the Himalaya is such that the process of mineral prospecting becomes a tortuous affair because of the discontinuities induced by thrusting and faulting. Systematic mineral exploration undertaken so far has been limited in geographical extent and much remains to be discovered about the mineral wealth of this vast and complex range. It may however be recalled here that export of mineral salt from Tibet is a very old practice. Although economic activity based on industrial minerals in the Himalaya has been marginal so far, the probability of low-volume high-value mineral deposits being located cannot be ruled out as exploration continues. At present the popular perception of natural resources in the Himalaya conspicuously underestimates this potential. To rectify this impression the location of some of the exploitable minerals in the Himalaya is sketched here.

Large deposits of boron, lead, lithium and caesium are located in the central parts of Tibet. Good deposits of coal are located in the upper Yangtse catchment while a big silver mine operates in Garze in Western Sichuan. Prospecting has led to mining for chromium north of Lhasa while a lot of marble is quarried a little to the east of that city. A big iron mine feeding an iron and steel plant operates in Dukou in Sichuan-Yunnan. In the eastern extremity of Tibet and in southwest Sichuan, ores of copper, tin, molybdenum, gold, silver, platinum and tungsten have been located. Northwest Yunnan has copper, zinc and lead in large quantities. In the lower parts of the Hengduan the possibility of locating gaseous hydrocarbons cannot be ruled out. Exploration in western Tibet is rather scanty. On the southern flanks of the Himalaya, coal, dolomite and base metals are available near Dedza in the eastern Himalaya while gold is located in the gravels of the Subansiri river. In Bhutan chemical grade dolomite, limestone and gypsum have launched the beginnings of a mineral economy. In Sikkim and the two Himalayan districts of the state of West Bengal, Darjeeling and Jalpaiguri, coal, dolomite, metal sulphides, graphite and tungsten occur. Mineral exploration in Nepal has not been undertaken very extensively yet but high-grade deposits of limestone in Udaipur and Jogimara and magnesite deposits at Kharidhunga and Kampughat merit a mention. Lead and zinc ores of high quality have been located near the Ganesh Himal area. Further west, in the Kumaon region magnesite and graphite, and in the Doon Valley limestone, magnesite and marble have been mined for some time. Himachal Pradesh has similar mineral resources, including gypsum and limestone while further west in Ladakh, chromite and fluorite are available. In the Hindu Kush mountains important minerals include marble, rock salt, limestone, gypsum and some iron ore.

In spite of such a spread and diversity in mineral resources the common image of resources in the Himalaya is dominated by renewable resources such as vegetation cover or water. As a result of their direct dependence on the climate and precipitation, the distribution and extent of both these resources are directly governed by the macro- and micro-climatic variations within and across the Himalaya. The wide variations in climate and precipitation thus govern the vegetation found of which there are hundreds of types throughout the region.

Even when an attempt is made to divide the forest types along the lines of the standard classifications of tropical, sub-tropical, temperate and alpine, they become inadequate to describe the rich diversity of the Himalayan forests. At one extreme are the cold and dry areas of the Hindu Kush where the vegetation cover is limited by the availability of water and there are a low number of plant species. On the other hand the rainy forests in the eastern Himalaya and the Hengduan have a much greater diversity. The number of plant species in Bhutan itself is reported to be 5 000 while for the whole of the eastern Himalaya it has been estimated at 9 000 or more.

It is difficult to make accurate quantitative estimates of forest areas in the region although efforts are continuing. The forests are most important as a repository of one of the world's richest stocks of biodiversity. They have also been used extensively for thousands of years as sources of food, fodder, fuelwood and other biomass by the Himalayan people thus giving the forests a key role in the agri-pastoral economy. Extensive commercial felling of forests for timber has gone on in the current century, especially in the last few decades when urban centres began to grow in areas near the forests. In this way Himalayan forests have played a very important role as a high value natural resource.

In line with the climatic divides the richness of the Himalayan forest cover declines from east to west and from south to north. Temperature and rainfall jointly determine the nature of available natural forest cover. Wet tropical evergreen forest occurs in the Chittagong area of Bangladesh, the lower foothills of Bhutan, the Sichuan and Yunnan areas of China, the lower parts of the eastern Himalayan foothills in India as well as in Myanmar (Burma) up to an altitude of 900 m. At the other extreme extensive natural climax grassland occurs in the northwestern half of Tibet where rainfall is scanty and temperatures are quite low. The various types of forests and their location are listed in outline in Table 4.1.

The climatic condition of the eastern Himalaya and most of western Sichuan and Yunnan provinces is suitable for climax natural forests. In most parts of western Tibet much of the dry uplands of the Hindu Kush do not support forest cover. For example, in Afghanistan permanent pastures and meadows account for 54.7 million ha of land while forests cover only 1.9 million ha. Extensive grasslands and shrubs dominate the landscape providing the resource base for one of the largest pastoral economies of the world, mainly run by a nomadic population. The extent of this economy can be estimated from the fact that in 1984 while agriculture accounted for 28 per cent of the total output in Tibet, animal husbandry accounted for 55 per cent and household production largely related to animal products accounted for another 15 per cent. Grasslands, as climax vegetation, occur under alpine and sub-alpine conditions. Some hillsides in the temperate midhills also support grasslands on dry and hot slopes together with climax forests on wet and colder slopes. In the context of the vegetation cover of the whole Himalayan region, a great deal of attention has been given to forest resources but it is the grasslands that are the more important. They are the resource base for pastoralism.

While the forests, farmlands and grasslands are of extreme importance for the agri-pastoral economy within the Himalayan region, the other renewable resource, water, has always been of central importance for the thickly populated plains to the east, south and west of the Himalaya. The rivers carried the fertile silt and irrigation water to these areas–this dependence of the neighbouring plains has led to the name "hydraulic society" being used to describe the South Asian civilization in the past and it is no less applicable even today.

The intense summer precipitation in the eastern parts of the Himalaya and the heavy snowfall in the western parts feed some of the longest glaciers in the world which provide the resource base for very important river systems. Notable

Forest types	Dominant species	Occurrence
I. TROPICAL FOREST GROUP		
a) Tropical Wet Evergreen/Semi evergreen Forest	Dipterocarpus, Artocarpus, Eugenia, Mesua, Terminalia, Lagerstroemia, Albizia, Schima, Quercus, Castanopsis, Phoebe, Homolium, Talauma	Chittagong, Bhutan up to 800 m, Yunnan, Xizang up to 450 m, Assam, Myanmar up to 900 m.
b) Tropical Deciduous Forest	Shorea, Terminalia, Lagerstroemia, Dillenia, Albizia, Bombax, Dalbergia, Tectona, Xylia, Anogeisus Ailanthus	Chittagong, Bhutan 500-1 000 m, Nepal below 1 000 m, Myanmar 900-1000 m, Uttar Pradesh , Jammu and Kashmir, Assam, Xizang, Sichuan, Yunnan 300-1 200 m.
II. SUBTROPICAL FOREST GROUP		
a) Subtropical Broad Leaved Hill Forest	Shorea, Terminalia, Michelia, Albizia, Schima, Bombax, Alnus, Castanopsis, Cedrela, Olea, Pistacia, Acacia	Chittagong, Bhutan, Nepal 100-2000 m; Myanmar 1 000-1 500 m, Sichuan, Yunnan 600-1 000 m, Assam, Punjab, Xizang.
b) Subtropical Pine/Dry Evergreen Forest	Pinus, Quercus, Schima, Castanopsis, Phyllanthus	Bhutan, Nepal 1 000-2 000 m, Myanmar 1 200-3 000 m; Sichuan, Yunnan, Xizang 1 000-2 000 m; Assam, U.P., Jammu and Kashmir, Punjab 1 000-2 000 m.
III.TEMPERATE FOREST GROUP		
a) Montane Temperate/ Himalayan Moist Temperate Forest	Pinus, Quercus, Acer, Betula, Machilus, Alnus, Quercus, Picea, Abies, Taxus, Tsuga, Rhododendron	Afghanistan 1 800-3 600 m, Swat, Hazara, Kashmir, Dir, Uttar Pradesh , Jammu and Kashmir, Assam; Bhutan 2 000-3 000 m, Nepal 2 000-2 800 m; Sichuan, Xizang, Yunnan 1 000-2 700 m.
b) Himalayan Dry Temperate Forest	Pinus, Picea, Cedrus, Quercus, Larix, Tsuga, Zizyphus, Acacia, Betula, Caragana, Juniperus, Populus, Salix, Fraxinus, Rhododendron	Afghanistan 2 100-3 600 m, Gilgit, Chitral, Nilana, Kagan, Jammu and Kashmir, Bhutan 2 000-3 000 m, Nepal 2 800-3 100 m, Myanmar 2 000-2 800 m, Xizang, Sichuan, Yunnan 2 700-3 000 m.
IV. ALPINE FOREST GROUP		
a) Sub-Alpine Forests	Junniperus, Picea, Abies, Betula, Tsuga, Rhododendron	Afghanistan 2 200-3 600 m; Dir, Swat, Gilgit, Chitral, Uttar Pradesh , Jammu and Kashmir, Nepal 3 400-3 900 m, Bhutan 3 000-4 000 m; Sichuan, Yunnan, Xizang 300-3 500 m.
b) AlpineShrub	Juniperus, Birch, Rhododendron, Tsuga, Betula, Berberis, Salix, Caragana, Hippophae	Afghanistan 2 400-2 600 m, Dir, Swat, Gilgit, Chitral, Uttar Pradesh , Jammu and Kashmir, Assam; Bhutan and Nepal above 4 000 m; Sichuan, Yunnan, Xizang 3 500-4 200 m, Myanmar 2 000-3 000 m.

Table 4.1: *Major forest types, dominant species and their occurrence in the Himalayan region*
Source : Bhatta, B.R. Unpublished ICIMOD (1992)

River	Measurement station	Total annual run-off ($10^8 m^3$)
Jinsha	Pingshan	1 437
Lanchang	Jing Hung	0 583
NuJiang	Dao Jeba	0 523
Yarlungtsangpo	Exit point from Tibet	1 395
Brahmaputra	Bahudurabad	5 104
Ganga	Hardinge Bridge	4 943
Indus	Near Arabian Sea	2 078

***Table 4.2:** Annual runoff of some rivers in the Himalayan region.*
Source: *Rivers and Lakes of Xizang (Tibet)* Science Press, Beijing, 1984; Sharma, C.K. "Water and Energy", *Resources of the Himalayan Block,* Sangeeta Sharma, Kathmandu, 1983

among the Himalayan rivers are Jinsha, Mekong, Salween, Irrawadi, Yarlungtsangpo-Brahmaputra, Ganga, Indus, Amu Darya etc. The river Jinsha, a tributary to the Yangtse in the upper catchment areas in the eastern slope of the Hengduan, after forming the boundary between Tibet and Sichuan for some distance, flows eastward towards the Pacific Ocean. Across the ridge of the Hengduan to the west flows the Lan Chang, as the Mekong is known before it leaves the Himalayan region in Yunnan, to flow to the Pacific Ocean through Laos, Kampuchea and Vietnam. Running literally parallel in the next valley westward across the Nu Shan mountains is Nu Jianag, as the Salween is named in the upper catchments in eastern Tibet. This river drains large parts of eastern Tibet between the Hengduan and the Nyainqentanglha mountains and passes through the deep and narrow valley between the Nu Shan and Gaoligong mountains in Yunnan. The northern parts of Myanmar, bounded by the Gaoligong Shan in the East, Naga Hills in the West and a branch of the Hengduan in the North, is the upper catchment of the Irrawadi draining into the Bay of Bengal through Myanmar. Bounded by the Naga Hills and the southern flanks of the Himalayan arc is the lower catchment of the Brahmaputra, which is one of the most rainy areas in the world. This part of the catchment includes Cherrapunji, the world's second highest rainfall area. The upper catchment of the river, named Yarlungtsangpo in Tibet, falls between the northern aspect of the Himalayan arc and the joint watershed boundary provided by the Gangdise and Nyainqentanglha mountains of Tibet. Most parts of the southern aspect of the Himalayan arc are drained by the Ganga while the rest of the southern aspect and the rest of the northern aspect are drained by the Indus. There are also a number of smaller rivers draining smaller parts of the Himalayan region that are not mentioned here. The combined water resource of all these rivers has not been not properly estimated but it may well be the highest water output from any one mountain range in the world. Table 4.2 gives the estimate of the annual runoff of major and some minor rivers as they drain out of the Himalayan region. This great volume of water and the energy latent in their flow are increasingly being exploited for hydropower generation and irrigation with the help of dams.

Other than rich water resources, vast extended grasslands and dense forests in some highland parts and in the foothills, the Himalayan region, like any other mountain area, has certain specific advantages which are no less important as a basis for economic activity. These are scenic beauty, salubrious climate, inaccessible wilderness areas and wide open spaces. In many mountain areas such as the Alps, where tourism has become the dominant element of the mountain economy, forests and pasture are becoming less and less utilized by the farmers.

The Himalaya, with all these specific advantages as well as the highest peak on Earth, surely has the resource potential for an equally prosperous tourist economy. This short account of the major resources of the Himalayan region must lead one to visualize the Himalaya, at least on the face of it, as a store-house of prosperity waiting to be exploited. It would have been a present reality but for some serious constraints enforced by the natural environment and by ecological processes. The whole issue of sustainable development hinges on the correct understanding of the potential of these resources and the constraints imposed by the environment on their utilization. ■

Environmental constraints on natural resource use

The rich forest, water, land and mineral resources, together with the mountain-specific advantages enjoyed by the Himalayan region can surely provide a stable foundation for many economic activities. It will however be unwise to assume that these resources can be utilized in just any way that the market or the interest of the state may determine or as people's basic needs may suggest. The emergence of an apparently dichotomous relationship between economic development and environmental conservation has been largely the result of the lack of understanding and recognition of the constraints that specific ecological features of the Himalaya impose on the economic exploitation of these natural resources. In the process of setting out the potentials and constraints for sustainable development in the Himalaya, it is necessary to have a closer understanding of these constraints. In the absence of such understanding ill-conceived programmes of growth and ill-informed and populist environmental opposition will continue to add to the dilemma. It is also worth recalling that the Himalayan region is characterized by the problem of poverty and population pressure. The evaluation of the carrying capacity and its possible increase are therefore issues which require a particularly clear knowledge of the environmental constraints.

The landscape of the Himalaya is founded on an immature geology and on unconsolidated rock systems. Problems thus arising are compounded by the heavy rainfall and fast-moving streams, and as a result the geomorphology of the Himalaya has changed and will continue to change in drastic ways. The long history of human occupation and survival in the Himalaya did not cause too many drastic changes in this delicate mountain ecosystem until very recently. Some recent economic and infrastructural activities have, however, been major interventions which have contributed to bringing these underlying constraints to the fore. Accordingly, these ecological weaknesses or sensitivities merit individual description so that the limits they impose may be clearly understood, at least at the qualitative level.

Seismicity

Seismicity is a term used to describe the form and status of earthquake occurrence and to indicate the probability and pattern of recurrence. The high seismicity of the Himalayan region is rooted in its recent orogenic evolution, as a result of which the Himalaya is still rising. Several estimates of this uplift have been made and they vary between 2 and 10 mm/year. Extensive studies on the Tibetan Plateau have shown a rate of about 5mm/year over the last 10 000 years. The total convergence between the Indian and the Tibetan (Eurasian) plates is estimated to be about 2 500 km of which about 500 km may have occurred along the Himalaya through repeated over-thrusting of the slices of the Indian crust on itself. In designing any structure in the Himalaya the implications of the resulting tremendous locked-in energy have to be taken into account

Table 4.3: *Some major earthquakes in the Himalayan region*

Year	Magnitude	Affected area	Nature of impact
1803	–	Garhwal	Immense loss of life. All construction destroyed.
1833	8.0	Sonming	Ground fissures, sand boils, many landslides.
1887	8.7	Assam	Landslides, debris flow, ground subsidence with heavy human casualties.
1920	8.5	Haiyuan	Numerous landslides with 200 000 deaths. Formation of big landslide dam lake.
1931	8.0	Quetta	Extensive damage to bridges and transportation systems with 30 000 human deaths.
1952	7.5	Lhasa	850 buildings destroyed, about 100 deaths.
1973	7.6	Luhao	20 km of highway destroyed, major rock falls and landslides.
1991	6.1	Uttarkashi	1 000 deaths, 50 000 homeless, 7 000 injured, damage to roads and bridges.

in the light of the progressive failures of slopes and the creation of landslides of large volumes. Whether it is road construction or dam building or house construction, ground tremors and movements along the faults constitute a very serious constraint. Earthquakes in the past have been disastrous because of human incapacity to anticipate their impacts. Just to indicate the scale of the constraint imposed by seismicity a few past Himalayan earthquakes are listed in Table 4.3. The question of the prevention of earthquake damage has come to the fore in the case of projected high dams in the region.

Mass wasting

Mass wasting is a very widespread constraint faced in all parts of the Himalaya. It is a general term to describe a variety of processes through which large masses of earth material move downhill under gravity, both in slow creeping mode or as rapid landslides.

Mass wasting is the most frequent and widely dispersed manifestation of the fragility of the Himalayan terrain and is basically a natural process, but man's activities can substantially aggravate its impact and scale.

Among the most important natural factors behind the widespread occurrence of mass wasting are:

i) steep slope with high relative relief
ii) seismicity
iii) groundwater flows accentuating landslips
iv) cloudbursts and intense rainfall
v) nature of the rocks (soft sedimentary, foliated metamorphic or fractured igneous)
vi) toe under-cutting by torrents and floods.

These are aggravated by anthropogenic factors such as:

i) loss of forest cover
ii) extension of agriculture onto steep slopes
iii) open-cast mining without environmental control
iv) roads built without regard for geological factors

Major mass wasting events, especially in narrow ravines, often result in the formation of a debris dam. Depending on the size of the obstruction, lakes are formed behind the dams which subsequently burst open under hydrostatic pressure. This is an essential geomorphological feature of the Himalaya and the resulting flash flood may cause catastrophe downstream, increase silt load drastically, bury agricultural fields or settlements, and damage the structure of dams and levees. To illustrate the nature of the hazard a few major landslides occurring in the Himalayan region are shown in Table 4.4. Mass wasting is a major constraint on road construction, the life of dam structures, heavy urbanization on the slopes and the establishment of terraced farmland.

Glacial lake outburst floods

The glacier lake outburst flood (GLOF) is the most devastating flood-producing phenomenon, which occurs in the Himalayan region from time to time. GLOF refers to the sudden outburst of lakes, dammed by glacier ice or moraines, producing flows of water that are often an order of magnitude greater than normal rain-derived peak flows and may travel tens of kilometres downstream, transporting colossal amounts of debris. The occurrence

Table 4.4: *An indicative list of constraints imposed by landslides*

Year	Affected area	Nature of damage
1893	Garhwal	Major rockslide caused a 1 500 m long obstruction which burst causing devastating flash-floods with huge loss of life.
1933	Sichuan	Flood from failure of landslide dam causing 2 500 deaths.
1968	Garhwal	40 m high blockage on Rishi-Ganga from deep-seated planer rockslide.
1970	Garhwal	Massive debris flow emerged from a tributary to the river Alaknanda causing a 60 m high dam. The burst caused flash floods that destroyed three bridges and triggered many more slides by toe-cutting.
1971	Yaan	Massive debris flow killing 114 people.

of GLOF in high mountains poses many problems for inhabitants and their infrastructure. First the loss of human life is extremely high, second agricultural crops and land are washed away on a large scale, third hydroelectric projects and roads arc totally destroyed or damaged, then rock-fill dams may be breached if the inflow of the torrent of debris cannot be accommodated over the spillway, and lastly large reservoirs are rapidly filled with sediment.

The bursting of moraine-dammed lakes is often due to the breaching of the dam by the erosion of the dam material as a result of overtopping by surging water or piping of dam material. Earthquakes leading to the slumping of dam material may also cause the bursting of the lake. The drainage of ice-dammed lakes may be due to:

i) flotation of the ice dam
ii) pressure deformation
iii) melting of tunnels through or under the ice, and
iv) drainage associated with tectonic activity.

The propagation of GLOF surges provokes landslides and bank erosion that temporarily block the surge waves and result in a series of surges as the landslide dams breach. The flood surge can propagate hundreds of kilometres below the glacier lake. Several empirical relationships have been developed from approximate computations of peak release discharges and they indicate that the moraine-dammed lakes may cause peak discharges which are 10 times higher than the ice-dammed lakes. The damage and constraints are similar to those as in the case of landslide dam bursts.

Although GLOFs have occurred with regularity, the devastation has been well documented in only a few cases. The Langmoche GLOF of 1985 which occurred on the river Bhote Kosi in Nepal is one of the few events for which a detailed account of the nature of damage downstream was made. This hazard of the high mountains is a particularly constraint on roads, bridges and hydroelectric installations downstream of glaciers.

Climatic extremes

The making of the Himalayan climate is a rather complex process. While the general pattern of climatic variation, both latitudinally and longitudinally can be explained, the understanding of climatic extremes such as cloudbursts, hailstorms, droughts etc., which play a crucial role as an environmental constraint at micro levels, is in a rudimentary stage. What is worse, due to inaccessibility, proper recordings and quantification of these events are very rarely found. Cloud bursts cause heavy damage and slope failures while hailstorms or drought inflict losses in agriculture. Shortage of space in this chapter makes detailed analysis of these problems for the Himalayan region difficult. Mention may however be made here of the most significant climatic extremes of heavy rainfall which are the root causes of devastating floods. Maximum observed 24-hour rainfall totals are given in Table 4.5 which follows the same pattern of rainfall in terms of spatial variation of intensity.

Erosion and sedimentation

The problems of erosion and sedimentation are the most well known and widespread environmental constraints in the Himalayan region. The relatively soft rock and the favourable climatic conditions are factors behind the quick weathering and production of soil. But the same factors make protection of the topsoil from erosion and subsequent deposition downstream a major problem, especially in agriculture and forestry because of that third, vertical, dimension to the landscape.

In the case of the Himalaya intense monsoonic rainfall has been an additional integral and important factor in excessive soil erosion. As a result of large scale mass-wasting and the

Table 4.5: *Maximum observed 24-hour rainfall at selected stations.*
Source: Bruijnzeel, L.A. and Bremmer C.N., ICIMOD Occasional Paper No. 11, Kathmandu, 1989

Station	24-hr rainfall (mm)
Cherrapunji	1 036
Dibrugarh	745
Darjeeling	640
Kathmandu	356
Butwal	403
Dhangadi	283
Almora	221
Dehradun	152

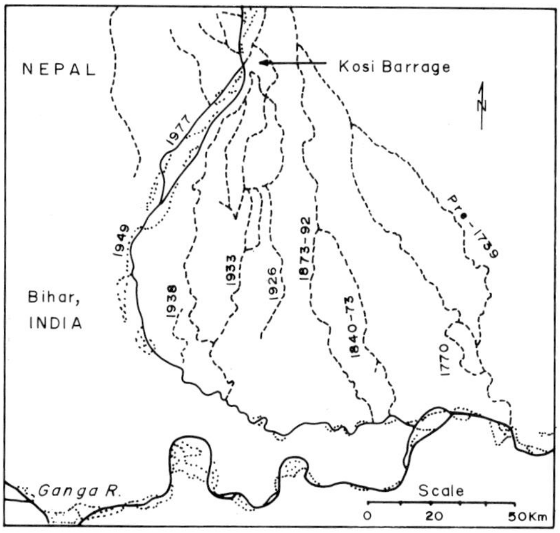

Figure 4.6: *Changes in the course of the River Koshi over its own alluvial fan (1736-1977)*

Table 4.6*: Sediment yields of selected Himalayan rivers.* Source: Holeman, J.N.,"Sediment Yield of Major Rivers of the World", *Water Resources Research* Vol. 4. No. 4. August 1968; Rivers and lakes of Xizang (Tibet) Science Press, Beijing, 1984

River	Station	Sediment yield t/ha/year
Indus	Kotri	5.1
Kabul	Nawshera	2.9
Chenab	Alexander Br	1.7
Jinsha	Batang	0.8
Jinsha	Pingshan	19.2
Lan Chang	Jiuzhou	2.5
Nu Jiang	Dao Je Ba	1.6
NianCu	Jiangza	1.5
Lhasa	Lhasa	0.4
Yarlungtsangpo	Nuxia	1.0
Brahmaputra	In Bangladesh	14.5
Ganga	In Bangladesh	15.7
Karnali	Chisapani	67.4
Narayani	Narayanghat	56.8
Bagmati	Chobar	30.3
Kankai	Mainachuli	48.4
Kosi	Chatra	31.3
Tamur	Tribeni	82.2
Teesta	Anderson Bridge	125.1

erosion-prone land surface, Himalayan rivers carry sediment loads which are among the highest in the world. Most of the sediments are carried during the three months of the monsoon period. In this respect the eastern half of the southern flanks of the Himalaya is the worst hit. The combined effects of mass-wasting and erosion processes generate relatively large particle size sediments which are deposited in the foothills. This provides conditions favourable to the shifting of the rivers as they reach the foothills. The extent of this process as a constraint is well illustrated by the case of the river Kosi which has shifted by about 150 km to the west during the geologically brief interval since records began two centuries ago (Figure 4. 6).

For the big rivers like the Yangtze, Brahmaputra, Ganga or Indus, measuring sediment load is full of difficulties and uncertainties. However, the measurements made are of extreme importance. Table 4.6 gives some selected sediment yield data for the Himalayan rivers which highlights the difference in the erosional status of the rain-rich windward slopes and the Trans-Himalaya. These estimates are not, however, totally representative of the sedimentation regime in the Himalaya and the quantification is only approximate. In addition they represent only the suspended sediments and very little information is available about the quantitative aspects of bed load which is equally important. In view of the dominance of mass-wasting processes as compared to erosion, Himalayan rivers are thus carriers of both water and silt to the plains. The high sediment load in the Himalayan rivers is a natural fertilizer for the flat plains and the creator of new fertile land. However, where dams obstruct the flow of the rivers, this high volume of sediment shows its negative side acting as a constraint by reducing the active life-span of the dams.

Floods

In recent years, the floods in the flat plains around the Himalaya, in particular in Bangladesh, have been linked, in popular writings, with the ecological degradation of the Himalaya, especially deforestation. A distinction, however, needs to be made between floods and the regular annual inundation resulting from heavy and intense rainfall.

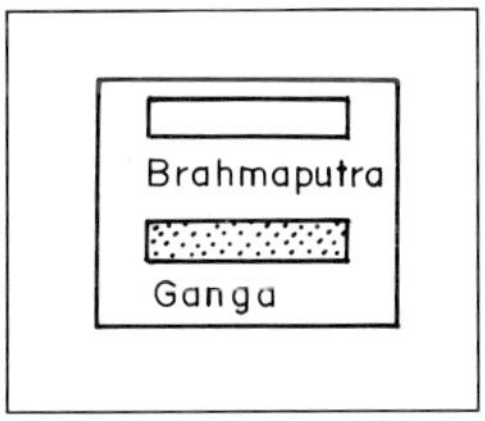

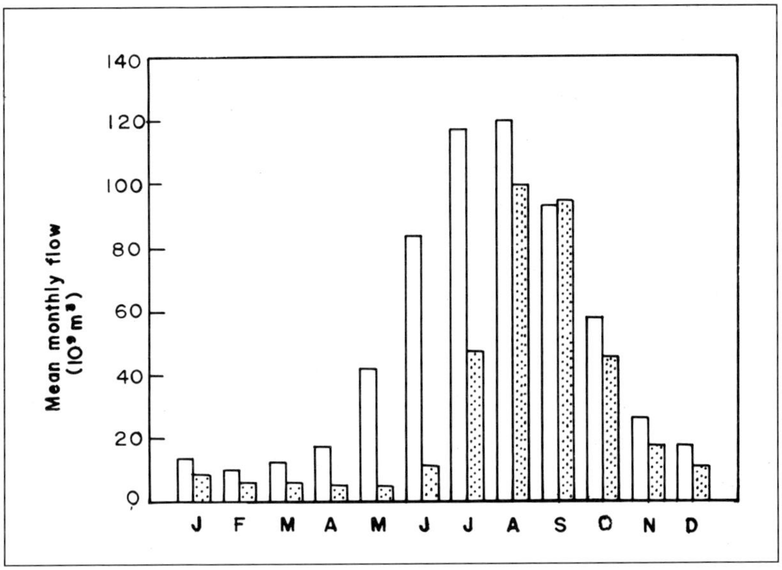

Figure 4.7: *Average monthly discharge of the Brahmaputra and the Ganga at Sara Bridge.* (Based on Rashid, Haroun er (1977) *Geography of Bangladesh*, University Press Ltd., Dhaka).

The seasonality of the rainfall and concentration of about 80 per cent of precipitation within 20 per cent of the year is an almost unsurmountable constraint to the utilization of the Himalayan water resources. The predominant outflow of the region takes place through the river Padma in Bangladesh, as the rivers Brahmaputra and Ganga are named below their confluence. The temporal variation of the flow of these two, the biggest rivers of the region, is shown in Figure 4.7. Note that the entry of huge volumes of water into Bangladesh is naturally to be expected during the peak monsoon months of August-September. The high probability of extremely heavy rainfall compressed within a period of hours makes the situation more acute. Water needs to be either stored upstream or led quickly out into the Bay of Bengal if flooding is to be avoided. Flooding imposes serious constraints on lowland settlements and agricultural choices. However, flooding or regular annual inundation, if taken up as a hydroecological inevitability and not as a disaster, may be looked upon as a less constraining phenomenon. The whole question is the subject of a great deal of current debate.

In the last few pages important constraints on the utilization of the rich natural resources of the fragile Himalayan region have been described. The inherent instability and the resulting constraints of the Himalayan region emerge quite sharply. In the next few sections the gradual growth in the utilization of natural resources in this region will be examined in a historical perspective. It will be evident how and why these constraints have led to environmental degradation in the Himalaya.

The growth of human economic activity in the Himalayan region is primarily based on the utilization of environmental resources. This might be called the people-environment-development relationship and will be analysed in the next section. ■

The people-environment-development relationship

Cultural diversity and the natural environment

Notwithstanding the fragility and hazard-proneness of the Himalaya, human existence in and movements through this mountain range have a very long history. In various ancient religious scriptures the Himalaya is frequently referred to. While the present issues in the people-environment-development relationship are of recent origin, the use of the fragile natural environment as a resource is as old as human existence in the Himalaya. As in the case of most mountains of the world, the population of the Himalaya is the product of a long and complex process of migration from almost all areas around, creating the condition for a high degree of ethnic and cultural diversity. The isolation of the human habitats and general inaccessibility of the terrain provided conditions favourable to diversity. The ethnic and cultural diversity of the Himalaya has, to some extent, been studied from the classical anthropological viewpoint and an indicative description is given in Table 4.7. Very little is documented, however, of these societies' rich knowledge of the fragile environment and of their strategies for the management of natural resources at the local levels.

Through their power of observation and their innovative capacities Himalayan people evolved their economic activities and management strategies to suit the characteristics of their specific natural environment. Whether it is the pastoral economy of cold and dry areas of Tibet, or the shifting agriculture of wet-tropical forests of Myanmar or the sedentary terraced agriculture in the mid-Himalayan region of Nepal, deeper enquiry reveals a logic behind indigenous practices, based on handed-down knowledge and aimed at sustainability. These strategies tacitly internalized the specific advantages and limitations of survival in small mountain watersheds. The knowledge that grew out of hundreds of years of experience is exemplified in the practice of shifting agriculture, terracing of farmlands, medicinal uses of plants, management of forest for maximum production of specific biomass forms (such as fodder), transhumant pastoralism, transportation and management of water and transportation based on animal power. In the attempt to understand the prospects and constraints for sustainable development, this heritage of local environmental wisdom should not be ignored.

On the other hand these local knowledge forms in the Himalaya have evolved in specific ecological situations and so are very diverse. In

Table 4.7: *Indicative list of ethnic and cultural diversity in the Himalayan region*

Country	Namesofethnic/linguisticgroups
Afghanistan	Baluch, Brahui, Gujar, Hazara, Kyrghiz, Kohistani, Moghol, Nuristani, Pariswan, Pushtun, Pamiri, Qizilbash, Tajik, Turkoman, Uzbek
Bangladesh	Chakma, Marma, Tripura, Mro, Bawn, Khumi, Khyang, Chaak, Thangxhangyas, Murung, Riang, Pemkhu, Lushai, Moghe, Kuki, Saka, Shandhu, Bonjugia, Pankhas
Bhutan	Drukpa, several groups of Nepali origin
China	Yi Bai, Hani, Lisu, Lahu, Jiangpo, Achang, Nu, Pumi, Derung, Miao, Dai, Naxi, Benglong, Tibetan (Zang), Sherpa, Loban, Hui, Han, Qiang, Wa, Menba
India	Adi, Angami, Ao, Batti, Bhotia, Chang, Dimasa, Dogri, Garhwali, Garo, Gorkhali/Nepali, Hmar Himachali, Kabui, Kashmiri, Khasi, Khezha, Khiemnungan, Konyak, Kumaori, Kuki, Ladakhi, Lahauli, Lushai, Lepcha, Bhotia, Tibetan, Vaiphei, Wanchoo, Yimchungre
Myanmar	Mao, Shan, Kachin, Burmese, Wa, Lisu, Lakhu, Han, Karen, Jingphaw, Atsi, Lashi, Maru, Kadu, Kanan, Naga, Pao, Palaung, Dhanu, Kaw, Lahu, Intha, Myaungi, Maingtha, Yinga
Nepal	Nepali, Maithili, Bhojpuri, Tamang, Awadhi, Tharu, Newari, Magar, Rai, Gurung, Limbu, Bhote, Hindi, Rajbansi, Satar, Sunuwar, Dannwar, Chepang, Dhangar, Thanri, Dhimal, Majhi, Thakali, Jirrel, Urdu, Dorai,Bodo.
Pakistan	Afridi, Khattak, Orakzai, Wazir, Mashud, Turi, Sinwari, Daur, Yusufzai, Kohistani, Kalash, Baltistani, Pathan, Baluch, Makrani, Boorishki, Brahui

spite of the romanticization of indigenous knowledge, it has been very little documented. One indisputable fact is that these knowledge systems were related to a low intensity of resource use when compared to the modern commercial use of resources with the new ease of accessibility. People did not transform the ecosystem in drastic ways. With these knowledge systems, Himalayan people evolved suitable management skills, which are related to local perceptions of ownership and responsibility, decision-making mechanisms and an executive structure for turning decisions into actions. The codes of behaviour towards nature and the logic behind certain behavioural patterns owe something to religious beliefs. Buddha's teachings are well known for their extreme sensitivity to ecosystemic stabilities and concern for vegetation. On the other hand, Shiva, the most worshipped Hindu god in the Himalaya, is himself an embodiment of the Himalayan ecology. His hair represents the forests and the river Ganga is held in check with its help, while the wildlife, represented by a living snake around his neck, is a part of his bodily decoration and ornament.

The sophistication of the indigenous strategies is not apparent since they are not recorded on paper. This is a constant excuse for development professionals who regard the strategies as "unscientific". Only in the last few years has this situation started to change. On this subject there are many interesting examples of the conflict of opinions. For centuries the people practising shifting agriculture in tropical and sub-tropical forests in the uplands of Bangladesh, Myanmar, southwestern China etc. have sustained a flourishing agri-horti-pastoral economy. Whether it was "scientific" or not has been repeatedly questioned by officials. The paddy farmers' keenness to maintain genetic variety *in situ* directly conflicts with the views of agriculture officials who support the green-revolution package. The herdsmen in northern Tibet are constantly told by officials that their unscientific management of pastures has led to the tragedy of the commons. These interesting and contradictory viewpoints are cited not to claim that indigenous knowledge is valid under all circumstances and under all intensities of resource use, but to stress the need to understand its evolutionary logic and to relate it to the ecological experiences of the people. Its utility in times of more intensive resource use need not always be denied in advance. However, it should also be stressed that indigenous cultures show an obscurantist rigidity especially when matters involve questions of social hierarchy. Thus any change may be obstinately opposed.

The multiplicity of ethnic and linguistic groups in all the nooks and corners of the Himalayan region may add yet another dimension to the problems of sustainability. The very diversity which, under conditions of peace, may be a positive resource for sustainable development can, under certain conditions, be the cause of widespread socio-economic instabilities which encourage hostility between the various mountain communities. Quick socio-economic transformations, insensitive to the fine structure of ethnicity and language in the Himalaya, run a grave risk of transforming diversity into fragmentation and generating ethnic conflicts. Once ethnic conflicts emerge as a dominant social process, concern for sustainable development becomes the first and easiest victim. Thus ethnic and cultural diversity in the Himalaya needs serious and positive attention not just because of the usefulness of indigenous knowledge for sustainable development, but because it is an important factor that can jeopardize the prospects of ever achieving it.

Accessibility, marginality and unsustainability

Himalayan indigenous knowledge and natural resource management systems evolved under conditions of relative inaccessibility and isolation. In the present century the introduction of mechanized transport, especially automobiles and aircraft, has changed the objective conditions for natural resource utilization in the accessible parts of the Himalayan region. It is therefore important to analyse the role played by the improved accessibility, either in bringing unsustainability nearer or encouraging sustainability.

Against the background of the geo-political history of the Himalayan region, the initial construction of the main trunk roads is better regarded as a political and military step than as any sort of development programme. The primary purpose was to enhance the presence of the institutions of state in the formerly inaccessible border areas. However, very quickly the main use to which the roads were put turned out to be non-military in nature. The connections established by roads or air links drastically reduced the spatial isolation or marginality of the mountain areas. And now the communication process no longer depends on the technologies of physical transportation. Even areas still highly inaccessible physically have been connected with instant electronic communications helped by satellite technology. So the psychological and cultural distances between the plains and the interior mountains have been greatly reduced, in spite of their spatial isolation. Such cultural changes, in turn, however, quickly generate popular aspirations for quicker physical means of transportation to and from less accessible areas. In this way whether it is the rich flat lands or the poor mountains, whether it is the powerful centre or the weak periphery, all want increased accessibility, albeit for different reasons. The less visible but real impacts of enhanced accessibility in the Himalayan areas are thus:

i) increased political integration with the powerful national state

ii) increased economic integration with the larger economies in the plains.

In this way, the new accessibility, when considered as a development measure in itself, runs the risk of simultaneously creating two major forms of marginalization, political and economic. When the mountain areas are connected by roads or airways, the new technologies of transportation are invariably controlled from the faraway and powerful centres in the plains. The mountain people largely lose the political autonomy that they enjoy under conditions of physical isolation. They also run the risk of becoming economically marginalized while competing with the much more organized market economies of the plains. Finally, they are also pushed to an intellectual or cognitive marginalization by the arrival of scientific experts either from the state or the market, who gather systematic information about important mountain resources like minerals, forests, water, etc. and then determine policies for their utilization either through the centralized state planning machinery or by the autonomous forces of the market. If there is any Himalayan dilemma, it is around this issue of the management of accessibility and ways of guarding against the marginalization of the Himalayan people.

Mobility for the people in the Himalaya needs to be an integral part of the development process. Recommendations for keeping the mountains inaccessible as a solution to the risks of marginalization have been made. But these are merely excellent examples of the plains bias among some urban conservationists unaware of the aspirations of the Himalayan people. Each individual in the mountain areas wants to have access to a larger space in shorter times, to take her/his produce to the market and bring in purchases at the earliest, to get away from the feeling of intellectual isolation and ignorance characteristic of inaccessible mountain areas, to take the injured or the sick to the medical centres as early as possible.

Today transformations in the Himalaya, or for that matter in any other of the world's mountain ranges, cannot be disconnected from those taking place in the plains. The question is, what is the nature of the link between them? Unless the specific advantages and disadvantages of the mountains are properly understood, and the advantages are put to good use and the disadvantages guarded against, there will always remain a strong probability that any new links will simply help to marginalize the mountain people. This does not have to be so and there are encouraging examples. Take the case of mushroom exports from the northern parts of the Hengduan mountain near the bordering towns of Ganze in Sichuan and Diqing in Yunnan. From government forests the indigenous Tibetan people individually collect the Matsutak mushroom which is a delicacy in Japan and hence has a ready export market. The mushrooms fetch a price of US$20 per kg as they are trucked away by road. The local forests are managed by the local communities. So clearly potential marginalization can be influenced by ownership and management policies and practices both at the local and national levels. Economic development in the Himalaya, then, should aim at diversifying opportunities for the people by improving accessibility whilst avoiding new agents of marginalization; by more intense and wise utilization of the natural resources and the mountain's specific advantages within the limits of ecological sustainability. New accessibility in

Namche Bazaar, Khumbu Himal, Nepal. Traditional Sherpa homeland and modern tourist Mecca

mountain societies speeds up socio-economic transformation, and controlling the rate of change may not always be easy. Under these conditions, the economic processes, even if they do not provoke marginalization, do often lead to ecological unsustainability. In order to understand the pressures which currently favour that unsustainability and the control mechanisms needed to foster the desirable converse, the existing environmental degradation in the Himalayan region will be briefly discussed together with its principal causes.

Prosperity, poverty and environmental degradation

With a basic assumption that the new accessibility means that economic development in the highlands cannot be disconnected from processes in the plains, a closer view will now be taken at the factors behind the present environmental degradation in the Himalayan region. Environmental degradation is basically a product of human exploitation of the various natural resources described above. The scale and dimension of degradation have been made worse by the ecological sensitivities, described as constraints, described in the earlier section. An effort will now be made to identify the reasons for unsustainability.

This analysis will not start with the premise that the poor people of the Himalayan region cause environmental degradation in this fragile mountain range. The most important reason for that is that neither poverty nor environmental degradation have been measured and correlated enough to justify such a definite conclusion. Instead, an effort will be made to identify basic features of environmental degradation in the Himalaya and to explore the causative forces. Part of the problem is that the impact of very rapid geomorphological changes which have been occurring for millions of years and human-induced ecological instabilities which are only a few decades old are often very difficult to distinguish from one another. Equally difficult is to quantify the state of poverty and prosperity in most parts of the Himalayan region because of the existence of barter trade and the predominance of common properties like forests and pastures as the main resource base for the local people. A mechanical dependence on the standard

Country	Region	Annual average income per capita (US$)	Literacy (per cent)
Bangladesh	Chattagram Hills	228 (1989)	16 (1989)
Bhutan	National	160 (1989)	10 (1982)
China	Tibet	88 (1985)	48 (1982)
India	Himachal Pradesh	166 (1982)	43 (1982)
Nepal	Dhadhing district	150 (1990)	25 (1990)
Pakistan	Baluchistan (rural)	72 (1988)	10 (1981)

Table 4.8: *Annual per capita income and literacy rates in some areas of the Himalaya (years for the data are given in brackets)*

econometric techniques may hide a real state of poverty in some cases or generate an illusion of poverty even among prosperous communities. This is an essential consideration for economic evaluation of inaccessible mountain areas. Thus, economic and social statistical estimates can at best serve as an approximate indication of the economic status of the Himalayan people. Table 4.8 presents the indicative picture of the state of poverty and literacy in some Himalayan areas.

Environmental writings on the Himalayan region have generally portrayed human-induced changes in the ecosystem as inevitably destabilizing. While such is generally true for the more recent and exogenous transformations, human interventions aimed at the reverse, at making the environment more resilient are also not difficult to identify. The experience of such intervention is important in facing the present challenge of achieving sustainability at high intensities of resource use. Economic activities and thus the nature of human-induced environmental degradation in the Himalaya can be divided into two separate, but interactive, groups. One is the continued use of land, forest, water resources etc. by the indigenous communities living in the Himalaya. The other is the result of the political-economic integration of the Himalayan areas with the national states or the larger economy of the plains. In this group, use of Himalayan resources is made to satisfy the needs of the state and the larger economy of the lowlands. In this group of resource use are to be found the older types, such as farming, or new ones, such as mining. Environmental degradation has been generated by both types, in the course of which the indigenous and the exogenous have sometimes collaborated, sometimes conflicted. Poverty, which is blatant and conspicuous by its presence in large parts of the Himalaya, should be seen as both a contributor to environmental degradation and a result of it.

The most visible and best-recorded natural resource degradation in the Himalaya has taken place in the forests. Both the poor and the prosperous need the forests and have, accordingly, degraded them by different means and in different ways. Pictures of poor people carrying headloads of tree branches have made the front cover of so many magazines that the other forces behind deforestation and the creation of environmental degradation have slipped from view. Most drastic changes in Himalayan forest cover have taken place at the areas bordering densely populated urban centres, in particular at the foothills of the Hengduan and the Himalayan arc. Incidentally, these are also the best-forested areas. Deforestation is directly linked with commercial logging, clearing for urbanization and clearing for farmlands but forest degradation arises from excessive and uncontrolled lopping by local rural people, damage to regeneration by burning and by cattle-grazing.

An example of the extent of the problem can be seen in the case of Nepal. The annual loss of forest cover (100 per cent canopy loss) has been estimated at about 44 000 hectares or 0.8 per cent of the total forest cover of the country. In the dry mid-hills of Nepal or the Kumaon-Garhwal region of India, the pressure of population has already damaged forests in the vicinity of the villages and women often have to spend 16-18 hours on a barefoot trek on risky mountain slopes to bring a headload of fodder or fuelwood often 1.5 times their body-weight from distant forests. In the dry areas of Tibet, men go with a small herd of yak for seven or eight days to collect fuelwood to last for some weeks.

In view of such inhuman hardships, if the poor people in the Himalayan region are destroying the forest resources, it is clearly out of desperation and not out of choice. In such conditions sustainability of the natural resource base can draw popular attention only when steps are also taken to ensure even a small reduction in this drudgery. The village population is also responsible for forest resource degradation by expanding farmlands at the expense of the forest. Under conditions of high population pressure on local subsistence agriculture, poor farmers have taken advantage of the poor demarcation of forest boundaries to denude the forests for farmland. Where agriculture is commercial, affluent farmers have similarly encroached upon the forests to bring additional land under profitable cultivation. On an even grander scale it is the official policies of settling people in the Terai region of the Sub-Himalaya, as has been done in India, Nepal and Bhutan, which have contributed most to deforestation.

The degradation of the grasslands and pastures has also been taking place at a high rate in all parts of the Himalaya. Grasslands have generally expanded into the areas of degraded forests. In fewer instances, the areas under pasture have also declined, giving way to farmlands. The pressure of an increased animal population is usually identified as the prime cause, while the visible effects of degradation are sharp decreases in highly nutritious and palatable grasses, the invasion of weeds, extensive coverage by non-palatable grasses, and the compaction of soil resulting in barren landscapes. At an aggregate level this degradation has reduced the total animal-carrying capacity of the Himalayan region significantly. The joint impact of the degradation of forest cover and pasturelands is seen in the degradation of farmlands due to the direct dependence of the latter on the former for nutrient and organic matter. In the case of the forests some quantitative data is available on the level of degradation. However, for the pastures and grasslands, which are ecologically more vulnerable to degradation, there is very little.

The other important land resource is the farmlands. In comparison with the common land resources, private farmlands are managed with greater concern for their sustainability. In the indigenous agriculture oriented to local consumption, sustaining the long-term productivity of the land has been the main aim and not maximization of production in the short term. While the degradation of common property resources like forests or pastures may be attributed to population and poverty, the degradation of farmlands is quite a different story.

Farming practices in the Himalaya have never been static but the recent phase of change under conditions of quickly improving accessibility can surely be called speedy, if not revolutionary. Traditional farming activities in the Himalaya were generally characterized by lower productivity and higher diversity as compared to the plains. New farming seeks high financial returns and low diversity. The introduction of the potato has made significant changes but probably the most important change has been a shift to horticulture dominated by apple cultivation. Special mention should be made of Himachal Pradesh and the Kashmir Valley in India, NWFP in Pakistan, MounKong in Tibet and Dali in Yunnan province in China, Jumla in Nepal and Thimphu district in Bhutan. In many areas this horticultural land became available through the clearing of natural forests. Other fruit trees encouraged include pear, cherry, walnut and chestnut. In areas close to large urban settlements, as near Kathmandu in Nepal or Dehradun in India, the change to vegetable cultivation has been more striking.

These various changes have degraded farmlands in two ways: one by intensification and the other by the increased fallowing of land. In areas of the Himalaya where the climatic and water resources have become increasingly significant and appropriate for commercial agriculture triggered off by new transport facilities, land use intensity has tripled. An increasing requirement for soil nutrients is then met by chemical fertilizers along with other elements of high-production agriculture, with their own problems of unsustainability. Another way that commercial agriculture has degraded land is by encouraging cultivation of land on steep hillsides. Under intense rainfall this results in the heavy erosion of soil nutrients. Land degradation in the Himalaya has also taken place through deliberate neglect and fallowing where climatic conditions and water

River	Damlocation	Approx.height (m)	Powerpotential (MW)
Kabul	Ambahar	281	1 270
Kabul	Bazargai	293	2 000
Jhelum	Kohala	–	2 000
Indus	Dhok Mila	–	1 200
Indus	Kalabagh	087	1 125
Jhelum	Mangla	116	1 400
Indus	Tarbela	142	2 500
Sutlej	Bhakhra	226	1 050
Beas	Pong	–	1 200
Parvati	Parvati	167	1 900
Yamuna	Lakhwar	204	300
Yamuna	Kishau	253	600
Yamuna	Kuwa-damta	200	126
Ganga	Tehri	260	2 200
Ganga	Koteshwar	104	–
Ganga	Kotlibhel	210	1 000
Mahakali	Pancheshwar	232	2 000
Karnali	Chisapani	270	10 800
Kosi	Barahashetra	230	3 600
Wangchu	Chukha I	–	336

Table 4.9: *Indicative list of constructed or planned dams in some areas of the Himalaya*

resources proved inadequate for high-intensity commercial farming. This is the case in mainly dry mid-mountain areas where new transport facilities have facilitated male migration to the plains. This includes both seasonal and permanent migration. Thus large areas of agricultural land are worked on only by the women, who are already overloaded. The result is a lack of maintenance of land, the collapse of terraces, the decline of soil nutrients etc. In this way, on all types of land, environmental degradation has brought about significant losses of productivity.

Land degradation has also been caused in some parts by instabilities arising from the large-scale expansion of new roads and open-cast mining. In the geological and climatic conditions prevalent in the Himalayan region the technology needed to construct roads which do not damage the environment is underdeveloped. Similarly, techniques of open-cast mining on Himalayan slopes have not attracted serious professional concern, nor have the rules and regulations for mining internalized the environmental constraints prevalent in the Himalaya. The problems caused by environmentally destructive surface quarrying in the rainy Doon Valley in the Indian Himalaya has brought this issue to the fore. Similarly the challenge of providing stable and dependable road transportation under all climatic conditions is felt most seriously in the Sichuan or Yunnan areas with problems arising from rain-induced landslides. On the Karakoram Highway difficulties due to slope instabilities are acute. These problems have caused increased mass-wasting and degradation of land by the inflow of mine or road-produced debris. Finally the large volumes of additional debris end up in the rivers and drastically affect the flow regimes.

In contrast with the land resources, which are extensively used by local people, the water resources of the Himalaya have started to be used extensively for purposes quite outside the area. The huge volume of water produced by the Himalaya, in particular during the three monsoon months of July–September, has always drawn the attention of dwellers on the flat plains below. Hill economies have made very little direct use of this water and all the river valley projects whether

Brilliantly engineered hillslopes of irrigation-fed terraces in Nepal's Middle Mountains are frequently damaged during heavy monsoon rains. They are also frequently repaired during the following dry season

constructed, under construction or under investigation, are mainly aimed at the satisfaction of electricity and water needs of the urban-industrial centres in the plains nearby. The dams in the region are mainly located in the Indus Valley and the western half of the Ganga Valley in the Himalaya. In the Hengduan mountains numerous smaller dams have been constructed, mainly for irrigation. Among the existing or planned major dams in the Himalaya the list contained in Table 4.9 will give an idea of the scale of the water resources utilization. This does not in any way present the totality of dam-building activity. The whole issue of big dams in the Himalaya has recently become a hotly debated one because of the threat of seismic activity in the region. The large-scale displacement of the people from the areas to be submerged and the environmental degradation which follows their rehabilitation has also become a crucial point in the debate about the Himalayan dams.

Tourism is another sector which has helped economic growth in parts of the Himalaya, while at the same time causing environmental degradation. The origin of Himalayan tourism was the British establishment of hill-towns all along the southern slope starting from Shillong in the east to Muree in the west. Before that of course there was pilgrimage such as visits to Lhasa for the Buddhists or to the temples of Kedarnath or Badrinath in Garhwal Himalaya, for the Hindus. However, with improving transport into the Himalayan region, tourism has successfully begun to capitalize on the specific advantages of the Himalayan landscape. For instance, in Nepal, tourism accounts for 23 per cent of the gross foreign exchange earnings. This growth, as in most other parts of the Himalaya, has come at considerable cost in environmental degradation.

Forest resources in the vicinity of the tourist routes and centres have been quickly destroyed. Pollution and littering have started even at the glacial sources of the rivers. It is estimated that about 50 tons of garbage is spread over and around the Mount Everest area. Notwithstanding the appreciable environmental damage caused by the various activities which generate economic growth but which have caused special hardships to the poor, their economic returns are often very skewed. For instance, in Nepal, less than 10 per cent of the growth generated reaches the poor rural people while the influential urban rich get the rest. Thus, the relationship of prosperity, poverty and environmental degradation in the Himalayan region is not a simple one and much deeper enquiries will be needed to determine ways of handling the issues. For this, the causes, nature and extent of environmental degradation in the Himalayan region will need to be investigated on a much larger scale.

Implications of environmental degradation

At a qualitative level there is already a good deal of knowledge. The implications of environmental degradation can be divided into three separate spatial categories, the local or micro-level, the regional or meso-level and the global or macro-level.

At the local level the implications are related to the slow and steady loss of the productivity of the common property resources of forests and pasturelands. For the rural people it means a vanishing resource base for their agri-pastoral economy: increasing hardship in the collection of fuel and fodder, decreasing standards of health etc. Such common property resources are vital for the majority of the rural people and it is they who are worst hit by their degradation. The world-famous forest protection movement "Chipko" or "Hug the trees" emerged as a response to such degradation of forest resources in the Garhwal Himalaya. The degradation of land resources can start the chain reaction by initiating a decline in local water resources. Early drying up of springs, which are the main water source for most Himalayan villages, has been reported and this causes further degradation in the physical quality of life. All these effects finally lead to a reduction in the total productivity of farmlands, causing a serious decline in food production and the rural economy in general. An essential starting point for the pursuit of sustainable development of these areas will be the regeneration of local common property resources and their appropriate management to ensure sustainable and high productivity.

At the regional level, environmental degradation in the Himalaya manifests itself mainly in the water resources: the innumerable rivers and rivulets emerging from the Mid-Himalaya into the Sub-Himalaya and the plains beyond. For millions of years floods have naturally been occurring in the Himalayan foothills, contributing rich and fertile silt. Over the past few decades, the speed of the flood and the nature of the sediment has reportedly changed. A farmer in the border area of Nepal and Bihar state of India described this experience of change in the following words: "Earlier the flood came silently like a small cat, touched our feet and went away in a few days, giving us fertile silt. Now it comes with the speed of a hungry tiger, takes away everything, covers the land with sand and does not want to go away."

This increased ferocity of floods may be linked with two independent factors. First, climatic change may have increased the probability of cloud-bursts during the usual continuous low-intensity rainfall. Second, land degradation in the Himalayan slopes described above has contributed to widespread changes in their hydrological characteristics resulting in heavier surface runoff and increasing the particle carrying capacity of the flood-water. Then follow droughts and scarcities of water. The great water resources of the Himalaya thus contribute to misery, suffering and poverty.

While dealing with the foothill floods, some reference must be made to the common misconception that land degradation in the Himalaya causes floods as far away as Bangladesh. Scientific literature on this issue increasingly demonstrates the logical inconsistencies associated with such a simple mechanical link of cause and effect. Floods at the common exit of two of the largest rivers of the world, Ganga and Brahmaputra, which drain some of the wettest areas of the world, need much deeper analysis and explanation than commonly supposed.

At the global or macro level, environmental degradation in the Himalaya has serious implications for biodiversity. The great climatic variation within small spatial distances, in particular in the eastern half of the Himalayan region, has provided the ecological basis for one of the richest zones of biodiversity in the world. Deforestation and forest degradation, especially in the eastern Himalayan foothills and the Hengduan, have already threatened biodiversity. It is not clear whether the losses are so grave that extinctions have occurred, but serious restrictions of location and species population have already taken place. Efforts at the conservation and protection of biodiversity have been made and a country breakdown of the protected areas is given in Table 4.10.

All these implications of environmental degradation in the Himalayan region have attracted the attention of environmentalists, scientists and people at large. Popular action on the protection on the Himalaya has been easily stimulated and the media have been extremely effective in raising discourse and debate on the state of the Himalayan environment. If any weakness exists, it is in the area of defining moves beyond, on the question of exactly how sustainable and participatory development are to happen.

An approach to sustainable development

The nature of environmental degradation coupled with the pressure of population in many parts constitute a serious problem. What is an even bigger problem is that in spite of a lot of general talk about sustainable development, it has not been possible to generate suitable options. Development continues within the framework of the dominant growth model. While it may take some time positively to define sustainable development, in view of the ecological fragility of the Himalaya, environmentally hazardous economic activities should be discouraged. An immediate need exists for institutional innovations to this end.

The starting point for the evolution of an approach to sustainable development is to bring to an end to the conflict between environment and development. The environment is a given natural resource,with its specific advantages and constraints. Development, if it has to be sustainable, must build on these advantages while guarding against the constraints. It is by a proper understanding of the scientific and economic dimensions of the constraints that unsustainability can be guarded against. Sustainable development cannot be immediately defined as a positive concept. At the moment the best way to define it is to use a double negative and say that it is what is not unsustainable in the long run. So a new approach to sustainable development has to be based on

a) improved accessibility without marginality; and

b) an intensification of natural resource use avoiding unsustainability.

This requires a continuous process of monitoring of socio-economic and environmental impacts.

The Himalayan region is not in a hopeless condition in spite of the pressure of population and the present resource degradation. Here is where the idea of sustainable development begins. However, it does need concerted efforts at all levels, from micro to macro, to face the dual challenge of acute poverty and the need for ecological rehabilitation. The rich natural resources and mountain-specific advantages of the Himalaya need wise utilization sensitive to needs at all levels.

The new and sustainable development will have to look for new ways to use resources with a proper recognition of the constraints, socio-economic as well as environmental. In terms of how this aim is to be achieved, the agenda for the Himalayan region can be divided in three levels, macro, meso and micro.

The natural resource dimension of the Himalaya extends beyond the eight countries of Asia within which it is physically located. By virtue of the present economic role and potential of its rivers, the Himalaya can be called the water tower of Asia. Ecological management and utilization of this huge water resource distributed by many international rivers is not just for any single country. The Himalaya needs a collaborative approach to its water resources. Information and data needed for ecological management of the Himalayan rivers needs to be collected and used in the larger interest of the people of the region. Hydrological and ecological information collected according to river basins, from the uplands to the plains, may be used for scientific understanding of the prospects and constraints of sustainable development. This collaboration at scientific level among the countries sharing the Himalayan rivers is urgent.

At the meso level, national agendas have to evolve towards enhancement of ecological research specific to the part of the Himalayan region within respective national boundaries. Conservation of biodiversity will be an essential part of the meso-level agenda for sustainable development. Equally important will be estimates of

	I		II		III		IV	
Category of protected area	Scientific Reserve/strict Nature Reserve		National Park		Natural Monument/ Natural Landmark		Nature Conservation Reserve/ Managed Nature Reserve/Wildlife Sanctuary	
Country (area 000 km^2)	No	Area (km^2)	No	Area (km^2)	No	Area (km^2)	No	Area (km^2)
Afghanistan (650)	4	1 310						
Bangladesh (143)							3	324
Bhutan (44.6)			4	8 337			8	1 168
Myanmar (677)								
China (9 561)	12	6 052					2+1*	1 097
Sichuan Province (570)	*11*	*4564*					*1+1**	*230*
Xizang Province (1 220)								
Yunnan Province (394)	*1*	*1488*					*1*	*867*
India (3 888)			10	7 174			70	8 971
*Arunchal *** (83.7)*			*1*	*1808*			*4*	*1474*
*Himachal*** (55.7)*			*1*	*1736*			*27*	*1726*
*Jammu & Kashmir***(222.3)*			*3*	*1051*			*27*	*1150*
Sikkim (7.1)			*1*	*850*				
*UP*** (294.1)*			*4*	*1729*			*12*	*4621*
Nepal (147)			6	8 246			6	1 687
Pakistan (775)			6	3 702			75+1*	5 301
Total **(5 265.5)	16	7362	25	27 459			163+2*	17 725

Table 4.10: *- Protected areas in the Himalayan region*
Source: Chalise S.R. (unpublished) ICIMOD, 1992

natural resource bases like forests, grasslands, soil, rainfall etc. on a regular basis. Much of the data and information base for the design of sustainable development can be generated by national institutions. The exact nature of the mountain characteristics can be determined only on the basis of a more complete database than that available today. Sensitization of senior-level administrators, planners and technocrats on ecological management in the Himalayan region will be the most vital step in fostering sustainable development. In this task, the media, which has played an important role already, must be expected to contribute more concretely in clearing up the confusion about ecology and sustainable development.

The last, and possibly the most important, segment of the Himalayan agenda for sustainable development is at the micro level. The present

V		VI		VII		VIII		IX		X	
Protected Landscape		Resource Reserve		Natural Biotic Area/ Anthropological Reserve		MultipleUse Management Area/Managed Resource Area		Biosphere Reserve		WorldHeritage site (natural)	
No	Area (km ^{2})	No	Area (km ^{2})	No	Area (km ^{2})	No	Area (km ^{2})	No	Area (km ^{2})	No	Area (km ^{2})
		5	3 140								
3	923							1	2 072		
2	*23*							*1*	*2072*		
1	*900*										
2	410										
2	*410*										
										3	3 100
1	0.6					70+2*	40 319	5*	n/a		
6	1333.6	5	3 140			70+2*	40 319	1+5*	2 072	3	3 100

* *area not available*
** *for China and India, only the areas of the related provinces have been added up*
*** *provincial area*

crisis and confusion in Himalayan development strategy is partly a result of the widespread exclusion and marginalization of the people from the decision-making part of the development process. The organization, knowledge and participation of the isolated local communities in the Himalaya will be needed to design sustainable development at local levels in association with the ecological scientists and planners working on larger geographical regions. In this respect the ecological scientists and planners will form the vital link spanning the micro level to the macro level. Any attempt to replace the micro-level actors by the macro-level ones will be a sure prescription for unsustainability, a luxury the Himalayan region cannot afford any more. ■

References

BANDYOPADHYAY, J. (ed.) *Beyond the Himalayan Dilemma* publication for ICIMOD, Kathmandu, forthcoming.

BLAIKIE, P., CAMERON, J. AND SEDDON, D. *Nepal in Crisis* Oxford University Press, New Delhi, 1980.

CHENG HONG AND MING TAO CHANG *Study on the Integrated Investigation of National Land-Resources and Strategies for Development in South-West China* (in Chinese). Science Press, Beijing, 1990.

IVES, J.D. AND MESSERLI, BRUNO *The Himalayan Dilemma* Routledge, London, 1989.

JODHA, N.S., BANSKOTA, M. AND PARTAP, T. (eds.) *Sustainable Mountain Agriculture* Oxford and IBH Publishers, New Delhi, 1992.

LALL, J.S. and MODDIE, A.D. (eds.) *The Himalaya: Aspects of Change* Oxford University Press, New Delhi, 1981.

Notes

Figures 4.2, 4.4 and 4.5

Source: Map of Nepal 1982, Atlas of Pakistan 1986, Social and Economic Atlas of India and Adjacent Countries 1979, Atlas of China 1989 and American Geographical Society of New York 1964. Area identification by Pitamber Sharma and Jayanta Bandyapadhyay, 1992

No boundaries shown on the maps in this section imply any judgement of their legal status.

5

Mountains North and South

The east slope of the dormant volcano Oraefajökull, South East Iceland

Introduction

Oriental societies have placed great importance on mountainous lands for thousands of years and mountains have been central to much Eastern theology and philosophy. In Western societies mountains were objects of fear and dislike until the dawn of modern science, especially natural science, at the beginning of the nineteenth century. This saw a dramatic change in perspective: mountains became a source of beauty, inspiration, and challenge. Exploration and mountaineering followed rapidly, leading to an elite tourism that laid the foundations for the present widespread popularity of mountain regions for mass tourism.

The age of exploration and reconnaissance mapping is now over, and with it the heroic age of mountaineering. However, the widespread realization that the mountain lands form the physical, and often the political, framework of an ever-shrinking world, ensures that interest in them will continue to grow. They have been pivotal to much research in the natural sciences–plate tectonics and seismology, botany and zoology, and climatology.

Perhaps of equal importance, mountains are increasingly perceived as high-energy landscapes in the sense that high altitude, steep slopes, running water, fluctuations of temperature across freezing point, and gravity combine to ensure that landscape-forming processes operate much more rapidly than in low-energy environments (areas of subdued relief). This in turn has led to the popular notion that mountains are very fragile and environmental disturbance upslope will invariably lead to catastrophic destruction downslope and out onto the plains. Herein lies a serious dilemma because, in a very general sense, this viewpoint is correct.

In detail, however, a simplistic conservationist approach has led to over-dramatization and risks causing more harm than good. This issue is treated extensively for the Himalaya by Ives and Messerli (1989) and is discussed repeatedly in the journal *Mountain Research and Development*. The problem has arisen because of the extreme difficulty of making generalizations about such complex regions.

The only safe generalization that can be made about mountains is that they are so complex, physically, and even more complex from the viewpoint of human adaptation and resource use, that simple conclusions must be avoided. This characteristic of the world's mountain landscapes–extreme diversity–is so important that the decision to represent five major mountain regions in this book runs the risk of not providing adequate representation for the mountain world at large.

This section has been added, therefore, so that at least an overview of some of the otherwise neglected mountain areas can be included. Even here, the range of diversity, both physical and cultural, is so great that only a random selection is feasible. Thus we have incorporated such widely contrasting areas as the mountain island of Hawaii (Big Island) replete with its highly active volcano, Grenada in the Caribbean, the remote arctic mountains of northeastern Canada, Iceland (an island nation of high mountains, plateaus and ice caps), New Guinea, an example of equatorial high mountains with an indigenous culture in transition, a section of northwestern Thailand with the remnants of hill tribe swidden subsistence, Lijiang Autonomous County with its Yulongxue Shan range in Yunnan, PRC, and the Sierra Nevada, USA.

The coverage of this book as a whole remains incomplete despite this approach. Even so, the region under consideration run the gamut from hot desert to equatorial forest, from Andean paramo to cold arctic desert, from cloud forest to puna to mid-latitude dark coniferous forest, from alpine meadow interspersed with sheer rock walls and glaciers to monsoon rainforest. In fact, the vast majority of the world's ecosystems adapted to either steep slopes or high altitude, their plant communities and associated faunas, are represented.

It is not surprising, therefore, that this selection embraces most of the world's national parks and biosphere reserves. It also contains an enormous range of cultures, from the high-tech winter recreation of industrialized countries to overpopulated subsistence agriculture of underdeveloped countries at the macro scale. At a more local scale it includes an almost infinite array of adaptations, from the nomads of western Tibet to Sherpas in transition to a mass tourism economy, from subsistence agro-pastoralists of the Andean puna to Yukagir reindeer herders of the northern Verkhoyansk Range of Siberia, from the second-home owners of the Swiss Alps to the mass water transfer technicians of California.

The difficulty of adequate representation of the mountain lands for study within the mandate of UNCED is not only the result of extreme diversity and global spread. It is also aggravated by large-scale gaps in knowledge and a severe shortage of reliable data. It is this realization that has prompted the proposal that a much more detailed and complete status report, data bank, and annotated bibliography become a high priority initial task for post-UNCED action. ■

Inugsuin Fiord at 70°N on Baffin Island's northeast coast

Mountains of the eastern Canadian Arctic

The northeast coast of Canada, between latitudes 55 and 83 degrees N, is a spectacular arctic mountain and fiord landscape. It is a remote land of stark beauty, lying almost entirely north of the arctic treeline; inland it slopes gradually down to the west, being transformed into a series of vast lake- and boulder-strewn plateaus. With a north-south distance of almost 3 000 km (more than the length of the main arc of the Himalaya), it must be classed as one of the great mountain regions of the world (Bird, 1967). This description will deal primarily with the Baffin Island and Labrador sections.

Labrador and Baffin Island represent the uplifted and block-faulted eastern edge of the Canadian, or Laurentian Shield, composed mainly of ancient Precambrian granites, gneisses, and metasediments. Differential uplift by as much as 1 000 to 3 000 m in the Tertiary Period of geological history caused accelerated river erosion followed by extensive and repeated glaciation (Bird, 1967; Hare, 1959). These processes, tectonic and erosional, have produced a mountain and fiord landscape with a topography comparable to the upper reaches of the Alps and Caucasus. Absolute altitudes attain 2 600 m with many rock spires and massive granite faces rising more than 1 600 m sheer from the fiord waters. The fiords themselves, many over 100 km in length, are up to 1 000 m deep.

The entire region is little visited and hardly known. There is no single name even for the 1 000 km length of mountains that form the northeast coastline of Baffin Island. Here numerous peaks exceed 1 800 m and inland the plateau is partially mantled by the 130 km long Banes Ice Cap, a relict of the last Ice Age (Ives and Andrews, 1963). Numerous small ice caps occur in the coastal mountains and many outlet and valley glaciers reach the vicinity of sea level. The Penny Highlands on the Cumberland Peninsula, transected by the Arctic Circle, constitute the highest and most impressive mountain block. Further south, in Labrador, the Torngat, Kaumajet and Kiglapait mountains fall progressively in height southward (1 600 m, 1 300 m, 1 000 m respectively).

Permafrost is everywhere continuous (Ives, 1974), and winters are long and severe with fast ice forming along the outer coast and the more northerly fiords retaining their ice until into July. In low-lying areas, dwarf willows, sedges, mosses, and a host of brightly flowering arctic-alpine perennials constitute the tundra vegetation. Because the Baffin Island and Labrador currents carry a mass of icebergs (mainly from Greenland) and sea ice southwards to Newfoundland, summers tend to have a high proportion of cold foggy and rainy days. Topographically, the region is similar to western Norway (although experiencing a much more severe climate for comparable latitudes), and the west and east coasts of Greenland.

A few hundred Inuit (Eskimo) in scattered hunting and fishing villages, together with the administrative centre of Frobisher Bay, constitute the sparse coastal population. Inland the area is totally uninhabited. Herein lies its attraction for modern adventure tourism and mountaineering.

It is an ultimate "wilderness"; one can spend three months in many of the fiords without seeing another human. Wildlife includes polar bears, caribou, wolves, foxes, black bears in the south, and numerous small arctic mammals, and a rich sea life, including seals, walrus , narwhales, whales, and a large variety of fish. The Penny Highlands, especially Pangnirtung Pass, has attracted mountaineering expeditions since the 1950s, and a large section was declared a national park (Auyuittuq National Park) in 1972 by the Canadian Federal Government (Mowat, 1965).

The Labrador section, especially the inland plateau which extends into Nouveau Quebec (Hare, 1959; Ives, 1957), has seen the development of numerous hunting (caribou) and fishing camps since the 1960s and this has already had a negative impact on the once extraordinarily rich freshwater fish and salmon populations.

This vast coastal mountain and inland plateau region first became known to European centres of civilization during the reign of Elizabeth I of England when the search for a Northwest Passage was seriously initiated. The major place names, Hudson, Frobisher, Baffin, Bylot, Davis, and Foxe, eloquently speak for this early exploration. Less well publicized, because of the nature of their trade, were the Scottish whalers

Baffin Island provides an Arctic mountain landscape, virtually untouched by man

who, together with their Dutch, Norwegian, Yankee, and other competitors, were responsible for almost eliminating the once magnificent populations of whale. Even before Elizabeth I, however, the Vikings had become familiar with much of the region. Erik the Red established the Greenland colonies between present-day Holsteinborg and Kap Farvel a thousand years ago. Southeastern Baffin Island and the Torngat Mountains of Northern Labrador are rivals for the Viking name Helluland (land of flat stones) sighted as the open boats sailed down the coast to Vinland (northern Newfoundland)(Mowat, 1965).

These historical attributes, together with the dramatic arctic wilderness setting and hard granite walls that make Yosemite's El Capitan look very modest, paint a picture of heroic exploration and expeditionary adventure in a land of midnight sun. While the number of visitors will likely remain modest because of expensive logistics, the very nature of arctic tundra plant and animal life, especially the extremely low biomass productivity, requires highly sensitive management. This is Inuit country and land-use conflicts between local communities and federal and provincial governments are already apparent. Efforts to create a Torngat Mountain National Park in Northern Labrador have remained incomplete because of this situation. The local people have a strong case for control over opportunities to increase their standard of living. Extreme remoteness, however, is no longer an adequate conservationist defence, and will become less so as adventure tourism continues to expand. ■

Grenada, West Indies

Grenada, the southernmost Windward Island, lies in the Caribbean Sea in the humid tropical zone of the northeast trade winds (latitudes 11.59 to 12.14 degrees N and longitudes 61.36 to 61.48 degrees W). 312 km^2 in area and dominated by mountains ranging from 680 to 840 m, this isolated region experiences the land-use constraints of an insular setting. The limitation of available agricultural land, most of which is steeply sloped, coupled with the demand for urban development and the tourist industry, has placed tremendous stress on the natural biosphere. Furthermore, these human activities on land directly affect the surrounding marine layer through polluted runoff and stream siltation. Because endemic plants, animals, and marine life face the detrimental effects of human activities, it is necessary to examine the island's current status and draw parallels with other tropical mountain islands and predict future trends.

The eastern slopes of Grenada are gradual with extensive coastal flats; therefore, this side constitutes the main growing area. Here, food crops such as maize, peas, sweet potatoes, yams, nutmeg, bananas and cocoa arc cultivated because the best soils (brown earths and sandy loams) are found between 150 and 300 m (Table 5.1; Ternan, et al., 1989). On the western side the mountainous terrain is deeply dissected with sharp divides only a few metres wide and forest covering nearly 4 000 ha (75 per cent located around the highest peaks at Grand Etang and Mount St Catherine Forest Reserves). This region is the location of the endemic Gommier (*Daccryodes excelsa*), blue mahoe (*Hibiscus elatus*), Mahogony (*Swietenia*), and the Caribbean pine (*Pinus caribaea*), all of which are threatened by increasing extractive land use pressures from farming and pastoralism. The soils of these steeply sloped areas are predominantly clay loams (84.5 per cent), which tend to be shallow, highly erosive, and have a low capacity to

Table 5.1: *Main types of land use and their area in Grenada based on Eschveiler, 1982*

Category	Total area (in ha) 1982
Food crops (Maize and vegetables)	4 160
Sugar cane	530
Tree crops	
Cocoa	4 460
Banana	3 560
Nutmeg and spcies	3 780
Coconuts	940
Fruit trees	930
Grassland (pasture)	170
Grassland and scrub	290
Total area in agricultural use	18 820
Forest	3 970
Woodland and scrub	5 270
Mangrove	190
Inland swamp	30
Other land	2 880
Total land area	31 160

Figure 5.1: *Length of growing period in days for various areas of Grenada*

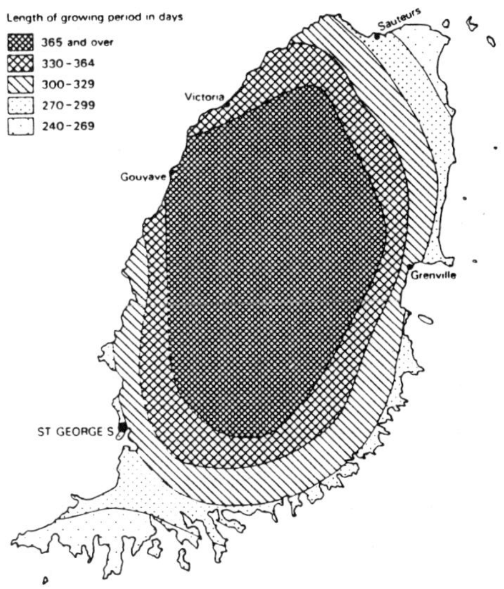

retain moisture, making them less conducive to agriculture (Figure 5.2). The climate and the topography, however, favour the cultivation of tree crops, which cover an area of 13 670 ha (70 per cent of the cultivated area), although tree crops are shallow-rooted and cycle the nutrients less efficiently than the original forest. As a result, erosion is enhanced, while the ecosystem becomes nutrient-deficient.

Probably the greatest nutrient losses occur where the forest is clear-cut for vegetable plots, grazing and other extractive measures. Trees are felled and burned to prepare the ground for planting or for grazing. Recent studies indicate that soil nutrients decline most rapidly after the first year of clearing (organic matter decreases by up to 40 per cent in the first year of cultivation). In Grenada this problem is compounded by the steepness of slope, in many regions in excess of 30 degrees. Deforestation increases erosion, and soils and nutrients are then transported downslope where eutrophication and siltation of river channels occurs. In turn, aquatic life is threatened, the tendency for flooding is enhanced, and the general water table for lowland irrigation is jeopardized. These watersheds, mainly from the central zone, also provide the main water supply for the capital, St George's, and tourist developments in the southwest of the island. As erosion increases upstream, siltation of water intake pipes becomes a recurring problem. In addition, high sediment concentrations discharged into the sea following rainstorms in the mountains affect the clarity of the water, and coral reefs south of St George's are degrading due to this reduced water clarity and sediment deposition. Extractive forest land uses not only upset the nutrient balance in the mountains but also displace the detrimental effects downstream to the plains and the adjacent marine ecosystem.

As the marine habitat continues to deteriorate and damage to the reefs begins to erode the beaches, the tourist industry, which is a major source of revenue, is threatened. In turn, the Grenadian government is calling for an effective land-use management scheme, which emphasizes the links between the sources of the erosion and the impacts downstream. Furthermore, reforestation efforts are currently underway because reports indicate that such conservation methods may reduce the total stream flow yield by 25 per cent and the stream flow may decrease by 50 per cent during minimum flow periods. Although these figures provide a positive outlook for the region as a whole, the losses in nutrient layer, endemic species of plants and animals, and marine habitat are irreplaceable. Once a mountainous area is cleared, to regain its natural state is virtually impossible. ■

Figure 5.2: *The soils of Grenada.*
Source: Ternan, et al., 1989

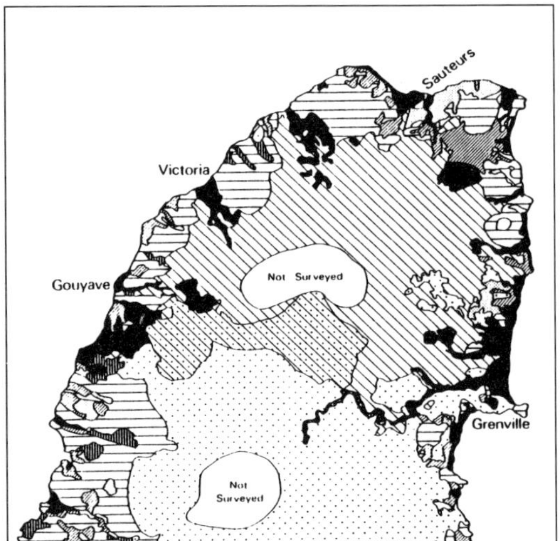

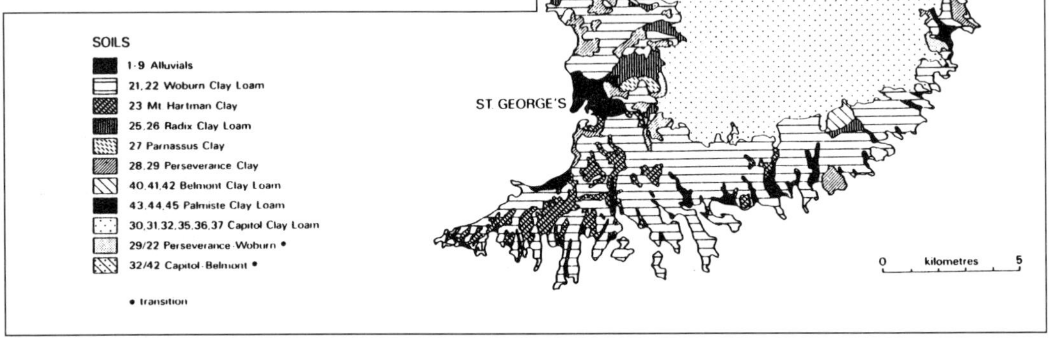

Hawaii–Big Island, USA

Introduction

The Hawaiian archipelago is one of the world's most isolated island groups. It is situated in the Pacific Ocean between latitudes 18 degrees and 22 degrees North at a distance of 4 000 km from the United States mainland. It also includes two of the world's major mountains: Mauna Loa (4 205 m), an active volcano, and Mauna Kea (4 205 m), an extinct volcano (Dinell 1987: 153).

Given the tropical, isolated island setting and great range of altitude and microclimates, it follows that the evolution of its flora and fauna resulted in the proverbial tropical island natural paradise. This extremely rich and diverse endemic flora and fauna was untouched by man until relatively recently. It is in this sense that the overused word "fragile" can be employed appropriately since, above all, evolution had occurred without adaptation to man or his domestic animals. The Big Island's present environmental status is the product of early pre-European impacts together with about 300 years of progressively more severe human pressure, leading both to large-scale species extinctions and the often equally disastrous introductions of exotic (alien) species. It is not only a question of the disruption of the integrity of many of the island's pristine ecosystems through introduction of exotic species. But through competition with and predation of native species, the direct human impacts have been augmented and accelerated. Thus, 70 per cent of all the native non-migrant birds have become extinct and half the survivors are now candidates for the Federal Endangered Species List. More than half of the native insects have been eliminated, together with an entire genus of land snails (Culliney, 1988: ix-x). Since a large proportion of these were endemic to Hawaii their extinction represents an absolute loss to the world's gene pool.

The reverse process–the introduction of exotics–is equally formidable. Thus more than 900 species of plants have been introduced (of which 91 are classed as pest); 15 birds; 18 mammals; and over 2 000 arthropods (Hamilton, 1991: interview).

While these figures refer to the island as a whole, because Big Island is essentially a tropical mountain island, they are relevant in their entirety. This section will seek to outline the causes for and the progression of these environmental losses and

Figure 5.3: *Principal Hawaiian islands*

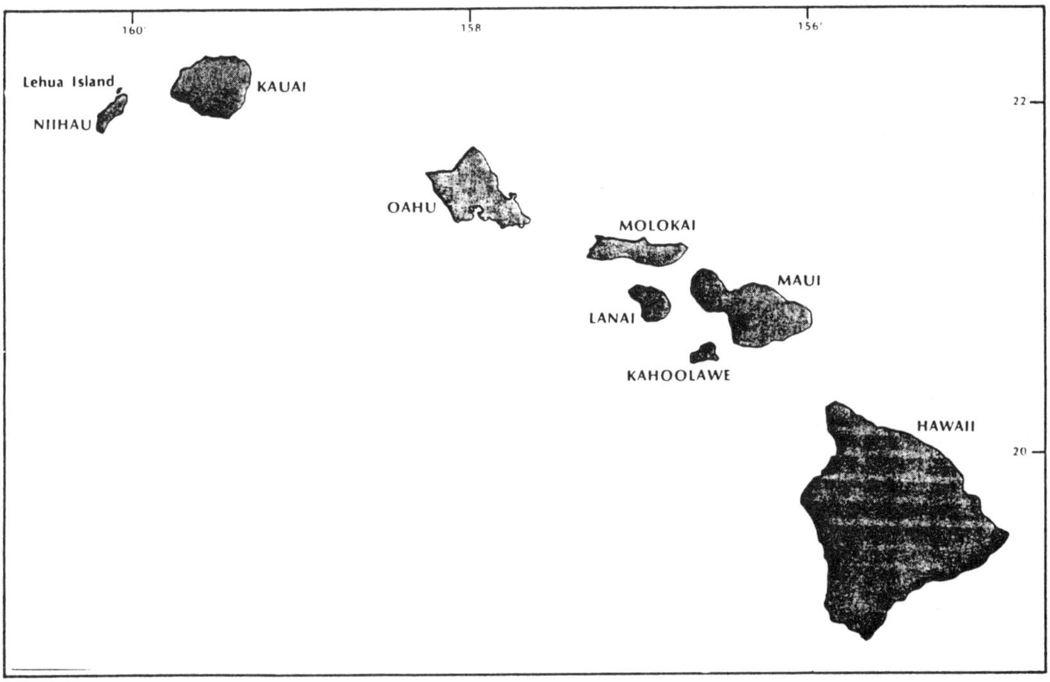

Figure 5.4: Hawaii Island

briefly review the efforts currently underway to slow down and reverse the process of destruction. It is also necessary to bear in mind that Hawaii retains much of its tropical island and mountain splendour. Mauna Loa and Kilauea are amongst the most active volcanoes in the world; they are producing new land and new habitats as molten lava continues to reach the sea. This, of course, is the primary tourist attraction. The fact that the Hawaiian Volcanoes National Park is both an international Biosphere Reserve and a World Heritage Site indicates the worldwide significance of the island.

The Big Island

Hawaii, with an area of 10 458 km^2, is larger than all the other islands in the archipelago combined (Figures 5.3 and 5.4; Morgan, 1983). It is dominated by the huge twin peaks of Mauna Loa and Mauna Kea, their long gentle slopes, extensively formed by recent unvegetated lava flows, sweeping down to the ocean through more than 4 000 m vertically. They are accompanied by several pronounced but lesser peaks, including Hualalai (2 521 m), Kohala (1 670 m), and Kilauea (1 248 m) and due to their location in the path of the tropical trade winds, their microclimates range from hot semi-desert to tropical rainforest (Juvik, et al., 1989: 3). Mauna Kea has the greatest biotic diversity found anywhere among the Hawaiian islands. Like most island systems concentric bands, corresponding with altitudinal gradients of temperature and precipitation, produce distinct ecozones on the mountain. For instance, the mamane-naio ecosystem comprises the highest forest zone on Mauna Kea (2 000 m up to the treeline at 3 000 m). Both the mamane (*Sophora chrysophylla*) and the naio (*Myoporum sandwicense*) are endemic trees with Australian and New Zealand affinities and bear seeds or fruits which are the principal food of a small endemic bird called the palila (*Psittirostra bailleui* [Juvik and Juvik, 1984: 192]).

The original human inhabitants, the Polynesian long-distance seafarers, are believed to have reached the archipelago between AD 200 and 400. Although it was previously believed that serious environmental impact awaited the arrival of the Europeans in the 18th century, it is now understood that the Polynesians effected dramatic changes. These resulted from their settlement pattern and modes of resource consumption, and fossil evidence proves that they certainly accounted for a number of extinctions amongst the native bird population. Much of their activity was in the coastal lowlands, and included the use of fire to clear land for agriculture. They also introduced rats and pigs, with far-reaching consequences for the native flora and fauna.

The first large-scale alteration of Hawaii's mountain ecosystems, however, followed European discovery in 1778. Initial impacts resulted from the introduction of cattle and goats and their extensive use for sale as provisions to early European mariners. This prompted widespread forest clearance to produce grazing lands and subsequent heavy grazing pressures. This process also saw the beginnings of the large-scale introduction of exotic species, both deliberately and inadvertently.

European demands for sandalwood (*Santalum*) quickly followed. Because they are root parasites, obtaining essential nutrients by penetrating the root networks of other species such as the koa, sandalwoods tend to be distributed in small, discontinuous groves that are associated with koa forests, including zones above and below the true rainforest belt. This genus is widely scattered throughout the Indo-Pacific region and the Chinese have demanded the fragrant heartwood of these trees since ancient times. Although the value of this endemic tree was recognized in the late 18th century, extensive trade did not begin until 1810, after which two decades of commerce practically destroyed the renewable resource. In the 1830s, as sandalwood harvesting slowed down, more systematic efforts toward deforestation began to take place. The demand for firewood increased as port towns were established for sugar production and whaling, and later for fuel for the sugar trains. In the 1840s and 1850s the cordwood industry dominated all islands. Not only was the resource potential exploited but the demand for cleared land by sugar planters and cattle ranchers was also considerable (Culliney, 1988: 203-206).

The first major logging operation was established on the Big Island in the koa forest on the western slopes of Mauna Kea above Waimea (between Makahalau at 1 218 m and Hanaipoe at 1 584 m). This valuable parcel of land was owned and operated by the famous Parker Ranch. Because koa became known as Hawaiian mahogany and the species was the second most abundant canopy tree in native island forests, harvesting was extensive. The major motive for forest clearance, however, was to provide land for ranching and agriculture. Soon this area became an eyesore as the koa lumber was stacked in lattice-like piles in lowland ridges and therefore became known by the local population as "Palihooukapapa" or cliffs of piled lumber. As the Parker Ranch and others expanded operations, however, methods of production attained greater efficiency and more tree species were consumed. A new technique called fluming enabled ohia lehua forests of the North Hilo District to be cleared swiftly to make way for large sugar plantations in the mid-19th century. The big wooden troughs, which were constructed to divert mountain streams, transported lumber as well as bundles of cane to the lowlands for processing and storage (Culliney, 1988: 207). In this case, not only were the forest ecosystems destroyed but the aquatic life was threatened in the name of big business and profit.

Another intensive industry which caused the deterioration of the mountain forests was the harvest of wild pulu around the Hilo District. This soft, dense wool covering, which grows at the bases of the leafstalks of hapuu ferns (*Cibotium*), was used for stuffing mattresses and pillows. Unfortunately, pulu gatherers destroyed extensive areas of the tree-fern understory by felling the entire tree in order to obtain the wool easily (Culliney, 1988: 208).

Clearcutting for grazing, and even selective logging, left bare random patches of the forest ecosystem and opened the Hawaiian biota to foreign invaders such as exotic weeds, insects and diseases. For instance, major weeds like the bamboo and passionflower vine (*Passiflora*) are most aggressive. These alien plants rapidly grow, smother and kill the understory and canopy species (Culliney, 1988: 213). In this way the forest's native flora was not only directly destroyed through industrial activities but was also left vulnerable by the resulting exposure due to human import of exotics.

Perhaps the most devastating disturbance came from livestock introduced by Europeans. By the mid-19th and early 20th centuries feral ungulates (sheep, goat, and cattle) grazed large, clearcut rangelands, especially on Mauna Kea; and caused destruction to the watershed through induced siltation and a threat to the native ecosystem in general. To make matters worse, many of these animals escaped to forested areas where the absence of predators allowed their numbers to increase dramatically. In the 1930s an estimated 40 000 feral sheep along with wild goats and cattle inhabited Mauna Kea. Government policy, aimed at eradication, focused on hunting, fencing, and stock drives. By 1950 the sheep population was reduced to 200 but the ecosystems had been badly damaged (Juvik and Juvik, 1984: 195). On Mauna Loa the goat population in the Hawaii Volcanoes National Park has now been eliminated. Pigs remain a problem.

Although the dry uplands were found highly suitable for grazing, the Europeans made a concerted effort to convert the middle elevations into rich agricultural lands for crops such as sugar, potatoes, taro, cotton, and pineapple. However, the damaged soils, due to uncontrolled grazing and poor land management, required the importation of fertilizer and the redirection of water. The most extensive irrigation development, called the Kohala Ditch, was built in 1906 on the Big Island and consisted of 14 101 m of rock tunnels, 7 005 m of open trench and 20 flumes. Not only did this project dewater the streams at higher elevations, but it exposed the few remaining wilderness regions to feral grazing as well. The outcome was a devastating blend of stream erosion and siltation, along with the destruction of native vegetation and in turn, the spread of weeds (Culliney, 1988: 231-232).

Today these established mountain land uses are merging with modern industries such as geothermal energy development, astronomical research, and military exercises, all of which involve new technology and further environmental degradation. The southeastern region of the Big Island, called Kilauea's Eastern Rift, is believed to contain an inexhaustible source of geothermal energy. Therefore, some entrepreneurs envision extensive development of heavy industry such as metallurgical refineries, which could threaten the balance between vulcanism and a naturally evolved landscape (Culliney, 1988: 356-357).

Mauna Kea is also experiencing modern-day human uses. With the construction of a jeep road to the barren volcanic summit in the 1960s came the realization that this mountain was the most suitable location in the northern hemisphere for a large-scale astronomical research station. This volcano is inactive and the summit is above the temperature inversion that confines clouds, moisture, and dust. In 1968 the University of Hawaii attained a lease to a four kilometre radius of land on the summit, upon which astronomical facilities could be constructed. By the end of the 1970s four optical telescopes with mirror sizes ranging from three to four metres in diameter were installed along with infrastructure including a highway. The director of this University of Hawaii Institute of Astronomy estimates the reserve may hold as many as thirteen telescopes by the year 2000. Conservationists fear the negative consequences of such large-scale technological developments to the existing natural ecosystem and the aesthetic impact since the summit is visible from many sea-level locations (Juvik and Juvik, 1984: 196). The summit area of Mauna Loa similarly is suffering increasing human scientific impacts. Ironically, the very observatories established in the 1950s to record progressive atmospheric pollution and to monitor climate change have significantly disturbed the volcano's environment.

Another modern ecological disturbance takes place high in the saddle region of the Big Island, between Mauna Kea and Mauna Loa. Here, the military causes obvious damage to the mountain landscape through its usage of modern technology, like tanks and artillery, and the mere presence of constant human pressures in the form of the infantry. These present-day factors contribute to the spread of foreign weeds and the burning of the dry forest (Culliney, 1988: 354-355).

The unique mountain habitats not only attract research opportunities but are also sought after as an oasis by the public. At the lower elevations resort facilities, golf courses and dude ranches are in great demand, in addition to subdivisions for second-home locations. These human pressures are altering the water table, as pollution enters and ultimately damages water purity of an already limited supply. Furthermore, as hundreds of hectares are divided, sold, and developed endemic plants and animals are lost and so is the evidence of the traditional Hawaiian culture. In terms of Hawaiian traditional culture, the very disturbance of the high mountain summits is regarded by many Hawaiians as an insult to their goddess Pele who is supposed to inhabit the active summit of Mauna Loa and to her sister, the goddess of snow, on neighbouring Mauna Kea.

The Big Island has been designated as having the greatest potential for development in the archipelago, except that its insular situation constrains expansion and multiple-use concepts and its water resources are limited. Land-use conflicts include that between the proponents of the elimination policy for the feral sheep, pig, and goat population and those advocating game hunting of these animals. Another dilemma involves massive agricultural expansion versus reforestation. And as improvements in vehicular mountain access occur, certain groups begin to compete for recreational use while others advocate regions of private research facilities (Juvik et al., 1989: 19).

As these various factions struggle to meet their interests, the environment continues to degrade to a point of irreversible deterioration. Current figures indicate that up to a third of the species and subspecies of flora and fauna endemic to Hawaii have become extinct and a majority of the existing native species are considered officially endangered under the United States Endangered Species Act of 1973 .

Most extinctions of biota are attributed to past and present agricultural and urban development and to the impact of competition and predation by plants and animals introduced in the post-European contact period.

Conclusion

Recent years have witnessed an increasing recognition of the extent of the damage that is occurring. The United States Endangered Species Act of 1973 and the large array of federal environmental legislation has provided an important base for effective conservation. The state has established a natural area reserve system and has enlarged the areas of the State Forests, although some areas are leased to ranchers and are not well managed. Nevertheless, efforts by the relevant state and federal authorities have been very much augmented by a variety of local and national organizations. The Nature Conservancy, the Hawaii Audubon Society, the Sierra Club, and the Conservation Council work together to identify threatened habitats and biota, document abuses to the Hawaiian cultural sites, publicize their findings, and lobby for the protection of these bio-regions. The *Islands of Life* campaign by the Nature Conservancy illustrates one small victory. Its strategy aims at identifying the few remaining, pristine wilderness areas and raising the assets to purchase them. In 1986 the Conservancy handed over the jurisdiction of an area of high mesic koa forest on Mauna Kea to the US Fish and Wildlife Service (Culliney, 1988: 364). Cooperation is crucial in an insular situation where the availability of options is constrained and the call for action is urgent. Only time will reveal whether the efforts towards preservation are quick enough to keep pace with the tremendous speed of modern human impacts. ■

Hengduan Mountains–Naxi, PRC

The People's Republic of China probably contains more mountain and highland territory than any other country in the world. These range from the high Himalaya, Pamirs, and Tien Shan, to the low coastal mountains of the southeast coast. From a climatic and vegetational point of view they range from subarctic in northeastern Manchuria, to extremely dry continental interior with no forest belt (for example, the Qilian Shan), to the tropical monsoon rainforest-covered middle hills of southern Yunnan. To select only one region, the Hengduan Mountains, and even then to emphasize a single small area, Naxi Autonomous District, once more illustrates the problem of representative coverage that afflicts the entire *Mountain Agenda-UNCED 1992* project.

The mountains of western Sichuan and northwestern Yunnan, in a general sense, are a southeastern extension of the Himalaya proper and the Tibet Plateau. They have a surface area of about 500 000 km^2 (about the size of France) and the two main culminations are the Gongga Shan, 7 556 m (Minya Konka), at about 30 degrees North and the Yulongxue Shan, 5 569 m (Jade Dragon Mountains), at about 27 degrees North.

The Hengduan Mountains have been known to a few Western travellers and scientists as some of the most difficult and complex country in the world. They are often referred to in the literature as the *River Gorge Country* or the *Transverse Mountains* (Rock, 1930; Kingdon Ward, 1960). The name *River Gorge Country* is derived from the gigantic sub-parallel gorges of the Irrawaddy, Salween, Mekong, and Yangtze (Jinsha Jiang) that, in their deepest sections have cut more than 4 000 m into the plateau surface.

The marked north-south topographical trend of the entire region, as well as the location of the river gorges, is a reflection of some of the more active seismic forces anywhere in the world. Actual fault scarps dominate large sections of the landscape, many of which are more recent than the maximum of the last Ice Age, and earthquakes occur frequently. The seismic activity, together with the considerable relief and steep slopes, deep subtropical weathering and, at higher levels, extensive glacial deposits, and rapid stream down-cutting, produce some of the world's most frequent high magnitude debris flows and landslides.

Maximum altitudes fall gradually from over 7 000 m in the north to 2 000–2 500 m in the south. The subtropical latitude and the monsoonal climate, together with the great altitudinal range, have produced a natural flora and fauna that ranks amongst the richest, most varied and complex in the world. Of particular importance, both in terms of commercial exploitation and urgently needed conservation, are the rich forests which, until recently, have sheltered a prodigious fauna. A single example of floral richness is the occurrence of more than 60 species of rhododendron; total species number in excess of 6 000.

For several thousands of years the Hengduan region has been inhabited by a large number of distinct mountain minorities. These include Bai, Naxi, Yi, Tibetan, in all more than 30 different nationalities with distinct languages, customs, and land management practices. Significant Han penetration occurred as recently as the 19th century. In contrast, substantial civilizations prospered in this rich region in the more distant past. For example, the Naxi claim that the origins of their written language predate Chinese; Dali, the capital of the Bai people with its magnificent pagodas, dates from the Three Nations period of the eighth and ninth centuries.

Since 1950 the entire region has been progressively integrated with the Chinese core area and a rudimentary road and railway network has been forged across some of the most technologically demanding terrain in the world. Han settlers have increasingly penetrated the region, especially during the last 100 years, occupying mainly the irrigable valley bottoms. Much of the region remains closed to the outside world and large sections have local government in the form of autonomous counties and districts. Dali was opened to visitors as recently as 1984 and Lijiang, capital of the Naxi nation, in 1986.

The combination of spectacular scenery, colourful minority people and rich architecture is resulting in a rapid expansion of many forms of tourism. Massive timber exploitation by the central government of the PRC and for local use has been an especially significant feature of the last 40 years. The region is second in importance for timber production in China. Consequently, it is not surprising that post-1979 assessments, from both

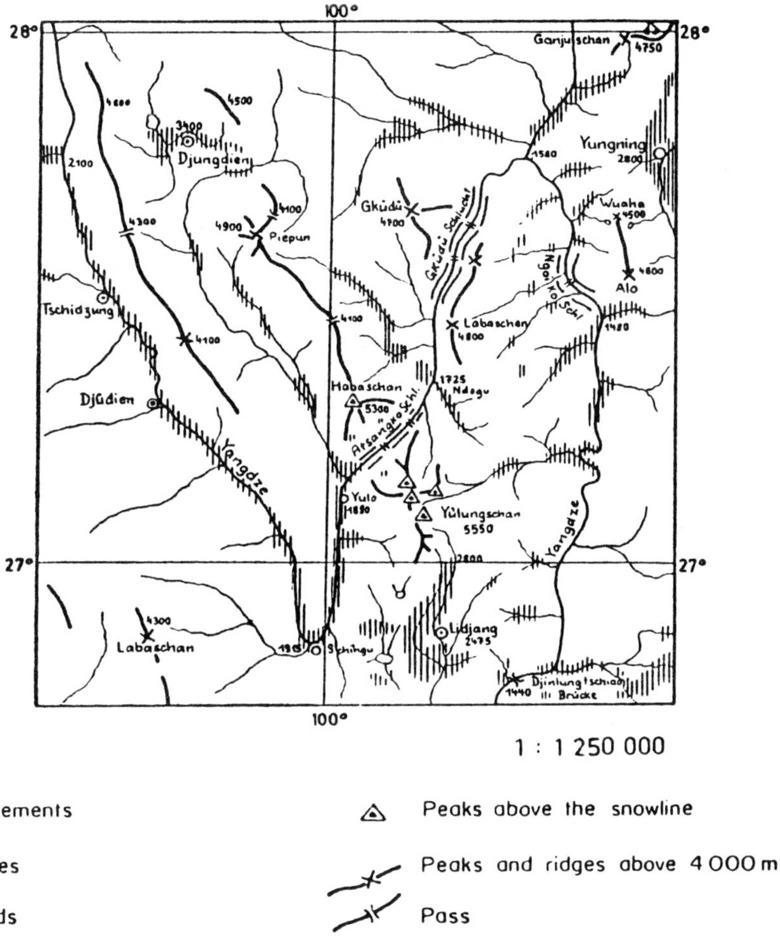

Sketch map from WISSMANN (1959, Abb. 1, p. 167).

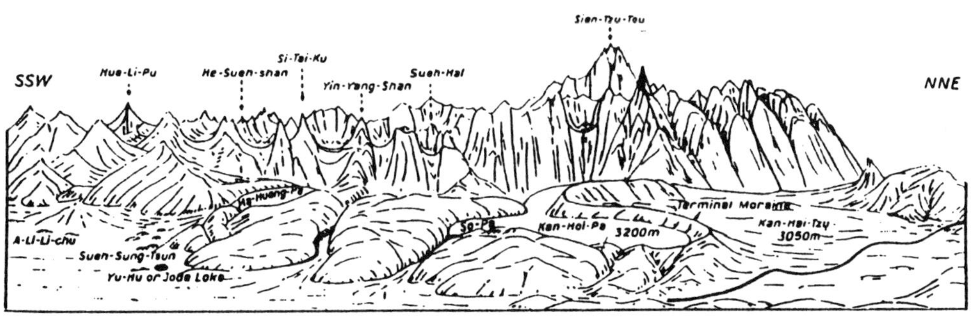

Figure 5.5: Top *Gongga Shan (7 556 m) and Yulongxue Shan (5 596 m)—geological observations. Eastern part of Yulongxue Shan* Source: sketch by H. S. Bao from Jen Mei Ngo (1958, Fig. 1)

Naxi highlander of the Yulongxue Shan (Jade Dragon Snow Mountains), Yunnan, People's Republic of China

The east face of the Yulongxue Shan, a gigantic fault scarp. The mountains support the most southerly glaciers and ice caps of Eurasia. Note the Naxi villages in the foreground

within and outside of China, lead to the conclusion that large-scale forest clearance on steep slopes is producing massive soil erosion, disruption of the hydrologic cycle, and downstream flooding and siltation. Southwest China (Hengduan Mountains) has produced its own equivalent of the *Theory of Himalayan Environmental Degradation* (Ives and Messerli, 1989).

The Lijiang-Yulongxue Shan region will be used to highlight the environmental and development issues of the Hengduan Mountains. It is transected by latitude 27 degrees North and lies in the great bend of the Jinsha Jiang at 100 degrees East. It is reached by road from Kunming, capital of Yunnan province, approximately 620 km to the southeast (Figure 5.5, Ives and Messerli, 1984: 61).

The Naxi Autonomous District has a total population of about 300 000 (1985); Naxi constitute the largest single group, with smaller numbers of Han, Bai, Yi, Tibetan, and other nationalities. Lijiang is the regional capital, a city of about 60 000 and lies at an altitude of 2 475 m. The highest summit of the Yulongxue Shan (Shan-Tzutou, 5 596 m) lies about 20 km due north of Lijiang and is the culmination of an impressive range of ice-capped limestone peaks extending NNE-SSW for about 25 km. The anomalous northward flow of the Jinsha Jiang cuts off the northern end of the range from the Habaxue Shan (5 396 m) forming one of the world's most spectacular river gorges (the Xia-qiao-tou, or Tiger Leap Gorge) giving a local relief in excess of 3 700 m in a horizontal distance of 6 km.

The character of the eastern face of the Yulongxue Shan is determined by a series of massive NNE-SSW faults causing the crestline to stand as much as 3 000 m above a line of tectonic basins (graben), the largest of which forms the Lijiang Plain, extending between 2 400 and 2 800 m. The line of hills forming the eastern margin of the graben only reach elevations of 3 400 to 3 500 m. The western face of the Yulongxue Shan is very difficult of access and was only partially observed from a distance.

Most of the region is underlain by limestone, Carboniferous to Devonian in age, metamorphosed to varying degrees, with some being marble. The result of weathering on the extensive limestone

exposures is a variety of karst phenomena, including lapies, dolines, and razor-sharp micro-fretting. There is also a general paucity of surface water, especially in the pre-monsoon season.

Above about 3 900 m the eastern side of the range is dissected by glacial cirques and by two large U-shaped gorges from which sizeable glaciers debouched during the last glacial episode, with termini extending down to at least 2 700 m. Today they are marked by huge end moraines. Several small cirque glaciers, ice caps, and hanging valley glaciers are active today with a regional snowline at about 5 000 m (cf. Shi, 1980; Ives and Messerli, 1984). Many of the peaks are unclimbed.

Between the upper timberline at about 3 900 m and the lower forest limit, at 2 600–2 650 m, is a series of distinct forest belts varying with aspect. These are primarily needle-leaf coniferous forests of *Abies, Picea* and *Pinus spp. Larix, Quercus*, and tree *Rhododendrum*, are locally important. Extensive areas, especially where disturbed by fire or clear cutting, support dense thickets of shrub oak, rhododendron, berberis and bamboo. Scattered groves of *Acer*, *Sorbus*, *Populus* and *Salix* occur within the coniferous forest belts. There are also some magnificent stands of evergreen oak (*Quercus*).

Below the lower forest limit the land is extensively cultivated. The presence of palms and bananas at the lowest levels indicates the range of vegetation belts from subtropical forest to alpine meadow, rock desert, and permanent snow in a very short horizontal distance.

Until recently the area contained tiger, leopard, snow leopard, two species of bear, wolf, deer, and a large number of other mammals. Excessive hunting has either eliminated these, or reduced them to very small endangered populations confined to the more remote areas. The same is true of a fascinating variety of pheasants. This region has long been famous for its endemic pheasants, several of which were believed to be extinct or exceptionally rare. However, discussion with local Naxi village elders in 1985 verified that several species, including *Chrysolophus amherstiae, Phasianus colchicus colchicus, Ithagenes kuseri Beebe,* and the very rare Yunnan white-eared pheasant, *Crossoptilon crossopitlon lichiangense*, are currently known to the local farmers. A specimen of *C. c. lichiangense* was taken for its plumage in early May 1985. Wolves were also being hunted in the vicinity of one of our mountain camps where they had killed two sheep (Ives, 1985: 382-383).

Sedentary human occupation is generally below about 3 000 m. The Yi cultivate barley up to this level, and rice is grown up to 2 700 m. The most conspicuous human activity, except for intensive irrigated farming in the lower Lijiang plain, is lumbering. Many mountain slopes are bare, or almost bare of trees, and indications of widespread soil erosion and gullying are readily apparent. Cut stumps, indications of forest fire over wide areas, and a stream of timber-laden trucks trundling south 24 hours a day lead to the supposition that environmental disaster is imminent.

The United Nations University and Chinese Academy of Sciences expedition of 1985 (Ives, 1985) was organized to undertake a first-level assessment of the degree of environmental instability. The observations quoted above, of course, are sufficient to indicate that sensitive resource management practices need to be developed. Nevertheless, the 1985 fieldwork (Ives, in press) indicated that the actual situation in Lijiang Autonomous District and surrounding areas is certainly not one of progressive environmental collapse. One of the major research tools used to reach this conclusion was to replicate a sample of some of the magnificent large-format landscape photography taken in the 1920s and 1930s by Joseph F. Rock (1947). Several thousand prints and photographic plates are in the archives of the National Geographic Society, Washington DC. A small selection was made available to the expedition courtesy of Dr Barry C. Bishop, Chair, NGS Committee on Exploration and Research. The admittedly limited, replication led to the following conclusions:

1) some areas today have a much better forest cover than 60 or more years ago;
2) some areas have a situation comparable to that of today;
3) some areas have been extensively over-cut.

These findings were further supported by extensive interviewing of local people and officials, survey of altitudinal transects through the forest belts to the upper timberline, and extensive reconnaissance dendrochronology. The above findings could then be supplemented as follows:

1) over the wider region between Lijiang and Kunming, much of the forest clear-cutting and soil loss down to bedrock is very old (i.e. hundreds if not more than a thousand years);
2) the local people have managed the lower forest belts such that although wide areas may have been fired and/or clear cut, natural revegetation is extremely rapid from the individual mature trees left as seed sources. In two instances, tree core examination demonstrated that a submature forest had become established following clearing that occurred some time after Rock's photographs were taken in the 1920s and 1930s.
3) initial search of other literature sources in other areas of the Hengduan Mountains, particularly in western Sichuan (Ives and Messerli, 1984) led to similar conclusions (cf. Imhof, 1974).

The above discussion is not intended to imply that the Lijiang-Yulongxue Shan area in particular and the Hengduan Mountain region in general is not subjected to enormous pressure on the natural resource base. Rapid population growth, large-scale extraction from the forests by a timber-hungry China, accelerating tourist impact, and general resource development all indicate the need for holistic resource management systems and for provision of the means for continued improvement of the well-being of the mountain peoples. However, as with most other mountain regions, a much better understanding of the cultural-natural relations dynamics is urgently needed to support rational development policy if sustainability is to be adequately taken into consideration. ■

Mountains of Iceland

Iceland, appropriately known as the land of ice and fire, is an island about the size of England (105 000 km^2) situated just south of the Arctic Circle in the North Atlantic Ocean. Physically it is composed of Tertiary and Quaternary basalt (lava) plateaus, shield volcanoes, strato-volcanoes, and ice caps (11 per cent of total area). Vatnajökull is the largest ice cap with an area of 8 400 km^2 and a maximum thickness in excess of 1 000 m; it extends to more than 100 m below sea level. The coastal climate is cold temperate maritime, but mountain slopes rise to over 1 000 m within a few kilometres of the coast. Hvannadalshnukur, the highest summit, is part of the crater rim of the dormant, ice-mantled volcano Öraefajökull, which rises to 2 119 m above the southeast coast and provides a mountain landscape almost alpine in scale (Figure 5.6).

With a current population of scarcely 250 000, Iceland is a very small, homogeneous nation state, with a predominantly subarctic mountain and high plateau landscape; it is also one of the most active volcanic regions in the world.

Although the Vikings were undoubtedly preceded by Irish monks, the effective history of the settlement dates from AD 871 and it originated from Norway. The original settlement was virtually complete by AD 930, with an estimated population of 30 000, which increased to about 75 000 by AD 1100 (Thorarinsson, 1960: 230). While the climate was probably warmer than today (870–1100), the dramatic change in the island's vegetation and soil cover over more than a thousand years is mostly due to human impacts, principally sheep grazing and secondarily fuelwood cutting. The natural climax vegetation, at least in those areas below 500 m, was birch forest *(Betula tortuosa)* on a rich and very deep volcanic soil supplemented by eolian deposition of volcanic ash and sands and loams picked up by the wind from the vast glacial outwash plains *(sandar)*. Large areas of the interior, however, were naturally barren.

Figure 5.6: Iceland's mountains

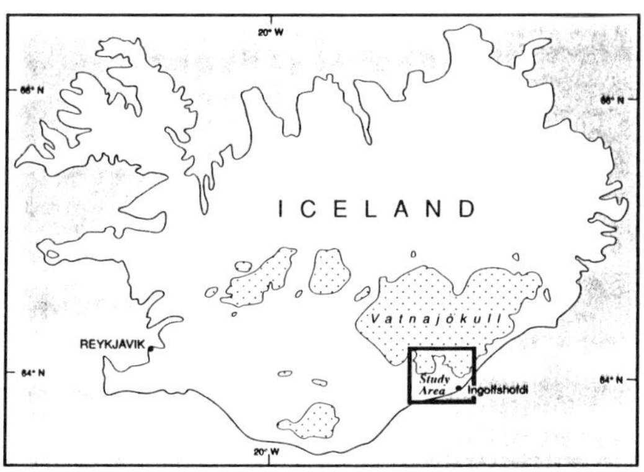

As the inhabitable lower land was settled overgrazing gradually increased. This was probably accelerated during the Little Ice Age (1500–1900) (Grove, 1988) when mean annual air temperatures were lowered by about 2.0 degrees Celsius thus restricting the biomass productivity of pastures and grazing lands (a reduction of 1 degree Celsius in mean summer temperature today will result in a 15 per cent reduction in crop yield [Fridriksson, 1969]). This climatic downswing was accompanied by increased volcanic activity, especially the Laki fissure eruption of 1783, and the Icelanders were brought to the brink of starvation to the extent that the Danish government contemplated total evacuation.

Today the Icelandic landscape is one of extensive open horizons, the greens of pastures and grazing land dominate the lower slopes and coastal plains, sparsely moss-covered and boulder-strewn terrain the middle slopes, and ice caps and block mountains occupy the distance. The original birch forest has almost entirely disappeared and with it more than half of the red volcanic soil cover. The signs of wind erosion under the pressure of grazing are everywhere apparent.

Despite this the countryside is one of the most starkly beautiful and dramatic in the western world. This, together with the remarkable history of almost legendary and heroic proportions and one of the world's most literary and artistic cultures, has ensured a progressive growth in tourism. While the absolute numbers will never rival those of the Alps or Rocky Mountains, at least partly on account of the uncertain, and often cold wet summer weather, in proportion to total Icelandic population the recreational impact is significant. Additionally, the younger generation of Icelanders have different attitudes toward material assets and Reykjavik, the capital, has grown from a small village with 1 200 people in 1850 to more than half the total population of the country in 1990.

Whereas 40 years ago most Icelanders took their holidays making hay on the farm of a family member, or on horseback camping trips into the interior, today four-wheel drive jeeps, all-terrain vehicles and dune buggies are having serious detrimental impacts on the vegetation as well as on the frequently vulnerable volcanic and glacial landforms.

Icelandic tourism is not well organized and insufficient accommodation and an unvaried diet are significant restraints. Nevertheless, the number of tourists has grown dramatically over the last 20 years and, as is common with tourism, a few localities receive concentrated attention. One such locality, the Skaftafell National Park, is used here to illustrate this.

Skaftafell is a tiny farming community lying under the loom of the 2 119 m summit of Öraefajökull and looking out across the great marshes, outwash plains and distant ice-capped volcanoes. Its origins date back to the early settlement period and it seems to have been farmed by the same family lineage since about AD 1400, and possibly for more than a thousand years (Ives, 1992). Until the 1950s Skaftafell could only be reached on horseback across dangerous glacier meltwater rivers. Visitors were few and very welcome. In 1969, with financial assistance from the WWF, the Icelandic government purchased the farms and made Skaftafell the centre of the country's first national park. In 1974 the major water obstacle to land transport, the river Skeidara, was bridged and Skaftafell became accessible from Reykjavik by a daily bus service. A park Visitors' Centre and camp ground were in full operation by the time the road was completed.

The first year (1974) saw 13 000 overnight stays. This fell to 4 000 in 1975 but increased steadily to exceed 24 000 by 1985. An increasing proportion were from overseas; foreigners exceeded 50 per cent by 1987. This growth of interest in Skaftafell was demonstrated by a 1987 hotel association questionnaire which indicated that it was the single most popular destination in Iceland.

Traditional Icelandic farmstead, with Iceland's highest summit, 2 119 m, the ice-capped dormant Oraefajökull volcano that last erupted in 1727 (Hvannadalsnukur)

Skardatindur, Southeast Iceland, Skaftafell National Park. It has been climbed only once, in 1954

There are two themes relevant to Skaftafell mass tourism:

1) visitor impact; and
2) type of management policy.

Undoubtedly the spectacular mountain scenery, high ice-covered volcano, and cascading glaciers constitute the main attraction. And while absolute numbers are small by Alpine standards, there were never more than three farms and the total area subjected to visitor impact is a few square kilometres. Modest hikes of 5–7 km bring the visitor over gentle heaths to dramatic glacier overlooks with thundering ice avalanches. Thus the physical impact is significant and spreading. While the Nature Conservatory has so far resisted pressures to permit park entry by four-wheel drive and other ATVs, these pressures continue to mount.

The second theme relates to the Nature Conservatory's attempt to restore the natural vegetation by eliminating sheep grazing from the surrounding hill and mountain slopes. There has been a significant increase in birch cover since the 1950s. Nevertheless, this policy has virtually eliminated the continued functioning of the farms. A national park policy based upon the United States tradition of assumed incompatibility between mountain park landscape and human occupation (especially farming)–the wilderness ethic–in an Old World setting can destroy rich cultural attributes. Additionally, the old turf-roofed farm buildings and tun (in-field), once emerald green and redolent with scythe-cut hay, is lost and with it the dramatic visual contrast between farm landscape, blue mountain in the distance, and sparkling ice field. Icelanders without sheep would certainly have succumbed to the Little Ice Age 200 years ago, as did their cousins in Greenland somewhat earlier. While erosion losses and vegetation rehabilitation are urgent management issues, perhaps there is still time for an effective compromise. And related to this, the weak Icelandic economy could be aided by fuller realization of the potential of appropriate and sustainable tourism. ■

Tateyama, Japanese Alps

Introduction

Japan has many developed mountain areas such as the Daisetsu Mountains in Hokkaido Island and the Northern and Central Japanese Alps. Parts of the Northern Japanese Alps belong to the Chubu-Sangaku National Park, among which the Kamikochi area has the most visitors (about 1 550 000 people in 1989 including about 480 000 people in August alone (Yamamoto, 1991). Similarly, the Tateyama range, north of the Yari-Hotake range, attracts numerous numbers of visitors; a combination of volcanic activity and snow/ice characterizes one of the alpine landscapes of Tateyama. Visitors enjoy hot springs, geysers and summer skiing as well as trekking and visiting shrines on the top of Mt.Tateyama (3 003 m).

Although the number of visitors to the Tateyama range is not the greatest in the Japanese high mountain areas, it should be emphasized that the area of Tateyama is only about 5 km^2. The visitor density to the area may have been the greatest in the world (Ives, 1982), and the environmental impacts and mountain hazards have been mitigated by gigantic engineering works. The Tateyama range was assigned to a part of the national park in December 1934. Since the area was developed mainly after the establishment of the national park, any developmental projects were required to be reviewed by the government.

Focusing on the Tateyama area, this section outlines the history of its development and increasing tourism, and examines the geomorphic processes changing the landscapes and the present situation of the human control of the landscape changes due to engineering work. Tateyama, which can be regarded as an extreme of developed mountain areas, will provide a good basis to discuss a future scenario in developing mountain areas of the world.

History of human use

This small area has been developed from two opposite directions; one from the west and another from the east. The former route from Toyama city to the Murodo railway station is called Tateyama Route, while the latter from Ohmachi city to the Murodo is called the Kurobe Route.

Parts of the Tateyama Route were first developed to transport materials for water-resource development, and also in anticipation of tourist use in the future.

First, a railway was constructed from Toyama to Tateyama station, and a cable car running from Tateyama station to Bijodaira began to operate in 1954. By June 1964, the public mass transportation system from Toyama city to the Murodo station was established. This transportation system enabled people to travel from Toyama city (nearly at sea level), to Murodo (2 450 m) in two to two-and-a-half hours and to summit of Mt. Tateyama (3 003 m) within four hours at off peak-times.

Visitors to Tateyama can use either public or private transport to the Tateyama station (475 m), but they then have to take a cable car and a licensed public bus to higher altitudes. No private cars are allowed to enter the high mountain area. This measure was adopted to minimize environmental impacts to the area.

The area along the Kurobe Route had not been used before a hydroelectricity development because of difficult access. The project plan was submitted to the government in 1955 to obtain special permission for development in the national park.

A new tunnel penetrating the Ushiro-Tateyama range was constructed in February 1958. Immediately upon the completion of this tunnel, trucks fully loaded with equipment and material, reaching a maximum of 600 per day, were able to reach the hydroelectric dam site. By the use of this new tunnel, the construction of the Kurobe Dam, with the maximum output of 335 000 kw, was completed in June 1963. The powerhouse building (approximately 120 m long, 20 m wide and 40 m high), transformer room, switch yard and related equipment are all located underground at a depth of 150 m in order to mitigate environmental degradation as well as to avoid frequent snow avalanches.

After the dam construction, the tunnel (5.4 km long) was modified and improved for tourist use: it is now used by trolley buses operated by electric power. Because of the steep slopes above the dam site, the construction of two more tunnels for a cable car (0.8 km) and a bus (3.6 km)

Mount Tateyama, Japan, is undergoing such devastating impact from millions of hikers that heavy machinery is used to build fieldstone footpaths and flights of staircases to the very summit. This is the ultimate technical solution to environmental protection, which itself constitutes a major structural disturbance

and a ropeway (l.7 km) was planned. Tateyama Tunnel penetrating the main part of Mt. Tateyama connected the eastern areas to the Murodo station in 1971.

Increasing tourism after 1971

The annual number of visitors to Murodo and the Kurobe Dam has been counted since 1964 by a local transportation company. The number of visitors to Murodo in 1970, before the completion of the entire transportation route, was 186 880, whereas in 1971, immediately after the completion of the entire route, the number rose to 527 240 (Tateyama-Kurobe Kanko Co., unpublished data). In other words, the abrupt increase in the number of visitors to the area in 1971 was attributed to the opening of the complete route to Murodo. The 1970s and the first half of the 1980s showed a fairly steady inflow, although in 1975 there was a slight decrease due to the so called "oil shock". Another accelerated increase in the number of visitors occurred in the late 1980s due to a business upturn and to more time for recreation. The number of visitors to Murodo and the Kurobe Dam in 1990 was 1 049 800 and 1 157 300 respectively.

The transportation system is open to the public from April to November. August is the most crowded month, with over 400 000 visitors to Murodo in 1990. The transportation at weekends during the peak season is rather like rush hour on commuter trains in Tokyo. Lining up in numerical order, visitors have to wait one to two hours to change from a cable car or a bus to go to the higher altitudes. These visitors concentrate in a tiny area of about 5 km^2 around Murodo-Tateyama.

The majority of visitors to the area seem to be more interested in climbing and trekking. The 1977 survey on why people visited the area revealed that only 0.7 per cent of the visitors intended scaling the summit of Mt. Tateyama to offer worship to the mountain god (Editorial Board of National Parks, 1978). Traditional, religious visits have recently greatly diminished.

Human control of landscape changes

Tunnelling and using a ropeway minimized the exposure of the artificial components above ground. This concept was also applied to the powerhouse of the Kurobe Dam, which was constructed inside the mountain. This method is thought to have succeeded in minimizing landscape changes as well as in avoiding the hazards of snow avalanches. In addition, using electric trolley buses (with no exhaust gases), instead of letting private vehicles enter into the alpine belt, helped not only to avoid the gas emission problem, but also avoided having to provide large parking spaces, which would have required further landscape changes.

The bus road to the Murodo station is paved. The road has concreted ditches at the shoulders to minimize the soil loss. Because the visitors concentrate in a tiny area round Murodo, trails for the visitors have been paved and staircased. Bare ground surfaces might have experienced some human-induced soil erosion, although no quantitative studies are available. The developmental project has tried to avoid soil loss around the bare ground by re-vegetating the surfaces.

Geomorphic processes

When the area was developed, the environmental assessment was made. Especially fragile alpine vegetation was the main object of interest for researchers and developers. Geomorphological work focused upon describing the distribution of the landforms (Fukai, 1975), but there was no process study. Unless the geomorphic processes are studied, it cannot be assessed whether human control in the area has been successful. For this purpose, we examine natural processes responsible for landscape changes in the Kuranosuke cirque, which has not been influenced by the human activities. The previous studies (Watanabe, 1985, 1989; Ono and Watanabe, 1986) show that rockfall, alpine debris flow and solifluction are the important processes. Also, snow avalanches are active in the cirque. These four processes, therefore, are briefly examined next.

Rockfall: Rapp (1960) divided rockfall into *pebblefall* and *boulderfall*. The present paper also uses the terms, *boulderfall*, which is defined as rockfall producing boulders and cobbles (>64 mm), and *pebblefall*, which denotes rockfall producing small-size debris (<64 mm).

The data on boulderfall debris was collected in June to August 1983. The total number of debris incidents observed on the snow from May to August was 325 (no rockfall had occurred before the beginning of May) and the total volume was 0.76 m^3 (Watanabe, 1989). The measurement in the autumn of 1988 led to the estimated total volume of 3.14 m^3 for autumn. The annual volume of debris produced by *boulderfall*, therefore, is 4 m^3.

The data on pebblefall was taken from 5 October 1982 to 9 October 1989. The area of the bedrock exposure which produces pebblefall debris in the cirque is approximately 1 500 m^2; the total annual amount to be produced by pebblefall from the bedrock surfaces is estimated as 24 m^3/yr.

Alpine debris flow: Ono and Watanabe (1986) and Watanabe (1985, 1989) described the alpine debris flow which occurred in the cirque in 1983 and 1985. Over the last 26 years (1965-90) it averaged 26 m^3/yr.

Solifluction: Repeat observations of twelve painted lines on the surface materials in the cirque for five to eight years indicate that the surface debris has moved downslope (16-37 degrees) at rates ranging from 2.6 to 19.2 cm/yr.

Snow avalanches: Many avalanches were observed in and around the cirque in the spring, but none of them has transported rock fragments. Snow avalanches are not effective as a geomorphic process, but are important as hazardous events: the former mountain huts in the Kuranosuke and Tsurugisawa cirques were destroyed and numerous climbers were killed.

Processes in the tephra-covered area: Although the Kuranosuke cirque is composed of granitic rocks, some parts of the surrounding areas, including Murodo, are covered with volcanic deposits. An unpaved trail on the tephra-covered slope west of Murodo, on which soil erosion is active, was observed in the field. The trail is not designed for public use and has been used only for mountain hut maintenance. It is not shown on an aerial photograph taken on 29 August 1969, but is clearly shown on an aerial photograph on 16 September 1977. This indicates that the trail has been de-vegetated in a short time. Some parts of the trail have eroded to 45 cm in depth. Compared with the paved trails around Murodo, this unpaved trail has been used less frequently. Nevertheless, soil loss along the trail is evident.

Conclusions

High mountain areas of the Japanese Alps have not been subjected to agricultural use or livestock grazing in historic times (Ives, 1982). Instead, many mountains have been worshipped and visited as sacred places. Mt. Tateyama had been regularly visited and worshipped as a sacred mountain as early as the eighth century (Tsukamoto, 1984).

From the foregoing examination, it is evident that the construction of the hydroelectric power station in the area led to the development of the mass-transportation system for tourism, thereby rapidly increasing the number of tourists. In addition, Tateyama has changed from a religious object to one of tourism.

Large-scale engineering methods such as tunnelling and using a ropeway enabled landscape changes to be minimized and so avoided mountain hazards such as snow avalanches, rockfalls and debris flow. Examination of the geomorphic processes in the Kuranosuke cirque showed that debris flow is very active on the bare ground. The paved and staircased trails around Murodo appear to have succeeded in mitigating soil loss, in contrast to the eroded unpaved trails observed in some sites. In these contexts, Tateyama can be regarded as a developed mountain area which has succeeded in minimizing the human impacts. On the other hand, it appears that the development project–spending huge amounts of money–has tended to rely on a massive engineering approach in order to handle the problems. As a result, the alpine area of Tateyama has some components of a "city landscape". Today, ptarmigans, which are protected from hunting as a "special natural monument", walk on the paved trails around Murodo.

Use of massive engineering methods is also applied to mountainous countries including Nepal. Both the Nepal Himalaya and Tateyama have water resources which, in the case of Tateyama, have already been developed but in the Nepal Himalaya are only now beginning to be developed. When the transportation system to the mountain areas of the Himalaya is improved, what could happen there?

References for this section are available from Dr. T. Watanabe, Graduate School of Environmental Science, Hokkaido University, Sapporo, Japan. ■

Northern Thailand

Northern Thailand comprises Region Five, the administrative division of the North, which includes the provinces of Mae Hong Son, Chiang Mai, Chiang Rai, Nan, Lamphun, Lampang, Phrae, and Uttaradit. This is a region of mountains and hills with relatively narrow valleys and occasional intermontane basins forming a highly complex relief merging across the borders of Burma and Laos, and further north into Yunnan, P.R. China. It represents a southern extension of the Himalaya and Hengduan Mountains with forested summits exceeding 2 500 m. Situated between latitudes 16 and 20 degrees N, it experiences a pronounced monsoonal climate with heavy summer rains (mid-May or June to October) followed by a cool dry season (October to February), then a hot dry season culminating in April/May with temperature maxima exceeding 40 degrees Celsius (Yoshino, 1980). The largest sector is drained by the main headstreams of the Choa Phraya southwards through Bangkok into the Gulf of Siam. The north-eastern sector drains into the Mekong, and the northwestern into the Salween and Irrawaddy.

The natural vegetation, in a broad sense, is tropical monsoon rainforest with distinct altitudinal belts. Above about 1 000 m to the summits a Lower Montane Forest predominates consisting of oaks, false chestnuts, laurels, and birches, amongst others. Overlapping its lower section and extending down to about 800 m is the Coniferous Forest belt (1 600–800 m). This is an edaphic community usually occupying steeper slopes and exposed ridges. It is dominated by two native pines, *Pinus merkusii* and *P. kesiya*, which provide the source for much of the on-going reforestation efforts. Oaks, false chestnuts, and other evergreen species occupy the understory while dipterocarps enter at lower elevations. Overlapping again, but forming a distinct lower altitudinal belt, is the Dry Evergreen Forest. This forest extends across the foothills and upper river terraces to the plains. It contains economically vital and seriously over-exploited teak and other commercial species.

Traditionally the lowlands and narrow valley bottoms have been characterized by the intensive irrigated rice culture of the ethnic Northern Thai centred on the northern capital of Chiang Mai, today Thailand's second largest city. The mountains and highlands, extending across vaguely defined international frontiers, have been the domain of the "hilltribes" comprising more than a dozen

Figure 5.7: *Schematic highland-lowland transect for northern Thailand*
From P Kunstadter et al., 1978

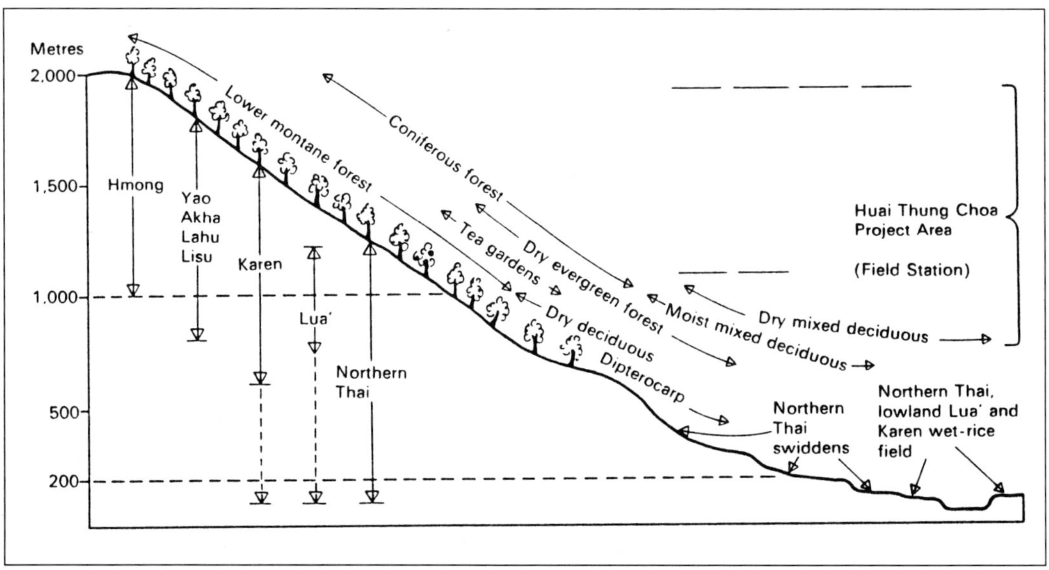

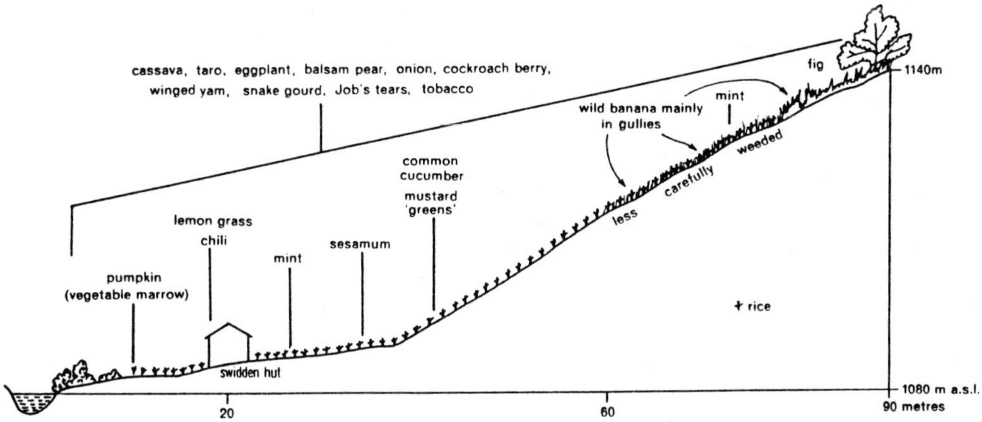

Figure 5.8: *Diagram showing position of crops in an actual Ban Hua Lao swidden, in relation to the swidden hut and slope, 1980*

ethnically distinct peoples. Living as farmers of the forest and practising various forms of swidden agriculture (Kunstadter, et al. eds. 1978) these peoples include Hmong, Lisu, Lahu, Karen, Yao, Akha, amongst others. There is a broad altitudinal distribution (Figure 5.7, Ives, 1980: 11) and until recently population densities have been very low and migration across the now more precisely defined international frontiers has been quite casual. The opium poppy has been a major cash crop and the larger area, extending into Yunnan, became known as the Golden Triangle. Until the 1950s, however, ethnic Northern Thai and hilltribes had very little contact, with the exception of the Karen, the largest individual group, many of whom transformed to a settled irrigated rice-based agriculture comparable to that of the Thais.

It has been argued (Kunstadter et al., 1978; Sabhasri, 1980; McKinnon,1983; Ives, 1983) that, given the traditional low population densities, swidden agriculture is a sophisticated, effective and ecologically balanced form of forest subsistence (Figure 5.8, Rajah, 1983: 354; Table 5.2, Chitman 1980: 77). This is contrary to popular belief since, the world over, slash and burn (synonymous with swidden) agriculture, by its very name, has been perceived as destructive. In Northern Thailand, this view has been exacerbated by ethnic divisions between Thais and hilltribals since the latter, according to the Thai constitution, are not literally human; more specifically, they cannot by law hold title to land. Nevertheless, comparative newcomers to the region, especially the Hmong, who use a long cultivation and very long fallow swidden system inhibit reversion to forest cover and have generated long-term degradation (Kunstadter et al., 1978: 10-11)

The last 40 years have witnessed rapid population growth amongst Thais and hilltribes alike. For the North as a whole sustained population growth of about 2.6 per cent per annum has been maintained over the last few decades, reaching in excess of 3.0 per cent per annum amongst the hilltribes. In absolute numbers, nevertheless, the hilltribes as a whole probably do not exceed a half million. However, the lowlands and valleys are heavily overpopulated and land-starved ethnic Northern Thais are pushing upslope and acquiring extensive tracts of formerly hilltribe land. This,

Table 5.2: *Slope and elevation for common crops*

Crop species	Elevation (m)	Slope (degrees)
Terraced rice field	500	15
Upland rice	550	30
Sesame	550-650	60
Soya bean	550-650	30
Sesame and maize	550-650	60

together with highland population growth has seriously unbalanced the hitherto sustainable swidden systems.

Swidden agriculture depends upon a significant time period for forest fallow, up to 20 years or more depending on the particular system and the forest type. During this time the small fields cut and burnt in the forest revert to closed-crown forest so that the process can continue indefinitely, as indeed it has done for centuries (Kunstadter et al., 1978). With post-1950 growing population pressures, the period of forest fallow has been progressively curtailed until the forest succession has been disrupted and the forest cover had been increasingly replaced by imperata grassland *(Imperata cylindrica)* and other biologically much less productive grasses.

Widespread destruction of forest cover on steep slopes is believed to have been the cause of rapidly accelerating soil erosion and gullying. Associated problems include disruption of the hydrological cycle, siltation of irrigation works in the valleys and lowlands, flooding in the rainy season with spread of infertile sands and gravels across the rice fields. This is compounded by ethnic distinctions and the perceived menace of opium growing.

During the 1970s the Vietnam War and its aftermath not only augmented a flow of hilltribals, especially Hmong, from Kampuchea and Laos into Northern Thailand, but led to increased ethnic tensions as the Thai government braced itself for the so-called "domino effect". Also pressure from the United States for curtailment of opium production and lack of normal relations with Burma contributed to setting the scale for enforced reforestation and actual military actions to control social unrest amongst some hilltribe communities which tended to be branded as communist insurgency.

Through the 1970s and 1980s numerous attempts via foreign and UN aid projects were initiated to:

1) curtail opium production; and
2) reduce forest loss and soil erosion.

Efforts to introduce alternative cash crops to opium included cut flowers, bulbs and seed production, potato cultivation and commercial forest plantation, as well as intensification of subsistence agriculture (Kunstadter et al., 1978; Andrews and Comudon, 1978; Andrews; 1983; Andrews and Kwaengsopha, 1979; Tiyavalee et al., 1979; Sabhasri, 1980; Chapman, 1980; Falvey et al., 1977; Gibson, 1983; Künzel, 1983; McKinnon, 1983). Many of these efforts were only partially successful, or else outright failures. A frequent obstacle was the inability to take into account the felt needs of the local people. In particular, a Thai National Forestry Service sense of urgency over the loss of tree cover led to extensive planting with pine seedlings. Since pine plantations severely impact hilltribal subsistence, accidental and/or deliberate firing (a normal form of relieving tension especially within what is basically a fire culture) has resulted in enormous forest plantation losses (Ives et al., 1980).

The many efforts to correct a perceived series of problems were in part futile simply because they were based upon several critical unproven assumptions. A United Nations University field investigation and series of workshops went some way toward clarifying a highly complicated situation. For instance, Hurni and Nuntapong (1983) and Rajah (1983) demonstrated that while conversion to a variety of subsistence-plus-cash crop intensified agricultural systems using hill terracing and other soil conservation techniques was physically feasible, socio-economic factors proved to be the effective obstacles. Thus a shortage of available labour amongst the hilltribes militated against the laborious process of terracing, while use of grant funds to provide wages produced an influx of ethnic Northern Thai.

These local problems are being exacerbated progressively by an enormous increase in tourism, with hilltribe opium-producing villages being major tourist attractions. Additionally tourist-induced local handicraft industries have augmented a movement of hill peoples to the lowland towns, and especially to Chiang Mai.

The United Nations University investigations led to the following statement of broad concerns:

1) existing Thai development policies may not be adequately based upon the behavioural patterns and perceptions of the local people;
2) the perceptions of highlanders by Thais and outsiders are not necessarily accurate, and in particular the ethnic Northern Thai are probably

Swidden agriculture with increasing population densities in northwest Thailand leads to progressive deforestation of steep mountain slopes. A Lisu maize field, northwest of Chiang Mai

responsible for much more of the loss of tree cover than are the highlanders;

3) the role of imperata grassland is not perceived clearly and the problems are neither technical nor scientific but social and economic;

4) agro-forestry, if appropriately applied to existing subsistence systems, has considerable potential for resolving the traditional conflict between forester and farmer (Chapman and Sabhasri, eds., 1983).

The overwhelming conclusion, however, was that the problems of the highlands of Northern Thailand are neither scientific nor technical. Rather they are people problems. Throughout the developing mountain world "solutions" imposed by outsiders will frequently fail; success will depend upon the degree to which the local people are able to take the initiative (Ives, 1983: 311). What is needed is a highlander's perception of the highlands (McKinnon, 1983).

This brief review of a relatively small mountain region in a developing country in the tropics, while incomplete, nevertheless, carries some important implications for many tropical mountain regions. Conflicts, or lack of understanding, between central governing elites, or majorities and mountain ethnic minorities, are central to any attempts to work toward sustainable development and environmental stability. Western expert perceptions will be unreliable bases for policy making in many instances. A large increase in development anthropology is needed. The experience gained by the Nepal-Australia Forestry Project (Griffin, 1988) in Nepal carries critical lessons worthy of general appreciation. If the goal of foreign aid is truly the well-being of the mountain minority peoples, their needs must first be identified and their contribution to all levels of project planning and implementation must be assured. Finally, institution-building is probably the single most difficult prerequisite (Griffin, 1987, 1988). ■

Papua New Guinea highlands

The island of New Guinea, which comprises the independent country of Papua New Guinea and Indonesian province of Irian Jaya, is located just south of the equator in the western Pacific, north of Australia. Along the centre of this tropical island, a significant mountain range extends an east-west distance of 1 000 km. As the highest and most heavily forested region between the Himalaya and the Andes, summits reach 4 510 m (Mt. Wilhelm) in Papua New Guinea to 4 884 m (Mt. Jaya) in Irian Jaya (Figure 5.9; Haberle, et al., 1991). Most mountains, however, have an elevation between 3 000 and 4 000 m and an average treeline at about 3 750–3 900 m (Haberle et. al., 1991: 25; Smith, 1985: 329; Brookfield, 1991: 203).

Human mountain settlement is predominantly in the highland valley systems between 1 500 and 2 500 m and the 2 million people (38 per cent of the total population for the entire island) who occupy these regions live at densities of 100 to 300/km^2 and have an annual population growth rate of 2 per cent (Grossman, 1984: 27). Consequently, forest clearance is most widespread in this altitudinal range. In the absence of human disturbance almost the entire island would be covered by rainforest; the only unforested sites would occur on mountain peaks, where grasslands and shrublands prevail above the upper treeline, and at lower elevations, where natural disturbances such as landslips are frequent. With widespread population increases resulting from the introduction of the sweet potato *(Ipomoea batatas)* in the 17th century, the colonization of the coasts and installation of cash-crop industries in the hinterlands by Europeans in the early 20th century (most intensively after 1960), and the subsequent advent of modern technology, forests are disappearing, causing erosion and loss of soil fertility. Unfortunately, current human activities are multifaceted and intensifying. Local subsistence populations, possessing modern tools and facing land shortages, encroach on the forest edge at accelerating speed. In addition, timber exploitation, mainly for export, results in vast forested areas being felled, with little evidence of forest regeneration efforts (Smith, 1985: 329-330; Brookfield, 1991: 204). Cash-crop industries, in the form of coffee plantations and smallholder cattle projects, also contribute

Figure 5.9: *Central highlands of Irian Jaya and Papua New Guinea*

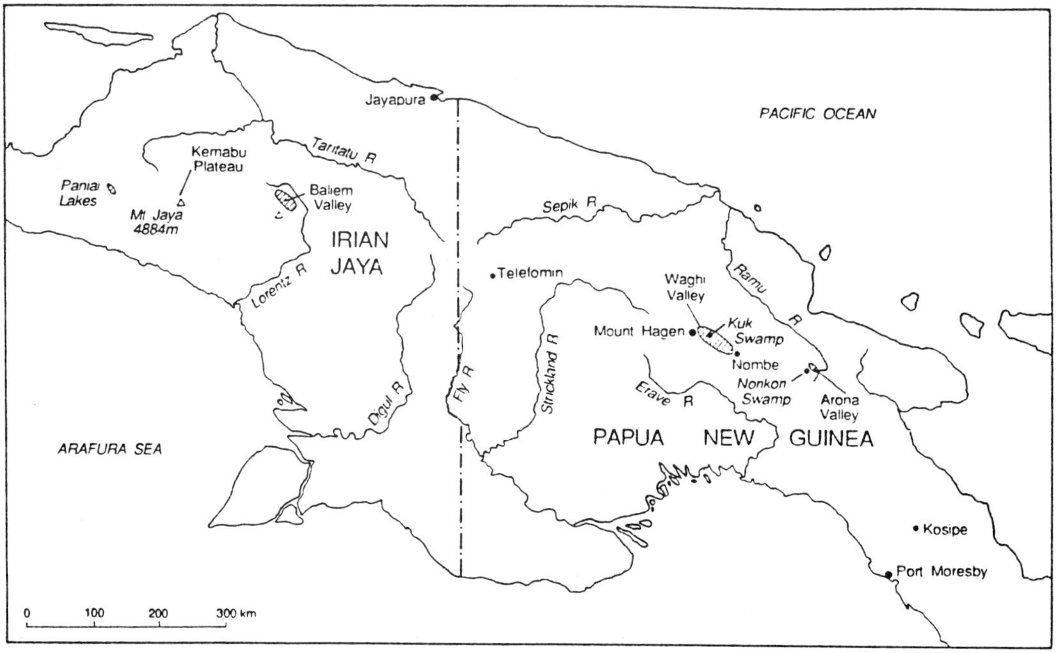

to environmental degradation because the returns to land and labour are often lower in commodity production and thus peasants must use more land and labour to support themselves where cash-cropping reduces subsistence output (Grossman, 1984: 8-9). Finally, the influx of tourism into the highland areas causes added environmental and societal stress in a region which is increasingly becoming dependent upon external factors for the basis of the local economy (Corlett, 1984: 843). Although these human pressures impact the entire island, emphasis will be given to Papua New Guinea due to the abundance of current data available, as opposed to the western portion of Irian Jaya which is closed to most foreign visitors (Brookfield, 1991: 203).

Papua New Guinea (PNG) lies in the western part of the Pacific and has a surface area of 461 700 km^2 between latitudes 0 degrees and 12 degrees S and longitudes 141 degrees and 156 degrees E. The climate is moist, tropical and humid, but as Jan Carstensz, a Dutch sea captain, in 1623 observed, the area includes "...a high range of mountains that in many places was white as it was covered with snow, which certainly is something strange to see on mountains so close to the equator" (Van Royen, 1980: 249). Indeed this region has prominent mountains, which kept the indigenous inhabitants free from external influence for at least 25 000 years. Initially, population densities were low until the 17th century when the sweet potato was introduced into the region via the Philippines and Indonesia, causing the number of people to increase dramatically (Gorecki, 1986: 160-161). Major European exploration, however, did not occur until the mid-1930s when Australian government patrol officers, missionaries and gold miners penetrated into higher elevations west of the established south-eastern coastal colonies. These European invaders discovered numerous, small-scale tribal societies at altitudes previously believed to be uninhabitable. For these highlanders, who based their subsistence on horticulture and pig husbandry, supplemented by hunting and gathering, contact with foreigners revealed a entirely new way of life: one of extensive environmental exploitation which would forever alter their native landscape.

Although forest clearance at high altitudes (approximately 2 000 m) had already occurred by 5 500 years BP and soil erosion on cleared hillslopes as a result of horticulture intensification is evident by 9 000 years BP, human impact did not threaten the carrying capacity of highland systems until the subsistence agriculture was placed in direct competition for local resources with commercial endeavours. Initially, humans ventured into these high altitudes only for short periods for hunting and cooking purposes. In order to alleviate population pressure on the valley floors, the sweet potato system allowed the permanent expansion of large communities toward the upper tree line, where clearance and burning quickly followed (Haberle et al., 1991: 25). Subsistence farming is still practised today but despite its relative efficiency, indigenous techniques are often blamed for the increase in downstream erosion, recent large-scale mass-wasting events, and infertile anthropogenic grasslands. This accusation, however, is far too simplistic. Environmental degradation has an extensive, historical complexity, ranging from ancient human settlement to contemporary industrial activities, which must be taken in account when searching for sustainable solutions. Humphreys and Brookfield (in press), for instance, indicate that many upland areas have been remarkably stable over the last 50 years (see below).

Steepland farming systems are a subset of those methods used in the adjacent, more gradually sloped areas. Commonly slopes of between 30 and 40 degrees and several hundred metres in length are under cultivation. Tillage, ditching, and fencing extend soil fertility by ridding excess water and retaining the topsoil. Some persistent fence lines even form *taluds* as high as two metres, separating cultivated land above from eroded area below. In this way, indigenous agro-technologies in combination with fallow periods, which range from only a few months to 30 years, are used in order to maximize the limited arable land (Humphreys and Brookfield, in press).

Unfortunately, this ancient agricultural practice is now coupled with contemporary motives for forest clearance, such as cash-cropping, logging and mining. In turn, undue pressure is being placed upon the environment, causing large areas to become infertile. Recently introduced commodity production–coffee growing and smallholder cattle projects–has resulted in extensive environmental deterioration for the benefit of a few urban elites, businessmen and major beneficiaries. Because almost all production is geared toward export, the expanded marketplace provides a strong demand for local output but places stress on the limited resource base. For instance, fallow periods are shortened and more marginal land susceptible to erosion is utilized. In addition, new cultivation methods, such as monocropping, mechanization, or the use of pesticides, frequently prove detrimental to the local environment. Therefore, not only is commodity production reduced but the potential productivity of subsistence farming is constrained as well (Grossman, 1984: 8-9).

Although today cattle are found virtually anywhere in Papua New Guinea, they are not native to the country. German colonists introduced them around the turn of the century and by the 1950s the cattle industry, along with coffee growing, was well established. Similar to cash-cropping, this commercial activity also has shown detrimental effects on the landscape. For example, a study conducted in the highland district of Kapanara reveals that overgrazing reduces the vegetation cover (in the overgrazed area approximate leaf cover is 50–60 per cent compared to vegetation cover of 88 per cent in an ungrazed location [Grossman, 1984: 127]) and trampling damages many plant species while compacting the soils; all of which alter the microclimate and accelerate soil erosion. Although compacted soils are more closely bound together, they have a greater potential for erosion because they are exposed to runoff. Current data shows that the weight under each hoof of a mature bovine is approximately 3.2 kg/cm^2 and the soil bulk density of the top 5 centimetres is 5 to 44 per cent higher in a heavily grazed site as opposed to a low stocked project (one animal per 8.5 ha [Grossman, 1984: 120,131]). Furthermore, grazing induces vegetation changes. Statistics show that in the highland Kapanara district palatable native grasses such as *Ischaemum barbatum*, *Capillipedium parviflorum* and *Ophiuros tongcalingii* have decreased in frequency; more specifically, the original 50 to 60 per cent cover of *Themeda* has gradually been thinned to less than 25 per cent. In turn, a host of weeds have invaded the patches of bare ground and remaining vegetation cover: *Hydrocotyle javanica*, *Oxalis corniculata*, and *Ageratum conyzoides*, which has achieved a leaf cover of over 25 per cent (Grossman, 1984: 125-127). Overgrazing is thus a serious problem which must be addressed, especially in light of the current problems associated with inadequate maintenance of enclosures. As more cattle escape and destroy gardens, people are forced to expand the realm of cultivation and the cycle of degradation is perpetuated.

Cattle grazing and agriculture are not the only contributors to forest clearance. While 200 000 ha are deforested annually through shifting cultivation, approximately 2.3 million ha have been felled by logging operations and between 60 000 and 90 000 ha through mining, urban, and infrastructural developments. Furthermore, the 1.4 million m^3 of forest products exported in 1989 yielded US$ 98 million, which represented 7 per cent of the country's export value (Saulei, 1990: 380). With 70 per cent (36.2 million ha) of the country's total land area (46.2 million ha) under some kind of forest cover, either lowland rainforests or highlands, and a local economy so dependent upon forest products, the pressure to exploit this resource base is inevitable (Table 5.3). However, the forest ecosystem, comprised of a dynamic mix of different plant and animal species, is not resilient to continued, intensive human disturbance.

As human activity increases and the exposed ground is leached and eroded by surface runoff, the soil nutrients decline. The resulting fallow grasslands (*Miscanthus floridulus* or *Imperata cylindrica*) grow progressively shorter and more depauperate, therefore minimizing their utility for grazing. Under agriculture *Imperata* soil even declines rapidly in nutrient status (acidification and base saturation levels often fall below 10 per cent), thus causing these areas to be of limited value without large artificial fertilizer inputs (Pain and Scott, 1981: 78).

In addition to the invasion of anthropogenic vegetation, human disturbance threatens wildlife as their habitat slowly shrinks. For example, the fauna species of the Gogol Valley total 251 with endemism ranging 36 per cent for mammals and 70 per cent for frogs. Sixty per cent of this wildlife is dependent on forests to varying degrees but the greatest effect of forest reduction is on birds. A number of species have become rare: *Cophixalus rostellifer*, *Gallicolumba beccarli*, *Hemiprocne mystacea, Peltops blainvillii* and *Harpyopsis novaeguineae* (kapul eagle) (Table 5.4 [Lamb, 1990: 55]).

Forest clearance threatens the natural ecosystem and alters the native landscape permanently. Watersheds are also negatively affected by human impact, with the consequences felt downstream far from the source. A recent study indicates that turbidity levels designated as "high" were recorded at 2–14 per cent in logged areas during the sample period, as opposed to 3–6 per cent in unlogged areas. This turbidity difference indicates changes in water quality caused by suspended sediment. Heavy sediment loads are a consequence of mass movement (e. g. from landslips), stream erosion, or surface slope wash, which explains the greater turbidity in impacted regions (Lamb, 1990: 131).

Mining is another commercial endeavour to cause problems for watershed quality and aquatic life. The copper mining of Mount Fubilan, for instance, involves the extraction of 1340 x 10^6 tonnes (t) of material, which is comprised of approximately 520 x 10^6 t of ore and 820 x 10^6 t of overburden, of which only a fraction is valuable metal. This mine and its process facilities are located at Folomian at an elevation of 1 600 m and approximately 1 000 river km from the Papuan coast. The watershed forms the catchment area (approximately 76 000 km^2) of the Fly River system, which drains a large part of southwestern Papua New Guinea. With the mining continuing at the rate of 150 000 t/day of ore and overburden (1989 estimate), high levels of erosion, turbidity, and particulates, such as cations, anions, heavy metals, will eventually make the aquatic environment uninhabitable, along with the surrounding embankments (Salomons and Eagle, 1990: 315). Also, many researchers fear the detrimental effects could cause damage as far as the coast.

As the demand for land increases with population pressure and the introduction of modern enterprises and technology, the need for conservation management becomes urgent. Tourism reached 40 000 in 1988, an increase of 85 per cent over the previous five years. While in total numbers Papua New Guinea does not rival most mountainous vacation destinations, such as the Alps in Europe or the Sierra Nevada in the US, local inhabitants are quickly recognizing the economic potential involved with tourism and are abandoning their subsistence lifeways. As a result, reliance on commercial enterprises and the export economy will increase dramatically. In accordance with this imminent danger, the government has established various research facilities in order better to understand future trends and to minimize potential environmental change.

The most effective management tool has been the establishment of the new Forest Research Institute in 1989, centralized at Lae. This institute has four branches: Botany, Management, Products and Protection, and is staffed by 55 officers of whom three are overseas advisors. Since its beginning, a number of achievements have been

	Area closed			Volume from productive forest	
Country	Total (000 ha)	Productive (000 ha)	Productive (ha/capita)	(10^6 m^3)	(m^3/capita)
PNG	34 230	14 085	4.5	1 817	586
Brunei	323	287	2.1	8.3	610
Indonesia	113 895	73 735	0.5	13 823	97
Malaysia	20 995	15 552	1.1	3 735	277
Peninsula	*7 578*	*5 807*	*0.5*	*1 422*	*125*
Sabah	*4 997*	*3 200*	*3.6*	*801*	*910*
Sarawak	*8 420*	*6 545*	*5.0*	*1 512*	*1 163*
Philippines	9 510	6 890	0.1	1 543	31

***Table 5.3:** Estimates of areas of closed forest (broadleaved and conifers) and standing volumes estimated for 1980 in Papua New Guinea and Southeast Asia (includes logged and unlogged forest).*
Source: FAO/UNEP (1981)

realized. The Botany Branch has collected and catalogued over 280 000 plant species and has stored them in the National Herbarium. The Forest Management Branch has successfully cultivated suitable species for reforestation on logged-over areas in plantations and then demonstrated agroforestry and forest pasture development techniques in highland communities. The Forest Products Branch has made progress in developing more efficient methods of wood preservation and, in turn, monitors and evaluates current sawmilling and seasoning practices. Finally, the Forest Protection Branch has conducted studies into the biology of the past and the present; more specifically, it has collected and preserved over 30 000 insect species (Saulei, 1990: 381). These accomplishments are the initial steps towards the environmental preservation and regeneration necessary to accommodate varying, conflicting interests. Furthermore, these successes illustrate how viable research and effective implementation are necessary in order to maintain an ecological balance, especially in an insular setting like Papua New Guinea.

The highlands of New Guinea are undoubtedly being disturbed and the pre-existing social systems continue to experience rapid modification. Nevertheless, Humphreys and Brookfield (in press) raise an extremely important question. Given the high population densities of their study areas, together with steep slopes and apparently minimal soil conservation practices, the rates of soil loss and degree of slope instability seem to be rather moderate. They demonstrate that the entire question of soil loss and sustainability, as in many mountain regions, requires an extensive historical perspective. Their studies show that population densities have fluctuated in the past and that they may have been reduced from a high level in the early part of this century. For instance, in 1960 the total population in the Chimbu (upper valley) near Mt. Wilhelm was about 29 000 on 220 km^2 of land below the upper treeline. By 1980 this had fallen to 24 000 due to substantial spontaneous outmigration despite high rates of natural increase. In many mountain areas of PNG there appears to have been no major environmental changes in the last half century.

These observations (Humphreys and Brookfield, in press) raise two issues:

1) the tendency to jump to conclusions should be resisted without a deep historical perspective and an understanding of indigenous land-use management;

2) in New Guinea, as in so many complex mountain regions, absence of an adequate database must be corrected as soon as possible. The long-term studies in PNG, being undertaken by the Research School of Pacific Studies, Australian National University and other universities and government agencies, are the types that are urgently needed in other regions. Brookfield's personal observational experience is already spread over 32 years (Humphreys and Brookfield, in press) and the results of the PNG studies have already forced some radical new thinking (Allen and Brookfield, eds., 1989). Individual research combined with governmentally sponsored team work will slowly reveal the intricate, historical background of highland degradation. This will facilitate a better understanding of the current complexities as a first step towards development of sustainable management practices. ■

Table 5.4: *Estimates of wildlife species present in the Gogol Valley.* Source: Liem (1978a)

Animalgroup	Total species	Endemic species no	Endemic species %	Species dependent on forest no	Species dependent on forest %
Mammals	27	10	37	20	74
Birds	167	77	46	102	61
Reptiles	34	19	56	15	44
Frogs	23	16	70	15	65
Total	251	122	49	152	60

The Polish Tatra

Apart from the Alps, the Tatra comprise the only mountain landscape of Central Europe with alpine, or high-mountain, attributes. They represent the culmination of the Carpathian chain centred on 49 degrees N and 20 degrees E, and rise to a maximum altitude of 2 663 m (Figure 5.10, Kotarba, 1992). Nevertheless, the total area is quite modest (600 km^2) and the crestline extends for only 57 km forming the frontier between Poland and Slovakia. Much the smaller part falls within Polish territory (150 km^2). The vertical relief between the northern foothills and the main crest, a horizontal distance of about 15 km, is 1 600 m., providing for a range of altitudinal geoecological belts from the beech forests of the foothills, across timberline at about 1 700 m, on to alpine meadows and the uppermost periglacial belt of rock faces, frost-shattered debris and occasional small permanent snow beds. The Tatra have no glaciers so they lack, unlike the Alps, the uppermost mountain (nival) belt (Figure 5.11; Kotarba, 1992).

The Tatra have a crystalline core, bordered to the north by a series of sedimentary nappes consisting of limestones, sandstones and flysch. They were uplifted during the alpine orogeny (contemporaneously with the Alps) and were subsequently glaciated on at least three separate occasions. Glacial erosion produced substantial valley widening and over-deepening and, in the upper parts, a series of cirque basins and knife-edged arêtes were formed. Dramatic cliffs up to 1 000 m in height have added to the area's high mountain character (Figure 5.12; Kotarba, 1992).

The onset of extensive human penetration into the Tatra Mountains dates back to the 15th century, but it was only in the 18th century that the Polish population at large became aware of their very exis-

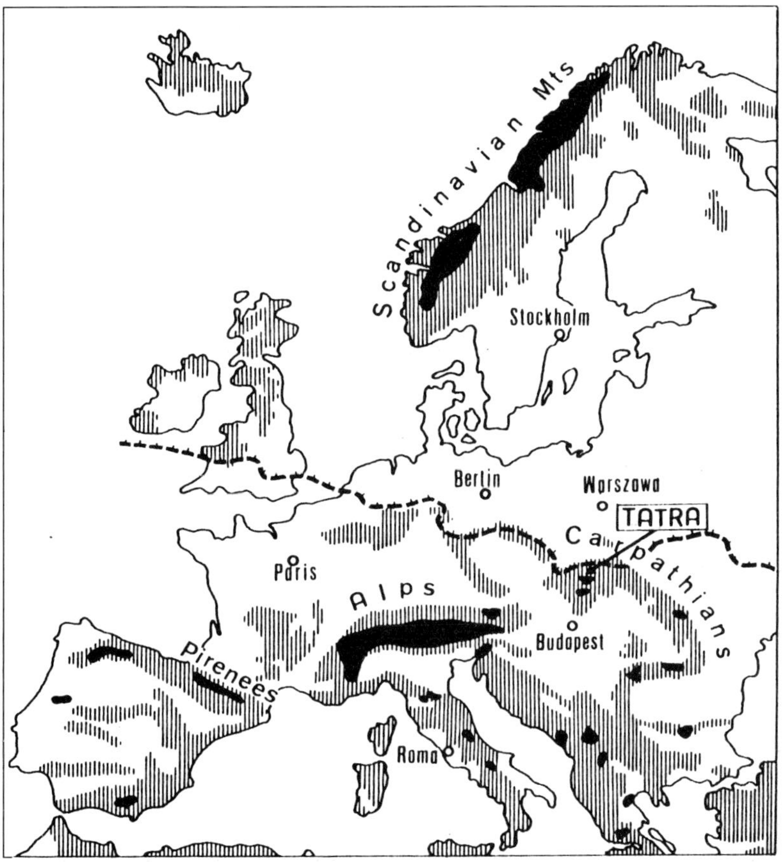

Figure 5.10: The Tatra mountains in relation to other European mountain groups

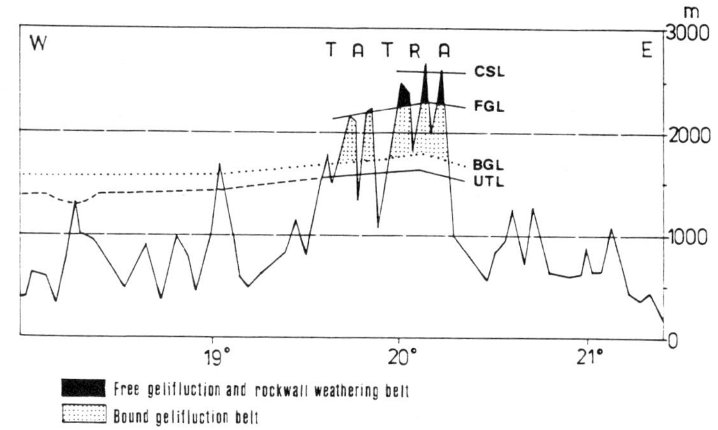

Figure 5.11: Transverse section of Tatra

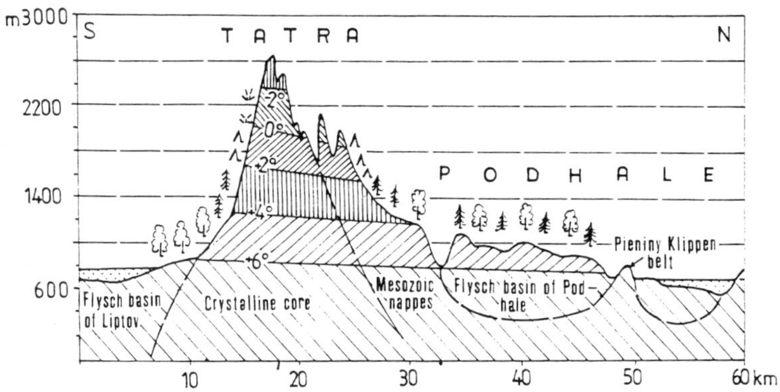

Figure 5.12: Erosion patterns in the Tatra

tence. It was mainly due to accounts by Western European travellers and scientists that the Polish people became informed about the outstanding natural history and folklore of the Tatra, and also about the already excessive hunting and overuse of the forests for mining, smelting and domestic fuel. By the mid-nineteenth century Krakow scientists began a struggle to protect the endangered animal species, especially chamois and marmot, and legislation was enacted in 1869, together with measures to ensure enforcement (Byrcyn, 1992).

The United States national park movement, culminating with the establishment of Yellowstone National Park in 1872, had repercussions in Poland and the following year a Tatra Association was formed. Its objectives included conducting research and popularizing the Tatra, together with nature protection. This was partly a response to the ongoing severe exploitation of the Tatra forests by local land owners. A proposal to establish a Tatra National Park was put forward as early as 1888 and an attempt was made to obtain funds so that local land owners could be bought out. Already in 1889 Count W. Zamoyski purchased a major part of the Tatra and rational forest management was introduced. Despite some successes, including an end to the opening up of new quarries and a block on construction of a cable car to the Swinica peak, extensive legal protection had to await Polish independence in 1918. Nevertheless, complex land tenure relationships ensured that discussions were protracted until 1939 when a small nature park was established.

The Second World War saw serious damage, even to this small park, because of poaching, timber felling and overgrazing, especially by sheep. The Tatra National Park (*Tatrzanski Park Narodowy*), with an area of 21 4000 ha, was finally established in 1954.

Present-day park functions

About a third of the park's total area is managed as a forest reserve. One of the primary objectives is to preserve existing old growth habitat and to reconstruct degraded stands. There is a strong research base and much historical data so that it is scientifically feasible to reconstruct Tatra forest habitats very close to formerly prevailing natural conditions.

Earlier forest degradation and the present-day impact of acid rain has weakened the forest structure over large areas. One consequence is the increasing susceptibility to wind-throw; others are the exacerbation of insect damage and spread of parasitic diseases. Thus a holistic approach to habitat reconstruction, including soils, is underway. Replanting is possible using the park's own nursery production of seed stock for most indigenous species, including stone pine, fir, spruce, yew and ash. Only beech seed is in short supply (Mirek and Piekos-Mirkowa, 1992).

Over the last five years 210 ha of partial reserves have been subjected to artificial reconstruction, which has included the planting of 980 000 seedlings: fir (47 per cent), spruce (22 per cent), beech (13 per cent), larch (9 per cent). Treatment of young stands was carried out on 568 ha, and occasional prescribed logging, including windthrows and dried-up trees, has yielded 50 000 m^3 timber.

Scientific activities have a very high priority with both pure research and applied objectives. After 1980 a third component–education–was added. From 1984 onwards a special educational component, the promotion of knowledge about the park as a national treasure, has been undertaken by the Tatra National Park Nature Museum. This involves topical museum exhibits and publications, including a popular journal.

Tourism and recreation

Tourist visits had reached 3.0 million per annum by 1980. Introduction of a permit system and associated measures had reduced this to 1.6 million by 1990. This is still considered to be beyond the park's long-term capacity, however, especially when the tendency towards concentration on a few popular areas is taken into account. The following types of recreational use are characteristic of the park: organized group sight-seeing, hiking, ski-touring, downhill skiing, mountaineering, and caving. There are nine tourist hotels and three other public facilities for overnight stays (total of 856 beds), four private recreation centres (601 beds), 61 houses, a sanatorium, two monasteries, three cable car stations, and two camp sites.

Other activities

Sheep grazing remains an important activity in the Tatra National Park. It has a tradition dating from the Middle Ages, with a rich shepherds' folklore characteristic of the entire Podhale Basin.

Sheep grazing reached a peak immediately after the Second World War with an estimated 27 000 sheep using the Polish Tatra, much beyond the region's regenerative capacity. By 1980 grazing was completely eliminated despite much local protest. The political changes in Poland as a whole in the 1980s, however, led to efforts to preserve local culture, which in turn resulted in the reintroduction of sheep grazing in the park. Nevertheless, the reintroduced grazing has been controlled. For instance, sheep are only allowed into areas ranked as partial reserves and flocks are restricted to 1 000 head under the guidance of experienced shepherds. Herein is a successful compromise between conflicting resource-use claims–economy and preservation.

As a next step, a joint proposal is being developed by the Tatra National Park and Czechoslovakia to include the entire Tatra Range in the global network of Biosphere Reserves. This will facilitate an international contribution to the UNESCO Man and the Biosphere (MAB) Programme of scientific research and environmental monitoring.

Such collaboration, should it materialize, will not come a moment too soon. Despite the relatively optimistic tenor of this report, it is necessary to reflect upon the careful assessment of the ecological status of the Tatra National Park undertaken by Mirek (1992, in press). The historical interventions of human activity, mining and metallurgy, sheep grazing and logging, certainly extracted their toll. Today, in addition to air pollution, increasing tourist pressures remain serious. There is uncontrolled human penetration of practically the entire park, accompanied by poaching, mushroom gathering, and berry picking, and especially the collection of rare plants. Nearly 80 per cent of the lower montane forest belt is occupied by secondary spruce monoculture that has replaced the native mixed beech-fir forest. Of the upper montane forest belt only about 27 per cent remains in a pristine condition. The upper timber-line has been lowered 100–200 m over about two-thirds of its length and about a third of the forest-tundra ecotone has been destroyed. About 10 per cent of the total plant species in the park have been introduced.

Air pollution has not only eliminated many terrestrial and epiphytic lichens, but about a third of all spruce trees bear traces of withering due to acid rain.

Comparable changes in the fauna have taken place. The marmot, especially, is endangered, with only about 300 individuals remaining. Despite official protection, the marmot is still poached for its lard, which is supposed to have medicinal properties. The otter (*Lutra lutra*), chamois (*Rupicapra rupicapra*), lynx (*Lynx lynx*), amongst others, face extinction. The insect fauna also have been seriously disturbed, and nutrient loading of fresh water bodies, especially alpine lakes, has seriously unbalanced their natural ecosystems.

Finally, tourist refuse has become a serious problem.

Conclusion

It is interesting to note that in August 1989, following a stiff legal struggle, Bieszczady National Park, at the eastern end of the Polish Carpathians, was tripled in size. This ended an effort to establish a major ski resort comprising a residential city with 5 000 beds for tourists, plus infrastructure for staff. Plans are also being developed to create an international park which will straddle the frontiers with Czechoslovakia and the former USSR. The Polish Tourist Society has been very instrumental in these developments (Dabrowski, 1991).

Thus, while serious management problems remain, the most intractable being pollution from sources outside the mountain region and heavy tourist pressures, it is remarkable that a country of Poland's political and economic fragility has been able to demonstrate such outstanding leadership in mountain ecosystem preservation, to the point of natural habitat reconstruction. This is a critical point for Mountain Agenda 1992, and UNCED as a whole: as a powerful international mountain network and agenda is established, so too can such success be enlarged and proliferated. ■

Figure 5.13: *The Spanish Pyrenees*

The shrinking of mountain glaciers has provided dramatic evidence of climate change, while on a longer timescale, glaciated valleys the world over show how climates have changed in individual regions, Central Pyrenees Spain

The Pyrenees

The Pyrenees, extending approximately 500 km from the Bay of Biscay southeastward to the Cape of Creus on the Mediterranean, constitute a topographic barrier between France and Spain (latitudes 42 to 43 degrees N and longitudes 2 degrees W to 3 degrees E). With the natural timber line at approximately 2 100 m (in the central region), this mountain chain reaches its highest level at 3 404 m (Pico de Aneto) which is moderate when compared to the Alps or the Himalaya. Nevertheless, the Pyrenees form a unique situation where Atlantic continental influences merge with Mediterranean components, resulting in a strong west–east gradient imposed upon a pronounced north–south topographic asymmetry. Because the axis lies oblique to the westerly wind belts, Atlantic storms penetrate from the northwest and their influence progressively weakens towards the southeast. The cool northern, or French, slope is steep due to its pronounced glacial morphology, with late-Cenozoic moraine complexes descending to 500 m. In contrast, the gradual southern, or Spanish, slope is sheltered from the northwestern Atlantic air masses, making this region warmer and more conducive to grain-based Mediterranean cultivation techniques. Here, human settlements are usually located on the broad interfluves of steep V-shaped fluvial valleys which occur because glacial erosion during the Ice Ages did not extend below 1 000 m. This variability in climate and topography has produced a marked diversity in the distribution of plants and animals and a variety of human adaptations to the resource base (Figure 5.13; Puigdefabregas, 1990: 197).

With the main passes located on either end of the chain close to the coast, each area has developed rather autonomously, under the political influences of their respective national governments. The Spanish side has experienced rapid social, economic, and ecological changes only in the last three decades, characterized by outmigration, agricultural abandonment and the introduction of modern technology. The French region has evolved more gradually, although ore-mining exploitation and tourist development have scarred the mountain landscape (Garrido, 1991: unpub.). This diverse ecological and historical development, characteristic of the mountain range, makes a comprehensive account of the environmental situation difficult. Nevertheless, an examination of the Central Spanish Pyrenees will

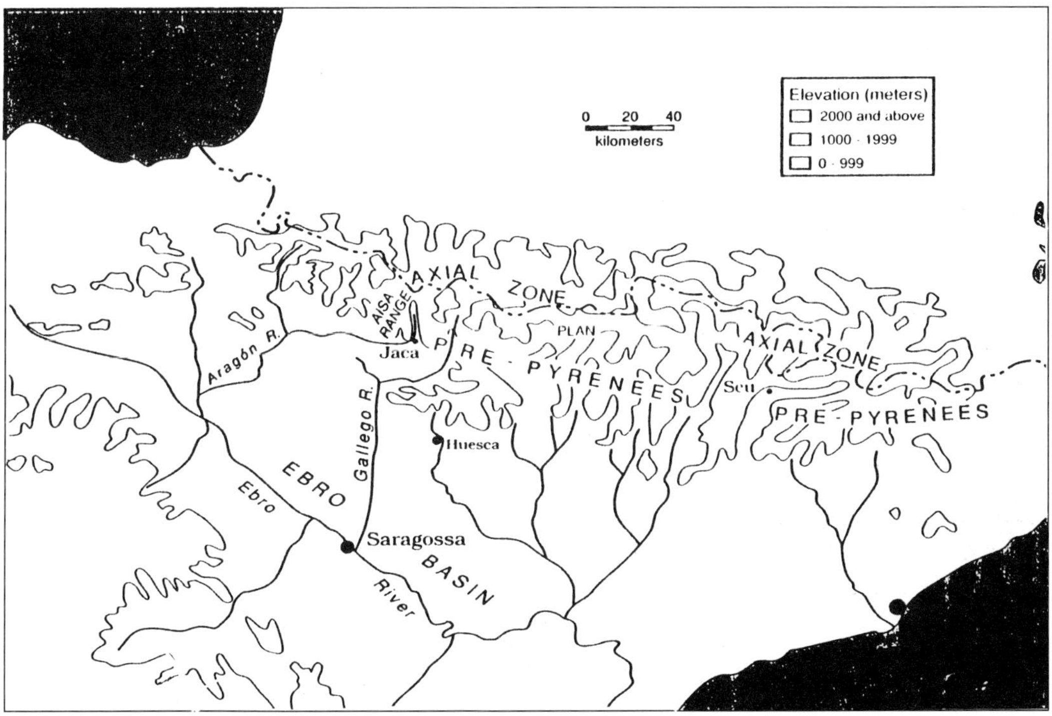

illustrate some of the common components affecting the region as a whole and should shed light on possible solutions.

The earliest forms of human adaptation to the Pyrenean environment were hunting and gathering, with pastoralism developing by about 500 AD in the Ebro Basin. Between 800 and 1000 AD these Mediterranean peoples began to migrate into the highlands to escape Muslim domination and to expand their agricultural activities. This highland area, supporting fine-textured soils (Eocene flysch, marls, and Oligocene clays) is highly erosive and difficult to work (Puigdefabregas and Fillat, 1990: 64) . Therefore, the inhabitants adapted to this low-energy mountain environment by developing an integrated system of grain cultivation combined with transhumance of the *inverse type*: the people lived in the highland valleys and grazed their flocks in the high mountain pastures in the summer and in the saline fields of the Ebro Basin in the winter (Puigdefabregas, 1990: Garcia-Ruiz and Lasanta-Martinez, 1990: 272). The main breed of sheep (*Rasa aragomesa*) was well suited to this pattern of resource use: its long legs, gregarious behaviour, and ability to thrive on short and dry pasture rendered it adaptable to steep slopes, alpine pastures, and the lowlands in the Ebro Valley, or the fallow areas following the harvesting of grain crops. Sheep were the main tool for interconnecting mountain subsystems by allowing maximum utilization of limited resources on a vertical scale, especially in light of population pressure. Furthermore, the wool economy provided a cash reserve in the case of catastrophic events, while the manure was used in the often arid environment (Puigdefabregas and Fillat, 1990: 66-67).

Risk-spreading adaptation ensured the success of this traditional integrated montane system. Crop diversification under different conditions, for instance, allowed the areas of cultivation to extend along sunny slopes of the flysch hills (rye), the lower reaches of the piedmonts and terraces (oats), and the outer edges of the valleys (wheat and barley). Also, wet years favoured terrace crops, while dry years favoured valley-bottom crops. Because cereal cropping was closely integrated with livestock husbandry, each village had grain fields grouped into two areas divided by a ridge or a stream; one was cultivated and the other was left fallow, opened to free grazing. The sheep provided the main source of manure (ashes of some leguminous bushes, such as *Genista scorpuis* were added) and germination of grains after harvest provided the main pasture in autumn. Because grain cropping in mountains accentuates soil erosion, terracing and water diversion reduced the risks but increased the dependency on labour. Two field types existed: the permanent fields which were subject to yearly crop/fallow rotation, and marginal fields where shifting agriculture was practised (*articas*). Once again, the latter may be identified as an adaptation to assure the population surplus necessary for the construction of conservation structures (trails, field walls, irrigation systems) and for coping with disasters, such as wars and sudden mortality of sheep (Puigdefabregas and Fillat, 1990: 67-69).

The traditional, labour-intensive society aimed to integrate all elements of the ecosystem to maintain a stable balance between population, resources and livestock. Unfortunately, the Spanish Pyrenees began to experience pronounced economic marginalization beginning in the 1950s and escalating by the 1960s. This led to the development of new structures of exploitation. Increased urbanization, better communication, and new technology triggered a mass rural exodus. Population densities fell from 10–15 people/km^2 at the beginning of this century to a present-day figure of 5 people/km^2 (Puigdefabregas and Fillat, 1990: 70). As with other temperate latitude mountain areas afflicted by population pressure (eg. the French Alps in the 19th century), outmigration and agricultural abandonment has led to mass wasting and extensive erosion, while modern enterprises, such as cattle grazing, hydroworks and tourism, are proving to be maladapted to the local resource constraints. As a result, the area of the Central Pyrenees is experiencing a decline in total population but an increase in broad-scale environmental degradation.

Due to the shortage of human resources, the traditional social organization began to disintegrate and, in place, management systems more adapted to the new demographic structure were introduced. Maintenance of drainage systems, terrace walls, and sheep management required an abundant supply of cheap labour. As old cereal fields were abandoned, mass wastage resulted from collapsed terrace walls and destroyed drainage systems. With improved means of transport and the buying of large quantities of fodder and cereal from other regions, cultivation became unprofitable (Garcia-Ruiz and Lasanta-Martinez, 1990: 272-273). Furthermore, the irrigation development in the Ebro lowlands resulted in a shortage of winter

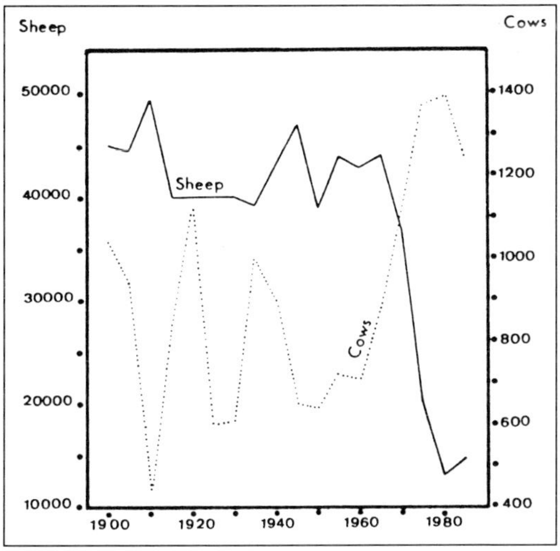

Figure 5.14: *Livestock changes in the Anso Valley*

Figure 5.15: *Land uses of the cultivated area in (A) 1957 and (B) 1981. The diagram below (C) shows the change of the old cereal fields (1957) into new land uses in 1981*

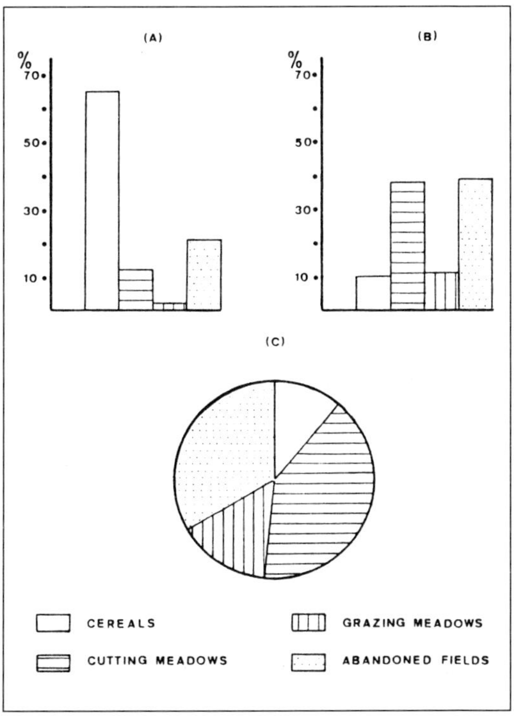

grazing grounds, thereby eliminating transhumance (Figure 5.14; Garcia-Ruiz and Lasanta-Martineż, 1990: 275). In turn, cattle grazing was introduced in the Pyrenees and this continued livestock pressure on high-mountain pastures contributed to the leaching of the upper soil layers, inducing the spread of mycotrophic low-quality plants, such as *Nardus stricta* or *Calluna vulgaris* (Puigdefabregas and Fillat, 1990: 70). As the reliance on sheep shifted to a cattle economy with an intensive forage-cropping agriculture in the valleys, the old grain fields above 1 000 m were transformed into meadows; however, the lower altitudes, hot summers and poor soils limited the transfer to irrigated agriculture, like alfalfa fields, used as a successful change-over technique (Puigdefabregas and Fillat, 1990: 71, Figure 5.15; Garcia-Ruiz and Lasanta-Martinez, 1990: 274).

Because the land-use system in low-energy mountain lands is complex, the introduction of non-rural activities, such as tourism and hydroworks, furthered the deterioration of the traditional, subsistence network and environmental stress. Beginning in the 1960s summer and especially winter tourism resulted in the take-over of land previously designated for winter food production. Winter grazing declined and hillslope abandonment accelerated. In turn, cattle farmers became more involved in the service sector (hotels, commerce, and retailing) and less engaged in slope management. An interesting study reveals a negative correlation between hotel vacancies and cattle production units per township. The most developed tourist areas are the least involved in livestock breeding; exemplifying the incompatibility between the two activities (Garcia-Ruiz and Lasanta-Martinaz,1990: 277-278).

Hydroworks, such as dam-building for water regulation of the irrigated plains and hydroelectricity, are another modern endeavour which has a detrimental impact on the mountain environment. Like the traditional mode of transhumance, cattle raising requires a balance between the highly productive meadows and the extensive pastures. The construction of dams and the resulting reservoirs destabilizes this land-use system by drowning villages and flooding fertile valleys where winter food reserves are grown (Tena Valley is the best example of a region exploited by tourism and dam construction [Garcia-Ruiz and Lasanta-Martinez, 1990: 279]). Not only has the traditional, subsistence structure disintegrated because of the inputs of modernization but the incompatibility between these new factors of exploitation has placed even greater pressure on the mountain ecosystem.

The present vegetation cover illustrates the extent of environmental stress. The original oak forests have been replaced largely by herbs and shrubs of the Euro-Siberian and Mediterranean varieties, which are most adaptable to disturbed sites. Likewise, grasslands occur in many disturbed areas *(Brachipodium ramosum, Festuca ovina, Koeleria vallesiana, Aphyllantes monspelliensis,* and *Genista scorpio),* while bushy vegetation characteristic of continental climates dominates also *(Buxus sempervirens, Juniperus communis,* and *Echinospartum horridum).* The *Pinus sylvestris* forests, underlain by calcareous rocks, often display a sub-Mediterranean understorey, which is considered a consequence of human disturbance of the natural biogeographical boundary (Gallart and Clotet-Perarnau: 1990, 219).

Vegetation change reveals the extensive pressure of human activities, past and present. This evidence, combined with the increasing lack of coordination among the different production modes integrated into the valley system, has led to the need for an urgent examination of new resource management techniques. Reforestation has been the preferred method used for resuscitating marginal regions associated with land abandonment and excessive erosion (Ortigosa, et al., 1990: 288). Because most of the human exploitation in the Central Pyrenees occurred on the mid- and high-valley slopes and in the south on shaded slopes, recovery of these abandoned lands is difficult due to extensive stony ground and lack of water-retaining properties of the soils. Nevertheless, the preferred tree species *(Pinus nigra* and *Pinus sylvestris)* are adaptable to the Pyrenean environment, where natural pine forests do exist (Ortigosa, et al., 1990: 282). Most reforested areas (70 per cent) are located below 1 100 m and approximately half (44 per cent) lie between 800 and 1 100 m, the region which experienced the most intensive exploitation. Reforestation effectiveness decreases with an increase in slope gradient (gradients of less than 10 per cent represent 42 per cent of the total). Reforestation on dam sites is aimed at reducing the sediment accumulation in the reservoir and thus prolonging the useful life of the dam (Ortigosa, et al., 1990: 284).

Although reforestation is geared towards ecological regeneration, socio-economic repercussions often counter the initial, intended aims. Land-use and grazing restrictions after plantation further accelerate outmigration. In turn, the growth of ungrazed *Brachypodium spp.* and other mat grasses increases the risk of fire, while lack of terrace maintenance enhances gullying or mass wastage by increasing infiltration rates. Also, slow-growing plantations on sunny slopes become endemic areas of the pine caterpillar *(Taumoetopoea pitiocampa)* with attendant major infestations (Puigdefabregas and Fillat, 1990: 70). Reforestation may alleviate the immediate problem of forest depletion. However, the negative impacts on the local people, such as the reduction in pasture area and quality of cattle fodder, has led to a reorganization of cattle grazing and subsequently, accelerated the population drift; both of these are correlated with land abandonment and erosion (Ortigosa, et al., 1990: 288).

The Pyrenees exemplify how population decrease and the incompatibility of modern activities lead to a deterioration of the highland ecosystem. As people abandon their subsistence life-styles, neglected lands are prone to erosion. Furthermore, the impact of modern industries places an enormous stress on the environment, one which cannot easily be alleviated. This situation shows that simply removing the source of human impact will not necessarily lead to recovery; rather, careful examination is required to instil unique solutions fitting the precise circumstances. One of the main challenges of contemporary mountain management is to incorporate the traditional notion of land-use efficiency with the retention of a minimum population number for conserving the present production structures (Puidefabregas and Fillat, 1990: 71). Only then can human activity continue with the environment relatively stable and the well-being of the people who live in the mountains respected. These general problems, of course, are exacerbated by the evolution of traditional independent or semi-independent ethnic groups, communities, and national minorities in hitherto much more isolated mountain regions. The Spanish Pyrenees are no exception, with the central government having to contend, not only with the Basque independence movement, but also the separatism of the Catalonians. Andorra remains a remarkable and special feature of this rapidly evolving mountain scene. Finally, the European Economic Community will likely affect the development of Pyrenean resource-use issues with increasing urgency in the future. ■

Sierra Nevada, USA

The Sierra Nevada range is an example of the types of environmental impacts that are common to most major mountain areas in North America (USA and Canada). Practically all have experienced a similar history of human impact, beginning with fur trapping, mining, especially gold and silver, and logging. Water diversions and hydroelectricity development followed. The most recent impacts are large- scale two-season mass tourism, and especially skiing.

The Sierra Nevada (latitudes 35 degrees to 41 degrees N; longitudes 118 degrees to 121 degrees W) is the longest, highest unbroken mountain range in the continental United States (Figure 5.16; Lantis et al., 1989: 415). The 640 kilometre-long stretch of mountain territory is slipped and tilted to create what is called a depressed "hinge" in California's Central Valley with gradual western slopes and a steep eastern upthrust high over the Nevada desert. The general elevation of the crestline is highest in the south (Mount Whitney, 4 414 m, is the highest mountain in the continental USA) and declines gradually northward to around 2 740 m. At the northern end of the range in the vicinity of Lake

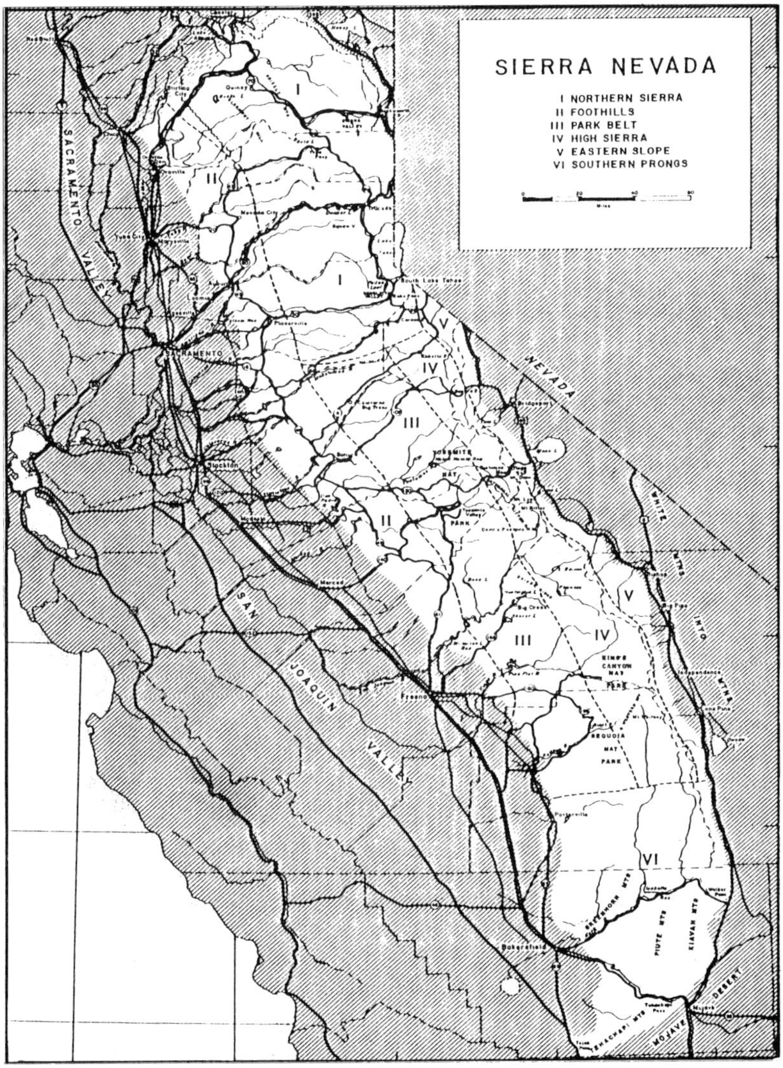

Figure 5.16: The Sierra Nevada can be considered to consist of five areas

Tahoe summits rarely exceed 3 045 m (Johnston, 1970: 3). The upper timber-line is irregular but in general it trends from about 3 500 m in the south to cover the summits at 2 740 m in the north (Arno, 1984: 135).

Covering 5.18 million ha, these mountains contain three national parks and eight national forests. These national forests account for 25 million visitor-days annually, which is one-eighth of the recreation use of all national forests in the nation. The Forest Service's Tahoe Basin Management Unit, which comprises parts of several national forests, alone records 2.8 million visitor-days a year, and Douglas Strong in his book *Tahoe, An Environmental History*, claims that the lake is visited by more people than any other natural scenic wonder of similar size in the United States (Palmer, 1988: ix-x, 46). In addition to recreational uses, timber harvesting, cattle grazing, dams, diversions of water, mining, and urban development are human activities that continue to make heavy demands on the limited resources of this diverse mountain environment. Unfortunately, the high concentration of human disturbance is not new. Indians, European explorers and missionaries, and early settlers left their imprint on the original landscape of the Sierra Nevada and, in essence, paved the way for the environmental degradation currently taking place.

Due to their small numbers, the Indians' impact was relatively insignificant although they used fire to clear brushlands in order to promote the growth of bulbous-rooted, seed-bearing plants and as a means of forcing out small animals to make their capture for meat and pelts easier; the fires were lit at intervals and only the small trees were cleared while the large trees were left standing (Storer, 1963: 35). By only extracting the resources for their subsistence needs and providing suitable conditions for regeneration, they did not drastically alter the ecological balance.

Spanish missionaries during the late 18th and early 19th century were responsible for the first major intrusions to the natural flora. The unique Californian flora composed of perennial and annual wild grasses and flowers was invaded by foreign varieties that arrived in the wool of sheep, in hay carried aboard ships for cattle feed, in droppings of domestic animals, in clothing, on implements, and mixed with seeds of garden crops. The constant trampling by large numbers of domestic sheep and cattle proved to be more destructive than that by wild animals and because the introduced annuals evolved over thousands of years in direct association with domestic grazing pressures, these foreign varieties had an advantage over the native species (Johnston, 1970: 9-11). Soon the exotic plants spread into the native vegetation. This invasion, combined with the extensive grazing practices, permanently transformed the Sierra Nevada foothills.

The largest influx of human settlement, however, occurred in the mid-1800s when gold was first discovered in the Mother Lode region (a 160 km stretch along the western foothills no higher than 305 m: the actual Mother Lode mine is located at 39 degrees 24 minutes N and 121 degrees 13 minutes W). The early hydraulic mining techniques used high pressure water jets to slough down hillsides and expose the gold-bearing quartz. The scars are still visible today along the Gold Run of Interstate 80 and California Highway 49. Another destructive practice involved mining gravel from creek beds, first with wooden troughs and later with large dredgers. The debris was discarded along the stream bottoms or as huge mounds of boulders on the embankments; these disfigurements are still evident today (Storer, 1963: 35-6).

The gold rush instigated the establishment of major enterprises in the region, such as timber production, livestock grazing, hunting and fishing. Initially, the ever-growing needs of the towns, comprised mostly of miners and their families, supported the lumber industry (Johnston 1970: 215). The lower western slopes were readily accessible and, therefore, logged most intensively. Controlled fires were often used at intervals in order to forestall the usual forest succession. The young hardwood trees were killed and the forest floor was opened to pine seedlings. However, many times the seedlings were either eaten or damaged by small animals and in turn the diversity of tree species was progressively reduced (Storer, 1963: 36).

By the 1860s the big Sugar and Jeffery pines of the Tahoe Basin were sought out because the First Continental Railroad was under construction.

Transportation of these logs proved difficult and the outcome was increasingly damaging. Either logs were moved via skid roads made of logs themselves down the eastern side or the sawmills were often located along a river front as in Truckee. The timber congested the river and the residual sawdust silted the streams, resulting in the destruction of spawning beds and the virtual extinctions of Lahontan cutthroat and the Tahoe trouts (Johnston, 1970: 216-217).

Overgrazing also devastated the watersheds by lowering the protective vegetation cover which inhibits downstream erosion. While the assimilation of the Swiss-style system, which consists of taking the cattle to the mountain meadows in the spring and returning to the lowland in autumn, allowed for the maximum exploitation of the high mountain grasslands, the short growing season meant recovery was slow and damage was permanent. As grazing occurred at increasingly higher altitudes, the natural evolution from meadow to forest was altered because the enhanced erosion by the hooves of the migrating livestock facilitated invasion by ferns and unpalatable weeds, further inhibiting natural succession (Storer, 1963: 37-41).

Fishermen and hunters also exploited the abundant variety of aquatic life and wildgame. Commercial fishermen extracted tons of trout from Lake Tahoe and collected vast amounts of trout eggs in the adjacent tributaries to be sent to other areas. This bounty did not last long. By 1916 commercial trout fishing stopped (Johnston, 1970: 218). Unfortunately, hunting for sport or profit continued and many wildlife species became endangered. The grizzly bear, which was native to the western slope, became extinct in 1924. Coyotes, wildcats, wolverines and martens, also originally common to the Sierra Nevada, were reduced to small numbers due to overhunting (Storer, 1963: 39).

Although the past inhabitants of the Sierra Nevada left permanent disfigurements on the mountain terrain and changes in the ecological balance, ongoing contemporary human activities continue to place the region in danger. Water diversion, transportation systems, and recreational use are components of the rapid urban development currently taking place. They not only have transformed the landscape, as did the earlier activities, but have also had irreversible biological effects.

Dams and artificial lakes have been constructed and continue to be proposed. On Forest Service land alone in the Sierra Nevada 467 dams have been built and the watersheds supply 130 municipal water systems; both of these extinguish other potential uses and wildlife in those streams (Palmer, 1988: 74). The most controversial reservoir is located in Hetch Hetchy Valley north of Yosemite. This area was acquired by San Francisco in 1907 for its water supply and resulted in one of the first major environmental struggles led by preservationists like John Muir (Storer, 1963: 42). A similar scenario developed in the Owens Valley where an aqueduct diverts the Sierra water south to Los Angeles. Pacific, Gas and Electric Company capitalizes on the hydroelectric power plants in the North Fork of the Feather River at the expense of the salmon runs. However, the problem of erosion has multiplied the detrimental effects associated with this form of exploitation. For example, 21 m of mud residual lies underwater behind the Pacific, Gas and Electric Company's Rock Creek hydroelectric facility. Similarly, in the Plumas National Forest 30 per cent of the water is so fouled by erosion that it no longer meets state quality objectives (*Sacramento Bee*, 9 June 1991: A4). In this way, valleys vanish, drainage networks are changed and aquatic life, in turn, is placed in jeopardy due to this water diversion and inefficient hydroworks.

Recently established industry may produce adverse biological effects, many of which are not easily noticed by the casual observer, but the initial entrepreneurial endeavours continue to present a threat to the region and their impact is highly visible and extremely detrimental. Logging continues on public land, 60 per cent of which is designated as "marginal", while an estimated 6.38 million m^3 of timber is either dead or dying, victim of air pollution, drought, or disease. From 1980 to 1989 the amount of wood cut from private and public lands in the Sierra jumped from 2.24 million m^3 to 3.72 million m^3 and the resulting logging roads comprise more than 30 400 km (about three-quarters the distance around the world) (*Sacramento Bee*, 11-12 June 1991: A10-11). Cattle grazing also is conducted precariously, frequently unconfined so that the wildlife habitat is damaged. In the national forests of the Sierra Nevada more than 1 784 585 ha are allotted to grazing, and in 1984, 32 019 cattle and 21 808 sheep grazed here for a total of 162 056 animal unit months (one AUM is one month of grazing by one cow, one horse, or five sheep over six months of age). No other activity in the mountains, or for that matter in the USA, uses as much land (Palmer, 1988: 193). These modes of decreasing the protective vegetation cover, that is, logging and grazing, lead to obvious soil loss and downstream erosion many times higher than normal (*Sacramento Bee*, 9 June 1991: A5). As lush forested regions are degraded, reservoirs become fouled, hydroelectric facilities damaged, and aquatic life reduced.

In addition to the extraction of valuable resources for the increased demand of the human population in the lower elevations, the establishment of a rapid transportation network makes the mountains readily accessible. The construction of roads and highways through dense forests allows for more direct sunlight and warmth; therefore, plants finding these conditions favourable adapt and proliferate while the ones requiring shade die. In addition the scraping of the sides of the road removes the plants already present and other species that succeed in disturbed soil thrive (Storer 1963: 40). This phenomenon is exhibited throughout the road network of the Sierra Nevada and is shown by the thick, dense pine tree cover along the highways. The vegetation cover is not only altered as a result of construction, but also is continually under pressure, due to vehicle maintenance. Carbon dioxide emissions from automobiles and the sodium chloride applied to highways as a de-icing agent severely damage vegetation, especially conifers. Studies indicate that de-icing salt causes damage as far as 18 m from the road but the most severe impact occurs within 5 m (Tahoe Regional Planning Agency, 1982: 31).

Along these same lines, industrial pollution and vehicle exhaust from the neighbouring Central Valley is creating a high acidic component in precipitation which is released onto land in the form of snow in the mountains. Because almost all the drainage networks funnel into lakes during snow melt, water contamination results in the loss of aquatic life and an increase in algae regeneration

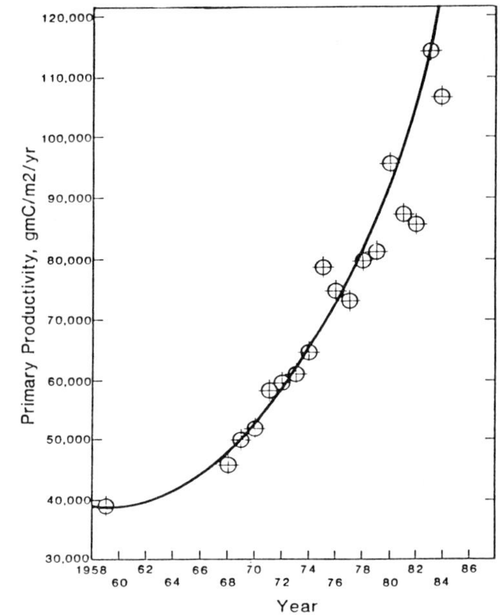

Figure 5.17: *Open water phytoplankton growth in Lake Tahoe* (Source:Tahoe Research Group 1985)

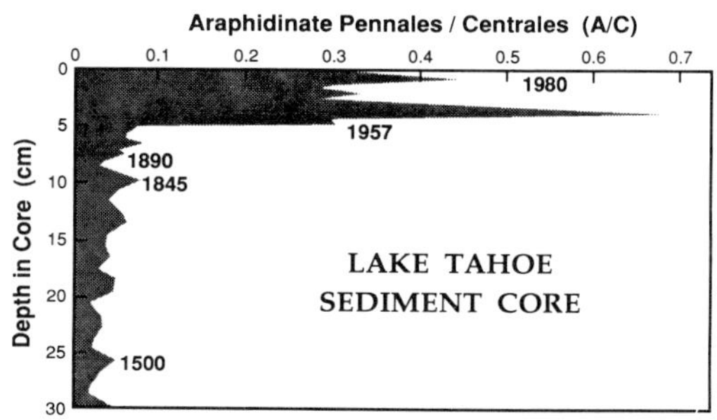

Figure 5.18 *Diatom algae ratio in Lake Tahoe*

Figure 5.19: *Lake Tahoe average annual transparency*

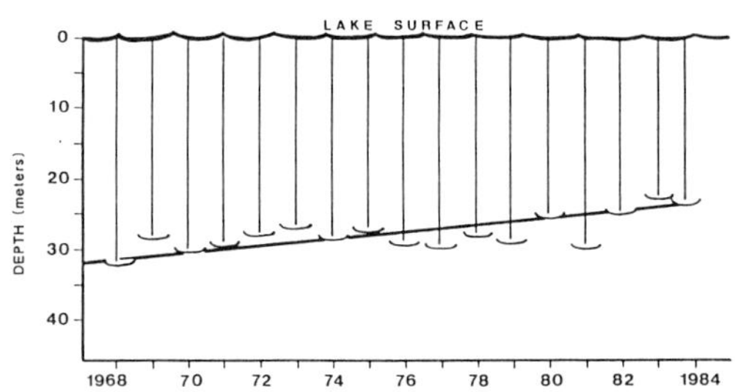

(Melack, 1983: 20). This transformation is most evident in the great lake itself, where depth visibility is rapidly decreasing. Crude statistics best illustrate Lake Tahoe's precarious situation.

Lake Tahoe is 19.3 km wide and 34.7 km long, with a surface area of 500 km^2 and holding 156 km^3 of water. The present mean depth of 313 m, with a maximum of 505 m, makes it the tenth deepest lake in the world. The average annual outflow of water is about 221.4 million m^3 and the 63 separate watersheds drain the basin directly into the lake, while one stream, the Truckee River, is the only outlet (Tahoe Regional Planning Agency, 1982: 8). Despite these grand dimensions, Lake Tahoe and the surrounding basin are showing detrimental signs resulting from human activity. For example, Tahoe Basin frequently exceeds the federal and state limits set on carbon monoxide levels in the United States. Carbon monoxide increased from 15.4 in 1981 to 16.3 ppm in 1985, when the Federal carbon monoxide standard was set at 11.3 ppm (recorded along the Highway 50 corridor on the South Shore during an 8-hour period). Because these pollutants entering the lake from the air contribute to the nutrient pool available to algae growth, Lake Tahoe's annual algae growth has increased from 35 g $C/m^2/yr$ in 1959 to 105 g $C/m^2/yr$ in 1984, with peak years of growth in 1975, 1980, and 1983 followed by brief periods of decline (Figures 5.17 and 5.18; Goldman, 1989: 5–7). More specifically, between 1970 and 1978 nutrients from erosion increased by 20 per cent , and algae grew by 150 per cent. From 1969 to 1983 freefloating algae doubled, increasing at an average annual rate of 5.5 per cent (Palmer, 1988: 54). Thus, Lake Tahoe's depth visibility is decreasing rapidly to a greenish tone. With the present clarity loss rate of about 0.4 m per year, Lake Tahoe has already lost more than 10 m of transparency over the last 30 years, and a straight line projection predicts that the lake could lose most of its transparency in forty years (Figure 5.19; Goldman, 1989: 27).

Figure 5.20: *Housing and population growth. Tahoe Basin since 1959*

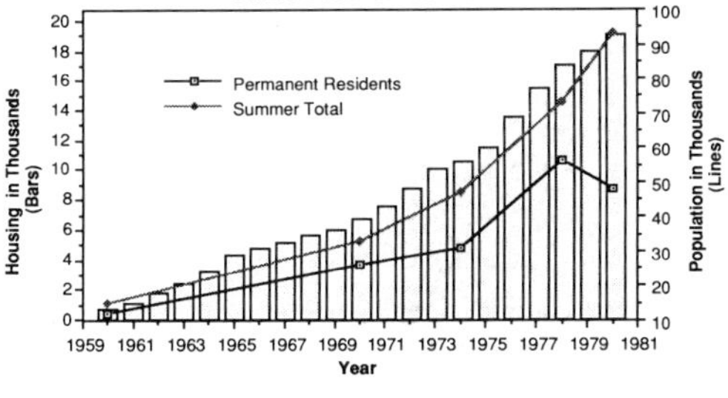

Lake Tahoe may appear green but the bluish tone of the trees in the basin indicates the extent of the air pollution associated with urbanization. Tahoe basin population has risen dramatically from about 10 000 in 1959 to 93 000 in 1980 (Figure 5 20; Goldman, 1989: 4). In turn, housing construction to accommodate these people has increased, making this region the most heavily developed area in the Sierra Nevada (Byron, 1986: 4). Consequently, urbanization has reduced the total hectares of marsh lands by 75 per cent, meadows by 50 per cent and riparian zones by 35 per cent according to the Western Federal Regional Council's Environmental Assessment; in other words, 1 400 hectares of natural stream zones or 12 per cent of the total (Tahoe Regional Planning Agency, 1982: 31, 84). Because tourism supports a large portion of the economy, much of the construction is geared towards visitor accommodation and recreational facilities. The average daily visitation is 33 000, in comparison to Yosemite Valley which has 20 000 people a day yet in a smaller space. Tourists can pick from 13 000 motel and hotel units within the greater basin area; South Shore, alone, houses 33 000 people and sleeps 9 000 at a given time (Palmer 1988: 46). Not only does the construction of recreational facilities, such as the clearing of vast hillsides for ski slopes like Squaw Valley, or the building of huge casino hotels like Harvey's South Lake Tahoe, destroy the natural landscape but once the urban visitors enter the region via rapid transit, their activities almost inevitably cause environmental damage. Wood burning stoves and car exhausts contribute to the high levels of airborne toxic chemicals. Hiking trammels the vegetation and increases soil erosion. With more people comes an increase in the tendency for litter accumulation and more fires caused by camp fires carelessly left unattended.

Regardless of the economic, political, or social motivation, industry, water diversion, and resorts all affect the native plant and animal species and change the natural landscape. For instance, at least four plant species are candidates for endangered species status *(paucifructus, Lewisia pygmaea longipetala, Draba asterophora v. macrocarpa,* and *Draba asterophora v. asterophora)* and one is already endangered *(Rorippa subumbellata)* (Tahoe Regional Planning Agency, 1982: 29). Four animal species, the American bald eagle, the peregrine falcon, the great grey owl and the wolverine, are officially endangered, while the foothill yellow-legged frog, the harlequin duck and the common loon are all slowly vanishing from their native habitat in the Sierra (*Sacramento Bee*, 11 June 1991: A12). Fortunately, conservation measures to combat the long history of environmental damage are slowly under way. Agencies and organizations are being established in order to allow for more public involvement in planning and management. For instance, the Tahoe Regional Planning Agency is among the many organizations which partake in the management of the region, along with the National Forest Service. A five-year moratorium on all new building is in effect in Tahoe, with only 300 permits allocated since 1987 in the Basin (League to Save Lake Tahoe, 25 July 1991: telephone interview). Hunting, fishing and hiking are also regulated by the acquisition of permits. Logging on state and federal lands is by selective cutting which takes out only a limited number of mature trees so that the open, sunlit places allow the small seedlings to grow; or "salvage logging", which is aimed at dead and dying timber (*Sacramento Bee*, 11 June 1991: A11). Perhaps the sudden concern for renewal and regeneration indicates that many people today are beginning to realize John Muir's declaration: "when you try to pick out anything by itself, you find it hitched to everything else in the universe" (Johnston, 1970: 239).

In conclusion it is emphasized that unsustainable resource use in the Sierra Nevada has produced major conservational disputes. The early work of John Muir and the founding of the Sierra Club in 1892 led to the establishment of Yosemite National Park, now famous worldwide. But the very success of this spectacular natural heritage has resulted in overuse and actual urbanization in the Yosemite Valley, its core area. Other particular pressures on the natural environment are the growth of Los Angeles and its insatiable demand for water and the transformation of the Central Valley from a semi-arid region into one of the most productive agricultural regions in the nation. Both of these developments require the extraction and diversion of vast amounts of water, primarily from the Sierra Nevada. The production of rice in the Central Valley (now one of the world's major rice-exporting regions) is only possible because of heavy federal and state subsidies of large-scale water diversions. This progressive development of large-scale agri-business dependent on mountain water is also leading to accelerating use of chemical fertilizers and pesticides with its attendant impacts on soil quality. It is unlikely that the present system will be sustainable over the next two or three decades. With the continued explosion of the population of California, now in excess of 36 million and growing at the rate of 2.6 per cent per annum, rational resource-use policies are urgently needed. The first step for this is more effective public education. ■

White avalanches bring death and destruction; they are also objects of great beauty. The example in this photograph is travelling at speeds of up to 160 km/hr

The Scottish Highlands

Background and context

Most of Scotland is upland in character and land use, but it is the highlands that command wider attention and interest for their mountainous qualities. The Scottish Highlands are the fragments of ancient fold mountain belts. Although they are modest in extent and vertical scale when compared with the geologically younger great ranges, they have great beauty and importance for recreation and conservation. But their future is not secure and the story of the pressures on this small hill range, close to urban populations, has general lessons for mountain conservation.

The scenic quality of the Highlands is founded on geological variety. But the low light of northern latitudes, the changeable weather patterns of an oceanic climate and the bareness of these hills all contribute to an austere northern beauty. Most of the original native tree cover has been lost through human action, but the tree line is low, and in the north and west it drops close to sea level, a measure of the harshness of the oceanic climate, which on high ground is quasi arctic in character. This arises from a compressed altitudinal zoning of climatic influence, so that with their modest elevation (most summits are around 1 000 m) there is high ecological sensitivity at relatively low altitude.

The value of these mountains to Britain's urban populations lie in their fine scenery, varied and internationally important wildlife and in providing accessible wild land. If not wilderness in an international sense, the wild land qualities of the Highlands are high, with significant blocks of roadless land where the visitor can experience challenge and hazard. These wild land qualities are important nationally, indeed beyond Britain, because there is little land of this kind left in the industrialized countries of Europe, except in Scandinavia. These wild land qualities are especially at risk from development pressures.

The social history of the Highlands is complex. This is land that has not always been without people, but chronic depopulation over the past century and a half has drawn people out of the glens (or valleys) leaving significant areas without or with minimal resident populations. The sequence of events in this story has left behind locally a strong sense of historical injustice that the people were dispossessed of their land and their local culture eroded.

For some people, part of this sense of injury is that the dominant pattern of land ownership in the main core of the mountains is the sporting estate, that is, large tracts from 5 to 20 000 ha in private ownership and with the main land use being game shooting, mainly of red deer (*Cervus elaphus*). This use of the mountain core evolved in the 19th century as a matter of fashion, and it had its heyday in the period before the First World War. But it continues as a dominant land use and has been reinforced recently because land of this kind is not easily acquired elsewhere in an open market. A representative of a major estate agency was quoted recently (*The Times* 3 January 92) as saying "...Scotland is still regarded as one of the last places in Europe in which large areas of natural wilderness can be bought and sold."

There has been a long history of public sector investment and effort to remedy the social and economic ills of the Highlands. This endeavour has included improvement of communications; investment in hydroelectric generation; support to the social needs of the population, and development agency investment in small-scale enterprise and major industrial ventures. A major programme of afforestation–mainly with North American conifers –has been promoted; fish farming has expanded greatly at coastal sites, and tourism is promoted heavily as it is now the main economic enterprise. Agriculture–largely pastoral and mainly sheep grazing–has long been a mainstay of the local economy and social structure and it has been the main route for government support to communities, through price-support mechanisms and grants. But this is very marginal agriculture and in the wider debate about over-production and European Community policies for agriculture, its long-term viability is uncertain, especially given the parlous state of upland farming in Scotland.

Conservation has become a major land use, with voluntary conservation bodies like the National Trust of Scotland and the Royal Society for the Protection of Birds now being significant owners of prime quality land. There is a plethora of designations to protect features of historic and archaeological interest, sites of nature conservation value and also to safeguard the natural beauty of the mountains. The process of designation has led to a good deal of complaint by landowners about the imposition of restraints on the use of their land and also by

Remnants of the old Forest of Caledon which formerly covered much of the Scottish Highlands

communities which perceive that conservation designations act against development.

The essence of the problem is that these mountain lands are not able to provide financial return through the traditional land uses that can provide standards of living locally, sufficient to match those enjoyed elsewhere in Britain. Also, the rural economy is marginal to the wider British economy and increasingly to the coming changes in Europe as enterprises bear costs in distance and scale that are disadvantageous. The outcome is significant social and economic tension amongst four main sectors: first, the legitimate interests of local communities in self-advancement; second, the interests of private landowners in exclusive use of their land; third, the pressures arising from development coming on the land from outside the area; and last, the wider national interest in conserving the fine qualities of the mountains and in making them available for public recreation. The local economy can only survive through continued subvention from the wealth of the wider nation, and the cost of managing private estates also requires continued support from the personal wealth of owners.

Present status

The future of the Highlands is uncertain. The long process of attempting to revitalize the economy of the area has had modest success, but it has been a hard road with many failures Depopulation overall has been reversed recently; there is now a healthier but still fragile economy, with most employment in services–mainly in tourism. The remnants of the local Gaelic culture are showing growth and there is more confidence in communities.

There is no comprehensive audit of change in the Highlands, but there is a long record of attrition of valued landscapes and conservation interests. This comes first of all through sustained overgrazing and burning of moorland vegetation, which has suppressed regeneration of native woodland and led to degradation in the quality of herbage. In the shorter term, there have been many significant impacts on valued landscapes: from afforestation, from hydroelectric development and more recently, in the coastal areas, from fish farming. Ugly bulldozed private hill roads give easy access for game shooting, and great improvement to and expansion of the public road network has led to much easier access to the mountains, and thus to greater recreational pressures from urban populations. These recreational pressures have had little management, so that footpaths in the hills are generally in poor condition and increased numbers of people walking in the mountains have put pressures on high montane habitats. These are very easily damaged and slow to recover (if ever) in some areas. Inexorably these pressures continue, some like growth in outdoor recreation being the outcome of changing social needs and greater mobility and wealth in society. Other impacts come from continued pressures for development, or the incursion of new or displaced land uses. The expansion of forestry is a case in point. At present the pace of afforestation has slowed down because of changes to the state's incentives for planting, which have led to a loss of confidence amongst forest owners. However, afforestation is bound to expand again particularly if the decline of hill farming releases more land into this use. But a key factor is that pressures to conserve the uplands of England and Wales have led to a major restriction on conifer planting there, and it is now government policy that expansion of the productive conifer estate will be in Scotland.

In a congested country like Britain which has most of its land in committed uses, the Highlands can be seen as being empty or available for the dispersal of activities that are not acceptable in the more crowded parts of the country. This land also has resources attractive to some developers, such as hard rock for the extraction of aggregates, minerals, deep water close to shore, unpolluted environments and remoteness from large populations. Pressures for exploitation in this way are as likely as not to come from government departments, some recent examples being pressures for the use of land for new military installations and the storage of nuclear waste. There is the continued prospect of further exploitation for energy, of a renewed demand for hydroelectric power or wind power installations.

The private sporting estate is an extensive and low-key land use that could be sustainable on poor mountain lands. Financial benefits come from the letting of sport shooting to clients, many of whom come from abroad and pay well for their sport. But there are tensions here also: the numbers of red deer are judged by informed opinion to be excessive (being estimated at 300 000 plus) and needing major reduction to achieve ecological benefits. But most owners are reluctant to reduce their deer numbers. There is a continued tension also between this exclusive sport and recreation in the mountains by the public, who seek and take access to this mainly private land on an unrestricted basis.

Approaches to solutions

This is a time of considerable debate in Scotland about the future use and care of Scotland's mountains, but the debate is complex in part because of the historic legacy and because of the range of interests to be accommodated in reaching solutions. These include the four sectors mentioned earlier, namely: the local community interests, the private landowners, the external development pressures and the national interest in conserving the quality of the mountains.

The Countryside Commission for Scotland (responsible for conservation of natural beauty and provision for the enjoyment of the countryside) in 1990 issued a major report on the conservation and management of Scotland's mountain areas. This aroused a wide range of reactions, from strong support for the report's analysis and proposals, to rejection of some of the solutions, including proposals for National Parks (Scotland never having adopted this protected-area mechanism).

In parallel with the preparation of the commission's report, government decided to merge that agency with the Nature Conservancy Council for Scotland, which has major interests in the Highlands by virtue of its mandate to conserve wildlife and its chain of national nature reserves and sites of special scientific interest. The new agency–Scottish Natural Heritage–is charged to continue the functions of its two predecessor bodies and it also has a statutory function to seek that activities within its remit be undertaken in a sustainable manner.

The wider debate about conservation of the natural environment and related changes in government policy have all influenced public agencies working in mountain lands. All now in one way or another espouse a conservation message; for example, the government's forestry policy has moved on from being mainly production-oriented to a more benign, multi-purpose woodland management approach. But it is too soon to discern a track record on the delivery of these new aims and as yet there is no indication that greenery is more than a gloss on present ways of working and no recognition that a new approach must mean much less intervention in fragile upland settings.

An end to the continued attrition of the qualities of Scotland's mountains will require first and foremost a better understanding and state of consensus between local and national interests. Key elements in the striking of such a bargain are as follows:

❑ Private ownership of mountain lands has often been protective of landscape and wild land because of a conservative style of management by owners, although there have been losses to such land from ugly bulldozed roads and afforestation. But a pluralist society can no longer be satisfied that land of highest national importance can be a matter of international trade and speculation with very wealthy owners able to ignore their responsibilities to local community and custom. A mechanism is needed that provides for accountability to society by large private estates and which allows for constraints on absentee ownership.

❑ Definition of a clearer national role for the mountains has to recognize their importance in providing recreation opportunities for urban populations in outstanding settings that inspire and provide for refreshment, challenge and personal self-development. Much of the land in the core mountain areas of Scotland now has recreation as its prime use.

❑ Development in Scotland's mountain areas has been led by public agencies in government departments and a more restrained and coordinated approach is needed in future, which better respects their recreational and conservation importance and which breaks down the barriers of present sectoral public policies.

❑ The way in which public funds are expended in mountain areas needs review. At present, agriculture and development uses take the lion's share, with recreation and conservation management being underfunded. This imbalance needs adjustment and incentives for land managers should be reviewed to assist them to satisfy the wider expectations that society now has for the better care of these areas.

❑ There is a wider responsibility falling on all visitors to the mountains to be sensitive to other land use interests, to show restraint in visiting sensitive areas and, in that use, to "tread lightly". Recreational enjoyment of these lands is the underpinning to conservation. In turn, recreation and tourism play a major part now in the economy of remote rural areas. This crucial interdependence between visitors, other land users and local communities, should be fostered.

A well-publicised issue in Scottish mountain conservation has been the long debate about the future management of the Cairngorms, a proposed World Heritage area. At the heart of this debate has been a lack of positive management for conservation and recreation, notwithstanding many different and often overlapping designations applied to these mountains. The sharp edge of the debate has focused particularly on proposals to expand the ski field at Cairn Gorm, the so-called Lurcher's Gully debate. The outcome of two separate bids for this expansion has been that the government has refused to sanction development, but this has created a strong view among the local community that conservation interests are unreasonably restraining proper exploitation of local resources. The conflict has also not been helpful in a wider sense by directing the spotlight on the Cairngorms and away from other pressing issues in Scotland's mountains.

In the wake of these debates and the setting aside of proposals in the Countryside Commission's Mountain Areas Report, the government has made a bold attempt to seek consensus in the Cairngorms by setting up a working party to debate the future management. This venture involves all parties to the debate and although not without some controversy, this Working Party (and a similar one for Loch Lomond) are crucial test-beds on which to seek accommodation between national and local interests in prime mountain land. The government's intention is to seek to use the voluntary principle, that is, to avoid imposing formalized management structures and to harness local management and commitment, both private and public sector. There is much uncertainty about this approach from observers who say that the voluntary approach has been tried in the past and failed dismally to deliver secure management for such land. But the present initiative must be given fair opportunity. If it does not deliver a significant advance in protection of these mountains then the debate will be renewed. ■

References

A Report on the Wilderness Impact Study: the effects of human recreational activities on wilderness ecosystems with special emphasis on Sierra Club wilderness outings in the Sierra Nevada, Palo Alto: Consolidated Publications, 1979.

AHLMANN, H. W., *Land of Ice and Fire*, London: Kegan Paul Truber, 1938, pp. 282.

ALLEN, B., and BROOKFIELD, H., (eds.), "Frost and Drought in the Highlands of Papua New Guinea", *Mountain Research and Development*, Vol. 9, No. 3, August 1989, pp. 199-334.

ALLEN, Barbara, and BARTOLOME, James, "Cattle Grazing Effects on Understory Cover and Tree Growth in Mixed Conifer Clearcuts", *Northwest Science*, 63 (5), 1989, pp. 214-220.

ANDREWS, A. C., and COMUDON, Y., *Results of Pasture Research by the Highland Agronomy Project. Third Report*, Thai-Australian Highland Agricultural Project, Chiang Mai University, 1978, pp. 25-34.

ANDREWS, A. C., and KWAENGSOPHA, S., *The Effects of Grazing and Fertilizer on Growth of* Pinus *and* Eucalyptus *species at Pa Kia. Fourth Report*, Thai-Australian Highland Agronomy Project, 1979, pp. 63-65.

ANDREWS, A. C., "Imperata cylindrica in the Highlands of Northern Thailand:its productivity and status as a weed", *Mountain Research and Development*, Vol. 3, No. 4, November 1983, pp. 386-388.

ARMSTRONG, R. Warwick (ed.), *Atlas of Hawaii*, Honolulu: University of Hawaii Press, 1973.

ARNO, Stephen F., and HAMMERLY, Ramona P., *Timberline*, Seattle: The Mountaineers, 1984.

BIRD, J., *The Physiography of Arctic Canada (with special reference to the area south of Parry Channel)*, Baltimore: The Johns Hopkins Press, 1967.

BRADFORD, G. R., "Are Sierra Lakes Becoming Acid?" *California Agriculture*, 35, pp. 6-7.

BROOKFIELD, Harold, "Research in the Mountains of the Island of New Guinea", *Mountain Research and Development*, Vol. 11, No. 3, 1991, pp. 203-211.

BYRCYN, W. G., "The Role of Tatrzanski Park Narodowy (Tatra National Park) in the Protection of the Tatra Mountains", *Mountain Research and Development*, Vol. 12, 1992 (in press).

BYRON, Earl R., and GOLDMAN, Charles R., "Sixth Annual Report Water Year 1985", *Lake Tahoe Interagency Monitoring Program*, Davis: Tahoe Research Group/Institute of Ecology, 1986.

CALLIES, David L., *Regulating Paradise*, Honolulu: University of Hawaii Press, 1984.

CHITMAN, Vanida, "Land Use and its Relationship to Agriculture in Pangsa, Chang Rai", Conservation and Development in Northern Thailand, *Proceedings of a Programmatic Workshop on Agro- Forestry and Highland-Lowland Interactive Systems, Held at Chaing Mai, Thailand, 13-17 November 1978*, Tokyo: United Nations University, 1980, pp. 75-81.

CORLETT, R. T., "Human Impact on the Subalpine Vegetation of Mt. Wilhelm, Papua New Guinea", *Journal of Ecology*, Vol. 72, 1984, pp. 841-854.

CREIGHTON, Thomas H., *The Lands of Hawaii: their use and misuse*, Honolulu: University of Hawaii Press, 1978.

CULLINEY, John L., *Islands in a Far Sea*, Sierra Club Books: San Francisco, 1988.

DABROWSKI, P., 1991, Letter to the Editor: "Struggle to protect the Bieszczady mountain chain in Poland", *World Mountain Network Newsletter*, No. 3: 10, 1991.

DILSAVER, "Population of a Mining Town in the Sierra Nevada", *Association of Pacific Coast Geographers-Yearbook*, 45, 1983, pp. 101-115.

DINELL, Tom, "Hawaii: Planning for Paradise", *Ekistics*, Vol. 54, No. 323-324, June 1987, pp.153-57.

DONALDSON, Mike and GOOD, Kenneth, *Articulated Agricultural Development*, Brookfield: Gower Publishing Co., 1988.

ELIAS, Thomas S. (ed.), *Conservation and Management of Rare and Endangered Plants*, Sacramento: The California Native Plant Society, 1986.

FALVEY, J. L., DAVIES, R. F. J., THANYALAPPITAK, E., and MIKLED, C., *Relationship between Weight, Girth, Height, and Age of Highland Cattle. Second Report*, Thai-Australian Highland Agronomy Project, 1977, pp. 26-30.

FARQUHAR, F. P., *History of the Sierra Nevada*, Berkeley: University of California Press in collaboration with the Sierra Club, 1965.

FERGUSON, D., *Sacred cows at the Public Trough*, Bend: Maverick Publication, 1983.

FRADKIN, Philip, "Eating of the West," *Audubon*, 81(1: 3), January 1979, p. 94.

FRIDRIKSSON, S., "The Effects of Sea Ice on Flora, Fauna, and Agriculture", *Jökull*, Vol. 19, 1969, pp. 146-157.

FURBISH, David and RICE, Raymond, "Predicting Landslides Related to Clearcut Logging, Northwestern California, U.S.A.," *Mountain Research and Development*, Vol. 3, No. 3, August 1983, pp. 253-259.

GALLART, Francesc and CLOTET-PERARNAU, N., "Geomorphic Systems on the Southern Margin of the Pyrenees", *Mountain Research and Development*, Vol. 10, No. 3, August 1990, pp. 215-226.

GARCIA-RUIZ, Jose M. and LASANTA-MARTINEZ, Theodore, "Land-Use Changes in the Spanish Pyrenees", *Mountain Research and Development*, Vol. 10, No. 3, August 1990, pp. 267-279.

GIBSON, T., "Toward a Stable Low-input Highland Agricultural System: ley farming in *Imperata cylindrica* grasslands of Northern Thailand", *Mountain Research and Development*, Vol. 3, No. 4, November 1983, pp. 378-385.

GILLIESON, D., OLDFIELD, F., and KRAWIECKI, A., "Records of Prehistoric Soil Erosion from Rock-shelter Sites in Papua New Guinea", *Mountain Research and Development*, Vol. 6, No. 4, November 1986, pp. 315-324.

GOLDMAN, Charles R., "Lake Tahoe: preserving a fragile ecosystem", *Environment*, Vol. 31, No. 7, September 1989, pp. 6-11.

GORECKI, Pawel P., "Human Occupation and Agricultural Development in the Papua New Guinea Highlands", *Mountain Research and Development*, Vol. 6, No. 2, May 1986, pp. 159-166.

GRESSITT, J. L. (ed.), *Biogeography and Ecology of New Guinea*, Junk: The Hague, 1982.

GRIFFIN, David M., "Implementation Failure Caused by Institutional Problems", *Mountain Research and Development*, Vol. 7, No. 3, August 1987, pp. 250-253.

GRIFFIN, David M., *Innocents Abroad in the Forests of Nepal*, Canberra: Anutech, 1988.

GRIFFIN, David M., "Intensified Forestry in Mountain Regions", *Mountain Research and Development*, Vol. 7, No. 3, August 1987, pp. 254-255.

GROSSMAN, Lawrence S., *Peasants, Subsistence Ecology, and Development in the Highlands of Papua New Guinea*, Princeton: Princeton University Press, 1984.

GROVE, Jean M., *The Little Ice Age*, London: Methuen, 1988.

HABERLE, S. G., HOPE, G. S., and DEFRETES, Y., "Environmental change in the Baliem Valley, Montane Irian Jaya, Republic of Indonesia", *Journal of Biogeography*, Vol. 18, 1991, pp. 25-40.

HARE, F. K., *A Photo-reconnaissance Survey of Labrador-Ungava*, Ottawa: Geographical Branch Memoir, No. 6, 1959.

HILL, Russell, *California Mountain Ranges*, Billings: Falcon Press, 1984.

HUMPHREYS, Geoff S., and BROOKFIELD, Harold, "The Use of Unstable Steeplands in the Mountains of Papua New Guinea", *Mountain Research and Development*, (in press).

HURNI, Hans, and NUNTAPONG, Sompote, "Agro-forestry Improvements for Shifting Cultivation Systems: soil conservation research in Northern Thailand", *Mountain Research and Development*, Vol. 3, No. 4, November 1983, pp. 338-345.

IMHOF, E., *Die Grossen Kalten Berge von Szetschuan*, Zürich: Stiftung für alpine Forschung, 1974.

IVES, Jack D., "Landscape Change and Human Response during a Thousand Years of Climate Fluctuations and Vulcanism", *Pirineos*, Skaftafell, Southeast Iceland, 1992 (in press).

IVES, Jack D., and ANDREWS, J. T., "Studies in the physical geography of north central Baffin Island", *Geographical Bulletin*, Vol. 19, No. 5, 1963, p. 48.

IVES, Jack D., and MESSERLI, B., "Gongga Shan (7556 m) and Yulongxue (5596 m). Geological Observations in the Hengduan Mountains of Southwestern China", *Erdwissenschaftliche Forschung*, Vol. XVIII, 1984, pp. 55-77.

IVES, Jack D., "Glaciation of the Torngat Mountains, Northern Labrador", *Arctic*, Vol. 10, No. 2, 1957, pp. 67-87.

IVES, Jack D., "Northern Thailand: the Problem", Conservation and Development in Northern Thailand, *Proceedings of a Programmatic Workshop on Agro-Forestry and Highland-Lowland Interactive Systems, Held at Chaing Mai, Thailand, 13-17 November 1978*, Tokyo: United Nations University, 1980, pp. 9-12.

IVES, Jack D., "Permafrost", in Ives, Jack D., and Barry, R. G. (eds.), *Arctic Alpine Environments*, London: Methuen, 1974, pp. 159-194).

IVES, Jack D., SABHASRI, Sanga, and VORAURAI, Pisit (eds.), Conservation and Development in Northern Thailand, *Proceedings of a Programmatic Workshop on Agro-Forestry and Highland-Lowland Interactive Systems, Held at Chaing Mai, Thailand, 13-17 November 1978*, Tokyo, United Nations University, 1980.

IVES, Jack D., "Yulongxue Shan, Northwestern Yunnan, People's Republic of China: A Geological Expedition", *Mountain Research and Development*, Vol. 5, No. 4, November 1985, pp. 282-385.

IVES, Jack, and MESSERLI, Bruno, *The Himalayan Dilemma*, New York: Routledge, 1989.

JOHNS, R. J., "The Influence of Drought on Tropical Rainforest Vegetation in Papua New Guinea", *Mountain Research and Development*, Vol. 9, No. 3, August 1989, pp. 248-251.

JOHNSON, H., *The Whistles Blow No More*, Glendale: Trans-Anglo Books, 1984.

JOHNSTON, Verna R., *Sierra Nevada*, Boston: Houghton Mifflin Co., 1970.

JONAS, W. J., "The Commercial Timber Industry in Colonial Papua New Guinea", *Pacific Studies*, Vol. 8, No. 2, Spring 1985, pp. 45-60.

JUVIK, James O., and JUVIK, Sonia P.,"Mauna Kea and the Myth of Multiple Use: Endangered Species and Mountain Management in Hawaii", *Mountain Research and Development*, Fort Collins: Pioneer Impressions, Vol. 4, No. 3, August 1984, pp. 191-202.

JUVIK, James O., JUVIK, Sonia P., and HAMILTON, Larry S.,"Altitudinal Resource Zonation vs. Vertical Control: Land Use Conflict on Two Hawaiian Mountains", *Man and the Biosphere Project 6A*, Tsahkadzor, U.S.S.R., October 1-5, 1989, unpublished.

KAY, E. Alison (ed.), *A Natural History of the Hawaiian Islands*, Honolulu: University of Hawaii Press, 1972.

KENT, Noel J., *Hawaii: Islands Under the Influence*, New York: Monthly Review Press, 1983.

KING, David, and RANCK, Stephen, *Papua New Guinea Atlas*, Hong Kong: Robert Brown and Associates, 1982.

KIRCH, Patrick V., "The Impact of the Prehistoric Polynesians on the Hawaiian Ecosystem", *Pacific Science*, Vol. 36, No. 1, 1982, pp. 1-14.

KOTARBA, A., "Natural environment and landform dynamics in the Polish Tatra Mountains", *Mountain Research and Development*, Vol. 12, 1992 (in press).

KUNIT, E. and CALHOON, K., *Landscape Preservation Study for the Sierra Foothills and Low Coastal Mountain Province*, Sacramento: California Department of Parks and Recreation, 1974.

KUNSTADTER, Peter, CHAPMAN, E. C., and SABHASRI, Sanga, *Farmers in the Forest*, Honolulu: The University of Hawaii Press, 1978.

KÜNZEL, Wieland, "Ethnic and Spatial Differences in Wage-Labour Employment and in the Introduction of Coffee at Huai Thung Choa, Thailand, 1979-80", *Mountain Research and Development*, Vol. 3, No. 4, November 1983, pp. 357-362.

LAMB, D., *Exploiting the Tropical Rain Forest*, Man and the Biosphere Series, Vol. 3, Paris: Parthenon Publishing Group, 1990.

LANTIS, David M., STEINER, Rodney, and KARINEN, Arthur E., *California: the Pacific connection*, Chico: Creekside Press, 1989.

LEAGUE TO SAVE LAKE TAHOE, CONSERVATION ORGANIZATION, telephone interview: 25 July 1991.

MCCASHION, John and RICE, Raymond, "Erosion on Logging Roads in Northwestern California: how much is avoidable?", *Journal of Forestry*, Washington: Society of American Foresters.

MCKINNON, John, "A Highlander's Geography of the Highlands: mythology, process, and fact", *Mountain Research and Development*, Vol. 3, No. 4, November 1983, pp. 313-317.

MELACK, J.M., *Assessment of Acidity of Lakes and Precipitation in the Sierra Nevada*, Santa Barbara: California Resources Center, 1983.

MEULLER-DOMBOIS, Dieter, "Vegetation Dynamics and Slope Management on the Mountains of the Hawaiian Islands", *Environmental Conservation*, Vol. 15, 1988, pp. 255-260.

MIREK, Z., and PIEKOS-MIRKOWA, H., "Flora and Vegetation of the Polish Tatra Mountains", *Mountain Research and Development*, Vol. 12, 1992 (in press).

MIREK, Z., "Transformations and Threats to Nature in the Tatra National Park", *Mountain Research and Development*, Vol. 12, 1992 (in press).

MORGAN, Joseph R., *Hawaii: a geography*, Boulder: Westview Press, 1983.

MOWAT, F., *Westviking; the ancient Norse in Greenland and North America*, Boston: Little Brown, 1965.

MUIR, John (Baron, Robert ed.), *The Mountains of California*, Golden: Fulcrum, 1988.

ORTIGOSA, Luis M., GARCIA-RUIZ, Jose M. and GIL, Eustaquio, "Land Reclamation by Reforestation in the Central Pyrenees", *Mountain Research and Development*, Vol. 10, No. 3, August 1990, pp. 281-288.

PAIN, Colin F., and SCOTT, G. A., "Highland-Lowland Interactions in Enga Province, Papua New Guinea", *Mountain Research and Development*, Vol. 1, No. 1, May 1981, pp. 71-78.

PALMER, Tim, *The Sierra Nevada: a mountain journey*, Washington DC: Island Press, 1988.

PETERSON, David et al., "Growth Trends of Whitebark Pine and Lodgepole Pine in a Subalpine Sierra Nevada Forest, California, USA," *Arctic and Alpine Research*, Vol. 22, No. 3, August 1990, pp. 233-243.

PUIGDEFABREGAS, J., "Preface", *Mountain Research and Development*, Vol. 10, No. 3, August 1990, pp. 197-199.

PUIGDEFABREGAS, Juan, and FILLAT, Federico, "Ecological Adaptation of Traditional Land Use in the Spanish Pyrenees", *Mountain Research and Development*, Vol. 6, No. 1, February 1986, pp. 63- 72.

RAJAH, Ananda, "Implications of Traditional Karen Land-use Systems for the Introduction of New Cropping Systems: Some Observations from Ban Hua Lao, Huai Thung Choa, Northern Thailand", *Mountain Research and Development*, Vol. 3, No. 4, November 1983, pp. 353-356.

"Regional Mercury Assessment", California Regional Water Quality Control Board, Central Valley Region, Sacramento.

REID, Robert, *A Treasury of the Sierra Nevada*, Berkeley: Wilderness Press, 1983.

ROSETTA, N., "Herds, Herds on the Range", *Sierra*, 70, March-April 1985, pp. 43-47.

SABHASRI, Sanga, "Research and Training in Southeast Asia in Relation to Priority Areas of the Programme on the Use and Management of Natural Resources", *Conservation and Development in Northern Thailand*, Japan, The United Nations University, 1980, pp. 83-86.

SALAMONS, W., and EAGLE, A. M., "Hydrology, Sedimentology and the Fate and Distribution of Copper in Mine-related Discharges in the Fly River System, Papua New Guinea", *The Science of the Total Environment*, Vol. 97/98, 1990, pp. 315-334.

SAULEI, Simon M., "Forest Research and Development in Papua New Guinea", *Ambio*, Vol. 19, No. 8, December 1990, pp. 379-382.

SHI, Ya-feng, *Glaciological Research of the Qinghai-Xizang Plateau in China*, Proceedings, Symposium Tibet Plateau, Beijing, Vol. II, 1980, pp. 1589-1597.

SMITH, James et al., *The Sierra Ecology Project*, Denver: Division of Research of the Office of Atmospheric Resources Management, 1978, Vol. 1-4.

SMITH, Jeremy, M. B., "Vegetation Patterns in Response to Environmental Stress and Disturbance in the Papua New Guinea", *Mountain Research and Development*, Vol. 5, No. 4, November 1985, pp. 329-338.

STONE, Charles P., and SCOTT, J. Michael (eds.), *Hawaii's Terrestrial Ecosystems: preservation and management*, Honolulu: University of Hawaii, 1985.

STORER, Tracy, and USINGER, Robert, *Sierra Nevada Natural History*, Berkeley: University of California Press, 1963.

STRONG, Douglas, *Tahoe: an environmental history*, Lincoln: University of Nebraska Press, 1984.

TAHOE REGIONAL PLANNING AGENCY, *Environmental Impact Statement for the Establishment of Environmental Threshold Carrying Capacities*, May 1982.

TAHOE REGIONAL PLANNING AGENCY, *Environmental Protection Fact Sheet*, September 1986.

TERNAN, J. L., WILLIAMS, A. G., and FRANCIS, C., "Land Capability Classification in Grenada, West Indies", *Mountain Research and Development*, Vol. 9, No. 1, February 1989, pp. 71-82.

THOMAS, Graham, "Tahoe Regional Planning", *Sierra*, 60, March 1975, pp. 25-31.

THORARINSSON, S., "Iceland", Chapter 10, pp. 203-233, in Axel Somme (ed.), *The Geography of Norden*, Oslo: J. W. Cappelens Forlag, 1960.

TONNNESSEN, K., and HARTE, J., "Acid Rain and Ecological Damage: implications of Sierra Nevada lake studies", *Public Affairs Report*, 23, pp. 1-19.

VAN ROYEN, P., *The Alpine Flora of New Guinea*, Vol. 1, Vaduz: Gantner, 1980.

VORAURAI, Pisit, IVES, Jack D., and MESSERLI, Bruno, "The Huai Choa Highland Project: Status and Opportunity", Conservation and Development in Northern Thailand, *Proceedings of a Programmatic Workshop on Agro-Forestry and Highland- Lowland Interactive Systems, Held at Chaing Mai, Thailand, 13- 17 November 1978*, Tokyo: United Nations University, 1980, pp. 105-111.

WALSH, A. Crosbie, *Migration and Urbanization in Papua New Guinea: the 1980 Census*, Research Monograph No. 5, National Statistical Office, 1986.

WARNER, Richard E., "A Forest Dies on Mauna Kea", *Pacific Discovery*, Vol. 13, March-April, 1960, pp. 6-14.

WEBSTER, Paul, *Understanding the Sierra Nevada*, Auburn: Webster Publishing Co.

WOOD, Andrew W., "The Humic Brown Soils of the Papua New Guinea Highlands: A Reinterpretation", *Mountain Research and Development*, Vol. 7, No. 2, May 1987, pp. 145-156.

YOSHINO, Masatoshi M., "Local Climatological Differences between Highlands and Lowlands in Thailand", *Conservation and Development in Northern Thailand*, Japan: The United Nations University, 1980, pp. 63-74.

6

The Andes:

geoecology of the Andes

Bolivian altiplano near Lake Titicaca and Cordillera Real

Introduction

Andean subject matter is, overall, immense and very complex. In the restricted space available here the characteristics of the Andes will be best conveyed by presenting a series of vignettes. These are introduced after a general treatment of the physical-ecological basis and will provide some examples of the current types of environmental and development issues. Several major themes can be identified that are particularly germane to the Andean problematique.

1) Prior to the Spanish Conquest (AD 1532) as most anthropologists, geographers, and ethnohistorians agree, Incan and earlier societies had evolved as highly sophisticated organizations that were able to produce significant surpluses based upon traditional agriculture and husbandry. In fact, the region between present-day La Paz and Cuzco, the core areas of Tiahuanaco and Incan empires, supported more people in a state of comparative well-being than occupy the same area today in poverty.

2) Following the sudden and spectacular collapse of the Inca, massive socio-economic and administrative changes were introduced. These were accompanied by the spread of European diseases and the incorporation of European domestic animals and crops and led to a population crash and severe societal disruption that reached its nadir about AD 1800.

3) Gradual recovery of the population (1820-1920) followed by explosive growth after 1920 accelerating to the present day has resulted in massive pressure on the highland resource base to the extent of triggering the greatest series of migrations in Andean history.

4) While this migration has been influenced by many factors, the main trends are conspicuously rural to urban and highland to lowland. For the Central Andes especially, this has set in motion some of the major problems that future strategies for sustainable development will have to face. The principal components of the migration dynamic include:

a) rapid expansion of urban centres, especially Lima, with overwhelming slum development;
b) loss to the highlands of some of the youngest and most able sectors of rural communities such that, in place, underpopulation is producing another kind of environmental stress;
c) environmental impacts in both source areas (highlands) and receiving areas (lowlands);
d) severe socio-economic and political unrest generated, in part, by points (a) to (c). A final phase of these processes relates to the widespread drug wars and destabilization of large areas by guerrilla activity.

The migratory processes, clearly identified by Escobar and Beall (1982) and Baker (1982), have been exacerbated by the manner in which traditional highland society, often non-Spanish speaking, has been denigrated by both national elites and international aid and development agencies alike. Thus, traditional farming strategies, crops, and domestic animals have been ignored or under-valued in preference to cash crops and imported technologies. Camino et al. (1991 unpub.) have emphasized, however, that recent work by anthropologists, biologists, and ethnohistorians has begun to record successes in turning this situation around. For instance, it is becoming widely recognized that the hitherto abandoned Incan irrigated terraces and ridged fields can be made productive at about 10 per cent of the cost of irrigating a comparable area in the arid coastal valleys.

These issues will all be treated more fully below. It remains to define and justify a division of the vast region of the Andes into reasonably manageable units. For this purpose the original Unesco MAB-6 delineation of Northern, Central, and Southern Andes will be retained, except that the Southern Andes needs to be extended south of the latitude of Valdivia (to include approximately latitudes 40 degrees to 55 degrees South). Thus the Northern Andes are contained within Venezuela, Colombia, and Ecuador: the agriculturally important humid equatorial Andes north of Peru. The Central Andes are characterized by a wide longitudinal extent with eastern and western cordillera and interior mountain blocks enclosing extensive high plateaus (altiplano) and supporting the world's largest high-altitude population: Peru, Bolivia, and the northernmost sections of Argentina and Chile. From about the latitude of Antofagasta (24 degrees) the Andes narrow into a single chain of high mountains of much simpler topography than further north. From the southern limit of the altiplano (Central Andes) the Southern Andes display some of the most arid landscapes of the entire Andean chain and are only very sparsely populated. With increasing latitude, however, precipitation increases until south of latitude 40-43 degrees South humid temperate forests and an increasing extent of ice cap and glacier dominate the landscape.

In addition to the High Andes, important non-Andean terrain must be included in any treatment of Andean environment and development issues. Thus the coastal lowlands, Caribbean and Pacific, are intimately related to Andean dynamics. The same is true of the eastern lowlands characterized by the selvas, or tropical rainforest of the upper Amazon and Parana-La Plata basins and, further south, the pre-Andean ranges, such as the Sierra de Cordoba on the Argentinian side. ■

A child from the High Andes, on the shores of Lake Titicaca; many mountain people migrate to the rainforests to the east or to a west-coast slum

The Andean region

The Andes Mountains extend through 70 degrees of latitude along the western margin of South America. They comprise a section of the 15 000 km New World Cordilleras and are 7 250 km in length; they occupy a continuous area in excess of two million km^2. The western, or New World, cordilleras are the longest north-south mountain system in the world and form a major barrier extending from the Antarctic far into the Arctic. Lying athwart the main global atmospheric and oceanic circulation systems they both extensively affect and are affected by world regional weather and climate. The Andean section of this gigantic mountain system extends from the coast of the Caribbean Sea in Venezuela and Colombia at about latitude 11 degrees North to Tierra del Fuego at about latitude 55 degrees South.

The Andes contain many peaks in excess of 5 000 m, together with the highest in the Western hemisphere–Aconcagua, on the border between Chile and Argentina in the latitude of Santiago, reaches an altitude just short of 7 000 m while 3 600 km further north, practically on the equator, the ice-enshrouded volcanic peak of Chimborazo rises precipitously above the Pacific coastal lowlands to 6 310m. Some of the world's most rugged mountain landscapes, although more moderate in absolute height, are located in the far south, in the Patagonian Andes (Fitz Roy: 3 375 m).

Given the enormous north-south length, extending through all climatic/vegetation zones between the equator and the Antarctic, the great individual summit heights and the unbroken high-crest altitude that produces some of the most dramatic rainshadow effects on earth, it is hardly surprising that the Andes can be claimed as containing the most extreme range of landscape types, climates, and vegetation communities in the world. These range from subantarctic and equatorial ice caps and active volcanoes to tropical rainforest, to high-altitude desert. They include the tree-like giant rosette plants of the paramos, the selvas, yungas, and cloud forests, and the almost lifeless salars of the Puna de Atacama, and the nothofagus evergreens of the south. On the Andean west flank above Arica in northernmost Chile 27 years have passed without measurable precipitation, yet on the west flank in southern Colombia precipitation amounts exceed 5 000 mm per annum, almost the highest in the world.

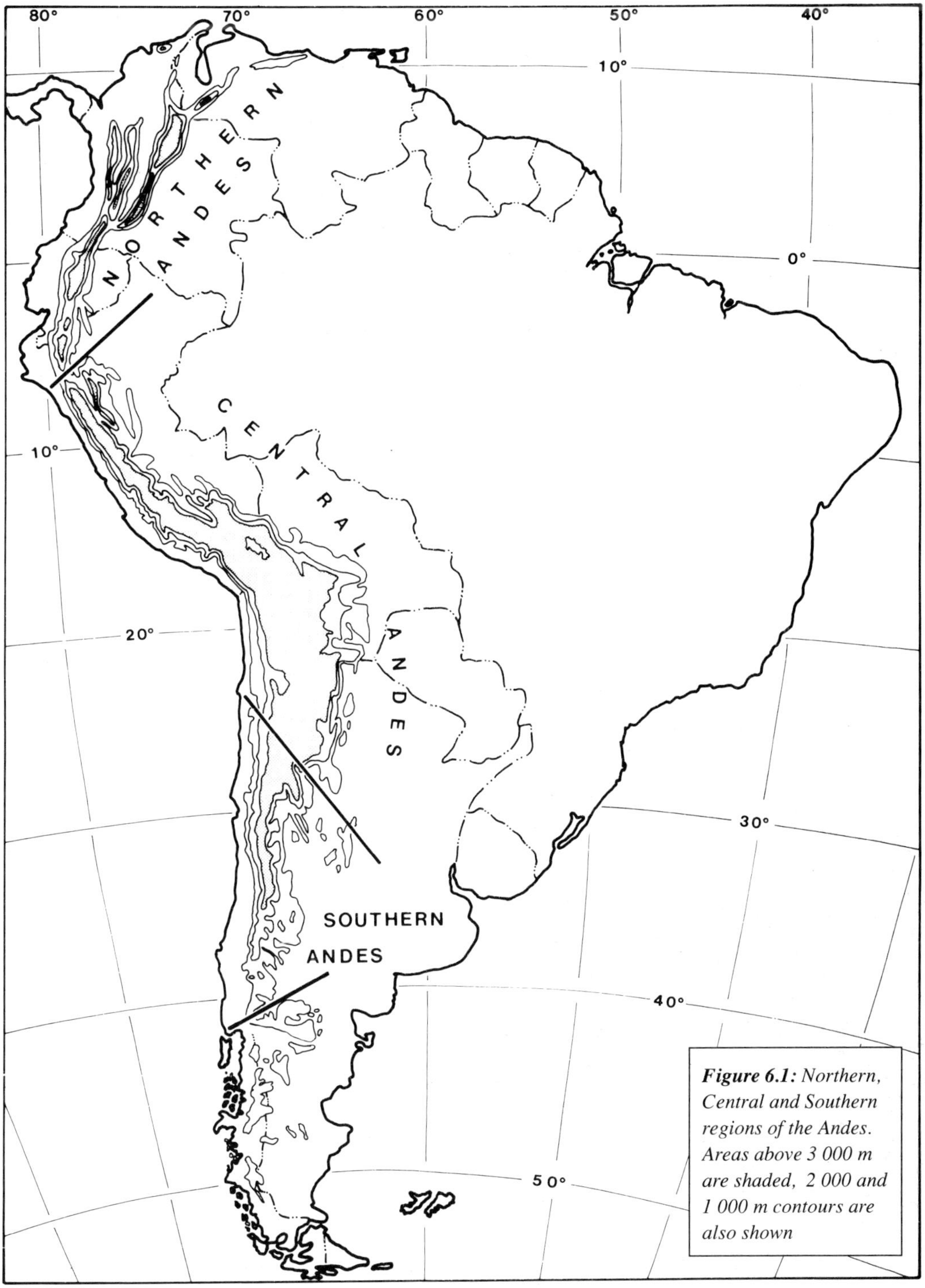

Figure 6.1: *Northern, Central and Southern regions of the Andes. Areas above 3 000 m are shaded, 2 000 and 1 000 m contours are also shown*

This extreme range of environmental types is greatly extended when the scale of perception is reduced to the micro level. This is especially true of the tropical and equatorial Andes where moisture and temperature gradients are abrupt, where a vegetation niche is demarcated by the shadow cast by a small rock, or where sensible temperature soars or plunges as a cloud passes across the face of the sun, where summer occurs every day and winter every night, in the high, thin hypoxic atmosphere.

From the foregoing it is possible to introduce a number of useful generalizations. Certain characteristics of the Andes make them unique among the high-altitude areas of the world. These include:

1) Abrupt changes in altitude resulting in a vertical succession of ecozones ranging from rainforest and desert at the lowest levels to mountain tundra and ultimately permanent snow and ice at the highest.

2) An enormous range of latitude, making for considerable variations in climate, soil, vegetation, and land use through the region.

3) The great longitudinal breadth of the Andes, particularly in Colombia and in the central subregion. The maximum width (more than 700 km) occurs between latitudes 15 and 20 degrees South at the Andean "knee" in Bolivia. (This area is also one of the highest in terms of mean altitude.)

4) The above three factors combine to give a picture of great massiveness. The total bulk of the Andean chain is about five million km^3.

5) Such ruggedness suggests very youthful mountains. In consequence, soils are immature and generally undifferentiated and biogeographical development is relatively recent.

6) Finally, the north-south barrier position of the Andes places it perpendicular to the great atmospheric and oceanic circulations. This creates considerable macro- and micro-climatic differences between the eastern and western slopes and the adjacent lowlands.

All these factors interact to produce a very complex set of climates and, therefore, a complex distribution of ecozones. Most important are the effects of latitude, altitude and topography.

The three main subregions are defined in Figure 6.1, so that they may serve as reference points for later discussion.

Northern Andes

The predominant characteristics of that part of the Andes situated between coastal Venezuela and northern Peru (Cajamarca) are its great diversity and its mosaic of ecosystems. The Northern Andes subregion is distinguished from the rest of the region by the higher relative humidity and by the greater climatic symmetry between the eastern and western flanks of the range. The large high plateaus found in the Central Andes do not occur.

This ecological diversity is dependent on the following variables: altitude, steepness of slope, precipitation and relative humidity, and synoptic climatology. The combination of these variables produces the broad range of diverse ecosystems in the Northern Andes which conventionally are grouped in the following ecozones:

Paramo or Tierra helada (land of frost)	4 500 to 3 200 m
Tierra fria (cool land)	3 200 to 2 200 m
Tierra templada (temperate land)	2 200 to 1 000 m
Tierra calienta (hot or warm land)	1 000 to 0 m

Further distinctions are usually made within these main ecozones according to differences in altitude, humidity, and steepness of slope. In terms of human use of these areas, these differences are often as important as the distinctions between the main ecozones.

The Northern Andean region is dissected by deep valleys running parallel to the main crest of the range and, therefore, the vertically arranged ecozonal belts occupy areas of comparable size. Accordingly, human occupation is not concentrated within any one belt, as it is on the high plateaus above 3 500 m in the Central Andes, and has to adapt to several altitudinal belts. At the upper levels a combination of high humidity and low temperature becomes the main limiting factor for human occupation of the Northern Andes. Consequently, the upper limit of cultivation is about 3 200 m, which is 1 000 m lower than in the Central Andes. Below this upper limit, agriculture and cattle-raising have become important in all ecozones. Nevertheless, there are two ecosystems which are more suitable for agriculture than the others and which at present have the highest population density. One of them comprises the less mountainous parts of the tierras frias where potato and crop cultivation, dairy farming, and increasingly, vegetable farming are found. The second is represented by those parts of the tierras templadas which have moderate humidity and excellent conditions for the cultivation of coffee, maize, and fruit .

Central Andes

The Central Andes, extending from Cajamarca, Peru, to Antofagasta in Chile and Catamarca (north of Belen) in Argentina, are characterized by a preponderance of large high plateaus above 3 500 m variously called "puna" or "altiplano". The puna vegetation of these high plateaus is a response to a short rainy season and low temperatures, particularly at night. It is further influenced by the specific effects of solar radiation, sharp variations in temperature, low humidity, and low oxygen pressure. The plateaus are surrounded and separated by higher mountain ranges and volcanoes. The western flank of these mountains and the coastal lowlands are dry, whereas the humid eastern flank is distinguished by a succession of vertical ecozones from the Zona Nevada rising up to 6 800 m to the tropical forests in the Amazon and Parana-La Plata basins. While the heights of these ecozones vary with latitude and slope aspect, the eastern escarpment generally shows the following relationship between altitude and vegetational belts:

Zona Nevada	6 800 to 4 800 m
Puna	4 800 to 3 500 m
Ceja de la montana (cloud forest)	3 500 to 2 000 m
Yungas (humid mountain forests)	2 000 to 1 000 m
Selva (tropical forests)	1 000 to 0 m

The high plateaus above 3 500 m in Peru and Bolivia are the most densely populated areas of the Andes. Four million people (33 per cent of the population) live in the Peruvian punas and 3.5 million (55 per cent of the population) in the Bolivian altiplanos. Some valleys in the central and eastern ranges of the Central Andes as well as on the eastern slopes are also densely populated. Consequently, 50 per cent of the population of Peru

The upper reaches of the Rio Beni valley, leading to a spectacular 5 000 m highway pass between La Paz and the Bolivian Yungas across the eastern escarpment of the Andes —a massive barrier overlooking the Orinoco and Amazon basins

and 90 per cent of the population of Bolivia live in mountain areas. Because of aridity the western slopes have low levels of human occupation. The coastal river valleys were densely populated even in pre-Colombian times and, because of the recent rapid growth of some urban centres, especially Lima, the population has increased considerably. Less than 10 per cent of the population of both countries lives in the eastern lowlands. The Central Andes were the heartland of the pre-Colombian indigenous empires and even today they represent the only area in the whole Andean region where the indigenous population exceeds 80 per cent of the total.

High-plateau residents grow potatoes, chenopodia, barley, and other frost-resistant crops. Their sheep, llamas and alpacas graze perennially even near the snowline. The extreme upper limit of potato cultivation is 4 200 m. In pre-Colombian times, most high-plateau communities possessed land rights and cultivated land at lower elevations in the areas with temperate and tropical climates on the eastern slopes of the Andes. In more recent times, escarpment communities often utilized multiple-altitude belts, but this system has been largely replaced by exchange between groups residing at different altitudes and by markets. The eastern border areas of the Andes in Peru and Bolivia, today more than ever, provide tropical, subtropical, and temperate zone products for markets in mountain areas.

Southern Andes

The Andean mountains extend to the southernmost tip of South America (Tierra del Fuego). The Southern Andes begin at the edge of the altiplano in Antofagasta and Catamarca and the altitude of the mountain summits decreases from north to south. The extent of dissection by valleys is very high and there are no high plateaus. The northern section is characterized by a dry or seasonally dry subtropical climate and also by an increased daily and seasonal temperature range. The latter becomes more pronounced with increasing latitude. The vegetation corresponds to the climate and the different altitudinal levels. Relatively humid forest ecosystems occur only in the extra-Andean coastal cordillera in Chile and the Argentinian Sierras de Cordoba. The xerophilic forest covers those parts of the eastern escarpments which receive at least 400 mm of rainfall. In the inner areas in the subtropical climatic zone, vegetation becomes extremely scarce. The limiting factor is aridity in the lower parts and temperature in the higher parts. South of an oblique line connecting Valdivia in Chile and Neuquen in Argentina both climate and vegetation cover change abruptly. The east-side arid to west-side moist assymetry is reinforced and temperate to subantarctic conditions prevail. The southernmost section is characterized by a pronounced glaciated topography to increasingly low altitudes, until, in southern Chile, glaciers reach tidewater in the spectacular fiords. On the Argentina side impressive glacial lakes also have ice calving into them. South of Aconcaqua mountain tourism, including skiing, becomes very important and a distinct set of environmental problems arise.

It is not surprising that the inner areas of the Andean range lacking exploitable vegetation are almost devoid of human occupation. The only exceptions are some isolated mining districts which are nevertheless of great importance. They are totally dependent on an external food supply, and water supply can also be a great problem.

However, important human settlements in this region are concentrated in the lower sections of major valleys and on the piedmont of both flanks of the Andes as well as in the lower parts of mountain chains parallel to the main range. These settlements are located in irrigated areas where maize and fodder crops are produced and where vegetable and fruit farming is important. Because of the availability of fodder crops and the exploitation of forests and grasslands as pastures, the raising of cattle, mules, and sheep is widespread. Important tourist settlements and infrastructures can also be found in the region, including the extra-Andean mountains. ■

Geoecology of the region

Geoecology is the study of interrelationships but, in order to understand the basic components—geology, climatology, biology—and to organize the information and facilitate its use for reference, the material in this section will be categorized and discussed under separate headings; some overlapping is unavoidable.

The geology of the Andes

The Andean Cordillera and the Peru-Chile Trench are part of the "ring of fire", a great band of volcanic and earthquake activity which circles the Pacific Ocean. The Peru-Chile Trench is a deep trough in the ocean floor which runs parallel to the mountain chain from latitude 4 degrees North to 40 degrees South. This trench is the site of tectonic-plate activity which provides new evidence for how the Andes Mountains were formed. Orogeny, the process of mountain-building, is now known to be closely linked with the volcanic and seismic activity which accompanies tectonic-plate collisions.

The lithosphere, the outer rock layer of the earth, is thought to consist of large tectonic plates which can be set in motion by the upwelling of volcanic magma along their margins from deep within the earth. This spreading motion moves the plates in one direction, causing the leading edge to be consumed (subducted) by bending down at the point of contact with another plate, thereby forming a trench. In the Andes, the two plates involved are the Nazca Plate (an oceanic plate) and the South American Plate (a continental plate). These two plates come together just beyond the present coastline to form the Peru-Chile Trench. The subduction of the Nazca plate is responsible for the geological history and present-day orogeny of the Andes (James, 1973).

The oldest rocks found in the Andes today are sedimentary rocks laid down in a great geosyncline (off what was then the coastline of South America) during the Palaeozoic era about 250-450 million years ago. Today, these sedimentary beds may be found far inland in the eastern ranges of the Andean Cordillera. At the end of the Palaeozoic era and the beginning of the Mesozoic, the supercontinent Pangaea began to show signs of breaking up. This period of disquiet set the plate-tectonic cycle in motion. The edge of the South American continent

Northward from Lake Titicaca the altiplano leads into narrow intermontane valleys. Sheep and llama are grazed at about 4 300 m below the glaciers of the higher mountains

became highly unstable, causing the geosynclinal layers to bend and buckle upward, forming the eastern ranges. At the same time, magma invaded these beds, creating batholiths and volcanoes.

During the Jurassic period of the Mesozoic (about 190 million years ago), the lithosphere began to crack along the continental edge and subduction of the Nazca Plate began, forming the Peru-Chile Trench. Magma welling to the surface east of the trench formed a line of offshore volcanoes. By the beginning of the Cretaceous period, Africa and South America had become separate continents and another volcanic arc formed east of the first one. By 50 or 60 million years ago, volcanic activity reached a peak and enormous quantities of magma invaded the crust, forming the great Andean batholith and pushing eastward to further fold and lift the eastern ranges.

The early part of the Cenozoic era was a time of considerable erosion of both eastern and western ranges. In the Central Andes, substantial quantities of sedimentary debris (up to 15 km in thickness) filled the area between the ranges to form the altiplano. During the Pliocene and Pleistocene epochs of the Cenozoic a period of uplift occurred which formed the mountains which exist today. The surface, which had been eroded to near sea level, was thrust up above 4 800 m with monadnocks up to 6 550 m. Folding and thrust-faulting created large basins. A vast lake (known as Lake Ballivian) was created during the Lower Pleistocene and then drained during final uplift of the Andes leaving Lake Titicaca as its present-day remnant (James, 1973; Winterhalder and Thomas, 1978).

Geomorphology and topography

The great diversity of relief in the Andean region today is a result of other processes in addition to tectonic-plate motion and its resultant orogenic processes. Two related geological forces which contribute to the landscape are volcanic activity and earthquakes. The igneous activity which is associated with mountain-building continues uninterrupted today, with volcanoes, both active and extinct, studding the mountain chain from Tolima in the north (Colombia) to Volcan Corcovado in the south (Chile). Some of the highest peaks in the Andes are volcanoes, such as Cotopaxi (5 896 m) in Ecuador, Tacora (5 950 m) in Peru, and Sajama (6 250 m) in Bolivia. South America boasts the world's highest volcanoes in three categories: possibly the highest extinct volcano (Aconcagua, about 7 000 m, in Argentina, also the highest peak in the Western Hemisphere), the highest dormant volcano (Llullaillaco, 6 750 m, on the Chile-Argentina border) and the highest active volcano in the world (usually considered to be Antofalla, 6 440 m, in Argentina, but more accurately Guayatiri, 6 060 m, in Chile which erupted in 1959).

The Andean region located near a tectonic-plate edge is thus subject to vulcanism and earthquakes. In addition earthquakes are frequently the cause of other disruptive natural events such as landslides, avalanches, and floods although these phenomena may also have other causes. An interesting comparison may be made between two earth tremors which struck the Andes in recent years: in May 1960 an earthquake registering 8.3 on the Richter scale hit southern Chile, causing about 5 000 deaths and considerable destruction in Valdivia and Puerto Montt; ten years later, in northern Peru, an earthquake of lesser magnitude (7.7 Richter) caused more than 66 000 deaths and destroyed the towns of Yungay and Ranrahirca and the city of Huaraz. The reason for this greater loss of life and property was that the 1970 tremor touched off an immense avalanche which inundated everything in its path (Robinson, 1967; Romero, 1972; Delury, 1977; Weil et al. 1972).

Topography: general

An overall picture of the variations in relief in the Andean chain is shown in Figure 6.2. The Andes are narrowest and lowest at the southern end and widest in the central section (Bolivia). A second broad area is at the northern end (Colombia and Venezuela) where the Andes fan out into four distinct ranges. Generally, the trend of the cordilleras is north-south, but at about latitude 18 degrees South the Andes turn westward to form a nearly semicircular curve parallel to the west coast. In southern Colombia the system divides into three distinct ranges, the easternmost of which bifurcates, one branch trending north along the Colombia-Venezuela border, the other northeast toward the Caribbean Sea. The Pacific coastal plain extends along the entire seaboard and in Ecuador the western range rises like a great wall abruptly from the broadened plain.

Detailed examination of the Andean chain shows that it is made up of many interwoven ranges which enclose high intermontane plateaus and valleys. The conjunction of two or more ranges is a nudo or knot; a number of these contribute to the constricted appearance of certain parts of the Andes, especially in the Northern subregion.

Topography: Northern Andes

In Venezuela, the most northern and eastern portion of the Andes, the mountains rise gradually from the Caribbean Sea and extend on either side of Lake Maracaibo toward the Colombia border. These ranges are in fact a structural continuation of the Caribbean islands. Two of Venezuela's mountain chains join to form Colombia's eastern range (Cordillera Oriental) while two other ranges rise parallel to it. These three distinct chains, separated by the great meridional valleys of Magdalena and Patia Cauca, meet at the Nudo de Pasto re-forming as two ranges. Here, in Ecuador, the Andean vault is at its narrowest, about 150 to 200 km, and is dissected by several perpendicular valleys. It is made up of two cordilleras and an inter-Andean valley between, where the city of Quito is located. From the Nudo de Pasto, Ecuador's ridges crowned with volcanoes branch southward to enclose the Ecuadorean Plateau, an

Figure 6.2: *Cross-sections through the Andes at several latitudes.*
Data from Bowman, 1924:48; Lewis et al., 1956; Marrero, 1964:48; Troll, 1968

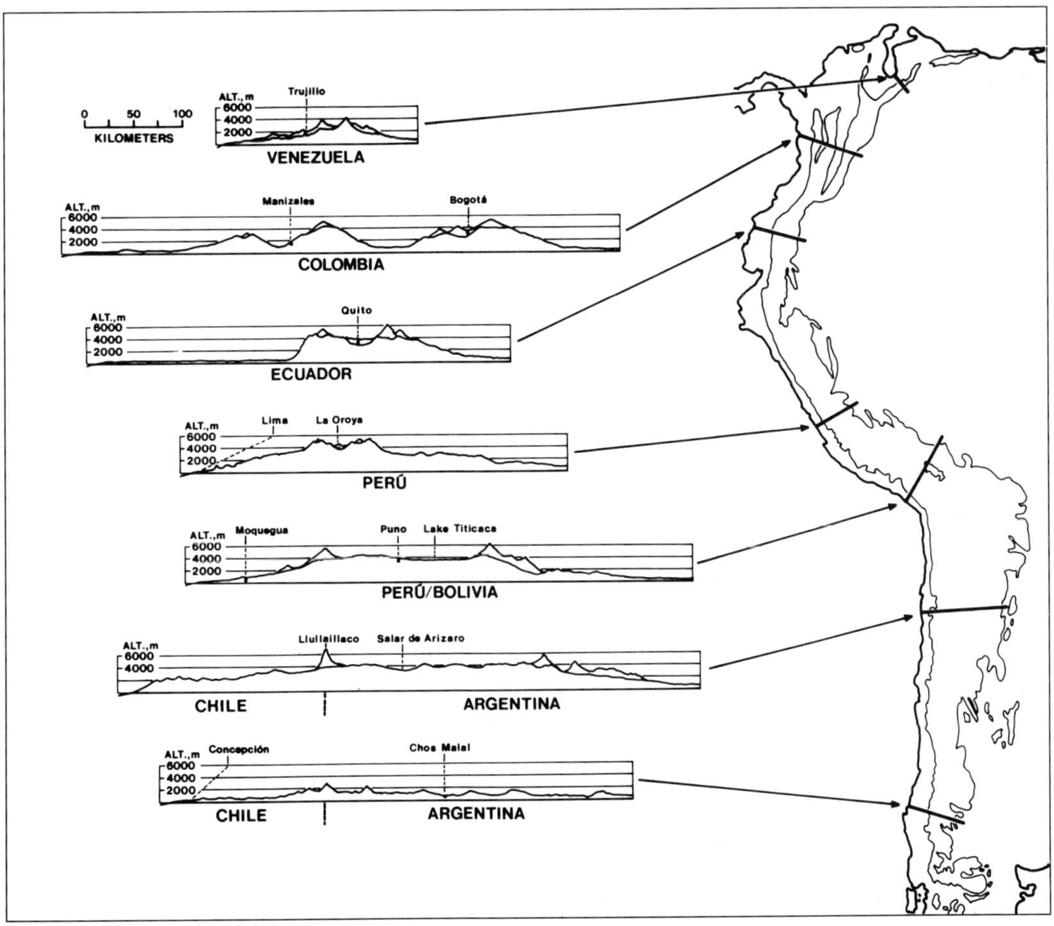

area studded with lacustrine basins (Marrero, 1964; Robinson, 1967)

From a structural viewpoint, the Northern Andes show a high surface-to-volume ratio as a consequence of extensive sloping surfaces. A second important feature is the scarcity of level surfaces (altiplanos) above 3 000 m.

Topography: Central Andes

Ecuador's ranges converge at the Nudo de Loja, and continue into Peru where three ranges are formed which come together at the Nudo de Pasco (as mentioned above). Here three mountain chains again arise which focus at the Nudo de Vilcanota. Further south at about latitude 14 degrees South the Andes diverge into two major ranges, enclosing the altiplano of Peru, Bolivia, and northern Chile and Argentina. The altiplano is the vast treeless and undissected tableland above 3 600 m which surrounds Lake Titicaca and Lake Poopo and which is characterized by interior drainage, windswept flats, salt marshes and saline lakes (Ogilvie, 1922; Sauer, 1950). The altiplano is extensively underlain by lava flows and Quaternary sediments. The Central Andes have a lower surface-to-volume ratio than the Northern Andes due to the great massiveness and high plateaus. In addition, there are a number of glaciated cordilleras and volcanoes exceeding 6 000 m.

Topography: the eastern flank

The eastern slopes of both the Northern and Central Andes show a great natural unity which is largely unaffected by subregional nuances. From the Venezuelan Andes to Bolivia, the eastern flank exhibits great geomorphological and ecological homogeneity. This immense fold, consisting of schists intersected with batholiths and dissected by deep valleys with humid-forest-covered slopes, extends over 3 500 km. Some ecosystems, such as the selva nublada, or cloud forest, are almost continuous from Venezuela to Bolivia.

Topography: Southern Andes

The southernmost portion of the altiplano extends into Chile and Argentina as the Puna de Atacama, a cold dry plateau dotted by salt flats which are fed by small streams. In much of Chile and the bordering areas of Argentina, the Andes form a single, narrow dominant range. However, in the northwestern provinces of Argentina the Puna de Atacama is bordered by a series of ranges which are functionally but not geologically related to the Andes. The orogenic activity which produced the main Andean chain buckled these outlying ranges into a series of long parallel north-south blocks enclosing high narrow basins. Regional seismic activity is intense in this area.

In Chile and along the western boundary of Argentina a single chain, deeply dissected by streams and lacking the level surfaces found in the Central Andes includes the highest summit in the continent, Aconcagua, 6 960 m. This dominant chain is separated from a lower coastal range by the Valle Longitudinal, a long depression about 20 km wide which becomes a string of small basins between Santiago and Coquimbo. Between latitudes 28 and 19 degrees South no permanent stream reaches the ocean. This lifeless coastal region is the Atacama Desert. Here in the northern coastal area are also the great nitrate basins of Chile (Sauer, 1950; Robinson, 1967; Miller et al., 1977).

Soils

Mountains and soil genesis

The process of soil formation is controlled by:

1) character of the bedrock
2) climate
3) living organisms
4) relief or degree of slope and
5) the time or duration that soil-forming processes have been proceeding without major disturbance (Retzer, 1974).

Parent material in high mountain areas is often high in volcanic, igneous, and metamorphic materials. Climatic characteristics at high altitudes include low temperatures and high wind speeds which increase mechanical weathering processes. Biotic communities within mountain systems are highly variable with much local differentiation; at very high elevations plant communities are limited by permanent frost and snow and ice cover. Relief brings into play the action of gravity and consequent downward movement of soil, detritus, and water. And, since prolonged time is needed for the development of mature soils, continual downslope movement and rapid soil depletion through erosion prevent this maturation.

It is the variation in elevation and slope that principally influence soil genesis over the mountain landscape (Buol et al., 1973: 116). Variations in elevation relate to climate and variations in slope relate to gravity; both have manifold effects.

The inverse relationship between temperature and altitude produces active weathering and soil-sorting by freeze-thaw cycles at the higher elevations (Corte, 1968; Fahey, 1973 and 1974; Mellor, 1979). Daily freezing and thawing, at elevations where night-time frosts occur throughout the year, produce a "diurnal solifluction" leading to the denudation of plant cover on slopes (Troll, 1968). Again, however, local landscape patterns influence conditions of removal and accumulation of deposits by wind action, drainage and erosion, and vegetation action on soil genesis (Buol et al., 1973: 117). Soil temperatures, which relate to biological activity and vegetation growth, are higher on north-facing slopes in the Southern Andes (southern hemisphere) and on south-facing slopes in the Rockies (northern hemisphere) (Buol et al., 1973:118). Pronounced relief and steep slopes are characterized by intensive erosion, creep of the regolith, and more dramatic processes such as free fall of materials, mudslides and avalanches. Such events are localized and may also be triggered by seismic or volcanic activity (Beek and Bramao, 1968). As Buol and his colleagues (1973: 119) note, the age of the soil is determined largely by the stability of the surface. Since marked relief produces unstable surfaces, mountain soils are usually young and shallow.

In general, soils show distinct altitudinal zonation from sea level to the level of permanent snow and ice (Bridges, 1978: 99). Most, but not all, mountain soils are of low fertility, shallow Lithosols, strongly acid, very stony, medium to coarse textured, and well-drained (Buringh, 1970: 97; Retzer, 1974).

Andean soils

Soil description and classification in the Andes is particularly difficult because of extreme altitudinal and latitudinal diversity. Hence, only soil systems in the broadest sense will be dealt with in this section.

Northern Andes: The humid climate of the Northern Andes produces a plant cover that is limited not by water, but principally by low temperature conditions which are a function of elevation. There are, however, many inter-Andean valley systems with sub-humid to semi-arid microclimates (Beek and Bramao, 1968). The semi-arid valleys are characterized by Sodic, or salt-containing, Solonetz soils, while the sub-humid valley systems tend toward the more mature Isohumic soils, with more rapid organic matter turnover, such as Brunizems and Chestnut soils. Stony Lithosols characterize the steep slopes while Acid Brown soils are more representative of gentler slopes. At the highest and treeless regions of the Northern Andes, soils are classified as Paramo humic or Andean humic soils (Cuatrecasas, 1968). These soils, which are highly fertile, are acidic, dark in colour, very deep and compact, and saturated with water. Paramo soils are rich in organic matter and predominantly Andosols, derived from volcanic material high in vitreous elements, and Alpine Rankers, derived from crystalline rock (Duchaufour, 1978: 28).

Central Andes: The western ranges of the Central Andes are relatively arid with desert-like soils. Beek and Bramao (1968) identify dominant soil types as Regosols (immature and limestone-derived), Lithosols, Alluvial soils, and the calcimagnesian Sodic soils known as Solonchak. The eastern Central Andean ranges are relatively more humid than the western ranges and have mixed Brown Forest soils, Lithosols, and heavy-textured Alluvial soils.

The altiplano can be divided into the seasonally dry northern plateau surrounding lakes Titicaca and Poopo and the semi-arid southern plateau of Bolivia, Chile and Argentina. Much of the area of the northern altiplano is covered with the sediments of shrunken or extinct lakes, including the great relic salars or salt flats (Beek and Bramao, 1968). Around Lake Titicaca Humic Gley soils are common; these are hydromorphic in nature and are characterized by temporary or permanent saturation of soil pores (Duchaufour, 1978: 103), which leads to slow decomposition of organic matter due to a soil oxygen deficit. Sodic soils such as Solonetz and Solonchak are present in depressed areas. By far the most prevalent soils are Chestnut soils, Rendzinas (alpine meadow soils), and Humic and Steppe Chernozems (Prairie soils). Winterhalder and Thomas (1978:28) identify the mineral fertility of some of these groups as good, since little leaching has taken place. In the semi-arid southern antiplano, soils are derived from volcanic ash with dark sandy topsoils. Dunes, salt flats and limestone-derived Regosols predominate further south.

Southern Andes: As Beek and Bramao (1968: 109) point out, "much of the northern sector is thickly mantled by layers of volcanic ash originating from a long chain of intermittently active volcanoes". Volcanic ash deposits in this sector are quite deep even on relatively steep slopes. In the northern and central areas of the Central Range, Lithosols and Brown Forest soils mixed with a volcanic ash mantle are common. Further south in the Central Range, volcanic-derived Andosols of low fertility, Lithosols, Alpine Rankers, and Podzols are the major soils. The western Andean foothills of Chile are characteristically Mediterranean in climate and soil types.

Hydrology

River drainage systems

The Andes serve to divide the South American continent into Atlantic and Pacific drainage systems. With a few exceptions, rivers draining the eastern ranges and slopes have perennial flows and are long; those draining the western ranges to the Pacific are short and many are seasonal (Robinson, 1967). Most of the eastward drainage of the Northern and Central Andes is via the three great river systems: Orinoco, Amazon and Parana-La Plata. Eastward drainage of the Southern Andes involves several river systems; westward drainage of the Andes, on the other hand, includes several hundred independent rivers.

Northern Andes: The Venezuelan Merida Cordillera has three principal drainage systems:
1) the Tocuyo River flowing north to the Caribbean Sea;
2) the Chama and Motatan rivers draining into Lake Maracaibo; and
3) numerous rivers, including the Uribante and the Bocono, which are a part of the Orinoco watershed.

Eastward drainage of the Colombian Andes is divided between the Orinoco and Amazon watersheds. The Central Cordillera feeds the Cauca and Magdalena rivers, which flow northwards to the Caribbean, whereas the Western Cordillera drains into several rivers including the Sinu, the Atrato, and the Patia. Ecuador's Cordillera Real has eastward flow to the Amazon and westward flow to a number of Pacific rivers including the Esmeraldas in the north and the Guayas in the south.

Central Andes: Northern and central Peru show a typical Amazon-Pacific drainage pattern. There are more than forty perennial or seasonal rivers that spill from the western flanks of the Cordillera Occidental. These rivers are used to irrigate the arid Pacific coast, producing fertile valleys where all major and minor population centres are located. The central and western ranges are dissected by rivers such as the Maranon and Huallaga in the north, and the Apurimac, Urubamba, and Mantaro in the south which flow northward into the Amazon. Further south, on the Peruvian/Bolivian altiplano, all drainage is internal and feeds large highland lakes such as Titicaca and Poopo and saline marshes such as the Salar de Uyuni in Bolivia. The Bolivian slopes of the altiplano are drained by the Pilcomayo river, the Parana system, and the Beni and Grande rivers of the Amazon system.

Southern Andes: Because the continent is narrow in the south, the rivers flowing to the east are considerably shortened. Rivers in northern Argentina lead into the Parana, while southern Argentine Andean drainage occurs through a series of southwest-flowing streams such as the Salado, the Colorado, the Negro, and the Chubut rivers. Numerous rivers drain the western slopes of the Chilean Andes. In northern Chile, where the coastal ranges reach the sea, many of the rivers are seasonal in flow. In central and southern Chile rivers are perennial and numerous.

Standing and stored water

High-altitude lakes, snowfields, and glaciers are important as sources of streams and as storage depots of fresh water (Löffler, 1968; Østrem, 1974). Ice and snow can modify the landscape, transform soils, influence the climate, and have a profound effect on living forms, particularly humans (Slaymaker, 1974; Mellor, 1979). Glacial lakes in the Andes often supply water for urban centres in nearby localities (Ogilvie, 1922:98).

In the Northern and Central Andes, the lower limit of permanent snow ranges from 4 600 m at the equator to more than 5 000 m in the latitude of La Paz, Bolivia (Schwerdtfeger, 1976). Very high lakes in the Andes are found at elevations between 4 000 and 5 000 m and many of these were formed during the last retreat of glaciers about 12 000 years ago, and, as Löffler (1968) notes, are still in direct contact with the ice. The damming of mountain lakes by glacial ice or glacial moraines produces instability with often tragic results. Kinzl (1968) cites cases of sudden discharges of glacial lakes leading to the loss of thousands of lives on numerous occasions in Peru.

With the exception of the very arid northern Chilean coast and the southern altiplano, the water supply in the Andes is sufficient for present needs. However, population pressure on existing water resources is now being felt in Bogota, which has the largest urban population in the Andes (Guhl, 1968). As urban centres, such as Bogota, Quito, Cuzco, and La Paz, continue to grow, glacial lakes and melt-water will become of increasing importance. Certainly, the expanding need for hydroelectric power will lead to more engineering works to exploit Andean waterway resources.

Climate and weather

Climatic variables, such as temperature, precipitation, air pressure, solar radiation and wind speed, are the "driving variables" that structure and influence the establishment of ecosystems. At a more fundamental level, there are several global determinants of climate that must be considered in any discussion of the climate and weather of a major geographic region. These are as follows:

1) latitude
2) magnitude or mass of land area and proximity to water bodies
3) atmospheric patterns, and
4) relief of the land mass (Robinson, 1967).

The Andes are characterized as:

1) primarily tropical and subtropical by latitude
2) in close proximity to the Pacific Ocean and at the western margin of a large continent
3) subject to the atmospheric conditions of the trade winds and equatorial intertropical convergence zone (ITCZ), and
4) having one of the highest and most massive mountain systems in the world (Eidt, 1968).

Mountain climates

Increases in altitude are accompanied by the lowering of air temperature and humidity and an increase in wind speed, air turbulence, and solar radiation. These altitude-related climatic features, together with variations in plant cover and topography, produce complex local and regional weather conditions.

Although there is an inverse relationship between temperature and altitude, there is no constant value for the temperature decline per unit elevation (lapse rate). The steepest lapse rates occur during the warmest months. For example, in the Alps each 1 000 m of elevation produces a 4.0 degrees C drop in temperature during January, whereas in July a 1 000 m rise gives a lapse rate of 6.25 degrees C (Geiger, 1965:444). Within the equatorial zone on the Peruvian altiplano, temperature gradients are very steep, at 10.5 degrees C per 1 000 m during the cooler season and 12.5 degrees C per 1 000 m during the warmer season (Little and Hanna, 1978). Seasonal temperature variation is less at higher elevations than at sea level. This is true for tropical highlands and even more so in temperate regions. There is, therefore, a trend from continental-type climates at sea level to maritime-type climates at high altitude. Seasonal variations at high elevations are minimized, and diurnal variations are maximized. Marked diurnal variation, as in deserts, results from high levels of long-wave radiation that occurs under cloud-free daytime skies and the rapid escape of this radiation under clear night-time skies. Under cloudy skies, the diurnal temperature range will decrease markedly.

Local variations in topography influence temperature and humidity, particularly with respect to diurnal ranges. Daytime temperatures of valley-slope-peak gradients decrease with increasing elevation. At night, however, there is a temperature inversion, where both valley and peak temperatures are low and slope temperatures are relatively high.

The same general pattern for the three relief features holds for humidity, except that humidity is maximal at night when temperatures are low. Therefore, valley floors, despite their relatively low elevation, tend to display the greatest diurnal temperature and humidity fluctuations.

Solar radiation, particularly short-wave radiation, increases with altitude because of the reduction in atmospheric oxygen, nitrogen, and ozone molecules which absorb and scatter radiation (Prohaska, 1970). Temperate highlands show most pronounced seasonal variation in solar radiation whereas in tropical highlands seasonal variation is less pronounced and more influenced by cloud cover, haze, and dust associated with dryness. Ultraviolet radiation at elevations greater than 3 000 m in the tropics is more than double that recorded at sea level (Buettner, 1969).

Andean climates

The atmospheric circulation, which transfers energy through the movement of air masses, controls the weather patterns of the Andes region. Figure 6.3 illustrates air-mass conditions over South America during December and January (Figure 6.3a–southern hemisphere summer solstice) and June and July (Figure 6.3b–southern hemisphere winter solstice). The dominant atmospheric features that influence South American climate are several high and low pressure "cells", the intertropical convergence zone (ITCZ), and the trade winds which converge toward the ITCZ. The ITCZ is a low-pressure trough which exchanges energy, through a vertical convection cycle (Hadley cell), with the trade winds. The equatorial position of the ITCZ contributes directly to the perennial humidity of southern Colombia and northern Ecuador (Sick, 1969). The seasonal shift of the ITCZ northward in June and July and southward in December and January dominates the seasonal rainfall patterns in the Central Andes.

Between July and January, the southern Pacific and southern Atlantic high-pressure air masses shift southward leading to a corresponding southward movement of the moisture-laden low-pressure ITCZ. This shift produces the Central Andean wet season in the highlands during the months of November to March when the ITCZ is in its southern position. The aridity of the Central Andean coastal zone is the result of mountain rain-shadow effect, the cold Pacific Humboldt current, and the southern Pacific high-pressure cell. The rain-shadow effect is produced by moisture-bearing air from the southern Atlantic high-pressure cell releasing its moisture as it ascends the eastern slopes of the Andes. As the already moisture-depleted air descends the western slopes, warming and the rise in

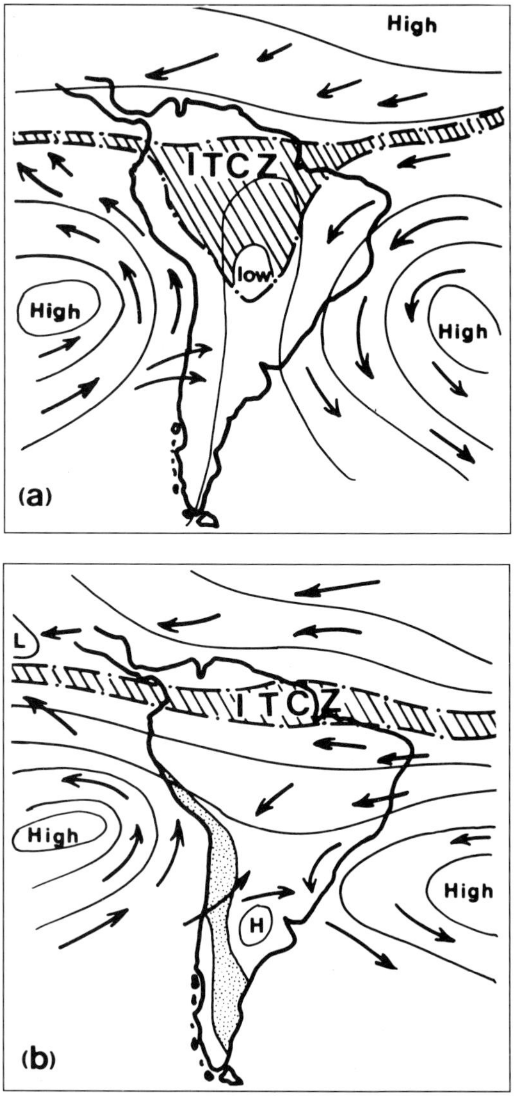

Figure 6.3: Atmospheric conditions in South America: (a) during the southern hemisphere summer solstice (December/January); (b) during the southern hemisphere winter solstice (June/July). ITCZ is the intertropical convergence zone; arrows signify the direction of air mass movements; the stippled area in the lower figure is the arid zone of the coast, altiplano, and Patagonia.

pressure increase the moisture-holding capacity of the air and precipitation is prevented. A rainshadow effect alone would not produce the extreme central coastal aridity—rather, the position of the Humboldt current adds a further dessicating feature to the coast. As the cold Humboldt current flows northward along the western coast, the cool-dry Pacific high-pressure air is cooled further as it crosses the Humboldt current and a very stable temperature inversion occurs in which rain is almost eliminated (Eidt, 1968). The El Nino upwelling current of warm water displaces the Humboldt current every few years, and gives rise to heavy rains and flooding along the otherwise arid coast. A shift in the ITCZ further south than normal has been suggested as one cause of the appearance of El Nino (Johnson, 1976).

Along the Chilean coast, south of the Atacama desert, the climate is influenced by polar maritime circulation patterns. In this area of central and southern Chile, polar air masses cross the coast and ascend the Andes with heavy precipitation resulting.

Precipitation

Rainfall patterns are illustrated for the Andes and adjacent coast in Figure 6. 4. In the north, precipitation is uniformly high throughout the year both in the highlands and on the coast. Southwards from central Ecuador, at about the latitude of Guayaquil, coastal aridity develops and increases, culminating in the totally dry Atacama desert of northern Chile. Central highland precipitation at parallel latitudes shifts into a seasonal pattern of rainfall where the annual totals are about half those in the Northern Andes. The arid puna of Bolivia, Chile, and Argentina occurs where the arid zone crosses the Andes (see also Figure 6.3b). The west-central coast of South America is an Andean rain-shadow

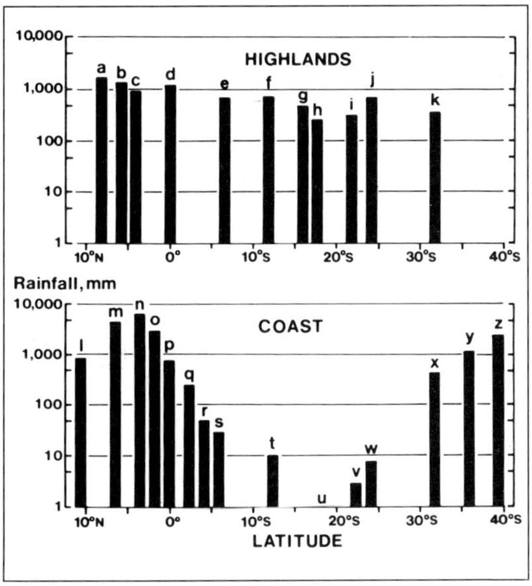

Figure 6.4: *Annual rainfall (in mm) along longitudinal gradients from 10°N to 40°S for the Pacific Coast and the Andean Highlands—expressed on a log scale.*
a. *Merida, Venezuela;* ***b.*** *Medillin, Colombia;* ***c.*** *Bogota, Colombia;* ***d.*** *Quito, Ecuador;* ***e.*** *Cajamarca, Peru;* ***f.*** *Cuzco, Peru;* ***g.*** *La Paz, Bolivia;* ***h.*** *Oruro, Bolivia;* ***i.*** *Cristo Redentor, Argentina;* ***j.*** *Salta, Argentina;* ***k.*** *Chos Malal, Argentina;* ***l.*** *Barranquilla, Colombia;* ***m.*** *Ciudad Mutis, Colombia;* ***n.*** *Buenaventura, Colombia;* ***o.*** *Tumaco, Colombia;* ***p.*** *Esmeraldas, Ecuador;* ***q.*** *Manta, Ecuador;* ***r.*** *Lobitos, Peru;* ***s.*** *Chiclayo, Peru;* ***t.*** *Lima, Peru;* ***u.*** *Arica, Chile;* ***v.*** *Iqique, Chile;* ***w.*** *Antofagasta, Chile;* ***x.*** *Valparaiso, Chile;* ***y.*** *Concepcion, Chile;* ***z.*** *Valdivia, Chile.*
Johnson,1976; A. Miller,1976; Prohaska,1976; Snow,1976

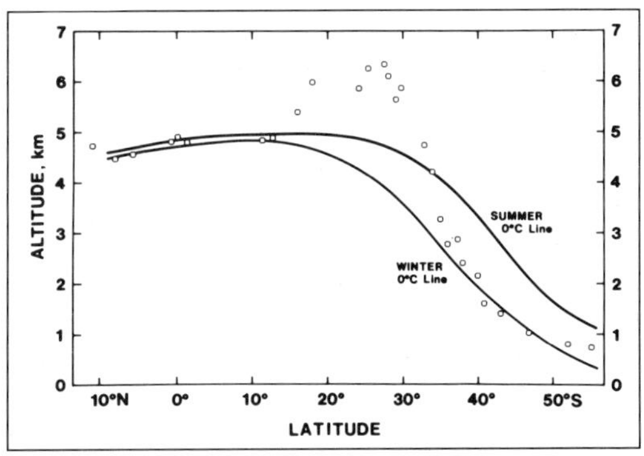

Figure 6.5: *Summer and winter limits of freezing temperatures (0°C lines) and altitudes of permanent snowlines (open figures).*
Modified from Schwerdtfeger, 1976

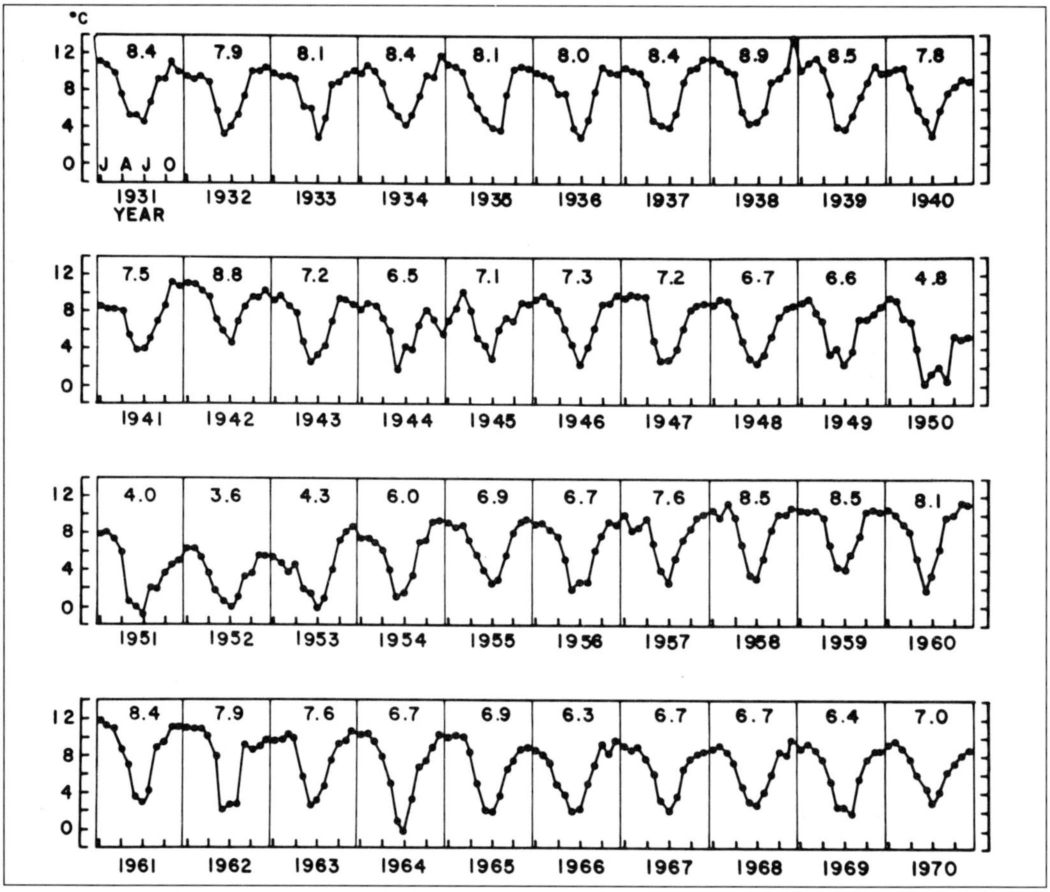

Figure 6.6: *Forty-year record of mean monthly temperatures (1931 to 1970) at Chuquibambilla, Peru (3910 m, 14°45' S lat.). Values at the top of each 12-month period are mean annual temperatures.* Modified from Little and Hanna, 1978

as precipitation falls on the eastern slopes; further south in Patagonia, the reverse occurs and the rain-shadow lies on the eastern slope. Valdivia, Chile, at about latitude 40 degrees South, is representative of this very wet region of the southern Andean coast. Particularly violent thunderstorms are common in the highlands, especially the central highlands. The snowline is given by latitude and altitude for the Andes in Figure 6.5. Deviations of the heights of permanent snow-fields from lines of freezing temperatures between latitudes 15 and 30 degrees South are caused largely by low precipitation. Precipitation in the form of snow or hail depends upon elevation, latitude and time of day. However, below the permanent snowline in the Northern and

Figure 6.7: *40-year trend in mean annual temperatures (1931 to 1970) at Chuquibambilla, Peru.* Modified from Little and Hanna, 1978

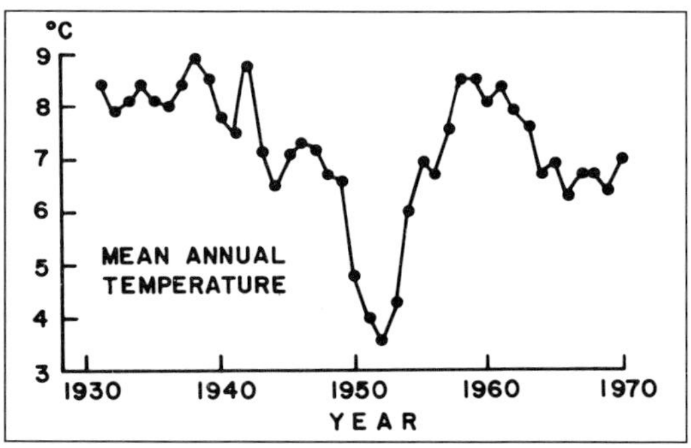

	Bogota		Quito		Cajamarca		Arequipa	
Latitude	4°38N		0°13S		7°8S		16°19S	
Altitude (m)	2 556		2 818		2 621		2 525	
Month	Daily mean	Daily range	Daily mean	Daily range	Daily mean	Daily range	Daily mean	Daily range
January	12.8	11	13.0	14	15.0	14	13.9	14
February	13.2	11	13.0	13	14.0	14	13.9	14
March	13.7	10	12.9	13	14.0	14	13.5	14
April	13.7	9	13.0	12	14.0	14	14.1	15
May	13.7	9	13.1	14	13.5	17	13.8	16
June	13.2	8	13.0	13	12.5	19	13.2	17
July	12.9	8	12.9	15	12.5	19	13.1	18
August	12.9	9	13.1	16	13.0	18	13.8	17
September	12.8	10	13.2	16	13.5	17	14.4	17
October	12.9	9	12.9	14	14.5	15	13.6	17
November	13.1	9	12.8	13	14.0	16	13.9	17
December	13.1	10	13.0	13	14.0	16	14.1	16
Annual	13.2	9	13.0	14	13.7	16	13.8	16

Table 6.1: *Temperature data (°C) at four sites of roughly equivalent altitude but different latitude in the Andes*

Central Andes, snow cover seldom persists into the late afternoon because daytime temperatures, even at 4 500 m, are well above freezing.

Temperature

Latitude, elevation and the Humboldt current are important determinants of Andean climate. However, latitude is only a minor factor in the Northern and Central Andes. Temperature lapse rates seem to range from 4 to 6.5 degrees C, but with much local variation (Johnson, 1976). The Humboldt current exerts a marked cooling effect on the Central Andean coast and western Andean slopes. In fact, temperatures may be warmer at 1 500 m on the western slopes than at sea level. This illustrates a reversal of the normal lapse rate pattern.

Daily temperature means and ranges at four locations are listed in Table 6.1. When altitude is held roughly constant latitude effects on mean annual temperature are minimal: Bogota, Quito, Cajamarca, and Arequipa, with a latitudinal spread of more than 20 degrees, show a mean annual temperature range of less than one degree C. What do become apparent are the southward trends of slight temperature seasonality and increased diurnal variation (Table 6.1).

Annual temperature values, however, can be misleading, since there is considerable year-to-year variation. Figure 6.6 illustrates a 40-year monthly temperature record at a site on the Peruvian altiplano. Seasonal variations at this site are principally the result of heavy cloud cover during the wet season and clear skies during the dry season (May-August). Annual variations in temperature range from a high of 8.9 degrees C in 1938 to a low of 3.6 in 1952. This remarkable amount of temperature variation is plotted in Figure 6. 7. The years from 1950 to 1953 must have been difficult ones for native farmers.

Barometric and oxygen pressures

No discussion on Andean climate would be complete without comment on altitudinal effects on air pressure. As altitude increases, barometric pressure decreases at a constant, but not linear, rate.

Oxygen pressure, which is a constant fraction of barometric pressure, decreases at the same rate. Accordingly, oxygen at 2 000 m elevation shows a pressure reduction of 20 per cent below sea-level values. At about 5 400 m elevation, there is a 50 per cent reduction in the available oxygen.

Vegetation

The distribution of climatic zones combined with altitude is the most important factor in determining the distribution of vegetation types. Similar plant communities may be found in widely separated parts of South America which have similar weather patterns. There are, however, other factors which influence vegetation which are not directly related to climate, notably soil type, slope, drainage, and human intervention (Robinson, 1967).

Plant life-forms show remarkable adaptations to the severe environments found in the Andean region. It is only the most extreme conditions that totally prevent plant growth such as the almost total dryness of the Atacama Desert and the permanent cover of snow and glaciers at higher altitudes.

A map indicating the major vegetation types of the Andes is shown in Figure 6.8. The terms given in the caption are largely those of Troll (1968) and are intended as descriptive labels. The vegetation belts to be described below are also shown in Figure 6.9, which is a schematic longitudinal section through the eastern and western cordilleras. The small inset map of South America indicates a line on either side of which the two sections are located.

This figure also includes many smaller areas too numerous to describe here, many of which result from sheltered conditions or special local climate factors. Figure 6.9 is particularly useful for comparing the symmetry or asymmetry of vegetation types to changes in moisture on either side of the Andes.

Northern Andes

Most of the Northern subregion can support a lush growth because of the high humidity. Tropical rainforests and other types of evergreen and deciduous forests dominate this subregion with considerable symmetry of vegetation types on the eastern and western flanks. On the lowest slopes are the tropical rainforests which support agriculture year-round, producing bananas, manioc, cacao and other crops.

Above the rainforest is the cooler cloud forest, called variously the tierra fria, selva nublada, Nebelwald, moss forest, or ceja de la montana; this last term is used primarily in eastern Peru and Bolivia. This belt consists of dense stands of ferns, epiphytes, and bamboo. Beyond the tree line is the paramo belt consisting of grassland and herbaceous plants (Sick, 1969; Weber, 1969), and above this is the snowline.

Central Andes

Here in the mid-section of the Andean Cordillera aridity begins to be a significant factor in vegetation patterns. Along the coastal plain, dryness increases southward to culminate in the Atacama desert, one of the driest places on earth. Except for riverine oases (where agriculture and large population centres are now found), desert types of vegetation predominate. These include thorn-bush and succulent deserts, and loma vegetation, which is supported by the garua, a heavy mist which moves north along the coast of Peru (Troll, 1968; Sick, 1969). The vast high plateau, or altiplano, exhibits what is called "puna" vegetation, but changes in humidity from north to south create three different puna types. Northernmost, but cutting across the Central Andes from northwest to southeast, is the humid or moist puna characterized by an uninterrupted carpet of grassy plants. Next is the dry puna where the bunch grasses called ichu (Festuca spp. and many others) and resinous Tola shrubs dominate. Desert puna, found in the Puna de Atacama of Chile and Argentina has typical xerophytic plants such as cactus and thorny shrubs (Troll, 1968). The puna area demonstrates most dramatically the arid diagonal of vegetation where zones extend inland rather than run parallel to the coast due to an increase in dryness from both north to south and east to west.

The eastern slopes of the Andes have a type of vegetation similar to that of the cloud forest of the tierra fria described above. In the Central Andes this region is called ceja de la montana (eyebrow of the mountain).

Southern Andes

The southern subregion of the Andes is situated largely in the temperate zone and temperatures

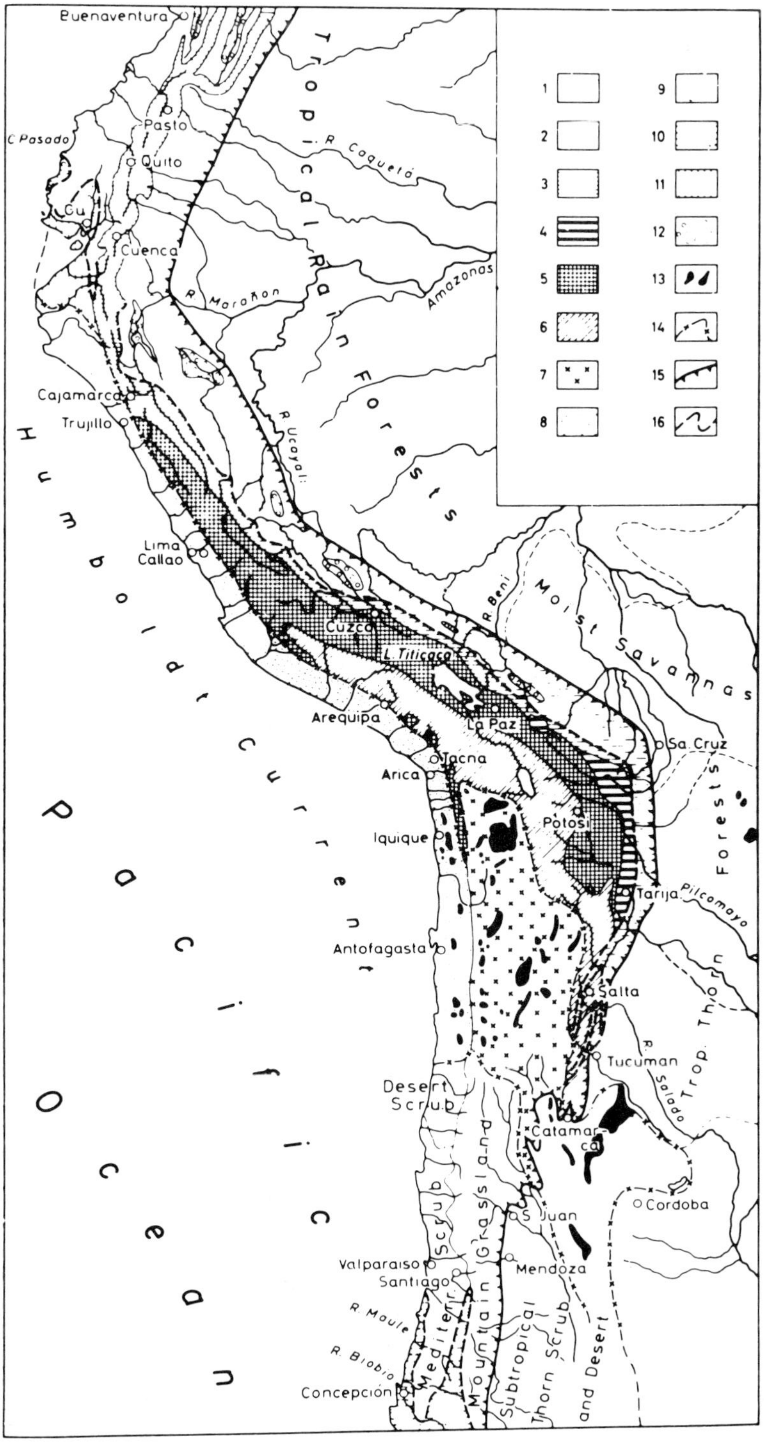

Figure 6.8: *Map of vegetation in the Andes from latitude 4°N to 37°S*

Vegetation belts and other symbols are:

1. *tropical rainforest (including montane forests);*
2. *tropical-subtropical semi-deciduous forests (Tucumano-Bolivian forests) including evergreen and deciduous subtropical montane forests;*
3. *equatorial paramo-belt and tropical semi-evergreen high mountain grassland (Pajonales);*
4. *subtropical mountain meadows;*
5. *moist or humid puna belt;*
6. *dry puna belt;*
7. *thorn and desert puna belt (Puna de Atacama);*
8. *coastal desert;*
9. *open savannas within the rainforests;*
10. *sclerophyllous woodland and shrubland of central Chile;*
11. *thorn savannas (forest and grassland) in the Ecuadorian and Peruvian coastal regions;*
12. *moist savannas (deciduous forest and grassland) along the coastal region of Ecuador;*
13. *salt pans or salares;*
14. *arid areas;*
15. *eastern margin of the Andes;*
16. *western boundary of hygrophytic vegetation areas.*

After Troll, 1968

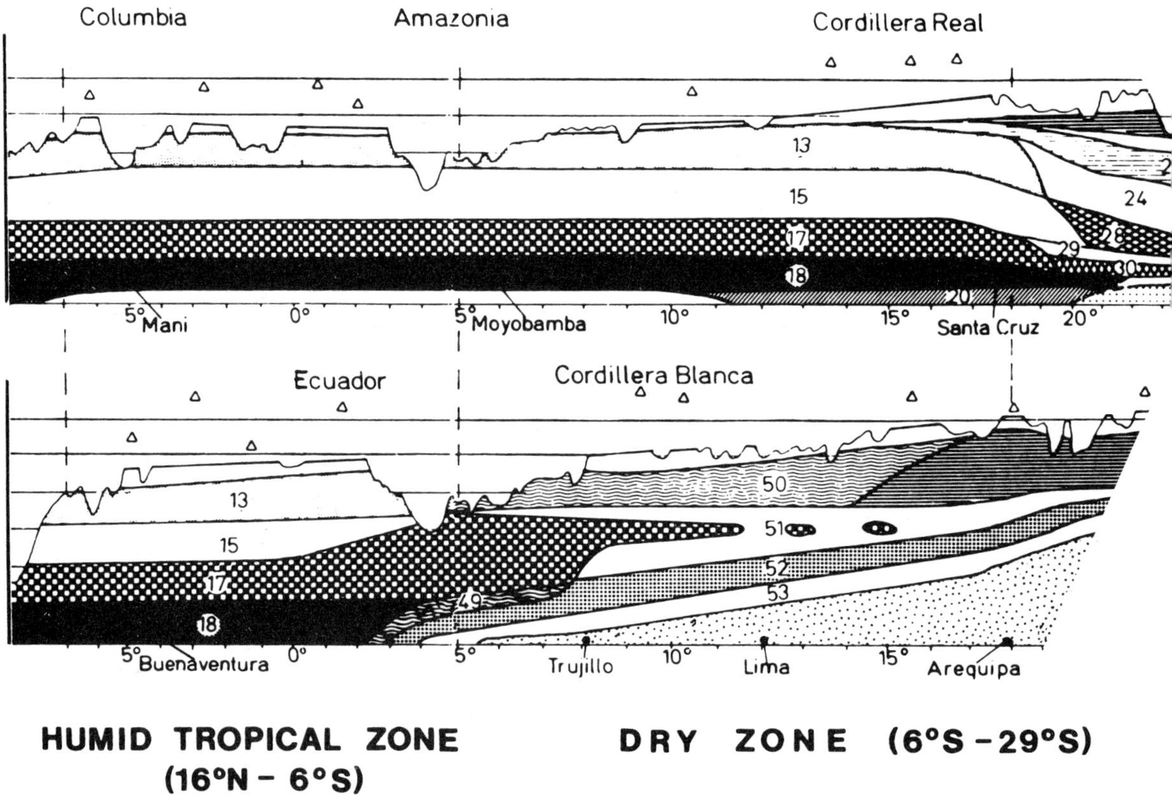

Figure 6.9: *Vegetation belts along gradients from Colombia to Tierra del Fuego. Longitudinal sections of the Andes are through the Oriental or Eastern (upper figure) and Occidental or Western (lower figure) cordilleras*

Cordilleras or ranges: triangles signify mountain peaks. Vegetation belts by altitude and latitude are identified by number in the figure. They are:

13. *microthermal tropical mountain grasslands (paramo);*
15. *mountain cloud forest;*
17. *tropical montana forest;*
18. *lowland wet tropical forest;*
20. *tropical moist savanna;*
21. *high mountain vegetation (puna);*
22. *mountain pastures;*
23. *mountain steppe;*
24. *tall grassland;*
25. *dry prairie;*
26. *patchy woodland;*
27. *subtropical thorn steppe;*
28. *subtropical aliso forest;*
29. *subtropical mirtaceas forest;*
30. *subtropical laurel forest;*
31. *subtropical pacara forest ecotone;*
32. *subtropical thorn savanna;*
33. *Patagonian mountain bushland;*
34. *mountain steppe with some timber;*
35. *mixed subantarctic forest;*
36. *subantarctic forest;*
37. *Patagonian steppe and bushland;*
50. *moist puna belt;*
51. *mesophyte bush vegetation;*
52. *succulent vegetation;*
53. *low thorn bush vegetation;*
54. *Peruvian desert and semi-desert with loma vegetation;*
55. *thorn bush and succulent vegetation;*
56. *wet temperate Chilean hardwood forest;*
57. *deciduous forest;*
58. *Valdivian forest;*
59. *Patagonian inland forest;*
60. *subantarctic evergreen forest.*

Modified from Czajka, 1968

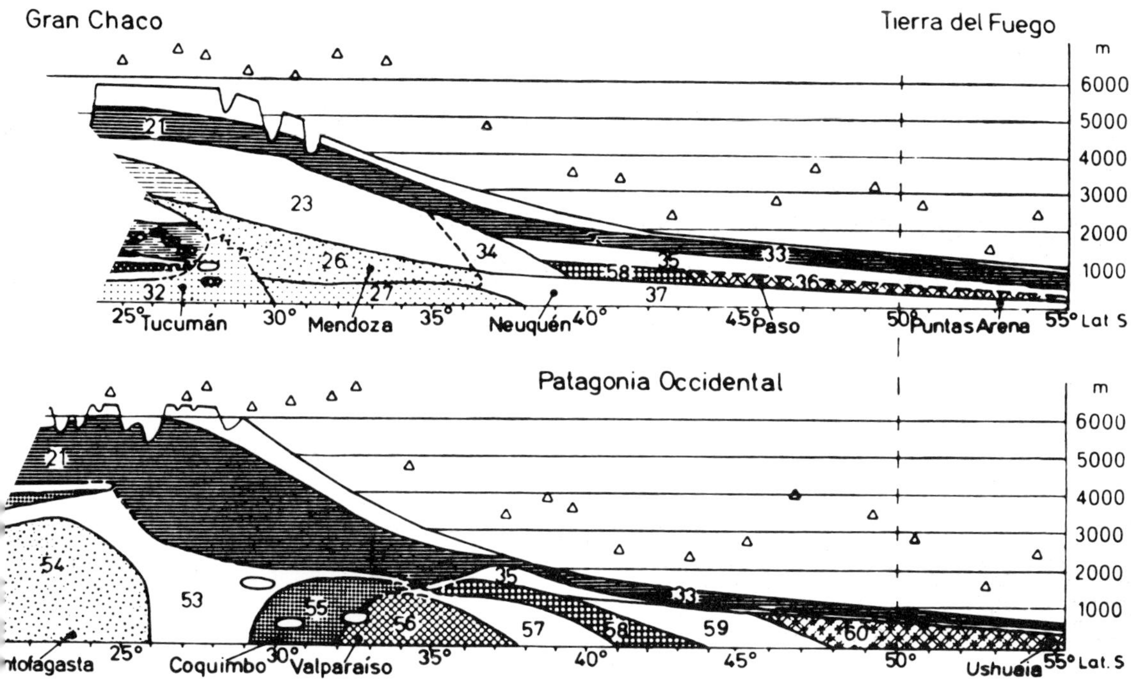

SEASONALLY DRY ZONE (29°S–40°S)

decrease southward. More important for vegetation, there is a change in the atmospheric circulation patterns which reverse the aridity pattern of the Central Andes; that is, increasing dryness on the eastern slopes and increasing wetness on the coast.

Along the coast, south of the Atacama Desert, is an area of thorn scrub. At about latitude 30 degrees South, westerly winds lead to an increase in moisture. In this area of central Chile there is cyclonic winter rain and summer dryness (Mediterranean-type climate), which produces a subtropical hard-leaf forest and scrubland. Extensive agriculture in the Longitudinal Valley depends on irrigation (Sick, 1969).

From north to south at higher altitudes is the Puna de Atacama, described above as having desert puna vegetation, succeeded by an area of mountain grasslands and mixed forests. On the eastern slopes, dryness gradually increases. In the northern part of the area, circulation patterns produce rain during the southern summer and, therefore, grasslands and some mixed forests. Southward, the vegetation gradually becomes scrubbier and more xerophytic.

TEMPERATE FORESTS AND DRY REGIONS (40°S–55°S)

The southern section of the Southern Andes, from about Valdivia southward, presents a contrasting set of environmental problems. On the Chilean side, the west slope is characterized by extensive Northofagus forest and other types of dense, cool temperate rainforest. Here, in a number of areas, massive extraction of lumber has become a serious problem.

At higher levels (e.g. San Carlos de Bariloche) ski resorts provide something approaching an Alpine flavour, together with associated environmental problems. This section of the Andes, on both sides, dependent upon access to utilization areas, will become increasingly important in terms of hydroelectricity production. The southernmost section on both sides retains much extremely rugged mountain wilderness grandeur. The Mount Fitz Roy region, in particular, has become increasingly attractive to the mountaineering world on account of the impressive vertical walls of solid rock.

Animal life

The native fauna of the Andes are rich and diverse with innumerable vertebrate and invertebrate species adapted to mountain ecosystems. Fittkau (1969) identifies South America as having the richest animal population of all continents. Certainly, the vast tropical forest contributes much to this faunal diversity; however, the importance of Andean forms should not be underplayed (Mann, 1968).

The zoogeographic divisions of the Andes are known as follows:

1) the *Patagonia-Chilea* subregion, from northern Peru to Tierra del Fuego (Central and Southern Andes), and

2) the *Guiana-Brazilia* subregion which includes highland Venezuela, Colombia, and Ecuador (Northern Andes).

Gilmore (1950) lists some of the characteristic fauna of the Patagonia-Chilea subregion as: opossums; some distinct armadillos; hystricomorph rodents (chinchillas), viscachas, maras, chinchilline rats, octodon rats, tuco-tucos); wild and domestic cavies (guinea pig); huemal deer; wild and domestic camelids (vicuna, guanaco, alpaca, llama); rheas; ducks, geese, condors, and many other birds. Excellent reviews can be found of Andean arthropods (Besch; Bucherl; Illies; Kuschel; Noodt; Schuster); of fish (Gery); of birds (Olrog); and of mammals (Simpson) in the second volume of *Biogeography and Ecology in South America* (Fittkau et al., 1969). ■

The famous Titicaca reeds, eucalyptus plantations and dry fields partitioned by possibly pre-Incan stone walls denote the climatological and agricultural importance of a large body of water on the high altiplano

Subregional ecology

Of all terrestrial composite ecosystems, the Andes are probably the most complex, since each altitudinal belt has its own structure, both vertically and horizontally, and plant and animal life is incredibly diverse. In general, the lack of integration among different environmental studies has resulted in partial and oversimplified approaches to Andean ecosystems. Such fragmented and oversimplified views have often led to environmental mismanagement.

Multiple and intensive use of Andean environments is inevitable in the future. Hence, the more thorough and comprehensive the knowledge of Andean environments is, the better the prospects for wise exploitation and long-term conservation of its natural resources. In the section that follows, a combined subregional (Northern, Central and Southern Andes) and altitudinal approach will be taken in order to deal with the manifold kinds of ecosystems found. Whereas the previous section dealt with environmental parameters in a very general way, an attempt will be made here to integrate environmental parameters and to provide more resolution and detail.

The Northern Andes

In this section, three main ecozones are discussed:
1) the cold paramo belt (tierra helada) above 3 000 m;
2) the intermediate, temperate belt (tierra fria) between 2 000 m and 3 200 m; and
3) the low elevation, warm belts (tierra templada and tierra caliente) below about 2 200 m.

Each of these Northern Andean ecozones is characterized by high precipitation and humidity, minimal seasonality in temperature and rainfall, and high primary plant productivity and species diversity.

Cold ecosystems: paramos

Paramos may be divided into "high paramo" (from 3 600 m to well above 4 000 m) and "low paramo" (from 3 000 m to 4 000 m) ecozones (Figure 6.10).

High paramos: This ecosystem is restricted to a few hundred square kilometres that are scattered on the uppermost levels of the Costa Rican mountains and the Colombian, Venezuelan and Ecuadorian Andes. Some paramo-like environments, however, are also found in the extreme northeastern part of the Peruvian Andes (Huanuco, approximately latitude 8° South): this environmental area is called Jalca. The high paramos are environments not greatly modified by human activities and may be considered as relatively stable under present conditions—cultivation and especially domestic animal grazing is beginning to extend upward into the paramos and annual firing is becoming a problem..

Mean annual temperature ranges between 3°C and 7°C with almost no seasonal variation. Conversely, daily variation, although largely tempered by the high humidity levels, may show a range as large as 23°C (from -3°C to 20°C) with a mean annual maximum of about 12°C, an absolute maximum of 20°C, and an absolute minimum of -3°C. Night and morning frosts occur on more than 150 days a year. Precipitation is fairly well distributed throughout the year, interspersed with two short, less humid periods: mean annual amounts range from 1 000 mm to 1 200 mm. Although precipitation usually takes the form of rain, it may also occur in the form of drizzle, fog, sleet, and snow. Atmospheric humidity normally ranges from about 75 per cent to saturation and heavy cloud cover is common throughout the year.

Paramos consist mainly of extensive, gently undulating surfaces. Topographically, they consist of either systems of regular and concave slopes (volcanoes' flanks) or successions of peat hollows and morainic mounds. These landforms were

Figure 6.10: *Vegetation belts in the Eastern Cordillera of Colombia*. After Van Der Hammen, 1968

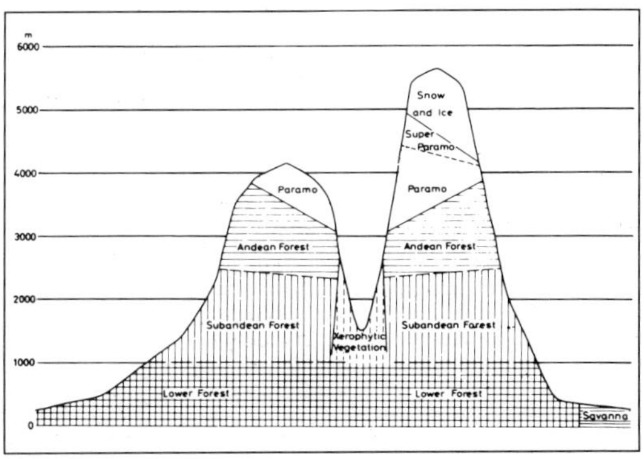

influenced by the glaciations of the Pleistocene epoch. Soils, therefore, are developed on both pre-glacial and glacial deposits.

Soils are generally acidic: according to Jenny (1948), pH ranges from 3.7 to 5.4. In a profile section, soils appear dark-coloured (due to the presence of organic matter) and water-saturated. The nitrogen content is high at 1.8 per cent (Jenny, 1948). On morainic debris, podzols have evolved, whereas in the hollows and foothills, soils develop normally into peat, gley, or pseudo-gley. The Unesco (1973) classification refers to paramos soils as Andosols with a low base status, that is, glacial, heavy clays, and peaty soils.

Vegetation consists chiefly of a low and open herbaceous formation. This is described by Unesco (1973) as tropical alpine open-to-closed bunch-grass communities with a woody sinusia of tuft plants (Espeletia spp), microphyllus to leptophyllus dwarf-shrubs, and cushion plants. Vegetation cover is almost continuous except in the upper part of the paramos where climatic conditions are severe enough to prevent plant establishment. Although not systematically studied, it seems that the composition of plant communities is largely governed by topography. The majority of species are evergreen, and paramos plant life is thus active throughout the year.

Cuatrecasas (1968) recognized three main plant formations:

1) A first level of bush formation, the subparamo, that is a transition between the forest and the paramo. Some of the shrubby genera that characterize this level are: *Hypericum, Aragoa, Arcytophyllum, Baccharis, Senecio, Diplostephium, Loricaria, Gynoxis, Stevia, Eupatorium, Ilex, Miconia, Brachyotum, Cavendishia, Vaccinium* and *Pornettya.*

2) The second formation is the paramo grassland which is the most typical landscape of the paramos proper. Here also some trees are to be found, such as *Polylepis* spp., *Gynoxis* spp. together with some tree-like shrubs including *Valeriana arborea, Senecio vaccinoides* and *Miconia summa.*

3) Above 4 500 m vegetation becomes rather scarce and the ground cover is intermittent. The most characteristic feature is the widespread presence of *Senecio* spp.

Landscape formation processes are slowed down by surface soil and overlying vegetation. Frost effects are thus mitigated by vegetation cover, and surface water runoff is reduced. On the slopes, however, interflow is slow but constant, and the high paramos play a spongelike role where the excess water is slowly but constantly returned to the ecosystems of lower levels.

The high paramo ecosystem is relatively stable under present conditions. Productivity is low and vegetation is not highly suitable for cattle in view of the species of plants which grow. As noted above, however, recent years have witnessed extensive burning and introduction of grazing.

Low paramos: These ecosystems constitute a transitional belt between a tropical humid subalpine forest and the high paramos. The changes in vegetation are chiefly denoted by an increase in woody species. In some places it is formed by open thickets of gnarled and twisted trees. Primary production is greater than in high paramos as a result of milder temperatures. The low paramo, of course, is most heavily affected by human activity.

The mean annual temperatures lie between 7°C and 11°C. Maximum average temperature is between 14°C and 18°C. The lowest temperature rarely falls below -3°C. Night and morning frosts are reduced to less than 50 per year. Annual precipitation varies from 800 mm to 2 500 mm and falls mainly in the form of a fine rain. In the lowest part of these environments and in the upper forest, hail may fall occasionally. Evapotranspiration is between 500 mm and 700 mm. As in the high paramos this altitudinal belt also transfers a significant water excess to the ecosystems at lower levels.

The abiotic substratum is largely composed of leached morainic material and fluvio-glacial deposits which on the slopes have been reshaped by solifluction. Geomorphological processes, as in the high paramos, are relatively slow: among the most frequent are solifluction and suffusion. Soils have developed largely into Podzols and Andosols (on volcanic ashes).

The vegetation is composed of several strata that include: low and knotty trees with lichens and epiphytes; large bushes several metres high, and shorter shrubs and grasses.

Human use of the paramos: Compared with other high-altitude environments, paramos might be considered unmodified. Unlike punas, the paramos have not had continuous and substantial occupation by human populations. Nonetheless, some of the paramos included territories of Chibcha Indian groups in pre-colonial times. Van der Hammen (1968) discovered by pollen analysis of paramo sediments that human activities appeared to begin about AD 1200.

Today, paramos are used mainly as grazing lands for sheep and cattle. In the low paramo, agriculture is practised, and potatoes, garden vegetables and some cereals are cultivated. The limit of agriculture in some areas extends to the high paramo. However, even the low paramo ecosystem is used by farmers and herders in a marginal way. The joint effects of cold and humidity produce conditions which are not conducive to agriculture, and, therefore, the upper limits for crops and pastoralism are 200 to 400 m below those of the Central Andes.

Fire is used as a "stimulating factor" for forage production. During the short, less humid periods, as a normal practice, peasants burn the grass-fields as well as the thickest patches of chusque (*Chusquea* spp.) to promote a regrowth response which yields suitable forage for livestock. Although little research has been done, it is assumed that these burning practices do not have major effects on soils, since the soils are wet enough to reduce damage from high temperatures. Human impacts increase toward the south.

In the Sierra Nevada of Santa Marta, Colombia, culture contact has led to increased exploitation of the paramos. Here, paramos are being used more frequently by certain groups of Indians as a result of competition for land resources. Non-Indian farmers, largely squatters in the mountains, have invaded Indian territories (Arwakos, Koggies) and the Indians are being pushed slowly up into the high-mountain ecosystems.

Temperate ecosystems: cloud forests and savanna

The temperate forest belt between 2 000 m and 3 200 m above sea level can be divided into two principal ecosystems:

1) the mountain cloud or humid forest with high annual precipitation between 1 500 mm and 3 000 mm, and

Cotopaxi (5 869 m), volcanic cone with permanent snow and ice, is one of the more spectacular summits south of Quito. The previous day's middle cloud is still subsiding into the valley while early morning clouds are already building up to obscure the high mountain. Extensive deforestation has occurred in the middle ground

2) the drier mesophytic forest with precipitation ranging from 800 mm to 1 500 mm a year. Two variant mesophytic ecosystems can be identified according to surface features: those on slopes and those on flat or undulating surfaces.

Humid or cloud forests: There are three important characteristics of these environments:

1) skies are almost continuously overcast with heavy cloud cover;

2) long and steep slopes predominate; and

3) there are powerful geomorphic processes which tend to be aggravated by environmental mismanagement.

On the steep slopes the uppermost layer of lithomass is waterlogged almost year-round. In some tropico-equatorial high-altitude environments, for instance, it has been recorded that chemical decomposition of crystalline rocks may take place to a depth of 80 to 100 cm (Birot, 1960). In the Andes, crystalline rocks are often brittle due to tectonic pressure. Therefore, even on slopes of 30 degrees, soils may reach depths of 30 to 40 cm. Soil formation and geomorphogenesis, however, are often opposing processes. On the slopes, powerful oblique leaching as well as the intense interflow limit soil formation. These leaching processes lead to podsolization.

Another dynamic feature is the occurrence of sudden mass movements such as landslides. They normally occur along ravines and water courses. Within these ecosystems mismanagement usually contributes to soil erosion; and, for instance, some of the roads that connect this altitudinal belt with the lower lands induce soil erosion.

Soil demineralization as an associated response to deforestation is another dynamic aspect to be considered within this environment. Salas and Folster (1976) found a considerable range of bioelements lost following clearing and burning of tropical forests. The replacement of those elements by natural processes is thought to occur within 10 to 20 years. The 1 300 to 1 400 kg of nitrogen (per field) which is lost above and below ground is replaced by nitrogen-fixation (at a rate of 100-150 kg/year).

In the upper levels of this altitudinal belt, vegetation is characterized by a mixed elfin forest of trees between 5 and 6 m tall (*Polylepis* spp., *Budleja* spp., *Vaccinium* spp).

According to Unesco (1973) this formation should correspond to a "tropical ombrophilous subalpine forest". In the lower part, trees become taller (15 to 20 m) and have slender boles, such as *Podocarpus* sp., *Weimmania* sp., and *Cecropia* sp. Mosses and lichens also are very abundant. Non-crustose lichens containing blue algae account for a total biomass of 5.7 kg/ha (Forman, 1975). This formation would correspond to "tropical ombrophilous cloud forest" (Unesco, 1973).

Mesophytic forests: These ecosystems occur largely on the inward-facing slopes of the Northern Andes, and have been profoundly modified by human activities. Therefore, most mesophytic climax forests are restricted to a few small areas. Human exploitation of these environments includes use of the cool slopes for cattle grazing and warm slopes for maize cultivation.

In Colombia, mesophytic flat surfaces, or rolling hills, include areas such as the Bogota savanna, the inter-Andean Narino basin, and the Antioquia region. In Ecuador, the inter-Andean corridor, where the city of Quito is located, lies in this ecosystem.

Warm ecosystems: tropical forests

Warm ecosystems are found between sea level and 2 200 m, where the upper level may be referred to as sub-Andean or tropical montana and the lower level as wet lowland forest. These regions are heavily populated, particularly in the "coffee belt" where densities up to 200 per km^2 are found.

Three main divisions are considered here: the upper montana slopes, the intermediate-level coffee belt, and the Andean foothills.

Montana slopes: The Unesco (1973) classification of this ecosystem is "tropical ombrophilous montane forest" with abundant vascular plants and epiphytes. These environments with their vast and dense forests have been rarely touched by man. There are, however, some timber areas where the exploitation of the forest has contributed to an increase of water runoff and erosion. Heavy precipitation occurs during the greater part of the year, amounting to over 4 000 mm per annum. Geomorphological processes are thus very intense, and solifluction carries off large amounts of colluvial cover which augments the sediment load of rivers.

Weathering processes and soil pedogenesis are also very intense. On the slopes oblique leaching gives way to soil ferrosilification, and evolution of kaolin-type clays. In hot and wet climates, however, desilification is also a characteristic feature of soil formation, as is suggested from the high concentration of silicon dioxide in tropical rivers (15-30 mg/litre). Thus, in those regions with a dry season, the soils show a strong tendency to laterization. High humidity and heat acting together produce high levels of bacterial activity, and mineral cycling as well as the turnover of organic matter are extremely rapid.

Coffee belt: This ecosystem has been profoundly modified by human activities, largely by coffee plantation agriculture. The best coffee soils are developed upon volcanic ash, which is very sensitive to erosion. In a comparative study of some Colombian soils, Jungerius (1975) found that soil erosion sensitivity is due to the combination of a very sandy A horizon and a predominantly clay B horizon on a clay subsoil of low resistance.

On certain coffee plantations, the heavy runoff may easily promote the removal of soils and development of ravines. Soil erosion still remains one of the key problems within these environments. At present, however, the high demands for coffee have led to the introduction of a new variety of coffee plant, caturra coffee, which needs no shaded areas for growing and, therefore, no protective canopy of trees. It has been suggested that forest canopy interception of rain may account for up to 35 per cent of total rainfall. Accordingly, the impact of the loss of canopy on soils in caturra coffee plantations should be investigated.

Low Andean foothills: In this relatively humid ecosystem the climate is similar to that of the coffee belt with a mean annual temperature above 24°C, high humidity, and rainfall usually above 2 000 mm. A deep mantle of laterite covers much of the area particularly cleared fields where maize, manioc, plantain, and cacao are cultivated.

Drier ecosystems in Colombia are found in the Magdalena Valley near Leyva, the Cauca Valley near Antioquia, and in some sections of the Patia Valley. These are geographically sheltered from the humid air masses, and are thereby frequently overheated by sunlight. The average temperatures are between 25°C and 29°C, with daily peaks of 40°C. Mean annual precipitation is below 1 000 mm, with a minimum during the periods of highest temperatures. There is, therefore, a high evapotranspiration rate and a strong water deficit lasting for several months. Dessication effects may be accentuated by dry "valley winds".

Vegetation is characterized by a formation with thorny trees and cacti. An understorey layer of grasses may appear during the rainy periods. The land is used either for cattle grazing or for the cultivation of rice and sugar-cane under irrigation.

The Central Andes

Of the three Andean provinces defined here, the Central region displays the greatest diversity and variety of ecosystems. It includes ice cap, tundra,

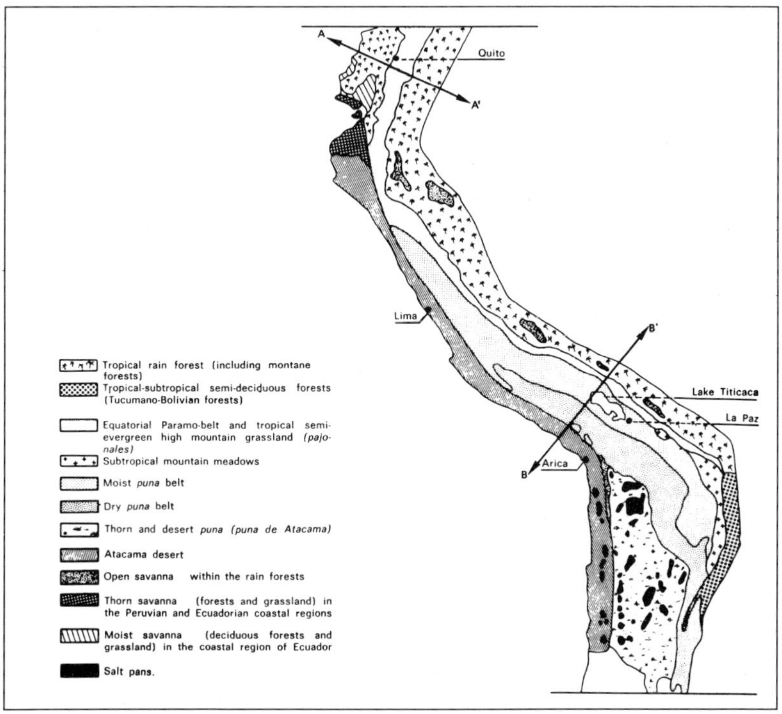

Figure 6.11: *Map of vegetation in the Central Andes.* Modified from Troll, 1968 by Thomas et al., 1977

desert, savanna, tropical wet forest, and puna ecosystems as well as numerous intermediate and unique montane formations. Figures 6.11 and 6.12 represent these diverse environments and vegetation belts.

The humidity gradient is also a major factor in ecosystem diversity throughout the Central Andes and an aridity grid must be imposed on the altitudinal belts. For example, the high punas will be discussed according to humid, dry, and desert conditions. Moreover, aridity gradients exist from east to west across the Andes as well as from north to south along the length of the chain.

Cold ecosystems: punas

The puna ecosystems extend over several hundred thousand square kilometres on the plateaus, high plains and slopes of the Andes between latitudes 8° and 27° South. These are the ecosystems of the prairies and high-altitude steppes where the precipitation is concentrated into a single wet season of variable length, yet remains within the range of 150 mm to 1 000 mm per annum. Puna lands are found at elevations between 3 700 m and 4 800 m in the Andes from latitudes 8° to 15° South, and at elevations between 3 200 m and 4 400 m further south. Mean annual temperatures are generally below 10°C, and frosts are common, especially during the dry season.

In contrast to the paramos, the punas have long been exploited by human populations—first by hunter-gatherers and then by farmer-pastoralists. Over a period of 12 000 years there has been a transition from a large herbivore biomass of herds of wild cervidae, equidae, and camelidae to one composed mainly of herds of domestic camelidae (llamas and alpacas), ovidae (sheep), and bovidae (cattle). There have been corresponding changes in the vegetation cover: possible regression, if not

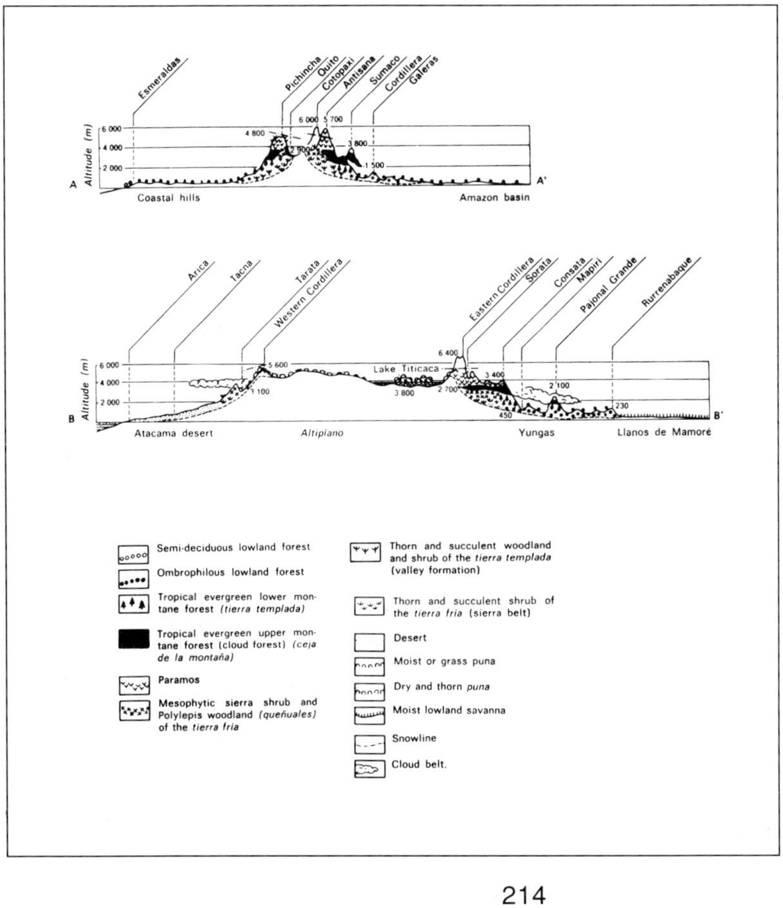

Figure 6.12: Vegetation belts in the Central Andes. Cross-sections through the Andes at the levels of Quito, Ecuador (A to A') and Lake Titicaca, Peru (B to B'). See figure 6.11 for positions of cross-sections.
Modified from Troll, 1968, by Thomas et al., 1977

disappearance, of open *Polylepis* woodland in the humid punas, and the beginning of overgrazing in the dry punas. The humid, dry, and desert punas are outlined in Figure 6.13.

Humid puna: Mean annual temperatures are between 3°C and 8°C, while absolute minima may be as low as -10°C. Static and dynamic frosts occur during the night and early in the morning, principally during the dry season, but occasionally also during the wet season. In the dry season, diurnal temperature range is considerable (15°C or more). The total amount of precipitation varies from 800 mm to 1 200 mm per year. Most of it falls during the months from November to April. One important feature of the puna ecosystems is the north-south climatic gradient noted above; in the south the rainy season is shorter. Thermal seasonality also becomes more pronounced toward the south, as does the water deficit. Variability of annual precipitation is another important feature that characterizes the southward trend, and one that clearly influences agricultural practices. Table 6.2 represents this trend. Quito, Cerro de Pasco, La Oroya, and Yauricocha have low coefficients of rainfall variation that are comparable to the wet tropical lowlands, whereas Cuzco, La Paz, and Oruro show the increased variation characteristic of the south-central Andes.

Puna vegetation is classified as tropical or subtropical alpine bunch-grass, with or without open stands of evergreen deciduous shrubs and dwarf shrubs. Floristically, humid and dry puna are closely related. The following variants can be recognized:

1) puna mat formed by densely packed mats of herbaceous vegetation, including cushion and rosette plants alternating with patches of bare ground
2) tussock grass communities in flats and more open areas

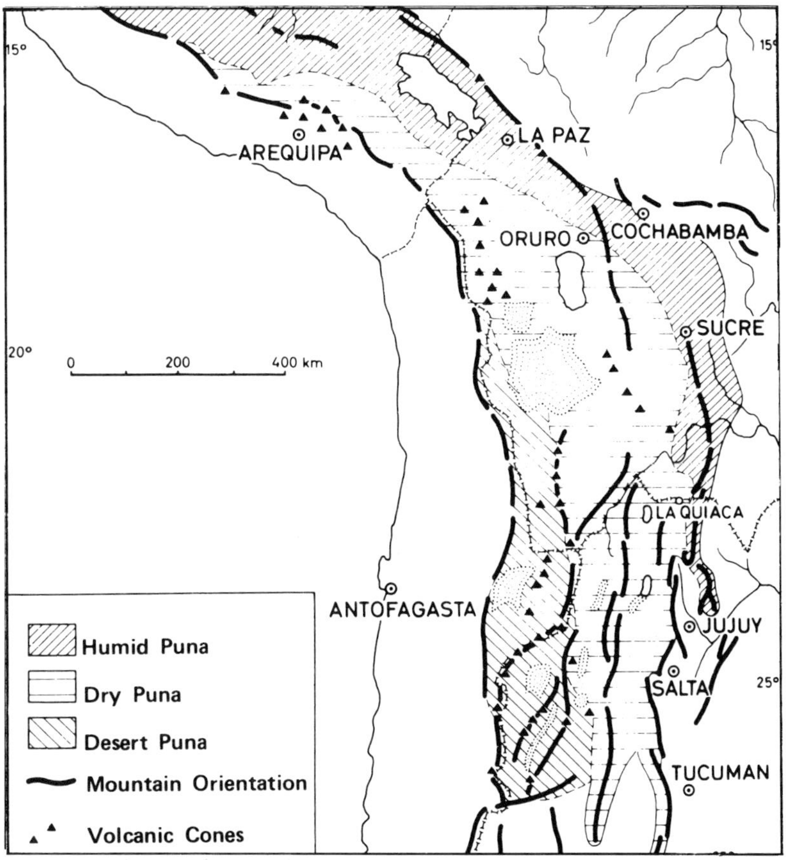

Figure 6.13: *Map of puna lands in the Central Andes.* Modified from Cabrera, 1968

3) distichia moor surrounding small lakes and streams and on more poorly drained soils
4) rocky areas where lichens, mosses and ferns are more abundant
5) groves of *Polylepis* spp., *Budleja* spp. and other woody species.

There have been changes in vegetation composition as a result of human activities. For example, there has been a severe reduction of elfin woodland into groves or thickets as a result of exploitation of wood for fuel, tools, and house construction. Fortunately, some recent experiences in stem cutting propagation with *Polylepis* (one of the endangered trees) has been successful in Huascaran National Park, Peru. The pressures of heavy grazing have contributed to decreases in palatable species, and increases in unpalatable species such as *Opuntia flocosa*, which is an indicator of grazing land deterioration. On the positive side, the introduction of seeded grass and clover in some areas has re-established palatable forage.

Dry puna: This ecosystem shows a greater contrast between seasons than the humid puna. Here, the rainy period becomes progressively shorter while the dry season is lengthened. Daily maximum temperatures will fluctuate between 15°C and 20°C, while the minima may fall as low as -10°C. Frost occurs on an almost daily basis. Here, as in most cold environments, cold and dryness interact to limit soil genesis.

Troll (1968) refers to dry puna as the "tola belt" due to the presence of evergreen bushes of which *Lepidophyllum quadrangulare* is quite common. The vegetation corresponds to bunch grass of varying coverage with dwarf shrubs and cushion plants. Ground cover ranges between 15 and 70 per cent, but in most cases it is less than 50 per cent. Within this ecosystem, the shrub communities, or tolares, become very apparent. The dominant species are shrubs from 0.5 m to 1 m in height. Although the spectrum of species composition varies, the most common ones are *Lepidophyllum quadrangulare*, *Fabiana densa*, and several species of *Baccharis*.

Desert puna: The southward position of the desert puna (Figure 6.13) contributes to even lower temperatures than other puna ecosystems. Moreover, the extreme aridity produces very marked diurnal temperature variation. This ecosystem is probably the most inhospitable in the Central Andes because of the combined climatic effects of hypoxia, cold and aridity. The desert puna is also the cross-over zone between the Atacama desert to the west and the Patagonian arid zone to the east. One of the essential features of punas, particularly desert punas, is internal drainage. With the exception of a few rivers in the southern part of the desert puna that feed the Rios Grande and Pilcomayo, rivers do not flow out of the puna ecosystems. Accordingly, the flat regions are dominated by large areas of ground coated with saline crust known as the "salares".

Vegetation cover does not usually exceed 15 per cent, although in isolated wet areas ("vegas") the coverage will be greater. The most diversified families of plants are *Compositae*, *Graminae*, *Leguminosae*, *Solanacae* and *Verbenacae*.

Site	Coefficient of variation in precipitation %	Altitude (metres)	Latitude and longitude
Quito, Ecuador	15	2818	0°S, 78°W
Yauricocha, Peru	10	4650	12°S, 76°W
Cerro de Pasco, Peru	11	4328	11°S, 76°W
La Oroya, Peru	14	3700	12°S, 75°W
Cuzco, Peru	27	3312	14°S, 72°W
La Paz, Bolivia	19	4105	16°S, 68°W
Oruro, Bolivia	28	3708	18°S, 67°W

Table 6.2: *Variation in precipitation along a southward trend in the highland Andes.*
Data from Johnson, 1976

Endemic genera include *Parastrephia, Lampaya, Chersodoma, Hemimunroa, Eustephiopsis, Anthobryum, Oreocerus, Chilio trichiopsis, Lophopapus* and *Urmeneata*. Most plants of the desert puna are adapted to frost, drought, and salt.

Puna altitudinal belts: Cabrera (1968) identifies two major puna altitudinal belts—the *punena* and the *altoandina*. The punena belt (3 700 m to 4 400 m) includes flat surfaces and foothills of the altiplano. The discussion of wet, dry, and desert punas has focused on Cabrera's punena belt. The altoandina belt is at higher elevations. Climatic conditions here are severe with mean daily temperatures normally near or below 0°C. Vegetation is characterized by low and open steppe of xerophytic grasses with some pulvinate dicotyledons. This belt is floristically related to the paramo and to Patagonia. Endemic genera include *Oxchloe, Patosia, Distichia* and *Werneria*.

Puna-temperate ecosystem: suni

This ecosystem marks the transition between the cold punas and the more temperate systems. The suni ecosystem is located between 3 600 m and 3 900 m at the lower edge of the punas. Two suni subsystems are the *altiplano suni* and the *suni of the slopes*.

Altiplano suni: This area surrounds Lake Titicaca and includes extensive flats at about 3 800 m. Vegetation is largely gramineae characterized by a wide variety of species. The prairie grasses can be as high as 60 cm in the most favourable sites. A few trees exist, especially around houses (*Polylepis*). Since the second half of the 19th century there has been widespread introduction of eucalyptus trees.

Exploitation of the region has been sustained and intensive. There have been modifications by the introduction of new animal species (sheep and cattle) and new cultigens *(Gramineae* and *Leguminosae)* following the Spanish conquest. Cultivated crops include potatoes, oca, olluco, quinoa and canihua (native chenopods), barley, oats, and onions. Around the margins of Lake Titicaca, giant reeds *(Totorales)* are used for building purposes and for fodder. Lake pastures are used for cattle which eat the algae *(llacho)* associated with small crustacea. The human population density surrounding the lake is as high as 100/km^2, in contrast to the haciendas beyond the lake on the altiplano where population densities are generally less than 10/km^2.

Slopes suni: These are the slopes at the borders of the puna lands and the low valleys and basins within the altiplano of Peru and Bolivia. The transition occurs from puna steppe and prairie to the shrub-covered heathland with grasses and many species of woody plants. In the wet season, the moisture allows the growth of mosses and a herbaceous ground cover that limits soil loss from heavy water runoff. In the dry season, there is rapid slope dessication. This and other climatic effects of topographic variation are pronounced. Examples of slope suni ecosystems are the La Paz basin and the eastern Andean slopes near Macusani, Peru.

Temperate ecosystems: intermediate elevations

These highly diverse ecosystems are found largely in Peru north of the altiplano at elevations between 2 200 m and 3 600 m above sea level. Three kinds of ecosystems can be identified:

1) the upper dry valleys and slopes of the western part of the Cordillera Occidental;
2) the upper reaches of the eastern escarpment of the Cordillera Oriental; and
3) the central system (between the two major cordilleras) of valleys and basins such as the Callejon de Huaylas, the Mantaro Valley and the Cuzco Basin.

Western slope ecosystems: The gradient from northern Peru to northern Chile is one of a relatively moist equatorial climate in the north to a very arid one in the south. In general, however, the climate is characterized by dry conditions, mainly as the result of the Andean rainshadow, with ecosystems of low primary plant productivity. Human population density is very low, in contrast to the eastern escarpment.

Eastern escarpment: The upper reaches of the eastern escarpment are moist and foggy and grade downward into the wet montana and tropical rainforest or selva. It is in Peru and northern Bolivia that the moisture asymmetry in cross-section is most pronounced. These high slopes are most similar to the humid or cloud forests of eastern Colombia and Ecuador. They are variously known as ceja de la montana, "high selva", pajonales, and tropical semi-evergreen high mountain woodland and grassland.

The slopes are steep and gravity plays an important role in water circulation and geomorphic processes. At the highest elevations gully erosion is common, but below this is somewhat limited by forest vegetation cover. The steep slopes also limit agriculture, despite highly fertile soils and abundant rainfall, and overland travel during the rainy season is often restricted by landslides and mudflows.

Central valleys and basins: This ecosystem corresponds to the *estepa montana* and *bosque humedo montano* of Tosi (1960). Mean annual temperature is between 10°C and 18°C, and only slight frosts occur during the dry season. The rains, which fall largely during the winter period, are often associated with adiabatic-convective storms leading to heavy downpours which contribute to erosion. Two major divisions are governed by topography: the slopes, and the basin and valley floors.

Slopes are often steep and, although some underlying rock outcrops, most of the surfaces are covered with colluvium. Soil formation is retarded by a lack of water in the dry season and by the loss of materials through runoff, solifluction, and landslides. Small and very localized earth-flows occur when the liquidity threshold of the clays in the colluvial cover is reached. There are, however, mass movements of surface materials that often have disastrous effects (Weil et al., 1972). Fortunately, such movements occur rarely.

Human activity in modifying the slope ecosystems has been intensive and sustained for more than a thousand years. A sophisticated system of irrigation and terrace construction dates back to pre-Inca times, but is still in use today. The terraces, irrigation channels and intensive agricultural practices have profoundly modified the structure of the surface colluvial cover and the topography. Accordingly, natural climax vegetation has almost disappeared. The human-modified mosaic of vegetation includes the following:

1) Dry-farming regions *(secano)* with long fallow periods. Farming may be carried out on terraces.

2) Shrub-covered heath lands grazed by sheep, goat and cattle. Most of the bushes (lignosae, lupins, berberis) have drought-adapted leaves and come into flower at the end of the wet season when the grass cover is most developed.

3) Regions of irrigated fields under continuous cultivation.

4) Ravines *(quebradas)* in which humid vegetation can be found.

5) Introduced species, especially stands of eucalyptus trees.

Deposits of alluvium containing abundant pebble and rock debris cover the floors of basins and valleys. The characteristic night-time thermal inversions that occur during the dry season are accompanied by very early morning frosts which are dangerous to crops above 3 000 m.

Agricultural exploitation is widespread and intensive, and geomorphogenetic processes are partly governed by agricultural practices. Erosion is less marked than on the slopes, but there is some lateral erosion by the rivers during flood stage which undercuts the alluvial terraces. Man-made terraces on the slopes and basin margins tend to inhibit soil loss from erosion.

Warm ecosystems: yungas, montanas and coast

These ecosystems are found at altitudes of between 800 m and 2 200 m and include slopes and valley floors. Mean annual temperatures range from 17°C to 23°C. The two primary categories of ecosystems at these low elevations are:

1) the montane forests and grasslands/shrublands of the low eastern Andean flank, and

2) the xeric vegetation of the low Pacific flank.

Precipitation is sparse throughout the length of the Pacific flank in the Central Andes. Along the eastern flank, precipitation is greater in the north than in the south (Figure 6.4).

A number of terms have been used to describe the eastern and western Andean flanks and foothills. Cabrera and Willink (1973) employ *humid yungas* for the eastern and *dry yungas* for the western flanks; Troll (1968) uses *ombrophilous lowland forest* for the east and *dry loma vegetation* for the west (Figures 6.8, 6.11, and 6.12); while Czajka (1968) uses a variety of terms (Figure 6.9). Another regional term for the eastern tropical forest slopes is montana.

Eastern Andean flank: In many ways, the eastern slopes are similar to the wet forests of the Northern Andes. Here, the Central Andes has a season of reduced precipitation. These slopes were originally covered with a dense ombrophilous forest (regions with heavy precipitation) or with deciduous forest (regions with seasonal dryness). Some small areas of savanna remain today. Valleys have been extensively cleared, mainly during the last hundred years.

Human exploitation falls into four classes:

1) cattle pastures with seeded grass which require careful attention to prevent invasion by shrubs and other non-palatable plants
2) shrub cultivation of coffee, citrus fruits, and coca leaves *(Erythroxylon coca)*
3) staple food cultivation of maize, cassava (manioc), and plantain bananas and
4) forest timber logging.

Western Andean flank: This ecosystem is characterized by a high level of sunshine and an exceptionally light cloud cover (more than 300 sunny days per year). These conditions are in marked contrast to the coastal lowlands where cloud cover is heavy, particularly during the winter. Temperatures are variable but frosts are absent. Precipitation is slight, variable from year to year, almost always below 500 mm and often below 250 mm. Evaporation potential, on the other hand, is greater than 1 500 mm; hence, there is a significant water deficit.

The slopes are either rocky or covered with a colluvio-torrential mantle which is discontinuous and of uneven thickness, with large blocks set in a consolidated sand and silt matrix. Soil formation is extremely slow. Vegetation consists of a broken steppe with extensive bare soil and includes various families of cactus, oreopanax, and acacias. Along the allogenous water courses are found alders and tall reeds in the lower regions. After the rains, grass growth is rapid and dwarf asters flower.

Human population density along the coastal flank is low, although goat herding is practised. The valley floors and land along the bottom of the slopes are irrigated by water from the numerous streams that drain the western Andes. These valleys, which are densely populated along the coast, support intensive, high-yield cultivation of cash crops including maize, rice, cotton, tobacco, garden vegetables, peppers, sugar-cane and fruit trees.

The Southern Andes

The distribution of major ecozones of the Southern Andes is shown in Figure 6.14. The coastal desert (Atacama) and the desert puna (indicated as areas 1 and 2 in Figure 6.14) overlap the dividing line between the Central and the Southern Andes. The greater part of the desert puna lies in the Central Andes, and was discussed above. The coastal desert will be examined in this section.

In the account of the ecology of the Northern and the Central Andes, organization of the ecosystems was based upon temperature and altitude gradients. This approach is less suitable for the Southern Andes due to the reduced influence of temperature and the increased importance of moisture. A simple organization based upon moisture and altitude will be used.

The Coast

Atacama Desert: Due to the pattern of atmospheric and ocean currents (notably the Humboldt current), much of the Pacific coastal plain is very arid and cooler than would be expected for such latitudes. The effect on temperature, in fact, is a moderating one, resulting in a series of similar mean temperatures all along the coast, despite a wide spread in latitude (A. Miller, 1976).

Moisture gradually decreases along the coast of Peru to reach an extreme of aridity in the Atacama Desert of southern Peru and northern Chile. Here, the mean annual precipitation (at Arica, Chile) is less than one millimetre, making it one of the driest places on earth. Mean annual temperature for this part of Chile is from 16°C to 19°C, with a yearly maximum of 31°C and a minimum of between 3°C and 8°C. Wind speed (2-6 m/sec) and direction (south to southwest) are constant.

Of the many streams which arise in the Andes of northern Chile, very few north of Copiapo reach the sea. So intense is the aridity that large areas are without visible plant life and, therefore, without animal life. In addition, the arid region extends to a greater height on the mountain slopes than it does in most of Peru (Sauer, 1950). Some agriculture is practised with the aid of irrigation near the more humid limits of this zone, but most of the economy of the area is based on its considerable mineral wealth (Robinson, 1967).

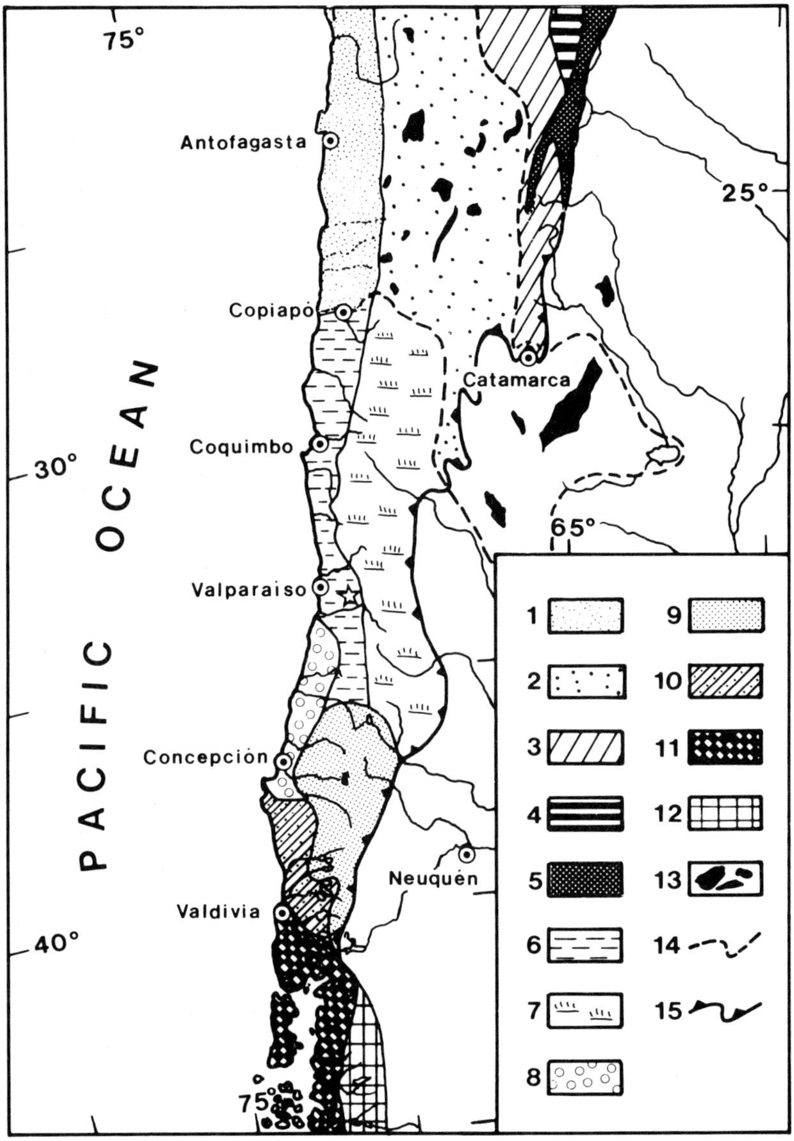

Figure 6. 14: *Map of vegetation in the Southern Andes. Vegetation belts and other symbols are: 1. coastal desert (Atacama); 2. arid or desert puna; 3. dry puna; 4. subtropical mountain meadows; 5. montane forests; 6. Mediterranean scrub; 7. mountain grasslands; 8. sclerophyllous woodland and shrubland; 9. Araucarian forest; 10. Nothofagus forest; 11 . Valdivian rainforest; 12. Patagonian deciduous forest; 13. salt pans or salares; 14. arid zone limits; 15. eastern Andean margin.*
Modified from Hueck, 1966; Troll, 1968

Mediterranean scrub ecosystem: In the southern portion of the Atacama Desert, south of Copiapo (latitude 27° South), the number of permanent streams increases and the vegetation (desert scrub and cactus) begins to indicate semi-arid conditions. At latitude 30° South (near Coquimbo and La Serena), there is a pattern of seasonal moisture. This is the Mediterranean zone, an area of summer drought and winter rain, or a reversal of the seasonal pattern in the Central Andes (this zone is indicated by areas 6 and 8 in Figure 6.14). Along the coast of Chile there is a gradual increase in rainfall from north to south, with winter precipitation and in the far south year-round rainfall. Between latitudes 27° and 31° South, the precipitation increases nearly tenfold from 25 mm to 200 mm annually and most of this falls in the winter months between June and August (A. Miller, 1976). At Valparaiso and

Santiago at about latitude 33°South, the annual precipitation ranges between 350 mm and 500 mm and in other areas of this region may reach 800 mm (P. Miller et al., 1977; A. Miller, 1976).

The Mediterranean scrub region of Chile is one of five such regions throughout the world; the other four are found as follows:

1) surrounding the Mediterranean Sea,
2) along the southwest coast of Africa,
3) in southern and southwestern Australia, and
4) in southern California.

All result from similar air and ocean circulation patterns and, as a consequence, are centred around latitudes 33° North and South and are usually on the western coasts of continents. Typically, Mediterranean scrub regions have warm or hot, dry summers and mild, wet winters with most of the precipitation resulting from a few intense winter frontal storms. Solar radiation and evaporation rates are high in summer and low in winter (P. Miller et al., 1977). Between Santiago and Coquimbo, soils are of the productive Chestnut-Brown type. Further south, especially beyond Concepcion, increasing podsolization lowers soil fertility (Sauer, 1950).

While the Mediterranean zone is basically a land of grass, cactus and scrub, the distribution of certain vegetation types within this ecozone is related to precipitation differences. The drier areas tend to have the most annuals (therophytes), the most succulents, the most drought-deciduous plants, the fewest woody plants and also desert shrubs with the smallest leaves. Moister areas are characterized by taller, woodier plants and by increasing numbers of sclerophyllous (hard-leafed) shrubs. Within the moist areas, low-elevation sites tend to have plants with large evergreen leaves and high-elevation sites tend to have winter-deciduous plants (Mooney et al., 1977). The term "moist" as used here is a relative one, since the whole Mediterranean zone has a range of life forms typical of arid and semi-arid regions.

Agriculture is very important in this part of Chile, which is the most populous and urbanized area of the country. Within the Longitudinal Valley, cereals (especially wheat), citrus fruits, grape vines, vegetables and fodder crops are produced. Despite the dry summers, extensive agriculture is possible because water supplies for irrigation from mountain streams are abundant. Between Santiago and Coquimbo and on the lower slopes of the Andes and the coastal range, livestock raising (especially sheep and goat) assumes greater importance than does cultivation (Robinson, 1967; Sick, 1969).

Wet forests: The Bio Bio River of coastal Chile may be used as a demarcation line between areas with dry and wet summers. North of this line, less than 5 per cent of the annual precipitation occurs during the summer months (December-February). South of the Bio Bio, the amount and frequency of summer rain increases sharply. By Puerto Montt, precipitation has become a twelve-month phenomenon with nearly 2 000 mm annually and forty days of rain during the summer. Wetter conditions south of the Bio Bio River are due in large part to the reduced effectiveness of the coastal range as a barrier to westerly air flow for it gradually becomes lower and less continuous. The rather dramatic change in precipitation pattern is reflected in differences in vegetation. The area of Mediterranean scrub, hard leaf vegetation and irrigated agriculture merges into a region of large evergreen forests, and cultivated wheat, oats, potatoes and apples (A. Miller, 1976).

In the Mediterranean scrub and hard-leaf forest areas of the west coast, a limited distribution of the *Nothofagus* (South American beech) genus occurs along the coastal range and in other areas where the annual rainfall reaches 750 mm or higher (P. Miller et al., 1977). As the frequency of hard-leaf vegetation diminishes southward there is a corresponding increase in *Nothofagus* forests. In the area north of Valdivia (area 10 in Figure 6.14) the deciduous species *N. obliqua* and *N. procera,* which may grow as high as 40 m, are the dominant trees. Other *Nothofagus* species grow much farther south, on the eastern side of the Andean cordillera bordering the Patagonian steppe (Weber, 1969).

South of Valdivia, the *Nothofagus* forest gives way to the Valdivian rainforest, an ecosystem characterized by a great number of species. The Valdivian area extends from the coast (at about latitude 40° South) up to 500 m altitude. Rain generally exceeds 2 000 mm/year and the mean annual temperature for Valdivia is 11.9°C, a degree or two less further south. No frosts occur in this area. Many of the trees are 40 to 50 m in height and most are evergreens. The frequency of epiphytes and lianas suggests a resemblance to the tropical rainforests of the Northern Andes. Some of the genera

At 5 400m in the Cordillera Real of the Bolivian eastern Andes, the limit of vegetation is almost reached. Small glaciers and permanent snowfields occur on the far ridge while temporary snowbanks occupy lee slopes in the middle ground

represented are *Aextoxicon, Laurelia, Nothofagus, Drimys* and occasionally *Podocarpus.* The bamboo-like *Chusquea* is found in patches throughout these forests (Weber, 1969).

The highlands

Mountain grasslands and scrublands: With the exception of the humid eastern slopes of the Sierras of extreme northwestern Argentina, in the highland areas of the southern subregion, temperatures and precipitation depend on the altitude and exposure to the west. Exposed areas have a smaller average diurnal range (e. g. Cristo Redentor, Argentina: altitude, 3 800 m, temperature range, 8°C) than do closed valleys within the cordillera which may have a range of 20° C or more. Precipitation increases with height up to the mountain crests with most high mountain areas receiving three or four times as much as the central valley at the same latitude. Between latitudes 30° and 35° South, precipitation increases north to south from less than 300 mm to more than 3 000 mm annually. Cloudiness and precipitation decline rapidly to the east everywhere south of 28°. The Argentine (eastern) slopes are quite arid, especially below 1 000 m. In highland areas, winds are frequent and commonly exceed 30 or 40 m/sec during storms. Heavy winter snow may make valleys and mountain passes inaccessible along the western slopes while the corresponding eastern slopes remain clear due to the asymmetry of precipitation in this area (A. Miller, 1976).

South of the desert puna ecosystem (Puna de Atacama) and north of latitude 37° South is a semi-arid area along the Andean cordillera where scrub vegetation occupies the lower slopes. At higher elevations, the vegetation consists mostly of coarse alpine grasses (Sauer, 1950).

Forests: South America has few species of needle-leaf trees and most of these are found in the southern half of the continent. The most abundant genera are *Araucaria, Podocarpus* and *Libocedrus.* The area south of the mountain grasslands is called the Araucarian forest ecosystem due to the frequent occurrence of *Araucaria araucana.* This conifer is found, either alone or with species of *Nothofagus,* between 600 and 1 800 m. On the eastern side of the cordillera, this forest belt borders the Patagonian steppe. Another important south Andean tree is *Libocedrus chilensis,* a cedar-type conifer. This species occurs in much the same area and habitat as *Araucaria araucana,* extending, however, further north and south and invading further into the eastern steppe (Weber, 1969). ■

Human populations in the Andes

Prehispanic populations

Despite the fact that the early prehistory of the Andes is just beginning to be defined, evidence is abundant for a considerable time depth of human habitation. Data from archaeological sites throughout the Andes suggest a pattern of continuous settlement that may date to as early as 15 000 or 20 000 years ago (Cruxent, 1968; Forbis, 1974).

Early peoples

Archaeological sites with reasonably accurate dates from 8 000 to 14 000 years ago (BP) are known from as far south as Fell's Cave (11 000 BP) in southern Patagonia, Chile (Bennett and Bird, 1960), and as far north as the El Jobo complex (13 000 BP) in northwestern Venezuela (Bryan et al., 1978). Between these two geographic extremes are sites in the highlands of Colombia (El Abra Cave), Ecuador near Quito (El Inga) (Mayer-Oakes and Bell, 1960), Peru in the Callejon de Huaylas (Guitarrero Cave) (Lynch and Kennedy, 1970) and in the central region (Lauricocha Caves), Argentina near Cordoba (Intihuasi Cave), and central Chile (Laguna de Tagua Tagua) (Montane, 1968). These sites are illustrated in Figure 6.15. Of greatest antiquity are cultural remains in association with extinct mammals from the Pikimachay Cave in the Ayacucho Valley, Peru. The lowest levels of Pikimachay Cave have been dated at more than 14 000 years ago (MacNeish et al., 1970; MacNeish, 1971).

Many of these sites are at very high elevations and this has some bearing on human adaptation to altitude stress. For example, El Inga near Quito is at an elevation of about 2 500 m above sea level, Pikimachay Cave is at 3 300 m, and the Lauricocha Cave site in central Peru is well above 4 000 m. Since this time range was one in which mountain glaciers were retreating, it is likely that the very high-altitude cave sites were only summer encampments (Lanning, 1967:47). On the other hand, many of the major valley systems in the Central Andes are between 2 700 and 3 300 m, so it is a safe assumption that some of these early populations were permanent high-altitude dwellers.

The earliest migrants to South America represented by the sites described above lived together in small, nomadic hunting and gathering bands. They entered the continent and probably proceeded south via the Andean highland valleys and western coastal regions (Newman, 1958; Sauer, 1944). Their stone tools were pre-projectile point and incorporated relatively crude flake, chopper, and biface traditions (Willey, 1971). Principal hunting was of large Pleistocene mammals such as the horse, ground sloth and mastodon. About 11 000 years ago, a new and more effective tool tradition arose in which bifacially flaked projectile points were manufactured. Willey (1971) calls this the "Old South American Hunting" tradition in which Pleistocene megafauna continued to be hunted. With the decline in large Pleistocene mammal populations about 9 000 BP, the "Andean Hunting-Collecting" tradition arose. This is a distinctly highland pattern of hunting deer and camelids such as the guanaco, and gathering plant foods. A pattern of transhumance, or regular human movements to follow natural food crops and wild animals, was probably practised; but at the least, as Willey (1971: 50) notes, "this period was characterized by a regional 'settling in' and specialized

Figure 6.15: *Early human habitation sites and several major prehispanic cities in the Andes*

subsistence exploitation of particular environments". The Andean Hunting-Collecting tradition of subsistence persisted in the Andean highlands until permanent settlements and plant and animal domestication were fully developed about 4 500 years ago (2 500 B.C.). Following this time, human settlements, technology and population grew rapidly (Lanning, 1974).

The earliest permanent sedentary villages known are in the coastal areas of Ecuador, Peru and Chile. There is little knowledge of the highlands, where hunting and plant collecting persisted much later than on the coast, and where population size was also low. By about 2 000 BC, small villages were found throughout the coastal valleys, in which fishing, shellfish gathering and plant domestication were principal subsistence modes (Lanning, 1967). Several hundred years later in the Central Andes, full-time farming villages developed as populations moved inland from the coast and no longer depended on littoral-zone foods. It was at this time that the earliest large-scale architecture (in the form of adobe pyramids) and pottery appeared in the Central Andes and coast. The period between 1 800 and 900 BC, as evidenced by monumental structures, was a time of rapid population growth, nucleated settlements, and the rise of a system of centralized political authority. Lanning (1974) identifies this as the period of incipient states and early civilization.

Advanced societies

There were three pan-Central Andean cultural traditions in the period between 900 BC and the Spanish conquest in AD 1532 (Figure 6.15). The first was the Chavin style as exemplified by the temple of Chavin de Huantar in northern highland Peru. Chavin persisted until about 200 BC. The second was the Tiahuanaco Empire that expanded north and south from its centre in the Bolivian altiplano, and its associated centres of Huari in southern highland Peru and Pachacamac on the central Peru coast (Lanning, 1974). These centres, which shared traditions and art styles, persisted from about AD 600 to 1000. Finally, after AD 1438, the Inca Empire, with its centre in the city of Cuzco in the southern Peruvian highlands, began its expansion (Rowe, 1946). The period between Chavin and the Tiahuanaco-Huari empires (200 BC to AD 600) was characterized by population growth and the first establishment of large cities (Huari, Pucara, and Tiahuanaco). The intermediate period between the Tiahuanaco-Huari empires and the Inca Empire (AD 1000 to 1438) was a time when the Central Andes was divided into small regional states in which there was extensive interstate commerce (Lanning, 1967).

At its maximum extent the Inca Empire incorporated highland and coastal zones of Ecuador, Peru and Chile, and highland zones of Bolivia and Argentina. The empire extended more than 3 000 km, but was limited in the north by the breakup of the Andes into separate cordilleras in Colombia, in the east by the montana forests, and in the south by the arid Gran Chaco of Paraguay and Argentina and Chilean grasslands and forests. Moreover, the Inca were able to incorporate only those peoples with a state political organization, agrarian-pastoralist subsistence base and folk-peasant culture. As Steward and Faron (1959: 116) point out, "The whole Inca subsistence pattern and the sociopolitical structure were highly adapted to an irrigation area and could not be supported in a tropical rainforest like that of the Amazon basin, in a steppe country like the Gran Chaco, or a mediterrean climate like that of Chile." Hence, it was a combination of environmental and socio-cultural factors that limited the expansion of the Inca Empire and not the first appearance of the Spanish.

Outside of the realm of the Central Andes were two broad categories of Andean populations: the chiefdoms of Colombia and northern Ecuador, and the southern Andean farmers and pastoralists of Chile and Argentina (Steward and Faron, 1959). The greatest chiefdom was that of the Chibcha, an organization of five states in the central Colombian highlands with the largest state at Bogota (Kroeber, 1946). The Chibcha practised intensive agriculture, had the most advanced civilization between Peru and Guatemala, and were exploited unmercifully for their gold by the Spanish. Societies in the Southern Andes were not as advanced in political organization, arts, crafts and architecture as the Chibcha. But they did practise intensive agriculture and herded llamas and alpacas, as in the Central Andes. The northernmost groups, Atacameño and Diaguita, were incorporated into the Inca Empire, whereas Araucanians further to the south in Chile were never fully subjugated by the Inca (Cooper, 1946).

Population

There is very little agreement among estimates of human population numbers in the Andes on the eve of the Spanish conquest (Denevan, 1976). Estimates of population are shown in Table 6.3 for Peru, the Central Andes, and the entire Andes. Some estimates represent much more careful calculation than others. One of the most detailed counts is by Stewart (1949) based upon compilations from the *Handbook of South American Indians*. The remarkable variance in the estimates in Table 6.3 can be attributed to the unavoidably crude extrapolation techniques chosen. Three basic ways of estimating numbers have been used:

1) native and Spanish tax registers and archival accounts of the numbers living in given areas;
2) calculation of population decline (ratios), due to the high mortality from epidemics, social disruption, and poor treatment of Indians by the Spanish (usually based upon late 16th century censuses or population nadir values); and
3) calculation of population densities for given areas or estimated densities and land carrying capacities. Most estimates are likely to exaggerate population numbers, although the range in estimates is testimony to the degree of uncertainty concerning pre-conquest population size.

What appear to be the most reasonable values for the Andes are listed in Table 6.4. Population density was greatest for the Chibcha who lived in a very wet and fertile area of the Colombian highlands. Highest densities for extensive areas were in the Central Andes, particularly Peru and Bolivia.

Spanish colonial times

The period immediately following the Spanish conquest of the Inca Empire in 1532 was one of rapid population decline and assimilation and acculturation of Indians throughout the Andes. There was, however, considerable variation in resistance to Spanish domination. For example, Chibcha defence against the Spanish was ineffectual, and this major chiefdom in Colombia was totally under Spanish control in 1541, just five years after its first discovery (Kroeber, 1946). In contrast, southern Chilean Araucanians fought doggedly, and often successfully, from the earliest Spanish settlement in 1541 and throughout the 17th and 18th centuries, and

Reference	Peru	Inca Empire or Central Andes*	Total Andes
Kroeber (1939)	-	-	3.00
Shea (1976)	1.34	2.03	-
Rosenblat (1954)	-	3.30	4.75
Bennett (1946)	-	-	4.50-7.50
Steward (1949)	2.33	4.08	6.27
Shea (1976)**	3.43	4.99	-
Rowe (1946)	-	6.00	-
Polo (1913)	-	-	10.00-12.00
Baudin (1961)	-	-	11.00-12.00
Sapper (1924)	-	-	12.00-15.00
Smith (1970)	-	***12.14	-
Dobyna (1966)	-	-	30.00-37.50

The Central Andes in the anthropological literature usually includes Ecuador, Peru and Bolivia, whereas the Inca Empire included parts of Chile and Argentina as well. A physiographic definition of the Central Andes excludes Ecuador.
***Shea's extrapolation backwards in time from data of Cook (1973).*
****Highlands or sierra given as 4.64; lowlands or coast given as 7.50.*

Table 6.3: *Estimates of native American population (in millions) in the Andes before the Spanish conquest of Peru in 1532.*
Modified from Denevan, 1976, with additions

***Figure 6.16:** Indian population change from 1520 to 1970. The geographic area covers the Audiencias of Lima and Charcas before 1800 and Peru and Bolivia after 1800.*
Data from Kubler, 1946, 1952 and Salzano, 1968

Area	Population (000s)	Land area (000 km ^{2})	Population density (persons/km ^{2})
Venezuela, North of Orinoco	144	320	0.45
Colombia, Chibcha	300	24	12.50
Other	700	358	1.84
Ecuador	500	180	2.78
Peru	2 330	596	3.91
Bolivia	1 170	300	3.90
Southern Andes			
Atacameno	40	301	0.13
Diaguita	41	316	0.13
Araucanians	1 050	374	2.81
Total	6 275	2 769	2.25

***Table 6.4:** Steward's (1949) estimates of native American population sizes and densities before the conquest*

were only completely "pacified" in 1883 (Cooper, 1946). Among the Quechua-speakers of the former Inca Empire, there was armed conflict with the Spanish, including the unsuccessful rebellion of Manco Inca in 1536-37 and the development of the Neo-Inca state which was conquered in 1572 (Kubler, 1946).

Spanish religious, socio-cultural, and economic institutions rapidly spread throughout the Central Andes after 1572. The Spanish, as the ruling class, exploited Quechua Indian labour through the system of *encomienda,* in which a Spaniard would be granted the rights to utilize the labour of a specific group of Indians (Steward and Faron, 1959: 151). Indians were used under this system as forced labour in agriculture and in the gold and silver mines. Such conditions contributed to very high Indian mortality, along with the successive epidemics of smallpox, measles, influenza and other diseases that struck the pristine Andean populations during the 16th and 17th centuries (Dobyns, 1963).

Another cause for high mortality of natives during the colonial period was the Spanish practice of replacing native cultivated foods with their own more familiar European foods. The replacement of maize, potatoes and quinoa with grapes, wheat and barley, which were not adapted to Andean soils and climate and not as productive cultigens, led to reduced food production and further stress on the Indians. Resettlement of the Indians from rural settings to villages and towns was also practised by the Spanish. This system of reurbanization was known as *reduccion* (Kubler, 1946). Each of these disruptive factors certainly contributed to states of social disorganization which aggravated the already poor conditions of hygiene and health, and which, in turn, led to the high mortality of the Andean native.

Figure 6.16 illustrates an approximation of Indian population changes from the years 1520 to 1970. These data are for the Audiencias of Lima and Charcas from 1561 to 1976, and are based upon tax registers and censuses (Kubler, 1946). The two Audiencias were Spanish colonial administrative units that corresponded to present-day Peru and Bolivia. The three estimates of pre-conquest population numbers represent several views of Andean population dynamics between 1520 and 1561. Smith (1970), and to a greater extent Dobyns (1966) argue that catastrophic population declines resulted from epidemics that struck Andean populations several years before and after the first direct contacts with the Spaniards in Peru. Kubler (1946) and Shea (1976), on the other hand, believe that epidemics were minor in their effects. Kubler (1946), however, accepts a value close to that of Steward (1949) and believes that Andean depopulation resulted from out-migration of Indians, perhaps to montana zones in response to the

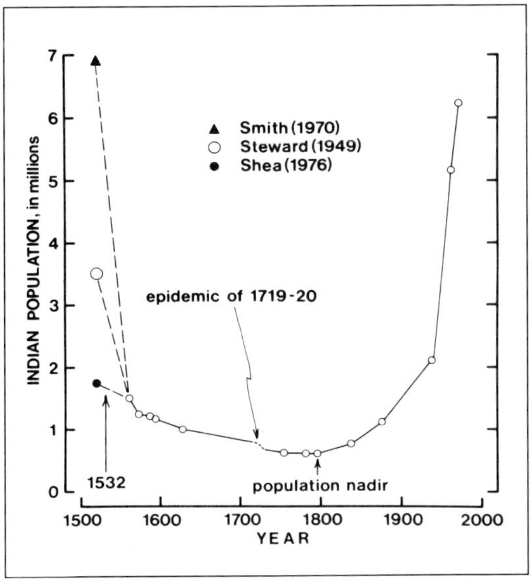

conquest. In any case, those who believe that epidemics were a major factor in Andean depopulation agree that mortality was much higher on the coast than in the highlands.

The trend of post-conquest native population decrease began to level off by the end of the 18th century. Since that time native Andean populations have increased dramatically; in 1970 the Indians of Peru and Bolivia probably exceeded pre-conquest numbers. Around the middle of the 20th century, Central Andean Indians began to lose their numerical majority over mestizos and hispanics. In 1940 the Indian population in Peru constituted 42 per cent of the total, a value that can be compared with 58 per cent Indian in 1795 and 95 per cent Indian in 1586 (Kubler, 1952). Therefore, the rapid population growth experienced by Andean Indians after 1800 has not been as great as the population growth rates of mestizos and hispanics.

Colonial conditions in Ecuador—the Audiencia of Quito—were quite similar to those in Peru and Bolivia to the south. Indians were exploited for labour in the gold mines and agrarian work, but it is likely that "more Indians were used in mining than in any other Spanish activity" (Murra, 1946: 816). The variety of distinct tribal languages of Ecuadorian groups were all lost during the 18th century, after which the dominant languages became Quechua and Spanish (Murra, 1946).

The republican period of the Andean nations following independence from Spain began in 1818 for Chile, 1819 for Colombia, 1822 for Ecuador, 1824 for Peru, and 1825 for Bolivia. Independence had only minor effects on the Indian and mestizo peasants of the Andes. The political power and authoritarian rule of the Spanish were transferred to the *caudillos* or wealthy landowners and to the Catholic Church (Pendle, 1967 :125).

Present population structure and distribution

Population values for the Andean nations in 1970 are given in Table 6.5. Of these seven nations, Colombia, Ecuador, Peru and Bolivia are, at the same time, nations with:

1) substantial numbers of individuals who reside in highland zones;
2) a large proportion of the population who are Indian (excluding Colombia); and
3) a sizeable rural population that is agrarian-based.

Concerning origins and present composition, populations from Venezuela and Colombia are principally mestizo; Chilean and Argentine populations are European; and Ecuador, Peru, and Bolivia are inhabited largely by mestizos and Quechua and Aymara Indians. The values given for high-altitude residents above 2 500 m are acknowledged to be gross estimates. Yet even with a 25 per cent overestimate, the total population number identifies the Northern and Central Andes as supporting the largest resident high-altitude population in the world.

From Venezuela in the north to Bolivia in the south, the highlands form the core of human settlement in these nations (Robinson, 1967). In Venezuela the extension of the Cordillera Oriental is at relatively low elevations and few people live at very high altitudes. Nevertheless, about 70 per cent of the population reside at moderate elevations in this northwestern highland area. In Colombia more than 75 per cent of the population dwell in the interior highlands and at considerably greater elevations than in Venezuela. The Cundinamarca upland basin with Bogota at its centre is the most densely populated highland area in the Andes (Guhl, 1968).

There are ten basins or valley systems between the eastern and western ranges of the

Andes in Ecuador. About half the population lives in these highland valleys. Within Peru slightly more than half the population resides in the six principal intermountain valley systems. In both Ecuador and Peru increasing population pressure in the highlands has produced substantial downward migration to the coast (Weil et al., 1972: 87). As a result coastal populations in both countries are growing at greater rates than highland populations, and there are major population shifts under way. As an example, the highland Peruvian Departments of Ayacucho, Cuzco and Puno showed an average population increase of 14 per cent between 1960 and 1970 in contrast to a 37 per cent increase for the nation (Wilkie and Reich, 1977: 81).The altiplano, or high plateau, which is the drainage basin of Lake Titicaca, encompasses parts of southern Perú and northern Bolivia. This vast expanse of land has a base elevation of about 3 800 m and supports large numbers of Bolivians, perhaps half the population. The altiplano is also an area of the Andes with a very large Indian population—largely Quechua and Aymara. About 80 per cent of the Peruvian altiplano population are Indian (Dew, 1967: 63).

Although the inhabitants of highlands of the Central Andes are predominantly rural, a considerable number live in large urban centres at high altitudes. Table 6.5 lists several large highland cities at elevations greater than 2 500 m: these support the population estimates given in Table 6.6. ■

Table 6.5: *Population of major Andean cities at elevations above 2 500 m.* From Wilkie and Reich, 1977: 84-85

City	Date	Population	Altitude, m *
Bogota, Colombia	1973	2 818 000	2 600
Quito, Ecuador	1972	565 000	2 800
Cuzco, Peru	1972	121 000	3 300
La Paz, Bolivia	1976	655 000	3 700
Cochabamba, Bolivia	1976	195 000	2 500
Oruro, Bolivia	1976	124 000	3 600
Total		4 478 000	

(All high-altitude cities are variable in elevation. For example, La Paz ranges from 3 230 m at its lowest level to the airport at 4 100 m* (Paz-Zamora et al., 1974)

Table 6.6: *Population values of Andean nations in 1970*

Nation	Total population* (000s)	% Rural population**	Population above 2500m***(000s)	% Population above 2 500 m
Venezuela	10 755	28	105	0.9
Colombia	22 160	42	5 666	25.6
Ecuador	6 028	54	2 047	34.0
Peru	13 586	51	5 774	42.5
Bolivia	4 658	65	3 676	78.9
Chile	9 780	30	55	0.6
Argentina	24 352	21	149	0.6
Total	91319	37	17472	19.1

* *From Organization of American States (1970).*

** *Rural areas are defined as settlements with less than 2 000 inhabitants.*

*** *Estimates of populations residing at altitudes greater than 2 500 m above sea level from Baker (1976); Venezuela estimate is based upon 5% of northern highland rural population* (Wilkie and Turovsky, 1976:80).

Stress and adaptation to high altitude

Human habitation and exploitation of the Andes has had its costs. These costs are in the environmental stresses felt by biological systems that reside at high elevations in any mountain zone. The stresses of high altitude arise from a number of sources, but the most serious, when compared with sea level, is the reduced amount of atmospheric oxygen associated with lowered barometric pressure. Such reduced terrestrial oxygen pressure is known as hypoxia.

High-altitude stresses

Hypoxia is an all-pervading stress that affects most systems within the human body. There are other climatic features of high altitude that stress humans independently of hypoxia, which may, in fact, also interact with hypoxic conditions. These are:

1) cold
2) low humidity
3) high wind flow, and
4) high levels of solar and cosmic radiation.

Associated with the geomorphology and topography of the Andes are problems for humans that include:

5) rugged and irregular relief
6) a monsoon pattern of rainfall with rain-shadow effects
7) rapid weathering and erosion, and poor development of soils, and
8) high amounts of terrestrial radiation.

All of these features lead to what Thomas and his colleagues (1976) have identified as "biotic communities with limited productivity". These environmental stresses and their effects on humans are discussed very briefly in the sections that follow.

Hypoxia

Reduced oxygen pressure from high terrestrial elevations is one of the most severe forms of climatic stress experienced by humans. Other forms of stress may be buffered by behavioural or cultural means, yet there are no effective ways of reducing hypoxic stress short of using bottled oxygen.

The effects of hypoxia are illustrated in Figure 6.17, which is a graph of the oxygen dissociation of haemoglobin in human blood. Oxygen is inhaled into the lungs where it passes into the bloodstream and is bound to haemoglobin (Hb). At sea level full saturation of haemoglobin with oxygen is about 97 per cent and each 100 ml of blood can carry about 19.5 ml of oxygen. This occurs at an oxygen pressure in the blood of slightly less than 100 mm Hg (or torr). The venous point, after oxygen is released to the tissues, involves a drop in pressure to about 40 mm Hg and a transfer of 5 ml of oxygen to the tissues. The broken line in Figure 6.17 indicates conditions in a newly resident individual at 4 000 m. With an oxygen pressure in the blood of only 57 mm Hg, haemoglobin is less than 90 per cent saturated with 17.5 ml of oxygen carried by each 100 ml of blood. Accordingly, the pressure drop to 40 mm Hg allows only 3 ml of oxygen to be delivered to the tissues, a value which is 60 per cent of that delivered at sea level. The adaptation of the respiratory, circulatory and oxygen transport systems to reduced amounts of atmospheric oxygen must take place for individuals to function at even close to normal levels at high altitude.

An elevation of 2 500 m is often taken as a "delimiter" of high-altitude stress (Pawson and Jest, 1978). This is an arbitrary choice of elevation, but one that is based upon the characteristics of the decline of the oxygen dissociation curve. For example, at 2 500 m, nearly all sea-level residents will experience some effects of the altitude, since arterial blood, at 93 per cent oxygen saturation, will

Figure 6.17: Oxygen dissociation curve of haemoglobin (Hb)

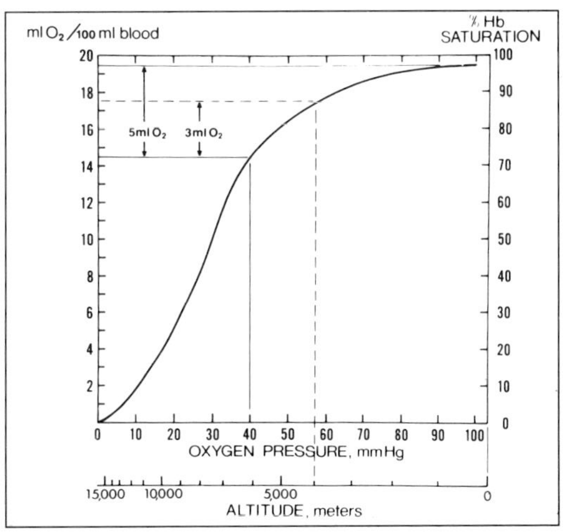

transfer only 4 ml of oxygen. Numerous studies have been conducted on how the body adapts physiologically to lowered atmospheric oxygen pressure. Of equal importance are studies of how hypoxia affects other systems in the body and how human behaviour is modified as an adaptive response to hypoxia.

Other climatic parameters

In tropical and subtropical highlands the occurrence of night-time frosts will vary from 0 to 100 per cent, depending on latitude and elevation. However, in most cases, diurnal temperature variation is large. The extent of night-time frosts is clearly a factor in cultivation, where either frost-resistant plants must be developed or cultivators must accept the risk of crop loss. At elevations where frost is common, a rare but unusually heavy snowfall may destroy crops despite their high degree of frost resistance. Other rare events, such as heavy wind flow with low temperatures, an unusually long dry season, or a prolonged drought will limit crop production and pasture for grazing animals. Despite the relatively well-watered conditions of the altiplano, a drought that struck Puno Department in Peru in 1956 contributed to crop losses of 80 per cent and cattle losses of 30 per cent (Dew, 1969: 89). Conversely, the monsoon rainfall pattern is accompanied by flooding during periods of heaviest precipitation.

Cold as a form of stress can be reduced by burning fuel for heat, by shelter, by clothing as insulation, and by biological adaptation of the individual. In high-altitude zones above 2 500 m fuel in the form of wood is limited or not present and principal reliance is placed upon effective shelter and well-designed clothing to combat the cold (Little and Hanna, 1978). Biological modes of adaptation to cold have been identified in the Andean native but of particular interest are the covariant stresses of cold and hypoxia which are known to interact and are more likely to increase the strain in the human biological system than hypoxia or cold alone (Little, 1976).

Radiation

Many forms of radiation are damaging to living tissues, from shortwave-length gamma and x-rays, to near-visible ultraviolet rays, and longwave microwaves. Terrestrial radiation in mountain regions in the United States is about 50 per cent greater than in lowland regions (Solon et al.,1960), and ultraviolet and cosmic radiation at 2 500 m or greater in the tropics is twice that at sea level (Buettner, 1969). Based upon the assumption that increased terrestrial and solar radiation at high altitudes should contribute to a high rate of mutation, Grahn and Kratchman (1963) conducted a study of neonatal death rates in the United States. Unfortunately, they were unable to control for terrestrial or solar radiation effects because of the covariant relationship between radiation, hypoxia and elevation. They did find a positive relationship between neonatal mortality and altitude.

Most highland populations are protected from the weakly penetrating ultraviolet radiation by adequate clothing, but the net effect of terrestrial and cosmic radiation on the high-altitude dweller is largely unknown. It may be that the total radiation exposure of the highland peasant, despite high levels, is still less than that received by the affluent sea-level resident with colour television, microwave oven and diagnostic x-rays.

Limitations to plant productivity

Hypoxia is relatively unimportant as a limiting factor to plant productivity at high altitude. Rather, it is the incidence of night-time frosts, moisture availability and soil properties that, if unfavourable, will limit productivity. Night-time frosts seldom occur below the elevation of 2 500 m from Colombia to southern Peru (Troll, 1968) At 4 000 m at least 80 per cent of the days of the year will have frost. Therefore, although latitude and local topographic conditions can influence frost rhythms, 4 000 m is close to the upper limit for most cultivated plants. There are some advantages to the pattern of mild, sunny days and cold nights below freezing that have been exploited by Central Andean natives. The preparation of chuno (dried potatoes) and charqui (dried meat) as forms of preserved food require a diurnal cycle of freezing, thawing, drying, and freezing again. Also, these foods can be preserved best under the dry conditions that exist between May and August in the Central Andean highlands.

The pattern of moisture availability for the Andes is indeed complex. There are, however,

East slope of the Bolivian Cordillera Real

some generalizations that can be made about precipitation. Within the highlands there is a gradient from well-watered in Colombia to very arid in northern Chile (Snow, 1976; Johnson, 1976). An associated north to south trend is: less seasonality of precipitation in wet areas and pronounced winter drought in arid areas. This trend is reversed in central Chile south of the Bio Bio River where winters are wetter and annual precipitation is high (Miller, 1976). The eastern slopes of the Andes are relatively wet, whereas the western slopes from Peru through northern Chile are arid.

Andean soils are highly diverse, but are subject to certain specific processes at high elevations. First, organic matter is often low because of slow decomposition rates in the cold. Second, solifluction can produce a denudation or total loss of vegetation from slopes (Troll, 1968). Third, steep slopes can easily lose thin layers of topsoil from solifluction, soil drift and erosion by torrential rains during the wet season. Preservation of the soil by construction of extensive terrace systems is a practice that dates back to antiquity in the Central Andes. Without terracing, extensive cultivation could only be practised in valleys and the agricultural productivity of the Andes would be severely limited. Simple earth terraces exist in Colombia, and stone-faced terraces are common in the Central Andes, northwest Argentina and northern Chile (Bennett, 1949).

Patterns of adaptation to high altitude

Many kinds of behavioural and biological adaptations are required for populations to survive and persist at high altitude in the Andes. Successful food production requires physical labour both in the fields and for animal herding. These physical activities require effective transport of oxygen and nutrients to working muscles to enable the worker to continue mandatory tasks under often harsh climatic conditions. Successful food production in the high Andes also demands a specialized knowledge of the ecosystem that is being modified in the process of growing animal or plant food. In order for a population to persist through time, reproductive capabilities must be maintained, and at least some children must be given the opportunity to reach adulthood in a relatively healthy state. These are some of the more obvious requirements in which it is clear that both behavioural or socio-cultural and biological adaptations interact in a high-altitude pattern.

Although the principal function of food production activity is to provide materials to satisfy a basic, human biological need, the activity itself involves knowledge of the ecosystem, learned behaviour and cultural traditions that play important roles in the development of specific resource exploitation strategies. A discussion of some of these strategies follows.

Resource exploitation and cultural adaptations

Several adaptive patterns or strategies were suggested by Brush (1976a) as characteristic of Central Andean populations. These are:

1) the presence of a mixed agricultural-herding or agropastoral economy;
2) the exploitation of several environmental zones at different elevations;
3) the support of vertical (altitude) and horizontal (area) trade networks; and
4) the current trend of migration from highland to lowland areas. The first three are traditional patterns that date back to prehispanic times, and influence the strategy of diversification and utilization of a variety of resources.

The effectiveness of the three patterns depends on the "vertical" structure of the highland environment where altitudinal belts produce an ecosystem gradient from tropical lowlands to alpine tundra. These belts are exploited by intensive agriculture and livestock herding: natural pasture exists above 4 000 m; tubers and some chenopod cereals (quinoa and canihua) are cultivated between 3 000 and 4 200 m; maize and other cereal crops are cultivated below 3 000 m; and rice, coca, fruits and other lowland foods are grown below 1 500 m.

At least two major types of exploitation of vertical gradients are practised. In the first case a community will have access to, or control over, lands spanning two or more altitudinal belts with members of the community moving among the belts as a part of their normal subsistence. Murra (1972), who developed the concept of "verticality" or "vertical control", described this system which was common during the prehispanic period; it is a refinement of Troll's earlier work on high-altitude geoecology. A modern example of this pattern was given by Brush (1976b) for the village of Uchucmarca in northeastern Peru. Uchucmarca's lands range across an altitudinal range of 3 500 m (800 to 4 300 m) or several belts. The Q'ero Quechua near Cuzco control lands between 2 000 and 5 000 m (Webster, 1971). Orlove (1977) described a system of agropastoral exploitation of two belts between 3 900 and 5 200 m in the province of Espinar in southern Peru which is similar to that practised on the altiplano (Thomas, 1976).

In the other case of vertical gradient exploitation, single belts are under control of individual communities which are a part of local and regional trade networks. This is a more common means today than in the past to gain access to the products of multiple belts without control of the land. Extensive trade networks and regional markets existed in the Central Andes even before Inca times and many prehispanic weekly and annual markets are still extant (Varcarcel, 1946).

The recent strategy of permanent or near permanent migration from the highlands to lowlands is being practised on an enormous scale in Ecuador, Peru and Bolivia. Largely because of population pressure and land shortage in the highlands, and perceived economic opportunity elsewhere, individuals are moving from rural highland areas to:

1) highland cities
2) coastal cities, and
3) rural areas of new settlement or colonization in the eastern lowlands.

Despite high rates of outmigration, few rural areas of the Central Andes are actually undergoing depopulation due to very high rates of population increase. Nevertheless, population growth of the highland areas is considerably slower than growth rates of eastern or western lowland areas (Wilkie and Reich, 1977). Slow growth alone would not be undesirable were it not for the unbalanced age and sex distributions produced by outmigration. Often the most dynamic and productive age classes are those that leave the rural community.

Major redistribution of high-altitude populations to the lowlands is likely to influence states of health in the new environment. Social alienation and isolation, unfamiliar foods, new disease environments, and changes in activity patterns predispose the migrant to a variety of stress-related diseases. In addition, movement from a hypoxic environment to the functional equivalent of a hyperoxic one appears to lead to respiratory and other health disorders (Dutt and Baker, 1978).

Biological adaptability

There are numerous approaches that can be taken to gain an understanding of the problems of human health and biology at high altitude. Three common approaches will be discussed here. They are:

1) adaptation/acclimatization approach
2) epidemiology approach
3) biological systems approach.

With the first approach a principal interest is in how homeostatic balance is maintained during hypoxic or hypoxic-related stress. Questions asked are: "Is normal function maintained?", "How is it maintained?", and "What biochemical or physiological feedback mechanisms control and maintain function under hypoxic conditions?" Studies have been conducted with visitors to high altitude to follow the time-course of acclimatization, with highland residents as functionally adapted models, and with downward migrants to follow the time-course of acclimatization to sea level (Velasquez, 1966; Nair and George, 1972).

A second approach (epidemiology) might be identified as a public health focus and concern with those pathologies that are aggravated by altitude or directly caused by altitude. Altitude-aggravated conditions include pneumoconiosis (Salguero-Silva, 1967) and gastro-duodenal ulcer (Hellriegel, 1967); altitude-induced conditions include chronic soroche (Monge and Monge, 1966) and pulmonary oedema (Coudert, 1972). Fertile areas for investigations are the patterns of interaction between high-altitude and respiratory disorders produced by infection, smoking, mining, industrial pollution, and allergies. Industrial pollution is rare at high altitudes in the Andes, because of a lack of industrial development. Bogota, Quito and La Paz are likely to be centres of pollution in the future.

A third approach deals with biological systems from cells and tissues to individuals and populations (Mazess, 1975). Here interest lies with how hypoxia produces strain in one or more systems of the body such as the reproductive system, and how the individual accommodates to impaired function or how function is restored. Studies of exercise and work impairment at high altitude have focused on the cardiovascular, respiratory, and musculoskeletal systems (Buskirk, 1976). Inspection of demographic variables and the human population system which is sensitive to high-altitude stress would fall within this approach (Baker and Dutt, 1972; Baker, 1978).

These approaches have a common concern with the range and limits of human adaptability to high altitude and many, if not most, investigations touch on more than one approach (Baker, 1976b). ■

Human biology at high altitude

For the sea-level resident, first exposure to high altitude above 2 500 m or 3 000 m is likely to produce one or more of these symptoms: shortness of breath, rapid pulse rate, headache, nausea, fatigue, mental disorientation, sleeplessness, and general malaise (Evans, 1966). As Frisancho (1975) notes, these symptoms will be felt at relatively low elevations during vigorous exercise, and at relatively high elevations symptoms will be experienced even during complete rest. With continued exposure to high altitude over several days, the sea-level resident will feel a decline in symptoms during rest, but a reappearance of some during moderate-to-light activity. After weeks or months at high altitude, the sea-level resident will reach a high degree of adaptation to hypoxia, but still will be unable to match the physical work abilities of the native born at high altitude. Many of these adaptations to hypoxia centre on how oxygen is transferred from environmental air to tissues in the body.

Physiological and biochemical adaptations to hypoxia

Transport of oxygen to tissues and cells from the lung requires a number of organ systems and specific processes. These are:

1) ventilation of air into the lungs;
2) pulmonary diffusion or transfer of alveolar oxygen in the lungs to blood in the pulmonary capillaries;
3) circulation of blood which carries oxygen bound to haemoglobin and dissolved in plasma;
4) diffusion of oxygen from blood capillaries to tissues;
5) utilization of oxygen by cells and subcellular components.

(Rahn, 1966; Lenfant and Sullivan, 1971; Frisancho, 1975; Quilici and Vergnes, 1978).

Ventilation and diffusion

The increased pulmonary ventilation of newcomers to altitude enhances diffusion of oxygen to the pulmonary capillaries. There are costs associated with this mechanism, since with hyperventilation, carbon dioxide will be lost from the lungs to produce a state of blood alkalosis. Other mechanisms, in turn, can compensate for alkalosis. Basically, however, the system is not very efficient. This theme of less efficient adaptive mechanisms of newcomers to high altitude compared with the more efficient mechanisms among permanent residents and natives is an important one. Among natives, there is a substantially reduced or "blunted" ventilating response that appears to develop after a childhood and adolescence at high altitude (Lahiri et al., 1969, 1976). The chest size and lung capacity of natives is great relative to body size and to size of lowland residents (Hurtado, 1932; Frisancho, 1969). This morphological adaptation, together with an increased oxygen diffusion ability of the lung, probably reduces the need for a ventilatory response in the high altitude native (Mazess, 1975). The larger chest size of natives also appears to be under developmental control (Frisancho, 1975; Lahiri et al.,1976).

Transfer of oxygen in blood and to tissues

Perhaps the most controversial adaptive mechanism in blood is the increased red blood cell production from renal erythropoietin production which stimulates erythropoiesis in bone marrow (Miller, 1974). Polycythemia (elevated red blood cell density) as a facilitator of oxygen-carrying capacity of the blood also produces greater blood viscosity which increases peripheral vascular resistance and the work that the heart must perform (Mazess, 1975; Garruto, 1976; Quilici and Vergnes, 1978). Therefore, polycythemia may be another example of an inefficient adaptation which is a good indicator of hypoxic strain and more characteristic of the immediate responses of newcomers to high altitude.

Of greater importance to the highland native is the Bohr effect of the oxygen dissociation curve of haemoglobin. The Bohr effect involves a shift to the right of the oxyhaemoglobin curve as the result of a lower tissue pH and produces decreased affinity of haemoglobin for oxygen (Lenfant et al., 1968). The advantage of the shift is that it facilitates greater unloading of oxygen in the systemic capillaries. Although the Bohr effect occurs in both high-altitude visitors and Andean native residents, the magnitude of the shift is much greater in the Andean native (Morpurgo et al., 1970). Andean camelids, on the other hand, have a higher oxygen saturation than humans at all levels of oxygen pressure from a left-positioned dissociation curve (Lenfant, 1973).

Other mechanisms that facilitate oxygen transport are:

1) increased density of capillary vessels to enhance diffusion of oxygen to organs and tissues, particularly working skeletal muscles (Miller, 1974);

2) increased heart rate and cardiac output, primarily during initial stages of exposure to hypoxia, which is thought to be yet another example of an inefficient "emergency" adaptation (Velasquez, 1976); and

3) pulmonary artery hypertension that is functional in that it leads to greater diffusion of oxygen from the lungs to the circulation (Arias-Stella, 1966).

Tissue and cell utilization

Less is known about tissue and cell adaptation than that of organs and systems. Myoglobin, which is a haem protein similar to haemoglobin but with a greater oxygen affinity, is found in heart and skeletal muscle. Its primary function appears to be to trap oxygen from haemoglobin and then to store it in muscle cells until needed. Myoglobin has been shown to be elevated at high altitude (Reynafarje, 1962). At high altitude, aerobic or oxidative enzyme systems are more active (Reynafarje, 1966, 1971), and anaerobic glycolysis (or conversion of glucose or glycogen to pyruvic acid and ATP) is improved (Barbashova, 1964). The evidence for adaptation to hypoxia at the tissue, cellular, and mitochondrial levels is considered by some as less convincing than evidence for adaptation at morphological or physiological levels (Miller, 1974). Others (Barbashova, 1964) argue on theoretical grounds that adaptation by physiological means alone is not adequate to explain complete adjustment to high altitude.

Influences of high altitude on normal function and health

High-altitude hypoxia influences many systems and processes in the body. The section that follows will discuss hypoxic stress and other influences on some of these systems. A caveat should be offered, however, in that these topics are extremely complex, each has a substantial scientific literature, and only superficial treatment can be given to each topic here.

Reproduction

Considerable research has been conducted on the effects of hypoxia and altitude on reproduction in laboratory and domestic animals and humans. Two comprehensive reviews have focused on human reproduction at altitude (Hoff and Abelson, 1976; Clegg, 1978) and another has dealt with maternal adaptation and fetal growth (Haas, 1979). Most data were drawn from Andean populations.

Recent interests in fertility at high altitude were stimulated by two events. The first was the publication of Carlos Monge's book (1948) on *Acclimatization in the Andes*. Monge cited early colonial archival material indicating that the Spanish had great difficulty maintaining their numbers by reproduction in highland settlements. The second involved a series of publications in the journal *Population Studies*. It began with Stycos's (1963) observation that fertility in urban, Quechua-speaking areas was lower than in rural Spanish-speaking areas of the Andes. This unusual demographic pattern was attributed by Stycos to late Quechua marriage and unstable unions. Later, Heer (1964) explained the low Quechua fertility as resulting from a high proportion of Quechua women in the labour force, and speculated on fertility limits from abortion and infanticide. When language was controlled statistically James (1966) found that altitude of residence and fertility were negatively related for each of three Andean nations (Ecuador, Peru and Bolivia). Heer (1967) concurred with James' analysis after reanalysis of his own data, but Whitehead (1968) criticized both by reference to the use of the child-woman ratio which is an insensitive measure of fertility. Whitehead argued that it was probably not the case that fertility was low at high altitudes, but rather that infant mortality was high. DeJong (1970) and later Baker and Dutt (1972) pointed out the limits to strictly social demographic analysis of census data and, instead, called for integrated biosocial research into the problems of fertility at high altitude.

Not a great deal is known about fecundity of permanent residents and visitors at high altitude. Studies with experimental animals, as Clegg (1978) and Mazess (1975) noted, have demonstrated only minor and transient effects with acute exposure to moderate hypoxia (4 000 m). Sea-level men were tested at 4 300 m for four weeks by Donayre and others (1968) for semen characteristics. The results of the study are given in Figure 6.18. Semen nutrients and pH had returned to normal after four weeks at high altitude, the percentage of abnormal cells and total cell count had levelled off, and only the percentage of motile cells was still declining. It appears likely that, with these values at the end of four weeks of altitude exposure, most of the subjects were sub-fertile or functionally sterile. However, Vander and co-workers (1978) found no changes in plasma testosterone, FSH, and LH in ten men who sojourned at 4 300 m for six days. Donayre (1966) also reported on sea-level women who were resident at 4,350 m. Nearly 60 per cent of the 29 women complained of menstrual problems, but 65 per cent of the women were using contraceptives. More systematically gathered data are available for eight university women who resided at 4 300 m for ten weeks (Harris et al., 1966). With the exception of menstrual flow, which was increased in one and decreased in five subjects, menstrual changes were minimal.

Among permanent residents several studies have been conducted to test for effects of hypoxia on fertility. Completed fertility of women at or beyond menopause was determined on three populations resident at 4 000 m or higher. Values were 6.7 and 7.7 children born to Quechua women from Nuñoa (Hoff, 1968) and Cerro de Pasco (CISM, 1968), Peru, and 7.3 children born to Aymara women from Huallatiri, Chile (Cruz-Coke, 1966). These values were intermediate for peasant populations that do not practise birth control or abortion (Baker and Dutt, 1972). Abelson and colleagues (1974) found a completed fertility of 8.5 among high-altitude migrants who migrated to sea level on the southern coast of Peru. He attributed the differences to an increase in fertility at sea level resulting from the release of hypoxic stress in a population attempting to maximize fertility. These lowered fertility rates appear not to be related to mid-term or late-term spontaneous abortions, which are extraordinarily low in native highland populations of Chile (Cruz-Coke, 1966) and Peru (Buck et al., 1968; Hoff and Abelson, 1976).

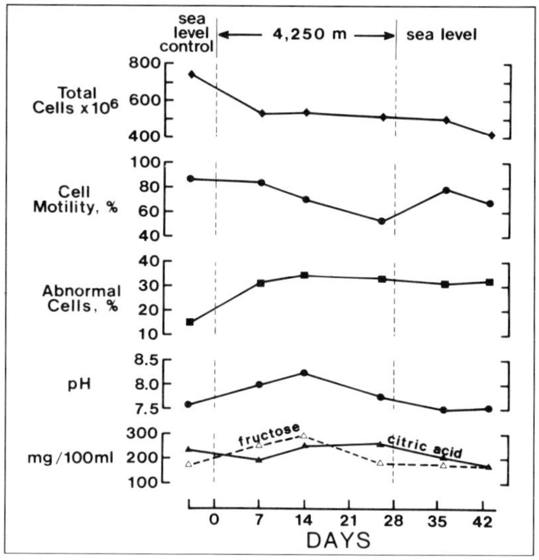

Figure 6.18: Semen characteristics of sea-level residents (nine men aged 18-22) at sea level (Lima), during four weeks at Cerro de Pasco (4 250 m), and upon return to sea level for two weeks.
After Donayre et al., 1968

The greatest strain on high-altitude reproduction is in mortality of perinates, neonates, and young infants. Infants born at high altitudes are at high risk of death, particularly during the neonatal period. Neonatal death rate (deaths within the first 28 days after birth) in 12 highland departments was greater than 5 per cent (52/1000 births) (Mazess, 1965) and in the district of Nuñoa, Peru, it was 6.7 per cent (Little and Baker, 1976). These values compare with neonatal mortality of between 2 and 3 per cent in lowland departments of Peru and less than 2 per cent in the United States. The probable cause of at least a part of the high mortality is the characteristic low birth-weight of infants born at high altitude (Haas, 1976). Low birth-weight, that is infants less than 2 500 g (approximately 5.5 pounds) is a factor in 75 per cent of neonatal deaths in the United States (McClung, 1969: 23), and is a likely factor in mortality of the newborn at high altitude. Whereas birth-weight of highland infants is low, placental weight is relatively high (McClung, 1969: 80), and provides a greater nutrient and oxygen supply to the infant. This suggests one way that the highland native has adapted to prenatal hypoxia. Another example is the heavier newborn infants born to Indian women in La Paz, Bolivia (3 700 m), when compared to the birth-weights of infants of European mothers (Haas, 1979).

Growth and development

Child growth in the Andes has been investigated in detail, with populations surveyed at a number of sites. These include: altiplano Quechua from Peru (Frisancho and Baker, 1970; Frisancho, 1976; Haas, 1976); altiplano Aymara from Chile (Mueller et al., 1978a); La Paz Aymara from Bolivia (Bouloux, 1968); downward migrants from high altitude to the southern Peruvian coast and coastal residents (Boyce et al., 1974; Haas, 1976; Beall et al.,1977); downward migrants from the highlands to the eastern montana or tropical forest (Hoff, 1974). Research has been designed to examine those parameters of life in the high Andes that can limit or inhibit normal growth processes (e.g. hypoxia, low temperatures, chronic illness, poor nutrition). Since a principal objective in many studies of human growth was to identify the effects of hypoxia, it was necessary to attempt to control the parameters noted above indirectly through identifiable statuses such as ethnicity, residence-elevation, residence-urban or rural, and occupation. Most studies used population comparison designs.

The child and adolescent growth of high-altitude Quechua and Aymara Indians tends to be slow, retarded and prolonged in contrast to comparable Indians at sea level. Differences between highland Indians and lowland Indians during growth to maturity are illustrated for stature or height in Figure 6.19. Birth-weights at altitude are low (McClung, 1969) and infant physical growth retardation during the first two years is clearly altitude-related (Haas, 1976). Adolescent growth is slow, and sexual dimorphism in size and body composition is not apparent until age 16 years (Frisancho and Baker, 1970). Menarche, which signals the beginning of sexual maturation in girls, is late at high altitude (Donayre, 1966; Clegg et al., 1970). Growth among highlanders of both sexes continues up to about age 22 years at which time full maturation of size is achieved. All systems and structures of the body do not, however, display a pattern of growth retardation in high-altitude residents. Some structures that are crucial for oxygen transport actually show allometric growth with tissue hypertrophy or hyperplasia.

First, there is the relatively large placenta in foetal growth at high altitude. The placental weight may be large in an absolute sense or the placenta may have a large surface area; but usually it is the placental ratio (placental weight/birth-weight) that is higher at altitude (McClung, 1969; Frisancho, 1970). Second, skeletal maturation parallels other indices of maturation and is retarded when compared with United States standards (Frisancho, 1976). Despite this pattern of slow growth of the skeleton, there is some increased growth in the form of bone marrow hyperplasia. Such cortical

Figure 6.19: *Growth in height of lowland (open symbols) and highland (black symbols) Indians. Data of Mueller and colleagues on Chilean Aymara Indians; all other data are on Peruvian Quechua Indians*

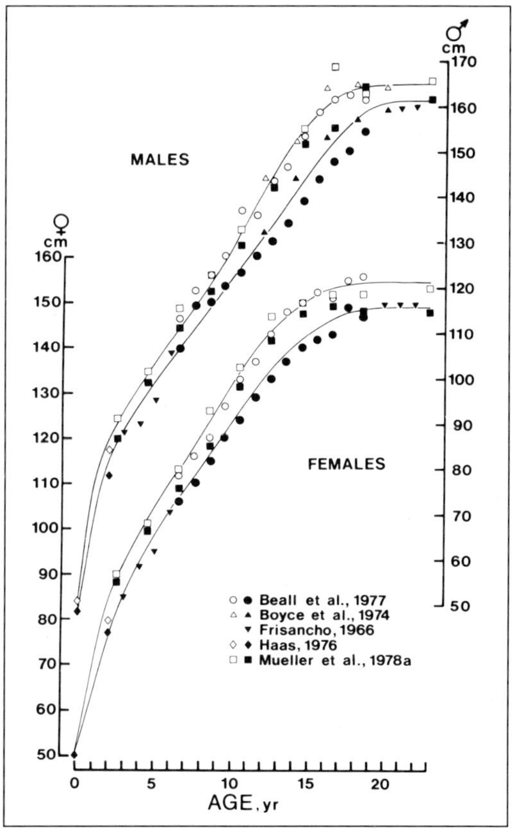

bone growth has been postulated as a response to increased haemotopoietic needs under hypoxic conditions (Frisancho et al., 1970). Third, because of an increased pulmonary arterial pressure in high-altitude residents, there is an enlargement of the right side of the heart (right ventricular hypertrophy). This functional hypertrophy first appears in very young infants and will only be manifest in individuals who have lived as children at high altitude (Penalosa et al., 1964; Penalosa, 1966). Finally, there is an increased size of the chest and associated pulmonary capacity of highland residents (Hurtado, 1932, 1964; Frisancho, 1969; Frisancho and Baker, 1970; Boyce et al., 1974; Beall et al., 1977; Mueller et al., 1978a, 1978b, 1978c, 1979). Relative chest size and shape (roundness) and measures of lung function (forced vital capacity, forced expiratory volumes) are consistently greater in native high-altitude populations. The postulated bases for the large thoracic cavity and other morphological adaptations will be discussed in a section that follows.

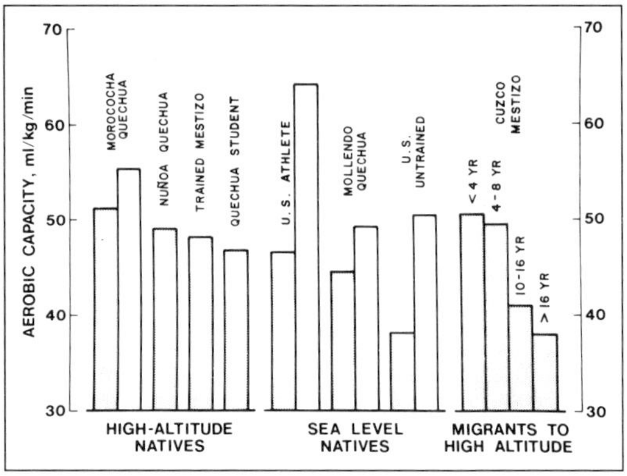

Figure 6.20: *Maximal work capacity (aerobic capacity in ml of oxygen consumed/kg of body weight/min) of several Andean and non-Andean populations. Dark columns represent exercise tests conducted at elevations between 3 400 m (Cuzco Mestizo) and 4 500 m (Morococha Quechua); light columns represent exercise tests conducted at sea level.* Data from Baker, 1969; Frisancho et al., 1973; Mazess, 1969; Velasquez, 1966

Physical activity and exercise capacity

One of the most important resources available to any given nation is its people, and the ability of its people to perform work or engage in physical labour. This is particularly so for the Andean nations with poorly developed technological and industrial bases, and where the economy is primarily agropastoral with minimal mechanization. Also of importance is a reduction in the ability to perform physical labour among newcomers to high altitudes, as in the Andes. In addition to hypoxia, there are numerous other factors that can affect work capacity:

1) chronic or acute illness (infections, parasites);
2) poor nutritional status (deficiencies, especially protein and calories);
3) body composition (low muscle mass);
4) age, sex and size;
5) physical conditioning or fitness level;
6) high air temperatures; and
7) motivation levels.

For example, the tropical lowland swidden cultivator of the eastern Andean montana may be limited in the agricultural work that he can perform by a heavy parasite load producing anaemia, a mild form of protein-calorie malnutrition, and the hot, humid ambient conditions. The high-altitude native is not likely to be limited in physical labour by heat or parasites, although respiratory infections and poor nutrition can play a role in addition to hypoxia. What is most limiting to work is, of course, hypoxia.

The most consistent measure of exercise capacity is maximal oxygen uptake (VO_2 max) or aerobic capacity, which is a measure of the absolute amount of oxygen that can be utilized by working muscle. This is a test in which individuals exercise to a state of exhaustion. Aerobic capacity values are presented in Figure 6.20 for natives, migrants and sojourners at high altitude. Natives at high altitude show maximal work capacity values that are equivalent to those of sea-level dwellers at their home elevation (Kollias et al., 1968; Baker, 1976a; Buskirk, 1976; 1978). Yet Quechua or Aymara ancestry does not appear to be required in order to work effectively at high altitude. Mestizos who have lived all their lives (Mazess, 1969), and those who migrated to high altitude before entering the second decade of life (Frisancho et al., 1973), are comparable to the highland Indian in aerobic capacity. Even United States highly trained runners from sea level approach the highlanders' capacities, but at great cost compared to the runners' sea-level performance (Buskirk et al., 1967). The only inconsistency within this pattern is the elevated aerobic capacity of the sea-level Mollendo Quechua Indians while at high altitude. Whereas all other responses suggest a hypoxic conditioning effect, either by physical training or developmental adaptation, the sea-level Quechua appear to manifest neither, which suggests a slight hereditary advantage.

Despite the adequate aerobic capacity of the high-altitude resident, few Andean cultivators or pastoralists engage in physical labour that ever approaches a maximal effort (Thomas, 1976), and aerobic capacity has been questioned as an appropriate measure of adaptation in peasant populations (Thomas, 1975). Rather, it is the case in the Peruvian Andes that submaximal activity predominates, and even pastoralists lead relatively sedentary lives (Thomas, 1976). An elevated aerobic capacity at high altitude *does* give the native a greater exercise "reserve" than is available to visitors, in that all activities are performed at a lower "relative work load" (Mazess, 1975).

It is quite clear that the adult sea-level dweller who visits or establishes permanent residence at high altitude will never achieve a work capacity equivalent to the lifelong, high-altitude resident. Moreover, there are good indications that, although aerobic capacity is increased slightly when high-altitude residents are tested at sea level, high-altitude migrants to sea level may suffer from respiratory disorders, anaemia and other ill- effects (Velasquez, 1966, 1970; Dutt and Baker, 1978). These variations in biological adaptability to sea level and high altitude may constrain movement of adults from place to place or contribute to unique problems in migrant peoples in the Andes.

Cold tolerance

Despite proximity to the equator, elevations above 3 000 m are often quite cold in the Northern and Central Andes. With increasing altitude, night-time frosts become common, and low temperatures begin to be felt in the late afternoon and persist into the early daylight hours. These cold conditions are especially stressful to the Andean native with little to combat the cold except shelter, homespun wool clothing, and the physiological and metabolic heat generating and conserving capabilities of the human body.

There are several poorly defined synergistic and antagonistic interactions between cold and hypoxia that may affect the high-altitude native. The Bohr effect or rightward shift of the oxy-haemoglobin dissociation curve is adaptive in the sense that it facilitates oxygen delivery at altitude. Low blood temperature produces a leftward shift in the oxyhaemoglobin curve which is maladaptive to hypoxia (Little, 1976). Under normal conditions, only blood temperatures of the fingers and toes will reach levels where tissue hypoxia may be aggravated (Jones et al., 1976). The "blunted" hypoxic drive or reduced ventilation of highland natives at rest and during work is synergistic with cold stress, since respiratory heat loss is controlled, at least when compared with that of sojourners. And increased capillarization of skeletal muscle in response to hypoxia may improve circulatory heat transfer within the body. Finally, the increased basal metabolism that characterizes some highland populations (Picon-Reategui, 1961; Mazess et al., 1969) requires increased oxygen consumption; metabolic rates during experimental total body cold exposures are maintained at high levels (Baker et al., 1967); and infants appear to be able to maintain elevated metabolism (Dufour et al., 1976). Accordingly, the adaptive mechanisms of oxygen transport in hypoxia are adequate to handle the metabolic needs for increased heat production as well.

The wool clothing of highland Quechua and Aymara Indians is well-tailored and designed for low temperatures (Hanna, 1976). Southern Peruvian houses of adobe or huts of stone afford more protection against chilling winds than low temperatures and are not heated. This protection against cold is even more limited during the rainy season when wet-cold becomes a problem.

Field studies of the altiplano Indian indicated that during day-to-day activities individuals were able to maintain warm deep body and skin temperatures (Hanna, 1970). Corresponding studies of sleeping conditions gave similar results

(Baker, 1966). Yet in both studies, children were documented as experiencing more cold than adults, despite attempts by adults to give children additional protection. Native children in other parts of the world are often more cold-stressed than adults because of their smaller body sizes (Little and Hochner, 1973).

From laboratory tests of highland Indians, several thermal and metabolic mechanisms of response to cold stress were apparent:

1) basal and resting metabolism was high during comfortable sleep (Mazess et al.,1969) and body cooling experiments (Baker et al., 1967; Mazess and Larsen, 1972);
2) deep body temperatures were higher than sea-level residents tested at high altitude (Baker et al., 1967; Hanna, 1970); and
3) during a variety of cold-exposure conditions, the highland Indians were able to keep hand and foot temperatures at high levels (Little, 1969; Little 1973; Little and Hanna, 1977).

Although genetic bases for some of these thermal adaptations are not discounted, the adaptations do appear to be developmental in pattern.

Nutritional status

There are a number of unique Andean characteristics that structure dietary intake and nutritional status of highland peoples. First, because of poor soils, aridity, steep relief and low temperatures, little land is arable, and what is arable is often of low agricultural productivity. Second, this condition is ameliorated somewhat by vertical belt exploitation and vertical trade of food products, but food energy requirements increase with the high activity levels required for transport of foods over different vertical belts. Third, there is some evidence that nutritional requirements are increased at high altitude as the result of cold and hypoxia. Fourth, there are nutritional deficiencies that are characteristic of highland areas resulting from soil quality, glacial and other weathering processes, and plant productivity. The material in this section will deal with a general survey of diet and nutrition at high altitude and discussion of the two latter points cited above.

Lowenstein (1968) reviewed the ICNND (US Interdepartmental Committee for Nutrition in National Development) surveys of the Andean nations. Protein-calorie malnutrition was widespread in preschool children from lower socio-economic classes, and particularly prevalent in Colombia and Peru. Stini (1969, 1972) documented the effects of inadequate nutrition in a Colombian peasant village (Heliconia) at 1 500 m where protein-calorie malnutrition is widespread among children. The result of malnutrition there was delayed skeletal maturation, reduced upper arm muscle circumference, and reduction in sexual dimorphism. The protein-deficient diet was derived from high-carbohydrates staples such as bananas, potatoes, maize, and sugar cakes. These and other refined, starchy, low-protein staples are common in the lower valleys and foothills of the Andes. Throughout the Andes from Venezuela to Bolivia, lowland staples are often high in carbohydrate and low in protein (bananas, rice, manioc, and sugar), although some animal protein is supplied by eggs, fish and insects in the wet lowlands of Peru (Buck et al., 1968:40) and Colombia (Dufour, 1979). At intermediate elevations in mountain valleys numerous cereal, legume, and vegetable crops can be cultivated whereas in the high punas above 4 000 m, only frost-resistant chenopods (quinoa, canihua) and tubers (potato, oca) can be cultivated (Picon-Reategui, 1976). It is at elevations above about 3 800 m that sheep and camelid pastoralism begin to predominate.

The dietary diversity observed in the Andes is substantial (Lowenstein, 1968), and the degree of nutritional adequacy of one settlement is not a good indicator of that of a neighbouring settlement (Picon-Reategui, 1978). Such a remarkable degree of dietary diversity was demonstrated for several altiplano communities within the same political district (see Table 6.7). Communities included a small town of about 2 500 persons, a native community (ayllu), a herding settlement (Gursky, 1969), and individual households in the countryside beyond the town (Mazess and Baker, 1964). Each community manifested dependency on different proportions of the basic staples of potatoes, chenopod grains, maize and European grains. Per capita daily intake by weight of food varied between slightly less than 500 g and about 1 500 g for the four communities (Picon-Reategui, 1976, 1978). It is likely, however, that some of the values underestimate the bulk of food and calories consumed. Protein intake did appear adequate in the Nuñoa communities but was lower in Vicos and Chacan (Picon-Reategui, 1978).

Although the effects of dietary protein at high altitude are not yet established, it is clear that dietary fat is deleterious, or at least poorly utilized, and dietary carbohydrate is beneficial. In balance studies conducted at 4 000 m, Picon-Reategui (1978) found a fat absorption of 56 per cent in Quechua Indians compared with normal sea-level standards of about 95 per cent absorption (Alfin-Slater and Aftergood, 1973). Earlier, the same investigator (Picon-Reategui, 1961) found a more effective tissue utilization of carbohydrate in the form of glucose at 5 600 m. Consolazio and others (1969) supported these findings by demonstrating improved work capacity

Table 6.7: *Foods consumed in g/day in six high-altitude communities in Peru.*
Compiled by Picon-Reategui, 1976, 1978

	Vicos* (2 750 m)	Chacan* (3 400 m)	Aylly** (4 000 m)	Town** (4 000 m)	Herding settlement** (4 300) m)	Surrounding households*** (4 000 m)
Fresh potatoes	347	202	94	11	94	741
Chuno****	-	32	141	41	18	470
Other tubers	217	115	81	-	-	28
Chenopod grains	-	24	259	77	107	90
Maize	151	251	5	114	-	25
Barley	52	40	226	40	15	53
Wheat *****	130	50	11	103	144	14
Rice	-	-	-	4	-	-
Beans	70	60	2	-	-	-
Vegetables	20	91	-	-	-	-
Garlic and onions	5	18	5	7	-	-
Fruits	-	-	-	9	-	-
Sugar	20	20	5	49	-	-
Meat	41	28	28	67	84	93
Fat and oil	5	3	38	8	3	5
Milk and cheese	-	3	-	15	-	-
Total (g/day)	1 058	937	895	545	465	1 519
Energy (kcal/day)	1 481	1 404	2 447	1 497	1 494	3 204

* *Data from Collazos et al., 1960*
** *Data from Gursky, 1969*
*** *Data from Mazess and Baker, 1964*
**** *Dried potatoes*
***** *Includes flour, kernels and bread*

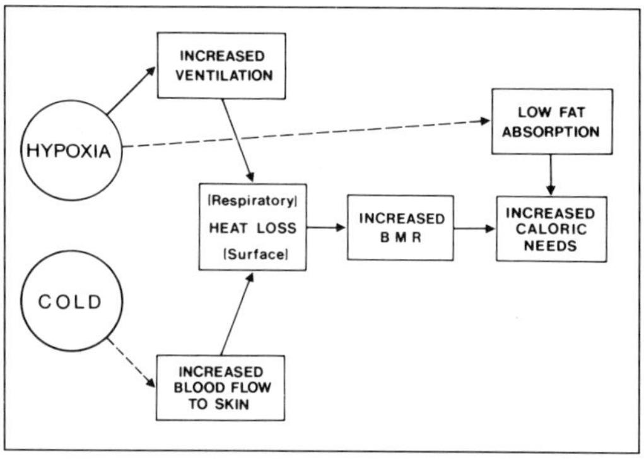

***Figure 6.21**: Relationships among hypoxia, cold, and caloric needs from food in high-altitude natives as suggested by Picon-Reategui (1978). Solid lines signify established associations; interrupted lines are not fully-established associations*

and reduction of high-altitude illness symptoms among subjects on a high-carbohydrate (68 per cent) and low-fat (20 per cent) diet while at 4 300 m. Therefore, the high-altitude resident is probably best served by his existing diet in which carbohydrates contribute between 70 and 85 per cent of total calories (Picon-Reategui, 1978).

Figure 6.21 is a diagram of high-altitude influences on food energy needs among native residents. Hypoxia stimulates increased ventilation at high altitude which is substantial in newcomers and slight in permanent residents. Increased ventilation produces an elevated respiratory heat loss that may be as high at 60 kcal per day for an average Quechua Indian male who weighs 55 kg (Velasquez, 1972). Low temperatures are associated with chronically elevated limb temperatures (Baker et al., 1967; Hanna, 1970; Little et al., 1971) which contribute to heat loss from the surface of the body. These two major avenues of heat loss are compensated for by an elevated basal heat production or metabolic rate that expends about 140 kcal per day in an average Quechua male (Velasquez, 1947; Picon-Reategui, 1961; Mazess et al., 1969). This increased heat expenditure must, in turn, be compensated for by augmented food intake to maintain the body in a state of caloric balance. Consolazio and others (1973) suggested other factors that might contribute to increased energy metabolism needs at high altitude. These included increased ventilatory work and work by the heart.

A few other unusual nutritional features of the Andes include the presence of endemic goitre from Venezuela to Bolivia. Goitre is common in mountain areas and results from glacial scouring of topsoil which removes iodine (Lowenstein, 1968). Other minerals and vitamins may be provided in the diet from unusual sources. Calcium is provided by powdered rocks mixed with a grain porridge and by ashed plant stalks for use with coca among the Quechua (Baker and Mazess, 1963). Moreover, coca itself provides several minerals and is also a source of protein (Dukeetal, 1975).

Health, morbidity, mortality and ageing

Patterns of health and illness in the Andes result from a complex interaction of sanitation, health care, nutrition, infectious disease vectors, and altitude. Modal socio-economic status of Andean populations is low, and many characteristic low socio-economic status indicators of poor health are widespread. These include high infant and child mortality, short life expectancy at birth, and infectious diseases as major causes of death (Wilkie and Reich, 1977). Influences of high altitude on morbidity and mortality may be covariant with or independent of socio-economic status. However, the common denominator of high-altitude pathology is any condition that impairs normal respiratory or cardiovascular function. The impairment of adequate transport of oxygen in the body carries a high risk of illness or death because of the already refined adaptation of the native to hypoxia.

The altitude-induced diseases of pulmonary oedema and chronic mountain sickness or soroche are probably independent of socio-economic status, may be triggered by fatigue or other factors, and are most effectively treated by movement to a lower elevation (Marticorena et al., 1964; Monge and Monge, 1966; Singh and Roy, 1969). These are the only serious diseases that are almost always high-altitude induced and they clearly carry a high risk of death because of their effects on the oxygen transport system.

Respiratory infections are in a category of disease that can severely limit the ability of the body to transfer oxygen from the lungs to circulating blood. Acute and chronic respiratory disorders are common at high altitude (Way, 1976). Hellriegel (1967) indicated a rate of 40 per cent acute respiratory tract diseases among hospitalized children at La Oroya, Peru (3 750 m), and a very high incidence of tuberculosis. Buck and others (1968:70) also found a high incidence of tuberculosis in the two high-altitude communities they studied. It has been suggested that high-altitude migrants to sea level are especially susceptible to tuberculosis (Baker, 1978). This may be an artifact of the high incidence of the disease in downward migrants from altitude and better diagnoses in sea-level medical facilities. Mortality from respiratory diseases is considerable in contrast to other infectious causes of death. In the district of Nuñoa, Spector (1971) found that respiratory disorders accounted for nearly 60 per cent of mortality at all ages, and Hoff (1968) found that between 28 and 47 per cent of all infant and childhood deaths in his sample were caused by the same disorders. The picture of high-altitude natives that arises is one in which the population is particularly hard hit by respiratory diseases and in which illness rates are followed by high mortality.

If the high rates of respiratory disease and associated mortality reflect an incomplete state of adaptation among high-altitude natives, then they fare considerably better with respect to cardiovascular health. Among adults who have resided at high altitude for a lifetime, hypertensive and coronary heart disease is substantially less common than at sea level (Marticorena et al., 1967a). Hypertension and hypercholesterolemia, predisposing conditions to heart disease, are correspondingly low in frequency among high-altitude natives (Buck et al.,1968:43; Hoff et al., 1972a; Watt et al., 1976; Maleka et al., 1978). Low systolic and diastolic blood pressure is characteristic of elderly individuals and few display the age-related increases that are so characteristic of sea-level residents from industrialized nations (Marticorena et al., 1967b; Baker, 1969). Even among high-altitude natives who migrate to sea level, systemic blood pressure is lower than in native lowlanders (Baker, 1978).

Low systemic blood pressure is clearly an advantage to the aged individual in reducing the risk of heart disease. And there is good evidence that a lifetime at high altitude predisposes an individual to low blood pressure. Leaf (1973) suggested that mountain regions such as the Andes may, in addition, contribute to longevity of their residents. Vilcabamba, Ecuador, was one of the mountain areas cited by Leaf as being populated by a sizeable number of aged individuals. In a recent conference on Vilcabamba reported by Mazess (1978a), cardiovascular health in the elderly population was shown to be excellent, including low heart rates, low blood pressure, and low blood cholesterol levels. Symptoms of bone mineral loss were reduced also among the Vilcabamba aged (Mazess, 1978b). These health status indicators gave a picture of aged individuals who were especially active and fit for their years. This was true despite the systematic age exaggeration uncovered by Mazess and Forman (1979) from studies of Vilcabamba censuses and genealogies. If high altitude does not contribute to a prolonged life span, at least it may contribute to a healthier life of more usual length.

Evolutionary and genetic implications

In the more than thirty years since Carlos Monge's (1948) book on "climatic aggression" leading to "the development" (evolution) of an "Andean man", minimal hard evidence has accumulated in support of this contention. A variety of research designs have been proposed to test for relative population fitness and selective advantage with little success (Harrison, 1966; Baker, 1971, 1976b; Haas, 1976; Schull and Rothhammer, 1977). Cruz-Coke (1978) argued that there has been insufficient time for selection to have acted effectively to modify the gene pool of highland populations in favour of enhanced altitude adaptation. However, even with a conservative estimate of 12 000 years of human habitation in the Andes, this is about 500 generations, which is sufficient generational time for genetic change to have taken place considering the severity of the selective pressure. Even gene flow, which has been estimated at 10 to 15 per cent for one highland community in Peru (Dutt, 1976), can be high between lowland and highland areas with selection still operating (Brues, 1972). Hence, despite negative results to date, the likelihood of some degree of genetic adaptation to altitude still exists.

Most of the attempts to identify hereditary characteristics that benefit highlanders have been in the realms of the following:
1) body morphology and growth,
2) physiological function and oxygen transport,
3) red blood cell enzyme and other blood and tissue polymorphisms.

This latter realm may be the most productive approach since blood biochemicals are usually under simple genic control. Modiano et al., (1972) and Yen (1972) surveyed red cell gene markers in Peruvian Quechua, and Ferrell et al., (1978) did the same in Bolivian Aymara. Erythrocyte enzyme variants of acid phosphatase (ACP) and 6-phosphogluconate dehydrogenase (6PGD) may be involved in altitude adaptation. Roberts (1977) found associations between 6PGD and blood pressure in women, and 6PGD and fasting cholesterol in men. In any case, a new variant form of 6PGD was found in both Bolivian and Chilean Aymara populations, although in low frequency (Ferrell et al., 1978). Schull and Rothhammer (1977) also noted the relationships between the Bohr effect and another erythrocyte biochemical polymorphism, 2,3-phosphoglycerate.

A great difficulty with identifying hereditary factors in body morphology and physiology is that genetic systems which control growth, structure, and function are usually polygenic, complex, and highly plastic in expression (Eveleth and Tanner, 1976:222; Roberts, 1977). For example, the hereditary or developmental basis for the large chest size of Central Andean natives has not been adequately resolved, despite considerable effort (Hoff et al., 1972; Beall et al., 1977; Mueller et al., 1978a). There may very well be a positive relationship between chest size (pulmonary capacity) and altitude, but in their study of "distance" relationships over a Chilean altitudinal gradient, Rothhammer and Spielman (1972) found that the major source of anthropometric variation was altitude and not genetic variation.

Finally, demographic investigations of fertility and mortality may provide some information on population genetics and altitude. The opportunity for selection through infant mortality (a significant selection factor in the pre-reproductive period) is greater than the opportunity through fertility among several high-altitude populations surveyed (Cruz-Coke, 1978; Garruto and Hoff, 1976). If a genetic characterization can be made between those who do and those who do not survive infancy at high altitude, then the direction and basis of Darwinian selection at altitude may be indicated.■

***Figure 6.22**: Population growth of Andean nations from 1920 to 1975*
Data from Celade, 1975

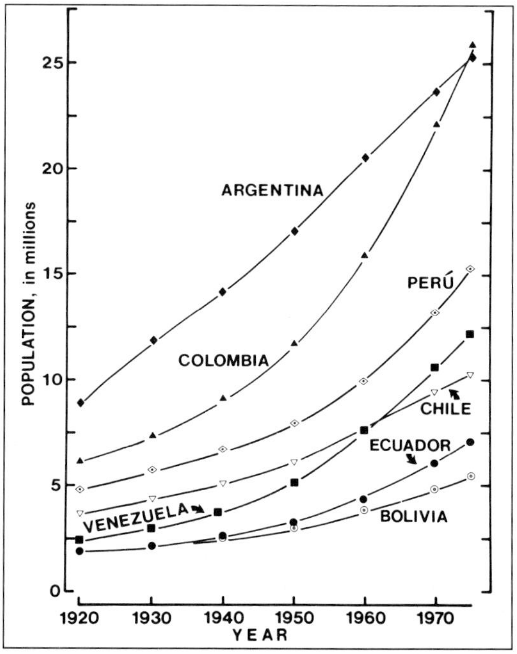

Continued settlement in the Andes

A number of demographic trends characterize developing nations in Latin America and other parts of the world today. The first is the dramatic and alarming increase in population numbers resulting from a high rate of fertility and low mortality rate (Stycos, 1968; Sanchez-Albornos, 1974). The second is the high rate of migration, both within and between national borders, that is unprecedented in the history of mankind (Davis, 1974). Third, the principal pattern of population movement and redistribution is one of migration from rural areas to urban centres, particularly large cities (Thomlinson, 1976: 313). Causes for the continuing streams of migrants today are manifold and complex (Lee, 1966) but include, at least, increasing population density, competition for dwindling resources in the area of origin, and perceived advantages in the area of destination (Gonzales, 1967). Another demographic trend, unique in the Andean nations, is the heavy migration from highland or sierra regions to the eastern and western lowlands (Weil et al., 1972; Crist and Nissley, 1973). A discussion of these population trends for the Andes follows.

Population growth and migration

Change in population numbers of the Andean nations from 1920 to the present is illustrated in Figure 6.22. With the exception of Argentina, all Andean nations show typical exponential growth functions produced by high annual growth rates. Table 6.8 lists crude birth and death rates and derived rates of annual growth for each of these nations. Three patterns of growth are current:

1) annual growth greater than 3 per cent from high fertility and low mortality (Venezuela, Colombia, Ecuador, Peru);

Nation	Birth rate (per 1 000)	Death rate (per 1 000)	Annual growth (%)	Doubling time* (years)
Venezuela	40.9	7.8	3.31	21
Colombia	44.6	10.6	3.40	21
Ecuador	44.9	11.4	3.35	21
Peru	41.8	11.1	3.07	23
Bolivia	43.8	19.0	2.48	28
Chile	33.2	10.0	2.32	31
Argentina	23.0	8.7	1.40	50

Table 6.8: *Crude birth and death rates (per 1 000 inhabitants) and annual growth rates (per cent) for Andean nations 1965-70.*
Data from CELADE, 1971

**At the present rate of growth*

Nation	1960	1970	1980**
Venezuela	37.1	28.1	21.2
Colombia	53.0	42.5	33.3
Ecuador	63.9	54.3	45.9
Peru	61.3	50.8	41.8
Bolivia	70.9	64.5	58.0
Chile	36.2	29.6	24.6
Argentina	26.4	21.1	17.0

** Settlements with less than 2 000 persons*
*** Projected*

Table 6.9: *Changes in percentage of population residing in rural areas in Andean nations.*
From Wilkie and Turtovsky, 1976:81

2) annual growth less than 3 per cent because of relatively high mortality (Bolivia) or low fertility (Chile); and
3) annual growth less than 2 per cent from low fertility and low mortality (Argentina).

These high rates of population increase do not affect all areas of the Andes equally because of migration. Rather, rural areas, from which there is substantial emigration, show relatively slow growth whereas urban centres, to which there is substantial immigration, show remarkably rapid growth. The trend of rural population decline as a percentage of total population is given in Table 6.9. Both lowland and highland cities are growing rapidly as the result of the influx of rural migrants. In the decade between 1960 and 1970, most large cities in Andean nations had annual growth rates between 4 and 7 per cent—well above national averages (Sanchez-Albornoz, 1974). The flow of migrants to cities cannot be assimilated easily, with the result that barriadas or suburban shantytowns have accumulated at the margins of urban centres (Mangin, 1959, 1960).

Migration to highland cities has contributed to their growth. However, with the exception of Bogota, most of the larger high-altitude cities (Quito, Cuzco, La Paz) have shown only modest growth. Rather than rural to urban movement in the highlands, the migrant has chosen to move downward, either to lowland cities or to homestead lands east of the Andes in the relatively uninhabited tropical forest (Dozier, 1969). The influence that downward migration has on population growth and distribution in Peru is represented by Table 6.10. From 1960 to 1970, the Peruvian population increased by 37 per cent, but the highland areas grew only by 18.8 per cent. Assuming roughly equal birth and death rates for the three regions, an estimated 735 000 persons migrated out of the highlands to the coast (660 000) and to the montana (75 000) during that decade. In one way, this pattern, which holds for much of the Northern and Central Andes, has protected the highland zones from the environmentally destructive effects of high population density. In another way, the depopulation in some highland areas and changes in age–sex composition of populations in other areas have socio-economic costs that may include reduction in productivity or in general adaptation to highland subsistence requirements.

Utilization of and further settlement in the Andes

Highland ecosystems are easily disturbed and are sensitive to natural and human-initiated destructive processes. Some of these include:
1) diurnal extremes of temperature, humidity and wind flow which accelerate mechanical weathering processes;
2) heavy seasonal rains following a dry season which produce gullying and rapid erosion;
3) poorly developed, shallow soils that are more susceptible to erosion because of 2) above and also because of steep slopes and the action of gravity; and
4) natural catastrophe such as earthquake, landslide or mudflow which can produce rapid and destructive changes in the mountain landscape (Billings, 1979; Ives, 1979).

Region	Population 1960 (000s)	Population 1970 (000s)	Population increase (000s)	% Increase
Eastern Lowlands*	632	938	306	48.4
Highlands**	4035	4792	757	18.8
Coastal Lowlands***	5240	7838	2598	49.6
Total Peru	9907	13568	3661	37.0

Table 6.10: Population growth in three Peruvian regions.
Data from Wilkie and Turouvsky, 1976: 75

* *Four, principally montana, departments.*
** *Nine, principally sierra, departments*
*** *Ten coastal departments and the province of Callao*

Superimposed on these natural processes are those activities of human populations (construction, cultivation, herding, mining) in which the impact upon the ecosystem is dependent upon human population density and technological application.

Concerns about the status of the Andes are usually directed toward the present and the future. It is quite clear, however, that dramatic modifications of the Andes took place long before the first contacts with Europeans. At some time in the past, the moist highlands below 4 000 m in Ecuador, Peru and Bolivia were covered with woodlands of sclerophyllous (*Polylepis* spp.) trees (Ellenberg, 1964). As population increased in the Central Andes and as extractive techniques improved, deforestation probably proceeded at a rapid rate. Prehispanic populations contributed to deforestation by elaborate and well-organized landscape remodelling of whole valley systems (Cook,1916; Rowe, 1946). Terraces, irrigation canals, roads, cultivation, grassland burning—each contributed to the modification of the settled valleys of the Andes. Construction of artificial, walled terraces, some of which are still used today, not only facilitated increased agricultural productivity but also prevented loss of topsoil. Hence, it should be clear that not all human modification of Andean ecosystems leads to direct environmental degradation.

There are, however, major differences between the prehispanic period when widespread ecosystem modification was conducted with relative success and conditions today. During the Inca period, the state had substantial control over major works, could easily marshal large labour forces to complete the work, and there is evidence that extensive planning was common (Rowe, 1946). Another difference between the two periods is that many of the socio-cultural adaptations that were effective in the past are being lost as hispanic and Western values and practices become a part of the highland pattern (Thomas, 1979). A detailed knowledge of an ecosystem and how it can be both managed productively and maintained without degradation is acquired over many generations. Time-tested practices of exploitation are changing more than ever, which leads to unstable patterns of adaptation. Finally, some current estimates place the Andean highland population at between two and three times what it was directly before the Spanish conquest (Baker, 1978). Increased population density is a major factor in processes of environmental change as greater pressure is exerted on the resources of the highlands.

A number of problems face Andean nations in the future. Major cities of between one-half million and two and one-half million inhabitants can be found in the highlands, and these cities with an incipient industrial base are growing at high rates. These few highland centres together with the numerous lowland cities are now absorbing at least half of the rapidly growing rural highland population. Yet this is only a temporary state, since the ability of lowland urban centres to accommodate highland migrants is limited. Resettlement efforts of governments probably will be redoubled to encourage pioneer migration to the eastern tropical lowlands of the montana, yungas and Amazon basin. Major migratory streams will then move from the western to the eastern Andes producing a marked shift in the geographical distribution of the population. This is already occurring in Bolivia where there is no effective western zone for downward migration. The effects of downward migration on the health and well-being of highland-adapted peoples is only beginning to be studied. Much more needs to be known about the human biology of migrant peoples in the Andes. ■

REFERENCES

ABELSON, A. E., BAKER, T. S., and BAKER, P. T., 1974: Altitude, migration, and fertility in the Andes. *Soc. Biol.*, 21: 1227.

ALFIN-SLATER, R. B. AND AFTERGOOD, L., 1973: Fats and other lipids. In Goodhart, R. S. and Shils, M. E. (eds.), *Modern Nutrition in Health and Disease*. Philadelphia: Lea and Febiger, pp. 117-141.

ARIAS-STELLA, J., 1966: Morphological patterns: mechanism of pulmonary arterial hypertension. In *Life at High Altitudes*. Pan American Health Organization, Scientific Publication No. 140, Washington, D.C., pp. 9-12.

ARIAS-STELLA, J., 1976a: Work performance of highland natives. In Baker, P. T. and Little, M. A. (eds.), *Man in the Andes: A Multidisciplinary Study of High-Altitude Quechua*. Stroudsburg, Pennsylvania: Dowden, Hutchinson and Ross, pp. 300-314.

ARIAS-STELLA, J., 1976b: Research strategies in population biology and environmental stress. In Giles, E. and Friedlaender, J. S. (eds.), *The Measures of Man*. Cambridge, Massachusetts: Peabody Museum Press, pp. 230-259.

ARIAS-STELLA, J., 1978: The adaptive fitness of high-altitude populations. In Baker, P. T. (ed.), *The Biology of High-Altitude Peoples*. Cambridge: Cambridge University Press, pp. 317-350.

ARIAS-STELLA, J., 1982: The Central Andes: environment, biology, and economic development: a perspective. *Mountain Research and Development*, 2(1): 127-140.

BARBASHOVA, Z. 1., 1964: Cellular level of adaptation. In Dill, D. B., Adolph, E. F., and Wilber, C. G. (eds.), *Handbook of Physiology Section 4: Adaptation to the Environment*. American Physiological Society, Washington, D.C., pp. 37-54.

BEALL, C. M., BAKER, P. T., BAKER, T. S., and HAAS, J. D., 1977: The effects of high altitude on adolescent growth in southern Peruvian Amerindians. *Hum. Biol.*,49: 109-124.

BEEK, K. J. and BRAMAO, D. L., 1968: Nature and geography of South American soils. In Fittkau, E. J. et al. (eds.), *Biogeography and Ecology in South America, Vol. 1*. The Hague: Dr. W. Junk N.V., pp. 82-112.

BENNETT, W. C., 1946: The Andean highlands: an introduction. In Steward, J. H. (ed.), *Handbook of South American Indians. Vol. 2, The Andean Civilizations*. Smithsonian Institution, Bureau of American Ethnology, Bulletin No. 143, Washington, D.C., pp. 1-60.

BENNETT, W. C., 1949: Engineering. In Steward, J. H. (ed.), *Handbook of South American Indians: Vol. 5, The Comparative Ethnology of South American Indians*. Smithsonian Institution, Bureau of American Ethnology, Bulletin No. 143, Washington, D.C., pp. 53-65.

BENNETT, W. C. and BIRD, J. B., 1960: *Andean Cultural History*. American Museum of Natural History, Handbook Series No . 15, New York.

BILLINGS, W. D. 1979: High mountain ecosystems: evolution, structure, operation and maintenance. In Webber, P. J. (ed.), *High Altitude Geoecology*. AAAS Symposium 12. Boulder, Colorado: Westview Press, pp. 97-125.

BIROT, P., 1960: *The Cycle of Erosion in Different Climates*. London: Fench.

BOULOUX, C. J., 1968: *Contribution a l'étude biologique des phénomènes pubèrtaires en très haute altitude* (La Paz). Centre d'Hematypologie du Centre National de la Recherche Scientifique, Toulouse, France.

BOWMAN, I., 1924: *Desert Trails of Atacama*. Special Publication No. 5, American Geographical Society, New York.

BOYCE, A. J., HAIGHT, J. S. J., RIMMER, D. B., and HARRISON, G. A., 1974: Respiratory function in Peruvian Quechua Indians . *Ann. Hum. Biol.*, 1: 137-148 .

BRIDGES, E. M., 1978: *World Soils, 2nd Ed.* Cambridge: Cambridge University Press.

BRUES, A. M., 1972: Models of race and cline. *Amer. J. Phys. Anthropol.*, 37: 389-400.

BRUSH, S. B., 1976a: Introduction to "Cultural Adaptations to Mountain Ecosystems". *Hum. Ecol.*, 4: 125-133 .

BRUSH, S. B., 1976b: Man's use of an Andean ecosystem. *Hum. Ecol.*, 4: 147-166.

BRUSH, S. B., 1977: *Mountain Field and Family: The Economy and Human Ecology of an Andean Valley*. Philadelphia, PA: University of Pennsylvania Press.

BRYAN, A. L., CASAMIGUELA, R. M., CRUXENT, J. M., GRUHN, R., and OCHSENIUS, C., 1978: An El Jobo mastodon kill at Taima-taima, Venezuela. *Science*, 200: 1275-1277.

BUCHERL, W., 1969: Giftige arthropoden. In Fittkau, E. J. et al. (eds.), *Biogeography and Ecology in South America, Vol. 2*. The Hague: Dr. W. Junk N. V., pp. 764-793.

BUETTNER, K. J. K., 1969: The effects of natural sunlight on human skin. In Urback, F. (ed.), *The Biological Effects of Ultraviolet Radiation*. Oxford: Pergamon Press, pp. 237-249.

BUOL, S. W., HOLE, F. D., and MCCRACKEN, R. J., 1973: *Soil Genesis and Classification*. Ames: Iowa State University Press.

BURINGH, P., 1970: *Introduction to the Study of Soils in Tropical and Subtropical Regions, 2nd Ed.* Centre for Agricultural Publishing and Documentation, Wageningen, The Netherlands.

BUSKIRK, E. R., 1976: Work performance of newcomers to the Peruvian highlands. In Baker, P. T. and Little, M. A. (eds.), *Man in the Andes. A Multidisciplinary Study of High-Altitude Quechua*. Stroudsburg, Pennsylvania: Dowden, Hutchinson and Ross, pp. 283-299.

BUSKIRK, E. R., KOLLIAS, J., AKERS, R. F., PROKOP, E. K., and PICON-REATEGUI, 1967: Maximal performance at altitude and on return from altitude in conditioned runners. *J. Appl. Physiol.*, 23: pp.259-266.

CABRERA, A. L., 1968: Ecologia vegetal de la puna. In Troll, C. (ed.), *Geo-Ecology of the Mountainous Regions of the Tropical Americas*. Bonn: Ferd . Dummlers Verlag, pp. 91-116 .

CABRERA, A. L. and WILLINK, A., 1973: *Biogeographia de America Latina*. Serie de Biologia, Monographia No. 13, Publicado por Secretaria General, OEA.

CAMINO, ALEJANDRO, 1981: Flexibilidad calendrica en la agricultura tradicional de las vertientes orientales de los Andes. In Letchman, H. and Soldi, A. M. (eds.), *La Tecnologa en el Mundo Andino*. Mexico: UNAM, pp. 169-194.

CAMINO, ALEJANDRO, 1989: Coca: del uso tradicional al narcotrafico. In Garcia Sayan, D. (ed.), *Coca, Cocaina y Narcotrafico*. Lima: Comision Andina de Juristas, pp. 91-108.

CEPAL (COMISION ECONOMICA PARA AMERICA LATINA Y EL CARIBE), 1988: *Gestin para el Desarrollo de Cuencas de Alta Montana en la Zona Andina*. Santiago de Chile: Naciones Unidas.

CISM, 1968: *Encuesta de Fecundidad en la Ciudad de Cerro de Pasco*. Centro de Investigaciones Sociales por Muestro y Ministerio de Trabajo y Communidades del Peru, Lima.

CLEGG, E. J., 1978: Fertility and early growth. In Baker, P. T. (ed.), *The Biology of High-Altitude Peoples*. Cambridge: Cambridge University Press, pp. 65-115 .

COLLAZOS, C., MOSCOSO. 1., BRAVO DE RUEDA, Y., CASTELLANOS, A., CACERES DE FUENTES, C., ROCA, A., and BRADFIELD, R. B. 1960: La alimentacion y el estado de nutricion en el Peru. *Anales de la Facultad de Medicina* (Lima), 43: 7-343 .

CONSOLAZIO, C. F., MATOUSH, L. 0., JOHNSON, H. L. KRZYWICKI, H. J., DAWS, T. A., and ISAAC, G. J., 1969: Effects of high-carbohydrate diets on performance and clinical symptomology after rapid ascent to high altitude. *Fed.. Proc.,* 28: 937-943.

COOK, N. D., 1973: The Indian Population of Peru, 1570-1620. Ph.D. dissertation, University of Texas, Austin.

COOPER, J. M., 1946: The Araucanians. In Steward, J. H. (ed.), *Handbook of South American Indians. Vol. 2, The Andean Civilizations*. Smithsonian Institution, Bureau of American Ethnology, Bulletin No. 143, Washington, D.C., pp. 687-760.

CORTE, A. E., 1968: Frost action and soil sorting processes. Their influence in the surface features of the tropical and sub-tropical high Andes. In Troll, C. (ed.), *Geo-Ecology of the Mountainous Regions of the Tropical Americas*. Bonn: Ferd. Dummlers Verlag, pp. 213-220.

CRIST, R. E. and NISSLY, C. M., 1973: *East from the Andes. Pioneer Settlements in the South American Heartland*. Gainsville: University of Florida Press.

CRUXENT, J., 1968: Theses for meditation on the origin and distribution of man in South America. in *Biomedical Challenges Presented by the American Indian*. Pan American Health Organization, Scientific Publication No. 165, PAHO/WHO, Washington, D.C., pp. 11-16.

CRUZ-COKE, R., 1978: A genetic description of high-altitude populations. In Baker, P. T. (ed.), *The Biology of High-Altitude Populations*. Cambridge: Cambridge University Press, pp. 47-63.

CUATRECASAS, J., 1968: Paramo vegetation and its life form. In Troll, C. (ed.), *Geo-Ecology of the Mountainous Regions of the Tropical Americas*. Bonn: Ferd. Dummlers Verlag, pp. 163-186.

DELURY, G. E. (ED.), 1977: *The World Almanac and Book of Facts*. Newspaper Enterprise Association, New York.

DENEVAN, W. M., 1976: Introduction to Part 1: Estimating the unknown. In Denevan, W. M. (ed.), *The Native Population of the Americas in 1492*. Madison: University of Wisconsin Press, pp. 1-12 .

DENEVAN, W. M., 1986: Abandono de terrazas en el Peru andino: extension, causas y propuenstas de restauracion. In de la Torre, C. and Burga, M. (eds.), *Andenes y Camellones en el Peru Andino*. Lima: Ministerio de la Presidencia and CONCYTEC, pp. 255-258.

DE NONI, G., NOUVELDT, J. F. and TRUJILLO, G., 1986: Estudio cuantitativo de la erosion confines de proteccion de los suedos: Las parcelas de Alangasi e Ilalo. *Centro Ecuuatoriano de Investigacion Geografica, Documentos de Investigacion*, no. 6: 35-47.

DEW, E., 1969: *Politics in the Altiplano: The Dynamics of Change in Rural Peru*. Austin: University of Texas Press.

DOBYNS, H. F., 1966: Estimating aboriginal American population, 1: an appraisal of techniques with a new hemispheric estimate. *Curr. Anthropol.*, 7: 395-449.

DONAYRE, J., GUERRA-GARCIA, R., MONCLOA, F., and SOBREVILLA, L. A., 1968: Endocrine studies at high altitude: IV. Changes in the semen of men. *J. Reprod. Fert.*, 16: 55-58.

DONAYRE, J., 1966: Population growth and fertility at high altitude. in *Life at High Altitudes*. Pan American Health Organization, Scientific Publication No. 140, Washington, D.C., pp. 74-79.

DUCHAUFOUR, P., 1978: *Ecological Atlas of Soils of the World*. New York: Masson.

DUFOUR, D. L., LITTLE, M. A., and THOMAS, R. B., 1976: Skin temperature at the nape in infants at high altitude. *Amer. J. Phys. Anthropol.*, 44: 91-94 .

DUFOUR, D. L., 1979: Insects in the diet of Indians in the northwestern Amazon, Colombia. *Amer. J Phys. Anthropol.*, 50: 434 (abstract).

DUTT, J. S., 1976: Population movement and gene flow. In Baker, P. T. and Little, M. A. (eds.), *Man in the Andes. A Multidisciplinary Study of High-Altitude Quechua*. Stroudsburg, Pennsylvania: Dowden, Hutchinson and Ross, pp. 115-127.

EIDT, R. C., 1968: The climatology of South America. In Fittkau, E. J. et al., (eds.), *Biogeography and Ecology in South America, Vol. 1*. The Hague: Dr. W.Junk N. V., pp. 54-81.

ELLENBERG, H., 1964: Montane vegetation and productivity in the tropics with special reference to Peru. In *The Ecology of Man in the Tropical Environment*. International Union for the Conservation of Nature and Natural Resources, No. 4, Morges, Switzerland, pp. 172-177.

ESCOBAR, Gabriel M. and BEALL, Cynthia M., 1982: Contemporary patterns of migration in the Central Andes, *Mountain Research and Development*, 2(1): 63-80.

FAHEY, B. D., 1973: An analysis of diurnal freeze-thaw and frost heave cycles in the Indian Peaks region of the Colorado Front Range. *Arctic and Alpine Research*, 5(3):269-281.

FAO/UNESCO/OMM, 1975: *Estudio Agroclimatologico de la Zona Andina*. Projecto Interinstitucional FAO/Unesco/OMM en Agroclimatologia. Informe Technico, Rome.

FITTKAU, E. J., ILLIES, J., KLINGE, H., SCHWABE, G. H., and SIOLI, H. (eds.), 1969: *Biogeography and Ecology in South America, Vol. 2*. The Hague: Dr. W. Junk N. V.

FORMAN, R. T. T., 1975: Canopy lichens with blue-green algae: a nitrogen source in a Colombian rainforest. *Ecology*, 56:1176-1184.

FRISANCHO, A. R., 1969: Human growth and pulmonary function of a high altitude Peruvian Quechua population. *Hum. Biol.* 41: 365-379.

FRISANCHO, A. R., 1975: Functional adaptation to high altitude hypoxia. *Science*, 187: 313-319.

FRISANCHO, A. R., 1976: Growth and morphology at high altitude. In Baker, P. T. and Little, M. A. (eds.), *Man in the Andes. A Multidisciplinary Study of High-Altitude Quechua*. Stroudsburg, Pennsylvania: Dowden, Hutchinson and Ross, pp. 180-207.

GADE, Daniel, 1975: *Plants, Man and Land in the Vilcanota Valley of Peru*. The Hague: Dr. W. Junk.

GARAY-COCHEA, Ignacio, 1986: Potencial agricola de los camellones en el altiplano puneno. In de la Torre, C. and Burga, M. (eds.), *Andenes y Camellones en el Peru Andino*. Lima: Ministerio de la Presidencia–CONCYTEC, pp. 241-252.

GARBELL, M. A., 1947: *Tropical and Equatorial Meteorology* New York: Pitman.

GARRUTO, R. M., 1976: Hematology. In Baker, P. T. and Little, M. A. (eds.), *Man in the Andes: A Multidisciplinary Study of High-Altitude Quechua.* Stroudsburg, Pennsylvania: Dowden, Hutchinson and Ross, pp. 261-282.

GEIGER, R., 1965: *The Climate Near the Ground.* Cambridge: Harvard University Press.

GERY, J., 1969: The fresh-water fishes of South America. In Fittkau, E.J. et al. (eds.), *Biogeography and Ecology in South America*, Vol. 2. The Hague: Dr. W. Junk N. V.

GONZALEZ, A ., 1967: Some effects of population growth on Latin America's economy. *J. Inter-Amer. Stud.,* 9: 22-42.

GOODYEAR, ALBERT C. et al, 1979. Laurens-Anderson Occasional Papers of Inst. of Archeology No.4 U of S Carolina Press.

GROSJEAN, M., GRAF, K., MESSERLI, B., ROMERO, H., SCHREIER, H., SCHOTTERER, V. and VUILE, M., 1992: Climate change and dynamics of natural resources in the Altiplano of Northern Chile during Late Glacial and Holocene Time: A first synthesis. *Mountain Research and Development*, 12(4), *in press.*

GUHL, E., 1968: Los paramos circundantes de la sabana de Bogota, 511 ecologia y su importancia para el regimen hidrologico de la misma. In Troll, C. (ed.), *Geo-Ecology of the Mountainous Regions of the Tropical Americas* Bonn: Ferd. Dummlers Verlag, pp. 195-212 .

GWYNNE, Robert N., 1992: Outward orientation and marginal environments: Growth and change in Chile's Norte Chico. *Mountain Research and Development*, 12(4), *in press.*

HAAS, J. D., 1976: Prenatal and infant growth and development. In Baker, P. T. and Little, M. A. (eds.), *Man in the Andes: A Multidisciplinary Study of High-Altitude Quechua.* Stroudsburg, Pennsylvania: Dowden, Hutchinson and Ross, pp. 161-179.

HARDEN, Carol P., 1988: Mesoscale estimation of soil erosion in the Rio Ambato drainage, Ecuadorian Sierra. *Mountain Research and Development*, 8(4): 331-341.

HARDEN, Carol P., 1991: Andean soil erosion: A comparison of soil erosion conditions in two Andean watersheds. *National Geographic Research*, 7(2): 216-231.

HARDEN, Carol P., 1992: Land use, soil erosion, and reservoir sedimentation in an Andean drainage basin in Ecuador. *Mountain Research and Development*, 12(4), *in press.*

HARRIS, C. W., SHIELDS, J. L., and HANNON, J. P., 1966: Acute altitude sickness in females. *Aerospace Med.*, 37: 1163-1167.

HARRISON, G. A., 1966: Human adaptation with reference to the IBP proposals for high altitude research. In Baker, P. T. and Weiner, J. S. (eds.), *The Biology of Human Adaptability*. Oxford: Oxford University Press, pp. 509-519.

HEER, D. M., 1964: Fertility differences between Indian and Spanish-speaking parts of Andean countries. *Pop. Stud.,* 18: 71-84.

HEER, D. M., 1967: Fertility differences in Andean countries: a reply to W. H. James. *Pop. .Stud.,* 21: 71-73.

HELLRIEGEL, K. 0., 1967: Health problems at altitude. Paper presented at the WHO/PAHO/IBP Meeting of Investigators on Population Biology of Altitude. November, Washington, DC.

HESS, Carmen G., 1990: "Moving up - moving down": Agro-pastoral land-use patterns in the Ecuadorian paramos. *Mountain Research and Development,* 10(4): 333-342.

HOFF, C., BAKER, P. T, GARRUTO, R., HAAS, J., and SPECTOR, R., 1972a: Variaciones altitudinales en pulso y presion arterial en nativos Andinos del Peru. *Archivos del Instituto de Bioloía Andina* (Lima), 5: 57-67.

HOFF, C. J. and ABELSON, A. E., 1976: Fertility. In Baker, P. T. and Little, M. A. (eds.), *Man in the Andes: A Multidisciplinary Study of High-Altitude Quechua.* Stroudsburg, Pennsylvania: Dowden, Hutchinson and Ross, pp. 128-146.

HOFF, C. J., 1968: Reproduction and viability in a highland Peruvian Indian population. Occas. Papers Anthropol. (University Park, Pennsylvania), 1: 85-161.

HUECK, K., 1966: *Die Walder Sudamerikas. Okologie, Zusammensetzung und Wirtschaftliche Bedeutung.* Stuttgart: G. Fischer.

HURNI, H., 1985: An ecosystem approach to soil conservation. Honolulu: *International Conference on Soil Erosion and Conservation*, 16-22 January, 1983, pp. 759-771.

HURTADO, A., 1932: Respiratory adaptation in the Indian natives of the Peruvian Andes: studies at high altitudes. *Amer. J. Phy. Anthropol.* 17: 137-165.

IVES, J. D., 1979: Applied high altitude geoecology. In Webber, P. J. (ed.), *High Altitude Geoecology*. Boulder, Colorado: Westview Press, pp. 9-45.

JAMES, D. E., 1973: The evolution of the Andes. *Scientific American*, 229(2): 60-69.

JAMES, W. H., 1966: The effect of altitude on fertility in Andean Countries. *Pop. Stud.*, 20: 97-101.

JENNINGS, J.D., (ed.) 1977 *Ancient Native Americans*. 2nd edn. Harper and Row, NY.

JOHNSON, A. M., 1976: The climate of Peru, Bolivia and Ecuador. In Schwerdtfeger, W. (ed.), *Climates of Central and South America. World Survey of Climatology Vol. 12*. Amsterdam: Elsevier, pp. 147-218.

KINZL, H., 1968: La glaciacion actual y Pleistocenica en los Andes centrales. In Troll, C. (ed.), *Geo-Ecology of the Mountainous Regions of the Tropical Americas*. Bonn: Ferd. Dummlers Verlag, pp. 87-90.

KOLLIAS, J ., BUSKIRK, E. R., AKERS, R. F., PROKOP, E. K., BAKER, P. T., and PICON-REATEGUI, E., 1968: Work capacity of long time residents and newcomers to altitude. *J. Appl. Physiol.*, 24: 792-799.

KROEBER, A. L.,1946: The Chibcha. In Steward, J. H. (ed.), *Handbook of South American Indians Vol. 2, The Andean Civilizations*. Smithsonian Institution, Bureau of American Ethnology, Bulletin No. 143, Washington, D.C., pp. 887-909.

KUBLER, G.,1952: *The Indian Caste in Peru, 1795-1940. A Population Study Based upon Tax Records and Census Reports*. Smithsonian Institution, Institute of Social Anthropology, Publication No. 14, Washington, D.C.

KUSCHEL, G., 1969: Biogeography and ecology of South American coleoptera. In Fittkau, E. J. et al., (eds.), *Biogeography and Ecology in South America. Vol. 2*. The Hague: Dr. W. Junk N. V., pp. 709-722.

LAHIRI, S., DELANEY, R. G., BRODY, J. S., SIMPSER, M, VELASQUEZ, T., MOTOYAMA, E. K., and POLGAR, C., 1976: Relative role of environmental and genetic factors in respiratory adaptation to high altitude. *Nature*, 261: 133-135.

LANNING, E. P., 1967: *Peru Before the Incas*. Englewood Cliffs, New Jersey: Prentice-Hall.

LANNING, E. P., 1974: Western South America. In Gortnstein, S, Forbis, R. G., Tolstoy, P., and Lanning, E. P. (eds.), *Pre-hispanic America*. New York: St. Martin's Press. pp. 65-86.

LENFANT, C., 1973: High altitude adaptation in animals. *Amer. Zool.*, 13: 447-456.

LENFANT, C. and SULLIVAN, K., 1971: Adaptation to altitude. *New Engl. J. Med*, 284: 1298-1309.

LENFANT, C., TORRANCE, J., ENGLISH, E., FINCH, C. A. REYNAFARJE, C., RAMOS, J., and FAURA, J., 1968: Effect of altitude on oxygen binding by hemoglobin and on organic phosphate levels. *J. Clin. Invest.*, 47: 2652-2656.

LEWIS, G. E., TSCHOPP, H. J., and MARKS, J. G., 1956: Ecuador. IN JENKS, W. E. (ed.), *Handbook of South American Geology: An Explanation of the Geologic Map of South America*. Memoir 65, The Geological Society of America, New York, pp.249-267.

LITTLE, M. A., 1969: Temperature regulation at high altitude: Quechua Indians and U.S. whites during foot exposure to cold water and cold air. *Hum. Biol.*, 41: 519-535.

LITTLE. M. A. and HOCHNER, D. H., 1973: Human thermo regulation, growth, and mortality. *Module in Anthropol.*, No. 36. Reading, Massachusetts: Addison-Wesley.

LITTLE, M. A., THOMAS, R. B., and LARRICK, J. W., 1973: Skin temperature and cold stressor responses of Andean Indians during hand immersion in water at 4°C. *Hum. Biol.* 45: 643-662.

LITTLE, M. A.,1976: Physiological responses to cold. In Baker, P. T . and Little, M. A. (eds.), *Man in the Andes: A Multidisciplinary Study of High-Altitude Quechua*. Stroudsburg, Pennsylvania: Dowden, Hutchinson and Ross, pp. 332-362.

LITTLE, M. A. and HANNA, J. M., 1977: Cold responses of high altitude populations . *Intl. J. Biometeor.*, 21: 123-134 .

LÖFFLER, H., 1968: Tropical high mountain lakes: their distribution, ecology and zoogeographical importance. In Troll, C. (ed.), *Geo-Ecology of the Mountainous Regions of the Tropical Americas*. Bonn: Ferd. Dummlers Verlag, pp. 57-76.

LOWENSTEIN, F. W., 1968: Some aspects of human ecology in South America. In Fittkau, E. J, Illies, J., Klinge, K., Schwabe, G. H., and Sioli, H. (eds.), *Biogeography and Ecology in South America*, Vol. 1. Monographiae Biologicae. The Hague: Dr. W.Junk N. V., pp. 389-412.

MACNEISH, R. S., 1971: Early man in the Andes. *Sci. Amer.*, 224(4): 34-46.

MACNEISH, R. S., BERGER, R., and PROTSCH, R., 1970: Megafauna and man from Ayacucho, highland Peru. *Science*, 168: 975-977 .

MANGIN, W. P., 1959: The role of regional associations in the adaptation of rural population in Peru. *Sociologus*, 9: 23-36.

MARRERO, L., 1964: *Venezuela y sus Recursos.* Cultural Venezolana, Caracas.

MARTICORENA, E., TAPIA, F. A., DYER, J., SEVERINO, J., BANCHERO, N ., GAMBOA, R., KRUGER, H., and PERIALOZA, D., 1964: Pulmonary edema by ascending to high altitudes. *Dis. Chest*, 45: 273-283.

MARTICORENA, E. A., SEVERINO, J., and HULTGREN, H. N., 1967: 1. Cardio-pulmonary pathology at high altitude. Paper presented at the WHO/PAHO/IBP Meeting of Investigators on Population Biology of Altitude. November, Washington, D. C.

MAYER-OAKES, W. J. and BELL, R. E., 1960: Early man site found in highland Ecuador. *Science,* 131: 1805-1806.

MAZESS, R. B., 1965: Neonatal mortality and altitude in Peru. *Amer J. Phys. Anthropol.*, 23: 209-214.

MAZESS, R. B. and BAKER, P. T., 1964: Diet of the Quechua Indians living at high altitude. *J. Clin. Nutr.,* 15: 341-351.

MAZESS, R. B., PICON-REATEGUI, R., THOMAS, B., and LITTLE, M. A., 1969: Oxygen intake and body temperature of basal and sleeping Andean Indians at high altitude. *Aerospace Med,* 40: 6-9.

MAZESS, R. B. and FORMAN, S. H., 1979: Longevity and age exaggeration in Vilcabamba, Ecuador. *J. Gerontol.*, 34: 94-98.

MCCLUNG, J., 1969: *Effects of High Altitude on Human Birth.* Cambridge, Massachusetts: Harvard University Press.

MCRAE, Stephen D., 1982: Human Ecological Modeling for the Central Andes. *Mountain Research and Development*, 2(1): 94-110.

MELLOR, M., 1979: Ice and snow at high altitudes. In Webber, P. J. (ed.), *High Altitude Geoecology* Boulder, Colorado: Westview Press, pp. 75-95.

MILLER, A., 1976: The climate of Chile. In Schwerdtfeger, W. (ed.), *World Survey of Climatology Volume 12 Climates of Central and South America.* New York: Elsevier Scientific, pp. 113-145.

MILLER, A. T., Jr., 1974: Altitude. In Slonim, N. B. (ed.), *Environmental Physiology.* St. Louis, Missouri: Mosby, pp. 350-375.

MILLER, P. C., BRADBURY, D. E., HAJEK, E., LAMARCHE, V., and THROWER, N. J. W., 1977: Past and present environment. In Mooney, H. A. (ed.), *Convergent Evolution in Chile and California. Mediterranean Climate Ecosystem.* Stroudsberg, Pennsylvania: Dowden, Hutchinson and Ross, pp. 27-72.

MONGE, M. C. and MONGE, C. C., 1966: *High-Altitude Diseases. Mechanism and Management.* Springfield, Illinois: C. C. Thomas.

MONTANE, J. C., 1968: Paleo-Indian remains from Laguna de Tagua Tagua, central Chile. *Science*, 161: 1137-1138.

MOONEY, H. A., KUMMEROW, J., JOHNSON, A. W., PARSONS, D. J., KEELEY, S., HOFFMANN, A., ELDYS, R. 1., GILIBERTO,J., and CHU, C., 1977: The producers—their resources and adaptive responses. In Mooney, T. A (ed.), *Convergent Evolution in Chile and California. Mediterranean Climate Ecosystems.* Stroudsburg, Pennsylvania: Dowden, Hutchinson and Ross, pp. 85-143.

MORPURGO, G., BATTAGLIA, P., BERNINI, L., PAOLUCCI, A. M., and MODIANO, G., 1970: Higher Bohr effect in Indian natives of Peruvian highlands as compared with Europeans. *Nature,* 227: 387-388.

MURRA, J, 1972: El *"control vertical" de un maximo de pisos ecologicos en la economia de las sociedades Andinas.* Visita de la Provincia Delcon de Huarnoco.

NEWMAN, M. T., 1958: A trial formulation presenting evidence from physical anthropology for migrations from Mexico to South America. In Thompson, R. H. (ed.), *Migrations in New World Culture History.* Social Science Bulletin 27. Tucson: University of Arizona Press, pp. 33-

NOODT, W., 1969: Die Grundwasserfauna Südamerikas. In Fittkau, E . J. et al. (eds .), *Biogeography and Ecology in South America*, Vol. 2, The Hague: Dr. W Junk N. V., pp. 659-684.

OGILVIE, A. G., 1922: *Geography of the Central Andes,* American Geographical Society of New York, New York.

OLROG, C. C., 1969: Birds of South America. In Fittkau, E. J. et al. (eds.), *Biogeography and Ecology in South America*, Vol 2. The Hague: Dr. W. Junk N. V., pp. 849-878.

ORGANIZATION OF AMERICAN STATES, 1970: *Datos Basicos de Poblacion en America Latina, 1970.* Departamento de Asuntos Sociales, Secretaria General de la. Union Panamericana, O.E.A., Washington, D.C.

Orlove, B. S., 1977: Integration through production: the use of zonation in Espinar. *Amer. Ethnologist*, 4: 84-101.

Pawson, I. G. and Jest, C., 1978: The high-altitude areas of the world and their cultures. In Baker, P. T. (ed.), *The Biology of High-Altitude Peoples*. Cambridge: Cambridge University Press, pp. 17-45.

Pendle, G., 1967: *A History of Latin America*. Middlesex: Penguin.

Peñalosa, D., 1966: Physiological patterns: cardiovascular characteristics of healthy man. In *Life at High Altitudes*. Pan American Health Organization, Scientific Publication No. 140, Washington, D.C., pp. 27-31.

Picon-Reategui, E., 1961: Basal metabolic rate and body composition at high altitude. *J. Appl. Physiol.*, 16: 431-434.

Picon-Reategui, E., 1978: The food and nutrition of high-altitude populations. In Baker, P. T. (ed.), *The Biology of High-Altitude Peoples*. Cambridge: Cambridge University Press, pp. 219-249.

Quilici, J. C. and Vergnes, H., 1978: The haematological characteristics of high-altitude populations. In Baker, P. T. (ed.), *The Biology of High-Altitude Peoples*. Cambridge: Cambridge University Press, pp. 189-218.

Retzer, J. L., 1974: Alpine soils. In Ives, J. D. and Barry, R. G. (eds.), *Arctic and Alpine Environments*. London: Methuen, pp. 771-802.

Reynafarje, B., 1962: Myoglobin content and enzymatic activity of muscle and altitude adaptation. *J. Appl. Physiol.*, 17: 301-305.

Reynafarje, B., 1966: Physiological patterns: enzymatic changes. In *Life at High Altitudes*. Pan American Health Organization, Scientific Publication No. 140, Washington, D.C., pp. 40-45.

Reynafarje, B., 1971: Mechanisms moleculares de la adaptacion a la hipoxia de las grandes alturas. *Archivos del Instituto de Biologia Andina (Lima)*, 4: 1-14.

Roberts, D. F., 1977: Methods and problems in physiological genetics. In Weiner, J. S. (ed.), *Physiological Variation and Its Genetic Basis*. London: Taylor and Francis, pp. 23-41.

Robinson, H., 1967 *Latin America. A Geographical Survey*. New York: Preager.

Romero, E., 1972: *Peru Una Nueva Geografia, Vol. 1*. Libreria Studium, Lima.

Rothhammer, F. and Spielman, R. S., 1972: Anthropometric variation in the Aymara: geographic and topographic contributions. *Amer. J. Hum. Genet.*, 24: 371-380.

Rowe, J. H., 1946: Inca culture at the time of the Spanish conquest. In Steward, J. H. (ed.), *Handbook of South American Indians. Vol. 2, The Andean Civilizations*. Smithsonian Institution, Bureau of American Ethnology, Bulletin No. 143, Washington, DC, pp. 183-330.

Salas, G. de la and Folster, H., 1976: Bioelement loss on Clearing a Tropical Rain Forest. Facultad Forestal, Universitad Distrital, Bogota.

Salguero-Silva, H., 1967: Summary of physiopathology in miners living at high altitudes. Paper presented at the WHO/PAHO/IBP Meeting of Investigators on Population Biology of Altitude. November, Washington, DC.

Salzano, F. M., 1968: Survey of the unacculturated Indians of Central and South America. *In Biomedical Challenges Presented by the American Indian*. Pan American Health Organization, Sci. Publ. No. 165, PAHO/WHO, Washington, D.C., pp. 59-66.

Sauer, C. 0., 1944: A geographical sketch of early man in America. *Geogr. Rev.*, 34: 529-573.

Sauer, C. 0., 1950: Geography of South America. In Steward, J. H. (ed.), *Handbook of South American Indians, Vol. 6, Physical Anthropology, Linguistics and Cultural Geography of South American Indians*. Smithsonian Institution, Washington, D.C., Bureau of American Ethnology Bulletin 143, pp. 319-344.

Schull, W. J. and Rothhammer, F., 1977: A multinational Andean genetic and health programme: a study of adaptation to the hypoxia of altitude. In Weiner, J. S. (ed.), *Physiological Variation and its Genetic Basis*. Symposia of the Society for the Study of Human Biology, Vol. 17. London: Taylor and Francis, pp. 139-169.

Schuster, R, 1969: Die terrestrische Milbenfauna Südamerikas in zoogeographischer sicht. In Fittkau, E. J. et al. (eds.), *Biogeography and Ecology in South America*, Vol. 2. The Hague: Dr. W. Junk N. V., pp.741-763.

SHEA, D. E., 1976: A defense of small population estimates for the central Andes in 1520. In Denevan, W. M. (ed.), *The Native Population of the Americas in 1492*. Madison: University of Wisconsin Press, pp. 157-180.

SCHWERDTFEGER, W., 1976: Introduction. In Schwerdtfeger, W. (ed.), *World Survey of Climatology Volume 12. Climates of Central and South America*. New York: Elsevier Scientific, pp. 1-12 .

SICK, W. D., 1969: Geographical Substance. In Fittkau, E. J. et al (eds.), *Biogeography and Ecology in South America*, Vol. 2, The Hague: Dr. W. Junk N. V., pp. 449-474.

SINGH, I. and ROY, S. B., 1969: High altitude pulmonary edema: clinical, hemodynamic, and pathological studies. In Hegnaur, A. H. (ed.), *Biomedicine Problems of High Terrestrial Elevations*. U.S. Army Research Institute of Environmental Medicine, Natick, Massachusetts, pp. 108-120.

SLAYMAKER, H. O., 1974: Alpine hydrology. In Ives, J. D. and Barry, R. G. (eds.), *Arctic and Alpine Environments*. London: Methuen, pp. 133-158.

SMITH, C. T., 1970: Depopulation of the central Andes in the 16th century. *Curr. Anthropol.*, 11: 453-464.

SNOW, J. W., 1976: The climate of northern South America. In Schwerdtfeger, W. (ed.), *Climates of Central and South America*. World Survey of Climatology Vol. 12. Amsterdam: Elsevier, pp. 295-403.

SOLON, L. R., LOWDER, W. M., SHAMBON, A., and BLATZ, H., 1960: Investigations of natural environmental radiation. *Science*, 131: 903-906.

STADEL, Christoph, 1986: Altitudinal patterns of agricultural activities in the Patate-Pelileo area of Ecuador. *Mountain Research and Development*, 6(1): 53-62.

STADEL, Christoph, 1989: The perception of stress by campesinos: a profile from the Ecuadorian Sierra. *Mountain Research and Development*, 9(1): 35-49.

STADEL, Christoph, 1991: Environmental stress and sustainable rural development in the Tropical Andes. *Mountain Research and Development*, 11(3): 213-223.

STAVER, C. P., BYERS, A. C., RAVELO, A. C. and DICKINSON, J. G., 1991: Refining soil conservation strategies in the mountain environment–the climatic factor: an Ecuadorian case study. *Mountain Research and Development*, 11(2): 127-144.

STEWARD, J. H. and FARON, L. C., 1959: *Native Peoples of South America*. New York: McGraw-Hill.

STINI, W. A., 1969: Nutritional stress and growth: sex difference in adaptive response. *Amer. J. Phys. Anthropol.*, 31: 417-426 .

STINI, W. A., 1972: Reduced sexual dimorphism in upper arm muscle circumference associated with protein-deficient diet in a South American population. Amer. J. Phys. Anthropol., 36: 341-352.

STYCOS, J. M., 1963: Culture and differential fertility in Peru. *Pop. Stud.*, 16: 357-370.

THOMAS, R. B., 1975: The biology of work. In Damon, A. (ed.), *Physiological Anthropology*. New York: Oxford University Press, pp. 59-79.

THOMAS, R. B., 1976: Energy flow at high altitude. In Baker, P. T. and Little, M. A. (eds.), *Man in the Andes: A Multidisciplinary Study of High-Altitude Quechua*. Stroudsburg, Pennsylvania: Dowden, Hutchinson and Ross.

THOMAS, R. B., BAKER, P. T., and HAAS, J. D., 1977: Man and the environment in the central Andes: a research prospectus. In Baker, P. T. (ed.), *Human Population Problems in the Biosphere: Some Research Strategies and Designs*. Man and the Biosphere Technical Notes 3, Unesco, Paris, pp. 33-52.

THOMAS, R. B., 1979: Effects of change on high mountain human adaptive patterns. In Webber, P. J. (ed.) *High Altitude Geoecology*. AAAS Symposium 12. Boulder, Colorado: Westview Press, pp. 139-188 .

TOSI, J. A., 1960: *Zonas de Vida en el Peru*. Instituto Interamericano de Ciencias Agricolas de la OEA. Zona Andina Boletin Technico No. 5, Lima.

TROLL, C., 1968: The cordilleras of the tropical Americas: aspects of climate, phytogeographical and agrarian ecology. In Troll, C. (ed.), *Geo-Ecology of the Mountainous Regions of the Tropical Americas*. Bonn: Ferd. Dummlers Verlag, pp. 15-56.

UNESCO, 1973: *International Classification and Mapping of Vegetation*. Unesco, Paris.

VALCARCEL, L. E., 1946: Indian markets and fairs in Peru. In Steward, J. El. (ed.), *Handbook of South American Indians:* Vol. 2, *The Andean Civilizations*. Smithsonian Institution, Bureau of American Ethnology, Bulletin No. 143, Washington, D C., pp. 477-482.

VAN DER HAMMEN, T., 1968: Climatic and vegetational succession in the equatorial Andes of Colombia. In Troll, C. (ed.), *Geo-Ecology of the Mountainous Regions of the Tropical Americas*. Bonn: Ferd. Dummlers Verlag.

VELASQUEZ, T., 1947: Metabolismo basal en la altura. Bachelor's Thesis, Facultad de Medicina, Universidad Nacional Mayor de San Marcos, Lima.

VELASQUEZ, T., 1976: Pulmonary function and oxygen transport. In Baker, P. T. and Little, M. A. (eds.), *Man in the Andes: A Multidisciplinary Study of High-Altitude Quechua*. Stroudsburg, Pennsylvania: Dowden, Hutchinson and Ross, pp. 237-260.

WAY, A. B., 1976: Morbidity and postneonatal mortality. In Baker, P. T. and Little, M. A. (eds.), *Man in the Andes: A Multidisciplinary Study of High-Altitude Quechua*. Stroudsburg, Pennsylvania: Dowden, Hutchinson and Ross, pp. 147-160.

WEBER, H., 1969: Zur naturlichen vegetationsliederung von Südamerika. In Fittkau, E. J. et al. (eds.), *Biogeography and Ecology in South America*, Vol. 2 , The Hague: Dr. W. Junk N. V., pp. 475-518.

WEBSTER, S. S, 1972: An indigenious Quechua community in exploitation of multiple ecological zones. *Actas y Memorias* del XXXIX Congreso Internacional de Americanistas, 3: 174-183.

WEIL, T. E., BLACK, J. K., BLUTSTEIN, H. I., MCMORRIS, D. S., MUNSON, F. P., and TOWNSEND, C., 1972: *Area Handbook for Peru*. DA Pam 550-42, US Government Printing Office, Washington, DC.

WHITE, Stuart and MALDONADO, Fausto, 1991: The use and conservation of natural resources in the Andes of southern Ecuador. *Mountain Research and Development*, 11(1): 37-55.

WILLEY, G. R., 1971: *An Introduction to American Archaeology. Volume II. South America* , Englewood Cliffs, New Jersey: Prentice-Hall.

WINTERHALDER, B. P. and THOMAS, R. B., 1978: *Geoecology of Southern Highland Peru: A Human Adaptation Perspective*. Institute of Arctic and Alpine Research, University of Colorado, Occasional Paper No. 27, Boulder, Colorado.

NB: Anyone requiring access to a more complete list of references should write to J. Ives, University of California, 280 Kerr Hall, Davis, California 95616-8604, USA.

7

Mountains of the Former Soviet Union:

value, diversity, uncertainty

The Caucasus resemble the Alps and were the target of pioneer mountaineers in the 19th century looking for new first ascents after climbing the last unconquered peaks in West Europe

Preamble

The state of the environment and the development of mountain regions of the ex-USSR in the last decade of the 20th century should be assessed in the context of the phenomenon of "perestroika". This was started by Gorbachev in 1985 and involved the following fundamental processes:

❑ the removal of the curtain of censorship ("glasnost") which concealed the real problems of the environment. Incidentally these are referred to in the ex-USSR as "ecological problems";

❑ the deepening of the economic crisis including recession in production, the destruction of the supercentralized system of management, and the overall reduction in the well-being of the population at large;

❑ the changes in the state establishment reflecting the desire of some republics to leave the USSR and the associated phenomena of separatism, confrontation and nationalism;

❑ the emergence of local inter-ethnic conflicts which in some cases assume the character of armed confrontation (for example in the mountain regions—Karabakh, South Ossetia in the Caucasus, and Fergana Valley, Osh in Soviet Central Asia).

Although they are each focused in specific areas, all these problems aggravate the general state of instability, both in the sphere of socio-economic relations, and in the rational use of natural resources and the conservation of the environment .

The areas of the territorial-ethnic conflicts shown by Figure 7.1 sharply illuminate the socio-political landscape of the mountain territories of the ex-USSR in the 1990s. Such is the background of the complicated and contradictory processes of regional development. The emergence of these destabilizing factors might be said, figuratively, to be due to "taking a lid off a pressure cooker". In addition these conflicts may have an ethnic, territorial, or economic character, although their roots go deep into history and are grounded in the struggle for living space and resources.

This extremely simplified scheme seems quite apparent in the case of the mountain areas of the ex-USSR, especially in the context of their marginal, peripheral location in relation to economically developed centres of the lowlands.

At the same time, the recent decades have been characterized by the stormy growth of "green" movements and more active research in key areas of ecological science under the major international programmes and projects: the International Geosphere Biosphere Programme (IGBP), "Global Change", Global Monitoring System, Climate Programme, Unesco's Man and Biosphere (MAB), etc. Thanks to the development of democracy in Soviet society in the last five years there is a real "boom" in cooperation with international and national governmental and non-governmental organizations. This is the dynamic landscape of the socio-economic development and research on the problems of sustainable environmental-economic development of mountain areas in the former USSR.

Author's note: *On 21 December 1991 the Union of Soviet Socialist Republics (USSR) was renounced. The leaders of eleven former Soviet Republics met in Alma Ata (capital of Kazakstan) and signed the Declaration which established the Commonwealth of Independent States including: Russia, Belarus, Kazakhstan, Ukraine, Azerbaijan, Armenia, Kyrghyzstan, Moldavia, Tajikistan, Turkmenistan, and Uzbekistan. Nine of these have vast mountainous areas.*

One of the world's largest states which occupied a sixth of the planet's land surface has split into 11 states with each a different history, different religions, cultures and economic situations, as well as natural features and resources. The geopolitical landscape of Eurasia has completely changed. This chapter was compiled in the summer of 1991 and regrettably, therefore, cannot reflect many of the subsequent political adjustments which in any case are subject to rapid evolution themselves.

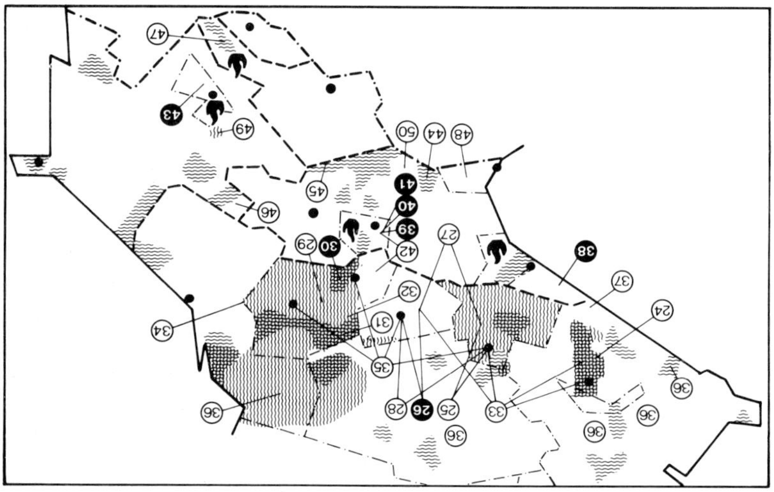

Figure 7.1: *Ethnic and territorial disputes mark the mountain areas of the former Soviet Union particularly in the Caucasus and ex-Soviet Central Asia where forced migrations in the past have also stored up tensions*

For key, see opposite

Details

I Caucasus area

II Soviet Central Asia

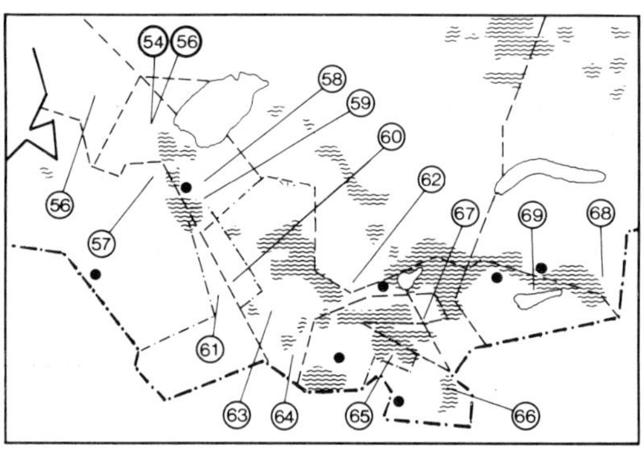

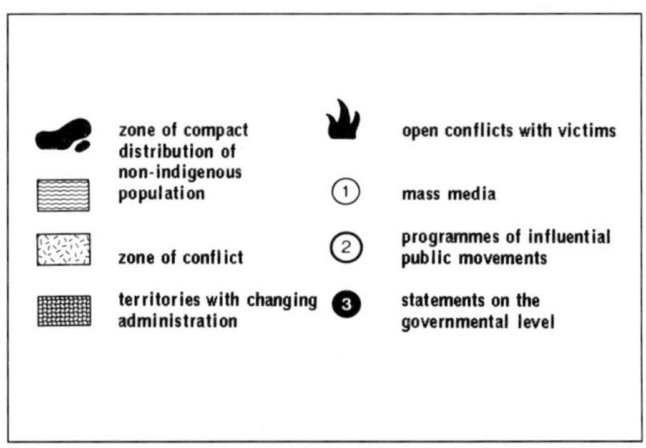

Territorial-ethnic conflicts

1 Murmansk Oblast of Russia—claims on Karelia;
73 Gorno-Altai Autonomous Oblast—on Tuva;
74 Krasnoyarsk Kray of Russia—on Tuva;
75 Aghinsk Buriat Auton. Okrug—on Buriatia (D);
76 Magadan Oblast—on Yakutia (A).

I: Caucasus

24 Krasnodar Kray on Adygheia (B);
25 Karachai and Cherkes Republics (C);
26 Kabardin and Balkar Republics (C);
27 Karachai-Balkar Republic (E);
28 Kabardin-Cherkes (E);
29 Restoration of autonomy of Ingushetia (D);
30 Eastern North Osetia—on Chechen-Ingushetia (C);
31 Part of Chechen-Ingushetia—on Kabardin-Balkaria (C);
32 Part of North Osetia—on Kabardin-Balkaria (C);
33 Establishment of the single Cherkessia (E);
34 Daghestan—on Chechen-Ingushetia (B);
35 Restoration of the Gorskaya (Mountain) Republic including the territories of Chechen-Ingushetia, North Osetia, Kabarda and Cherkesia (D);
37 The Larger Sochi—on Georgia (A);
38 Secession of Abkhazia from Georgia (G)
39-42 Secession of South Osetia from Georgia (G);
43 Nagornyi Karabakh—to Armenia (E);
44 Southwest of Georgia (Javakheti)—on Armenia (B)
45 Southwest Georgia—on Azerbaijan (B)
46 Southwest of Azerbaijan—on Georgia (B);
47 South of Armenia—on Azerbaijan (B);
48 Abolition of the Ajarian Auton. Republic (G);
50 Re-emigration of the deported Turks-Meskhetians to Georgia (B)

II: Soviet Central Asia

63 Zeravshan Valley (Uzbekistan)—on Tajikistan (F);
65 Southern mountain regions of Kirghizia—on Tajikistan (F);
66 Part of the Pamirs (Tajikistan)—on Kirghizia (F);
68 Southern regions of Kazakhstan—on Kirghizia (F);
69 Northern regions of Kirghizia—on Kazakhstan (F);

A–change of boundaries;
B–former or current areals of ethnic groups;
C=A+B;
D–past change of the status of autonomy;
E–historical, ethnic and/or economic integrity;
F=B+E;
G–revival or suppression of national self-identification.

Introduction

The Soviet Union accounted for one sixth of the world's land surface, and nearly 30 per cent of this territory is highlands and mountains. Mountain ridges over 1 500 m in altitude account for 12 per cent of that and constitute both high middle-mountains and high mountains.

Thanks to wide coverage of the latitudinal zones and the high and dissected topography of mountain countries, the USSR's mountains are characterized by great natural diversity and have most of the world landscapes except for humid tropics and mountain-savannah tropical biomes of low and equatorial latitudes. From the nival-glacial landscapes and polar mountain permafrost deserts of the North (Polar Urals and Byrranga Mountains) to mountain xerophytous subtropical forests in the south (southwestern Tien Shan), from mountain mixed coniferous and broad-leaved forests in the west (Carpathians, Caucasus) to mountain grasslands and elfin woodlands in the oceanic zone and dark-coniferous boreal forests in the Far East (Kamchatka, Sikhachi Alin)–it is impossible to cover at a glance all the diverse mosaic of the mountain world of this country!

The dramatic and centuries-long history of the Russian Empire, and in recent decades of the Soviet Union is the story of the "accretion" of national territory in the shape of the far-off marginal lands including mountains and highlands, thanks to the courage and enterprise of the Russian explorers and merchants who sometimes used force of arms. At the turn of the 20th and 21st century this story of colonization is showing up, as if cast from a mould, in the network of the administrative establishment of the USSR.

Of the total number of 15 Union Republics, 5 are predominantly mountain countries: Armenia, Azerbaijan, Georgia, Kyrghyzstan, Tajikistan, and 3 Republics–Russia, Kazakhstan and Ukraine–all have a high proportion of mountain areas. Mountains are less densely populated than lowlands, but even so over 20 per cent of the USSR population lives in mountain regions. The ethnic, cultural, and historical diversity of the USSR mountain areas is just as great (or even greater) than their natural diversity. It may be mentioned that the most ancient world civilizations of Central Asia, the Caucasus and the Altai are within the "Soviet ecumene".

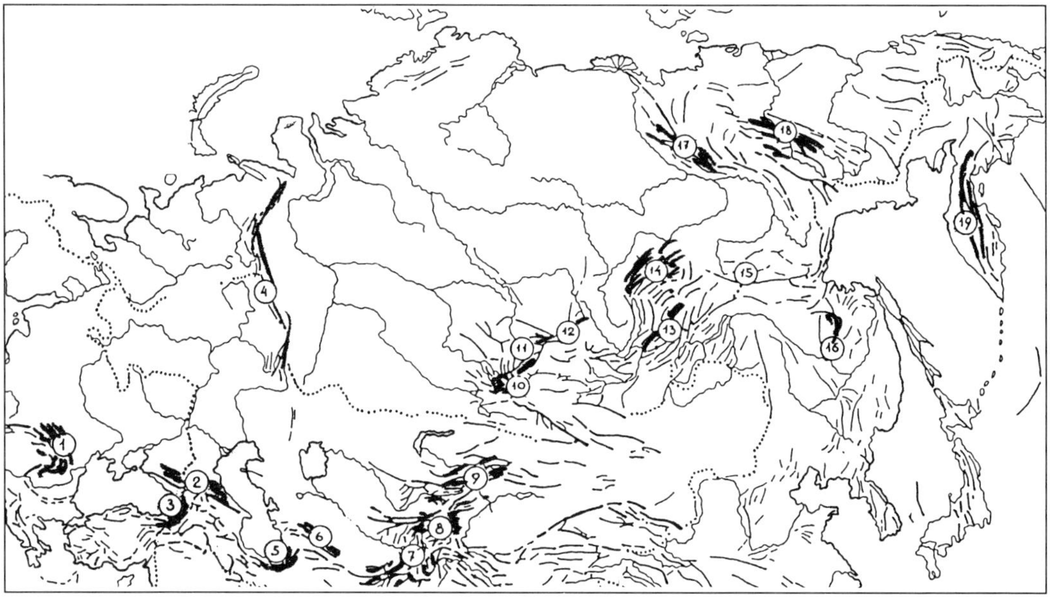

***Figure 7.2**: The major mountain ranges of the ex-USSR*

1.	*Eastern Carpathians*	*7.*	*Hindu Kush*	*13.*	*Yabloncvyi Ridge*
2.	*Greater Caucasus*	*8.*	*Pamirs*	*14.*	*Stanovoe Upland*
3.	*Pontian Mountains*	*9.*	*Tien Shan*	*15.*	*Stanovoe Ridge*
4.	*Urals*	*10.*	*Altai*	*16.*	*Burey Ridge*
5.	*Mt. Elbrus*	*11.*	*Western Sayans*	*17.*	*Verkhoyan Ridge*
6.	*Kopet Dag*	*12.*	*Eastern Sayans*	*18.*	*Cherskiy Upland*
				19.	*Sredinnyi Ridge*

Here is the list of only the major language-ethnic groups inhabiting this enormous mountain space:

- the Iranian group (Tajiks and Pamir Tajiks: Yazguliom, Bartang, Rushan, Shugnan, etc., Kurds, Talysh, Tats, Ossetes);
- the Armenian group
- part of the Indo-European family.

The Caucasian family is represented by:

- the Kartveli group (Georgians, Ajars),
- the Adigei-Abkhazian group (Abkhazians, Kabardians, Circassians and Adigeis),
- the Chechen-Daghestan group (Chechens, Ingush, Daghestans, Avars, Laks, Darghins, Tabasarans, Lezghins, Aguls, Rutuls, etc.).

The Ural family includes:

- the Finn group (Karels, Saami, Komi-Permiak, etc.),
- the Samodi group (Nenets, Nganasans).

The most ancient and diversified Altai family embraces:

- the Tiurk group (Karachai, Balkars, Azerbaijanians, Turkmens, Uzbeks, Kazakhs, Kirghiz, Altai, Khahas, Tuva and Tofalars, Shorets, Yakuts, Dolgans),
- the Mongol group (Buriats),
- the Tungus-Manchurian group (Evenks, Amur people: Nanai, Ulcha, Oroks, Udeghe, Oroch),
- the group of paleo-Asian people (Chukcha, Koriaks, Itelmen, Yukaghirs).

The centuries-long isolation of mountain peoples, severe environments for human life on the periphery of more developed and fertile lowlands (mountains are often the last shelter for refugees from lowlands), strong blood ties–all this gave rise to the phenomenon of a common mountain culture independent of the geographical location of human habitat. In architecture this is reflected in the type of housing and fortified towers; in rock paintings a horn of mountain goat is a symbol of the tribe of mountain hunters (it is found from Scotland and the Alps to the Pamir and the Karakoram). Up to present times many mountain regions (especially the remote ones) are nothing less than living ethnographic museums.

After the Revolution of 1917 the whole mosaic of unique cultural-historical landscapes of mountain areas with their different levels of economic development was overlapped by the unitarian system of planning and development.

The supercentralized structure of power and management ("a single plant with one office") has permeated the whole living body of the Soviet society from the top of the pyramid in Moscow to the remotest mountain kishlaks and auls.

Certainly, one should not underestimate the significant successes of power-executing governmental structures in upgrading the level of education, health care and communication in mountain areas. But because they neglected the role of local communities in the management and development of resources, in the conservation of traditions, the centralized political and economic establishment of the country gave birth to numerous conflict situations. These clearly showed up in mountain regions in the ethnic riots of the last decade (Karabakh, South Ossetia, Osh), in the protests and demonstrations of the "greens" against major engineering projects (Rogoun Hydro Power Plant in Tajikistan, Katoun Hydro Power Plant in Altai, the Transcaucasian railway, etc.). The soil in which they grow is the few, but absolutely fundamental, problems of mountain communities, namely:

- competition for natural resources, limited living space,
- desire to protect the unique culture and age-long traditions of their kin,
- traditionally conservative perceptions of "innovations from outside" a kind of adaptation mechanism for survival in the conditions of isolation.

The mechanisms and institutions of this adaptation differ from region to region: via religion, blood-kin relations ("kunaks", clans), systems of economic relations (exchange of goods with lowland communities), family establishment and land legacy.

At the same time, both the mountain environments and the mountain communities are highly sensitive and fragile under impact, that is to say the existing stability (adapted to the environment) is easily substituted by instability and unsustainability in relation to invading endogenic disturbances.

Many scientists emphasize that mountain regions belong to zones of high risk for human life and economic activity. Everyday reality for mountain people is the threat of natural hazard (earthquakes, landslides, mudflows), the loss of soil and crops, the struggle for domestic fuelwood.

Life cycles in mountains are closed and dynamic.

Starting from the 1920s most of the mountain regions of the Soviet Union have been subject to the powerful pressure of actively developing industrial society which has meant mining, hydro power industry, the construction of transportation facilities, forestry, agro-industry, and so on. Table 7.1 generally describes the most important natural and labour resources and their use in the major mountain regions of the former USSR.

The Soviet economy is characterized by a monofocal spatial structure: the European part is economically more advanced and sucks in like a vacuum cleaner the resources of the peripheral areas (Siberia and the Far East, Soviet Central Asia and Kazakhstan and the North). The mountain areas geographically situated on the outskirts of the "parent state" function predominantly as donors of resources. The hypertrophied centralization of planning, the sectoral approach to development and the unlimited power of the ministry monopolists are the three whales on whose backs the Soviet economy lay for 70 years.

This approach to development seriously harmed the mountain regions of the USSR, and with the depletion of the easily accessible resources of the lowlands in recent decades, there is a continuously expanding invasion of remote mountains; most probably, this trend will continue in the foreseeable future.

The results of this process show more and more vividly.

- The clearing of mountain forests and mining for minerals sharply accelerates the erosional processes, and increases the frequency of disastrous

Resources development	Mountain regions,						
	High latitude mountains	Carpathians -Crimea	Caucasus	Central Asia, Kazakhstan	Urals	Altai, Sayans	East Siberia, Far East
1. Mineral resources/mining	++/++	+/+	++/++	++/++	+++/+++	++/++	+++/++
2. Water resources/ hydropower	+/+	+/+	++/++	+++/++	+/+	++/++	+++/++
irrigation	-	-	++/++	+++/+++	+/+	++/+	+++/+
3. Biological resources/ forests/forestry	-	++/++	++/+	(+)/	+/+	++/++	+++/+++
rangelands/ animal breeding	-	++/++	++/+++	+++/+++(+)	++/+	+++/++	+/+
land/cereals	-	++/++	++/++	+/+	++/+	++/++	++/+
furs/hunting	-	?	+/+	+/+	+/+	++/++	+++/++
medicinal plants/ pharmaceuticals	?	++/++	++/++	+++/+	+/+	+++/++	+++/+
4. Recreation/tourism	+/(+)	+++/+++	+++/+++	+++/++	+++/+	++/++	++/+
national parks, reserves	(+)	+++	+++	++	++	++	+
5. Labour resources	(+)	++	+++(+)	+++(++)	++	++	+

Table 7.1: *Natural and human resources in the mountains*

Potential/utilization

+	*low/limited*	+++(+)	*surplus of labour resources*	(+)/	*critical state of resources*
++	*moderate/moderate*	+++	*high/excessive*		

events such as floods, mudflows, and landslides. Annually, the total damage inside the country is assessed at several billion roubles.

❑ Unjustified increase of livestock has brought critical pressures on mountain rangelands. In Kyrghyzstan in the last decade the sheep population increased from 1 to nearly 10 million.

❑ Lack of any long-range strategy of support for the mountain communities (via investment and tax subsidies) has resulted in large-scale outmigration of the mountain people to cities, the destruction of the traditions of mountain agriculture and of cultural value systems–as they were in Armenia and Georgia, and continue to be in the republics of Soviet Central Asia.

This process of depopulation of mountains was complicated by the forced migration of mountain peoples in the 1930s, 1950s and 1970s down to the lowlands as labour for the irrigated monoculture of cotton in the republics of Soviet Central Asia and Azerbaijan. The tragic page in the history of mountain people of the Caucasus was the expulsion by Stalin during the Second World War of the "guilty" peoples from the Caucasus and Crimea. Turks-Meskhetians, Chechens,Balkarians, Crimean Tatars and others were moved away in a few days to Kazakhstan, Central Asia, and Siberia. The consequences of this act of violence are evident in the tragedies of the 1990s:

❑ the number of refugees is increasing dramatically, territorial-ethnic conflicts are becoming more heated, and a whole people, the Turks-Meskhetians, are to this day devoid of a national area.

❑ the processes of depopulation in mountains are taking place simultaneously with powerful demographic explosions in some republics, especially those with Islamic populations. Thus, Tajikistan has the world's highest population growth rates–3.5-5.0 per cent. If these rates continue, in 15-17 years the population of this small republic will double.

Besides contributing to the instability of society, against the background of the economic crisis of the 1990s, the migrations and demographic processes in mountains are increasing population pressure in mountain areas. There is population pressure on protected areas (nature reserves), and many of them are the foci of the biological diversity and are stores of endemic plant and animal species.

In the 1930s Academician N.Vavilov referred to several mountain regions of the USSR, the Pamir and Transcaucasia, above all, as the most important focus of the ancestors of several crops of world significance: wheat, pulses, drought-resistant almonds and wild pistachio. The mountains of Tajikistan were the original habitat of pistachio, in his opinion.

Many animals and birds of the mountains are rare or close to extinction (for example, the Marco Polo goat). To save these species requires efforts from far beyond national boundaries. Protected mountain areas are their last refuge, and the guarantee of survival.

However, today mountain reserves (numbering about 70 and including biospheric reserves) and sanctuaries (over 50) are hardly sufficient to ensure conservation of the diversity of mountain ecosystems and threatened plant and animal species. The balance between protected and developed areas is clearly shifting towards the latter. Since the end of 1970s protected areas which have a mixed regime of reservation and "soft" mountain tourism–the National Parks–started to develop in the USSR. National Parks were created in the Carpathians and the Caucasus, and currently being established is the huge (over 1 million ha) Pamir National Park. For the Altai region the conception of the South-Altai Ecological Region is being developed. It should integrate recreation and tourism for visitors from the industrial regions of Siberia and Urals with soft forms of agriculture specializing in ecologically-clean production and in medicinal plants. This initiative stems from the Parliament of Russia and the Eurasian Ecological Centre.

One can hardly overestimate the role and significance of the mountain areas for the socio-cultural development and the geopolitical situation of the former USSR.

Bordering the south-western, southern and eastern rims of the "parent state" the mountain territories provide resources for the common economic and political space of the country. On one hand they are rich in minerals, power sources, biological resources but on the other hand, being stores of water and biological diversity, the mountains strongly influence the natural and human cycles of both the nearby and the remoter lowlands. Their role as the environment-forming factor is immeasurably important.

As for national-cultural and historical diversity, or the geopolitical landscape of the mountainous border of the country, one should keep in mind that mountain areas play several roles. On the one hand, mountains are citadels of limited accessibility, but on the other hand–and this role is most important–mountains are a kind of membrane (or even a catalyst) filtering and controlling the cultural, economic and social flows between civilizations and nations. One illustration is the Great Silk Road that functioned for centuries, and is now being rehabilitated by joint activities by many countries, including the USSR as a special project at the initiative of Unesco. This is the inherent and unique feature of mountain areas.

However, the role and functions of mountain areas were underestimated and not fully appreciated by the Soviet political and ideological leadership. Mountain Republics were in some cases perceived as "dead ends", i.e. as republic-citadels, republic-fortresses, their major role being that of defending barriers against neighbouring countries. Vivid examples of such are Tajikistan and Kyrghyzstan which were developing in such a way as to be orientated exclusively towards the "parent state" (the centre). They had no developed relations with their eastern and southern neighbours. They were not integrated into the economic space of Central Asia, China, and India, which are close to them in culture, traditions and religion.

The state establishment even today has no specialized "mountain institutions" (commissions, councils of Parliament) to develop strategies for the development of the former USSR's mountain areas, to work out the laws and regulations to

The Pamir mountains of eastern Tajikistan are the highest in the territory of the former Soviet Union

maintain sustainable development in the marginal mountain areas. This is one possible explanation for the numerous conflicts and the instability of the 1990s in the Caucasus, Central Asia and Tuva. Only recently was there some progress in the situation in general, although the development scenarios and orientations of these extremely diverse mountain areas of the ex-USSR are still very unclear and uncertain.

However, the priority task of today that cannot be delayed is the critical reassessment of the current status of the mountain areas of the country. What are the spatial dimensions of the "hot" environmental and socio-economic problems? What are their historical roots and future trends? What is our level of knowledge in these fields, what are the gaps and uncertainties?

The limited space in this chapter does not allow even a brief coverage of the totality of the environmental and economic problems of the ex-USSR mountain areas, which range from the Arctic zone to the southern mountains of Altai and Soviet Central Asia. Our analysis will concentrate on one major mountain system: the Pamir and its bordering ridges.

Why was this particular region chosen?

First of all, this is the centre of ancient human development with an extreme diversity of environmental and cultural-historical situations which have many different impacts.

Secondly, the valleys and foothills of the Pamir have comparatively dense populations of diverse ethnic composition, traditions and culture.

And last, but not least, this region is an arena of sharp conflicts, even fighting, and a zone of the utmost political and social instability because of the unprecedented population growth rates and the negative consequences of the former supercentralized planning and management regimes. ■

The Pamir and its setting

Introduction

The Pamir (mountain massifs of the Tien Shan and Pamir-Alai) constitute the highest mountain regions of the Soviet Union. In the current administrative system they mostly belong to Tajikistan, though in the historical-ethnographic and religious-cultural perspective they belong to the vast environmental-economic space of Central Asian highlands which include Afghanistan, Pakistan and parts of China.

The Pamir is the area which gives rise to the main rivers of Central Asia–Syr Darya and Amu Darya. According to N.I.Vavilov it is also one of the world's foci of the ancestors of cultured crops and mountain agriculture; it is itself the node of the numerous historical and socio-economic problems of Central Asia.

The ridges of the highest mountain systems of the Western Pamir, Hindu Kush, and Himalaya block moisture transported by winds from the Indian and Atlantic Oceans, and thus form the continental (arid) climate which has sharply contrasting temperature regimes (difference between the mean temperatures of January and June is from 27 to 32 degrees C) and a marked seasonality of precipitation. These environmental conditions and historical processes lasting many centuries have formed the distinct *ethnos* of Mountain Tajiks–settled cultivators of irrigated lands and animal-breeders. Long isolated from the more prosperous civilizations of the Turan Lowland in the west, from the ancient Indo-Aryan civilizations developing in the oases of Merv, Khiva, Bukhara and Samarkand, the Mountain Tajiks have up to present times kept much of their unique culture and tradition. The area populated by Mountain Tajiks includes parts of Afghanistan, Pakistan and China, and has a mosaic of languages and dialects. The inhabitants of neighbouring valleys are often unable to understand each other's speech (Yazguliom and Vanch, for example).

After the establishment of Soviet power in Tajikistan in 1924, and the delineation of the

Figure 7.3: *Situation of Tajikistan in the Karakoram-Hindu Kush system*

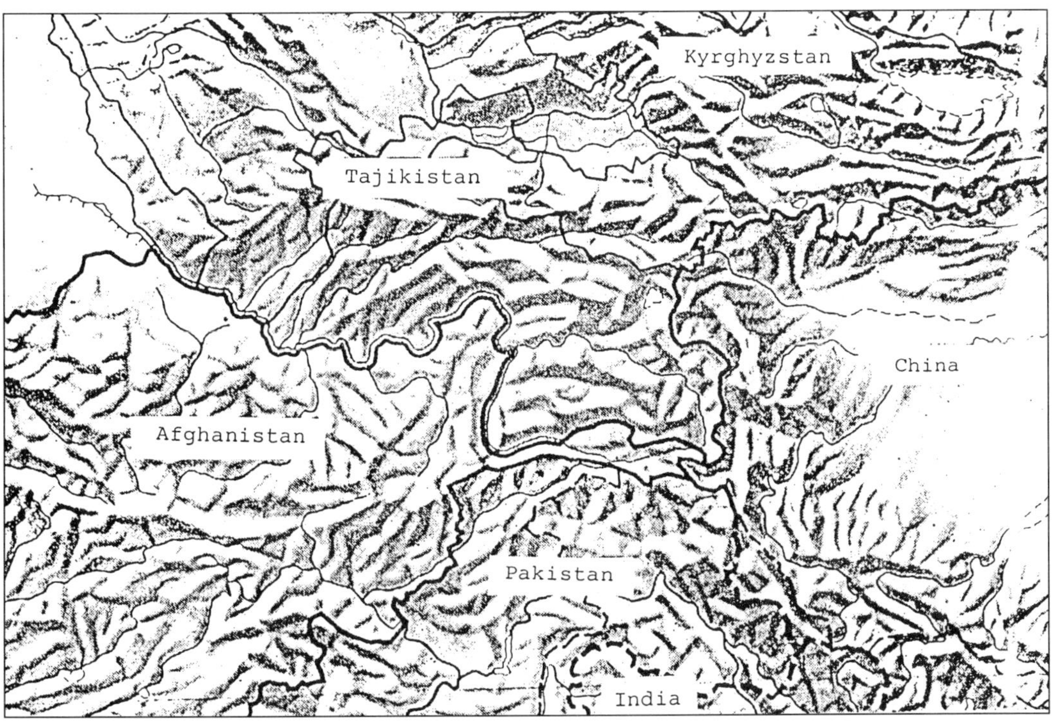

national republics of Soviet Central Asia in 1929, the Mountain Tajiks were incorporated into the different, though related ethnic area of the Lowland Tajiks, and acquired a common status in the Tajik Soviet Socialist Republic–one of 15 Soviet republics of the ex-USSR.

Modern Tajikistan is located in the south of the Soviet Union between latitude 36°40' and 41°05' N and longitude 67°31' and 75°14' E. Its area stretches 700 km from west to east, and 350 km from north to south. In the north, Tajikistan has wedges of territory protruding into part of Uzbekistan, and part of neighbouring Kyrghyzstan in the western part of the Fergana Valley.

From the total 3 000 km of its boundaries 1 460 km are boundaries with foreign states: 430 km with China, 1 030 km with Afghanistan. In the southeast, Tajikistan is separated from India and Pakistan by a narrow strip of Afghan territory 15 to 65 km wide. The area of Tajikistan is thus 143 100 km^2 and constitutes 0.64 per cent of the total of the former USSR's territory. Its population (1989) is 5.2 million

The ethnic structure of the population is as follows: Tajiks–58.8 per cent, Uzbeks–23.0 per cent, Russians–10.4 per cent; there are also: Tatars, Kyrghyz, Ukrainians, Kazakhs, Turkmens, etc. These data are from the early 1980s. Now there is strong outmigration of the non-indigenous nationals. The main religion is Islam.

The Tajiks belong to the most ancient settled nations of Central Asia. The ancestors of Tajiks–the East-Iranian tribes and people of various nationalities who populated the territory of Central Asia–developed as early as the Bronze Age an indigenous and advanced civilization with the major cities of Bukhara, Samarkand, Balkh, Merv, Nishapur, Khogent, and others. The final phase of the formation of the Tajik nation coincided with the establishment of feudalism in the Early Middle Ages in the 7th to 10th centuries AD. Sogdians, Baktrians, Ustrushans, Fergans–these were the ethnic groups that formed the Tajik *ethnos* or nation. With the advent of Arabs in Central Asia in the 7th to the early 8th century, Islam replaced Zoroastrism, Buddhism and other religions, and firmly established itself, replacing the Greek-Baktrian and Hellenic culture by Islamic traditions. The abundant archaeological monuments in Tajik territory are the silent witnesses of the dramatic history of this country. In the middle of the 19th century Central Asia and Tajikistan were the arena of competition between the British and Russian Empires for the domination of this part of Central Asia. In 1867 the establishment of the Turkestan General Province completed the process of colonization of Central Asia by Russia.

After the October Revolution of 1917 and the Civil War which ended in Central Asia in 1926, Tajikistan entered upon the period of Soviet development. Tajikistan is, as a matter of fact, a perfect model of the development of a mountain country which leapt, in the 1920s, from feudalism to socialism (in its Soviet interpretation that is: rigid centralized planning, state ownership of resources and production facilities, dictatorship by the Union Ministries in the use and distribution of resources).

The Soviet period of development of Tajikistan despite undoubted socio-economic and cultural achievements was marked by abundant problems and the conflicts of development that are common to the whole of the ex-USSR in the 1990s. However, the specific natural environments (93 per cent of the territory is mountainous) and the cultural-ethnic features formed a peculiar Central Asian phenomenon in this region, namely the Soviet Muslim world.

The general common feature of these problems is "dualism". On the one hand, there are the problems of an industrially developed country, and on the other hand, the spectrum of problems typical of Third World countries. These latter problems include explosive population growth, resource-oriented development and dependence on the industrially more developed centre.

The current socio-economic situation of the mountainous Tajik Republic can be characterized as a period of untying existing complicated political and socio-economic knots and of a search for a long-term development strategy in conditions of transition to a market economy and independence.

Natural environments and resources

Tajikistan is a typical mountain country with absolute elevations ranging from 300 to 7 495 m and is part of the Pamir-Alai and Tien Shan mountain systems. Nearly a half of Tajikistan is above 3 000 m. Topography is deeply dissected and

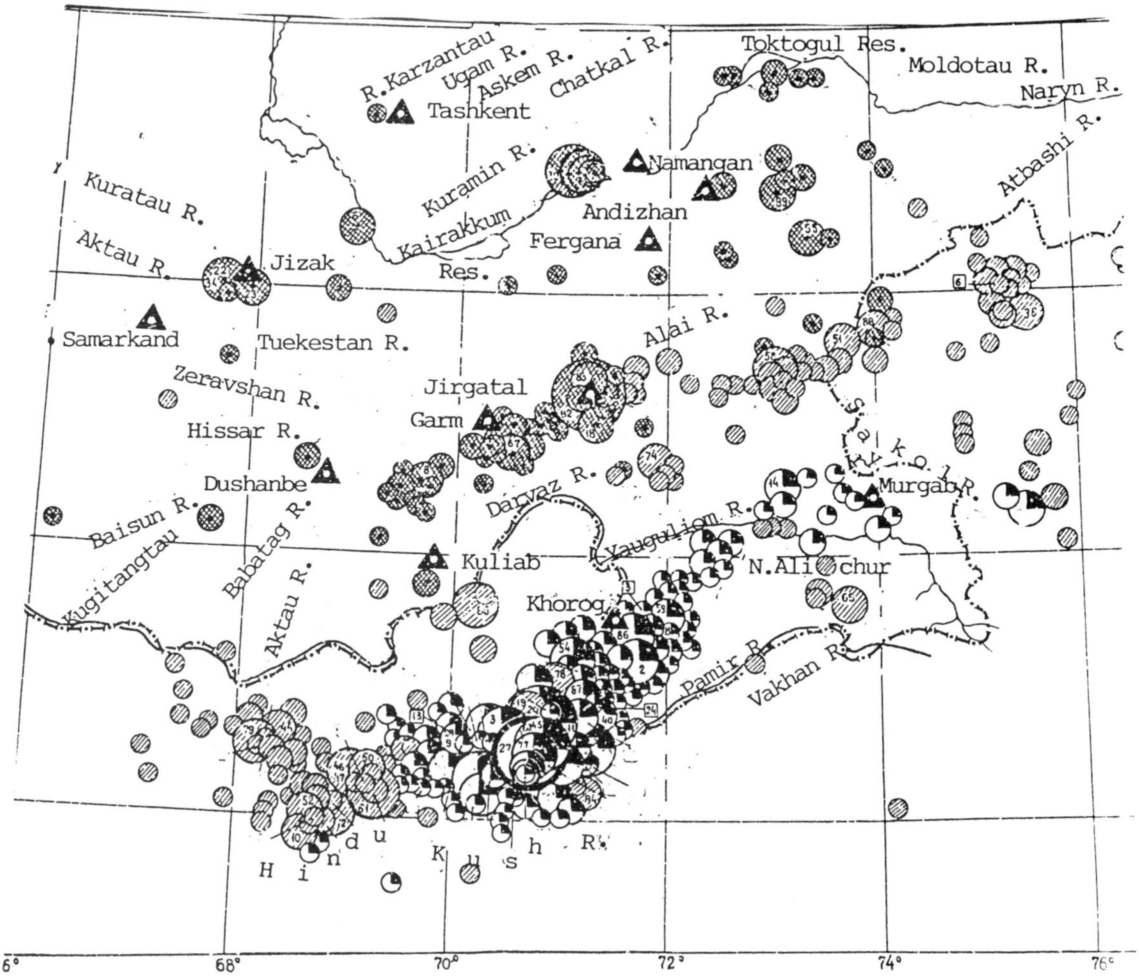

Figure 7.4: *Epicentres of earthquakes in Central Asia and Kazakhstan*

marked by abundant canyons and gorges. Plains in the southwest (the Vaksh Valley) and northwest (the Fergana Valley) are represented by broadened parts of river valleys or extensive depressions filled by alluvial-proluvial deposits.

The modern relief of Tajikistan is the product of joint action of alpine tectonic crustal movements and denudation processes. There are no volcanic phenomena in the mountains of Tajikistan, but earthquakes are common. This is a zone of extremely intensive seismic processes.

The topography of Tajikistan is the dominant factor behind the diversity of landscapes and local climates, and it strongly influences settlement systems and the pattern of economic activities of the population. Of equal importance for the latter is the availability of natural resources and their geographical distribution.

A LAND OF HIGH RISK

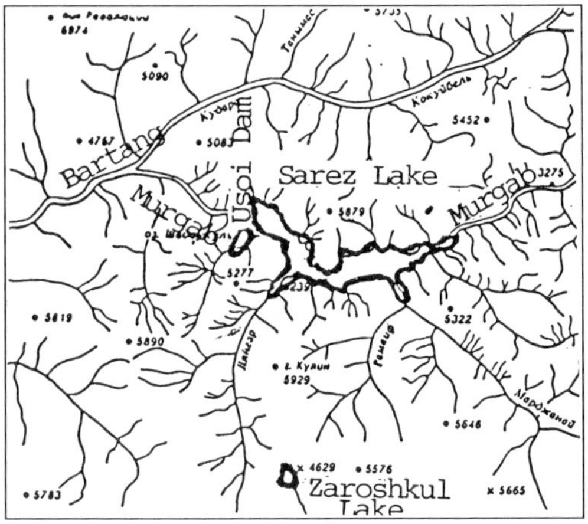

Figure 7.5: The Sarez Lake area

40 km

Since the beginning of the 20th century over 500 earthquakes with magnitude of greater than Richter 5 were registered in Tajikistan; three of them were catastrophic: the Karatag (1907), Sarez (1911), and Khait (1949) earthquakes.

In 1911 in the Western Pamir a powerful earthquake triggered a landslide of a block of mountain rocks over 6 billion m^3 which blocked the Murgab Valley and engulfed the kishlak (village) of Usoy. This natural dam about 1 km high formed the huge Sarez Lake; its surface level was at an altitude of 3 239 m, its length was 75 km, its surface area was 86.5.km^2, maximum depth was 505 m, and its volume, 16-17 km^3. The water level of the lake rose most rapidly in the period 1911-1914 at 79 m per year. Then as water started to filter through the dam the rate of rise decreased to 13.5 m per year, and after the earthquake of 1943 (one of many), loose rock in the dam consolidated and the oscillations of level stabilized. Currently, the rise of the level of the Sarez Lake continues; the mean annual rise of its surface is 20 cm per year.

Down the Bartang and Pianj Valleys numerous kishlaks are under threat of flooding if the Usoy dam breaks, though according to hydrological observations made many times a year over many years the lake is in a quasi-equilibrium state. However, there are several scenarios of a possible catastrophic water outbreak: either as a result of the sliding of other unstable mountain blocks and the "jumping" of the resultant wave over the dam, or because of overfilling of the lake depression and the consequent erosion of the upper unconsolidated rocks of the dam. Scientists and engineers have developed a proposal for the artificial draining of the Sarez Lake which would solve two problems: eliminate the risk of a catastrophic outbreak, and fill the drying Aral Sea by moving this water volume via the Pianj and Amu Darya channels.

Other similar dammed lakes, though not so huge, are found in Tajikistan (Yashilkul, Iskanderdul, several lakes on the River Shing, etc.) and are a permanent warning of the risk factor for life and economic activities of the people of the mountains and the adjacent lowlands.

Other risk factors that arise with the high seismicity of the region are rockfalls and the sliding of large rock masses from unstable slopes. The sliding of a gigantic block of rocks–one of several landslides and mudflows triggered by a strong earthquake–was the origin of a tragedy in 1949. This land mass covered in an instant the regional centre Khait which had a population of over 24 000. This event was in the same year as the notorious Ashkhabad earthquake with over 100 000 victims. But the Khait tragedy was little known even inside the USSR; behind Stalin's iron curtain such tragedies were hidden under the security classification "secret". Now there is a small memorial at the location of the buried kishlak.

The risk of such catastrophic events triggered by earthquakes is increasing many times due to mistakes in project design, both in the mountains and in the piedmonts and lowlands. In 1989 (one month after the catastrophic Spitak earthquake in Armenia) a huge loess landslide buried the Sharora kishlak in the Hissar area only 30 km from Dushanbe, the capital of Tajikistan. A minor earthquake stripped off a mass of loess overmoistened by waters filtering from a permeable irrigation canal. The loess body accumulated over 50 million cubic metres of water. Victims of the "engineer's mistake" were numbered in hundreds, and thousands more became homeless.

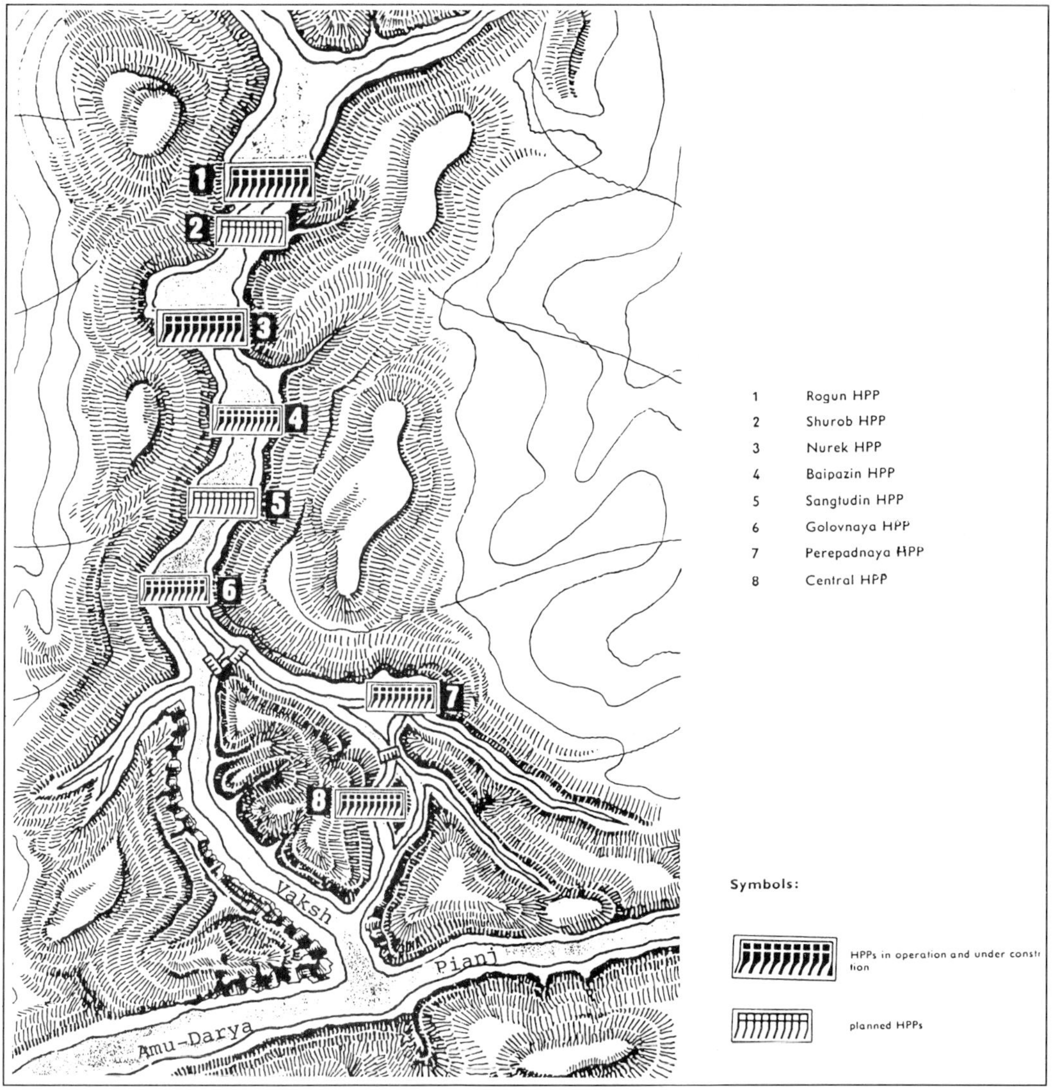

Figure 7.6: *Layout of the Vaksh cascade of hydroelectric power plants*

Water resources, as in all arid countries, are the main wealth of Tajikistan. Water is indispensable for agriculture and is a huge hydroelectricity resource making it the basis of industrial development.

Rivers, defined as water courses more than 10 km long, number 947 and their total length adds up to 28 500 km. They constitute the two major river systems of Central Asia–Amu Darya and Syr Darya.

Most rivers belong to the Amu Darya basin; the major ones are the Pianj (920 km long), the Vaksh (643 km long) and Kafirnigan (382 km long). The Syr Darya River (total length from source to mouth 2 684 km) has only a small catchment area in Northern Tajikistan. In between the Amu Darya and Syr Darya channels and parallel to them is the Zeravshan River, 640 km long. The river runoff is supplied by glacial and snowmelt,

THE ARAL CRISIS

A fishing fleet high and dry underlines the extent of recession of the Aral Sea

In the 1950s and the early 1960s the USSR government decided on a large-scale expansion of the irrigated areas of Soviet Central Asia. It pursued the following targets:

1) To increase cotton production, and achieve "self-reliance in cotton" for the USSR.
2) To supply meat and rice.
3) To provide employment.
4) To increase production of vegetables and fruit, and to transform the region into "the All-Union orchard and kitchen-garden".

Since the early 1950s the irrigated area expanded (in thousand ha):

- in Uzbekistan from 2 200 to 4 100;
- in Tajikistan from 361 to 675;
- in Turkmenia from 454 to 1 200.

The large-scale withdrawal of water for irrigation has influenced the volume of river runoff. As compared to 1911–60 when 120 km^3 of runoff formed in the mountain areas of the Pamir-Alai and Tien Shan and 56 km^3 reached the Aral Sea, by the middle of the 1970s the inflow to the Aral had fallen to 7–11 km^3, and in the 1980s it had practically stopped altogether. The runoff of the Amu Darya and Syr Darya is drawn down by an irrigation network 150–200 000 km long or 10–15 times longer than the major rivers of this zone.

The cotton monoculture required the application of large amounts of fertilizers: this quantity increased 3.5–6 times, and was 2.5–3 times higher than the national average.

The demographic situation was characterized by explosive population growth throughout the region; population increase in the last 17 years was 2.3 times in Uzbekistan (from 8.1 to 19 million), 2.2 times in Turkmenia (from 1.5 to 3.36 million), 3.2 times in Tajikistan (from 1.5 to 4.8 million). This gave rise to the most acute social and environmental crisis. The major features are:

- the destruction of the ecosystem of Aral and the adjacent territories;
- a fall in the level of the Aral Sea from 53 m above sea level in 1960 to 40.3 m in 1987;
- a reduction in the area of the sea from 67 000 to 41 000 km^2;
- a reduction in its volume from 1 064 to 404 km^3.

Salinity increased from 10 to 28–30 parts per thousand; climate in the whole region became more continental; dust storms are more frequent and transport salt from the dried-up Aral Sea floor to the vast cultivated areas under cotton and other crops; in the Murgab and Tejen oases the groundwater level is rising. The result is salinization of soils and their withdrawal from cultivation.

The degradation of the environment in the Aral Sea and the Aral area inflicts huge economic losses: N.F. Glazovskiy estimates the necessary investment for rehabilitation of the region at about 37 billion roubles. This assessment gives the approximate economic loss due to "development" according to the scenario of the 1960s.

Another dramatic situation is that of the Karakalpak people who have lived since ancient times along the shores of the Aral Sea: in 10 years the mortality among Karakalpaks increased 6 times, cancer of the oesophagus 7–10 times; 64 per cent of examined children have health problems; social and national tensions have increased in the region; the erroneous strategy of socio-economic development has led to what amounts to the "hidden" genocide of the whole Karakalpak nation!

rainfall, and groundwater flow (the latter accounts for 25-30 per cent of annual runoff). Mountain glaciers cover about 6 per cent of the area of Tajikistan (8492 glaciers of total area 8 476.2 km^2). The glaciers accumulate 456.9 km^3 of water and it is this which is the real wealth of the arid Central Asia region.

The annual runoff of 61.8 km^3 of water from the mountain areas of Tajikistan through the dry lowlands of the Aral area is the life support of many millions of people in Turkmenia, Uzbekistan and Karakalpakstan.

The hydropower potential of the river network of Tajikistan is over 64 million kW. The republic was second only to Russia in this resource in the Soviet Union. In the 1930s the first minor hydro station was commissioned in the Varzob Valley to provide power for the Dushanbe Industrial Agglomeration; since then hydro power plants have been constructed in many regions of Tajikistan. The most intensive development of hydropower resources was in the Vaksh Valley; there a series of hydro plants is being constructed in the main channel, along with large reservoirs which are also used for the irrigation of new lands for (first and foremost) cotton production.

The Nurek and the Rogoun (under construction) hydro plants hold the world record for the height of their man-made groundfill dams (330 and 335 m, respectively).

These gigantic projects have imposed several social and environmental problems: among them are large-scale flooding of agricultural areas that are in short supply in the mountainous country and are insufficient for the needs of the rapidly growing population, and the need to move people from their customary environments to the newly developed agricultural areas in the lowlands. It is expected that from 22 to 40 thousand rural people will have to be moved from the zone flooded by the Rogoun water reservoir. Construction of this hydro development is already in full swing, though no solution to the social conflict has been found yet.

Another factor that adds to the social and partly political conflict which also acquired a nationalistic aspect is the policy of exporting

Figure 7.7: Tajik SSR: Resources of minerals and raw materials

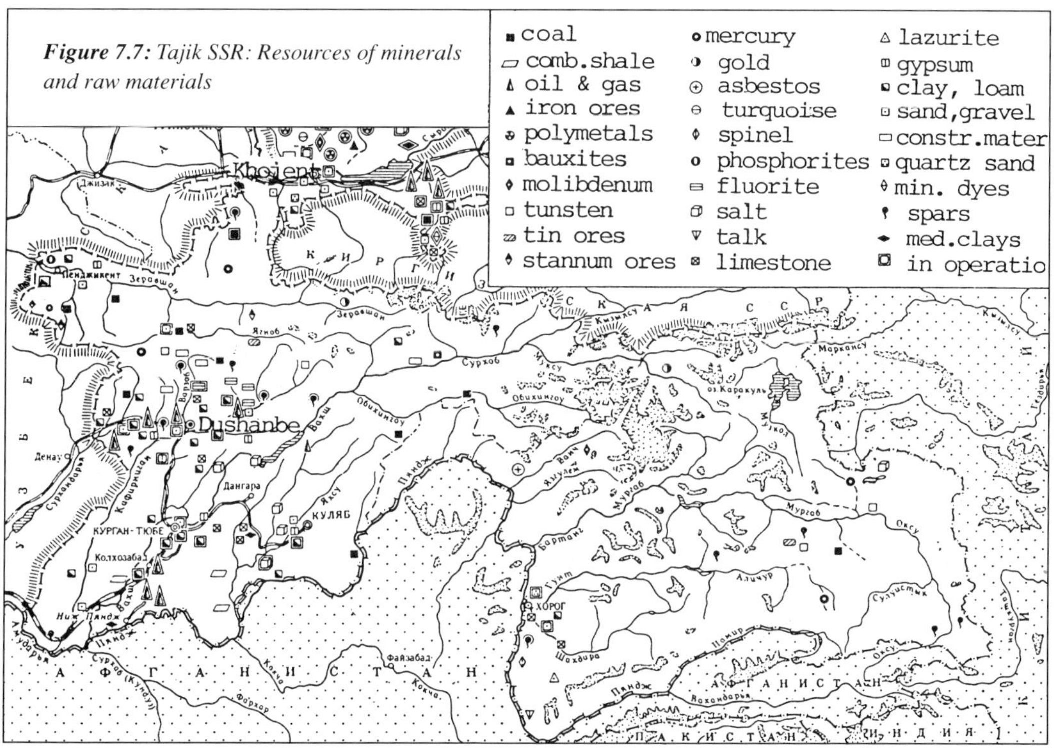

hydropower to other Union Republics, although many mountain kishlaks in Tajikistan have no supply of electricity themselves.

Development of minor ("pocket-size") hydro plants that would have met the demands of rural communities was abandoned in 1950s in favour of the giant power plants on the major rivers.

The mistakes in the use and management of the rich water resources of the region have caused an actual water shortage and have given rise to the absurd idea of diverting the rivers of Siberia to the Central Asian region. An evil chain of conflicts has thus developed: economic, social, environmental and political conflicts between both republics and nationalities. To undo this complicated knot of problems it is necessary to change the system of resource management and the general orientation of economic strategies in favour of sustainable development.

Mineral resources include a wide range of ore-bearing and other minerals. Mining sites for lead, zinc, gold, spinel and lazurite have been known since long ago. But before the 20th century mining was a small-scale industrial activity in a predominantly agrarian country. In the Soviet period over 300 sites of various mineral deposits were discovered. 100 of them were opened up to extract over 36 useful constituents.

One should mention here a characteristic of the centralized management system: the development and exploitation of mineral resources is in the hands of the Union Ministries which actually hold a full monopoly of mining in the area. Their investment for the development of local communities is limited and small. Traditionally the priority activities of the local population have always been agriculture, small-scale commerce, and crafts; therefore, labour for the mining industry was always imported from elsewhere, for example from Russia or the Ukraine. This process lasted for decades, and by the early 1990s led to a conflict between the people of indigenous nationalities and the immigrants: localities of mining enterprise were never really integrated into the surrounding socio-economic and cultural landscape.

Large-scale outmigration from the republic in the 1990s of the Russian-speaking population has led to a paradoxical situation: against the general background of explosive population growth and increasing unemployment, in some industries, including mining, there are abundant vacancies. The indigenous population is not inclined to change the values of pastoralism and its cultural traditions for unwonted employment in the industrial sector, even though the latter provides many material advantages.

There, then, is another knot of development problems to be undone at the turn of the century.

There are two kinds of mineral resources that integrate quite well now with the local national traditions: minerals for jewellery and handicrafts, and the various vitreous silicates and carbonates known to miners as "spars", fluorspar, feldspar etc.

The Pamir jewellery minerals–"Badakshan lals" (spinel), turquoise, amethyst, rock crystal, etc.–have been known since ancient times and were highly valued in Central Asia and in India. The traditions of Mountain Tajiks always included the mining and cutting of jewellery minerals (Porshnev kishlak in the Pamir). A continuation of these traditions can provide additional income to the mountain dwellers if this sector is disengaged from the state monopoly.

The unique spas of Khoja Obigarm, Obigarm, Garmchashma, which have medicinal uses, possess great potential for development in combination with the recreational industry. Being "environmentally safe", these resources can be the basic elements for profitable and conflictless development of many remote and currently underdeveloped regions of Tajikistan.

Land resources are the most deficient element in the resource potential of Tajikistan. Most of its territory is mountain ridges with eternal snow, glaciers, rocks and talus. Nearly half of the area is dry cold desert of the Eastern Pamir Upland (3-4 000 m in altitude).

Of the total area of Tajikistan (14 255 000 ha), agricultural lands are 4 415 300 ha, including: rangelands–344 800 ha, cultivated lands–819.3 ha (irrigated–570.8), hay cropping land–30.1 ha, perennial orchards–30.1 ha, fallow lands–22 800 ha. A total of 92 per cent of agricultural lands is owned by state and collective farms.

Along with the general trend for expansion of cultivated lands, there is a reduction of irrigated land area per rural dweller–0.15 ha in 1970, 0.11 ha in the 1990s. This trend is enhanced, on the one hand, by rapid population growth (3.5 per cent

Erosion from irrigation water is common in the cotton fields of the Vaksh and Hissar valleys

annually), and on the other, by the monoculture of cotton which has become the social evil of the Central Asian republics: it has forced out many agricultural crops and promoted the shrinking of winter pastures. The problem of winter pasture stands apart: overgrazing (by sheep) occurs everywhere in Tajikistan and is the cause of rangeland degradation including erosion, and invasion by weeds.

Nearly 30 per cent of the irrigated cotton fields of the Vaksh and Hissar valleys are eroded by water and a significant area is salinized. Because of the intensive application of pesticides (over 5 kg per ha) on cotton fields the residual concentrations of chemicals in soils are 3.1 times higher than health standards require.

In view of the rugged topography of Tajikistan the main agricultural pressure is on the Vaksh Valley lowlands (southwest) and the Fergana Valley (north). In recent decades these territories (7 per cent) have developed into a zone of persistent "critical ecological and social problems" that coincides with the most densely populated areas (up to 200-300 rural inhabitants per km^2).

Since the 1970s dry horticulture on "adyrs" (loess foothills) started to develop widely. Being one of the world foci of the origin of pistachio, almonds, apricots and other horticultural crops, Tajikistan has great potential for this branch of agriculture. This activity also agrees well with the cultural traditions of local people; therefore, it can be the basis for a new scenario of development. The restructuring of land use (the reduction of the area under cotton) can ensure socio-economic sustainability and eliminate many of the above-mentioned conflicts and contradictions.

Tajikistan is the least forested even of the Central Asian republics–forests account for little more than 3 per cent of its area.

Forest resources of the republic are state-owned and amount to 1 800 000 ha; 1 200 ha are on long-term lease from the state to collective and state-owned farms and are used as rangelands. This leaves no chance for forest regeneration, because grazing by animals destroys both undergrowth and shrubs. This is a conflict due to "double" land ownership.

Since the late 19th century there has been a steady trend towards the shrinking of the forest area through clearance in all Central Asian republics. Thus, the areas under valuable archa primeval forest in the region (archa is a form of juniper) have been reduced from 2 million to 460 thousand ha, or to a quarter of what they were. Deforestation in the area encourages widespread erosion on slopes and more frequent natural hazards (mudflows, landslides, rockfalls, etc.) with the high seismicity of the region making things worse.

This problem, too, is part of the array of mountain and foothill problems of the Western and Southwestern Pamir, Hissar and Zeravshan Ridges.

Climate is the second influence after topography which is decisive for human environment and the local economy: for the settlement system, the distribution of production and land use systems. All the socio-economic landscape is to a certain degree adapted to local climates which are a mosaic of differences. Strongly linked to the topography, there are five major climatic zones in Tajikistan.

1) the zone of dry climate with hot summers, mild winters and moderately mild autumns (south of the Vaksh Valley, 400-800 m);
2) the zone of low-humidity climate with hot summers, mild and moderately mild winters (Hissar Valley, Western Pianj Valley up to 1250 m);
3) the zone of low-humidity climate with warm summers and moderately mild winters (mountain areas up to 2000-3500 m);
4) the zone of low-humidity climate with moderately warm summers, moderately mild to moderately severe winters with abundant snow (high areas of the Hissar, Zeravshan, Turkestan, and Kuramin Ridges);
5) the zone of dry climate with moderately warm summers and moderately severe winters (highlands of the Western Pamir). The high plateau of the Eastern Pamir (above 4 000 m) belongs to the zone of dry climate with cold summers and severe low-snow winters.

The geographical position of Tajikistan inside Eurasia is what decides the high continentality of its climate with characteristically accentuated seasonal and daily fluctuations in meteorological conditions. The relatively cold winter is abruptly terminated by a rainy spring, and, just as rapidly, changed to a dry practically rainless summer (except for the Pamir Highlands).

The southern location of Tajikistan (in the same latitudes as Turkey and the Mediterranean) accounts for the high position of the sun in the sky: 28° in winter, 45° in summer, and the high total annual solar radiation inflow (insolation): from 151 (Fergana Valley) to 176.1 Kcal/cm^2 (Fedchenko Glacier).

Depending on local climates, there is different duration of vegetation growth period and different patterns of agricultural cropping.

Decisive for climatic conditions in Tajikistan are the air masses that are predominantly brought by the western drift from the Atlantic, the Mediterranean and the Siberian sector of the Arctic. The tropical summer flows from the west (North Africa, Iran, Turan) strongly dominate the air flows from the Indian Ocean which are interrupted by the mountain ridges of the Himalaya and Karakoram.

In geological times the climate of this region was mild and humid owing to the monsoon from the Indian Ocean. This gave rise to subtropical landscapes that have left some relics even to the present day. In the Holocene the pattern of atmospheric flows changed, and an arid climate was established. Mountain glaciation shrank, and the aridity of landscapes became clearly pronounced. The global warming expected in the beginning of the 21st century will greatly transform the local climatic situations.

What will be the specific changes in the Central Asian region, in the mountains of the Pamir and Tien Shan? What will be the responses of glaciation, and, correspondingly, of runoff to these climatic changes? What adaptation mechanisms in nature and the economy will be at work in the rapidly changing environment? All these questions are now relevant not only for academic researchers, but equally for the practitioners engaged in the formulation of long-term development strategies.

Even now regional changes of local climates are being registered in Tajikistan. Three categories of changes are identified:

1) changes of radiation budget on irrigated lands;
2) changes of meteorological regimes in the areas of the major water reservoirs; and
3) pollution of the atmosphere in large urbanized zones by dust and other agents.

Irrigation in dry climates results in a tremendous increase of heat loss in the process of evaporation (due to the latent heat of evaporation) and this usually exceeds the input component of the radiation budget. The irrigation of vast areas has significantly modified the processes within air masses, bringing about changes in temperature and humidity patterns in the lower atmospheric layers.

Meteorological characteristics	V	VI	VII	VIII	IX	X
Difference (°C) of air temperature in irrigated and non-irrigated areas	−1.8	−2.0	−2.6	−2.8	−2.2	−1.0
Difference (%) of absolute air humidity in irrigated and non-irrigated areas	2.2	3.8	4.2	3.0	1.7	1.0

Table 7.2: *Air temperature and humidity differences 2m above the surface of irrigated and non-irrigated lands in Tajikistan*

The results of Studies of heat budget and of microclimates in the Vaksh Valley have clearly demonstrated that evaporation is the decisive factor in the hydrometeorological regimes of the irrigated areas. Mean annual total evaporation from cotton fields is shown to be about 1 000 mm, while from non-irrigated areas it is only around 340 mm. In July, when evaporation from a cotton field is found to be at a maximum–about 200 mm–a non-irrigated plot evaporates no more than 30 mm.

The major water reservoirs that are being constructed as elements of hydro plants are also changing the microclimates of the surrounding land areas. Thermal radiation inflow to the water surface goes mostly to evaporation, and to turbulent heat exchange between water surface, atmosphere and deeper water layers. Depending on the depth and surface area of the reservoir about 60-95 per cent of radiation inflow is spent on evaporation, and 5-40 per cent on heat exchange with the atmosphere.

Owing to that, the air temperature on the shores of water reservoirs in the warm season is significantly lower than in remote areas away from water surfaces (see Table 7.3).

Because water surfaces are smoother than land surfaces, wind velocity in the areas of water reservoirs is higher, especially in the autumn (fall) season when water is cooler than air, and there is turbulent exchange above the water surface.

In recent decades more dust has been coming into the atmosphere from cultivated fields thus bringing about smogs and reducing short-wave radiation and light inflow.

In the areas with mountain relief in Tajikistan, disturbances of the radiation budget are often facilitated by temperature inversions. Pollution of the atmosphere increases the condensation of water vapour, cloudiness, and rainfall. The late 1980s to the early 1990s had (as compared to the multiannual means) unusually intensive rains with hail and strong winds in the beginning of the vegetation growing period (April-June). Besides damage to agriculture, these phenomena inflicted numerous landslides and mudflows in the area.

Are those phenomena the portents (and indicators) of imminent global climatic changes? This question has no answer yet.

Science has not yet developed a system of regional and local models of climatic changes. This field of knowledge is characterized by uncertainty, though it is now an object of study for several disciplines. Coinciding in time with the contradictory trends of the socio-economic situation in the region, the problem of the assessment of alternative scenarios is a challenge for the scientific community.

Table 7.3: *Air temperature inland (Buston) and reservoir shoreline (Kairakkum) sites and differences (°C)*

Ste	I	II	III	IV	V	VI	VII	VIII	IX	X	XI	XII	Mean annual
Buston	0.7	4.6	8.6	15.7	21.8	27.8	29.3	27.1	21.8	14.8	5.9	1.7	15.2
Kairakkum R.	0.6	4.0	8.7	15.6	21.2	26.4	28.2	25.9	21.0	14.7	6.2	1.6	14.4
Difference	0.1	0.6	−0.1	0.1	0.5	1.4	1.1	1.2	0.8	0.1	-0.3	-0.1	0.8

To understand the extreme complexity of the task, let us try to assess in the most general form the diversified mosaic of the natural and socio-economic landscape of Tajikistan.

The territory of Tajikistan is very diversified in ethnographic situation, topography, climate and the combination of landscapes. Established as a state in 1929, Tajikistan incorporated within its boundaries several territories that differed tremendously in their natural and cultural-historical features:

- The plateau of the Eastern Pamir with its nomadic Kyrghyz population (Karakiyghyz means Black Kyrghyz), and the Lower Fergana Valley with a high proportion of the Uzbek *ethnos*;
- The highlands of the Western Pamir–Badakhshan–populated by Mountain Tajiks, and;
- The Amu Darya Valley in the south with its mixed Tajik-Turkmen population.

The role of administrative and state boundaries in Tajikistan deserves a special discussion.

Under the Inter-Republican Treaty on the Delimitation of the former Autonomous Turkestan Republic (before 1918 the Turkestan Province of Russia) and on the order of the central government in Moscow, the boundaries of the republics were delineated on a subjective basis often ignoring the natural features, and–what is even more important–without due account of the history and ethnic patterns of populations. That was the time that the seeds of the inter-ethnic conflicts and conflicts for resources which came to the surface in the 1990s were planted: the claims of Tajiks on Uzbeks for Samarkand and Bukhara, the disputed eastern areas of Tajiks and Kyrghyz, etc.

The administrative divisions inside the Tajik Republic (over 45 regions, three oblasts, and one autonomous unit–Gornyi [Mountain] Badakhshan) were implemented on uncertain grounds which took little account of the ethnic and cultural diversity. Established by bureaucratic methods, the regions are unable to form a working framework for the territory which would ensure the sustainable development of the communities. This is the explanation for the insignificant role of the local population in choosing the patterns of development, and for the complete dependence on central administration in material and financial spheres. Several areas that have major industrial enterprises (mining, power production) were entirely dependent on Union Ministries which had no strong interest in the development of the social life of local communities: this is the conflict of periphery versus centre.

A powerful destabilizing factor superimposed on the natural and ethnic diversity of the territory was the demographic explosion of the 1970s.

The mean annual rates of population growth in the republic are 3.5 per cent (in some regions up to 5 per cent!), and in this index the republic is at the head of the table in the ex-USSR and, possibly, in the world as well. In the decade of 1979-89 the population of Tajikistan increased by 34 per cent or by 1 311 000 people and, according to the census of 1989, has reached 5.2 million (in the 1920s there were less than 1 million people). If these trends persist (presently there is no indication of significant change), in 15-17 years the population of the republic will double! The proportion of families of 10 and more persons is constantly increasing, having reached over 14 per cent in the 1980s.

During the Soviet period the settlement system in Tajikistan developed under two driving impulses: the political-economic factor and the environmental factor.

Since 1930s the strategy which was imposed "from above", from the centre (Moscow), was the specialization of the republic's economy in cotton-growing.

It required the migration of abundant labour to the newly irrigated lands of the Vaksh Valley. The source of cheap and unskilled labour was found in the population of the remote mountain kishlaks which were assumed to be "unpromising" in respect of socio-economic development. (This is a specific Soviet cliche, that first appeared in 1930s and has been applied to rural settlements remote from the larger central settlements of collective and state farms, which were thus declared to be economically inefficient).

Three waves of forced migration in the 1930s, 1950s and 1970s have fundamentally transformed the historical pattern of population settlement that has been formed (and controlled) by the environmental conditions of specific areas.

Thus, in the intramontane valleys of Hissar, Zeravshan Ridge, Peter the Great Ridge and, particularly, in the Western Pamir (Vanch, Yazguliom, Bartang Valleys) small kishlaks were located on taluses and formed a specific "island" pattern of settlement.

The process of forced redistribution of population within the republic's territory aggravated the inherent polarization of the marginal mountain regions and of the more economically advanced lowlands which got most of the available material resources and investments. In the late 1980s this man-enhanced polarization has shown its reverse side: the former mountain inhabitants started spontaneously to return to the abandoned kishlaks, but most of their lands were already fully occupied by the rapidly growing population that had stayed on in these self-same kishlaks.

Thus a complicated and often contradictory history created the specific socio-economic landscape of Tajikistan of the late 20th century. Its spatial image can be described in the following everyday notions.

The Gornyi (mountain) Badakhshan autonomous oblast–Pamir

This oblast has an area of 63 700 km^2 (44 per cent of area), 3.3 per cent of the population, and a mean population density of 1.9 persons/km^2. A high mountain zone (3.5-7 km above sea level) it can be regarded as a kind of "'fridge" with frozen mineral and recreational resources, on the one hand, and as a water tower feeding water to Amu Darya and Vaksh, on the other hand. This zone is clearly peripheral to the economically more developed centres of Dushanbe and the Vaksh Valley. Pamir is isolated from the latter for 6–7 months a year when snow closes the passes on the direct road Dushanbe-Khorog. All life-supporting commodities (fuel, food) are transported from the centre via Osh (Kyrghyzstan) using the Pamir highway from Osh-Khorog with passes above 4 000 m. The oblast is fully dependent on resources of the centre and got subsidies from the republic and from the Union Government.

The majority of the population of the Eastern Pamir (a high plateau with an extreme natural environment) are Kyrghyz who, up to the Soviet

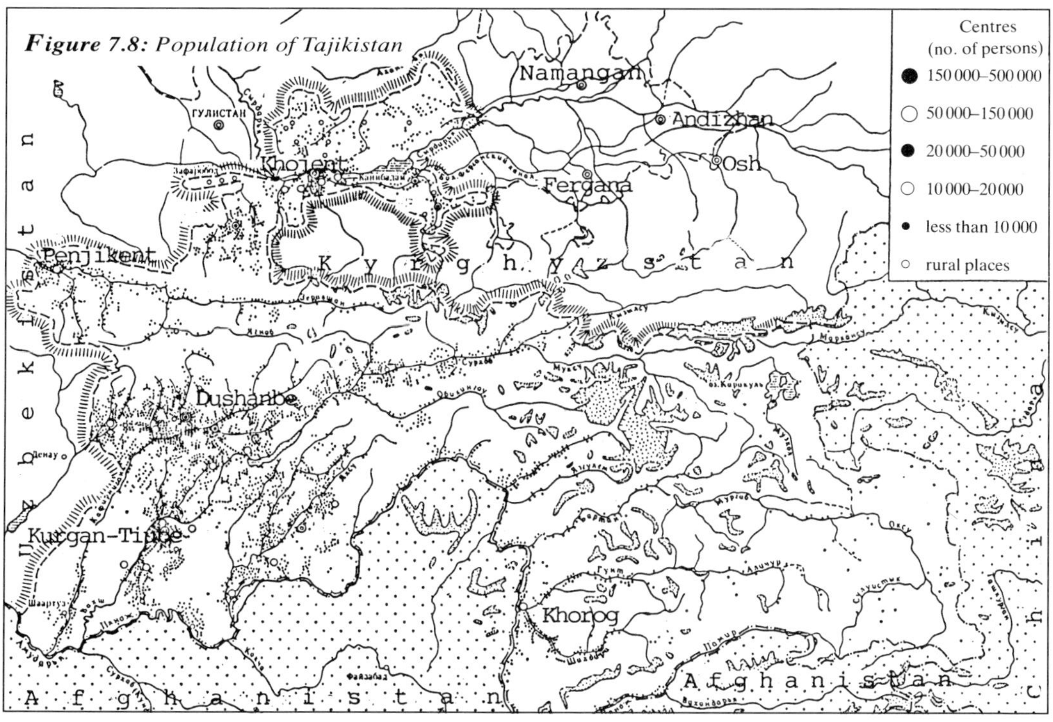

Figure 7.8: Population of Tajikistan

Tradition dictates not just the calendar and styles of dress but the shapes of even the commonest agricultural tools

period, were nomadic herdsmen. The narrow valleys of the Western Pamir-Badakhshan: Vanch, Yazguliom, Bartang, Ishkashim–are populated by Mountain Tajiks who are land cultivators and animal-breeders close to the cultural-ethnic area of Karakorum; they represent the Ishmailite branch of Islam. Up to the present day some remote mountain kishlaks maintain the traditions of mountain agriculture: the archaic practices of hand-hoeing and hand-threshing. The ethnic traditions clearly show in the devices for load carrying by men. Isolated valleys have their specific adjustments: in Yazguliom, Vakhan and Ishkashim men put both hands and shoulders into straps, while the left hand stays free. The technique of load transportation in baskets is similar, the carrier putting his hands and shoulders into basket straps (Western Pamir, Afghani Badakshan and Nuristan, Hunsa). In Nepal such baskets have no straps for the hands, but only one strap which is put on the carrier's head and held on the forehead by the hands.

Old men in distant mountain kishlaks still use the folk cultivation calendar that strictly regulates all cycles of agricultural practices. The solar calendar "isobi mard" is widespread; time is measured according to "the movement of the sun over a man's body": in the last winter month "khut" (fish) the sun moves to "darmon" (guts)–9 days–then to "pourouk" (ribs)–3 days–and to "dil" (heart)–9 days. This is the period for spreading manure, repairing tools, feeding oxen to get them strong for ploughing; the women prepare for the New Year Festival, Navruz.

In such way the whole year was "preset", the calendar was fully adjusted to the cultivation cycle. These centuries-long traditions were adapted to local environmental conditions and used to regulate all the relations of man with his environment.

New technologies introduced in the Soviet period were mostly brought from the lowlands of Western Tajikistan and from the European centre. They entered into conflict with the fragile system of cultivation of the highlands: bulldozers started to operate along ancient irrigation systems to widen the main canals, steep slopes were undercut and lost stability, erosion and landslides became more active. But the heaviest blow to mountain agriculture was given by one hundred per cent collectivization of small farms and the organization of large state and collective farms. The younger generations have lost the feeling that land belongs to them and that small plots have to be cared for. The centuries-old traditions of regulated use of natural resources sensitive to weather changes were replaced by a unified indefinite system of five-year planning of yields. For the fragile balance of the mountain areas this system turned out to be a destabilizing factor.

The demographic explosion of the 1960-70s has not spared the Pamir mountain areas, and employment problems have become very serious.

To these destabilizing factors one should add the phenomenon of the "dead end" location of the Pamir: the state boundary with the areas of China and Afghanistan also populated by Mountain Tajiks has separated the economic and cultural life of this single ethnic and economic space of Central Asia. To find a way out of this "dead end of development" at the turn of the 20th century, to re-establish cultural and economic links–is the key problem for the sustainable development of this vast mountain area.

The cotton lands

Southwestern Tajikistan includes the lower parts of the Vaksh, Pianj, and Kafirnigan valleys. This area is the major cotton-growing region–the Soviet "cotton field". It concentrates one-quarter of the population of the Republic, and the mean population density is 30-50 persons/km^2. It was the area to which the people of the mountain kishlaks were moved in the middle of this century. In the course of this forced migration many people became ill and even died under the stress of unaccustomed climatic conditions (scientists have no data, because accurate statistical information was never made available).

There, in the Amu Darya Valley, the most ancient civilizations of Central Asia once existed: in the 7-6th centuries BC there was Baktria, a slave-owning state that comprised northern Afghanistan, and southern Uzbekistan. This was an area of rich material culture as evidenced by the archaeological findings of golden coins in sections of Kabadian. The authority on antiquities, Kvint Kurtsiy Ruf, has written: "The nature of Baktria is diverse; vines produce big and sweet fruit; abundant water irrigates hot soil; the most fertile lands are cultivated for cereals, other lands are turned into rangelands for cattle, but most of the land is unproductive plain."

Ancient records tell us that Baktria was "the country of a thousand cities".

In the 4th century BC after conquest by Alexander the Great, Baktria became part of his vast empire which "fused together" the Hellenic and Central Asian cultures. It was an intricate mixing of the traditions and religions of West and East: Zoroastrian beliefs and Buddhism which had penetrated Central Asia via Afghanistan. In the course of its long historical development this area was a focus of cultural and trade connections, for it was squarely on one of the Ancient Silk Roads.

In the middle, and especially in the last half of the 20th century the Vaksh Valley became one of the most critical "hot zones" of Tajikistan. The main reason was the monoculture of cotton. This area contains one third of all the irrigated lands of the republic, and 37.6 per cent of ploughed irrigated lands; it produces 50 per cent of all fibre cotton, and 94 per cent of the most valuable fine-fibre cotton. The orientation to extensive cotton production in combination with high population density has produced a cat's cradle of problems and conflicts. Water infiltration has led to loss of water and salinization of soils; pesticides and herbicides are penetrating groundwater of which some is used to supply drinking water. The low quality of drinking water, inadequate sewage and sanitation in settlements –about 40 per cent of rural citizens take drinking water from aryks (open canals)–result in a high incidence of typhoid, viral hepatitis and bacterial dysentery. These diseases are respectively 15, 12 and 3 times more frequent than the national average.

The local people who produce the so-called "white gold" and ensure cotton self-sufficiency for the Soviet Union are paying a high price with their health for this development orientation which was forced on them from outside. Even the successes of growing citrus plants and orchards on slopes with investment from the state do not compensate for the social and economic losses. The unprecedented growth rates of population (in some areas they approach 5 per cent!) make this situation fraught with social outbursts.

This region of Tajikistan can be compared to a pressure cooker without a safety valve. To find a way out of this situation and reduce social pressures in the region is the major problem of policy-makers in the government of the republic.

After the clearing of the endemic tugai (floodplain) forests in the Amu Darya and Pianj valleys, floods and bank erosion have become much more frequent. The dammed Sarez Lake in the Western Pamir (17 km^3) and the sporadically emerging glacial lakes blocked by periodic advances of Pamir glaciers constitute a permanent threat to the people living several hundreds of kilometres away from these risk zones. The principle of the interaction of highlands and lowlands is eminently demonstrated in this region.

The capital agglomeration of Dushanbe

This urbanized industrial zone is spontaneously spreading outwards from the alumina-producing complex of Regar in the west to the "warehouse of the republic"–Ordjonikidzeabad–in the east. This is evidently a centre with all a capital's functions and problems: growth of urban population, of unemployment, of environmental degradation and declining quality of life. This zone contains nearly one fifth of the population of Tajikistan.

What will be the consequences of changes in management and power due to "perestroika" ?

This is a good question to which the answers are now uncertain. Will reorientation of the economy and society towards free markets contribute to more sustainable development? What will be demographical and settlement policy in the traditionally authoritarian management system? These are the key problems facing Tajikistan at the end of the 20th century.

Northern Tajikistan

This zone is isolated from the central capital zone and develops rather autonomously. It accounts for a sixth of the area and contains a third of the population, with a density of 50-100 persons/km^2. The passes across the Hissar and Turkestan Ridges of the highways connecting Dushanbe to Northern Tajikistan are closed for five–six months a year. Located in the mouth of the Fergana Valley where it opens to the Aral lowlands, the zone's boundaries contain the conflict-prone ancestral homelands of several ethnic groups: Uzbeks, Tajiks and Kyrghyz. There, the density of rural population is the highest in the ex-USSR: 350-400 persons/km^2.

Due to its trans-boundary situation, Northern Tajikistan is oriented in its development policy towards integration into the economic space of Uzbekistan. It should be mentioned that nearly 50 per cent of the population of Northern Tajikistan is Uzbek. The Khojent Oblast (administrative division coinciding with Northern Tajikistan) ranks next to the Dushanbe Agglomeration in its degree of economic development, specifically in agriculture, mining and the processing of agricultural raw materials.

The valley of Zeravshan

The subject of cultural and historical claims by Tajiks and Uzbeks as the ancient capital of Sogdiana, this narrow valley opens in the west onto the oasis of Samarkand–the cradle of the Tajik nation. The valley is a buffer between Northern and Southern Tajikistan. The closing of the passes cuts the Zeravshan valley from the north and south of the republic for five–six months a year and its social and economic life is oriented towards Samarkand–a major city of Central Asia and a tourist Mecca for visitors from all over the world.

Further north and parallel to the Zeravshan Valley is the unique Yagnob Valley that has conserved the relics of the Sogdian *ethnos* pushed out from other areas to the remote mountains by the invasions of Alexander the Great and later of Arabs. Before 1966 the population of the valley was only 1 500 and most of it was moved out to the steppes of Zafarobod to cotton areas. The language of the Yagnob population is considered to be a relic Sogdian dialect, and only 30 per cent of its words are Tajik.

Being fully isolated from other regions of Tajikistan, the Yagnobs have kept alive the traditions of primitive mountain agriculture: they cultivate small terraced plots with oxen and use the *omach* (a primitive plough). The threshing of the main crops, wheat and barley, is also done with the help of oxen. The *aivans* (open galleries) have conserved the unique architectural patterns of carved doors, ceilings and pillars.

Local people believe themselves to be Muslims, but forbid blowing out a fire and worship wild rose bushes and old poplars. The names of their kishlaks–Imbef, Mujif, Pishanza, Morghib–show ancient Sogdian roots and traces of Zoroastrianism.

Thus a marvellous fragment of the ancient Central Asian world is to be found only a few tens of kilometres from mining combines and crowded tourist sites around the Iskanderkul Lake (the Lake of Iskander or Alexander the Great). It is a small *ethnos* or nation on the brink of extinction. Here then are some questions to be answered. Could it be conserved by the establishment of an ethnographic reserve? What would be efficient legal and ethical mechanisms?

The Vaksh Valley

Watered by the right tributary of the Amu Darya, this valley has a particular place in the geography of Tajikistan. Crossing the republic from northeast to southwest it forms "the environment-economy axis" of the interactive system of the Pamir and Darvaz highlands and the lowlands of the Vaksh Valley. This zone has an extremely important role in the history of the economic development of the area: it was one of the branches of the Silk Road connecting Central Asia to western provinces of China via the Alai Valley (Kyrghyzstan).

Notwithstanding the ethnic conflicts of Kyrghyz and Tajiks that existed in the historical past (mostly over resources), this zone attracted population from the Fergana and Zeravshan valleys, and from Western Tajikistan. The specific and sustainable settlement system that developed was focused on stock rearing (in mountains) and land cultivation (cereals, vegetables, fruit) in the valleys and middle mountains.

In the Soviet period the development of this zone was contradictory. On the one hand, thanks to the development of transportation infrastructure (the Dushanbe-Khorog Highway, the Pamir Highway) and the introduction of potato-growing and horticulture, the middle-mountain areas of Garm and Komsomolabad became important exporters of the products of land cultivation and animal breeding to Dushanbe and the Vaksh Valley. On the other hand, the great hydropower potential of the Vaksh River and the need to control runoff for the irrigation of the vast cotton areas of Southern Tajikistan and Uzbekistan accounted for the construction, since the 1930s, of the Vaksh system of hydro power stations with big water reservoirs (on a stretch 300 km long, 9 dams were constructed or are being constructed; they have vast water reservoirs stretching for a total of 80 km of the channel). This construction was being carried out by the USSR Ministry for Power Production, and has given rise to a sharp conflict over the withdrawal of agricultural lands and the need to move out about 40 000 people to other areas of the republic. Against the background of huge population growth and the deepening economic crisis of the 1990s this contradictory pattern of regional development was strongly criticized on social grounds by citizen action movements, and above all by the greens. At the focus of this conflict is the territory that is to be flooded by the water reservoir of the Rogoun hydro power plant (under construction). There is an obvious conflict of interest between the central management and local communities, the interests of the latter being ignored by the planned economic projects. One can say, metaphorically, that the vascular system (the Vaksh River), which functions as a life-supporting linear structure in the system of economic and cultural highland-lowland interaction, is blocked by clots of dams and reservoirs.

It should also be mentioned, that the urban and industrial centres taking shape in the hinterland of the hydro power plants are not integrated into the local agrarian economic space. They have no function even as second-rank centres supporting development of local communities. The need to find ways to integrate different types of economic activity within certain areas is another problem to be resolved. What are the possible compromises that could lead to sustainable development and a reduction of social tensions?

Population, activities, traditions

Tajikistan belongs to the regions of rapidly growing population. In 1897 within the present-day boundaries there lived 811 000 people; about 70 000 of them were urban craftsmen and merchants. During the 20th century the population increased 6 times, and according to the Census of 1989 it was 5.2 million In the period 1939-59 the mean annual growth rate was 1.5 per cent, in 1959-80 it was 4.7 per cent, 3.8 times higher than the USSR average. Population grows mostly as a result of natural processes, and the rural population increases at high rates (Table 7.4).

In 1897 the urban population accounted for 7 per cent, in 1913 it was 9 per cent. The ratio of urban to rural population was practically stable before the Soviet period.

Significant growth of the urban population started in the 1930s with the general industrial

***Table 7.4:** Dynamics of population in Tajikistan SSR*

Year	Population(thousands) Total	urban	rural	As per cent of total urban	rural
1913	1034	95	939	9	91
1940	1525	293	1232	22	78
1959	1981	646	1325	33	67
1966	2556	921	1625	37	63
1970	2900	1077	1823	37	63
1980	3901	1349	2552	35	65
1983	4239	1437	2802	34	66

***Table 7.5:** Dynamics of the ethnic population structure of Tajikistan SSR*

	1959		1970		1979	
	thous.pers.	%	thous.pers.	%	thous.pers.	%
Total population	1980.6	100	2900	100	3801	100
Tajik	1051.1	53.1	1629.9	52.2	2237	58.8
Uzbek	455.0	23.0	665.7	23.0	873	23.0
Russian	262.6	13.3	344.1	11.9	395	10.4
Tatar	56.9	2.9	70.8	2.4	80	2.1
German	32.6	1.6	37.7	1.3	39	1.0
Kyrghyz	35.7	1.3	35.5	1.2	48	1.3
Ukrainian	26.9	1.4	31.7	1.1	36	0.9
Kazakh	12.6	0.6	8.3	0.3	10	0.3
other	55.5	2.8	75.4	2.6	83	2.2

development of the republic. The highest proportion of urban population is in Northern Tajikistan and the Hissar Valley, the lowest is in mountain and foothill regions of the Pamir, Garm and Zeravshan zones.

The process of formation of the urban population is governed by several major factors: immigration from outside, mostly from the European USSR; forced emigration of people from mountain kishlaks; and natural growth. The increase of urban population was a reflection of the strategy of the republic's government to promote urbanization and the enlargement of rural settlements. Until recently this policy was implemented by way of so-called "organized resettlement"; what that actually meant was forced migration. Thus, in 1950-69, 15 500 farms were abandoned; in 1939-59 the population of the mountain areas, which was never large, decreased by nearly 100 000. Several hundred kishlaks were abandoned with their developed traditions of mountain cultivation. The ecological balance of lands which appeared to belong to nobody was completely destroyed.

Since the middle of the 1960s–the years of demographic explosion–63 per cent of the total population increase in the republic was due to rural increase. In rates of rural population growth Tajikistan was the leader in the USSR. The share of the rural population in the total population of Tajikistan is the highest among the Union Republics–66 per cent. Inside Tajikistan the highest percentage of rural population is in the Pamir mountain area (86 per cent); at the same time the number of mountain kishlaks decreased by one third in the last three to four decades as a result of the state policy of settlement.

In the traditions of the Tajik and other local nations the rural way of development was always dominant. The traditions of seasonal migration were also strong: in between the agricultural seasons thousands of "dehkans" (farmers) sought employment in the Fergana Valley and Samarkand in cotton factories and in construction. This income was invested in farm and family. Such an age-old system supported, though at a low level, the system of farm economy, the traditions of rural communities and established land use.

Multi-ethnic structure

Tajikistan displays multi-ethnicity to a marked degree. Developing for millenia within a rather limited area, the territory has accumulated a wide range of nationalities and cultures that can hardly be imagined in other, more spacious regions of the country: Tajiks and Uzbeks, Arabs and Berbers, Gypsies, Jews, and later introductions of Russians, Ukrainians, and Germans (Table 7.5).

Of considerable interest is one of the first distribution maps of the ethnic groups in Tajikistan compiled in the 1930s by the "Complex Expedition" of the USSR Academy of Sciences which surveyed the regions of the republic (Figure 7.9). This map provides a kind of base line for the analysis of changes in the ethnic diversity of Tajikistan consequent on the establishment of Soviet power in this multi-ethnic feudal country. This primitive map-scheme is the only document that reflects the ethnic structure in the 1930s. More recent maps reflect the outcomes of complex migration processes (including forced migrations) and national policies; they show quite a different pattern of ethnic groups, and some ethnic areas have completely disappeared (for instance, the Turkmen area in Jili-Kul, from where the Turkmen population was expelled in the 1950s.

The diversity of the national traditions of the ethnic groups is clearly shown in the patterns of construction (Figure 7.10) and of dressing (Figure 7.11).

Recent years are characterized by the enhancement of national self-identification and the restoration of Islamic fundamentalism; this explains the increased emigration of the Russian-speaking population. Earlier (in the 1980s) a rather large German community practically disappeared from Tajikistan where it had lived since the middle of the 1940-50s after deportation from the Volga region. In the 1990s emigration processes are active again in Tajikistan, as in all ex-Soviet Central Asia, and the future trends of these processes can hardly be predicted.

However, there is already one negative result: despite rather high unemployment in the urban areas, the positions freed by outmigrants in industry and in the social services are not being filled by the local population. The traditional

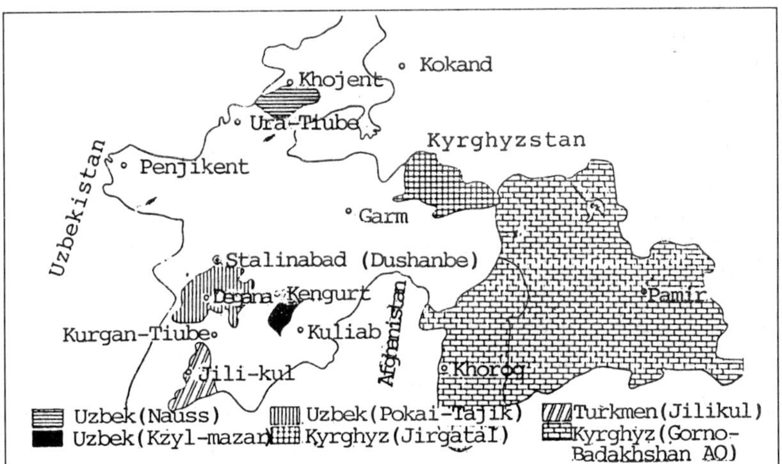

Figure 7.9: *Scheme of the regions of national minorities in Tajikistan SSR.* After S.M. Abramzon, 1934

Figure 7.10: *Construction patterns in regions of Tajikistan.* Above: *Anini district. Mosque in the mountain village Zerobod.*

Left, below: *Pendjikent district. Mountainous settlement in Kshtut canyon.* Drawings by E. Ierzovski

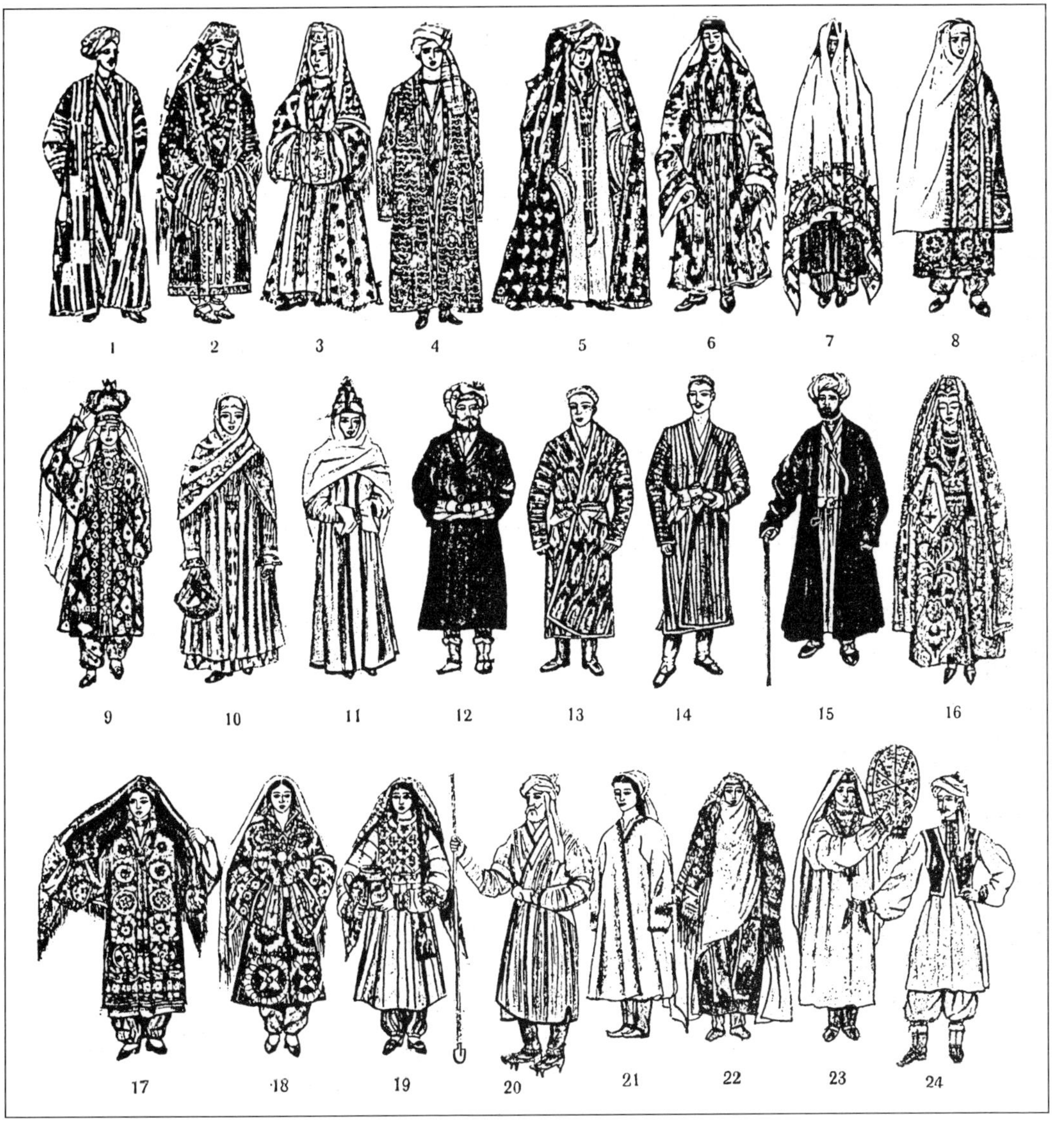

Figure 7.11: *Traditional Tajik dress*

1.	*Ura-Tiube*
2-5.	*Bukhara*
6.	*Karatag*
7-8.	*Kuliab*
9.	*Darvaz*
10.	*Lowlands*
11.	*Northern Tajikistan*
12.	*Shugnan*
13-14.	*Leninabad*
15.	*Urban*
16.	*Samarkand*
17.	*Kalaikhum*
18.	*Karateghin*
19-20.	*Darvaz*
21.	*Rushan*
22.	*Shugnan*
23-24	*Ishkashim*

national and Islamic orientation towards agricultural activities, servicing and trade is winning over the attraction of employment in the non-traditional spheres.

Lately, a new development was the phenomenon of the tourist boom. The local population and policy-makers strongly support development of the tourist industry as a source of income (in hard currency, preferably) to the state budget. Many small cooperatives have been established with a view to servicing foreign tourists. However, this activity has not yet become really efficient, because there is still no tourist infrastructure or tradition of service corresponding to Western standards.

Motivation of tourism by the still intact beauty of natural landscapes has not yet produced the desired effect: those who have come so far are mostly small groups of mountain tourists and mountain climbers. But the most serious threat to the development of the tourist industry comes from the monopolistic claims of the central governmental structures.

The local population finds itself excluded from this economic sphere and, naturally, shows no interest in work for massive tourism developments. In the future the Nepalese scenario of mountain trekking might be possible. But now in some places the "tourists in shorts" enter into conflict with the "pilgrims coming to worship sacred places" (such as the Obi-Mazar Valley, or the ruins of Khozrati Burkh Mosque). Another problem for tourism development is the depletion of the environmental quality in recent decades. This is a result of intensive development of industry, hydro power production, and population growth which have combined to increase pressures on vulnerable recreational resources and in some places to exceed critical levels and undermine the tourist-attracting resources.

The environments of Tajikistan, many of them unique ones, and its rich biodiversity are inadequately protected by a net of reserved territories. There are only three nature reserves: Tiger Balka (Tiger Valley) in the Amu Darya Valley, Romit mountain reserve in the Hissar Ridge, and Dashti-Jum reserve in Southern Tajikistan. Their area is rather limited (up to 50 000 ha), and they are all under threat from anthropogenic interference from the adjacent territories. These "islands" of more or less unmodified ecosystems are in no way able to protect the whole biodiversity of the unique nature of the region.

The Pamir National Park, which is now in the planning phase, should have an area of over 1 million ha, and should play an outstanding role in the conservation of nature in the highlands. However, there are still several problems to solve: accommodating the return migrants from the Vaksh Valley who lived in this region before the 1950s, finding a compromise for hunting the Marco Polo goat (the licences for hunting are now sold with much profit to Western hunters by state and cooperative organizations), and finding the mechanisms to control "wild" tourism and harmonious relationships with local mountain communities.

Transport infrastructure

The economic development of the region requires a sound infrastructure but what is in place is inadequately developed and unevenly spread: the mountain areas of Western Pamir, Darvaz-Karateghin, and Zeravshan are separated throughout the winter season by passes which are closed to the highways from the industrially advanced centres of Dushanbe and Khojent. In the conditions of centralized supply of commodities and other life-supporting items for mountain communities, this factor has a negative impact on their socio-economic prospects and their level of well-being. Mountain roads are often cut into landslide-prone slopes and are under permanent risk of destruction in the season of rain and floods; this threat is very serious even for the major highways: Khorog-Kulaikhumb, Dushanbe-Garm, Dushanbe-Aini. The high seismicity of the region provokes rockfalls, landslides and mudflows and adds one more element to the array of transportation problems.

The network of secondary unasphalted roads connecting kishlaks and rural production facilities is developing spontaneously to meet local demands. The mountain slopes undercut by networks of rural roads are subject to intensive erosion. There is absolutely no protection of slopes by engineering techniques or by afforestation; thus, the resource basis for cereals, vegetable-growing and animal-breeding is being steadily undermined.

The expansion of transportation networks to the marginal mountain areas, now a spontaneous process, conflicts with the sustainability of the resource potential and the mountain environment. It is obvious that, in a situation of rapid population growth and return-migration to mountain areas, high-quality roads become a priority need.

The provision of health care and education services to remote kishlaks is a major factor for advancement of the mountain communities. Tajikistan does have a well-developed network of air transportation, but it is unable comprehensively to resolve all the transport-related problems of sustainable development for the republic.

Conclusion

At the turn of the second and third millennia, ancient Tajikistan is facing difficult problems and seeks the strategies for long-term development. The Soviet period of developments which is still historically brief but packed by events, has led to fundamental restructuring of the socio-economic and cultural life of Tajik society. The natural and agrarian landscapes of the territory have also been significantly transformed.

The key question for Tajikistan and, primarily, for its governing establishment and policy-makers is: will the environmental and resource capacity of the territory be sufficient to provide living space and meet demands of the rapidly growing population of the republic? The solutions and scenarios of development lie within a kind of Bermuda triangle, of which the apexes are: population growth–availability of (land) resources–conservation of unique environments.

There are abundant uncertainties hindering the selection of the optimal scenarios for development: although the territory is well studied, there is no reliable and easily available information on environment and resources. This information is dispersed in many institutions and departments, and it takes much effort to aggregate and handle. This paradox is due to the planning system, which is both supercentralized and sectoral. The interests of ministries and departments (at the levels of the USSR and of the republic) were never integrated in specific localities. Local communities had no voice in the planning process and in the development of their own habitat.

Added to all that is the future climatic change. What will the responses of the nival-glacial zone of the Pamir and Pamir-Alai be to a global warming of 1.5–2.5 degrees C expected by 2020–2030? What transformations will take place in the hydrological regimes and erosion processes? Will the economic system–water reservoirs, irrigation network–manage to adapt to these rapid (in one to two generations) changes? These and many other questions should be kept in mind by the policy-makers responsible for long-term development scenarios.

To ensure the reliable and science-based character of these scenarios, they should be founded on fundamental knowledge. The first priority should go to a system of comprehensive monitoring and information bases with the employment of modern computer technologies. Jointly, this should provide the support system for decision-making on sustainable development. At the end of the 1990s the republic is at a crossroads. The "perestroika" of former President Gorbachev is the greatest and most recent (during the last 70 years) impact on the whole socio-economic, resource-environmental, and political system of Tajikistan. Will Tajikistan integrate in the future into the economic and cultural space of Southern Asia, or will it continue as a dead-end, resource-producing peripheral to the USSR or whatever succeeds it?

This was written in the summer of 1991 in the picturesque Surkhob Valley on a spur of the Peter the Great Ridge in a field camp near the Sarinai kishlak. Further down, in the Surkhob Valley which spreads wide at this site, life is slow, full of the tense everyday labour of people, and of women above all. The opposite slope of the Surkhob Valley is the site of the former Khait kishlak buried by a landslide. In its stead, a new settlement is growing, though much smaller than the former one.

In ancient times, this valley was one of the numerous "streams" of the Great Silk Road that connected the civilizations of the Mediterranean, Central Asia, and China. Close to this site was the Khait Fortress that protected the Tajik cultivators from the invasions of bellicose Kyrghyz. Land cultivation, trade, wars–they were always together in this valley. What does the 21st century hold for the Tajiks–a people of unsurpassed hospitality–living in the small Sarinai kishlak in the Surkhob Valley?

There is a possibility of the development of an international tourist centre at Jirghital connected by a motorway or auto route to Beijing–Urumchi, to Dushanbe and Samarkand. Or, as before, in the long winter season when two metres of snow cover hides every thing in sight, men will take their time in the chaikhana (pub) enjoying green tea and shurpo (hot meal), while women take care of their 6-10 children in their poor houses. What awaits this marvellous country in the near future? The responsibility for the optimal strategies is not only with scientists and policy-makers, but with the local communities, as well. ■

Figure 7.12: *The Caucasus population, settlement and transportation. 1979.* Modified from *Atlas of the World Nations* 1964

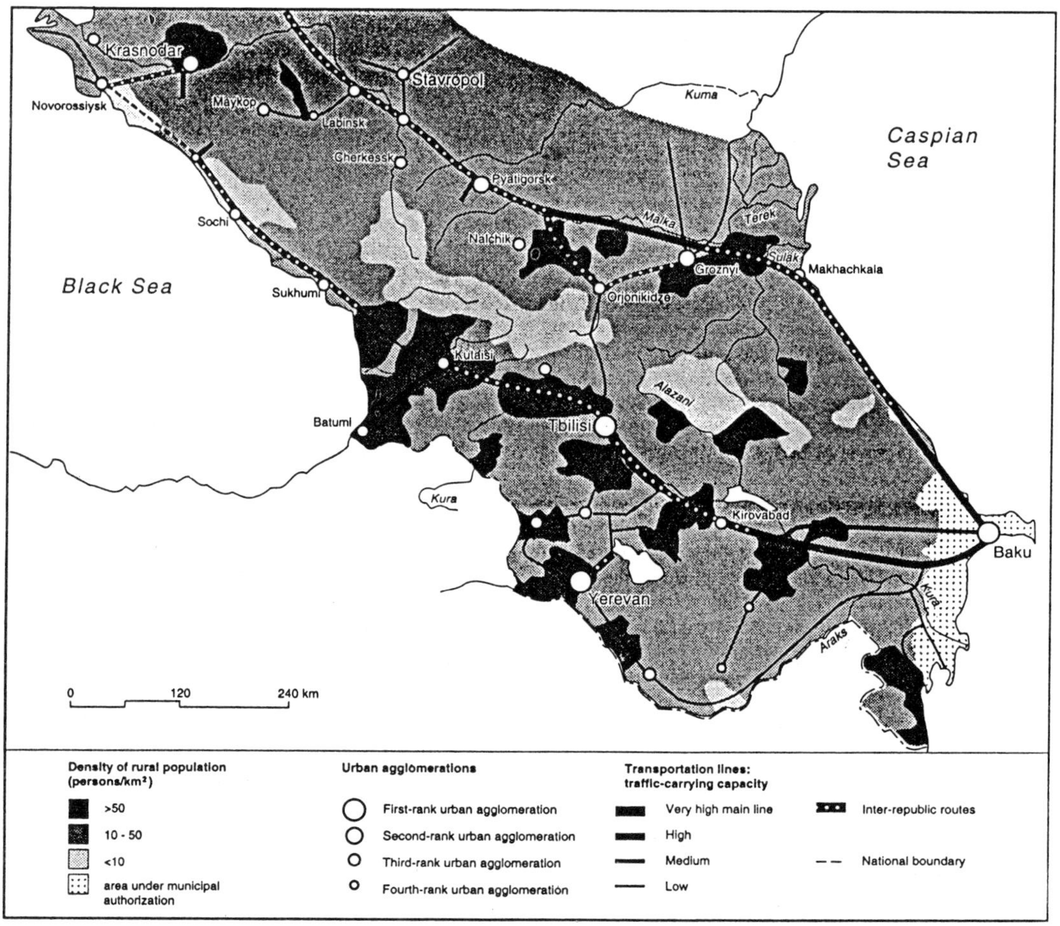

Scenario for the development of the mountain regions

The search for strategies in the uncertain situation

At the divide of the 20th and 21st century the future development of the mountain regions is hidden in a fog of political and economic uncertainty. The very membership in the USSR or its successor of several mountainous republics–Georgia, Armenia– is an open question. In general, the territories of Caucasia and Transcaucasia in the 1990s are in a state of instability and political and economic crisis: new states–Georgia, Kabardino-Balkaria, Ossetia, etc.–are being formed, economic and cultural links are being disrupted, massive migrations of nations and ethnic groups are taking place. There is a difficult process of change in the forms of property–from state and public property to private and cooperative forms; the economy is adopting a market orientation. These large-scale processes of structural reform have, undoubtedly, a powerful impact on the environment and resources of mountain areas. However, because of the specific character of these processes one should expect, at least in the early phases, that they will enhance the negative consequences of environmental and resource-base degradation. One can state with some certainty that in the next decades development of these mountain regions will take place in a situation of economic crisis and instability. As an illustration, one can cite the case of the destruction of the transport, communication and economic links between the republics of Transcaucasia.

As a result of inter-ethnic conflict between Azerbaijan and Armenia, aggravated by the rigid (separatist) position of Georgia, the Armenian Republic has become an "island" state within the USSR, having no real connections with the centre. Railways and highlands, oil and gas pipelines are blocked. One can easily imagine that this situation will increase pressure on its natural resources (forests, rangelands) that are already in a depressed state. For the same reasons, the damage caused by the Spitak earthquake of 1989 is still not restored: many urban and rural sites are in ruins, despite the large-scale assistance provided by the world community.

Another illustration of the disruption of economic links is Altai, southern Siberia. The proclamation of the independent Republic of Mountain Altai within the boundaries of the former Altai Kray of the Russian Federation has resulted in the destruction of the classical system of highland (Altai Mountains) and lowland (Ob Valley) interactions. The ambitions of the local leaders have disrupted the single economic and cultural environment: the rich recreational and tourist resources of the Altai Mountains have been separated from the agricultural and mining resources of lowlands and foothills which were the main contributors to the local budget.

The clear orientation of the local administration to the independent planning of development of the new (artificial) territorial formation will inevitably lead to economic and social losses, and higher instability. It is quite obvious that the future of sustainable development in the Altai region is in the integration of agriculture, soft tourism, and mining in a single "highland-lowland" complex.

There is a perfect historical example of such: the ancient Chuy Way efficiently supported the natural and human system of Altai which connected the highly developed agricultural regions of southern Siberia, Inner Mongolia and China. The recently commissioned grandiose Baikal-Amur Main Railway (BAM) can be interpreted as a modern Soviet version of the colonization "of the wild west". Crossing the sparsely populated territories of Siberia and Yakutia this transportation artery has opened access to the fuel and mineral resources of the huge region. However, really to develop the resources of this area given the extremely severe natural conditions of the North-Baikal and Stanovoy Uplands, sparse population, and undeveloped economic and social infrastructure requires grandiose investments not only from the former Soviet Union, but also from other countries. There is a need for a new wave of pioneers to develop these new lands! This supertask of development of the BAM zone would require the efforts of several generations of the Soviet people in the situation of the 1990s economic crisis and environmental constraints.

The above-cited problems of development in the mountain regions of the USSR suggest several principal conclusions on the situation and trends in the mountain areas in the near future:

❑ in the political and socio-economic crisis in the ex-USSR in the beginning of the 1990s it is the factors of uncertainty and instability which will decide the processes of development in the decades to come;

❑ the demographic explosion in the mountainous republics of Soviet Central Asia and Azerbaijan which began in the 1970s is the long-term dominant that will have formed the "problem" and "conflict" areas at the beginning of the 21st century;

❑ the issues of global climate change are outside the perspective of the policy-actors and policy-makers. In view of the first and second issues above, the distant effects of the climate change are perceived as too abstract and irrelevant for management.

Recommendations

In the situation of the foreseeable uncertainty of development of the ex-USSR mountain areas a heavy burden of responsibility falls on science.

What is implied by that?

It should be mentioned that the Russian academic tradition–in geography, geology, ecology, ethnography and other branches–puts special emphasis on mountain studies. Thanks to that, the level of knowledge on mountains of the ex-USSR can be assessed as relatively high. However, priority was given to the narrow professional, sectoral studies. The integrated regional projects were very few and had a secondary role. There are several exceptions: a splendid integrated study on Tajikistan was implemented by the USSR Academy in the 1930s; the Caucasus was comprehensively studied by the Institute of Geography in the 1970s. Still, despite the Everest of information accumulated in many decades for most of the former USSR mountain regions, there is a very clear shortage of integrated regional studies, especially of those supporting regional development. Therefore, an important task faced today by the scientific community is the assessment of the new realities of the mountain world in the ex-USSR. Of particular importance is the employment of modern techniques of environmental and resource monitoring, geo-information systems, and the system of support for decision-making in the environmental field.

The theoretical studies should give priorities for the development of the models and scenarios taking into account the history and traditions, the global climate changes, and new economic and geopolitical realities. Mountains–a cradle of humanity–are today the remote margins of civilization in most countries. The mountains of the Soviet Union are no exception. Conservation of their unique nature and rich abundance of cultural values, fragile and vulnerable, is not only nostalgia for "the lost countryside of childhood." To use the pragmatic language of the end of the 20th century: the mountains are the resource and economic guarantee for the future, and also the key factor in the sustainability of the development of the nations and countries in plains and lowlands. ■

Major publications

AGAKHANIANTZ, O.E. (1981). Arid mountains of the USSR. Moscow.

AVAKIAN, G.E. (1989). People and mountains. "Mysl", Moscow.

BADENKOV, Yu.P., et al. (1990). Caucasia. In: "The Earth as transformed by human action" Cambridge Univ. Press with Clark University.

CHUPAKHIN, V.M. (1987). Altitudinal-zonal geosystems of the Soviet Central Asia and Kazakhstan. Alma-Ata.

GVOZDETSKIY, N.A. (1963). The Caucasus. Moscow.

GVOZDETSKIY, N.A. (1968). The Pamir. Moscow.

GVOZDETSKIY, N.A., GOLUBCHIKOV, Yu.N. (1987) Mountains. "Mysl", Moscow.

JUMAEV, T. (1989). Mountains of Uzbekistan. Tashkent.

KOTLIAKOV, V.M. (1977). Mountains, glaciers, hypotheses. Leningrad.

MAMYTOV, A.M. (1987). Mountain soils of Soviet Central Asia and Kazakhstan. Frunze.

BADENKOV, Yu.P., KOTLIAKOV, V.M., LOSEV, K.S. (eds.) (1988). Mountain territories: rational use of nature, economic development and settlement. Moscow.

FERSMAN, A.E., VASILIEV, V.N., et al., (eds.) (1933) Problems of Tajikistan. vols. 1 and 2. ANSSSR, Leningrad.

SCHUKIN, I.S., SCHUKINA, O.E. (1959). Life of mountains. Moscow.

STANIUKOVICH, K.V. (1973). Vegetation of mountains of the USSR. Dushanbe.

GERASIMOV, I.P. (ed.) (1980). The Alps–the Caucasus. "Nauka", Moscow.

GERASIMOV, I.P. (ed.) (1984). The Greater Caucasus–Stara Planina (Balkans). "Nauka", Moscow.

LUKINOV, I.I., BRYK, M.V., GOLUBETS, M.A., et al., (eds.) The Ukrainian Carpathians. vol.1."Nature", (1988); vol. 2."History" (1989); vol.3."Economy"(1988); vol. 4."Culture" (1989). "Naukova dumka", Kiev.

Appendix 1

Population and environment conservation in mountain regions

(all areas in thousand km^2)

	High latitude mountains	Carpathians, Crimea	Caucasus	Central Asia, Kazakhstan	Urals	Altai, Sayan	N-E Siberia, Far East
Mountain area	350	17.7	178.8	521.8	96.3	372	3 812.8
Number and area of nature reserves	2/10.74	4/0.29	30/7.5	16/7.78	5/8.57	3/13.06	11/30.58
Number and area of sanctuaries authorized by the Republic	7/0.095	13/2.32		30/16.87		2/4.7	4/3.8
Per cent of protected area	2.3	2.0	5.5	4.7	8.8	4.7	0.9
Mountain population (thousands)	120.6	936	7 687	11 217	665	640	1 715.6

Appendix 2

Mountain regions of the USSR

(Administration, highest summits)

I. Mountains of high latitudes

- Franz-Jozef Land and Novaya Zemlya (Russia) 620 m and 1547 m
- Khibins (Russia) 1 191 m
- Polar Urals (Russia) 1 895 m
- East-Arctic Isles (Russia) 1 096 m
- Byrranga and Putorana (Russia) 1 664 m
- North-East Siberian Mountains (Russia) 3 147 m, Mt. Pobeda
- Far-North-Eastern Mountains (Russia) 2 562 m, Mt. Ledianaya

II Caucasus

- Greater and northern Caucasus (Russia, Kabardino Balkaria, Ossetia, Checheno-Ingushetia, Daghestan) 5 642 m Mt. Elbrus
- Transcaucasian mountains (Georgia, Armenia, Azerbaijan) 4 090 m Mt. Aragats

III. Carpathians

- (Ukraine) 2 061 m Mt. Goverla

Crimea

- (Ukraine) 1 545 Mt.Roman-Kosh

IV. Soviet Central Asia and Khazakhstan

- Island mountains of Kyzylkum desert (Turkmenia) 920 m
- Balkhans and Kopet Dag (Turkmenia) 1 880 m Mt. Arlan, 2 912 m Mt. Shakhshakh
- Saur and Tarbagatai (Kazakhstan) 3 816 m Mt. Muztau, 2 992 m Mt. Tastau
- Low hills of Central Kazakhstan (Kazakhstan) 1 566 m Mt. Kyzyltas
- Manghyshlak upland (Kazakhstan) 556 m Mt. Besshoky
- Jungar Alatau (Kazakhstan) 442 m Mt. Besbaskal
- Tien Shan (Kyrghyzstan, Kazakhstan, Uzbekistan) 7437 m Mt. Pobedy
- Hissar Alai (Uzbekistan, Tajikistan, Kyrghyzstan) 5621 m
- South-Western Pamir-Alai (Tajikistan)
- Pamir (Tajikistan) 7 469 m Mt. Peak Kommunizma

V. Alta-Sayans

- Salair Kriazh and Kuznetskiy Alatau (Russia) 2 178 m
- Altai (Russia) 4 173 m Mt. Munku-Sardyk
- Mountains of Tuva (Russia) 3 970 m Mt. Mongun-Taiga

VI. Mountains of eastern Siberia and the Far East (Russia)

- Yenisei and Angara Kriazh 1 104 m
- Mountains of Baikal Area 2 758 m Khangarul Ridge
- Mountains of Southern and Eastern Transbaikal Area 2 519 m Mt. Barun-Shabartuy
- Baikal-Stanovaya Area, 2 999 m Mt. Kodara
- Okhotsk Sea Area 2 889 m Yudomskiy Ridge
- Amur Area Mountains 2 384 m Taikanskiy Ridge
- Sikhachi-Alin 2 077 m Mt.Tardoki-Yani
- Sakhalin Mountains 1 609 m Mt.Lopatin
- Kamchatka 4 750 m Mt.Kliuchevskaya Sopka
- Kuril islands 2 339 m Alaid Volcano

VII. Urals (Russia)

- Polar Urals 1 895 m Mt.Narodnaya
- Middle Urals 724 m
- South Urals 1 640 m Mt.Yamantau
- Mugojary 657 m.

Appendix 3

Population and indigenous peoples in mountain regions

Region and indigenous nationality	Total population of the indigenous nationality (thousands)	Persons living within their national administration unit (thousands)	Persons living in mountain areas (thousands)
HIGH-LATITUDE MOUNTAINS			
Komi	345	292	5.0
Nenets	35	30	1.0
Dolgan	6.9	4.9	1.0
Nganasan	1.3	-	0.3
Enets	0.2	-	0.2
CARPATHIANS, CRIMEA			
Karaims	2.6		
Krymchak	1.4		
Crimean Tatars	272		
Ukrainians		-	860
SOVIET CENTRAL ASIA AND KAZAKHSTAN			
Tajik	4 215	3 172	2 690
Kyrghyz	2 529	2 230	2 230
Kazakh	8 136	6 535	634
Uzbek	16 698	14 142	1 300
Turkmen	2 729	2 537	37
URALS			
Bashkir	1 449	864	195
Tatar			200
Chuvash			25.4
Komi-Permiak	152	95	11
Khanty	23	12	0.4
Mansi	8.5	6.6	0.2
Nenets	35	30	1.0
ALTAI, SAYANS			
Altai	71	59	59
Tofalar	20.0		2.0
Tuva	207	198	198
Khakas	80	63	63
Shorets	17		17
Kazakh			8.7

Population and indigenous peoples in mountain regions

Region and indigenous nationality	Total population of the indigenous nationality (thousands)	Persons living within their national administration unit (thousands)	Persons living in mountain areas (thousands)
CAUCASUS			
Georgian	3981	387	1628
Abkhaz	105	93	47.4
Ossetian	598	400	160
Armenian	4623	3084	3084
Azerbaijan	6770	5805	1150
Takysh	22		22
Tat	31		31
Kurd	153		153
Adyghei	125	95	17
Mountain Jew	19		19
Abazin	34		
Avar	601	496	290
Agul	19	14	
Balkars	85	71	60
Darghin	365	280	
Ingush	237	164	66
Kabardin	391	363	80
Karachai	156	129	120
Lak	118	92	
Lezghin	466	204	
Persian	40		
Rutul	20	15	
Tabasaran	98	78	
Tsagur	20	5	
Circassian	52	40	20
Chechen	957	735	290

Population and indigenous peoples in mountain regions

Region and indigenous nationality	Total population of the indigenous nationality (thousands)	Persons living within their national administration unit (thousands)	Persons living in mountain areas (thousands)
SIBERIA, FAR EAST			
Buriat	421	341	140
Khalkha-Mongols	3.0		
Yakut	382	365	47.0
Aleut	0.7		0.4
Itelmen	2.5		
Ket	1.1		
Koriak	9.2	6.6	4.0
Nanaets	12		3.6
Negidalets	0.6		
Nivkh	4.6		1.8
Orok	0.2		0.06
Oroch	0.9		0.3
Selkun	3.6		
Udeghei	3.2		1.0
Ulcha	23		7.0
Chuvan	1.5		
Chukcha	15	12	10.8
Evenk	30	3	0.3
Even	17		10.2
Eskimo	1.7		1.5
Udin	8.0		3.2

8

The Appalachians of North America:
marginal in the midst of plenty

Classical Appalachian countryside: arctic flora left from the Ice Ages is frequently found near the summits

Introduction

This part of the Global Report is about the Appalachian Mountains which dominate the eastern half of North America. The purpose is to encourage discussion on these mountains specifically, and on mountain issues generally.

Most mountain systems are isolated from major population centres and from significant industrial growth. The Appalachians are not. Surrounded by more than half the population and two-thirds of the industry of North America, the Appalachians have experienced in full force the impact of Homo sapiens on a mountain ecosystem. But despite major environmental stresses, the Appalachians have not been domesticated as has the rest of the eastern part of the continent. Their ecology has rebounded, and continues to diversify as the contemporary inhabitants of the Appalachian region seek new ways to integrate conservation and development needs.

Because the natural history, cultural heritage, and historical development of the Appalachian Mountains have been well documented, the region may provide an historical model for other mountain ranges currently undergoing environmental and cultural change. It is within this context of environmental and social change that we describe the Appalachian Mountains, their physical environment, natural resources, cultural setting, and the past and present trends in development. And the Appalachians, it should be noted, are one of the few examples worldwide of a post-development mountain system.

The Appalachians in outline

The Appalachian Mountains stretch as a range 2 600 km from the St Lawrence River of Canada southwestward to Georgia and Alabama in the USA, covering 18 degrees of latitude–nearly the entire east coast of North America. This physical barrier exercised a dramatic affect on nearly everything but the continental glaciers that ground over the northern section before retreating 12 000 years ago. This impact of the Appalachians plays a central role in the biological differentiation of the eastern United States; they are a pivotal influence on the weather experienced not only within the mountains but also throughout the east coast of the continent; they have a historic role in the settlement of both Native American populations and the ecologically much more disruptive European populations; and, finally, they may serve to demonstrate how a mountain ecosystem can recover after ecological and developmental trauma.

Biogeography

Biologically, the Appalachian Mountains are the primary determinant of the ecology of eastern North America. These mountains are central to shaping weather patterns, generating large areas of heavy precipitation on the west and rainshadows on the east. Low human population density and less accessible terrain allow the mountains to remain predominantly forested, serving as a significant refuge for a diversity of natural flora and fauna adjacent to an increasingly domesticated half of the continent. The ecological diversity preserved by the mosaic of habitats in the mountains creates a biological species variety not present elsewhere in temperate North America.

The relict ridge-top tundra of the northern Appalachians and ridge-top spruce-fir forest of the central and southern areas are today's reminder of the glacial tundra and dark blanket of boreal forest that retreated slowly northward with the glacial ice. This boreal mix, today called the Appalachian Extension, still ties the Appalachians biologically not just to Canada but also to the northern ranges of Asia and Europe. Following the retreating spruce came the warmer, lighter green, and ecologically richer hardwood forests that are familiar today, with mesic (moist land) mixtures of great variety on the wetter western slopes and xeric (dry land) mixtures on the drier eastern slopes. The highly varied geology of the range–predominantly sedimentary to the south, becoming igneous and metamorphic to the north–combines with precipitation, temperature and slope to allow a rich variety of habitats. Ecologically the Appalachians are one of the most diverse areas in the global Temperate Zone. At the southern end the Great Smokies section alone possesses a greater species mix than any other American area north of the tropics.

Settlement

The influence on humans of the mountains arose from the way the barrier slowed down the Native American migration eastward during the Paleo,

Archaic and Woodland phases just as it later slowed European movement in the opposite direction. Extensive Native American communities developed much earlier in the western Mississippi Valley than along the east coast. Once eastward penetration was achieved and migration began, these early Americans used the mountains intermittently and variably as the climate and their cultural development permitted. The dominant groups rarely inhabited the rougher sections unless forced to by another group–thus presaging Euro-American use and settlement of these mountains.

Initial European exploration of North America occurred in the early 1600s with the Dutch trading up the Hudson River for fur, the English settling farmland north in New England and south in Virginia, and the French circling the north end of the Appalachians via the St Lawrence River and the Great Lakes for fur trading. Dutch traders going up the Hudson and Mohawk Rivers very early bisected the Appalachians almost exactly where geographers would later divide the northern and central-southern sections. The boundaries drawn early on by the fur trade dictated European penetration of the mountains for a century or more until European disease and technology overwhelmed Native American populations beyond the Allegheny Front. The French traded down the western flank of the mountains into the midwest, forming alliances with the Iroquois Confederacy, alliances that would eventually plague the English settlers headed west, ending in the French and Indian War. Then European, mainly English and Scotch-Irish settlers, invaded the central-southern Appalachians and made the land their own. In the northern Appalachians less organized tribes sometimes survived but were pinched between the French in the north and the English in the south and had no opportunity for refuge in the cold peaks of the Whites, Greens, or Adirondacks. However, near Katahdin in Maine, the Passamaquoddy and Penobscot Tribes managed to hold on to an existence in the spruce woods.

Resource extraction

Resource exploitation began in the northern Appalachians where there was more effective access from the coast on both sides of the mountain range, the French northward, the English southward, and where easy river access up the Hudson and Connecticut Rivers allowed better interior access. In the northern region central Maine and the heart of the Adirondacks remained relatively untouched until the late 1800s.

The resources of the central and southern Appalachians far exceeded, in economic value, the resources of the northern section; but these resources were low in value without the organizational, financial, and technical resources required to extract them. During the early 1800s coastal forest resources dwindled, while population was augmented by on-going immigration from Europe, and the technology of the Industrial Revolution developed. Then in the mid-1800s the remaining northern spruce forests, Katahdin and the Adirondacks, were entered with dam-building technology allowing river transport for the timber. New railroad technology brought development to the Pennsylvania coalfields. In 1852 the eastern seaboard became linked with Ohio. Finally, in 1874, a mainline railroad was built over the rugged Allegheny Front from Virginia to Ohio, opening up the heart of what became known as Appalachia. The age of resource extraction developed quickly and boomed for only forty years before beginning a steady decline that is either continuing or stable today depending on how it is measured. Where logging operations cut and moved on, often with massive fire in their wake, the land was almost without value. The lower slopes were usually settled and the higher slopes tended to eventually come under government reclamation as National Forest or state preserves. In a few cases extreme inaccessibility or a surveyor's mistake left old-growth forest standing.

Environmental resilience to the extraction period has been uneven but sometimes remarkably good in this temperate climate, though few areas have recovered their climax communities, and the massive fires after the logging changed the biology of some areas dramatically. Logging continues but on a localized scale. The disruptive impact still goes on as coal mining also continues as a widespread industry, utilizing strip-mining technology which disrupts large areas and requires a smaller workforce than before. Newer environmental problems are becoming apparent and, while not as immediately dramatic as mass logging or mining, may be more pervasive. Atmospheric pollution, including acid rain and heavy metal deposition, reaches every part of the biosphere from twig end to root tip, from eagles to soil bacteria and permeates the chemical reactions of life. Widespread chemical application to forest and farm, including pesticide, herbicide and fertilizer, is deeply implicated in runoff into Appalachian rivers and groundwater, and results in contamin ation of human water supplies in the mountains and downriver in the lowlands. In some local areas, acid mine drainage poses an additional problem.

Cultural development

The culture of the Appalachians developed with some common threads and, depending on the catharsis of change experienced, with some different results. In a dominantly agricultural society, people who settle mountains accept: second choice in land; frugality of lifestyle; and isolation from outside contact. As a result, from the north through the south in the Appalachians, agricultural cultures predominated with farm families cobbling together subsistence livelihoods through a combination of seasonal opportunities rather than any single livelihood. These might include cropping, herding, hunting and gathering, logging, trapping for fur, and distillation of whiskey from cropped grain. Fur and whiskey were the earliest value-added cash crops from the mountains, more easily transported to markets than lumber or coal. Indeed, the sale of Appalachian whiskey was so successful that it sparked the first non-Native American challenge to the authority of George Washington's fledgling United States government, when Pennsylvania mountain farmers challenged the excise tax on their main cash crop in the Whiskey Rebellion. The federal government prevailed but affirmed in the mountain people a hostility to government that persists to this day through much of the Appalachian range.

Appalachian culture was initially not unlike the rural culture of the lowlands where it originated. After several generations, however, isolation fostered both independent development and insulation from the changes of the lowlands. A relationship developed between Appalachian people and the land and forest that was nurturing in both economic and emotional ways. Given the knowledge the people developed of how to utilize the land, with minimal cash income a farm family could carve out a livelihood. The timber and coal extraction era of the late 1800s and early 1900s broke this isolation for a while, but by then the culture for the most part was entrenched. Even today from New England through the southern Appalachians–outside the coalfields –farming, frugality, and multiple small-scale income sources are cultural traditions.

Mechanical coal extraction, early 1900s

The coalfield experience during the extraction period was different, and the trauma that occurred to both the people and the land lasts to this day. The land and forest became not nurturing but threatening. Where logging camps came and left, coal camps came and stayed; where the settlement of forests and farmland was gradual, the settlement of coal camps was a sudden and massive influx of workers. Pennsylvania coalfield development occurred before the Civil War on what became Union territory. Coalfield development southward, in West Virginia, Kentucky and Tennessee, occurred after the Civil War in what had been Confederate territory.

In the southern fields the coal developers were mostly northerners with finance, technology and legal sophistication behind them. There land ownership was a mix of large patents dating from the Revolutionary War plus land held by southerners desperately impoverished by the Civil War, individuals often having little appreciation of the implications of the technology or of legal manoeuvring. Control of the land and resources shifted even further to large holdings which were controlled by corporations, and they increasingly exercised this control from outside the coalfields. Coal towns were populated primarily by immigrants from Europe and the eastern United States, largely from the still depressed south. This workforce spent long days working under dangerous conditions with lives oriented by, and family economics frequently controlled by, the mining companies. The coal miner's life was hardly the independent yeoman's existence of the nearby areas. Housing was normally set on steep hillsides or in narrow valleys near the mines where instability or flooding were common. In these areas the industrial operations of mining (mainly coking) polluted the soil, air and water.

A mine family's interaction with the land and forest (contrasted with the farmer's) was frequently negative. The focus of a miner's life was within the rhythms of an industrial operation that responded to a national economy, not the farmer's rhythms of sun and season that were buffered by their greater self-sufficiency from the boom and bust of the national economy. By economic measure the miner earned much more than the farmer, but the miner's overhead expenses were far higher, his life's options fewer, and his job security lower. The miner's answer to this outside control was to form unions to confront the companies; and even today, in an overall Appalachian culture of independent, stubborn people, unions are found mostly only in the coalfields from Pennsylvania to Kentucky.

Economic development

Economic development after the extraction period has been uneven for most of the Appalachian range and to a great extent has been a function of the relationship between the mountains and the lowlands, where dense settlement, intense development and financial power are more characteristic. The relationship is one of interdependence, but the greater power is invested in lowland culture, both overt, as in political and financial power, and indirect as in better formal education and access to information. The mountain realm has become for the lowlands a useful extension, a place to gain raw materials, find cheap labour, seek recreation, and most recently to dump garbage. Today resource extraction, mainly coal, oil and gas, and timber, represents the economic base of part of the range. Manufacturing and tourism have become the main economic base of most of the rest. The current national shift from manufacturing to a service economy means a net loss of jobs in these mountain areas. Agriculture, once universal through the Appalachians, is currently unimportant in formal economic measures but remains a critical part of the informal economy and, possibly more important, of the economic and emotional buffer of the culture in the face of broader economic boom-bust cycles.

Improved roads and widespread broadcast reception, especially through satellite TV, have substantially lowered the feeling of isolation in the mountains and raised the question of to what extent economic development is compatible with cultural preservation. Mountain people, in common with most people, want better lives. Now, their attempts to define what "better" means are heavily influenced by the consumer-oriented society surrounding them and the temptation of higher wages in jobs away from their land.

Meanwhile, land values in many areas have increased, sometimes dramatically, in response to tourism and recreation. A few benefit in the short term, but absentee ownership and control have increased. Many people in mountain communities can no longer afford even land for housing. This slow subtraction of land from the cultural equation invites further dissolution of the traditional relationship. Cultural resilience becomes lowered in a way analogous to lowered environmental resilience in the face of atmospheric pollution.

In conclusion, despite all the changes now affecting the Appalachian Mountains, perhaps their dominant feature is their resilience. Environmentally, the Appalachians have been assaulted by agriculture, by timberin, and by mining. Despite major soil erosion in some regions, typically less than one hundred years after this assault the mountains recover with remarkable vigour. Culturally there is also remarkable resilience. In a continent that has absorbed wave after wave of migrant peoples and melded diverse cultures into an American culture, the Appalachian culture remains surprisingly distinct and intact, a cohesive culture surrounded by the enormous population, dynamism and economic pressures of the East Coast of the USA. How long the biology of these mountains or the culture of their peoples can continue to be so resilient is a major question given the new and perhaps more pervasive impacts of influences now entering these mountains. ■

Questions raised in the global context

As a mountain range within a highly industrialized region, and as a range in which environmental and social changes have been extensively documented, the Appalachian Mountains experience offers lessons relevant to conservation and development initiatives within the range in addition to parallels to post-development forces at work in other ranges of our world. The following points are advanced not as conclusions but as the basis for a longer-term Appalachian analysis:

1) The Appalachians are a mountain range with a 200 plus year history of wholesale resource (renewable and non-renewable) extraction by outside interests with little regard for environmental and social impacts or for the future. Most of the profits from this resource extraction were removed from the mountain communities and little was replaced in the way of physical and social infra structure. Are the Appalachians a useful case study for "development" based on resource extraction currently taking place in other regions of the world?

a) By and large the Appalachian Mountains are recovering without the assistance of large-scale reforestation projects and systematic land use management. Is such natural recovery possible only in wet, temperate environments? And further, what is the relationship between recovery and soil erosion?

b) Coal mining has resulted in severe environmental degradation (deforestation, soil erosion, acid mine runoff, valley flooding, and the presence of unstable slag heaps and sludge ponds). Mining also caused extreme socio-economic hardship for local and migrant communities during the 20th century. Is this a parallel for intensive extractive development in other mountain regions?

c) The Appalachian Mountains are a region in which present environmental problems are related primarily to pollution from extraction and poor agricultural practice and only secondarily to internal population pressure. Is the absence of population-driven problems characteristic or atypical with regard to other mountain ranges?

2) Social and environmental problems within the Appalachians have been and are being

addressed almost solely by federal and state agencies. Nonprofit organizations such as churches, clubs, institutes and universities have had a relatively small impact compared with their role in the rest of the United States. How does this diminished private sector role parallel the experience of other mountain regions?

a) The Tennessee Valley Authority (TVA) and the Appalachian Regional Commission (ARC) have conducted what may be two of the largest and most expensive integrated, centrally funded development projects ever undertaken in any mountain range in the world. What have been the results of these large-scale projects? And should these projects be imitated by agencies and organizations in other mountain ranges of the world?

3) The Appalachian socio-economic experience typically took one of two forms: either a serf-like existence within a company town, where land, housing, commerce, work and opportunity were controlled by one economic force, the company; or an independent yeoman-like existence with agricultural families drawing on diverse skills and resources to create a livelihood. Is this bipolar experience typical for other developing mountain areas?

a) The Appalachians and its resources are owned and managed by a bewildering mosaic of absentee and local commercial interests, government agencies, small landowners, and nonprofit organizations. How do these outside land ownership and resource management patterns affect the design and direction of local development projects?

b) The Appalachians contain abundant renewable and non-renewable natural resources such as water, petroleum, timber and coal. Is this resource base capable of sustaining a standard of living characteristic of the rest of the continent? What are the limits to growth in the Appalachians?

4) After initial isolation, the mountains, mountain people, and mountain resources have been developed mostly by forces from the surrounding lowland areas, becoming a well-used extension of the nearby industrial and population centres. What is the real cost mountain communities and environments must pay for the growth and maintenance of adjacent lowland society?

a) Tourism is the most rapidly growing industry in the Appalachian Mountains; and tourism is often promoted as a means of diversifying mountain economies and providing employment. How should this recreational utilization of the mountains by surrounding society be guided? Who should own and manage these industries?

b) The lower population densities and open land in the Appalachians have begun to attract the attention of hazardous, commercial, and residential waste management interests in the industrialized areas near the mountains. Can waste dumping in the Appalachians coexist over the long term with other uses such as recreation, water supply, lumbering, and farming?

c) The Appalachian mountain communities and the adjoining more densely populated areas have historically been perceived and functioned as a "world apart", with cultural isolation enforced by both physical and perceptual barriers. Is this separation a typical experience for mountain communities elsewhere? What are the consequences for Appalachian culture as these barriers drop and isolation recedes?

d) The Native American populations of the Appalachian region either died from warfare and disease or were removed or restricted to reservations as a result of European immigration. Many of their Euro-American successors later also faced loss of autonomy and self-reliance when their largely agricultural way of life was disrupted by an economy based on large-scale resource extraction controlled by outside interests. Is this pattern of one group supplanting a previous group typical in other mountain ranges? ■

Physical and cultural profile of the Appalachian Mountains

Physiographic, political and cultural divisions

The Appalachian Mountains span 2 600 km as a great barrier chain that parallels the east coast of the North American continent. Geologically, the Appalachians can be traced around the North Atlantic to a geologic unity with the hills of Iceland, Scotland and Ireland. Culturally, this link across the oceans was also made later when the Scotch-Irish played a large role in the Appalachian settlement.

The Appalachian Mountains, as with all mountain belts, are divided into regions in order to clarify physical and cultural diversity, and for planning purposes. These include geographic and political versions, as well as cultural perceptions.

The most generalized, a geographer's definition, is a *physiographic system* dividing the Appalachian Mountains into northern, central and southern regions (Figure 8.1). The northern Appalachians lie in northern New York State, New England and along the St Lawrence River in Canada. The central Appalachians lie from southern New York State to an imaginary line which trends due west at latitude N 38 degrees (south of Washington, DC). The highest mountain in the central Appalachians is the 1 482 metre Spruce Knob in West Virginia. The southern boundary of the southern Appalachians lies within Georgia and

Figure 8.1: *Physiographic divisions of Appalachia.*
Source: Raitz and Ulack, 1984; *National Atlas of the US*, 1970

1) Laurentian Mountains
2) Notre Dame Mountains
3) Katahdin Mountains
4) White Mountains
5) Green Mountains
6) Adirondack Mountains
7) Taconic Mountains
8) Catskill Mountains
9) Reading Prong

Appalachian Plateau
consisting of:
10) Glaciated section,
11) Conemaugh section,
12) Kanawha section.
13) Cumberland Section,

14) Ridge and Valley
15) Blue Ridge Mountains

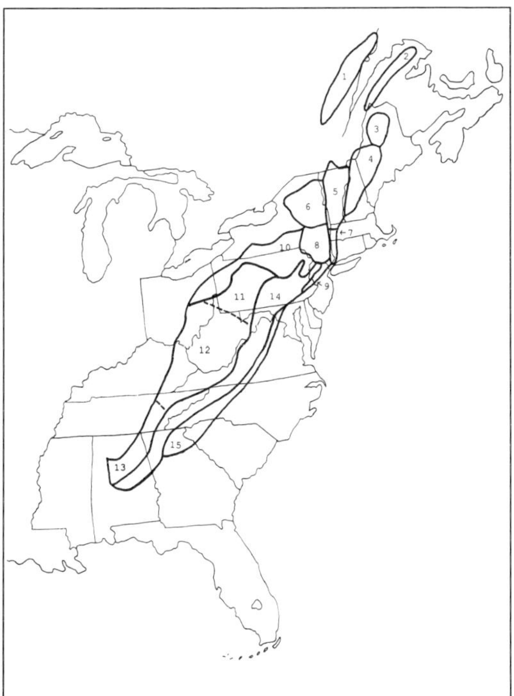

Figure 8.2: *Appalachia as defined by the Appalachian Regional Commission.*
Source: Guiness and Bradshaw, 1985

Alabama where the mountains meet the coastal plains of southeastern North America. The highest peak of the entire Appalachian Mountains, Mt. Mitchell (2 037 m), lies near the southern end. Mountains included are the southern Allegheny Mountains in the east and the southern Allegheny Plateau (locally, the Cumberland Plateau) in the west.

The central and southern Appalachian Mountains are further subdivided into several *physiographic regions* or "provinces". These provinces are, from west to east,

1) the Appalachian Plateau
2) the Ridge and Valley
3) the Blue Ridge, and
4) the Piedmont, an associated area sometimes included (Figure 8.1).

The Appalachian Plateau Province is an uplifted plateau dissected by deep river valleys lying to the west from New York to Georgia.

The Ridge and Valley Province lies east of the plateau, starting with the high backbone of the Allegheny Front. It extends from southern New York to northern Georgia and is characterized by a trellis drainage of northeast-southwest trending valleys and ridges whose orientations have been determined by the structure of the underlying folded and faulted sedimentary rocks.

The Blue Ridge Province is a range of mountains stretching from southern Pennsylvania to northern Georgia and standing out in clear relief between the Piedmont to the east and the Great Valley to the west.

The Piedmont ("foothill") Province is a region characterized by flat to rolling uplands, which lie between the coastal floodplains of the eastern United States and the rugged mountains of the Blue Ridge.

Appalachia, as a *political designation* (Appalachian Regional Commission; Raitz and Ulack, 1984), is the area starting in the north with two counties of the Allegheny Plateau in western New York, and stretching southward through the central and southern physiographic regions on into surrounding lowlands of Mississippi in the southwest and the Piedmont along the southeast flank (Figure 8.2). The Appalachian Mountains as a *cultural,* or *local,* definition of region is sometimes ill-defined or conflicting in its boundaries. Some generalizations are appropriate to understanding the Appalachian range and the people who live in the mountains.

In the northern Appalachians the major cultural definitions coincide with the mountain ranges because of the dividing rivers or lowlands. Moving southward the Catskill Mountains of southeast New York are geographically isolated by the Hudson, Susquahanna and Delaware Rivers and are locally distinct. Westward and southward of the Catskills the cultural boundaries are less easily defined and seem to be based on distance on the north-south axis (along the ridges) and geography on the east-west axis (across the ridges).

Also used are the terms north, central, and south Appalachians to refer to general areas of the entire range. There is, in this case, no relation to physiographic provinces.

Statistics about and references to "Appalachia" are sometimes difficult to compare because of the different definitions used for that region. Only valid comparisons have been attempted here.

Geology and geomorphology of the Appalachian mountain range

Geology

The physiographic provinces of the Appalachian mountain range have been determined primarily by the geologic history of the region, including both the Paleozoic, Mesozoic and Cenozoic tectonic history of the Appalachian mountain belt, and the Pleistocene and Holocene glacial and post-glacial history.

The present-day geological structure of the Appalachian Mountains is the result of three continental collision events that occurred during the Paleozoic era, between 570 and 245 million years ago: the Acadian, Taconian and Appalachian orogenies (mountain-building events). Most of the New England and Canadian region of the northern Appalachians is underlain by metamorphic and igneous rocks of primarily Precambrian to Middle Paleozoic age, including the granites of the Adirondack, Green and White Mountains, and the slates of the Green Mountains (Figure 8.3). This "Appalachian" metamorphic and igneous belt can be traced through the Blue Ridge Province to northern Georgia and eastern Alabama

(Figure 8.3). This belt extends eastward into the Piedmont. Motion along a fault between the Piedmont and the Blue Ridge mountains is responsible for the Blue Ridge Front which divides the two regions (Figure 8.3).

West of the Blue Ridge mountains lies the inner fold and thrust belt of the Ridge and Valley Province. The rocks of this region are sedimentary rocks of Paleozoic age. Differential resistance to erosion between the different types of layered sedimentary rocks within the fold and thrust belt is responsible for the "Ridge and Valley" character of this province. In some regions (e.g. the Grandfather Mountain region of North Carolina) metamorphic rocks of the Blue Ridge Province have been thrust over the sedimentary rocks of the Ridge and Valley Province, and erosion through the overlying metamorphic rocks has resulted in tectonic windows. Differential erosion of the metamorphic and sedimentary rocks in these regions has resulted in the formation of valleys known locally as "coves".

West of the inner fold and thrust belt of the Ridge and Valley Province, and south of the Adirondacks metamorphic complex, lie the Allegheny and Cumberland Plateaus. Together they form the Appalachian Plateau, which is underlain by gently folded and faulted Paleozoic platform sediments deposited on the eastern margin of the North American crust during the Paleozoic era. These Paleozoic sedimentary sequences include the coal-bearing strata of the Pennsylvanian period (approximately 320 to 285 million years ago) and the oil and gas-rich strata of the Eastern Overthrust Belt in the Allegheny Plateau.

Stretching of the North American continental crust, associated with the opening of the Atlantic Ocean during the Triassic period, resulted

Figure 8.3: *Geology of the Appalachian Mountains.*
Source: *National Atlas of the US*,1970

1) Quaternary
2) Tertiary and Cretaceous
3) Jurassic and Triassic
4) Upper Paleozoic
5) Middle Paleozoic
6) Lower Paleozoic
7) Precambrian

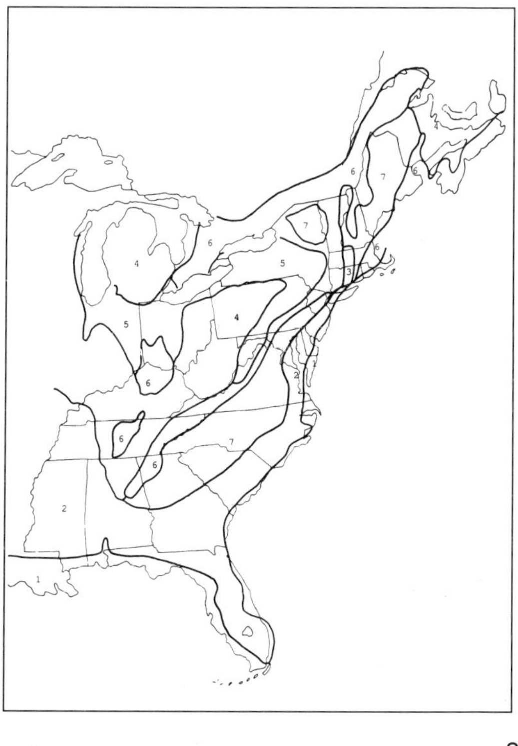

Figure 8:4: *Limit of continental glaciation.*
Source: *National Atlas of the US*, 1970

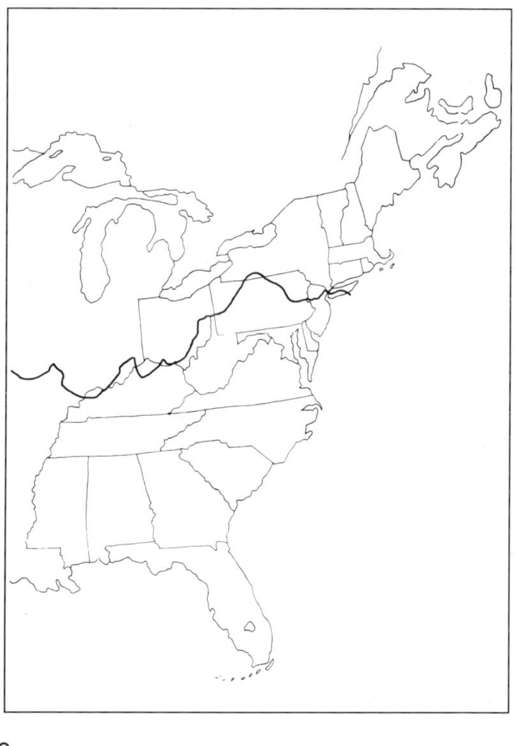

in the formation of fault-bounded grabens, or depressions, which were filled with sedimentary rocks. The St Lawrence, Hudson and Connecticut River valleys of the northern Appalachians have formed along these depressions.

Geomorphology

The most striking geomorphological division within the Appalachian mountain range is that between glaciated and non-glaciated regions. Between approximately 500 000 and 10 000 years ago much of the North American continent was covered with ice sheets up to one mile thick. At the southern margins of the various ice sheets that advanced during the Pleistocene, large terminal moraines were deposited. The Ohio River marks the approximate southern limit of ice in the west.

One result of the Pleistocene glaciation is that the geomorphology of the northern Appalachians is strikingly different from that of the central and southern Appalachians. The northern Appalachians are characterized by glacially carved mountains and valleys: mountains and mountain ranges are generally rounded and oriented in a north-south direction (the direction of advance and retreat of the glaciers), and the valleys generally display the classic U-shape of glacially carved regions. Cirques or cwms are also present. The lowlands of the northern Appalachians often have a hummocky nature due to underlying glacial sediments deposited during the retreat of the glaciers. This hummocky landscape, along with the high clay content of the glacial sediments, is responsible for the numerous low-lying wetlands found in the northern Appalachians.

Another characteristic geomorphological feature of the northern Appalachians is the presence of numerous lakes which are now an important part of the tourist industry in the northern Appalachians.

South of the limit of glaciation the geomorphological character of the Appalachians has been defined by the action of water on a geologically highly varied landscape. The different erosion-resistant properties of the metamorphic rocks of the Blue Ridge Province and sedimentary rocks of the Ridge and Valley Province are responsible for the present northeast-southwest orientations of ridges and valleys throughout the rest of the Appalachians.

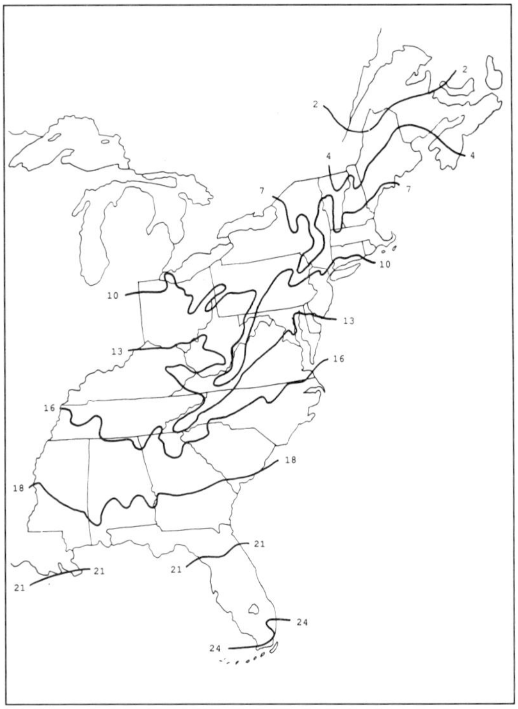

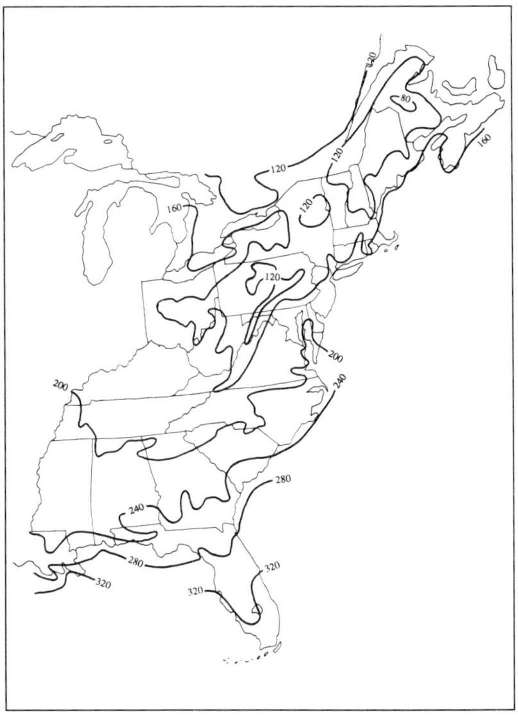

Climate

As a result of its northeast-southwest orientation and its topographic relief, the Appalachian mountain range displays great climatic variation. Between northern Alabama (USA) and the St Lawrence River (Canada), the Appalachian Mountains span almost 18 degrees of latitude. Average annual temperatures range from 18 degrees Celsius (C) in the highlands of Alabama to 4 degrees C in the Katahdin and 2 degrees C in the Notre Dame Mountains (Figure 8.5). Average January temperatures range from 7 degrees C in northern Alabama and Georgia to only minus 23 degrees C in the far north. Of greater importance to agriculture is the variation in the growing season, or the average number of frost-free days between the last frost in the spring and the first frost in the fall. The growing season varies from 210 days in the highlands of northeast Alabama to less than 90 days in the mountains of the northern Appalachians (Figure 8.6).

Figure 8.5: *Average annual temperature.*
Source: *The Weather Handbook*, 1963

Figure 8.6: *Average frost-free period.*
Source: *The Weather Handbook*, 1963

Figure 8.7: *Average Annual Precipitation.*
Source: *The Weather Handbook*, 1963

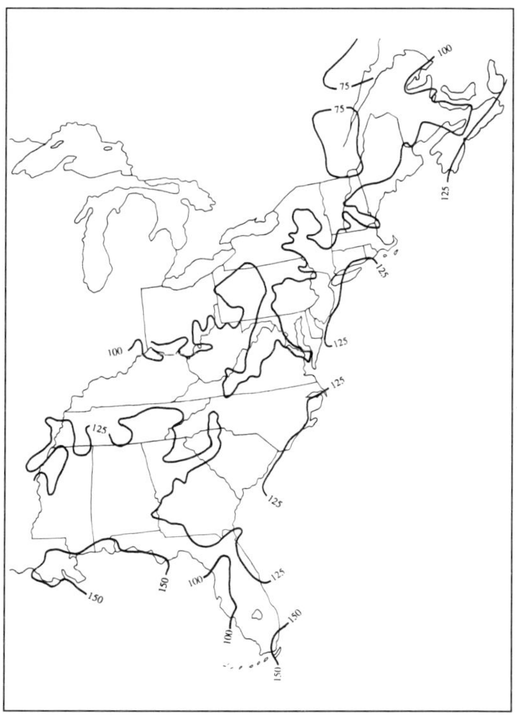

The Appalachian Mountains are blessed with a fairly abundant and constant precipitation as either rainfall or snow, which is evenly spaced throughout the year. Average annual precipitation ranges from about 70 to 170 cm per year, showing a decrease to the west across the Allegheny Plateau and to the north up to the Adirondacks. Local variations can be dramatic, however, because of the rainshadow effect caused by the high ridges of the Ridge and Valley. Pickens, West Virginia, receives over 260 cm annually while Upper Tract, West Virginia, 80 km east, receives about 84 cm. Spruce Knob, highest of the Ridge and Valley peaks, lies between the two places.

The Adirondacks and the ranges through New England to the Notre Dame Mountains of Canada endure a combination of precipitation from the Great Lakes (the "lake effect"), the tendency of North American continental weather patterns to funnel through the northeast, and proximity to the Atlantic Ocean on the south. Local humour revolves around how fast the weather changes, the prevalence of fog, and the accumulation of snow.

Winters in the northern Appalachians are significantly more severe than those of the central and southern Appalachians. While virtually none of the precipitation in the valleys of the far southern Appalachians occurs as snow, in the mountains of the northern Appalachians annual snowfall averages of over 300 cm are common, and peaks of over 600 cm annually occur at Tug Hill on the west of the Adirondacks and in Quebec west of the Notre Dames, both attributed to lake effect. While the severe winters of the northern Appalachians make for a shorter growing season, they are also responsible for the booming ski industry of the Green and White Mountains of Vermont and New Hampshire. Snowfall along the Blue Ridge of North Carolina in the southern Appalachians is only 36 cm per year. However, despite low annual snowfalls, there is a developing ski industry in the

Ridge and Valley supported by artificial snow-making equipment and cold winters.

Variability, mentioned above in relation to northeastern weather, is also a characteristic of weather southward along the mountains, though it does not appear as clearly in charts as it is experienced by mountain dwellers. Mountains are the playground of weather systems. The Appalachian Mountains bear the interplay of cold, dry Arctic air from the north and warm, moist ocean air from the south, intermixed with a prevailing weatherstream from the west. The prevailing westerly weatherstream brings the midwestern pollution stream through the ranges as well, with increasingly severe consequences to forest and human communities over the years.

While tropical storms (e.g. hurricanes) rarely reach into the Appalachian Mountains, when they do they may result in extremely heavy rains which, in turn, may cause floods, landslides and debris avalanches.

Biogeography

The geologic, geographic and climatic variables discussed above through 2 600 km of the Appalachian Mountains from Alabama (USA) to Quebec (Canada) generate a great mosaic of habitats. Factors determining specific habitats and their biotic communities are numerous and sometimes quite subtle. Their interplay is very complex and in many aspects still poorly understood. This constant, slow interplay continues and changes through time. All through the mountains as glaciers come and retreat, erosion wears away the land, and climate changes. The southern half of the Appalachians were likely to have been tundra, while the northern ranges were under ice (Strausbaugh and Core 1970). The tundra retreated slowly northward with the ice, followed by a dark green wave of spruce forest, and finally by the hardwood forest communities more familiar to us today. Relict colonies exist in West Virginia, North Carolina and elsewhere consisting of Canadian plant associations assumed to have been left behind with the retreat of last glaciers (ibid.). Some examples are Cranberry Glades, a rare West Virginia bog-like habitat; Ice Mountain, a West Virginia sandstone cliff where ice persists into and sometimes through the summer, supporting several Canadian plants; and possibly the ridge-top spruce and heath communities that exist as far south as North Carolina.

Biogeographical changes up to 1600 (before Euro-American settlement) normally occurred very slowly, over millennia. Catastrophic fire may have played a significant role in coniferous forests, where dead needles are held on the tree for a time in many species, and crown fires spread in the tight stands. In hardwood forests fire was not considered to be a major factor but rather a very localized one (Shelford, 1963).

Biogeography in the mountain environment is thought not to have been significantly affected by Native Americans with the possible exception of the grass "balds" and heaths discussed below. Euro-American settlement and a new level of tool technology brought changes at a much swifter pace starting in 1700s. Changes really gained momentum in the 1800s. First impact was on the Canadian and New England ranges, where the mountains are closer to the coast, river access is more immediate, and a burgeoning industrial economy needed fuel and material. Further south the forests of the broad coastal plain and Piedmont, and the agricultural economy buffered the mountain forests a few years longer. In 1852 the Pennsylvania coalfields were reached by a railroad, which was pushed on west to Ohio. By the mid-1800s, the blast furnaces of western Virginia's iron mines had depleted the available forests for charcoal, railroad technology had advanced enough to consider building on across the mountains via the New River to the Ohio River, and the more efficient band sawmill had been developed. In the 1870s simultaneous wholesale logging and coalfield development began in the central and southern mountains, a little later than in the Pennsylvania fields. The forests were said to be growing faster than they could be cut, but in little over a generation there were only remnants left: a surveyor's mistake at Gaudeneer, West Virginia; some inaccessible coves that became Great Smokey Mountains National Park in North Carolina; and a few others (Clarkson 1964). The chestnut blight, discussed below, was introduced by Euro-American activity and wiped out the dominant tree of a widespread forest community during the early 1900s.

Forest communities develop through successive seres (sequential developments of groups of plants at the same place over a period of time). Within a particular climax region, all seres on different habitats converge into the same general climax community given enough time (Shelford, 1963). Thus maple-beech forests are found on soils ranging from limestone, granite and shale to sand and peat. Much of our Appalachian forest today is a sere of the original climax type, for instance after logging, pin cherry is common in the south and paper birch in the north.

Three major human factors affecting recent great change in Appalachian forests and specific habitats are site history, current management, and pollution (Shelford 1963, Bormann, 1982). Throughout the Appalachians the forest conditions that existed before 1600 are almost entirely gone with some biotic communities existing in remnant but incomplete form and some not at all (Shelford 1963).

Site history includes past logging, agriculture, fire and management practice including re forestation. Management can have widespread and sometimes unpredictable results, delaying sere progression toward climax community at unwanted stages that may degrade economic usefulness, ecological diversity or both. Wild animals such as squirrel and deer have been shown to have very high impact on forest regeneration, consuming in some cases nearly all a seed crop on a regular basis and browsing seedlings of preferred species to extinction. Thus managing for deer can influence forest development in major ways that are often detrimental to climax species (ibid.). Allowing domestic animals to graze in forests, traditionally an Appalachian practice, has high impact in similar ways, and has long been discouraged by the Soil Conservation Service. Except for some early selective cutting of white pine in New England for ships' masts, logging practice historically through most of the Appalachians has been to clearcut anything of economic value. Fires of heroic proportions often followed, burning out seed stock, mother trees, saplings and even soil. Reforestation efforts in the 1930s frequently used Scots pine *(P. sylvestris)* in both the north and the south of the Appalachians, a tree now considered inferior to native species for both lumber and wildlife (Little, 1980).

Current management practice mirrors the discussion under site history except that selective cutting and modified clearcutting are also now widely practised, whereas the scale of logging is small and localized.

Pollution, in a regional form such as acid rain (Figure 8.7), is increasing and can affect whole forest sections. It is being investigated for its effects on the root and foliage zones particularly of the northern coniferous forests, the resultant spruce budworm infestation of stressed trees, and death of great stretches of forest (Mello, 1987). Decline in the sugar maple forests, with resultant impact on the maple syrup industry, has been linked to acid rain.

Five separate plant-forest community types are generally recognized in the Appalachian Mountains. These communities are as follows:

1) the alpine tundra
2) the boreal forest
3) the transition forest
4) the mixed deciduous (mesophytic) forest
5) the Appalachian oak forest (Figure 8.8) (Daubenmire, 1978; Sutton and Sutton 1988).

1) The alpine tundra: Alpine tundra in the Appalachian Mountains is restricted to portions of the northern Appalachians that lie above 1 500 metres. Common plants of the alpine community, which are generally outliers of the arctic tundra, include various blueberry-cranberry shrubs (*Vaccinium*), mountain heather *(Phyllodoce caerulea)*, willows (*Salix*), and mountain alder (*Alnus viridus*). Attempts are being made to protect these high mountain regions.

2) The boreal forest: The boreal forest of the Appalachian Mountains is primarily a spruce-fir association that covers the Notre Dame Mountains in Canada and much of northern Maine, including the lowlands. The black bear and the raven are associated through most of the range. In the north the association consists of white spruce or red spruce and balsam fir *(Picea glauca, Picea rubens, Abies balsamea)*, with moose and black bear as dominant animals.

Along the Extension white spruce fades out in favour of red, and near Spruce Knob, West Virginia, the last of the balsam fir gives way to Frazer fir *(Abies fraseri)*. This southern association exists in intermittent form on peaks to Mt. Mitchell in North Carolina. Deer replace moose south of the Adirondacks. The once extensive red spruce forests of the Appalachian Extension, comprised of dense stands of large trees often one metre in diametre, have been removed. Most of that original spruce range is occupied by transition forest.

3) The transition forest: The transition forest, or the Northern Hardwoods and Spruce Forest, was originally the dominant forest type of the lower elevations in the Adirondack, Green, White and Katahdin Mountains (Figure 8.8). These forests are dominated by sugar maple (*Acer rubrum*), birch (*Betula*), American beech (*Fagus grandifolia*), balsam fir (*Abies balsamea*), balsam poplar (*Populus balsamifera*), and eastern hemlock (*Tsuga canadensis*). Red spruce at one time was also common in the transition forest. All but perhaps 5 per cent of the original forests of New England have been logged.

4) The mixed deciduous forest: The mixed deciduous, or mixed mesophytic forest covers the Allegheny and Cumberland Plateau regions from western Pennsylvania, through West Virginia to Kentucky and Tennessee (Figure 8.8). These forests include mixed stands of beech (*Fagus*), sugar maple (*Acer saccharum*), basswood (*Tilia americana*), yellow poplar or tulip tree (*Liriodendron tulipifera*), red oak (*Quercus rubra*), white oak (*Quercus alba*), hickory (*Carya*), magnolia (*Magnolia*), birch (*Betula*), and white ash (*Fraxinus americana*).

Of particular interest in the southern Appalachians are the virgin forests found in "coves", historically inaccessible valleys generally above 1 500 m. These "cove forests" were spared by the lumber industry due to their inaccessibility and were later protected in scattered regions of the central and southern Appalachians, including the Great Smokey Mountains National Park. Within these forests several species of trees from the eastern US attain record size, and some trees are as old as 500 years. These indicate the nature of the old-growth forest that once covered the western Appalachians. These forests include yellow poplar (*Liriodendron tulipifera*) up to 10 m in circumference, eastern hemlock (*Tsuga canadensis*) up to 6 m in circumference, yellow buckeye (*Aesculus octandra*) up to 5 m in circumference, yellow birch (*Betula alleghaniensis*) over five m in circumference, and sugar maple (*Acer saccharum*) up to 4.5 metres in circumference. White ash, beech and northern red oak are also of unusual size and age in these forests.

5) The Appalachian oak (chestnut) forest: The Ridge and Valley and Blue Ridge Provinces were once covered by the oak-chestnut forest (Figure 8.8), which included chestnut (*Castanea dentata*), red oak (*Quercus rubra*), chestnut oak (*Quercus prinus*), white oak (*Quercus alba*), and tulip tree (*Liriodendron tulipifera*). White oaks were dominant in the valleys, while chestnut dominated the hillsides up to 1 500 to 1 700 m, at which point the northern hardwood forest of beech, sugar

Figure 8.8: *Forests of the Appalachian Mountains.*
1) Alpine tundra (not shown)
2) Boreal forest (spruce-fir)
3) Transition forest (northern hardwoods and spruce) (includes small beech-maple section)
4) Mixed deciduous forest (mixed mesophytic)
5) Appalachian oak (chestnut) forest
6) Grass bald, heath barren, glade (not shown)
Source: *National Atlas of the US*, 1970

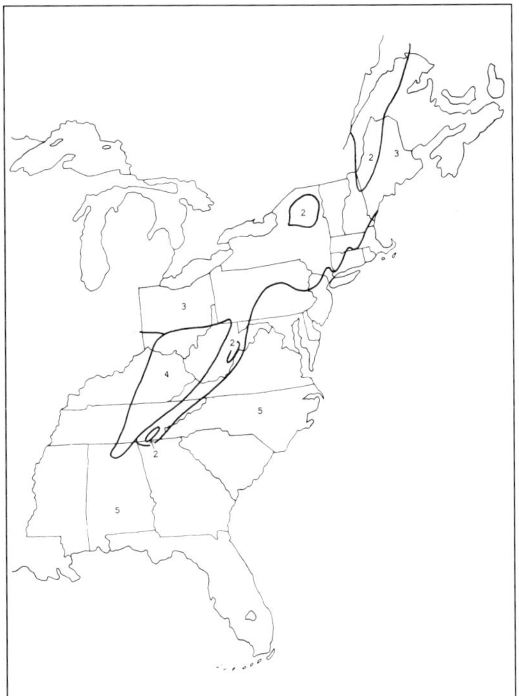

maple and birch became dominant. During the early 20th century the imported chestnut blight killed most stands of chestnut in the Appalachian Mountains. The chestnut, as a once dominant species in the Appalachian oak-chestnut forest, has never recovered (Irland, 1982). As with most of the Appalachian Mountains the oak-chestnut forests were almost entirely cut over. The only virgin oak-chestnut forest left is found in the Shenandoah National Park of Virginia.

Cultural geography of the Appalachian Mountains

Humans have lived in the Appalachian Mountain region and used its natural resources for almost 12 000 years. From the time of the first Native Americans through to our present era, the mountains have fostered cultures and lifestyles different from, but interrelated with those of the adjoining lowlands. Many writers have characterized mountain life as isolated, and a debate over whether the Appalachians should be considered a separate culture has been ongoing for over a hundred years (Billings et al., 1986). However, a true cultural geography of the Appalachian Mountains region must take into account the highland-lowland connection.

Also of importance in the cultural study of any mountain system is the concept of verticality, first elaborated for cultural systems by the Andean archaeologist John Murra (1972). Simply put, verticality holds a correspondence between marked changes in elevation, ecological zones and human resource use.

Ethnicity, religious belief, political organization, social customs–all are interwoven into a cultural fabric that offers a distinct history and future possibilities. It is far too easy, when considering challenging or harsh environmental zones like mountain systems, to reduce cultural practices to adaptive strategies or responses to environmental dictates. For this reason, the following human geography of the Appalachians is organized around cultural periods. ■

The people of the Appalachians: the Native American presence

Until 15 years ago little attention had been given to the question of Native American settlement in the Appalachian Mountains. Conventional wisdom held that the high elevations were themselves too rugged to foster use and that the lower elevations were only sporadically used for hunting. Indeed textbooks in North American archaeology had little to say about the region of, and more often than not, maps of native cultural areas did not address this eastern region, except as "unnamed tribes of the interior" (Kroeber, 1939). However, these blank areas were more attributable to research bias than to non-use–literally, few archaeologists had studied the mountains due to heavy vegetation cover and limited access. Mandates for environmental impact studies on Federal lands forced archaeologists into US Forests in the highlands of the central and southern Appalachians, and researchers in the northern region also began to focus on their highlands. This research generated so much interest in the archaeological community that a regional conference, Upland Archeology in the East, is devoted to the study of prehistoric Native Americans in the Appalachians, and smaller conferences regularly see papers on the subject.

The prehistory of Eastern North America is generally divided into three major cultural periods based on lifeways: Paleoindian (9500 BC to 8000 BC); Archaic (8000 BC to 1500 BC); and Woodland (1500 BC through historic contact at ca. AD 1600). While dates for these periods vary according to latitude, and various names are given them by archaeologists, they represent three major shifts in subsistence and social complexity: a nomadic, hunting focus; a semi-nomadic, generalized hunting and foraging lifeway; and a settled, agricultural focus.

The Paleoindian period represents the first human incursions in the region. Undisputed archaeological data place the beginning of this period at 9500 BC, although earlier claims have been made for the eastern United States (Gardner, 1989). The period is most easily recognized by its diagnostic artifact, the Clovis spearpoint, a beautifully made long thin blade almost always manufactured from microcrystalline lithic material (jasper, chert, flint). Climatic studies indicate that although the Pleistocene glaciation was waning, the colder wet climate was still a reality for these early pioneers.

The Paleoindian tool kit reflects a dependence on hunting, and the settlement pattern indicates a fairly nomadic existence, probably in small groups. However, at the western base of the Virginia Blue Ridge is the Flint Run Complex, a series of Paleoindian sites on the Shenandoah River near Front Royal that give evidence of seasonal permanence surrounding a jasper quarry. Evidence of a structure from the lower levels of the site may represent the earliest "house" in eastern North America (ibid.).

The Archaic period includes a long stable adaptation to an environment that offered a host of plant and animal resources. The early period probably saw a continuity with the Paleoindian lifeway, as the toolkit still shows a dependency on hunting; however, this gave way to generalized foraging by the middle of the period (6500 BC) when moderating temperatures encouraged the replacement of the coniferous forest with a more modern deciduous one in the Appalachians. Along with this came a plethora of small mammals, fowl, mast, riverine plants, and finally fish runs by about 3500 BC, all of which are thought to have been utilized by Native Americans. By the middle of the period, the toolkit reflects foraging focused on specific resources and perhaps a shift to a technology that relied more on wood. New artifact types include grinding stones, axes, stone flake tools for woodworking, basketry, and net sinkers for fishing. Settlement pattern studies indicate that these people were less nomadic than their Paleoindian ancestors, moving on a seasonal basis that included time spent in the mountains.

That population during the Archaic period grew in the Appalachians is based on an increase in the number of sites dating to this period. Interestingly, the high elevations do evidence human use, beginning with the Early Archaic in the central and southern Appalachians, and spearpoints dating to about 8000 BC have been recovered from the Blue Ridge from Maryland through the south. The dominant species of the forest, the chestnut, provided tremendous quantities of food for humans and animals, alike.

In the north high elevations were being used by about 7500 BC. By the latter part of the period, movement was probably reduced even more, with large base camps in the lowlands and highlands encouraging shifts twice a year. In the winter and spring the floodplains of major river systems were used by extended family groups, and large fire hearths yield evidence of fish processing. In the summer, these groups appear to have broken apart into smaller groups, perhaps hunting and gathering plants but coming together at upland base camps for the fall nut harvest. This focused foraging way of life was pan-regional, with similar settlement patterns being seen throughout the Appalachians.

The Middle and Late Archaic periods signaled a population explosion, the beginning of social complexity and perhaps territoriality among native peoples, with trade in non-local materials such as soapstone, rhyolite and greenstone becoming prevalent in the central and southern Appalachians. Also at this time is the appearance of stone bowl technology to provide storage, an indicator of long-term settlement.

The Woodland Period in eastern North America is tremendously complex, including permanent settlement and probably warfare, the Adena-Hopewell Mound Builder Cultures of the Midwest, the Mesoamerican influences of the Mississippian Cultures of that region and the Southeast, and the development of chiefdoms on the eastern flanks of the Appalachians. Fuelling much of this complexity were technological changes, particularly plant domestication and agriculture and storage technologies. Ceramics became a common addition to the toolkit by the Early Woodland period. There is little doubt that populations increased exponentially in the Midwest, beginning with the Middle Woodland period so that by about AD 900, Cahokia, a city of over 60 000 people, sat on the banks of the Mississippi at St Louis. This had important implications for the Appalachians, which may have functioned as a barrier from eastern expansion until about AD 1200.

By the late Woodland, the Ridge and Valley Province of the southern Appalachians was included in the Mississippian tradition, based on maize agriculture, bottom-land farming and compact towns. These populations were the direct ancestors to the Creek, Choctaw and Chickasaw of the early historic period. The high elevations were probably still used on a seasonal basis, but the

Little Ice Age of this period (AD 1300-1700) may have reduced the success of agriculture, forcing a renewed dependence on hunting. The mountains are filled with small hunting camps dating to this period.

When Cahokia fell between AD 1300 and 1400, massive migrations eastward resulted in the replacement or assimilation of long-lived Proto-Siouan indigenous populations and cultural traditions in the central Appalachians. A new tradition became prevalent in the region, including villages surrounded by fortifications, new ceramic traditions that mirrored those of the Midwest, and new storage technologies (large underground pits). These indigenous peoples of the Blue Ridge had formed confederacies by the end of the prehistoric era, possibly for protection against both the Iroquois and Europeans.

The history of what is now the most famous native group of the Appalachians, the Cherokee, is difficult to trace into the prehistoric period. Their way of life was dramatically altered with European advancement toward the Appalachians in the early 18th century as were the lives of all native peoples throughout the Appalachians.

(Sources: Trigger, 1978; Ritchie, 1971; Kinsey et al., 1972; Gardner, 1986; Lewis and Kneberg, 1958; Chapman, 1985; Goodyear et al., 1979; Jennings, 1977; Friggin, 1980.)

The early historic era: The native population, fur trading and European exploration

After the arrival of European explorers in the western hemisphere during the late 15th century, the native populations had only about 200 years before their numbers declined to near extinction in some cases, primarily due to diseases such as smallpox. The Appalachians provided a refuge for populations that were able to survive as remnants, but even before actual Europeans made their way to the mountains in the 17th century, their diseases had preceded them via trade routes, and it is now believed that the massive die-off of the native population began years before European settlement.

At AD 1600, the Appalachians were home to the speakers of five major language families: Iroquoian, Susquehannocks, Shawnee (Central Algonguin), Siouan, Iroquois (Cherokee) in the south-central Region; and Muskogean in the southeast. The Iroquois Confederacy may· have numbered 20 000. The Susquehannocks have been estimated at 15 000 for this early period, The Cherokee controlled the area from southwest Virginia through north Georgia, possibly numbering 22 000 in 1650.

One historical fact about this period stands out above all else when considering the European impact on the native populations of the Appalachians: the fur trade. Furs and pelts, including beaver, fox, deer, bison, otter and mink, were in great demand by European markets, and almost as soon as Europeans established themselves in eastern North America they began trading with native peoples. The Appalachians were rich with wildlife, and trade routes among native peoples were quickly established into the interior. The Iroquois and Cherokee, in particular, coalesced their power because of the control they maintained over the interior fur trade.

By the first half of the 16th century, four European nations, the Swedish, Dutch, French and English, had placed settlements on the Atlantic seaboard with the French and English making headway into the interior by that time (Figure 8.9). The first European to explore what is now western Virginia, John Lederer, noted that in 1671 there were few natives in the Piedmont, and virtually none in the Shenandoah Valley. Early historic records indicate conflict between the Algonquins, Iroquois and Shawnee in Pennsylvania and West Virginia during this early period. By the late 17th century only remnant groups lived in Pennsylvania. Refugees from the Iroquois allied with the Dutch and French as well as the English. The Iroquois were able to maintain their control over restricted tribal lands with small state reservations today in upstate New York. Indeed these people including the Mohawk are highly visible in the Native American Rights movement and have been recently involved in legal battles over land rights.

The Cherokee had gained considerable power in the southern Appalachians, but they were forced to cede territory in South Carolina to the English in the 1720s, a process which continued throughout much of the 18th century. By 1791 they had ceded all land in the Blue Ridge east to the foothills as well as much of Tennessee and were forced to emigrate west along the Trail of Tears by 1838. Those who still remain in the mountains of North Carolina today on the Qualla Reservation are the descendants of a thousand refugees who escaped the forced removal and hid in the highlands.

The dynamics of Native American politics and cultural alliances were very complex during the early historic period, but one outcome was common–most Native Americans died from disease and to a certain extent warfare and the remainder were highly restricted by the new American government or completely removed to yet unsettled parts of the west. With the approaching quincentenary of the Columbian exploration of the western hemisphere, the American populace as a whole will be faced with difficult questions concerning the modern Native American presence. The Appalachian Mountains afforded some groups refuge until the mid-19th century, but little is left of their native lifeways today.

European settlement in the Appalachians

After the initial years of colonizing the eastern seaboard and trading in the interior, the English began settling the Piedmont and Ridge and Valley from New York south through Georgia by the late 17th century. The French placed sporadic settlements in the interior to facilitate trading, and the north Appalachians were initially influenced by their culture. German immigrants fleeing Europe for religious and political freedom began settling the Great Valley from Pennsylvania south through North Carolina during the first quarter of the 18th century. But the mountains themselves were not truly opened up for settlement by Euro-Americans until after the Revolutionary War (Figure 8.9). The reasons that the mountainous region was not opened up for settlement until that time may be traced to the Proclamation of 1763, a British proclamation coming in the aftermath of the French and Indian War, which forbade all European settlement beyond

Figure 8.9: *Major European immigration.*
Source: *The Atlas of North American Archeology*, 1988

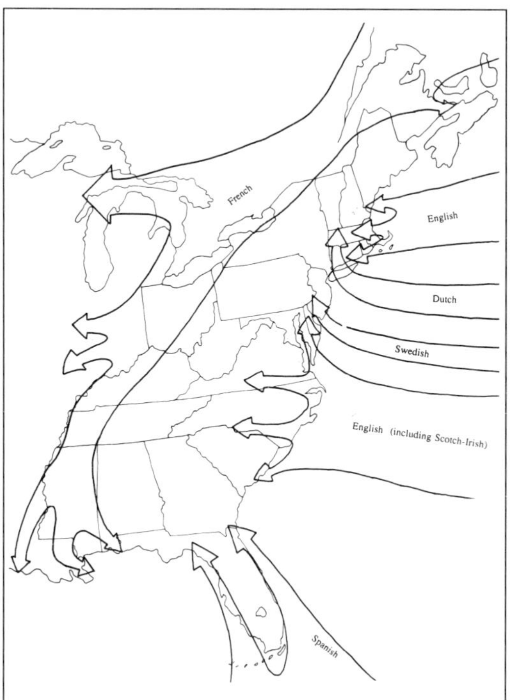

Figure 8.10: *Advance of the Frontier.*
Source: *The Atlas of North American Archaeology*, 1988

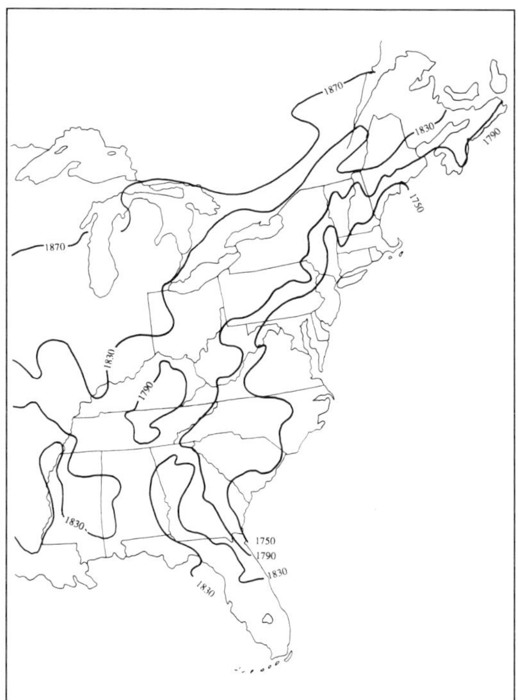

the Appalachian Front (Raitz and Ulak, 1984) (Figure 8.11). The westward land was set aside as Indian territory as compensation for the Native assistance during the war. However, some settlers defied the line, especially in the South, and this may have been the cause of many Native groups siding with the British during the Revolutionary War. Whatever the reason, the mountains were not secured for Euro-American settlement until the beginning of the 19th century.

Euro-Americans in the Appalachians

Appalachia has been referred to as a mosaic of cultures, comprised of peoples of various ethnic and religious backgrounds. Geographers point to three cultural hearths out of which the Euro-Americans who settled the Appalachians came: New England, Middle Atlantic, and Chesapeake Tidewater (ibid.). These were quickly joined by Germans and Scots-Irish in the early 1720s and were later joined by Welsh, French, Huguenots, Irish and Swiss in the central and southern Appalachians. The Hudson Valley was a hearth for English and Dutch in New England, and the Middle Atlantic was nurtured by English and German religious refugees. By 1727 over 20 000 Pennsylvania Dutch, the German groups that originated in the Palatinate, were living in the lower Susquehanna Valley. Some began to move west along with thousands of Scots-Irish Presbyterians. Each group brought with it cultural traditions expressed in architecture, farm layout and agrarian practices. While the Germans seemed to prefer the valley floors of the mountainous regions, the Scots-Irish settled on mountainsides with small farmsteads (ibid.). Their migration into the central and southern mountains resulted in perhaps the most enduring association of a cultural group with a geographic region in American history. The mid-18th century marks the beginning of what has been called "Appalachian Folk Culture", and the isolated Scots-Irish farmsteads in the Appalachian

Figure 8.11: *Proclamation of 1763.*
Source: *The Atlas of North American Archaeology*, 1988

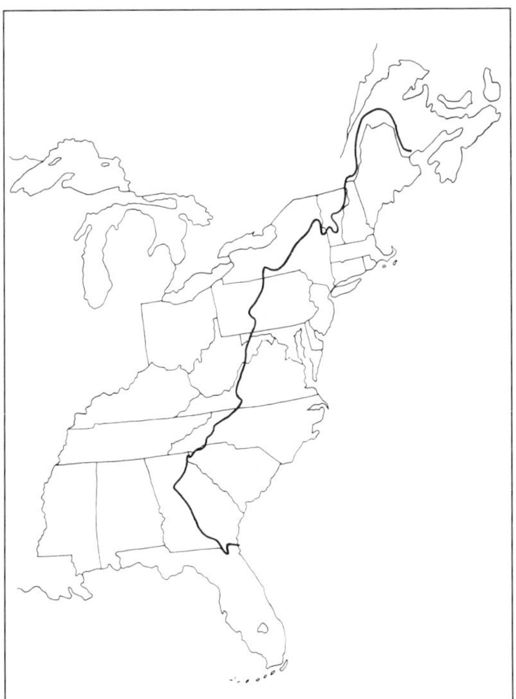

Figure 8.12: *Generalized routes of Scotch-Irish immigration, 1700s.* Source: Raitz and Ulack, 1984

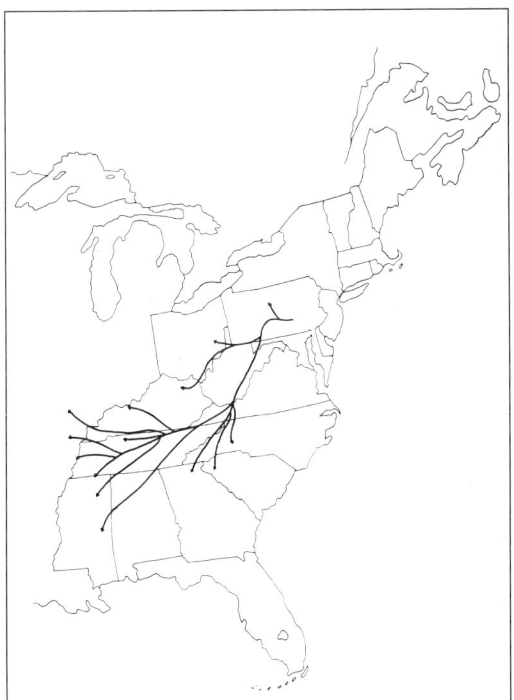

highlands are cultural icons today. These are the people who in large part became the miners and loggers of Appalachia in the late 19th century.

The 50 years between 1725 and 1775 saw German and Scots-Irish expansion south through the Great Valley into the Carolina frontier, a trend which resumed after the American Revolution. However, with the Potato Famines of the 1840s, large numbers of Irish began coming to the north-central Appalachians for mining jobs. Western Pennsylvania in particular became a core of Irish immigration. With the growth of the anthracite coal and steel industries in this region during the late 19th and early 20th centuries, eastern European immigrants from the Ukraine and Hungary began to arrive in large numbers, some settling in West Virginia. Unlike their western European predecessors, these immigrants came to company towns, not farms. They eventually settled surrounding towns in the anthracite region, and many later moved to major industrial cities such as Pittsburgh.

The underdevelopment of the central Appalachians

Almost thirty years of research and massive financial support from public and private agencies have been directed toward the study of social problems, poverty in particular, in the central and southern Appalachians. "Appalachia", the cultural area defined as being centred in the coalfields and isolated hamlets of this region, sprang into the American consciousness in the early 1960s when the social welfare programmes of the Kennedy and Johnson administrations exposed the impoverished economic and health conditions of the "Mountain People". Indeed, in the minds of many people, the term "Appalachia" is synonymous with the Appalachian Mountains, so that the cultural term is confused with the geographic region and poverty is assumed throughout (Raitz and Ulak, 1984; Precourt, 1983).

However, Appalachia as a cultural area has a specific history dating to the mid-19th century, and its social problems connected with poverty have followed it since that time. Today it is agreed by many who live there, including social scientists who study the region and public officials who govern on both the local and federal level, that chronic economic and human despair have persisted here to the present day. "Today Appalachia is in a state of economic crisis that is as deep as the one which called the War on Poverty into being more than twenty years ago" (Gaventa, 1987). The number of central and southern Appalachia residents living in poverty increased by 2.5 million between 1979 and 1983, "bringing the poverty rate in the region to almost 20 per cent" (ibid.).

Given the amount of attention focused on the region and the establishment of a federal agency, the Appalachian Regional Commission, to oversee development and renewal, why has poverty continued to shape this region? In part, the answer lies in the way in which the central Appalachians have been characterized by those who control the funding for development and renewal projects. The models that have been used to explain why poverty persists have failed to consider the sheer complexity of variables that contribute to the history and will shape the future of the region.

History of Appalachia as a cultural area

The history of the Appalachia as a "cultural region with inherent social and economic problems" (White, 1978) began after the Civil War. At the end of Reconstruction, signalled by the Compromise of 1876, the South and other rural areas were devastated by the post-war recession. The compromise, which encouraged business expansion at the expense of federal intervention on the local level, generated great interest in the mineral wealth of the mountains. With non-interference being the order of the day, there was little if any regulation concerning how land and mineral rights were obtained and the descendants of Scots-Irish immigrants compensated.

As early as the 1890s, popular articles appeared in the print media about the "southern Mountaineers", one in *Atlantic Monthly* going so far as to characterize them as "Our Contemporary Ancestors" (Frost, March 1899). Their legendary feuds were followed in newspapers with little mention that these disagreements often arose over questions of land rights. Their settlements, based on extended kinship and separated by the geography of the mountains, lent themselves to isolation and local autonomy, a characteristic "typical of most preindustrial rural communities" (White, 1987) but interpreted by the new outsiders as "backward", and in some instances "less than human" (Precourt, 1983) for not participating in progress. Some authors attributed their lack of integration into society at large as a sign of genetic deficiency (Raitz and Ulak, 1984), speculating that their ancestry could be traced to convicts and indentured servants.

Their largely agrarian way of life was rapidly replaced by one in which their livelihood was dependent on single industries such as mining and timbering, as well as the accompanying marked fluctuations. The labour wars of the early 20th century in the region are testimony to attempts by miners to gain just compensation for their work, and many historical accounts of the coal towns and timber camps reveal the poverty and poor health conditions of the region. By the 1930s the first large-scale federal assistance programmes were implemented under the National Recovery Act to alleviate some of the social and economic problems, but there is little evidence demonstrating success (ibid.). From the period of the 1930s through the early 1960s the region became more removed from the rest of the country, and new businesses did not move into the region due to geographic isolation and lack of infrastructure. With the 1960s came a new round of large federal programmes, including the Appalachian Regional Development Act of 1965, which created the Appalachian Regional Commission (ARC) to deal with the problems of the region.

Just how bad is it today?

Studies conducted in the mid-1980s indicate that the central Appalachians or more specifically the 85 counties whose economy is based in the coal industry in southern West Virginia, southwest Virginia, north central Tennessee, and eastern Kentucky have recovered little since the implementation of 1960s social welfare programmes. In nearly one-half of the counties per capita income was less than 60 per cent of the United States average (*Appalachia*, March 1985). During the worldwide recession between 1981 and 1983 central Appalachia lost more than 500 000 jobs, many in the mining and manufacturing sector. According to the ARC in the first four years of the decade the Appalachian region lost two and one-half manufacturing jobs for every one that had been created in the 1970s (Gaventa, 1987). Between 1982 and 1987, 250 textile mills closed in the southern Appalachians. Unemployment rose to 16 per cent, over one-third higher than the national average (*Appalachia*, March 1985). In the coalfields unemployment officially peaked at 30 per cent, but this rate is not thought to represent the real rate, which should

The 19th-century railroads did little to combat the feeling of isolation from the rest of the country increasingly apparent since the Second World War

include those who have dropped out of the labour market or have taken part-time jobs for lack of full-time employment (White, 1987).

Recent conversations with Dr Cecil Bradfield, a sociologist who conducts programmes out of the Red Bird Mission in Clay County, Kentucky, reveal that the real unemployment rate there was estimated at 40 per cent in mid-1991. Of the population 60-70 per cent is living in sub-standard housing. Concomitant with these figures is the increasing problem of domestic violence believed by social workers to be the result of frustration on the part of unemployed males whose wives find employment in the service sector.

The figures for education are not encouraging. It is estimated that in many central Appalachian counties less than one-third the populations have a high school diploma (*Appalachia,* December 1984), and drop-out rates were near 30 per cent as of 1985 (Appalachian Data Bank Report No.1). Functional illiteracy rates affect 30 per cent of adults in this region, and almost half of the unemployed adults are considered functionally illiterate (ibid.).

In 1985 the House Select Committee on Hunger held hearings on the continued problem of hunger in the central Appalachians (White, 1987). It was determined that federal budget cuts of the early 1980s for revenue sharing programmes were particularly damaging to the small communities in this region, reducing assistance to health clinics and other social services.

Clearly, the War on Poverty in the central Appalachians was not won during the 1960s, and impoverished conditions continued in the region. Solutions to these problems have been proposed over the years by federal, regional and state agencies, non-profit service organizations and other groups, and many of these programmes have taken as their starting point the identification of the sources of poverty. Through the 1980s two models were used to pinpoint the sources–the Culture of Poverty model and the Colonialism model. Both assess blame, the former placing it with the poor of the Appalachians; the latter with external interests that control the resources of the region. Both, however, are inadequate for describing the difficulties facing the central Appalachians.

The Culture of Poverty

First developed in the mid-1960s by anthropologist Oscar Lewis to describe the generational poverty of Puerto Rico, the Culture of Poverty model was applied to the central Appalachians to describe what was believed to be a similar lifestyle and outlook. According to Lewis, chronic poverty engenders the development of a culture and a personality that perpetuates failure and non-integration (1966). Upward mobility, a desired trait in the culture at large, is inhibited. An attitude of fatalism pervades the community outlook. Kinship ties are the core of the community and family members dependent on each other for economic, and emotional support find migration an impossibility, even if work becomes available in other areas. The poor accept their lot in life, taking solace in religious promises of a hereafter in which they will be rewarded for their early suffering. Thus, poverty becomes both the fault and the solace of the poor, who are passive but deviant carriers of their culture. According to analysts, the underdevelopment of the central Appalachians becomes a function of Appalachian character (H. Lewis et al., 1978).

This model has since been heavily criticized on several fronts. Most obvious is the point that Oscar Lewis's model was first developed in an urban setting and is not indiscriminately applicable to rural areas. The misuse of the model relies on an unstated but accepted universal standard of poverty and implies that those who do not attempt to "pull themselves up by their bootstraps" are somehow deviant. Wright (1971) notes that in rural communities, members view interdependence and loyalty to family as positive traits that have historically been characteristic of rural life. H. Lewis and Knipe (1978) argue that the Culture of Poverty model exaggerated the negative aspects of Appalachian culture and held what is really a sub-culture to definitions more applicable to the culture at large.

It has also been pointed out that the poverty is itself a stigma, and a community's self-image, once stereotyped by negative traits such as "poor" or "backward", is damaged in a fundamental way (Precourt, 1983). Due in part to the realization that the culture at large either holds them in contempt or feels pity for them, the "poor" lose what control they feel they have over their lives and come to mistrust and withdraw from their labellers. The literature of the Appalachians is filled with anecdotes by residents of the central region who were told in the early 1960s that the lives they led were miserable. Precourt recounts the experience of John Stephenson, now Director of the Appalachian Centre at the University of Kentucky, who remembers, "I, like so many people raised near the Appalachians, was not so aware that we had such problems until someone informed me....In truth, I still think of the mountains as a corner of heaven first and a national disgrace second."

However, it is important to note that no critic of the Culture of Poverty model denies the impoverished conditions of the region. A call for the proper study and understanding of the Appalachian culture is not the refusal to recognize real problems. In fact the greatest challenge to the Culture of Poverty model comes from those such as H. Lewis et al., (1978), who argue that the blame for the impoverished conditions of the central Appalachians is not with those who live there, but rather those of absentee status who own and control the resources of the region. This shifting of blame to external sources resulted in the Colonialism or Exploitation model.

Colonialism in Appalachia

Throughout the 1970s and early 1980s the Colonialism model held sway in the regional conceptualization of poverty. According to Lewis (1978), "Appalachia is a good example of colonial domination by outside interests" (read: coal, timber and manufacturing interests, as well as the federal government), who exploit the natural resources and people of the mountains through the complete control of their livelihood and environment. This model points to the historical domination of the region by outside corporations, whose irresponsibility to workers and the natural environment have left the region with little, as well as the taking of land by the federal government, which displaced families who had lived in the mountains for generations.

According to the Colonialism model, the issue is one of power and decision-making which, once removed from the hands of those who live in the region, are turned on them for the sake of capital accumulation. In its most extreme form, the Colonialism model advocated "throwing the invaders out" by returning the control of the region to its residents through land and tax reform. In its more moderate form, the model pointed out that many economic undertakings in the Appalachians, including tourism, TVA development, coal mining, timbering, extractive enterprises and the "Colony of Appalachia", (which provided the fuel for the Industrial Revolution in the United States), always subjected the area to the removal of its wealth and left behind little for the people who lived there permanently.

Whether extreme or moderate, all researchers who propose the Colonialism model as applicable to the central Appalachians agree that poverty and underdevelopment are functions of "the exploitative conditions institutionalized in the region" (ibid.). In this way, fatalism and passivity are seen as adaptive traits that make sense in a cultural milieu in which individuals have no control over their lives. These characteristics, typed as deviant by the Culture of Poverty model, are viewed as predictable responses in a colonial situation.

The Colonialism model included four components which its adherents argue are characteristic of the central Appalachians:

- a forced, involuntary entry;
- the impact on the native culture is greater than should be expected through acculturation;
- a rapid modification in the way of life of the colonized; and
- a condition of racism used by those in dominant positions to control the colonized (Blaunder, 1968 in Lewis and Knipe, 1978).

The Colonialism model was proposed not only because its adherents sought to correct the ethnocentrism of the Culture of Poverty model but also because they were interested in offering scientific explanations for the true causes of poverty. The psychologism inherent in the Culture of Poverty model was seen as very unscientific (Lewis et al., 1978), made up of the tools of other colonials whose work supported the exploiters of Appalachia. This new explanatory tool of the 1970s was also developed by researchers who had either been raised in Appalachia, educated elsewhere and returned, or had worked there long enough to see the unfairness in the negative stereotyping that was part of the Culture of Poverty model. Indeed, there is a strong sense of advocacy on the part of these researchers to correct common misconceptions about "hillbillies". There is also a tremendous sense of anger directed toward the agencies of the federal government and corporate interests that have historically caused the impoverishment of the Appalachians.

Unlike the Culture of Poverty model, the Colonialism model has not been rejected by professional academics and locals. Various formulations of it are found in much of the contemporary analyses of the Appalachians. However, the agreement on a major cause of poverty has evidently not been effective in solving the problem, and there is dissatisfaction on the part of some researchers that the Colonialism model does not completely account for the experiences of those living in poverty. In the late 1980s a new model was proposed by David White (1987), a social psychiatrist and professional social worker whose research focused on the economic distress of the central Appalachians.

His Social Epidemiological model draws from both of the previous models and proposes that any comprehensive look at the region must admit that single causes for poverty misrepresent the complexity of the problems facing the people who live there. He calls for a holistic approach which includes a "diagnosis" of endemic "disease", the acceptance of multiple causes for chronic poverty, and the development of "prevention" strategies. While it is not yet clear how much success this model has met with or how widely accepted it is, it appears to be a more realistic assessment of poverty in the central Appalachians.

The Social Epidemiological model

According to White, the economic and social wellbeing of the Appalachian people (host of the disease) is "the predictable consequence of political and economic arrangements" (the agent of disease) interacting with the history and culture of the region. In this characterization alone, poverty is seen as part of a system in which both internal and external forces are joined. While the major problems are still identified as absentee land ownership, extractive industries and exploitative relationships, and an ineffective Federal policy for the region, these must be considered in the context of the host–the social, geographical, and cultural realities of the central Appalachians. The agent is the precipitating factor necessary to cause the disease but is not sufficient in itself. The expression of the disease results from the interaction of the host and agent.

White's model includes the people of Appalachia as contributing to their disease, thus allowing them some control over their lives but does not engage in "blaming the victim", the drawback of the Culture of Poverty model. The Social Epidemiological model clearly accepts the Colonialism model's assessment of the external cause of poverty but is more interested in determining the importance of *multiple* external causes not simply an ambiguously defined sector of colonialism. White argues that this approach avoids "the 'all-or-nothing' characteristic of a single causative model" (ibid.). Thus, the Culture of Poverty model is useful for explaining the role of the host in perpetuating the disease but views the way of life associated with poverty as an perennial effect not an original cause of the disease. Precourt (1983) makes a related point in noting that many of the characteristics of the mountaineers once viewed as virtuous, independence, self-sufficiency, resoluteness, are the same traits that led to their undoing by reinforcing isolation in the face of a situation that probably called for aggressive, united action, against the extractive economies of outside interests that overtook the region in the later 19th century.

At the same time the major contributing factor to the disease is the hundred-year history of extraction and its environmental and social consequences. While this has been described elsewhere in a larger paper, thus making a chronology redundant here, it is important to note that the contemporary expression of the disease (poverty) is traced by White to very specific causes: inadequate local tax revenues and services in coal-bearing regions due to a structure that does not properly assess absentee owners; lack of economic development and diversification; loss of agricultural lands; and lack of sufficient housing (1987). He points out that more than 77 per cent of the coal-rich acres of central Appalachia are owned by out-of-state corporations that take little responsibility for the areas they control and have been successful in manipulating local and Federal policies in their favour. In addition, the Federal government returns inadequate compensation in the form of *in lieu* payments to counties in which it holds lands and where it is exempt from taxation. In his analysis of contemporary poverty in the central and southern Appalachians, Gaventa notes: "The wealth produced in Appalachia has not come back to develop Appalachia" (1987), as more and more companies are disinvesting in the region, moving textile factories to Mexico where operating costs are less, or expanding international energy speculation while closing mines and steel plants in Appalachia.

White offers several levels of solution for the problems he diagnoses, ranging from curbing to curing to preventing the return of disease. Above all, he proposes that social policy makers "must be made conscious of the realities of domination and power in the region" (1987) and that programmes of land and mineral tax reform and political realignments be implemented. The hosts themselves are called on to participate in adult education programmes and social action to see to it that the needed reforms are begun. He also calls for cooperative self-determination on the part of Appalachian residents by way of community development. Thus, there is a move away from large-scale, regional efforts to those that are specifically tailored to the needs of individual communities. However, White is not proposing that "trickle-down" social programmes based on private enterprise are all that is needed to heal Appalachia. The federal presence is still very necessary to the reform, including the enforcement of reclamation laws and commitment to rebuilding social and health programmes that were undermined in the early 1980s.

In a sense, White is calling on the people of the Appalachians to reclaim as strengths the cultural traditions that have been subverted into negative stereotypes by the culture at large. The question of community autonomy is central to the debate as is education. He is also calling on local and state governments to fulfil their missions as protectors by enforcing existing laws and reforming those that have contributed in large part to the poverty of the region (e.g. tax laws). He is calling on external corporate interests to admit their responsibility to the region and people that have supplied their wealth. This is a major healing process but one that must be undertaken by both agent and host if it is to succeed. ■

Natural resources, land use, and mountain development in the Appalachians

Overview

The history and development of Europe through the 1700s and 1800s is deeply intertwined with resource and land use of the North American coastal plain, the Piedmont, and soon after, the Appalachian Mountains. By 1700 the natural resources of Europe had long since been tapped, and some were running low given the resource extraction technology of the day. Resource control was power in a competitive Europe. The early coastal settlers found resources in forest, water power, agricultural land and minerals that were untouched. Initial exploitation of the coastal resource base buffered the wholesale exploitation of much of the Appalachian resource base for nearly two centuries. Early Appalachian settlers were concerned mainly with clearing agricultural land in river bottoms, and some of the best timber in the mountains was probably lost to bonfires (Clarkson, 1964). Lacking the technology of processing and transport, the scale of resource extraction was small. Nearby and accessible mountains such as the Catskills and Taconics along the Hudson River, the Notre Dames along the St Lawrence River, and the Greens and Whites along the Connecticut River were tackled first. The great spruce forests of interior Maine and the core of the Adirondacks awaited a more developed level of technology, manpower and management, as did the coalfields and forests of the more southern ranges.

The ruggedness of much of the Appalachians held resource exploitation at bay until the mid- and late 1800s, barely over a century ago. By then the Industrial Revolution had developed mechanical and steam power, a facility at managing large tasks and groups of workers, a capital finance system to fund large projects, and an appetite for raw materials. The national political climate was expansionist and developmental, and an immigrant workforce was flooding in from an overcrowded Europe.

These all became focused on the Appalachian forest and mineral, mainly coal, resource base. In Maine and much of the Adirondacks dam building technology played a critical role, and the logs were floated to mills and on to the sea for transport. In the more southern mountains, heavy railroads across the mountains were the key to reaching the forests and coalfields. In both cases the steam winch and the newly developed band sawmill were important to mass extraction. Forests "unbroken to the eye growing faster than they could be cut" (Clarkson, 1964) disappeared between 1880 and 1920. The trauma of coal extraction continues even today with constantly improving technology. The Appalachians were changed utterly.

Land and resource use and ownership today, discussed at length in a later section, extend from the wholesale extraction period. Early settlers, where there were any, were few and unsophisticated in matters of politics and law. Land ownership was not necessarily a matter of record, boundaries were sometimes ill defined for there had been no need, and the resources themselves were of low value unless the capital and technology were available for extraction and transport (Tams, 1963). Much of New England, the Catskills and the far northern end of the Appalachian Plateau had been settled and developed early on.

Interior Maine, the Adirondacks and much of the great forest and coal land through the rest of the Appalachians was obtained by corporate interests through money, manoeuvre and intimidation in the mid and late 1800s. Much of the forest land, after cutting, fire and abandonment, became the large state holding we see today in the Adirondacks and the federal forest holdings southward on the ridges of the Ridge and Valley Province. The spruce lands of Maine and the coalfields of the Allegheny Plateau remained valuable to corporate interests and so have remained as large corporate holdings. Smallholders predominate in most cases only where resource extraction occurred extensively but on a small scale over time and early in the settlement period, or where exceptionally good agricultural land was developed early, or where the resource was depleted and the land abandoned.

Forest resources

The forests of the Appalachian Mountains, both hardwood and softwood, are one of the great renewable resources of the eastern United States. The history of forest use in the Appalachian Mountains until recently has generally been one of complete disregard for the future.

Throughout most of eastern North America forests were indiscrimately cut-over and/or burned during the last two to four centuries. Land was cleared for agricultural use, or to use the timber for ship-building, the production of charcoal (a particularly consuming practice), and the building of railroads. Charcoal production alone caused the early stripping of much of southern New England and western Virginia forests to feed the forges, mills and smelters nearby (Shelford, 1963). Subsequent demand for coal and more timber was part of the development pressure on the less accessible areas in the mountains. White pine was so useful to the early settlers of New England that almost all of the native stands of the tree had been cut by 1900 (Sutton and Sutton, 1988). Likewise, red spruce, which was a preferred lumber for ship masts and general construction, was so intensively logged that by 1930 almost one million acres of red spruce had been destroyed in New England (Irland, 1982) and adjacent Canada and a like amount in the Appalachian Extension (Shelford, 1963; Strausbaugh and Core, 1970).

It is estimated that only 5 per cent of the original forests of New England have not been logged (Irland, 1982; Sutton and Sutton, 1988). Similar patterns of clear-cutting, with no regard for the regeneration of forests or the preservation of soils, were common throughout the central and southern Appalachian areas during the late 19th and early 20th centuries after the railroads were built (Clarkson, 1964; Raitz and Ulack, 1984; Clark, 1984).

Timber clearance during the 19th and 20th centuries in the highlands of the Appalachians apparently resulted in accelerated soil erosion, unchecked runoff, increased flooding and the siltation of streams and rivers. In 1929 an estimated 40 million acres of land was "wasting away" as a result of land abandonment and erosion in the southeastern United States (Clark, 1984). In the Tennessee River watershed clear-cutting during the early part of this century caused flooding and extensive siltation in the Tennessee River, making navigation impossible and prompting the Tennessee Valley Authority (TVA) and the Civilian Conservation Corps (CCC) to undertake extensive reforestation projects during the 1930s, 1940s and 1950s. At the present time thousands of acres of once-forested hillsides in the mountains of Tennessee are presently covered with only "rock cobbles", and "scrub brush is all that will grow" (Wallach, et al., 1970).

The general trend of deforestation and rampant clear-cutting throughout the Appalachians was reversed during the 1930s and 1940s. Extensive deforestation prior to this period, coupled with a reduced demand for wood products from the Appalachian Mountains now that the forests of the northwestern United States were supplying much of the timber consumed in the United States, and active reforestation projects carried out by the Tennessee Valley Authority, the Civilian Conservation Corps and the US Forest Service, were responsible in part for this change. In New England the abandonment of farms and pastureland since the turn of the 20th century resulted in an increase of 8 million acres of forest land, over one quarter of the present forest land in the region.

By the mid-1950s 84.5 per cent of Maine and 83.9 per cent of New Hampshire were covered with forest (Watson, 1967). At the present time more than 75 per cent of New England is forested with most of northern Maine and the Green and White Mountains of Vermont and New Hampshire covered with spruce and pine. Maine is now "the most heavily forested state in the nation" (Daniels et al., 1990), and New Hampshire and Vermont rank with Maine as among the four most extensively forested states in the United States (Mitchell, 1981). Presently 75 per cent to 80 per cent of the Appalachian Mountains of Virginia, Kentucky and West Virginia are forested as well (Raitz and Ulack, 1984).

Forest product use varies within the Appalachian Mountains. Approximately two-thirds of the wood harvest of the central and southern Appalachian mountains including the Piedmont Province is currently processed by local sawmills, while about one third is processed as pulpwood to be made into paper and fibre products (Raitz and Ulack, 1984). Southern forest product industries, comprised of lumber and pulp, are concentrated not in the Appalachians proper but in the Piedmont regions of Virginia through Alabama, with some in northern Pennsylvania (Raitz and Ulack, 1984). Central and southern Appalachian counties showing comparatively minor lumber and pulp production are generally located in regions with the best agricultural land (e.g. in the Shenandoah Valley of Virginia), in rugged mountain regions (e.g. the Blue Ridge Mountains of the southern Appalachians), and in counties where much of the forested land is owned by energy and coal companies (e.g. in southern West Virginia and eastern Kentucky). Energy and coal companies, though owning vast tracts of forest land in the coal-mining districts of the central Appalachians, are generally not interested in utilizing their forest land for the extraction of lumber and/or pulp (see section below on Land and Resource Ownership and Management in the Appalachians).

In New England the pulp and paper industries dominate the forest resource-based industries. The value of the paper and pulp industries here are almost four times that of the lumber industries (Irland, 1984). In fact the largest white-paper mill in the United States, owned by International Paper Company, is situated on the Androscoggin River in Maine. Interestingly, New England produces only 5 per cent of the nation's pulpwood but is responsible for 14 per cent of the nation's paper production (Irland, 1982). Much of the pulpwood used for paper production in New England is imported from the southeastern United States and from Canada.

With the exception of a few localized regions within the Appalachian Mountains, such as the pulpwood production centres in northern Maine, the contribution of the forest and lumber industries to the economy of the Appalachian Mountains is not great. In New England wood-based industries account for only 2 per cent of total regional employment and personal income (Irland, 1982). In New York state, lumbering employs only 0.12 per cent of the state labour force (Thompson, 1966). Wood-based manufacturing employment, as a percentage of overall manufacturing employment, is 3 per cent to 4 per cent in Pennsylvania, 5.5 per cent in Massachusetts, 6.7 per cent in Vermont, and 30 per cent in Maine (Irland, 1982; Raitz and Ulack, 1984; Meeks, 1986). The percentage of people employed in wood-related manufacturing, however, can vary considerably from region to region.

The present degree of forest utilization or "underutilization" in the Appalachian Mountains is in part the result of past and present land-ownership patterns. In the northern part of the central Appalachians, 89 per cent of the forested land belongs to non-forest industry private landowners including farmers, 4 per cent is owned by forest industries, and 7 per cent is publicly owned (eg. by National and State Forests) (Raitz and Ulack, 1984). In West Virginia the average forest land-holding is 10 acres or less, and 63 per cent of the forested land is owned by private land owners, 29 per cent by corporations, and 8 per cent is public land (DeVore and Kahn, 1986). Private individuals own 62 per cent of the New England forests, most of whom own 50 acres or less. The lumber industry owns 32 per cent of the New England forests, mostly in Maine, and 6 per cent of the New England forests are publicly owned (Mitchell, 1981; Irland, 1982). The small and fragmented parcels of land found throughout much of the Appalachians prevent effective forest and watershed management and the efficient utilization of forest products other than home-cut firewood in many regions (Daniels et. al., 1990).

Government policy and planning along with forest management has a major influence on the way forest lands are used in rural America (Daniels et. al., 1990). This is particularly true of forest and woodland taxes. In West Virginia for example, the lack of interest by small land-holders in maintaining woodlands for timber use is certainly encouraged by the state tax structure in which forest industry land is taxed 50 per cent higher than "farm woodland". The small farmer, on the other hand, is encouraged in his operation.

The future of the forest industry in the Appalachians is and will continue to be dependent on a large number of internal and external forces, including the national and international markets for forest products, the present patterns of land ownership including degrees of absentee, foreign, and corporate control, government policies, and internal ecological factors. External control should not be underestimated. The present Japanese dependence on US and Appalachian wood is in part the result of their own past forest policies and land use patterns. Internal ecological factors which may affect or alter the future of the Appalachian forests and forest-product industries include the presence of insects and diseases; the Dutch elm disease and the chestnut blight have radically altered the eastern hardwood forests since the turn of the 20th century, and the spruce-budworm presently threatens much of the northeastern softwood forests (Irland, 1982). Air pollution stress may eventually result in the loss of sensitive forest species, including red spruce, aspen, white and yellow birch, red and white pine, black willow, white ash, white oak, tulip poplar, honey locust and sycamore (Bormann, 1982). In addition today's Appalachian forests are a "complex transitional mixture", and it is therefore not clear what the forests of the Appalachian Mountains will look like in 50 years (Irland, 1982).

In the opinion of Raitz and Ulack (1984), these problems:

> ...place substantial constraints on the development of commercial forestry as an important element in regional development. In Appalachia the scientific management of the region's forests, the sustained yield of high-quality timber products, and employment by primary and secondary wood-processing industries do not seem to be a possibility except in localized areas.

This negative attitude towards the future role of forests and forest-products in the Appalachian Mountains, however, is not shared by all (see Mitchell, 1981; Irland, 1982; and Clark, 1984). In fact forest resources, being renewable, may be the most important of all the natural resources in the Appalachian Mountains to be developed in the future.

The low measure of formal contribution to the Appalachian economy, however, belies the strong contribution the forest makes to the people who live in the mountains in emotional and informal economic ways. The early settlers throughout the Appalachians tended to be, as noted earlier, poor and of independent mind. A subsistence existence that was initially enforced by physical and economic barriers became a lifestyle practised to this day by mountain dwellers even as these barriers are lowering. Hunting and fishing represent a combination of recreation and food for the larder. Firewood for heating is readily available, obviating the need to buy fuel oil, and is also a product for urban market. Fur trapping and herb gathering, principally ginseng in the south, supply seasonal income, as does itinerant logging on the smallholdings noted above. None of these activities alone can be shown to have great formal economic impact, but in the aggregate they provide the following:

1) part-time income on a seasonal basis;
2) a lowering, sometimes dramatic, of the overhead costs of living; and thus
3) an informal but effective safety net of sorts during bust cycles of the formal economy;
4) recreation on a regular basis; and
5) a place where a disempowered populace can find temporary empowerment, thus an emotional safety net.

The value of the forest resource throughout the Appalachians thus goes beyond even the informal economy to a nurturing relationship developed over generations. This relationship seems to endure even natural disaster. A consequence for people leaving the mountains is the loss of both the informal economic support and the nurturing systems of the forest resource for a life outside that has better formal economic measure but often lower actual quality. This same difference is seen in the coalfields and is discussed in the appropriate section.

The wise use of Appalachian forests also requires taking into account such diverse aspects as their scenic beauty, which is partially responsible for the "booming" tourist and outdoor recreation industry in the Appalachians, the potential for wood-based (biomass) energy, and the importance of forests in controlling runoff, erosion, flooding, water and air quality, and in maintaining biodiversity (Bormann, 1976; Mitchell, 1981; Irland, 1982; Clark, 1984).

The ecological importance of forests is difficult to assess using standard methods of economic analysis but must be considered in any local or regional forest and watershed management policy. In fact the interrelationships between fossil fuel use and the health of forest ecosystems suggests that forests should be considered in regional and national energy policy as well (Bormann, 1976; 1982). Bormann (1982, p. 91) points out that "...man-made substitutes [for the forest] require a considerable capital and energy expenditure to maintain functions formerly provided on a continuing basis by natural ecosystems using free solar power".

Mineral resources

The northern appalachian area

Mineral resources in the Catskills, Adirondacks and northeastward are extremely limited and have played only a minor role in the economic development and settlement of the region. Organic fuels are absent in New England, and large deposits of metallic minerals are uncommon. Mining in the northern Appalachians is restricted to quarries of granite, (the largest granite quarry in the world is in Barre, Vermont), slate, limestone, clay, and sand and gravel; and to mines of iron ore (e.g. Old Forge in the Adirondacks), garnet (for sandpaper and emery board), talc and soapstone, wollastonite and zinc.

In pre-industrial times local granite quarries were common through New England, and the technology and investment needed were very small. Quarrying was a seasonal activity (usually winter, because frost was used to pry the granite) that could be fitted into the year's work cycle to patch together a living. Prior to the 1970s asbestos was also mined. Now even in Vermont the importance of mining is both small and decreasing. In 1970 employment in the mining industry accounted for only 0.7 per cent of the jobs in Vermont (Meeks, 1986). Mining then cannot be expected to play much of a role in the future development of the northern part of the range.

The central and southern Appalachian areas

Mining in the central and southern Appalachian Mountains ("Appalachia") has been extremely important in the economic, industrial and social development of Appalachia, and the industrial eastern and Midwestern United States. Continued extraction of zinc and copper, and particularly of coal, oil and gas, will have large impacts on the future of the central and southern Appalachians and surrounding regions.

The mineral resources of the central and southern Appalachian Mountains include metallic and non-metallic minerals and organic fuels. The non-metallic mineral resources include limestone and sandstone, which are quarried for construction and mining; gypsum, quartz and slate. Eastern Pennsylvania is one of the largest slate-producing regions in the country.

Metallic minerals extracted in Appalachia in the past have included gold, iron, copper and zinc. Only copper and zinc are currently mined in sizeable quantities. Some of the largest zinc orebodies in the United States are found in eastern Tennessee, which in 1970 produced 29 per cent of the nation's zinc. Mining and the refinement of copper sulphides, though relatively unimportant from an economic point of view in the Appalachian Mountains, have had enormous environmental impacts in the Ducktown and Copper Hill regions of eastern Tennessee.

The copper sulphide refinement process in these regions has spewed large quantities of sulphur dioxide into the air resulting in the destruction of virtually all the vegetation in "wide areas" surrounding the Ducktown refining plant (Raitz and Ulack, 1984) and in the denudation of "...hundreds of thousands of square kilometres of the landscape" in the Copper Hill area (Bormann, 1982, p.110). This loss of vegetation has further resulted in extensive sheet and gully erosion and the heavy silting of surrounding streams (Raitz and Ulack, 1984). The Copper Hill and Ducktown "Deserts" are perhaps the most obvious and distressing cases of acidic air pollution in the United States.

Figure 8.13: *Coalfields.*
Source: *National Atlas of the US*, 1970

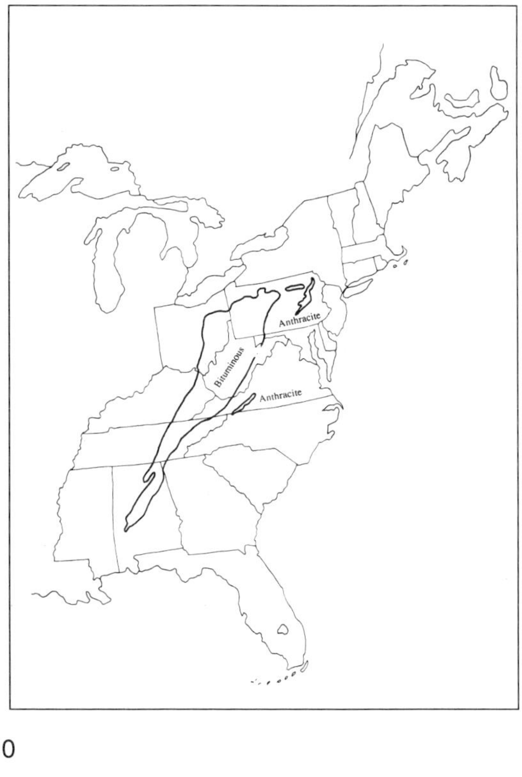

Of the mineral resources extracted from the Appalachian Mountains it is the extraction of organic fuel deposits, particularly coal, which has had the greatest social, economic and environmental impacts on the region, and organic fuels will continue to play a major role in the development of Appalachia. Coal is the most abundant and valuable resource in the central and southern Appalachians. In the 1960s coal accounted for 80 per cent of the mineral production in Appalachia. In 1977 the central and southern Appalachians accounted for 71 per cent of the coal production in the United States (Raitz and Ulack, 1984).

Mining of coal in Appalachia is concentrated in the Plateau Province, both Allegheny and Cumberland (Figure 8.13). Anthracite is mined in eastern Pennsylvania while bituminous coal is mined in western Pennsylvania, West Virginia, Kentucky, Tennessee and Alabama (Figure 8.1, Divisions 11, 12 and 13). The "Appalachian coal mining communities" referred to in much of the literature are concentrated in eastern Kentucky, western Virginia and southern West Virginia (Figure 8.1, Division 12).

Coal production in the central and southern Appalachians increased by 27 per cent between 1960 and 1978, with the greatest increase occurring in Kentucky (165 per cent increase). Unfortunately, increased mining production in Appalachia and in the United States as a whole is not an indication of economic well-being in the coal mining communities. As a result of improved mining technology, the increased expense of mining equipment, and the large capital expenditures required to increase efficiency, most small coal-mining operations have closed in recent years, and the coal industry has become dominated by large corporations (Appalachian Land Ownership Task Force, 1983; Raitz and Ulack, 1984; Gaventa et al., 1990; Yarrow, 1990).

Mining operations are becoming increasingly localized in regions where modern mining techniques and strip-mining are most effective (Appalachian Land Ownership Task Force, 1983; Branscome, 1990). The net result of the increased mechanization and consolidation of the coal mining industry has been increased production and fewer coal-mining related jobs. Between 1954 and 1968 bituminous coal production in the United States increased by 40 per cent but coal-related employment decreased by 42 per cent (Raitz and Ulack, 1984). Between 1948 and 1969 mining employment in West Virginia dropped from 138 000 to 47 000 (Raitz and Ulack, 1984), a decrease of 66 per cent!

Within the last decade employment in the coal-mining industry of the United States has decreased drastically, primarily as a result of increased international competition (Gaventa et al., 1990; Yarrow, 1990). Since the "mini-boom" in the coal industry in the late 1970s, which followed the OPEC oil embargo of the early 1970s, employment in the coal-mine labour force and in coal-dependent communities has dropped 40 per cent nationwide (Gaventa et al., 1990; Yarrow, 1990). In the metallurgical coalfields of southern West Virginia and western Virginia employment shrank by 83 per cent between 1980 and 1990 (Yarrow, 1990). The effects this drop in employment has had on the coal mining communities of Appalachia has been "devastating" (Yarrow, 1990).

The social and environmental problems associated with the coal-mining industry are multifaceted and in cases overwhelming. The boom-bust cycles of the coal industry, coupled with the removal of coal profits from the coal-mining communities, has resulted in recurring unemployment, poverty, and depression throughout much of Appalachia, and in particular in the coal communities of Pennsylvania, West Virginia and Kentucky (see for instance, Caudil, 1962; Lewis et al., 1978; Gaventa, 1980; Gaventa et al., 1990; and Yarrow, 1990). There have been few if any attempts by the coal companies to reinvest coal profits within the mining communities, and the result has been extreme poverty amidst some of the richest natural resources in the country (Appalachian Land and Resource Ownership Task Force, 1983; Gaventa et al., 1990). (This subject is discussed further in the section on Land Ownership and Resource Management in the Appalachians.)

One of the cultural contrasts in the central and southern Appalachians is between the communities of the coal areas and those of the adjacent agricultural areas. Both were settled at roughly the same time by culturally similar migrations. Hill farms developed though there was very little good agricultural land in what became the coalfields.

The great timbering of the mountains occurred to both areas, but the advent of mass coal extraction changed settlement patterns, land ownership, and the culture's very relationship with the land in the coal areas.

In a real sense, the massive influx of labour to the mines supplanted and obliterated the then dominant culture of the area, and the formerly nurturing relationship of the culture and the land changed. When a miner left for his shift (women were not allowed in the mines), he might not come home. Rains washed the valley bottoms, the only building ground. The nurturing support felt by the hill farmer was lacking for the miner.

Revd. Michael Curry, growing up in the heart of the West Virginia coalfields, remembers that the land was considered a threat to life and property. This relationship with land is discussed further in the section on Agricultural Resources, but it should be noted here that the substantially higher income of the miner was not enough to compensate for the informal economic support systems available to the hill farmer.

Since the early 1960s there has been a sharp increase in the amount of coal obtained by strip mining. Between 1960 and 1978 the amount of strip-mined coal in West Virginia increased by almost 130 per cent (Appalachian Land Ownership Task Force, 1983). Strip mines are only second to forest land in land surface cover in Wise County, West Virginia (Appalachian Land Ownership Task Force, 1983). In eastern Kentucky 53 per cent of all the coal mined in 1975 was taken from strip mining, and in seven counties surveyed in eastern Kentucky by the Appalachian Land Ownership Task Force (1983) 70 per cent of the total coal production in 1978 came from strip mining. Large-scale strip mines throughout the coal-mining districts of western Virginia, southern West Virginia and eastern Kentucky are planned for the future.

Environmental problems associated with strip mining have become acute in the central Appalachians. These problems include the removal of forest and top-soil from strip-mined areas; increased frequency and intensity of floods; siltation of streams and reservoirs due to increased run off and erosion; increased probability of landslides; pollution of streams and rivers due to acid run-off and the leaching of toxic metals (e.g. nickel, aluminium, and manganese); groundwater pollution (due to acid drainage); lowered water tables (resulting from decreased percolation of rainfall); the destruction of floodplain farmland through the deposition of clays and acid water during flooding; air pollution from dust and debris; and the loss of natural habitat and beauty (Appalachian Land Ownership Task Force, 1983; Raitz and Ulack, 1984; Harvey, 1986). The intensity of the Tug Fork flood of 1977, in which 4 700 homes and 200 miles of highway and railroads were destroyed at an estimated cost of US$ 200 million, is believed to have been in part the result of strip mining in the Tug Fork watershed (Appalachian Land Ownership Task Force, 1983; Raitz and Ulack, 1984).

In addition, the construction of sludge reservoir dams above mining communities presents a major threat to property and life. One such dam burst in 1972, flooding Buffalo Creek in Logan County, West Virginia, and killing 120 people. A slag dam in Harlan County, Kentucky, burst in 1981 and the "black ooze" which flowed down the valley killed one woman and destroyed many homes (Raitz and Ulack, 1984). Ironically, the Tennessee Valley Authority (TVA), which spent 30 years working towards the prevention of soil loss, river siltation, and flooding in the Tennessee Valley watershed, has been partly responsible, through its coal-purchasing policies, for the strip mining of large tracts of land in Kentucky (Clark, 1984; Branscome, 1990).

The Surface Mining Control and Reclamation Act (SMCRA), signed into law by President Carter, after being vetoed twice by President Ford in 1974 and 1975, was meant to reduce the environmental effects of strip mining. However, unreclaimed "orphan land" is widespread across the coal-mining districts of Appalachia. Approximately 7 per cent of the land surface of Mingo County, West Virginia, has been strip-mined, of which only half has been reclaimed, and 24 000 acres of strip-mined land in western Virginia were stripped prior to the passage of strip-mining laws (Appalachian Land Ownership Task Force, 1983). According to Harvey (1986, p. 112): "A large portion of the Appalachian land surface mined prior to the 1970s remains unreclaimed. Nutrient deficiencies, physical factors and high concentrations of toxic ions make the reclamation of such orphan lands exceedingly difficult." In addition, there is a loophole in the SMCRA which allows mountainsides to be returned to their "original contours" through the use of "longwalls", and which allows the removal of entire mountain tops without restoration to original contours.

Overall the history of mineral-resource extraction in the Appalachian Mountains has been one in which little thought has been given to the impact of the mines and mining methods on both the people who work for the mining companies and the local environment. Raitz and Ulack (1984) suggest "one must seriously question whether coal will have a positive long-term effect on employment, gross income, or investments in most counties where it is mined, or whether the region can create and maintain a stable economy if its future employment is based exclusively on coal". History does not suggest that coal mining will have a positive effect on the economic, social and environmental well-being of the central and southern Appalachian Mountains in the future.

Oil and gas together are the second most valuable mineral resource in the central and southern Appalachian Mountains, with the deposits concentrated in the "Eastern Overthrust Belt," which runs from Alabama to New York (Figures 8.14 and 8.15). The first well drilled specifically for oil was in 1859 in Pennsylvania, and the Appalachian Plateau Province was a major oil-producing region until the turn of the 19th century. At the present time there is active exploration for oil and gas within the Eastern Overthrust Belt, and in recent years there has been extensive leasing of oil and gas rights by major oil companies in the region.

However, since oil and gas exploration and production requires large capital expenditures, and since the industry is controlled by corporations whose financial and production centres are based outside of the Appalachian Mountains, there is little reason to believe that the presence of oil and gas in the

Figure 8.14: *Oil fields (may also produce gas).*
Source: *National Atlas of the US, 1970*

Figure 8.15: *Natural gas fields.*
Source: *National Atlas of the US*, 1970

Appalachian Mountains will radically alter the economic and social development of the region. Rather, it appears that the extraction of oil and gas will continue the present land ownership and tax structures already present in Appalachia which to date have left many energy-resource rich counties examples of extreme poverty (Appalachian Land Ownership Task Force, 1983).

Water resources

As in most mountain ranges water is one of the important renewable resources of the Appalachian Mountains. Water is used for domestic and industrial consumption, recreation, irrigation, transportation, waste disposal and power generation. Water rights, management and use, as well as pollution, are major issues and problems throughout the mountains and adjacent lowland regions.

Historically, transportation was the primary river use throughout the Appalachians. The Hudson and St Lawrence Rivers were the earliest access routes into the new American vastness, and the Mohawk (and its Erie Canal), a Hudson tributary, became the first major route to the opening Midwest. Later, the Susquehanna and Potomac systems became major settlement routes, and one of the first comprehensive surveys west from Virginia was conducted by (later President) George Washington, attempting to define a canal and river route based on the New River to the Ohio. In Maine and the Adirondacks, logging centred around log drives floated by dam-released water, and in the central and southern parts of the range, spring high-water log floats were the only mass means of timber transport before the railroads.

In later times, primary river use in the Appalachian Mountains has been electrical power generation. Large and small-scale hydroelectric power plants are scattered throughout the northern Appalachians (including the Adirondack Mountains), and dams have been built for electrical generation and flood control on "just about every river system in Appalachia" (Appalachian Land Ownership Task Force, 1983, p. 133). Most of the large dams and hydroelectric plants in the Appalachians were built during the 1930s, 1940s and 1950s by the US Army Corps of Engineers, the Tennessee Valley Authority, and assorted state agencies and utility companies.

It is along the Tennessee River where the hydroelectric potential of the Appalachian Mountains has been developed to its greatest extent. Under the Tennessee Valley Authority (TVA), established in 1933, 33 large dams and five hydroelectric plants were built along the Tennessee River and its tributaries. However, despite the large generating capacity of the TVA hydroelectric plants, 80 per cent of TVA power is presently generated at thermal plants (nuclear and coal-fired). The TVA is the largest consumer of coal in the United States (Guiness and Bradshaw, 1985; Branscome, 1990).

In the two coal-producing states of West Virginia and Kentucky, where coal is used to generate 98 per cent and 90 per cent, respectively, of these states' electric power (Raitz and Ulack, 1984), the use of Appalachian rivers as an energy source has clearly never been seriously entertained. Bluestone Dam, near Beckley, West Virginia, built in the 1930s, is only now being considered for conversion to hydroelectric generation. Whether the industrial northeastern United States chooses to use hydroelectric power imported from Canada for its future energy needs, or whether it obtains its energy from coal-fired electric power plants in West Virginia, is a decision which will have a major impact on the economies of West Virginia and Kentucky and on air quality throughout Appalachia (Sayre and Calzonetti, 1989).

"Pumped storage facilities" are the newest and most controversial issue in the development of hydroelectric generation in the Appalachian Mountains. The use of pumped storage facilities involves pumping water from a lower reservoir to a higher reservoir during low energy consumption periods (e.g. at night), and during high energy consumption periods the water is run back downhill through turbines to generate electricity. The upper reservoir is thus used as a giant storage "battery" for electricity. Pumped storage facilities are used primarily in conjunction with nuclear-powered electric plants, a controversial issue on its own throughout the United States, which cannot be "turned down" during low consumption periods.

A pumped storage facility was proposed for the New River in West Virginia, though the plan was abandoned after Congress designated the New River Gorge as a National River, part of the

National Park System. Other proposed locations for pumped storage facilities have included Powell Mountain and Brumley Gap in Virginia, the former since dropped after opposition by local and environmental groups; and in the upper Canaan Valley of Tucker County, West Virginia. Bath County in Virginia, on the West Virginia border, presently contains one of the largest such facilities in the world (Daniel Taylor-Ide, personal communication).

The building of large storage reservoirs may in cases involve the flooding of towns, farmland and ecologically unique or scenic regions. The power generated by such facilities is and will be "exported" to meet the needs of urban and industrial areas outside of the Appalachians (e.g. the east coast of the United States). The construction of these facilities thus raises the following question: what must the nation's rural mountain communities pay in order to meet the nation's energy needs?

Large supplies of water are essential for many industrial uses, and the availability of water may be one of the determining factors in the location of industrial plants. For instance, between 25 000 and 80 000 gallons of water are used in the production of one ton of paper. Thus most of the large paper mills in the eastern United States are situated on Appalachian rivers, such as the Androscoggan in Maine and the Pigeon and Tennessee rivers of the Piedmont in North Carolina and Tennessee. Industrial pollution associated with paper production is a major problem in these rivers, making them unfit for recreational uses, and expensive treatment may be required prior to the use of the water for other purposes.

Perhaps the most extensive system of polluted rivers in the Appalachians is found in and below the coal-mining districts of Pennsylvania, West Virginia, and Kentucky (Appalachian Land Ownership Task Force, 1983; Raitz and Ulack, 1984; Harvey, 1986). Mining in iron-sulphide bearing strata and the mining of coals with high sulphur contents, along with high rainfalls and runoff, due to strip mining; and the low natural alkalinities of many Appalachian rivers, results in highly acidic river waters. The Susquehanna, Monongahela and Ohio rivers have been particularly affected by acid drainage (Raitz and Ulack, 1984).

Agricultural pollution of waters, due to the influx of herbicides, pesticides and fertilizers is also a problem in many Appalachian rivers. The leaching of nitrogen and phosphorous into the Susquehanna River from the manure of dairy cattle in the highlands of Pennsylvania is believed to be partially responsible for the eutrophication of

Symbol of old West Virginia–turn of the century steam locomotives

Chesapeake Bay (*Washington Post Magazine*, 7 July 1991).

Following domestic and industrial consumption and the generation of hydroelectric power, the use of water resources for recreational purposes including fishing, boating and swimming is probably the most economically important use of water in the Appalachians. This is particularly true of the large TVA reservoirs found along the Tennessee River and the numerous natural lakes scattered throughout the glaciated northern Appalachians. Additional reservoirs have been built in the lake-scarce central and southern areas. Unfortunately, acid and toxic metal precipitation in the northern Appalachians may be seriously impairing the quality of stream and lake waters there (Bormann, 1982; Sayre and Calzonetti, 1989). According to Bormann (1982, p. 130) "many lakes over an enormous area of northeastern America have undergone severe deterioration and tens of thousands more are progressively moving toward that state".

Agricultural resources

As in most mountain ranges the large variety of terrains, climate and soil types found in the Appalachian Mountains results in highly varied agricultural systems. Despite the differences in farming throughout the region, however, agricultural trends are strikingly similar between the northern, central and southern Appalachians.

The late 19th century was the "peak" period of Appalachian agriculture, when much of the mountain region was covered with farmland. Farms at this time were primarily subsistence farms. Individual farmers grew grains, fruits and vegetables, raised livestock and poultry, and produced butter, cheese, honey and maple syrup for home consumption and sometimes for sale. Horses and mules were an integral part of the farm and were used for ploughing the mountainous fields and hauling goods. A farm family's life was an individualized combination of cropping, herding, and other usually forest-based activities such as logging, hunting, trapping and

Figure 8.16: *Precipitation acidity 1955–56.*
Source: *Atlas of US Environmental Issues*, 1990

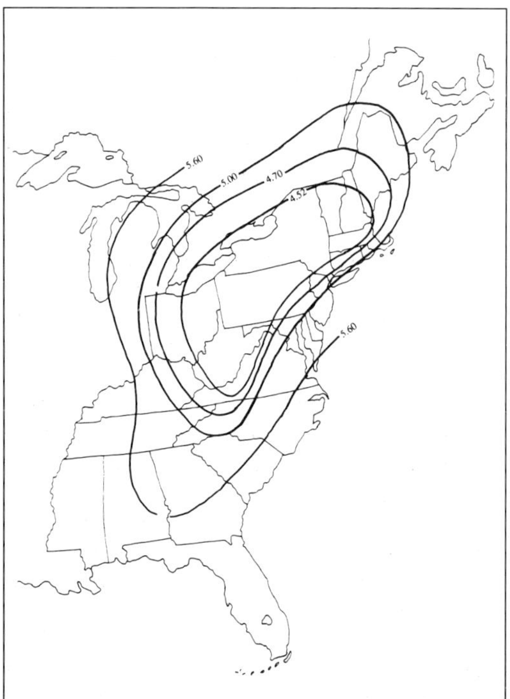

Figure 8.17: *Precipitation acidity 1986.*
Source: *Atlas of US Environmental Issues*, 1990

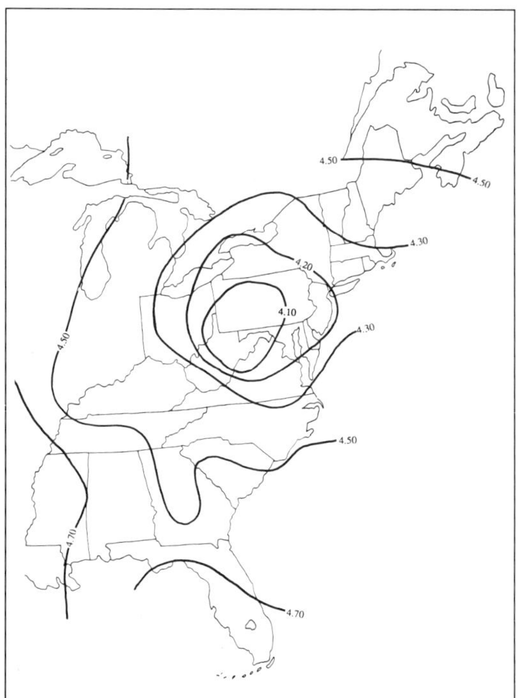

gathering. Whiskey or applejack, discussed later, were sometimes important products.

The period from settlement to timber and coal extraction was formative for the culture of Appalachians. The extraction period of the late 1800s and early 1900s brought cultural catharsis, especially to the coalfields (Tams, 1964); and the culture we know as Appalachia today is a combination of farm culture in some areas and coal communities in others. Timber extraction probably had less long-term social impact than coal extraction because in the main small farms and landholdings continued to exist outside the corporately held coal lands. A farming tradition continued as noted earlier with subsistence farms on the hillsides and more productive farms in the valley bottoms. The farm family, whether in New England or the more southern parts of the range, could be said to have had low overheads as their chief means of livelihood.

Coal communities, by contrast, were very different from the subsistence farms and communities regionally adjacent. The boom time of coalfield development required a massive influx of labour unavailable from within Appalachia (Tams, 1964). Much of this pool had no agricultural or forestry background. They were from a wide range of ethnic backgrounds heretofore unrepresented in the mountains. They came to an area with little or no farmland; they were frequently economically locked for long periods to a coal company, and in the characteristic boom and bust cycling of a commodities industry such as coal, they were tied to the fate of the national economy (Tams, 1964). Besides, corporate and large landholders, as noted earlier and detailed later, owned most of the land and had no interest in surface development. Aside from small garden plots, coalfield dwellers did not have the emotional and informal economic support of the farm and forest felt by the adjacent non-coal areas. They could not depend on staying in one place for very long and so might not even feel the continuity of life in one community.

Since the late 19th century there has been a drastic reduction in the amount of utilized farmland and in the number of active farms in the Appalachian Mountains. During the 1800s agriculture was the primary use of land in all of the New England states except Maine, where forestry was the dominant use of land. By 1940 only Vermont was predominantly agricultural, and by 1970 Vermont's agricultural land had been reduced to only 32 per cent of the total land in the state (Lapping, 1982). In New England as a whole, between 1880 and 1970, the number of active farms decreased from over 200 000 to less than 30 000 (a decrease of over 85 per cent) and utilized farmland decreased from 21 million acres to approximately 5 million acres, a decrease of over 75 per cent (Lapping, 1982). Between 1900 and 1982 the number of farms in Vermont decreased from more than 33 000 to 6 315, a reduction of 80 per cent, and between 1920 and 1982 the percentage of Vermont's land utilized for agriculture dropped from 73 per cent to 26.5 per cent (Meeks, 1986).

Similar trends in farm numbers and utilized farm land were seen in each of the other northern Appalachian states, and in the central and southern Appalachian states. In the southeastern United States as a whole the number of farms decreased from over 3 million in 1920 to about 1 600 000 in 1959, a decrease of almost 50 per cent in less than 40 years (Kirby, 1987). In the six states surveyed by the Appalachian Land Ownership Task Force (1983), between 20 per cent and 32 per cent of the farms in the study region went out of production between 1969 and 1974, and between 11 per cent and 28 per cent of the utilized farmland (over 1 million acres) went out of production during the same period of time.

These trends in decreasing utilized farmland and decreasing number of farms have been accompanied by sharp decreases in the number of people employed in farm labour with simultaneous increases in agricultural output and the value of agricultural products. Between 1958 and 1978 farm employment in New England dropped 54 per cent; cash receipts from farm products increased by 81 per cent in the same region between 1964 and 1978 (Lapping, 1982). The farm population of Vermont dropped from almost 125 000 in 1920 to less than 20 000 in 1982, a drop of over 80 per cent (Meeks, 1986).

In the Tennessee Valley Authority (TVA) management region agricultural employment, as a percentage of all employment, dropped from 62 per cent to only 6 per cent between 1933 and 1973 (Branscome, 1990). In the 80 counties surveyed by the Appalachian Land Ownership Task Force (1983) 26 per cent of the farming population left farming between 1969 and 1974!

These trends in agriculture are the result of several factors common to the entire Appalachian mountain range and to much of the United States. The first has been the increased mechanization of farming methods and the technological "improvement" of farming and farm production during the 20th century through the use of fertilizers, herbicides and pesticides, and through the introduction of new strains of plants and animals. These "improvements" have resulted in an increased need for capital expenditures in order to maintain or begin farming operations.

Expenditures for farm machinery, buildings, food storage facilities, sanitation equipment, fertilizer, hybrid seed, fencing and livestock are often extremely high. In 1979 the average annual expenses for a Vermont dairy farm with 66 cows was approximately US$100 000. The net average income for the same size dairy farm was only US$115 000 (Meeks, 1986). In addition while mechanization reduced the manual labour necessary to work farms in the large valleys of the Appalachians (e.g. the Shenandoah Valley of Virginia and West Virginia and the Champlain Valley of New York and Vermont), new farm machinery was often unsuitable for the farms which operated on the steeper hill slopes (e.g. in the Allegheny Mountains of West Virginia). The small "marginal" farms (e.g. those on the steep hill slopes), often operating on low budgets and receiving small incomes, have been squeezed out of operation by competition with the larger, more mechanized farms operating on "prime" farmland.

The second reason for the decrease in farms and farmland in parts of the Appalachian Mountains has been the gradual "urbanization" of rural lands during the last several decades. As farmland becomes more useful for non-farming and non-forestry purposes, such as the building of homes, factories, shopping centres and roads, farmers are tempted to sell their farms and farmland, which often provide only minimal or part time incomes anyway. Because the construction of factories, roads, businesses and homes is often done on the relatively productive floodplains, the process of "urbanization" often removes prime farmland from agricultural production. According to the Appalachian Land Ownership Task Force (1983) survey, 123 181 acres of "prime farmland" was lost to "urban sprawl" in the 80 county survey region of 13 million acres between 1969 and 1979.

Land speculation, which involves purchasing land in the hopes of increased land value over a short period of time due to urbanization pressures, recreational development, or resource extraction, has also contributed to the reduction of utilized farmland and the abandonment of farms in the Appalachians. Figures show an increase in farmland values of selected counties in Vermont between 1954 and 1982.

Excessive land values ranged from 17 per cent in Addison County, a county in which there was little land speculation going on at the time the estimates were made, to 176 per cent in Bennington County, a county proximate to the Boston metropolitan area and containing a college community. McDowell County, West Virginia, a county undergoing rapid development for second and vacation homes, had average land values of approximately US$3 000 per acre in the mid-1980s, the highest average land values in the central and southern Appalachian Mountains and values well above the standard agricultural worth of farmland within Appalachia, which was as low as US$650 per acre in the Plateau regions of Kentucky at the same time (Raitz and Ulack, 1984). Land values in the mountains of North Carolina, another region undergoing rapid second, vacation, and retirement home development, often exceeded US$2 000 per acre in the early 1980s.

High land values for often small and marginal farms are the direct result of land speculation by recreational developers and of land purchases for second and vacation homes in the tourist regions of the Appalachian Mountains. However, in the coal counties of Kentucky and West Virginia farmland values are generally related to energy development. Land speculation in coal counties may increase farmland values by up to five times (Appalachian Land Ownership Task Force, 1983).

Urbanization and land speculation are generally more intense in the vicinity of large urban centres (e.g. Boston, New York, Washington, DC), though the building of large interstate highways has resulted in greater urbanization and land speculation in regions, which were once difficult to reach from these urban centres. For example, in western Windsor County, Vermont, which can now be reached by interstate highway, 43 per cent of the land is now owned by non-residents (Meeks, 1986). The percentage of farmland owned by farmers in New England ranged from a low of 3.8 per cent in Rhode Island to a high of 55.4 per cent in Vermont, the latter only slightly above the national average of 53.6 per cent (Lapping, 1982). With the exception of Vermont, in New England farmers "have become minority owners of the region's farmlands" (Lapping, 1982).

Another reason for the abandonment of marginal and small farms in the Appalachian Mountains has been competition with other farming regions of the United States. Farm products from the Appalachians must compete with apples from Washington, grapes and vegetables from California, melons and cotton from Texas, and butter and cheese from Wisconsin and Minnesota. The fluid milk market, which accounts for most of the agricultural income of Vermont, Pennsylvania and New York, is protected from both United States and international competition by federal and state regulations.

The poor resource base of many Appalachian farms (e.g. poor soils, steep terrain and cold climates), along with the small size of most Appalachian farms, land tenure systems, and poor market access, have all hastened the abandonment of farms throughout the Appalachians. "Fragmented neoplantation", a common situation in the Appalachians in which dispersed fields are rented or leased to be operated by a single farmer or farming operation, tend to be inefficient and non-competitive. An extreme example of "fragmented neoplantation" occurs in the Champlain Valley of New York and Vermont where up to 40 per cent of the agricultural land is rented or leased. This changed relationship with the land among large numbers in the mountains may portend a fundamental change in the culture of various parts of the Appalachian Mountains.

While large highways connecting Appalachian farm communities with the urban centres of the east coast and the Midwest increase the value of farmland and increase the likelihood of urbanization and land speculation, they also increase the accessibility of urban markets to farms. Improved access to urban markets generally results in the diversification of farming and a greater concentration on fresh fruits and vegetables (Lapping, 1982).

It should also be noted that federal legislation, tax structures, agriculture and labour polices, and the research orientation of the US Department of Agriculture and the State Land Grant Colleges, have encouraged and rewarded large farm operators and agricultural corporations, and have hastened the decline of small farms during the 20th century (Lapping, 1982; Appalachian Land Ownership Task Force, 1983; Kirby, 1987). The top 20 per cent of the southern producers of tobacco, traditionally considered a "small farmer's" crop, received 53 per cent of all government subsidies (Kirby, 1987).

Many if not most of the farms in the Appalachian Mountains are non-commercial farms. Commercial farms were defined by the US Census of Agriculture as farms which had annual incomes of US$20 000 or more in 1978. Commercial farms may also be considered to be those farms which are run by "full-time" farmers. General trends in Appalachian agriculture have been not only towards fewer and larger commercial farms but at the same time increased numbers of part-time farmers whose incomes are only in part obtained by farming. In 1978, 45 per cent of all the farms in the United States were considered to be commercial farms by the US Census of Agriculture, while only 18.6 per cent of the farms in the central and southern Appalachians were considered commercial farms.

Large numbers of commercial farms are clustered in specific Appalachian regions, such as on the uplands of Pennsylvania and New York where dairy products are extremely important. The Plateau regions of West Virginia and Kentucky, where farmland is generally of low quality and where coal mining is common, have the lowest number of commercial farms in Appalachia. In Vermont, the most "agricultural" state in the nation (Daniels et al., 1989), close to 43 per cent of the state's farms made less than US$10 000 in 1983, and the average income of a Vermont farm was only US$9 086 during the same year (Meeks, 1986), an amount hardly able to sustain a farm family.

As a result of generally low farm incomes throughout the Appalachian region, part-time farming is common. In 1969, 65 per cent of the farms in Vermont were classified as "part-time" farms (Meeks, 1986). In 1982, 42 per cent of all Vermont farmers worked off the farm for 100 days or more (Meeks, 1986). By county, the lowest figures are found in the northeastern and northern counties where the finest pasture land in the state is located and which are farthest from industrial and tourist centres. Similar figures are seen in West Virginia where 48 per cent of the farmers worked off the farm for 200 days or more in 1978. Unfortunately for the full-time farmers, part-time farmers make it more difficult for commercial farms to compete and survive in a country where viable commercial farms are on the decline.

The "industrialization" and mechanization of farms throughout the Appalachian region has also had a number of serious environmental side effects. These include the following:

1) the loss of soil through erosion;

2) soil compaction, due in part to the use of tractors and in part to the use of chemical fertilizers rather than natural compost; and

3) soil and water pollution from the increased use of fertilizers, pesticides, herbicides and defoliants. Natural waste products from large farms, in particular cow manure from the large dairy farms of New England, New York and Pennsylvania, are partially responsible for the increased phosphate and nitrate contents of Appalachian river systems and downstream bodies of water, which in turn has resulted in the eutrophication of rivers, lakes, reservoirs and bays (e.g. the Chesapeake Bay) (Berry, 1981; *Washington Post Magazine*, 7 July 1991).

Modern farms are also increasingly dependant on non-renewable petroleum products to run farm machinery, to heat farm buildings, and to use for fertilizer. In the United States 3 per cent of all the fossil fuels consumed are used directly in farm production; 16 per cent of the nation's fossil fuel consumption is related to food systems, including farming, transport and food preparation (Berry, 1981; Lapping, 1982).

The overall ecological deterioration of farmland and the increased mechanization and competitiveness of farming has been accompanied by the depopulation of rural communities as people abandon their farms and head to the city to find jobs in the industrial sector (Berry, 1977; 1981; Lapping, 1982; Meeks, 1986; Kirby, 1987). According to Berry (1977, p. 41) the modernization of agriculture in the United States has led to the "forcible displacement of millions of people" and the "disintegration of the culture and communities of farming".

Finally, it must be pointed out that even in Vermont, agriculture was responsible for only 5 per cent of the gross state product, and agricultural-based industries are worth less than the ski industry. In addition 80 per cent of all foodstuffs consumed in New England are imported from other regions of the United States or from abroad. A dependence on "imported" foods is common throughout the Appalachian Mountains (Berry, 1977, 1981; Lapping, 1982; DeVore and Kahn, 1986). Agricultural revitalization in the Appalachians would, it is to be hoped, reduce the dependence of Appalachian communities on outside agriculture.

Farm products of the Appalachians

Much of the early settlement of the mountains was subsistence-based, but these farms did have basic needs and wants, tools and some staples being a minimum, and did produce product for trade and sale. Usually a farm family cobbled together opportunities that varied with the time of year, the climate and their luck. Products had to be capable of preservation and light enough to transport.

The very earliest product was fur from trapping. After the early boom and the Native American trade discussed earlier, trapping has remained until recently a minor but regular source of income throughout the range. The fur market has deteriorated in the face of animal activist activity and a move toward synthetics. Gathering herbs has also been a minor but regular activity, best represented today by the ginseng harvest of the central and southern areas.

One of the best known mountain products in the central and southern mountains has been whiskey ("moonshine"), around which has formed cultural lore, many songs, and in George Washington's time, the first challenge to the authority of the newly formed American government, the Whiskey Rebellion. Whiskey was probably the first value-added product of the mountains. Instead of hauling grain to market, the farmer could distil it down to a much lighter and more valuable product, which was also much more easily preserved than the grain. The Rebellion was a reaction by mainly Scotch-Irish farmers of western Pennsylvania, for whom whiskey was the principal farm product, to the federal attempt to enforce an excise tax. The government's power to enforce its laws was proved, but the frontier farmers' hatred of federal authority was affirmed and has had long-lasting political consequences (Baldwin, 1939). Illicit whiskey production for sale continued well into this century. Some of the early race car drivers acknowledged learning their skills running moonshine on mountain roads. Even today, moonshine is available in small quantities in the central and southern mountains, but arrests for sale are rarely reported. Legal whiskey production centres in Kentucky and Tennessee.

In the northern end of the Appalachians, whiskey was produced from apples ("applejack"), sometimes distilled by freezing the water out and decanting the alcohol. Apple whiskey gained the potency but never the notoriety of moonshine.

Today throughout New England, as well as in New York and Pennsylvania, agriculture is dominated by dairy production. Dairy products account for almost 79 per cent of Vermont's agricultural income, 48 per cent of New Hampshire's agricultural income, and 26 per cent of Maine's (Meeks, 1986). Individual counties in New York and Pennsylvania obtain 65 per cent to 70 per cent of their incomes from dairy farming (Raitz and Ulack, 1984). It is above all the fluid milk production in these states which is important, most of which is consumed in the nearby cities (e.g. Boston, New York and Philadelphia) (Lapping, 1982).

In Vermont cheese production also consumes large quantities of milk. The Krafts Cheese Plant in Middlebury, Vermont, uses more than half of New England's Class II milk (milk not used for direct consumption) and produces 20 million pounds of cheese per year (Meeks, 1986). In general, then, farm policy in New England has been and will be primarily concerned with the maintenance and promotion of dairy farms (Lapping, 1982). In fact, protectionist measures have been in place in New England for some time to ensure a market for New England dairy farmers. The future of New England's dairy farms and farmers is at the present time dependent on such protectionist agricultural policies.

Originally a common product of almost all New England farms, maple syrup is now produced primarily for the "luxury" market and is responsible for 1.8 per cent of Vermont's agricultural receipts (Meeks, 1986). In 1980 Vermont produced 38 per cent of the maple syrup sold in the US with New York following at 26 per cent (Meeks, 1986). Nursery and greenhouse products, including Christmas trees, are important in a few places, particularly near urban centres. Other significant New England fruit crops include apples, pears and peaches.

Agricultural production in the central and southern Appalachians is quite different from that of the northeastern United States and varies between the different physiographic provinces of the region. Most of the large and successful agricultural communities of the central and southern Appalachians are found in the Great Valley, including the Shenandoah Valley of Virginia. Both the Plateau Province and the Ridge and Valley Province west of the Great Valley, with their steep hill slopes and poorly developed or extensively eroded soils, are the least productive regions for crop farming. Animal husbandry, however, has been an integral part of the hill farming system from settlement onward, tending to be another of the cobbles in the opportunistic lifestyle of the hill farmer and often part of the informal economy.

Locally poultry and eggs are extremely important in the southern Appalachians. In some southern Appalachian regions poultry farming is responsible for as much as 90 per cent of a county's agricultural income (Raitz and Ulack, 1984). Elsewhere fruits and nuts (primarily apples, peaches and pecans) are important. In Berkeley County, West Virginia, located within the Shenandoah Valley, 55 per cent of the county's agricultural income is derived from fruits and nuts. Henderson County, North Carolina, is the seventh largest producer of apples in the United States (Raitz and Ulack, 1984).

Corn, tobacco, and cotton are also grown commercially within the southern Appalachians. Apples and corn may be the most widespread edible crops common to the Appalachian

Mountains, tying New England to North Carolina. Possibly a more widespread crop of recent years has been conifers planted and pruned as Christmas trees on land that has been removed from tillage or pasture from Maine to Georgia.

Appalachia contains only 3 per cent of the United States vegetable acreage, though there is probably great potential to increase the vegetables grown for the large, nearby urban populations. Other opportunities lie in fish farming, especially when value-added aspects such as smoking are undertaken. Deer ranching (based on red or fallow deer and the New Zealand experience), grape and wine production, organic farming, herb production, mushroom growing, and intensive niche farming are now important only in local areas but show potential for wider application as education, awareness and technology develop.

Tourism and the recreation industry

The tourism and recreation industry, including the ownership of second (vacation) and retirement homes, has had a long history in the Appalachian Mountains and has had significant environmental, social and economic impacts on the mountains and mountain communities throughout the region. The tourist industry of the Appalachian Mountains is based upon its scenic attractions, the presence of natural features suited to outdoor recreational activities, and the accessibility of the Appalachians to large numbers of urban dwellers in both the eastern and midwestern United States. In fact 70 per cent of the population of the United States (or approximately 175 million people in 1990) live within a one-day drive of the Appalachian Mountains (Raitz and Ulack, 1984). The most inaccessible region in the Appalachian Mountains, the Mt. Katahdin Massif of Baxter Park in northern Maine, is only 6 hours from the Boston metropolitan region.

Tourist and recreational attractions in the Appalachian Mountains include the following:

1) large bodies of water, which in the southern Appalachians are generally man-made reservoirs and in the northern Appalachians are generally natural lakes formed by glacial activity;
2) scenic uplands;
3) large forested regions;
4) ski-slopes; and
5) regions of historic interest.

The "scenic uplands" of the Appalachian Mountains include the region's three National Parks: the Great Smoky Mountains National Park, which straddles the Blue Ridge Mountains of North Carolina and Tennessee; the New River Gorge National River; and the Shenandoah National Park on the Blue Ridge of Virginia. The Blue Ridge Parkway, administered by the National Parks System, connects the Shenandoah and Great Smoky Mountains National Park. More than 27 million people visit these Appalachian National Parks per year, and the Great Smoky Mountains National Park has more visitors per year than the three most popular western national parks, Yosemite, Yellowstone and Rocky Mountain National Parks, combined (Raitz and Ulack, 1984). Some predict that visits to the New River Park will exceed that to the Smokies by the end of the decade (New River Headquarters, personal communication).

National forests, state forests, and state parks are scattered throughout the Appalachian Mountains and provide scenic locations for recreation. The Adirondack Park, managed by the state of New York, is the largest state or federal park in the United States at 5 700 000 acres, 40 per cent of which is state-owned forest preserve land (Liroff and Davis, 1981; Jamieson, 1964). Baxter Park in Maine is the largest wilderness area in the eastern United States (Irland, 1982). In the northern Appalachians, ski slopes, owned and operated by private corporations but generally located on National Forest Land, provide economically the single most important recreational activity.

Visits to the Appalachian Mountains by "tourists" began as early as the late 18th century and the first tourist "boom" was precipitated by the building of railroad lines into the mountains in the mid-19th century (Raitz and Ulack, 1984; Meeks, 1986). Tourism was generally restricted to the summer months, and the main purpose for coming to the mountains was to escape the summer heat and disease of the eastern seaboard and to soak in the "mineral" or hot springs.

Major mineral spring resorts in the central Appalachians included the White Sulphur Springs of Greenbrier County, West Virginia; and Hot Springs, Bath County, Virginia, both located in the Ridge and Valley Province. The state of Vermont was peppered with "mineral spring" resorts in the late 19th century (Meeks, 1986). The Blue Ridge Mountains of North Carolina, the Catskill and Adirondack Mountains of New York, and the Green and White Mountains of Vermont and New Hampshire were major destinations for the middle and upper classes of the east coast during the latter half of the 19th century. Tourism declined throughout the Appalachians during the depression years and Second World War but picked up again with the increase in privately owned cars and paved roads built in the mountains.

Until the 1960s the "tourist industry" helped "ease the social transition" from the declining agricultural and forestry sectors in the northern Appalachians (Meeks, 1986). Change associated with tourism, prior to the 1960s, was gradual and apparently had "minimal effects" on land use patterns, community infrastructures, social patterns, and the environment (Meeks, 1986). In fact the detrimental environmental and social impacts of tourism were significantly lower than those of the mining and forest industries. However, the "new recreation industry" of the 1960s, 1970s and 1980s, based on capital-intensive resort development and land speculation, has had significant impacts on local and state-wide economies and has, in some cases, threatened already unstable economies, communities and natural environments.

Tourism in the Appalachians has often been considered an important means of diversifying local and state economies. In fact in the northern Appalachians, tourism has allowed the diversification of previously single-resource based economies. In 1972 three northern Appalachian states belonged to the top 10 states in the nation in travel (tourist) expenditures relative to gross state product (GSP). Tourism accounted for 13 per cent of New Hampshire's GSP, 15 per cent of Vermont's GSP, and 27 per cent of Maine's GSP (Meeks, 1986). For each of these states tourism was more important to the state economy than either forestry and forest-based manufacturing or agriculture (Meeks, 1986). Locally, large percentages of a town's income may be derived from tourism, such as in Gatlinburg, Tennessee and Cherokee, North Carolina. Both are towns on the edge of the Great Smoky Mountains National Park and thus both "parasitic" on the natural beauty of the park (Raitz and Ulack, 1984; Meeks, 1986). However, elsewhere, such as in the vicinity of some of the TVA reservoirs, recreational income may contribute as little as 2 per cent to the total income of a town or county (Raitz and Ulack, 1984).

In Vermont the single most important recreational activity for the state's economy is skiing. In 1982 Vermont received US$260 million from the ski industry. However, even in Vermont the summer recreation industry is worth more than the ski industry, the state of Vermont receiving US$320 million from tourism in the summer of 1982. In 1970 hunting and fishing in Vermont accounted for 14 per cent of the state's recreational income, though with decreasing deer herds and fish populations this percentage is expected to decrease (Meeks, 1986).

In regions where second (seasonal or vacation) homes are common, such as in the Blue Ridge Mountains of North Carolina, in the Ridge and Valley Province of western Virginia and West Virginia, and in southern Vermont, the presence of homes owned by non-residents may substantially increase the tax base of the communities. A number of the seasonal-home communities in Vermont receive over 50 per cent of their tax revenues from out-of-state property owners. North Carolina and the northern Appalachian states, excluding New York, receive 5 per cent to 10 per cent of their tax revenues from out-of-state property owners. There is disagreement, however, as to whether the increased tax revenues outweigh or are outweighed by the costs in social amenities provided to nonresident land owners and visitors (Appalachian Land Ownership Task Force, 1983; Raitz and Ulack, 1984; Meeks, 1986).

One of the major problems associated with recreational development and the increase in seasonal homes is the attendant increase in land values and land taxes. In some regions of the Blue Ridge Mountains of North Carolina land prices rose from US$100 to US$1,000 per acre, a 10-fold increase, in just five years following recreational development (Appalachian Land Ownership Task Force, 1983). A similar 10-fold increase in land values was experienced in Cumberland County, Tennessee, though over a

15 year period (Appalachian Land Ownership Task Force, 1983). In Warren, Vermont, land values increased from US$6 million to US$451 million, a 75-fold increase, between 1960 and 1976. Large increases in land prices elsewhere in southern Vermont, and in the mountains of Maryland and West Virginia, have been noted in the above section on agricultural resources and farming.

Increased land prices often make it impossible for young local families to purchase land or homes, resulting in outmigration from the community. As a direct result of increased tax pressure local landowners are often forced to sell their land and move, or to subdivide their land and sell it in small parcels (Lapping, 1982; Appalachian Land Ownership Task Force, 1983; Raitz and Ulack, 1984; Meeks, 1986).

Subdivision of land by either farmers or developers results in a patchwork of small land parcels which are unsuitable for other uses (e.g. farming or forestry). Subdivided lots are generally not resold to local, resident land owners but tend to be sold to other urban dwellers who are able to pay higher prices for the land (Lapping, 1982). It is unlikely then that subdivided land, sold for seasonal or retirement homes, will be available for other uses in the near future. As pointed out by Irland (1982, p. 121) "the owners of many small tracts [of land] seem uninterested in investing in wood-growing, in selling timber, in allowing public recreation, in managing for wildlife, or even tolerating hunters".

The state of Vermont has attempted to stem the tide of outmigration, loss of agricultural land, and the growth of recreational sub-divisions by implementing environmental and land use laws (Act 250) (Daniels et al., 1989), and by implementing a "negative" capital-gains tax in which land taxes decrease the longer a piece of land is owned (Lapping, 1982). However, it appears that the state of Vermont's attempts to prevent or slow down land speculation and sub-divisional developments has, to date, been less than successful (Daniels et al., 1989).

Problems of pollution often attend recreational development and tourism. Water pollution is a major problem in many growing recreational communities which do not have land use regulations. The inability to deal with and/or treat sewage is perhaps the major cause of water pollution in the newly developed recreational and retirement communities (e.g. Massanutten Mountain in the Shenandoah Valley of Virginia)(Raitz and Ulack, 1984). As a result of land clearance for building homes and roads, large construction projects often cause serious hillside erosion, siltation of streams, and flooding. Aesthetic "blight" (e.g. billboards) often accompanies recreational development and tourism as well, making the local environment less appealing to permanent residents and at the same time partially destroying the scenic beauty which is often responsible for the tourism in the first place.

Tourism clearly can be a mixed blessing, but for a rural economy whose other choice is poverty and a slow dwindling away of population, tourism is an appealing alternative. Employment in the recreation sector is generally seasonal and wages tend to be low (Appalachian Land Ownership Task Force, 1983; Raitz and Ulack, 1984; Meeks, 1986). But seasonal employment is a traditional mountain characteristic. In Stowe, Vermont, the number of persons employed in the first quarter of 1970 averaged 1 097, while in the second quarter, following the ski season, the number of persons employed averaged 622 (Meeks, 1986).

Throughout the Appalachian Mountains the lowest wages are paid by the tourist industry (Appalachian Land Ownership Task Force, 1983; Raitz and Ulack, 1984; Meeks, 1986). The result is often low-wage employment in high-cost environments. However, while seasonality of the recreation industry is generally considered to be a "problem", in Vermont where winter is a slack time for many workers in the agriculture and forestry sectors and where tourism was initially a primarily summer industry, the seasonal work offered in the winter by the ski industry has helped many local economies (Meeks, 1986).

Many large recreational developments are built by "outside" businesses, such as major national or international hotel chains, and are financed by "outside" institutions. Both construction companies and construction crews may be brought in from elsewhere. In many cases large developments, which may include shopping centres, large retail businesses, and franchises force the smaller local businesses to close. As pointed out by the Appalachian Land Ownership Task Force (1983, p. 89):

> What appears to be occurring today in the recreation areas of Appalachia is a process similar to that which occurred decades ago in the Central Appalachian coal fields. There, with the development of an energy industry, the people were displaced from their land and turned into the miners needed for industrialization. Today, in recreation...areas, people are also being displaced, often to provide cheap labor...for the support services necessary for recreational development.

Finally, "outsiders", either as seasonal visitors or new residents, generally alter the social and political character of local communities. In some cases, as when doctors move into a small rural community, the "newcomers" may improve and/or increase the services available to the community. In other cases a two-tiered society of wealthy, often educated and professional "newcomers" and less-wealthy, less-cosmopolitan "locals" is formed (Irland, 1982; Raitz and Ulack, 1984; Meeks, 1986).

It is generally agreed upon by scholars (not businessmen) that due to its seasonal nature and low-wage workforce "recreation alone can almost never provide a base for a viable economy" (Appalachian Regional Commission Res. Report No. 2, 1966, quoted from Irland, 1982, p. 90). However, with local land use regulations and environmental legislation in place, tourism may be beneficial for Appalachian communities that wish to diversify their economic base.

Manufacturing

Manufacturing is an extremely important part of many Appalachian Mountains community economies. In the central and southern Appalachians as a whole, manufacturing industries employed roughly 25 per cent of the civilian labour force in 1980, while mining and agriculture together employed only 7 per cent of the labour force in the same year (Raitz and Ulack, 1984). In two of the states that lie entirely within the Appalachians, Vermont and West Virginia, manufacturing industries employed 25 per cent of the state workforces in the early 1980s (Meeks, 1986; DeVore and Kahn, 1986). While manufacturing accounted for 27 per cent of Vermont's GSP in 1982, mining and construction accounted for only 5 per cent of the GSP, and agriculture accounted for only 4 per cent.

The importance of manufacturing to local economies, however, varies considerably within the Appalachian Mountains. Within the central and southern Appalachians manufacturing is essential to some economies but relatively unimportant in the coal-mining counties of Kentucky and West Virginia. In Mingo County, West Virginia, manufacturing employed only 7.4 per cent of the working population in the early 1980s (35 per cent were employed in mining). In Harlan County, Kentucky, only 5 per cent of the workforce was employed in manufacturing in the early 1980s (38 per cent were employed in mining); and in Martin County, Kentucky, there were no manufacturing industries at all in the early 1980s (Appalachian Land Ownership Task Force, 1983).

Manufacturing in the Appalachian Mountains has traditionally been based upon the region's available natural resources and has included the wood, textile, iron and steel, ceramic and glass, tobacco, and paper industries. In the northern Appalachians wood and textile industries have been the most important of the manufacturing industries. Iron and steel industries in the Appalachians have been centred in western Pennsylvania and northern Alabama. The Appalachian aluminium industry, requiring vast quantities of cheap electrical power, is centred around the Tennessee River Valley where the Tennessee Valley Authority (TVA) was active in building hydroelectric power plants in the 1930s and 1940s. Tobacco manufacturing industries are common in the Appalachian regions of Virginia and North Carolina. Machine tools and stone products have been important components of Vermont's manufacturing economy. Interestingly, in 1982 an estimated 5 per cent of Vermont's manufacturing economy was based upon the recreation and tourist industry (Meeks, 1986).

In the early 20th century the production centres of the United States textile industry shifted from New England to the southern Piedmont of the Carolinas and Georgia, primarily due to the following:

1) the change in the location of the textile markets from the previously dominant markets of the Northeast to a more scattered distribution throughout the United States;
2) the presence of cheap hydroelectric power in the southeast;

3) the presence of cheaper labour in the southern states than in the northeast; and

4) the fact that southerners, in the early to mid-20th century, were less inclined to join labour unions than their fellow labourers in the northeast. During the late 1980s, 27 per cent of the workers in the Tennessee Valley Authority (TVA) region were employed in the textile industry (Branscome, 1990).

In the 1980s, for the same reasons that the textile industry moved from the Northeast to the South, the textile industries now shifted their production centres to foreign countries (e.g. Taiwan, South Korea and Mexico), and some populations could be subjected to a displacement equivalent to that experienced by the New England textile towns and communities in the early 20th century.

Many of the industries found within the Appalachians are small-scale industries; in the early 1980s 58 per cent of Vermont's manufacturing plants employed fewer than 10 people (Meeks, 1986), and 62 per cent of West Virginia's manufacturing plants employed less than 20 people (DeVore and Kahn, 1986). Within the mountain regions many of the industries are also low-wage, low capital-investment and "slow-growth" industries (Meeks, 1986; Raitz and Ulack, 1984). In Vermont, however, a number of "high-tech" industrial plants have been built in recent years, including the electronics and computer plants of IBM, Digital Equipment, and General Electric built in Burlington. It is not presently clear whether or not more large electronic firms will decide to locate branches in the Appalachian Mountains in the future.

Throughout the USA the 1980s have seen a gradual shift from a manufacturing-based economy to a "service" and "finance-based" economy. During the early 1980s the "service sector" was already more important than manufacturing to the economies of both Vermont and West Virginia (Meeks, 1986; DeVore and Kahn, 1986). The "service-finance sector" was the most economically important sector of Vermont's economy in the early 1980s, with manufacturing and tourism ranking second and third in importance, respectively. It should be pointed out, however, that a large percentage of the service and finance sectors in the Appalachians is based upon the tourist industry. In Vermont in 1982, 35 per cent of the service sector was based upon the recreation industry; 25 per cent of retail and wholesale trade was based upon the tourist industry; and 15 per cent of the finance, insurance and real-estate sector was based upon the tourist industry (Meeks, 1986). Unfortunately for the rural communities of the Appalachians, much of the service-sector growth in the United States is taking place in urban centres (Gaventa et al., 1990).

The general decline in manufacturing throughout the United States during the 1980s has been caused by these factors:

1) a shift of manufacturing plants to overseas locations where labour is cheaper;

2) the automation of manufacturing; and

3) the closing of less profitable manufacturing plants in the United States.

This decline has been detrimental to manufacturing communities and labourers throughout the United States, but the steel towns of northern Appalachia, the coal communities of central Appalachia, and the mill towns of the southern Piedmont have been particularly hard hit (Gaventa et al., 1990). According to the US Office of Technology Assessment only 60 per cent of the manufacturing workers who lost jobs nationwide, due to plant closures during the 1980s, were able to find new jobs (cited in Gaventa et al., 1990). Should these trends in the decline in manufacturing continue many Appalachian communities could experience serious economic decline. In the opinion of Gaventa et al. (1990: 3) the future of manufacturing in Appalachia appears "grim", and "hazardous-waste disposal is one of the few industries even considering [locating in the Appalachians]".

Land and resource ownership and management

In order adequately to understand the development of the Appalachian Mountains in the past, and in order to plan effectively for the future development of the Appalachians, it is essential to understand the patterns of land ownership, mineral and water rights, and land management in the region. In fact the ownership of land and its present use will certainly "effect the options available for future developments" (Appalachian Land Ownership Task Force, 1983, p.1). The subject of land ownership and its effect on the past and future development of the Appalachians has already been discussed to a certain extent in reference to forest and agricultural resources and the tourist industry. However, the patterns of land and resource ownership, resource utilization rights, and land use management in the Appalachians are discussed further here. Much of the discussion is based upon the monumental and ground-breaking work of the Appalachian Land Ownership Task Force (herein referred to as the ALOTF), the findings of which were published in the book *Who Owns Appalachia* (1983).

The largest single land owner within the Appalachian Mountains is the United States federal government, and most of this land is owned and managed by the US Forest Service (Kahn, 1978; ALOTF, 1983). Other federal government agencies which own large tracts of land in the Appalachians include the National Park Service, the Tennessee Valley Authority (TVA), the US Army Corps of Engineers, the Department of Energy (which owns the nuclear processing plants at Oak Ridge, Tennessee), and the Bureau of Indian Affairs which holds land "in trust" as the Cherokee Indian Reservation in North Carolina. Most of these federal land holdings are located in the central and southern Appalachians (Figure 8.18). Federal land holdings are continuously expanding (e.g. the recently created New River Gorge National River), often to the anger of local citizenry (Kahn, 1978; ALOTF, 1983).

Figure 8.18: *Federal and state government land-holdings.*

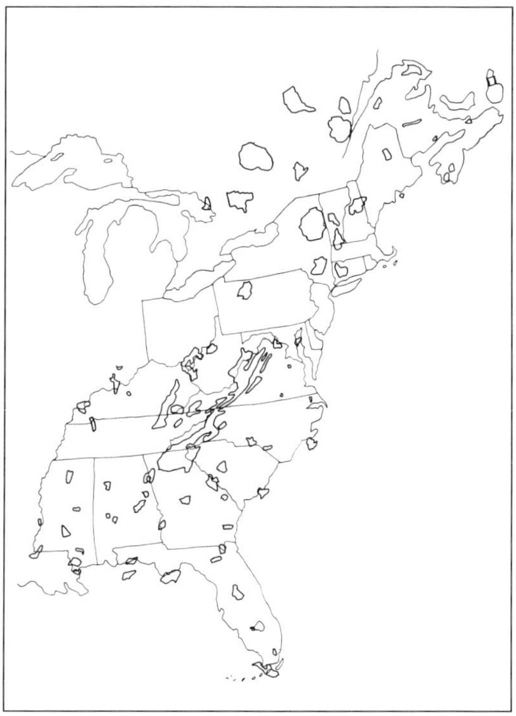

Large tracts of land in the Appalachian Mountains are also held by state governments in the form of State Forests and State Parks. Baxter Park in Maine, for instance, is a state-run park located in a state where federal government land holdings are negligible. Interestingly, the 200 000 acres of land which make up the Baxter Park were donated by a one-time governor of Maine, Percival P. Baxter. The land is not, strictly speaking, owned by the state of Maine but is held in trust by the state for the people of Maine (Irland, 1982). Other state governments with major land holdings in the Appalachians include Tennessee, Kentucky and Virginia (Figure 8.18).

There are numerous private, non-profit organizations which own land in the Appalachian Mountains as well, including environmental organizations (e.g. the Nature Conservancy and the National Audubon Society), churches, institutes and universities. In Buncombe County, North Carolina, there are over 8 000 parcels of land held by tax-exempt organizations that claim religious purposes (ALOTF, 1983). Such organizations may also hold mineral rights. The largest such holding in Appalachia includes over 11 000 acres of oil and gas rights in Johnson and Martin Counties, eastern Kentucky, held by Harvard University (ALOTF, 1983).

Apart from the conflicts that arise over the use of public land (e.g. between environmental groups and corporations with mineral rights or timber companies with permission to clear-cut on public land), one of the major issues surrounding public and private, non-profit land and mineral rights ownership is that of tax revenues. Kahn (1978) points out that within the central and southern Appalachians US Forest Service ownership of land may account for up to US $10 million dollars per year in lost county tax revenues which are desperately needed by Appalachian communities to pay for schools, roads, health programmes and other public services. Swain and Clay Counties in North Carolina, in which 86 per cent and 73 per cent of the lands within the counties respectively are owned by government and non-profit organizations, have been particularly hard hit by the loss of tax revenues (ALOTF, 1983). Kahn (1978) also points out that the US Forest Service manages the Appalachian forests for the benefit of Appalachia's "large surrounding population" of "city dwellers and nearby residents" (US Forest Service *Guide for Managing the National Forests in the Appalachians*, quote taken from Kahn, 1978). More recently (in 1989) the Forest Service was directed to undertake rural economic revitalization programmes in or within 100 miles of National Forest lands. Paradoxically, this includes Washington, DC and other urban centres.

Another aspect of land ownership patterns in the Appalachians that affects development and land use management is the preponderance of corporate and absentee owners of land and mineral rights. Large land-holders in the Appalachians include timber and paper, coal, energy, steel, railroad, chemical and utility companies. Real estate and recreation development corporations, along with financial corporations, are becoming increasingly important in land ownership patterns in many regions of the Appalachians (ALOTF, 1983; Raitz and Ulack, 1984; Meeks, 1986). The findings of the Appalachian Land Ownership Task Force (1983) show that of the 13 million acres of land surveyed in West Virginia, Virginia, Kentucky, Tennessee, North Carolina and Alabama, 40 per cent of the land surface and 70 per cent of the mineral rights were owned by corporations, while 72 per cent of the land surface and 80 per cent of the mineral rights were owned by absentee owners. Of the top 50 land surface owners in the sampled region, 46 were corporations (ALOTF, 1983, Appendix 2).

Concentration of ownership and particularly corporate ownership in Appalachia is directly related to the presence of coal reserves. In four West Virginia counties surveyed by the Appalachian Land Ownership Task Force (1983) almost 90 per cent of the land sampled (two thirds of all the land in the four counties) was corporately held. Concentration of ownership is lowest in agricultural counties. Absentee ownership, however, "is pervasive throughout the region, regardless of the rural economic base" (ALOTF, 1983, p. 20). Absentee owners include coal and energy companies, timber companies, federal and state governments, second-home owners, and recreation developers.

While there have been no studies in the northern Appalachians which have been as thorough as that of the Appalachian Land Ownership Task Force (1983) in the central and southern Appalachians, there is evidence to suggest similar, though not exactly the same, patterns of ownership. In 1969 a study using 30 sample towns found "53.3 per cent of Vermont's privately owned land area was probably owned by out-of-state interests" (Meeks, 1986, p. 249). Out-of-state ownership in the northeast, however, is apparently dominated by second-home owners, recreation developers and timber companies (Irland, 1982; Meeks, 1986). For instance 96.8 per cent of Bloomfield Vermont is owned by an out-of-state company, the St. Regis Paper Company (Meeks, 1986).

Agricultural communities in Vermont generally show less out-of-state ownership than do forested regions, regions with poor farmland, and ski-area towns (Meeks, 1986). Estimates suggest that 52 per cent of Maine's land surface is owned by a dozen pulp and paper companies (ALOTF, 1983). As with the counties in which large tracts of land are held by governments and non-profit, private organizations, ownership of large tracts of land by absentee and corporate landholders also generally results in low average tax revenues (ALOTF, 1983).

There are several explanations for this finding. First, many of the large land holdings owned by timber, coal and railroad companies were obtained during the 19th century or at the turn of the 20th century. Thus, the "market approach" to land valuation, based on recent sales of land, are rendered ineffective. Second, most absentee landholders, and especially the companies which are already paying low taxes and wish to hold their land for future mineral extraction, but also including holders of small tracts of land (e.g. second-home owners), do little to improve their properties. As taxes on property are generally based in part on land and building improvement, permanent residents often pay higher taxes than absentee land-holders. A third reason is the "misuse" of the "use" principle in tax assessment (ALOTF, 1983): farmland and woodlands held for speculation or future mineral extraction are taxed at the low farmland and woodland rates. Finally, the Appalachian Land Ownership Task Force (1983) suggests that organized political pressure by large and corporate land-holders is used to keep taxes low on land owned by outside interests (e.g. those lands owned by coal energy and timber-paper companies).

The irony of pouring federal and state subsidies into regions with rich natural resources and the problems associated with present tax structures throughout most of Appalachia is stated in the following paragraph taken from the Appalachian Land Ownership Task Force publication of 1983 (p. 63):

> The paradox of ailing, underfinanced school systems amidst highly valuable property resources is only one of the many symptoms of inadequate property taxation in Appalachia. The larger the owner of the region's land, the less the proportionate taxes paid. Gross under-assessment of mineral resources...adds to the lack of tax revenues. In many counties, massive federal or non-profit holdings also contribute to the fiscal crisis. As a result of the inequities of the property tax system, the larger owners–usually absentee corporations–go under taxed, while federal and state subsidies are poured into these "needy" Appalachian counties to provide a minimal level of services. Even with the intergovernmental subsidies, impoverished schools and inadequate services continue amidst growing, relatively tax-free, exploitation of the region's wealth.

Land ownership patterns and the problems associated with low tax revenues make it difficult for many Appalachian communities to diversify their economic structures. It is often difficult for new industries to purchase land in counties where much of the land is tied up by absentee owners with no interest in selling, and it is often difficult for older industries to purchase land for expansion (ALOTF, 1983). The lack of available infrastructure (e.g. water and sewage systems, roads and schools) generally discourages new industries from locating in Appalachian communities as well.

Ironically, in the Appalachian Mountains, which are relatively uncrowded, there are regions where there is a shortage of land for housing, and in Appalachia housing "has long been recognized as a national disgrace" (ALOTF, 1983, p. 95). Again, this is in part due to land and mineral ownership patterns and land speculation. In the coal counties of central Appalachia, land for housing may be impossible to buy or outrageously expensive, almost all of the land being held by coal and energy companies for future mineral extraction.

In the Appalachian coal counties the only land available for building may be in the flood plains, the most dangerous place to live in the strip-mined, flood-prone mountains. In addition, it is often extremely difficult to obtain loans to buy or improve land and homes in regions where the underlying mineral rights are owned by a second party, particularly in regions where owners of mineral rights have priority in the use of land (ALOTF, 1983).

Throughout the Appalachians there are large numbers of active government agencies and non-government (often political) interest groups which are concerned with the preservation and/or development of natural resources. Federal government agencies which have been, or are involved in land-use regulation and/or development in the Appalachian Mountains, and which do not actually own or administer land, include the following: the Environmental Protection Agency (EPA), the Soil Conservation Service (SCS), the Appalachian Regional Commission (ARC), the US Bureau of Mines Office of Surface Mining Enforcement (charged with implementing the Surface Mining Control and Regulation Act), and the Economic Development Administration (EDA), to name just a few. There are also large numbers of state and local government agencies charged with planning, administration and regulation working within the Appalachians. One result of multiple government agencies working within the Appalachian Mountains is "fragmentation, conflict and slow progress" (Daniels et al., 1990) in regional and local land use planning.

Non-governmental organizations active in preventing, regulating, or promoting development in the Appalachian Mountains include the National Audubon Society, the Appalachian Mountain Club, the Adirondack Mountain Club, the National Coal Association, The National Coal Lessor's Association, Woodlands Mountain Institute, and the Maine Woodsman's Association, to name just a few.

Coordinating the activities of government agencies and non-government organizations and resolving conflicts between organizations working in the Appalachian Mountains will be essential for the organized preservation and development of the Appalachian Mountains in the future. ■

References

APPALACHIAN CENTRE, 1985. *Dropout and Functional Illiteracy Rates in Central Appalachia*. Appalachian Data Bank Report No.1, University Press of Kentucky, Lexington, Kentucky, March.

Appalachian Journal. Journal published by Appalachian State University, Boone, North Carolina.

APPALACHIAN LAND OWNERSHIP TASK FORCE, 1983. *Who Owns Appalachia; Landownership and its Impact*. University Press of Kentucky, Lexington, Kentucky, 235 pp.

APPALACHIAN REGIONAL COMMISSION. Illiteracy: an everyday problem for millions, *Appalachia*, 18 (1-2), pp.21-28.

APPALACHIAN REGIONAL COMMISSION. Two decades of change in the region, *Appalachia*,15(3), pp. 41-88.

BATTEAU, A. (ed.), 1983. *Appalachia and America, Autonomy and Regional Dependence*. University of Kentucky Press, Lexington, Kentucky, 286 pp.

BAYFIELD, N. G., and G. C. BARROW, 1985. *The Ecological Impacts of Outdoor Recreation on Mountain Areas in Europe and North America*. Recreation Ecology Research Group, Wye College, Ashford, UK.

BERRY, W., 1977. *The Unsettling of America: Culture and Agriculture*. Avon Books, New York, 228 pp.

BERRY, W., 1981. *The Gift of Good Land; Further Essays, Cultural and Agricultural*. North Point Press, San Francisco, 281 pp.

BORMANN, F. H., 1976. An inseparable linkage: conservation of natural ecosystems and the conservation of fossil energy. *Bioscience*, vol. 26, pp. 754-760.

BORMANN, F. H., 1982. The landscape: air pollution stress and energy policy. In Reidel, C.H. (ed.) , *New England Prospects, Critical Choices in a Time of Change*, University Press of New England, Hanover, New Hampshire, pp. 85-140.

BRANSCOME, J., 1978. The federal government in Appalachia: TVA. In Lewis, H. M., et al. (eds.), *Colonialism in Modern America: The Appalachian Case*, Appalachian Consortium Press, Boone, North Carolina, pp. 283-293.

BROOKS, M., 1965. *The Appalachians*. Houghton Mifflin Co., Boston, 346 pp.

BROWN, L. R., and P. SHAW, 1982. Six steps to a sustainable society. *Worldwatch Paper 48*, Worldwatch Institute, Washington, DC, 63 pp.

CALZONETTI, F. J., T. ALLISON, M. A. CHOUDHRY, G. G. SAYRE, and T. S. WITT, 1989. *Power from the Appalachians; A Solution to the Northeast's Electricity Problems*? Greenwood Press, New York, 234 pp.

CAMPBELL, J. C., 1921. *The South Highlander and His Homeland*. University Press of Kentucky, Lexington, Kentucky.

CAUDIL, H. M., 1962. *Night Comes to the Cumberland*. Little, Brown and Co., Boston.

CHERNIAK, M., 1986. *The Hawks Nest Incident, America's Worst Industrial Disaster*. Yale University Press, New Haven, Connecticut, 194 pp.

CLARK, C. D., 1984. *The Greening of the South: The Recovery of Land and Forest*. University Press of Kentucky, Lexington, Kentucky, 168 pp.

CLARKSON, R. B., 1964. *Tumult on the Mountains: Lumbering in West Virginia, 1770-1920*. McClain Printing Co., West Virginia.

CLOKE, P. J. (ed.), 1989. *Rural Land-Use Planning in Developed Nations*. Unwin Hyman, London, 289 pp.

COLE, L. A., 1984. *Forest Resource Planning: State of the States*. The Council of State Governments, Lexington, Kentucky. 13 pp.

COLLIER, C. R., et al., 1964. Influences of strip mining in the hydrologic environment of parts of Beaver Creek Basin, Kentucky, 1955-1959. US Geological Survey Professional Paper 627 (A-C), Washington, DC.

CUNNINGHAM, R., 1987. *Apples on the Flood, The Southern Mountain Experience*. University of Tennessee Press, Knoxville, 214 pp.

DANIELS, T. L., M. B. LAPPING, and J. W. KELLER, 1989. Rural planning in the United States: fragmentation, conflict and slow progress. In Cloke, P. J. (ed.), *Rural Land-Use Planning in Developed Nations*, Unwin Hyman, London, pp. 152-177.

DAUBENMIRE, R., 1978. *Plant Geography; With Special Reference to North America*. Academic Press, New York, 338 pp.

DEVORE, P. W., and J. H. KAHN (eds.), 1986. A plan for sustainable small community development in West Virginia. Unpublished Manuscript from the Technology Education Program, West Virginia University.

FORD, T. R. (ed.), 1962. *The Southern Appalachian Region: A Survey*. University of Kentucky Press, Lexington, Kentucky.

FOSTER, C. H. W., 1984. *Experiments in Bioregionalism: The New England River Basins Story*. University Press of New England, Hanover, New Hampshire.

FROST, William G. 1989. Our contemporary ancestors in the southern mountains. *Atlantic Monthly*, 43(3), pp. 311-319.

GARDNER, T. W., and W. D. SEVAN (eds.), 1989. Appalachian geomorphology. Special Issue of *Geomorphology*, Vol. 2, No. 13.

GARDNER, W. M., 1986. *Lost Arrowheads and Broken Pottery: Traces of Indians in the Shenandoah Valley*. Thunderbird Publications, Manassas, Virginia.

GAVENTA, J., 1980. *Power and Powerlessness: Quiescence and Rebellion in an Appalachian Valley*. University of Illinois Press, Urbana, Illinois, 267 pp.

GAVENTA, J. 1987. The poverty of abundance revisited. *Appalachian Journal*, 15(1), pp. 24-33.

GAVENTA, J., B. E. SMITH, and A. WILLINGHAM (eds.), 1990. *Communities in Economic Crisis; Appalachia and the South*. Temple University Press, Philadelphia, 301 pp.

GEISLER, C. C., 1983. Introduction to *Who Owns Appalachia; Land Ownership and its Impact*. University of Kentucky Press, Lexington, Kentucky, pp. ix-xxv.

GRAHAM, F., 1978. *The Adirondack Park, A Political History*. Alfred A. Knopf, New York, 314 p.

GRIFFIN, J. B., 1943. *The Fort Ancient Aspect: Its Cultural and Chronological Position in Mississippi Valley Archeology*. Univ. of Michigan Press, Ann Arbor.

HARVEY, C. E., 1986. *Coal in Appalachia, An Economic Analysis*. University of Kentucky Press, Lexington, Kentucky, 219 pp.

IRLAND, L. C., 1982. *Wildlands and Woodlots, The Story of New England's Forests*. University Press of New England, Hanover, New Hampshire, 217 pp.

JENNINGS, J. D.,(ed.), 1983. *Ancient Native Americans*. 2nd edn., Freemen, New York.

KAHN, S., 1978. The forest service in Appalachia. In Lewis, H.M., et. al. (eds.), *Colonialism in Modern America, The Appalachian Case*, Appalachian Consortium Press, Boone, North Carolina, pp. 85-107.

KENT, B. C., 1989. *Susquehanna's Indians*. Anthropological Series No. 6, Pennsylvania Historical and Museum Commission, Harrisburg.

KINSEY, W, F. III et. al., 1972. *Archeology of the Upper Delaware Valley*. Anthropological Series No. 2, Pennsylvania Historical and Museum Commission, Harrisburg.

KIRBY, J. T., 1987. *Rural Worlds Lost; The American South, 1920-1960*. Louisiana State University Press, Baton Rouge, Louisiana, 390 pp.

KOCH, S. G., 1980. *Water Resources Planning in New England*. University Press of New England, Hanover, New Hampshire, 185 pp.

KRICHER, J. C. and G. MORRISON, 1988. *Eastern Forests of North America*. Houghton Mifflin Co., New York, 368 pp.

LAPPING, M. B., 1982. Toward a working rural landscape. In Reidel, C. H. (ed.), *New England Prospects; Critical Choices in a Time of Change*. University Press of New England, Hanover, New Hampshire, pp. 59-84.

LEE, H., 1982. Energy: the challenge. In Reidel, C. H., (ed.), *New England Prospects; Critical Choices in a Time of Change*, University Press of New England, Hanover, New Hampshire, pp. 141-177.

LEWIS, H., L. JOHNSON, and D. ASKINS, 1978. *Colonialism in Modern America: The Appalachian Case*. Appalachian Consortium Press, Boone, North Carolina, 370 pp.

LEWIS, Oscar. 1966. The Culture of Poverty, *Scientific American*, 215, pp. 19-25.

LIROFF, H R. A., and G. G. DAVIS, 1981. *Protecting Open Space; Land Use Control in the Adirondack Park*. Ballinger Publishing Co. Cambridge, Massachusetts, 302 pp.

LITTLE, E. L., 1980. *Field Guide to North American Trees, Eastern Region*. Alfred A. Knopf, New York, 714 pp.

LOVINGOOD, P. E., 1985. *Emerging Patterns in the Southern Highlands: A Reference Atlas*. Appalachian Consortium Press, Boone, North Carolina.

MEEKS, H. A., 1986. *Time and Change in Vermont, A Human Geography*. The Globe Pequot Press, Chester, Connecticut.

MELLO, R. A., 1987. *Last Stand of the Red Spruce*. Island Press, Washington, D.C., 199 pp.

Mineral Resources of the Appalachian Region. US Geological Survey Professional Paper no. 580, Washington, DC.

MITCHELL, J. G., 1981. Whither the Yankee forest. *Audubon*, Vol. 83, pp. 76-99.

MOORE, J. R., 1967. *The Economic Impact of TVA*. University of Tennessee Press, Knoxville, Tennessee, 163pp.

MUSE, W. V. (ed.), 1968. *Business and Economic Problems in Appalachia*. Ohio University Division of Research, College of Business Administration, vol. 1., Athens, Ohio, 60 pp.

National Atlas of the United States, 1970. US Geological Survey Special Publication, Washington, DC.

OGBURN, C., 1975. *The Southern Appalachians, A Wilderness Quest*. William Morrow & Co., New York, 245 pp.

PATRIC, J. H., 1980. Some environmental effects of cable-logging in Appalachian forests. Forest Service General Technical Report NE-55; Northeastern Forest Experiment Station, Upper Darby, Pennsylvania.

PHOTIADIS, J. D., and H. K. SCHWARZWELLER (eds.), 1970. *Change in Rural Appalachia, Implications for Action Programmes*. University of Pennsylvania Press, Philadelphia, 265 pp.

PRECOURT, Walter, 1983. The image of Appalachian poverty. In Batteau, A. (ed.), *Appalachia and America: Autonomy and Regional Dependence*, University Press of Kentucky, Lexington, Kentucky.

RAITZ, K. B., and R. ULACK, 1984. *Appalachia, A Regional Geography; Land, People and Development*. Westview Press, Boulder, Colorado, 396 pp.

REIDEL, C. H. (ed.), 1982. *New England Prospects; Critical Choices in a Time of Change*. University Press of New England, Hanover, New Hampshire, 206 pp.

RICE, O.K., 1985. *West Virginia, A History*. University Press of Kentucky, Lexington, 326 pp.

RITCHIE, W. A., 1969. *The Archeology of New York State*. Natural History Press, Garden City, New York.

SAYRE, G. G., and F. J. CALZONETTI, 1989, The politics of acid rain and Canadian power imports. In Calzonetti, F. J. et al. (eds.), *Power from the Appalachians, A Solution to the Northeast's Electricity Problems*? Greenwood Press, New York, pp. 29-144.

SHACKELFORD, L., and B. WEINBERG (eds.), 1977. *Our Appalachia, An Oral History*. Hill and Weng, New York, 397 pp.

SHELFORD, V. E., 1963. *The Ecology of North America*. University of Illinois Press, Urbana, 610 pp.

SICAMA, T. G., 1974. Vegetation, soil and climate on the Green Mountains of Vermont. *Ecological Monographs*, Vol. 44, pp. 325-349.

STRAUSBAUGH, P. D. and E. L. CORE, 1970. *Flora of West Virginia*. West Virginia University Bulletin, Morgantown, 560 pp.

SUTTON, A., and M. SUTTON, 1988. *Eastern Forests*. Alfred A. Knopf, New York, 638 pp.

TAMS, W. P., 1983. *The Smokeless Coalfields of West Virginia*. West Virginia University Press, Morgantown, 106 pp.

THOMPSON, J. H. (ed.), 1966. *Geography of New York State*. Syracuse University Press, Syracuse, New York, 227 pp.

TRIGGER, B. G., 1978. *Handbook of North American Indians (Northeast)*. Smithsonian Institution, Washington.

TRIMBLE, G. P., Jr., 1974. Some options for managing forest land in the central Appalachians. Forest Service General Technical Report NE-12, Northeastern Forest Experimental Station, Upper Darby, Pennsylvania.

VANCE, R.B., 1935. *Human Geography of the South; A Study in Regional Resources and Human Adequacy*. University of North Carolina Press, Chapel Hill, 596 pp.

WALLACH, B., 1981. The slighted mountains of upper east Tennessee. *Annals Assoc. American Geographers*, Vol. 62, pp. 666- 670.

WALLACH, B., J. N. KACHENDERFER, and J. H. PATRIC, 1970. Effects of clear-cutting, past and present, on water resources of the Monangahela National Forest. *West Virginia Agriculture and Forestry*, Vol. 3.

WATSON, J. W., 1967. *North America, Its Countries and Regions*. Frederick A. Praeger, New York, 881 pp.

WELLER, J. E., 1965. *Yesterday's People, Life in Contemporary Appalachia*. University Press of Kentucky, Lexington, Kentucky, 163 pp.

WHEELER, J. H., 1950. Land use in Greenbrier County, West Virginia. University of Chicago Department of Geography Research Paper No. 15, 180 pp.

WHITE, David B., 1987. A Social Epidemiological Model of Central Appalachia, *Arete: Journal of the College of Social Work, University of South Carolina*, 12(1), Summer, pp. 47-66.

WOODRUFF, J. F., 1971. Debris avalanches as an erosional agent in the Appalachian Mountains. *Jour. Geography*, Vol. 70, pp. 399-406.

WRITER'S PROGRAM OF THE WORKS PROJECT ADMINISTRATION IN THE STATE OF WEST VIRGINIA, 1940. *West Virginia, A Guide to the Mountain State*. Oxford University Press, New York, 559 pp.

YARROW, M., 1990. Voices from the coalfields: how miners' families understand the crisis of coal. In Gaventa, J., et al. (eds.), *Communities in Economic Crisis, Appalachia and the South*, Temple University Press, Philadelphia, pp. 38-52.

ZELLER, A., and R. W. MILLER (eds.), 1968. *Manpower and Development in Appalachia; an Approach to Unemployment*. Frederick A. Praeger, New York, 270 pp.

ZINN, G., and K. JONES, 1985. Forests and the West Virginia Economy. West Virginia University Agricultural and Forestry Experiment Station, Vol. 3, bulletin 691.

ZWINGER, A. H., and B. E. WILLARD, 1986. *Land Above the Trees, A Guide to American Alpine Tundra*. Harper and Row, New York, 487 pp.

NB: Not all text references are in this limited bibliography. A full list is obtainable from the Woodland Mountain Institute, Franklin, West Virginia, 26807, USA.

9
Mountain Protected Areas

The Torngat Mountains, North Labrador, where a balance has been reached between native rights and a national park

The special significance and characteristics of mountains require in many instances that major portions of them be afforded extra care or protection. Designation of areas as parks, reserves, sanctuaries and thc like has recognized these special qualities and "senses of place".

Some reasons for protected area status and a few examples follow:

❑ Mountains are often associated with "sacred" aspects of nature. There may be pilgrimage to holy hills, or taboo places of fear that present unusual management situations (e.g. Maria Lionza, Huang shan, Bromo-Tengger-Sumeru).

❑ Mountains have a mystique for scholars, visitors, and the general public. This has plus and minus effects (e.g. Kilimanjaro, Elbrus, Lorentz).

❑ Traditional, indigenous groups with threatened cultures often occupy or use the areas. They add greatly to the interest, can contribute much, represent a clear case for cultural diversity conservation. Cultural diversity may be more threatened than biodiversity (e.g. Pico de Neblina, Annapurna).

❑ They are headwaters of valuable surface water resources. Special care is needed to safeguard water quality for all downstream sites. The few remaining economically feasible water storage reservoirs for water and power are in mountain valleys. Of particular significance is cloudforest, which has endemic species and hydrological resources (e.g. Mount Kinabalu, Australian Alps).

❑ Mountain biota, under climatic stress at the best of times, are particularly vulnerable to climate change from increasing greenhouse gases, as well as from exogenous air pollution. Protected areas crossing several altitudinal belts are needed. They offer great possibilities for global climate change and air quality research and monitoring (e.g. High Tatras, Great Smokies).

❑ Mountains are a last refuge for many rare plants and animals displaced or eliminated from more transformed lowlands. They are vital to biological diversity conservation. Freestanding mountains become biological islands (e.g. Taranaki, Mount Apo).

❑ These are dynamic landscapes of relatively rapid change. Volcanism, uplift, erosion, glacial outbursts, seismic activity, avalanches, torrents all contribute to significant, rapid alternations in topography, vegetation, and land use. These are high-energy environments where some control over human alterations is often needed (e.g. Hawaii volcanoes, Tongariro).

❑ There is a concentration of high scenic value, attractions for tourists and recreational use. Management is needed to maintain these values (e.g. Mount Cook, Hohe Tauern).

❑ The concentration of recreation/access in confined corridors demands a proactive policy and management approach to avoid overcrowding, degradation of access routes and campsites (e.g. rubbish, sanitation) (e.g. Himalayan parks, Tasmanian/New Zealand national parks, Huascaran).

❑ Mountaineering expedition pressures demand positive control to avoid site degradation and require that equipment/materials/garbage brought in be taken out (e.g. Sagarmatha [Everest]).

❑ Mountain ranges often form country boundaries, and thus offer opportunities for the establishment of international border parks, peace parks and cooperative international action (e.g. Pyrenées Occidentales and Ordesa, Sagarmatha and Qomolangma, and the proposed Mont Blanc Park and convention on the conservation of the Alps).

Previous chapters have documented the threats to mountain biophysical environments and to mountain societies in some of the major mountain ranges of the world. There are possibilities for mitigating the negative impacts and enhancing some of the values, if the watchword is *sustainable* mountain development. This requires some degree of conservation control over the exogenous and endogenous driven actions affecting mountain land, water and people. One of the most useful institutional inventions is the designation (followed by implementation) of formal "protected areas".

"Protected areas" are defined as formally designated areas over which some degree of control of human activity is exerted in order to conserve species, ecosystems and cultures, while producing in perpetuity a flow of ecosystem services or products, both tangible and intangible. They range in character from a strictly protected nature preserve to a national or state forest where harvesting is regulated to produce timber or non-wood forest products, to a cultural landscape where human activity is very much in evidence, but

***Table 9.1:** IUCN Categories of Protected Areas*

I. Strict Nature Reserve. To protect areas and maintain natural processes in an undisturbed state in order to have ecologically representative examples of the natural environment available for scientific study, environmental monitoring, education, and for the maintenance of genetic resources in a dynamic and evolutionary state.

II. National Park. To protect outstanding natural and scenic areas of national or international significance for scientific, educational, and recreational use. These are relatively large natural areas not materially altered by human activity where extractive resource uses are not allowed.

III. Natural Monument/Natural Landmark. To protect and preserve nationally significant natural features because of their special interest or unique characteristics. These are relatively small areas focused on protection of specific features.

IV. Managed Nature Reserve/Wildlife Sanctuary. To assure the natural conditions necessary to protect nationally significant species, groups of species, biotic communities, or physical features of the environment where these may require specific human manipulation for their perpetuation. Controlled harvesting of some resources can be permitted.

V. Protected Landscapes and Seascapes. To maintain nationally significant natural landscapes which are characteristic of the harmonious interaction of man and land while providing opportunities for public enjoyment through recreation and tourism within the normal lifestyle and economic activity of these areas. These are mixed cultural/natural landscapes of high scenic value where traditional land uses are maintained.

VI. Resource Reserve. To protect the natural resources of the area for future use and prevent or contain development activities that could affect the resource pending the establishment of objectives which are based upon appropriate knowledge and planning. This is a "holding" category used until a permanent classification can be determined.

VII. Anthropological Reserve/Natural Biotic Area. To allow the way of life of societies living in harmony with the environment to continue undisturbed by modern technology. This category is appropriate where resource extraction by indigenous people is conducted in a traditional manner.

VIII. Multiple Use Management Area/Managed Resource Area. To provide for the sustained production of water, timber, wildlife, pasture and tourism, with the conservation of nature primarily oriented to the support of the economic activities (although specific zones may also be designated within these areas to achieve specific conservation objectives).

Two additional categories are international labels which overlay protected areas in the above eight categories:

IX. *Biosphere Reserve.*To conserve for present and future use the diversity and integrity of biotic communities of plants and animals within natural ecosystems, and to safeguard the genetic diversity of species on which their continuing evolution depends. These are internationally designated sites managed for research, education and training.

X. World Heritage Site. To protect the natural features for which the area is considered to be of outstanding universal significance. This is a select list of the world's unique natural and cultural sites nominated by countries that are party to the World Heritage Convention.

where practices are controlled so as to be sustainable. The World Conservation Union (IUCN) recognizes and defines ten categories of protected areas. Their classification is under revision and may result in five categories and a special class under international instruments. The long-used ten categories and definitions are given in Table 9.1.

The most recent list of protected areas published by IUCN includes information for categories I through V (IUCN, 1990). It covers only areas larger than 1 000 hectares, except for offshore or oceanic islands of at least 100 ha where the whole island is protected. There were, in 1990, 6 940 areas covering 651 467 597 ha. There were in addition 282 Biosphere Reserves and 82 World Heritage Sites where natural elements were paramount.

A data bank on Categories I through V, which are the categories of paramount interest to IUCN's Commission on National Parks and Protected Areas, is maintained by the Protected Areas Data Unit (PADU) of the World Conservation Monitoring Centre in Cambridge, UK. From that data bank, Thorsell and Harrison (in press) have compiled a list of mountain protected areas. In order to do this, certain minimum criteria had to be set. First of all, it was decided to include only categories I through IV. The minimum size was set at 10 000 ha. The most contentious issue was establishing a minimum relative relief criterion of 1 500 m. This leaves out many protected areas in what are locally considered as mountains (e.g. the Scottish Highlands, Wales, the Urals, the Jura and many Australian mountains). Even so, Thorsell and Harrison identified 432 mountain protected areas in 63 countries. Table 9.2 presents the results of their compilation based on the Biogeographical Realms of Udvardy (1975).

This list includes high dissected plateaus such as the Grand Canyon, Ethiopian Highlands and Yunnan Plateau because of a greater relief than 1 500 m. All biogeographical realms are represented, although due to the large size of the Greenland National Park at 97 million ha, the Nearctic Realm alone has 63 per cent of the total land area of all the mountain protected areas. If the minimum relative relief had been lowered to 1 000 m (not an uncommon height criterion for defining a mountain) the list would have been expanded by another 200 sites.

There are 25 of these mountain protected areas in 15 countries that have been considered to be of such global natural significance that they have been inscribed on the World Heritage List. They include such outstanding areas as Virunga National Park in Zaire, Huascaran NP in Peru, Sagarmatha NP in Nepal and Hawaii Volcanoes NP in the USA. UNESCO's Biosphere Reserve Programme has recognized 67 mountain protected areas in 26 countries in a world network of sites where research and monitoring are often linked in comparing natural areas with human use areas.

This inventory is being refined and in general increased, as more data are forthcoming and as other compensatory criteria come into play. Of substantial relevance in improving the information is an effort at regional directories of protected areas. The World Conservation Monitoring Centre

Biogeographical realm	Number	Total Area (ha)
Nearctic	93	152 707 666
Palaearctic	146	30 120 611
Afrotropical	35	10 986 512
Indomalayan	53	8 811 898
Oceania	8	3 598 032
Australia	4	1 840 459
Antarctic	11	2 086 861
Neotropical	82	30 392 615
Total	432	240 544 654

Table 9.2: *Inventory of most of the world's mountain protected areas*

has produced a large directory, *Nature Reserves of the Himalaya and the Mountains of Central Asia* (Green, in press). Other regional directories dealing with other major mountain ranges might well be warranted. More than inventories and lists of declared areas is needed however. Analysis is required as to how well these parks and reserves of various kinds are being managed or controlled to fulfil the purposes for which they were designated. These special mountain areas, like all mountain areas, are experiencing increasing pressures from competing uses and from sheer number increases in visitors and users. Many have been ill conceived in design (especially to meet the stresses associated with any climate change or increased air quality deterioration), have no adequate management plans, are under-funded, and have little or no control or surveillance mechanism. IUCN's Commission on National Parks and Protected Areas periodically proclaims a list of threatened protected areas, and unfortunately mountain protected areas are too often highly represented. For instance on the most recent listing (1990) Pirin (Bulgaria) and Montes Azules (Mexico) were added to an existing list that includes such perennial parks in peril as Mount Apo in the Philippines.

It is probable that more international and national attention will be focused on mountain protected areas in view of a late 1991 initiative for a mountain programme centred in IUCN's Commission on National Parks and Protected Areas. Certainly planning funding and management need improvement universally. Somehow locally affected people inside and adjacent to protected areas and to some extent users, even though far removed, need to be brought into the planning and management process. Cultural values need to be accorded a recognition along with biological values, commensurate with their importance in the specific area. Improvement is needed in many areas. Moreover additional areas are needed in many mountain ranges or individual mountains. Coverage is needed in the Atlas Mountains, Antarctica, the Alps, Papua New Guinea, the Hindu Kush and the mountains of Myanmar and Laos. And greater attention should be paid to the possibilities of establishing parks on adjacent country borders, since mountain crest lines frequently mark territorial limits. Transfrontier or border parks have served as peace parks, and, at a minimum, offer opportunity for international collaboration for more effective conservation. Thorsell and Harrison (in press) list 24 mountain transfrontier reserve complexes, four in North America (e.g. Glacier, USA - Waterton Lakes, Canada), six in Europe (e.g. Tartrzanski, Poland - High Tatra, Czechoslovakia), four in Africa (e.g. Volcanoes, Rwandi - Virunga, Zaire - Gorilla, Uganda), six in Latin America (e.g. Sajama, Bolivia - Lauca, Chile) and one trans-state border park in Australia, Australian Alps, involving New South Wales, Southern Australia, Victoria and Australian Capital Territory. A number of others have been proposed.

References

GREEN, M.J.B., (in press). *Nature Reserves of the Himalaya and the Mountains of Central Asia.* World Conservation Union/World Conservation Monitoring Centre. 481 pp.

IUCN. 1990. *United Nations List of National Parks and Protected Areas.* IUCN, Gland Switzerland, and Cambridge, UK. 284 pp.

THORSELL, J. and J. HARRISON, (in press). National parks and nature reserves in the mountain regions of the world. In *Proceedings of Parks, Peaks and People International Consultation.* Edited by S. FULLER. East-West Center/World Conservation Union. 37 pp.

UDVARDY, M.D.F., 1975. *A Classification of the Biogeographical Provinces of the World.* IUCN Occasional Paper 18. Morges (now Gland), Switzerland. 48 pp. 1990.

IUCN. 1990. *United Nations List of National Parks and Protected Areas.* IUCN, Gland Switzerland, and Cambridge, U.K. 284 pp.

10

Climate Change in the Mountains

Morsarjökull, southeast Iceland, Skaftafell National Park. The glacier has been thinning and retreating since the late 19th century due to climate warming, with a short period of readvance, 1970 to present

Introduction

Scope of the problem

Our knowledge of the climatic characteristics of mountain regions is limited by both paucity of observations—short records that seldom span one hundred years and a sparse station network–and insufficient theoretical attention given to the complex interaction of spatial scales in weather and climate phenomena in mountains. Meteorological research has tended to focus on the upstream and downstream influences of barriers to flow and on orographic effects on weather systems (Smith, 1979), rather than on conditions in the mountain environment. Atmospheric phenomena themselves display a hierarchy of spatial and temporal scales as illustrated in Table 10.1. Microscale features of the atmosphere—wind gusts, for example—are superimposed on larger scales of motion and are not fixed in place, whereas small-scale elements of the landscape surface, such as vegetation canopy, large rocks and hollows, can create microclimatic contrasts in surface heating, soil moisture or snow-cover duration that have longer–lasting significance. The role of sunny (adret) and shaded (ubac) slopes in the Alps in influencing land use and settlement location has been long recognized (Garnett, 1935). Local wind systems, generated by radiational and thermal contrasts in complex terrain, are best developed when synoptic-scale pressure gradients are weak and there is little cloud cover; hence, they are intermittent components of the climate. Synoptic-scale systems—mid-latitude cyclones, for instance—are extensively modified as they move across a mountain barrier. Modifications occur on a large scale in terms of changes in frontal structure and cloud systems, and on a local scale in terms of wind systems, such as Föhn (Chinook) occurrence, or precipitation intensity. Isolating these processes in order to understand their operation is vastly complicated by the inadequate database for most mountain areas of the world.

Mountain influences on climate and related environmental features are a result of four basic factors: altitude, continentality, latitude and topography, each of which affects several important meteorological variables. The role of these factors, detailed in Barry (1981), are summarized schematically in Table 10.2 where the effects refer to responses to an increase in the factor listed. In turn, these climatic differences are expressed in vegetation type and cover, geomorphic and hydrologic features. The particular influences of topography are complex and worthy of further discussion. At a primary level, we need to distinguish between isolated peaks, mountain ranges that are large enough to modify the upstream and downstream airflow substantially, and extensive high plateaus that create major barriers to air motion and generate their own climates. Tabony (1985) notes that high peaks experience similar temperatures to the free air of the same altitude. However, elevated plateaus are heated in summer and cooled in winter by radiative processes. Valleys within uplands have 'enclosed' atmospheres that are diurnally modified by nocturnal cooling, especially in winter, and enhanced daytime heating.

Table 10.2 identifies one area important for human activities in high mountains, namely, the physiological stresses imposed by climate. The primary factors are reduced air pressure, which limits oxygen intake and working capacity, and

Table 10.1: *Scales in mountain weather and climate*

	Micro-scale	Local-scale	Regional-scale
Meteorological phenomena	Turbulent motion (gusts)	Slope and valley winds; fall winds	Thunderstorm cluster; synoptic system
Landscape elements	Rocks; vegetation clumps	Terrain elements (slopes; valleys)	Mountain range; plateau
Climatic features	Snow patches	adret/ubac radiational contrasts; thermal belts	Plateau; monsoon

Factors	Primary effects	Secondary effects
Altitude	reduced air density, vapour pressure; solar radiation receipts; lower temperatures	increased wind velocity (mid-latitudes); increased precipitation (mid-latitude); reduced evaporation; physiological stresses
Continentality	annual/diurnal temperature range increased; cloud/precipitation regimes modified	snow line altitude rises
Latitude	daylength and solar radiation totals vary seasonally	snowfall proportion increases; annual temperatures decrease
Topography	spatial contrasts in solar radiation/ temperature regimes, and precipitation as a result of slope and aspect	diurnal wind regimes; snow cover related to topography

Table 10.2: *Climatic effects of the basic mountain climate*

low temperatures, which necessitate adequate clothing and shelter and place limits on crop production potential. However, these primary factors differ in their significance. Low air pressure is a permanent unavoidable condition, whereas low temperatures can be counteracted. It is also worth noting that for a given altitude, say 4 000 m (neglecting the small numerical difference between geopotential and geometric height), the corresponding standard atmosphere value of pressure is approximately 630 mb at latitudes equatorward of 30 degrees, but at 60 degrees N latitude ranges between 593 mb in January and 616 mb in July (Sissenwine, 1969). Thus, at an equivalent height, the effect of reduced air pressure is substantially greater in middle and high latitudes, particularly in winter. The passage of a cyclonic system could further lower the pressure by some 20-30 mb, equivalent at the given altitude to a height difference of 250-375 m. Such latitudinal and seasonal effects may be important for visitors to high mountains, as well as in terms of high-altitude settlements and work enterprises in mid-latitudes.

Specific mountain climate data

1) *The European Alps* are by far the best-known mountain area of the world in terms of weather and climate and related environmental characteristics. Several summit observatories have records spanning 100 years and there is a dense network of regular observing stations and precipitation gauges. Detailed climatic atlases exist for the Tirol (Fliri, 1982) and Swiss Alps (Kirchhofer, 1982). Complementary information exists on Alpine glaciers (Haeberli et al., 1989), hydrologic regimes (Baumgartner et al., 1983), forest growth (Aulitsky et al., 1982) and other more specific topics. The Alps have also been the locale for the meteorological research programme ALPEX (Alpine Experiment) of the Global Atmospheric Research Programme (GARP) of the World Meteorological Organization, conducted between September 1981 and November 1982 (Smith, 1986), and many university research projects. Extensive studies also exist for the Carpathian Mountains (Obrebska-Starkel, 1990).

2) *The island of Hawaii* is well-known climatically through observations made at Mauna Loa Observatory since 1967 and various research programmes conducted on the windward and leeward slopes of the mountains in Hawaii and other islands. Similar data exist for *Mt. Fuji, Japan*, which also has a summit observatory. Most of the detailed studies on Mt. Fuji's climate are published in Japanese.

3) The climatic features of the *Rocky Mountains* and *Coast Ranges* in North America and the *mountains of Scandinavia* are known primarily through specialized university and other agency research programmes. Experiments on winter cloud-seeding and mountain lee-wave phenomena have been of particular importance in North America. Mountain-valley winds and orographic precipitation have been investigated in both Europe and North America. The station networks in these countries are moderately good but permanent mountain observatories are lacking. Detailed glacio-hydrological records are also available for

Norway, in particular. The Colorado Rocky Mountains and Scandinavian mountains have also been sites of ecological research under the International Biological Programme's Tundra Biome studies in the 1970s and, in the former area, related work has continued through Long-Term Ecological Research Program activities (Barry, 1986). A similar level of information is available for the *Greater Caucasus* in terms of climate and glacio-hydrological topics, but almost all of it is in Russian language articles and monographs.

4) A moderate level of information on the climate of very high mountains is available in the case of the *Northern Andes* and *Nepal Himalaya* The former area has a reasonable station network, including some high-altitude stations; microclimatic studies, related to ecological conditions, have provided valuable supplementary information (Monasterio, 1980). The major lack is aerological sounding data for information on free-air conditions. The large-scale climatic controls of this area are still poorly defined. In the case of Nepal, most stations are in the Himalayan valleys, but short-term measurements, particularly by recent Japanese glaciological expeditions, have provided additional information (Barry, 1981, Chapter 5). For the adjacent *Tibetan (Qinghai- Xizang) Plateau* there is now a growing meteorological literature, although several key studies are available only in Chinese.

5) Mountains where there have been discontinuous research programmes and only a sparse station network is available include such diverse areas as New Guinea, Ethiopia (Hurni and Stahli, 1982), Mt. Kenya, the Hoggar and the Mt. St. Elias Range. In New Guinea, where there is only one permanent station above 2 000 m, information on mountain environments (Barry, 1980) has focused on ecological conditions (Smith, 1975) and on the glaciers of Mt. Carstenz in Irian Jaya (Hope et al., 1976). More recently, frost occurrence and agroclimatic variability in the New Guinea Highlands have been analysed intensively (Brookfield and Allen, 1989).

Selected issues

This section provides a brief review of some selected topics of particular importance in mountain climatology. They are issues in the sense that incomplete knowledge of them may present problems in attempting to mitigate their consequences for the mountain environment and its inhabitants.

Orographic precipitation

Precipitation forecasting in mountain regions is nowadays performed using a combination of model prediction and near-real time radar measurement of precipitation falling, wherever such technology is available. Various numerical models are available to calculate precipitation rates for air ascending adiabatically over a mountain slope (Sarker, 1966) and incorporating "spill-over" effects (Colton, 1976). The concept can also be extended for snowfall (Rhen, 1978) and for convective precipitation (Georgakos and Bras, 1984). Hydro-climatological research has identified four factors that determine precipitation amount: rate of ascent, water vapour supply, wind direction and wind speed (Browning, 1980). Topographic variables that interact with the meteorological factors are: elevation, relative relief, aspect (orientation) and slope angle.

Calculations of the influence of mountainous terrain in England and Wales on air streams from different directions, with specified wind speeds and moisture contents, are illustrated by Hill (1983). Similar calculations of orographically-induced vertical motion for different wind directions have been made for Kyushu, Japan, using a three-dimensional numerical model with a 10 x 10 km topographic grid. The patterns of vertical motion compared satisfactorily with storm event precipitation similarly stratified by wind directions (Oki et al., 1991).

In the western United States there have been a number of pilot studies and operational programmes aimed at increasing winter snowfall by orographic cloud seeding. These include work in the Rocky Mountains of Colorado and in the Sierra Nevada. The seeding is carried out using silver iodide either from aircraft or, more cost-effectively, ground generators. Experiments near Climax, Colorado, with careful statistical control, indicated that a 25 per cent precipitation increase was achieved during southwesterly flow at 3 km with relatively high temperatures at 500 mb (Mielke et al., 1981). However the effect on seasonal totals is usually much less pronounced. Nevertheless, related studies in the San Juan Mountains, Colorado, (Steinhoff and Ives, 1976) and the Sierra Nevada, California, have sought to evaluate possible ecological impacts of increased winter snow pack and of silver iodide on flora, fauna, hydrological and sedimentation processes. The studies in Colorado included intensive plot studies where snow pack was increased several fold by the use of snow fences.

One of the major issues relating to precipitation is the recurrence of extreme events. An intense storm in July 1976 was responsible for the "Big Thompson" flood in the Colorado Front Range that caused at least 139 deaths and US$35 million property damage (Maddox et al., 1978). Jarrett (1990) shows that flooding in basins above about 2 400 m altitude in Colorado is related to snow melt, whereas at lower elevations, floods result from intense rainstorms. These appear to be both slow-moving summer thunderstorm systems and synoptic-scale cold lows, mainly in spring and autumn. At the higher elevations, storm precipitation is about an order of magnitude less than in the foothills (Figure 10.1). This result contradicts earlier ideas derived from simple transposition of storm models over the higher terrain. It has importance for structures; thus, reservoirs and culverts at higher elevations may have been overdesigned.

Figure 10.1: *Relation between precipitation and elevation, including envelope curve, for large storms in Colorado.* From Jarrett, 1990

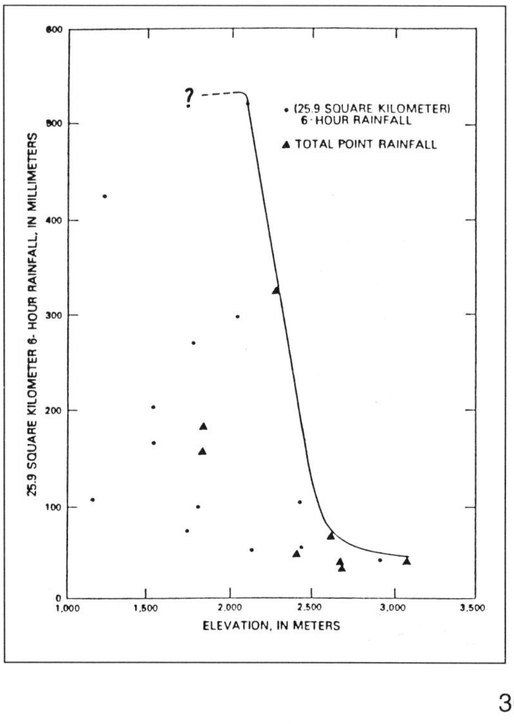

Extreme precipitation events have geomorphological significance in the Himalayas where they may cause widespread slope failure. Froehlich et al. (1990) show that storm events of 60-100 cm magnitude recur 2-4 times/ 100 years at Darjeeling, where the annual totals average 260-400 cm with extremes of 600 cm. In October 1968, at the end of the monsoon season, such an extreme storm event resulted in modifications to about one quarter of the cultivated area around Darjeeling (Starkel, 1972). The issue of the response of hydrological systems, erosion processes and sedimentation to climate change has been examined for mountains of western Canada by Slaymaker (1990). He outlines the type of impacts likely to result from climate warming, but notes that shifts in the limit of periglacial erosion, permafrost and forest vegetation will be slow.

Air quality and pollution deposition

Many mountain valleys are increasingly subject to the effects of air pollution originating from local settlements, industrial plants and automobiles, as well as from the regional transport of pollutants into the mountains from industrial conurbations. The diurnal wind regime in mountain valleys, during intervals of weak regional-scale pressure gradients, gives rise to upvalley and upslope motion by day that may transport pollutants into the mountains. At night the circulations are reversed but, typically, inversion conditions in valley bottoms and basins can lead to high concentrations of pollutants at low-levels (Hanna and Strimaitis, 1990). In winter, when solar heating is insufficient to remove them, such inversions can persist for most of the day.

Pollutants reach the surface by any deposition and washout. In mountain areas, the orographic enhancement of precipitation rates can lead to increased washout. Forland and Gjessing (1975) report that washout rates (relative to dry deposition) for Mg, SO_4 and Ca were 5-15 times greater on the 600 m high mountains around Bergen, Norway, than in the city itself.

Afforestation/deforestation of slopes

Studies of the effects of forest cover on local climate have received considerable attention, often showing conflicting results (Penman, 1963). The effects of differing vegetation cover on catchment hydrology have been studied for many years in Europe, North America and elsewhere (Bosch and Hewlett, 1982). Studies of upland moorland areas transformed by coniferous plantations have also been made in Great Britain. In a survey of94 paired catchment experiments, where trees were either removed by cutting or burning, or killed by applications of herbicides, or the area was planted, Bosch and Hewlett (1982) conclude that the direction and magnitude of changes in water yield can be predicted with fair accuracy. Many of the experiments were at elevations of 1 000 m or more in middle mountain terrain. Pine and eucalypti forest types give a change in annual water yield of about 4 cm per 10 per cent change in forest cover, while deciduous hardwoods cause a 2.5 cm change in yield per 10 per cent change in cover. The changes are largest in areas of higher rainfall. Increases in water yield following forest cover reduction are longer-lived in drier climates as the vegetation recovers more slowly. A change in vegetation cover from forest to grassland increases surface albedo, but reduces aerodynamic roughness and precipitation interception, all of which affect evaporative losses. Increased albedo lessens the absorbed solar radiation, but surface temperatures are higher at the surface of a grassland. Reduced roughness lowers the turbulent flux of moisture from the surface to the atmosphere. A multilayer simulation of interception by a pine forest, compared with grass, indicates that the latter intercepts only one quarter of the amount in a pine forest (Sellers and Lockwood, 1981). Using meteorological data from Oxfordshire as input, they calculate total annual evapotranspiration losses of 555 mm from pine versus 398 mm from grass (a 28 per cent reduction) and corresponding annual runoff values of 152 mm and 303 mm, respectively. Simulated peak flows were also 33 per cent greater for the grass cover. In mountain areas, a further consideration is that winter snow packs are generally greater in forested areas than in clearings and they persist longer in the spring.

In some tropical and Mediterranean climates, forested slopes can increase the available moisture through fog drip as a result of the vegetation removing cloud droplets from the airflow. This is an important determinant of the distribution of montane cloud forest, for example (Cavelier and Goldstein, 1989). However, the possible management of this moisture source appears to have received little attention until now. ■

Mountain glaciers in Baffin Island. Retreating glaciers have long been one of the most obvious signs of changing climates

Past climate

Sources of evidence

The major types of evidence for past climatic conditions are briefly summarized. Details of the techniques used to extract such information are available in the references cited.

1) Glacial geomorphology and glaciology. Numerous studies are available in the various mountain areas of the world on glacier variations and past glacier extent (Röthlisberger, 1986; Karlen, 1988; Haeberli et al., 1989). The lower altitudinal limits of ice cover can be mapped and dated by carbon-14 techniques for the last glaciation and by lichenometric methods for the last few centuries. For the more recent glacial advances or still stands, ice thickness, and therefore volume, may be estimated from trimlines on the valley sides. These changes in ice extent and inferred changes in snow line altitude can be interpreted in terms of likely changes in ablation-season temperature and winter accumulation, although unique solutions cannot be derived. Some attempts have been made to model ice volume changes in terms of climatic forcings, such as the work of Allison and Kruss (1977) for Irian Jaya (New Guinea). More recent studies on glacier climate modelling for the Alps have been carried out by Kuhn (1989), Oerlemans and Hoogendorn (1990) and others (see Oerlemans, 1989). Statistical analyses of glacier data indicate that in western North America cumulative deviations of mass balance from the mean value for each glacier are strongly correlated up to about 500 km distance, implying that useful regional climate information can be inferred from glaciological observations (Letréguilly and Reynaud, 1989).

2) Ice cores. The extraction of climatic and other atmospheric signals from ice cores has considerable potential in high-altitude ice bodies above the zone of melting (Thompson et al., 1984a). Falling snow traps air that is sealed off when ice is formed at about 60-100 m depth. The ice preserves records of atmospheric gas concentrations, aerosols, pollen and volcanic dust, as well as isotopic composition of the snow (related to crystallization temperature of the atmospheric water vapour) and net accumulation rate. In zones of high accumulation rate, annual layers can be distinguished for up to about 10 000 years, but in Alpine glaciers the records span at best a few thousand years. Ice core studies in mountain areas include those on Quelccaya Ice Cap, Peru; Colle Gnifetti and Mont Blanc, Alps; and Dunde Ice Cap, western China (Wagenbach, 1989). Drawbacks are the limited number of suitable cold firn sites and the rather short records available from Alpine ice bodies. The information is representative of a regional-scale area and this may be valuable in assessing regional anthropogenic effects, especially for pollution by heavy metals such as lead.

3) Paleoecology. Evidence of past climates is also obtainable from several biological sources of which pollen and dendrochronological records are the most important. Pollen records extracted from lake sediments and peat bogs can provide information on ecological changes at the genus, or occasionally the species, level for the last 10 000 to 100 000 years and in some instances longer. However, pollen may be transported long distances, the vegetational composition is not always fully or proportionately represented, and the ecological record must be converted to climatic information by some form of transfer function (Webb and Clark, 1977). For Pleistocene materials, an additional problem is caused when former plant assemblages lack a modern analogue. In mountain regions, local wind systems complicate the problem of interpreting the local versus regional pollen rain (Markgraf, 1980). In particular, Solomon and Silkworth (1986) draw attention to the "mixing lid" formed by valley inversions that may act as a strong barrier to upslope transport of lower-montane pollen. Thus, pollen embedded within the valley circulations may be isolated from that in the airflows above the ridge line. Hence, altitudinal shifts of species are hard to isolate. In this respect, pack-rat middens are useful, in the western United States for example, in providing specific plant macrofossil information (Betancourt et al., 1990). Further difficulties in the utilization of pollen data are the necessity to date the sediments by carbon-14 and the relatively coarse temporal resolution that is usually available, given the intervals between such dates, their standard errors, and variable sedimentation rates. Fifty to 200 years is the typical resolution over time intervals of 1 000 to 10 000 years, respectively.

Dendrochronology has several advantages. It provides annual, or even seasonal, resolution over hundreds to a few thousands of years. Two distinct techniques provide climatic information. The first, widely employed, dendroecological method is to measure annual ring width and the second is to analyse wood density (Fritts, 1976; Schweingruber et al., 1979). Ring width, when corrected for age trend, varies strongly in response to summer temperature towards the polar and upper altitudinal tree lines, and to summer moisture near the lower altitudinal tree line in arid regions. Detailed quantitative interpretation of the ring width or wood density information involves the development of numerical transfer functions, analogous to those for pollen studies, based on climatic records at nearby stations. Tree ring studies can also be used to determine fire histories and volcanic eruptions, as well as streamflow condition using ring width-runoff calibrations.

4) *Historical records.* Direct reports of weather-related conditions are contained in personal diaries and official records in European countries, China, Japan, and elsewhere from the 16th-17th centuries, as interest in natural science developed, or even earlier in association with documentation of agricultural production for taxation purposes. In the Alpine countries, Britain and Scandinavia, in particular, some of these sources provide information on the climatic deterioration in mountain and upland areas during the Little Ice Age, AD 1650-1850, compared with the Medieval Warm Period (Lamb, 1977; Parry, 1978; Pfister, 1985a; 1985b; Grove, 1988; Zumbühl, 1988). Extraction of quantitative material from such sources requires skilled knowledge of historical document interpretation (the necessity for primary sources, content analysis, and consistency checking) and means of standardizing incomplete or short-period records from a particular location with modern data.

5) *Instrumental observations.* The origins of mountain meteorology can be dated to the work of Horace-Benedict de Saussure in the Alps (Barry, 1978). In August 1789, he and his son maintained hourly weather observations for two weeks on the Col du Géant, Mont Blanc. Systematic observations at mountain observatories, however, did not begin until the late 19th century (Barry, 1981, Table 1.1). Diaz and Bradley (1991) identify some 22 stations in Europe, 8 in Asia, and 37 in the USA above 1500 m with long-term (+30 years) records. However, not all of these are mountain stations; some are on high plateaus and others in mountains valleys. Second-order and auxiliary stations with shorter records are perhaps ten times more numerous.

6) *Remote Sensing.* Remote sensing, by aerial photography beginning in the 1930s and satellite sensing beginning in the late 1960s, provides spatially extensive views of surface conditions at specific time intervals. Examples of useful records include air photographs of glacier extent in remote alpine mountain areas (Allison and Peterson, 1976) and global satellite mapping of snow cover since about 1970 (Wiesnet et al., 1987). However, the latter data are suitable only for analyses of large regions. Operational snow mapping of 28 river basins in western North America is performed by NOAA/NESDIS using daily-coverage GOES 1 km-resolution data. Daily AVHRR data from NOAA polar-orbiting satellites are also used by many countries for similar purposes (Rango, 1985). In both cases, such data are usually supplemented by airborne gamma-radiation measurements and/or ground observations of snow depth and water equivalent. Cloud cover is always a problem in using visible and infrared satellite data, but passive microwave data can assist in solving this problem, albeit with a lower spatial resolution (Rango et al., 1989).

Past conditions

1) *Last glacial maximum.* For the last glacial cycle, global climates have been reconstructed by several groups using a variety of paleoclimatic data extracted from cores of ocean sediments, lake and bog sediments, ice layers, tree rings, etc. (CLIMAP Project Members, 1976, 1981; COHMAP Members, 1988). Ocean temperatures estimated for the last glacial maximum, about 18 000 BP, based on planktonic foraminifera, show either modest cooling (< 2 degrees C) or even warming of ocean surface waters in most low–and subtropical–latitude areas. In contrast, glacial-geomorphologic evidence of former glacier extent and downward displacement of vegetation zones in tropical mountain areas of the order of almost 1 km imply substantially greater cooling of 5-6 degrees C. This pattern has, for example, been found for New Guinea (Bowler et al., 1976) and Hawaii (Porter, 1979).

Webster and Streten (1978), Rind and Peteet (1985), and LaFontaine (1988) discuss the

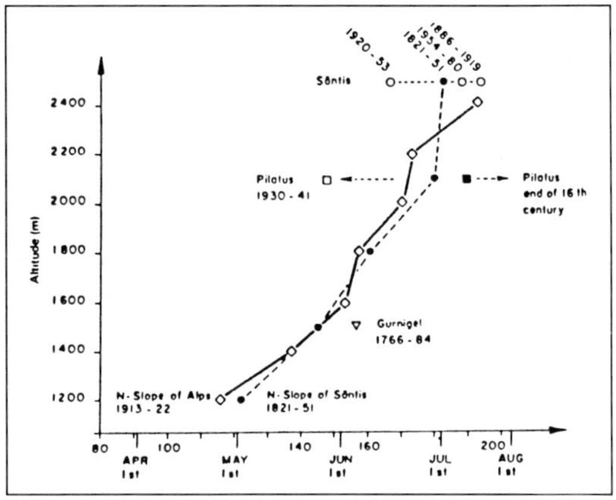

Figure 10.2: *Changes in date of snow melt at locations in the Swiss Alps.* From Pfister, 1985b

evidence and possible explanations, if the interpretations of the paleoclimatic records are assumed to be reliable. They suggest several physical causes: the atmospheric temperature lapse rate may have been steeper than now, or more frequent incursions of upper level cold troughs from middle latitudes may have increased snowfall and lowered temperatures. Simulations of snowline lowering using the CLIMAP-reconstructed sea surface temperature data and Goddard Institute for Space Studies climate model (8 degrees latitude x 10 degrees longitude resolution) indicated lowerings only half (or less) of those observed, implying that the CLIMAP data may have a warm bias (Rind and Peteet, 1985). Subsequently, Rind (1988) has shown that model results must be used with great caution. By using a finer-grid resolution (4 degrees x 5 degrees) than in the previous study, he demonstrates that more atmospheric cooling and snow line lowering is simulated for the Last Glacial Maximum in the Hawaiian region, although little change occurred in the other tropical mountain areas (Colombia, New Guinea and East Africa). The improved fit is attributable to the effects of the grid resolution on moist convection in the model. However, Rind emphasizes that better agreement between model and observations may not necessarily imply that the model results are more realistic!

2) *Little Ice Age.* Geomorphological studies show that there have been numerous advances and retreats of glacier margins since the large-scale retreat at the end of the last glacial maximum, dated around 18 000 years ago. The best known of these is the Little Ice Age of the 16th-19th centuries in Europe (Grove, 1988), where there is supporting documentary and observational evidence (see above). However, similar fluctuations are reported in most mountain areas of the world, with slight differences of timing. As for the glacier fluctuations identified in major mountain regions during the Holocene period (10 000 years before the present until now) by Röthlisberger (1986), there are broad similarities, and the more detailed records of the last 1 000 years (dated mainly by lichenometry in New Zealand) indicate a general pattern resembling that of the Alps, but with a major 14th-century interval of advance (Gellatly et al., 1988). In the central Asiatic mountains of the Russian Confederation Kotlyakov et al. (1991) also find that there were important advances in the late 15th century and early 16th century. The glaciological expression of climate fluctuations depends strongly on the continentality of the climate. For example, the equilibrium line altitude was lowered only 50 m in the drier Tien Shan and Altai during the 13th century, but 150 m in the more humid Caucasus. Similar effects are evident in recent glacier fluctuations.

Apart from Alpine glacier information, records of snow cover have been assembled for the Alps by Pfister (1985a; 1986b). He reports that altitudes above 1 800-2 000 m in the vicinity of Mt. Santis became snowfree three to four weeks earlier in 1920-53 than in either 1886-1919 or 1954-80. The period 1920-53 experienced warm spring to early summer months. However, the later melt in 1954-80 was related primarily to 5 per cent more water precipitation (falling as snow). In 1886-1919 there was an 8 per cent increase in spring precipitation. Surprisingly, 1821-51 was less extreme than either of these periods. Other records for Mount Pilatus, near Lucerne (Figure 10.2), show a six-week difference between the 1930s and the end of the 16th century.

Pfister (1985b) shows that the climatic response to a given synoptic pattern may be quite different in the lowlands from that at higher altitudes. In winter, storm systems from the west bring rainfall and induce snow melt in the lowland but snowfall in the Alps, whereas during anticyclonic situations inversions with fog may maintain lowland snow cover, but permit melt above the inversion on south-facing slopes. In spring, the increased amounts of precipitation fall as snow above 2 500 m, but only 50-60 per cent of the precipitation falls as snow at 1 200 m. As a result of these complexities, changes in snow cover at lower elevations are often poorly correlated with those on neighbouring mountains. Thus, Figure 10.2 shows little difference between the dates of snow melt at 1 200 m for 1821-51 and 1913-32 on the north slope of Santis and the Alps, respectively, in contrast to the situation at higher elevations.

3) *The observational record.* It is of interest to know what changes mountain regions have experienced. Mountain observations can provide an indication of changes in the free atmosphere for a much longer period than sounding data, but up to now, such records have received limited attention. Measurements on the Zugspitze and Sonnblick in the Alps provide such long-term series, but even at these stations there are problems of data homogeneity due to changes or instrumentation or observing practice. Nevertheless, the unique 100-year record on the Sonnblick, Austria, (Auer et al., 1990) shows the well-known early 20th century warming between 1900 and 1950 of about 2 degrees C in spring and summer and 2.5 degrees C between 1910 and 1960 in October (Figure 10.3). In winter, however, no clear trend is apparent although the 1970s were warmer than the early part of the century. This contrast with the general northern hemisphere trend, where the warming is most pronounced in winter, may reflect the free-air lapse-rate conditions at the mountain summit. Records for five valley stations in the Canadian Rocky Mountains covering a common period of 1916-88 show important topoclimatic differences according to Luckman (1990). Only Banff, with almost a 100-year record, shows an overall positive trend in mean annual temperatures.

The records from mountain observatories also enable us to compare the degree of parallelism and relative amplitudes of trends in the mountains and on the adjacent lowlands. Analyses illustrating trends of sunshine and snowfall in lowland and mountain regions of Austria (Steinhauser, 1970, 1973) are among the most complete such records available. Annual sunshine totals at Sonnblick (3 106 m) and Villach (2 140 m) show fluctuations similar in timing and amplitudes to those at four lowland stations. This agreement holds also on a seasonal basis, except in winter as a result of inversions associated with lowland fog and stratus. Variations in snow cover duration in Austria since 1900 show inter-regional differences, with stations in western Austria and the southern Alps displaying patterns that are different from those in the northern Alpine Foreland and northeastern Austria. Temperature trends at Sonnblick for 1887-1979, compared with Hohenpeissenberg (994 m) and lowland stations in the surrounding region suggest that differences between them reflect spatial gradients rather than altitudinal contrasts (Lauscher, 1980).

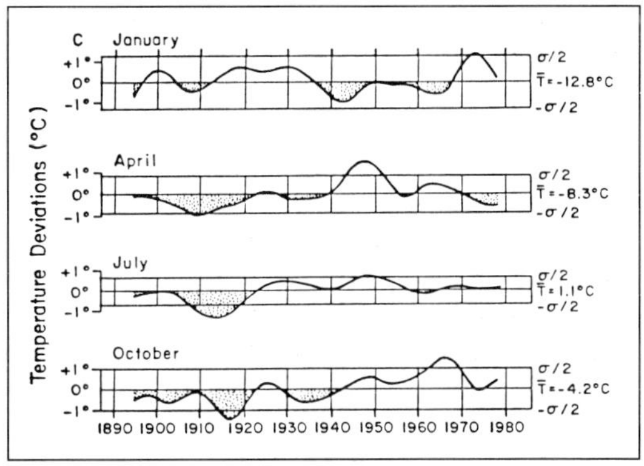

***Figure 10.3**: Temperature departures from the mean for 1887-1986 at Sonnblick (3 106 m) for January, April, July and October. Departures are smoothed by a 20-year Gaussian moving average. Monthly mean values (°C) and the standard deviation (σ)/2 are indicated.* After Auer et al., 1990

For many Alpine areas there are numerous observations of changes in ice masses. Retreat of glacier fronts and negative mass balances characterized most glaciers in the Alps (Figure 10.4) and other Alpine areas from around 1900 until the 1960s-1970s with only brief interruptions (Wood, 1988; Hastenrath et al., 1989). Smaller glaciers in the European Alps underwent some advance in the 1980s, in response to increased winter accumulation and slightly cooler summers, but this interval appears to have ceased (Patzelt and Aellen, 1990). Maritime glaciers in west coast areas of

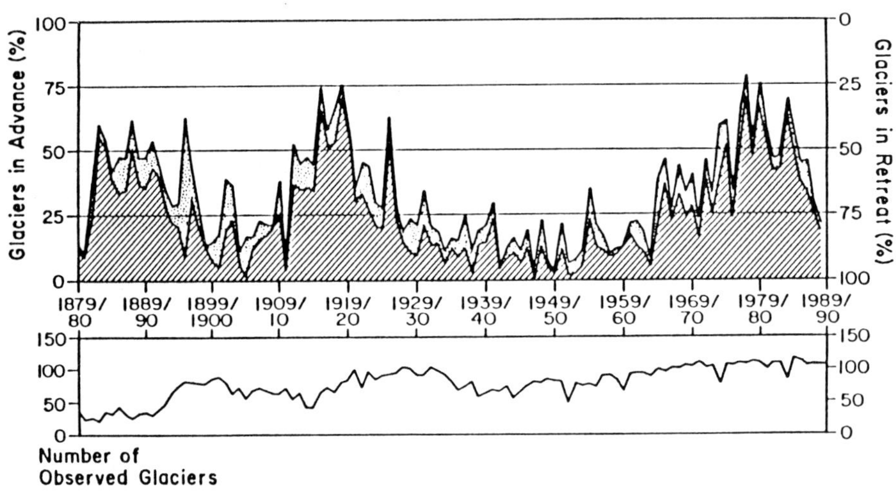

Figure 10.4: *Percentage of glaciers advancing, retreating or stationary in the Alps.*
From Patzelt and Aellen, 1990

North America and Scandinavia showed similar advances associated with precipitation increases during the 1980s whereas glaciers in continental interior locations mostly continued to retreat (Makarevich and Rototaevn, 1986).

The century-long meteorological records in the European Alps can be usefully compared with observations of changes in Alpine glaciers. Chen (1990), for example, reconstructs the balance of eight glaciers using summer temperatures and annual precipitation records. For 1864-1987, he finds an area-weighted mean-annual mass balance of -287 mm. The annual mean air temperature (at 25 stations in or near the Alps) rose more than 0.6 degree C from the 1850s to 1988, culminating in the late 1940s with subsequent weak cooling. Chen and Funk (1990) demonstrate that the mass balance of the Rhone Glacier, which has been studied more or less continuously since 1974, responds primarily to summer temperature with sensible-heat flux and net radiation contributing almost equally to the energy input required for ablation.

Temporal changes of climate variables in the Alps show some interesting contrast with altitudinal effects. At Sonnblick (3 106 m) the average number of days with snow cover during May-September decreased from 82 days for 1910-25 to only 53 days for 1955-70 (Bohm, 1986). During the same interval, mean summer temperatures rose about 0.5 degree C. However, if we compare the difference in days with snow cover over an altitude difference of 100 m (corresponding to a mean lapse rate of 0.5 degree C/100 m), a decrease of 10-11 days, rather than 29 days, would be expected in the eastern Alps. Evidently, nonlinearities associated with snow melt effects and summer snowfalls must be involved.

There are quite long records of snow depth data at mountain stations in the Alps and at snow courses in the North American Rocky Mountains and Cordillera. However, in only a few instances have these been digitized and archived. Consequently, these records have been underutilized for climatic analyses of temporal change. Two recent studies using such data illustrate the potential complexity of spatio-temporal changes.

Snow depth data at Davos (1 540 m) Switzerland, are available since 1892. Fohn et al., (1990) show, using 5-year running means, that snow depth on 1 January increased from < 60 cm in the 1890s to 80-90 cm around the 1920s, and declined to about 30 cm in the mid-1930s. Subsequently, depths increased again and have been more or less constant, around 50 cm, up to

1990. Nevertheless, snow pack water equivalent on 15 April has substantially exceeded that on 1 January since about 1975, whereas the two values were similar from 1950 to 1965 (Fohn et al., 1990) indicating more snowfall in late winter. In the southern and western Alps, 1988 and 1990 were particularly poor snow seasons in the early winter but the century-long Davos record shows that such short-term anomalies are recurrent and need not indicate a warming trend.

Snow course records on 1 April at 275 high-elevation sites in Idaho, Montana, Wyoming, Colorado and Utah for 1951-89 have been analysed by Changnon et al. (1991). They find that a shift in the north-south distribution of snowpack occurred in the mid-1970s. Winter seasons with heavy snowfall in the "northern" Rockies and low snowfall in the "southern" Rockies were confined to the period 1951-73, while seasons with the opposite pattern were likewise confined to the 1976-89 period. This appears to be a natural fluctuation associated with a change in the frequency of depression tracks. Similar north-south contrasting patterns were identified in precipitation studies by Bradley (1976).

A different source of long-term information for the high Andes is provided by ice cores collected from the Quelccaya Ice Cap in southern Peru (14 degrees S, 71 degrees W), 5 670 m above sea level. Annual layers for the last 1 500 years suggest that a recent decrease in precipitation may be associated with more frequent El Nino events in the western Pacific. The interval AD 1500-1720 was identified as the wettest part of the record (Thompson et al., 1984b; 1985). ■

Future climate

Assessing future climate

Assessments of potential future climatic conditions can be made by following three approaches:

1) *Analogues.* Until recently, the most commonly adopted method was an empirical study using analogues of previous events identified from observations, historical or geological records. For example, warm/cold years or wet/dry years have been grouped either from individual extreme years or longer intervals of one or other regime as a basis for scenarios of regional conditions (Jager and Kellogg, 1983; Lough et al., 1983). However, the observational record is considered too short to represent adequately potential future changes induced by greenhouse gases. The mid-Holocene and even Tertiary intervals have also been examined as possible analogues of greenhouse warming, but Crowley (1990) concludes that none of these provide satisfactory analogues, especially for regional conditions.

2) *General circulation models (GCMs).* GCMs can be used to simulate the effect on global climate of various changes in climatic forcing (e.g., in solar radiation, greenhouse gas concentration, surface boundary conditions due to deforestation and desertification). They can incorporate the major physical processes that interact to determine regional climates. Nevertheless, many of the processes involving ocean-atmosphere interactions and biogeochemical interactions are still treated rather crudely. Computing limitations also necessitate relatively coarse spatial resolution (equivalent to about 5 degrees latitude typically) and therefore mountain terrain is often greatly smoothed. This is known to produce errors in the simulated wind fields and therefore in the distribution of clouds and precipitation in particular. Moreover, model climate outputs are conventionally presented for sea level and ignore conditions at the surface over elevated mountainous regions. To address this problem, local climatic conditions may be assessed empirically using statistical relationships for the observed present climate (Giorgi and Mearns, 1991). This assumes that similar relationships would still obtain under a different global regime. Brazel and Marcus (1991) illustrate an attempt to compare temperature observations in a

mountain area of Kashmir and Ladakh with standard GCM simulations of present climate.

3) *Nested models*. Recently, attention has turned to using a high-resolution limited area model nested within a GCM to examine regional climate change (Giorgi and Mearns, 1991). GCM output is used to provide the boundary conditions for a limited area model that can provide a resolution of 10-100 km over areas of 1-25 x 10^6 km^2. The results of such studies are illustrated by Dickinson et al., (1989) for the western United States and by Giorgi et al., (1990) for western Europe. Investigations of regional greenhouse-gas-induced climate change scenarios are planned for the near future.

Climate scenarios and potential impacts

Up to now there have been a limited number of studies concerned with potential future climatic conditions in mountain regions. Attention has mainly focused on changes in glacier runoff. A glacier-climate model study of the Hintereisferner, Austria, suggests that over a 60-year period increasing greenhouse gas concentrations could increase runoff by 11 per cent, but the calculations assume the same summer radiation regime and neglect possible changes in cloudiness and precipitation (Grenell and Oerlemans, 1990). As illustrated in Figure 10.5, the possible hydroclimatic effects of greenhouse gases are likely to be complex.

Studies of changes in the hydrology of a medium-sized catchment in California, based on GCM simulations (Gleick, 1989; Lettenmaier and Gan, 1990) indicate some of the likely general characteristics that may be anticipated for a global warming. These include the following:

1) decreased winter snowfall and reduced spring-summer runoff and soil moisture and

2) increased winter runoff, due to more winter rainfall and earlier snow melt.

The seasonal distribution of runoff in watersheds with seasonal snow cover is mainly sensitive to temperature, which accelerates snow melt. However, total annual runoff is more sensitive to precipitation changes. Such investigations need to be carried out for mountain watersheds in other parts of the world.

Potential significance of changes in climate for mountain environments

Mountain snow packs are of major significance in a number of respects. First, they are a primary water resource for adjacent lowlands in terms of agricultural use (irrigation), industrial use and drinking water, as in the western United States where about 70 per cent of the water required by agriculture originates from mountain snow packs. A different water usage exists in Norway, for example, where snowmelt runoff is utilized for hydropower generation. Second, adequate snow depths and duration of snow cover are the essential elements of winter sports developments, now widespread in alpine regions of both hemispheres. Third, the snow pack characteristics are important in providing habitat for small animals and in creating a mosaic of microenvironments for plant cover

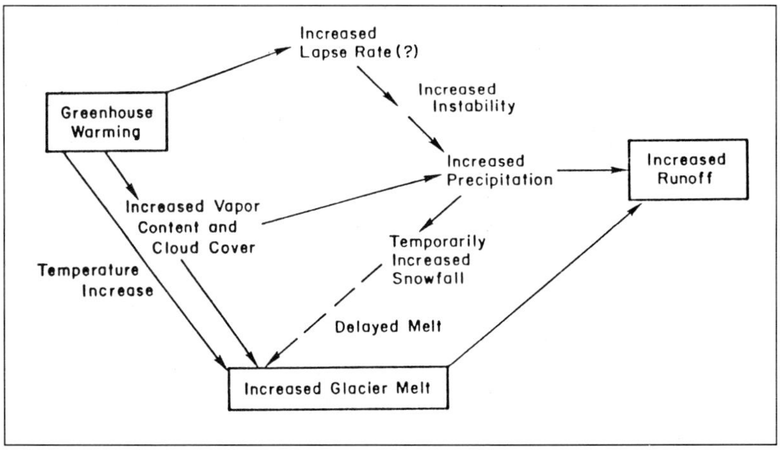

***Figure 10.5**: Schematic diagram of possible greenhouse-gas-induced warming effects on climate and hydrology in mountain areas.*
From Barry, 1990

in mountainous terrain. In human terms, the snowpack properties and climatic elements also determine the potential for avalanche occurrence and for drifting and blowing snow. Climatic factors that may cause significant changes in mountain snow cover are now considered in the context of the above concerns.

1) *Snow cover duration.* The duration of continuous snowcover (D) typically varies linearly with altitude (h) since it depends mainly on mean temperature. The following relationships are cited by Slatyer et al. (1984):

$D = 0.173\,h - 204.3$ for the Australian Alps (36°S)

$D = 0.122\,h - 23.1$ for the Swiss Alps (47° N)

$D = 0.155\,h + 11$ for Britain (63° N)

where D is in days, h is in metres.

Slatyer et al. (1984) note that the area that has 90 days of snow cover in Switzerland (above 930 m) extends over nearly 22 900 km^2 while the corresponding area in Australia (above 1 700 m) covers only 40.5 km^2. A modest rise in mean snow line with a shorter snow cover duration would virtually eliminate the season for winter tourism in the Australian Alps (Galloway, 1988). Meteorological factors combined with the modest elevation of the latter area also give rise to a large year-to-year variation in snow depths (Budin, 1985). Strong westerly regimes give snowy winters due to orographic uplift over the Australian Alps, whereas warm dry winds suppress snowfall when the subtropical ridge of high pressure is located over southeastern Australia, as during El Nino-Southern 0scillation (ENSO) warm phases.

The criterion used for assessing snow cover suitable for skiing in Canada is the percentage probability of a day with at least 5 cm snow cover, a maximum temperature less than 4.6 degrees C and no measurable liquid precipitation (including freezing precipitation). Conditions are considered unreliable if this percentile value is <50, marginally reliable if it is 50-74, and reliable if it is >75 (Crowe et al., 1977). Using climate simulations from two GCMs for $C0_2$ -doubling, and climate data for two downhill skiing centres in Ontario, Harrison et al. (1986) conclude that the ski season at Lakehead on the northwest shore of Lake Superior could be reduced 31-44 per cent with economic losses approaching $2 million (Canadian) while in the Georgian Bay area further south, downhill skiing would be virtually eliminated. The Georgian Bay skiing resorts could lose $37 million annually and the service centre a further $13 million (Canadian). Such conditions occur there at present during mild winters.

2) *Snow depth.* For Switzerland, Witmer et al. (1986) provide a detailed analysis of snow depths in relation to altitude and aspect. They use data for 20 or 30 years for 209 stations between 200 m and 2 800 m, although only five stations are above 2 000 m. Particularly interesting for applied studies is their analysis of slope-aspect differences in snow depth. Compared with a horizontal surface, depths in late March are twice as great on a 20 degrees north-facing slope, but only 30 per cent of horizontal on a 20 degrees south-facing slope. Such aspect differences need to be considered in any assessment of potential future changes in snowfall amount and snow cover duration. Less readily detectable in standard climatological records would be the character of recent winter seasons in the European Alps where the snowfall shows little change in amount but the timing of significant accumulation is delayed beyond late December to early January (Fohn et al., 1990). Such shifts could have major effects on winter sports.

3) *Snowmelt runoff.* Since most precipitation at high elevations falls as snow, the timing of runoff is primarily determined by snow melt and therefore spring temperatures and solar radiation. European runoff studies deal primarily with partly glacierized basins. Collins (1987; 1989), for example, shows that discharge from tributaries of the upper Rhone are inversely correlated with mean summer temperatures at valley stations such as Sion. A one degree C lowering in mean May–September temperature at Sion between 1941-50 and 1968-77 was associated with a 26 per cent reduction in mean summer discharge. Reductions in the glacierized area of a drainage basin such as the upper Rhone were investigated by Kasser (1973). A decrease in ice cover of 165 km^2 (from 16.8 per cent of a ~ 220km^2 basin in 1916 to 13.6 per cent in 1968) caused an estimated reduction of ~140 kg/m^2 in the April to September runoff at Porte du Scex compared with a mean for 1916-55 of 887 kg/m^2.

Direct anthropogenic impacts versus global climate changes

The relative importance of climatic factors versus human influences in causing environmental change is generally difficult to disentangle. This is illustrated by arguments over the nature and causes of desertification (Hare, 1983), for example. However, the removal of vegetation cover, particularly forests, by logging, and changes in species composition due to agriculture and grazing are more apparent. In a case study for the northern slope of the central Caucasus, Krenke et al. (1991) attempt to calculate the relative effects of anthropogenic versus natural changes on heat and water budgets. Between the second half of the 19th century and the 1980s, the forested area decreased from 32 per cent to 14 per cent in the Kabardin-Balkaria foothills between Mt. Elbrus and Nalchik, and the snow/ice covered area shrank as the equilibrium line altitude rose. In the nival-glacial belt, a decrease in runoff has resulted mainly from an 11-12 per cent reduction in precipitation. In the formerly forested areas, now steppe or meadow, where precipitation amounts have increased by 5-10 per cent, evaporation has also decreased and runoff increased. At lower altitudes, anthropogenic impacts are more significant than the natural changes, whereas the converse is true at higher altitudes. ■

Status of knowledge and recommendations

Data

This survey indicates that there are significant gaps in the available database on mountain climates. First, there is no convenient inventory of existing (or former) mountain climate stations, much less a catalogue of data collected by them. Assembling such information from national archives would be tedious but of modest cost relative to the value of a well-documented, accessible (computer-compatible) database. It would need to be updated annually. Second, there are many mountain areas, notably in the North and South American Cordillera, with very few permanent mountain stations. This situation will not be easily remedied, although automatic weather stations offer a possible solution, at least on a field "campaign" basis.

Understanding of processes

Theoretical studies of mountain meteorology have focused on the synoptic-scale effects of mountain terrain (cyclone and precipitation modification on the windward slopes; and lee cyclogenesis downstream), or on meso-scale features such as local winds and lee waves. Studies within mountain regions have concentrated heavily on mountain-valley winds, the effects of topography on radiation, and weather modification. Many basic questions concerning the altitudinal variation of water balance components and energy budget components, for example, have been relatively neglected. Such questions are of great importance if climate model results are to be interpreted properly within areas of complex terrain.

Mesoscale numerical models suitable for studies of local circulation, diffusion and air quality, as well as of precipitation prediction, are well developed and have been applied to many regions of complex terrain, if not to high mountain areas. The problem of using GCMs for climate change scenarios may be capable of resolution via the nested model strategy, but such work is only just beginning. The availability of suitable observational data for the validation of such analyses is likely to be a serious deficiency.

Constraints

The limited progress in climatological studies in mountain regions is attributable primarily to insufficient funding. This has affected not only the maintenance of high-altitude stations, especially observatories, but also the training of scientific personnel. There has been a failure to recognize the need for climate studies in areas of complex terrain, where measurements may be difficult to interpret in a regional context and where operational costs may be high. Nevertheless, modern automatic weather stations and data loggers powered by solar panels are now available at modest cost and can operate reliably, unattended for long periods. Most climate research in mountain areas has been carried out in connection with the assessment of prediction of water resources, forestry management, and pollution monitoring. Biological and physiological studies of altitudinal and climatic effects on flora, fauna and human populations have also been performed in several areas, although these have generally been short-term programmes.

Needed actions

Several recommendations can be made based on this review and assessment of the status of mountain climate research. The following tasks are essential:

1) A thorough inventory of existing (or previously completed) climate observation programmes should be made. This survey should identify existing data, their period of record and variables measured, and the location and availability of existing data sets.

2) These data should be compiled, quality controlled and made widely available on convenient media (diskettes, tapes and/or CD-ROMs) preferably by a single centre working with various institutions that may hold some of the records.

3) The importance of sustained measurement and monitoring programmes in mountain regions needs to be communicated to appropriate national and international agencies, especially those concerned with global change related studies. These agencies include national programmes concerned with climate, water resources and environmental quality, and international agencies such as the United Nations Environment Programme, the Man and Biosphere Programme and the Global Environmental Monitoring Programme of UNESCO, the World Climate Programme of WMO, and International Geosphere Biosphere Programme of ICSU.

4) Building effectively on such measurement and research programmes will necessitate that efforts be made to develop the entire infrastructure of education and training programmes for mountain studies including building and maintaining appropriate facilities in mountain locations. One or more Regional Research Centres for the IGBP could, for example, be devoted to problems of mountain environments. ■

References

ALLISON, K. and KRUSS, P. 1977. Estimation of recent climatic change in Irian Jaya by numerical modelling of its tropical glaciers. *Arct. Alp Res.*, 9: 49-60.

ALLISON, K. and PETERSON, J.A. 1976. Ice areas on Mt. Jaya: Their extent and recent history. In: G.S. Hope, J.S. Peterson, I. Allison and U. Radok (eds.) *The Equatorial Glaciers of New Guinea*. A.A. Balkema, Rotterdam, pp. 27-38.

AUER, I., BOHM, R. and MOHN, L.H. 1990. Die tropospharische Erwarmungsphase die 20.Jahrhunderts im Spiegel der lOO jahrigen Messreihe des alpinen Gipfelobservatoriums auf dem Sonblick. In: *Proc. 20th Internat. Tagung fur Alpine Meteorologie, 1988* (Sestola, Italy). Rome, Italian Met. Service, in press.

AULITSKY, H., TURNER, H. and MAYER, H. 1982. Bioklimatische Grundlagen einer standortgemassen Bewirtschaftung des subalpinen Larchen - Arvenwaldes. *Eidg. Anst. forstl Versuchswes. Mitteilurgen*, 58(4): 325-580.

BARRY, R.G. 1978. H.B. de Saussure: the first mountain meteorologist. *Bull. Amer. Met. Soc.*, 59: 702-705.

BARRY, R.G. 1980. Mountain climates of New Guinea. In: P. van Royen, (ed.) *The Alpine Flora of New Guinea*, Vol. I, General Part. J. Cramer, Vaduz, Liechtenstein, pp. 75-109.

BARRY, R. G. 1981. *Mountain Weather and Climate*. Methuen, London.

BARRY, R.G. 1986. Mountain climate data for long-term ecological research. In: *Proceedings of International Symposium on the Qinghai-Xizang Plateau and Mountain Meteorology*. Science Press, Beijing pp. 170-187.

BARRY, R.G. 1990. Changes in mountain climate and glacio-hydrological responses. *Mountain Research and Development*, 10: 161-170.

BAUMGARTNER, A., REICHEL, E. and WEBER, G. 1983. *Der Wasschausshalt der Alpen*. R. Oldenbourg, Munich, 343 pp.

BETANCOURT, J.L, VAN DEVENDER, T.R. and MARTIN, P.S. (eds.), 1990. *The Last 40 000 Years of Biotic Change*. University of Arizona Press., Tucson, 467 pp.

BOHM, R. 1986. *Der Sonnblick. Die 100 jahrige Geschichte des Observatoriums und seiner Forschungstatigkeit*. Vienna, 0sterreichischer Bundesverlag, 224 pp.

BOSCH, J.M. and HEWLETT, J.D. 1982. A review of catchment experiments to determine the effect of vegetation changes on water yield and evapotranspiration. *J. Hydrol.*, 55:2-23.

BOWLER, J.M., HOPE, G.S., JENNINGS, J.N., SINGH, G., and WALKER, D. 1976. Late Quaternary climates of Australia and New Zealand. *Quaternary Research*, 6: 359-399.

BRADLEY, R.S. 1976. *Precipitation History of the Rocky Mountain States*. Westview Press. Boulder, Colorado.

BRAZEL, A.J. and MARCUS, M.G. 1991. July temperatures in mountainous Kashmir and Ladakh, India. *Mountain Research and Development*, 11: 76-86.

BROOKFIELD, H. and ALLEN, B. 1989. High-altitude occupation and environment. *Mountain Research and Development*, 9(3):201-9.

BROWNING, K.A. 1980. Structure, mechanism and prediction of orographically enhanced rain in Britain. In: R. HIDE and P.W. WHITE (eds.) *Orographic Effects in Planetary Flows*. GARP Publ. Series No. 23, WMO, Geneva, pp. 85-114.

BUDIN, A.R. 1985. Interannual variability of Australian snowfall. *Austral Met. Mag.*, 33:145-139.

CAVELIER, J. and GOLDSTEIN, G. 1989. Mist and fog interception in elfin cloud forests in Colombia and Venezuela. *J. Trop. Ecol.*, 6: 309-322.

CHANGNON, D., MCKEE, T.B. and DOESKEN, R.J. 1991. Climate variability of mountain snowpacks in the central Rocky Mountains. In: *Proc. 15th Annual Climate Diagnostics Workshop*. NOAA, US Dept. of Commerce, pp. 384-389.

CHEN, J.Y. 1990. *Changes of Alpine Climate and Glacier Water Resources*. Doctoral dissertation No. 9243, ETH, Zurich, 178 pp.

CHEN, J.Y. and FUNK, M. 1990. Mass balance of Rhonegletscher during 1882/83-1986/87. *J. Glaciol.*, 36:199-209.

CLIMAP PROJECT MEMBERS, 1976. The surface of the Ice Age earth. *Science*, 191.

CLIMAP PROJECT MEMBERS, 1981. *Seasonal reconstruction of the earth's surface at the last glacial maximum*. Geological Society of America, Map Chart Series, MC-36.

COHMAP MEMBERS, 1988. Climatic changes of the last 18,000 years: observations and model simulation. *Science*, 241: 1043-1052.

COLLINS, D.N. 1987. Climatic fluctuations and run off from glacierized alpine basins. In: S.I. Solomon et al. (eds). *The Influence of Climate Change and Climatic Variability on the Hydrologic Regime and Water Resources*. Internat. Assoc. Hydrol. Sci., Publ. No. 168:77-89.

COLLINS, D.N. 1989. Hydrometeorological conditions, mass balance and runoff from alpine glaciers. In: J. Oerlemans, (ed.), *Glacier Fluctuations and Climate Change*. Kluwer, Dordrecht, pp. 305-323.

COLTON, D.E. 1976. Numerical simulation of the orographically induced precipitation distribution for use in hydrologic analysis. *J. Appl. Met.*, 15: 1241-51.

CROWE, R.B., MCKAY, G.A. and BAKER, W.M. 1977. *The Tourist and Outdoor Recreation Climate of Ontario. Vol. 3*, Atmospheric Environment Service, REC-1-73, Downsview, Ontario.

CROWLEY, T.J. 1990. Are there any satisfactory geologic analogs for a future greenhouse warming? *J. Climate*, 3: 1282-92.

DIAZ, H.F. and BRADLEY, R.S. 1991. Long-term variations in temperature at high-elevation sites in the northern hemisphere. *Internat. J. Climatol.* (in review).

DICKINSON, R.E., ERICO, R.M., GIORGI, F. and BATES, G.T. 1989. A regional climate model for the western United States. *Climatic Change*, 15: 383-422.

FLIRI, F. 1982. *Tirol-Atlas*. D. Klima. Universitatsverlag Wagner, Innsbruck, 23 plates.

FOHN, P. et al., 1990. Schnee und Lawinen. In: D.D. Viahcher (ed.) *Schnee, Eis und Wasser der Alpen in einer warmeren Atmosphäre*. Mitteilungen 108, Versuchsanstalt für Wasserbau, Hydrologie und Glaziologie, ETH, Zurich, pp. 33-48.

FORLAND, E.J. and GJESSING, Y.T. 1975. Snow contamination from washout/rainout and dry deposition. *Atmos. Environment*, 9:339-52.

FRITTS, H.C. 1976. *Tree Rings and Climate*. Academic Press, New York.

FROEHLICH, W., GIL, E., KASZA, I. and STARKEL, L. 1990. Thresholds in the transformation of slopes and river channels in the Darjeeling Himalaya, India. *Mountain Research and Development*, 10: 301-12.

GALLOWAY, R.W. 1988. The potential impact of climate changes on Australian ski fields. In: G.I. PEARMAN (ed.) *Greenhouse: Planning for Climate Change*. CSIRO, Aspendale, Australia, pp. 428-437.

GARNETT, A. 1935. Insolation, topography and settlement of the Alps. *Geog. Rev.*, 25: 601-617.

GELLATLY, A.F., CHINN, T.J.H. and ROTHLISBERGER, F. 1988. Holocerle glacier variations in New Zealand: a review. *Quat. Sci. Rev.*, 7:227-42.

GEORGAKOY, K.P. and BRAS, R.L. 1984. A hydrologically useful station precipitation model. *Water Resour. Res.*, 20:1685-1610.

GIORGI, F., MARINUCCI, M.R., and VISCONTI, G. 1990. Application of a limited area model nested in a general circulation model to regional climate simulation over Europe. *J. Geophys. Res.*, 95: 18, 413-431.

GIORGI, F. and MEARNS, L.O. 1991. Approaches to the simulation of regional climate change: a review. *Rev. Geophys.*, 29: 191-216.

GLEICK, P.H. 1989. Climate change, hydrology and water resources. *Rev. Geophys.*, 27:329-344.

GRENELL, W. and OERLEMANS, J. 1990. Energy balance calculations on and near Hintereisferner (Austria) and estimate of the effect of greenhouse warming on ablation. In: J. OERLEMANS, (ed). *Glacier Fluctuations and Climate Change*. Kluwer, Dordrecht, pp. 305-232.

GROVE, J.M. 1988. *The Little Ice Age*. Methuen, London, 498 pp.

HAEBERLI, W., MULLER, P., ALEAN, J. and BOSCH, H. 1989. Glacier changes following the Little Ice Age. A survey of the international data base and its perspectives. In: J. OERLEMANS (ed.), *Glacier Fluctuations and Climate Change*. Kluwer, Dordrecht, pp.77-101.

HANNA, S.R. and STRIMAITIS, D.A. 1990. Rugged terrain effects on diffusion. In: W. Blumen, (ed.) *Atmospheric Processes Over Complex Terrain*. Meteorol. Monogr. 23(45), American Meteorological Society, Boston, MA, pp. 109-143.

HARE, F.K. 1983. Climate and desertification. A revised analysis. WCP-44. *World Climate Program. Geneva: World Meteorological Organization/UNEP*.

HARRISON, R., KINNAIRD, V., MCBOYLE, G.R., QUINLAN, C. and WALL, G. 1986. The resiliency and sensitivity of downhill skiing in Ontario to climatic change. In: *Proc. 43rd Annual Meeting, Eastern Snow Conference*, pp. 94-105

HASTENRATH, S., ROSTOM, R. and CAUKWELL, R.A. 1989. *Variations of Mount Kenya's glaciers*, 1963-87. Erdkunde, 43:202-210.

HILL, F.F. 1983. The use of average rainfall maps to derive estimates of orographic enhancement of frontal rain over England and Wales for different wind directions. *J. Climatol.*, 3:113-129.

HOPE, G.S., PETERSON, J.A., RADOK, U. and ALLISON, I. (eds.) 1976. *The Equatorial Glaciers of New Guinea*. A.A. Balkema, Rotterdam. 244 pp.

HURNI, H. and STAHLI, P. 1982. Das Klima von Semien. In H. Hurni, *Hochgebirge von Semie-Athiopen Vol. II Kaltzeit bis zur Gegenwart*. Geogr. Bernensia 13, Univ. of Bern, Switzerland, pp. 50-82.

JAGER, F. and KELLOGG, W.W. 1983. Anomalies in temperature and rainfall during warm arctic seasons. *Climatic Change*, 5: 39-60.

JARRETT, R.D. 1990. Paleohydrologic techniques used to define the spatial occurrence of floods. *Geomorphologie*, 3: 181-195.

KARLEN, W. 1988. Scandinavian glacial and climatic fluctuations during the Holocene. *Quat. Sci. Rev.*, 7: 199-209.

KASSER, P. 1973. Influence of changes in the glacierized aren on summer run-off in the Porte du Scex drainage basin of the Rhone. In: *Symposium on the Hydrology of Glaciers*. Publ. no. 95, Internat. Assoc. Sci. Hydrol., pp. 221-225.

KIRCHHOFER, W. (ed. in chief.) 1982. *Klimaatlas der Schweiz*, Part 1 (and subsequent parts). Schweiz. Met. Anst., Zurich.

KOTLYAKOV, V.M., SEREBRYANNY, J.R. and SOLOMINA, O.N. 1991. Climate change and glacier fluctuations in the southern mountains of the USSR. *Mountain Research and Development*, 11: 1-12.

KRENKE, A.N., NIKOLAEVA, G.M. and SHNMKIN, A.B. 1991. The effects of natural and anthropogenic changes on heat and water budgets in the central Caucacus, USSR. *Mountain Research and Development*, 11 (in press).

KUHN, M. 1989. The effects of long term warming on alpine snow and ice. In: *Landscape Ecological Impact of Climate Change on Alpine Regions with Emphasis on the Alps*. Agricultural Univ. of Wagenigen, Netherlands, pp. 10-20.

LAFONTAINE, C.V. 1988. *Comparison of the Rimulated climate and geological observations from equatorial land regions for the past 18,000 years*. M.S. thesis (Meteorology). Center for Climatic Research, University of Wisconsin, Madison, 62 pp.

LAMB, H.H. 1977. *Climate Past, Present and Future Vol. 2. Climate History and the Future*. Methuen, London, 835pp.

LAUSCHER, F. 1980. Die Schwankungen der Temperatur nuf dem Sonnblick seit 1887 im Vergleich zu globalen Temperatureschwankungen. In: *16 International Tägung fiir Alpine Meteorologie (Aix-les Bains)*. Soc. Meteorol. de France, Boulogne-Billancourt, pp. 31-319.

LETREGUILLY, A. and REYNAUD, L. 1989. Spatial patterns of mass-balance fluctuations of North American glaciers. *J. Glaciol.*, 35(120):163-168.

LETTENMAIER, E.P. and GAN, T.Y. 1990. Hydrologic sensitivities of the Sacramento-San Joaquin River basin, California, to global warming. *Water Resources Res.*, 28:69-86.

LOUGH, J.M., WIGLEY, T.M.L. and PALUTIKOV, J.P. 1983. Climate and climate impact scenarios for Europe in a warmer world. *J. Clim. Appl. Met.*, 22: 1673-84.

LUCKMAN, B.H. 1990. Mountain areas and global change: A view from the Canadian Rockies. *Mountain Research and Development*, 10: 183-195.

MADDOX, R.A., HOXIT, L.R. and CARACENN, F. 1978. Comparison of meteorological aspects of the Big Thompson and Rapid City floods. *Mon. Wea. Rev.*, 106: 375-389.

MAKAREVICH, K.G. and ROTOTAEVN, O.V. 1986. *Present-day fluctuations of mountain glaciers in the northern hemisphere.* Data of Glaciological Studies Publ. No. 57. Soviet Geophysical Committee. Academy of Sciences of the USSR, Moscow, pp. 157-163.

MARKGRAF, V. 1980. Pollen dispersal in a mountain area. *Grana,* 19:127-46.

MIELKE, P.W., Jr., BRIER, G.W., GRANT, L.O., MULVEY, G.J. and ROSENZWEIG, P.N. 1981. A statistical reanalysis of the replicated CLIMAX I and II wintertime orographic cloud seeding experiments. *J. Appl. Met.,* 20: 643-659.

MONASTERIO, M. (ed.) 1980. *Estudios Ecologicos en los Paranlo Andinos.* Ediciones, Universidad de los Andes, Merida, Venezuela, 312 pp.

OBREBSKA-STARKEL, B. 1990. Recent studies on Carpathian meteorology and climatology. *Internat. J. Climatol.*, 10: 79-88.

OERLEMANS, J. (ed.) 1989. *Glacier Fluctuations and Climate Change.* Kluwer, Dordrecht.

OERLEMANS, J. and HOOGENDORN, N.C. 1990. Mass-balance gradients and climatic changes. *J. Glaciol.*, 35:399-405.

OKI, T., MUSIAKE, K. and KOIKE, T. 1991. Spatial rain-fall distribution at a storm event in mountainous regions, estimated by orography and wind direction. *Water Resour. Res.,* 27:359-369.

PARRY, M.L. 1978. *Climatic Change, Agriculture and Settlement.* Dawson-Archon Books, Folkestone, England, 214pp.

PATZELT, G. and AELLEN, M. 1990. Gletscher. In: D.D. Vischer (ed). *Schnee, Eis und Wasser der Alpen in einer warmeren Atmosphäre.* Mitteilungen 108, Versuchsanstalt für Wasserbau, Hydrologie und Glaziologie, ETE, Zurich, pp. 49-69.

PENMAN, H.L. 1963. *Vegetation and Hydrology.* Commonwealth Agricultural Bureaux. (Tech. Comm. No. 53, Commonwealth Bureau of Soils). Farnham Royal, Bucks, England 124 pp.

PFISTER, C. 1985a. *Klimageschichte der Schweiz, 1525-1860.* Vol. 1, Academia Helvetica 6. P. Haupt, Bern, 151 pp. and appendices.

PFISTER, C. 1985b. Snow cover snowlines and glaciers in central Europe since the 16th century. In: Tooley, M.J. and Sheail, G.M. (eds.), *The Climatic Scene,* London, G. Allen and Unwin, pp. 164-74.

PORTER, S.C. 1979. Hawaiian glacial ages. *Quaternary Research,* 12: 161-187.

RANGO, A., 1985. A survey of progress in remote sensing of snow and ice. In: B.E. GOODISON (ed.) *Hydrological Applications of Remote Sensing and Remote Data Transmission.* Internat. Assoc. Hydrol. Sci. Publ. no. 145, Wallingford, England, pp. 347-359.

RANGO, A. MARTINEC, J., CHANG. A.T.C., FOSTER, J.L. and VAN KATWIJK, V.F. 1989. Average areal water equivalent of snow in a mountain basin using microwave and visible satellite data. *IEEE Trans. Geoscience and Remote Sensing,* 27: 740-745.

RHEN, J.O. 1978. *Orographic precipitation model for hydrometeorological use.* Atmos. Sci. Paper no. 287, Colorado State Univ., Fort Collins.

RIND, D. 1988. Dependence of warm and cold climate depiction on climate model resolution. *Journal of Climate,* 1: 965-997.

RIND, D. and PETEET, D., 1985. Terrestrial conditions at the last glacial maximum and CLIMAP sea-surface temperature estimates: Are they consistent? *Quaternary Research,* 24: 1-22.

RÖTHLISBERGER, F. 1986. *10 000 Jahre Gletscher-geschichte der Erde.* Verlag Sauerlander, Aarau and Frankfurt, 416 pp.

SARKER, R.P. 1966. A dynamical model of orographic rain. *Mon. Wea. Rev.*, 94:555-72.

SCHWEINGRUBER, F.H., BRAKER, O.U. and SCHAR, E. 1979. Dendroclimatic studies on conifers from central Europe and Great Britain. *Boreas,* 8: 427-52.

SELLERS, P.J. and LOCKWOOD, J.G. 1981. A computer simulation of the effects of differing crop types on the water balance of small catchments over long time periods. *Quart. J. Roy. Met. Soc.,* 107: 395-414.

SISSENWINE, N. 1969. Standard and supplemental atmospheres. In D.F. REX, ed., *Climate of the Free Atmosphere*, World Survey of Climatology Vol. 4 (H.E. Landsberg, ed. in chief) E1sevier, Amsterdam, pp. 5-44.

SLATYER, R.O., COCHRANE, P.M. and GALLOWAY, R.W. 1984. Duration and extent of snow cover in the Snowy Mountains and a comparison with Switzerland. *Search*, 15: 327-331.

SLAYMAKER, 0. 1990. Climate change and erosion processes in mountain regions of western Canada. *Mountain Research and Development*, 10: 171-182.

SMITH, J.M.B. 1975. Mountain grasslands of New Guinea. *J. Biogeog.*, 2, pp. 27-44 and 87-102.

SMITH, R.B. 1979. The influence of mountains on the atmosphere. *Adv. Geophys.*, 21:87-230.

SMITH, R.B. 1986. Current status of ALPEX research in the United States. *Bull. Amer. Met. Soc.*, 67: 310-318.

SOLOMON, A.M. and SILKWORTH, A.B. 1986. Spatial patterns of pollen transport in a mountain region. *Quatern. Res.*, 26:150-62.

STARKEL, L. 1972. The role of catastrophic rainfall in the shaping of the relief of the lower Himalaya (Darjeeling Hills). *Geogr. Polonica*, 21: 103-60.

STEINHAUSER, F. 1970. Die sakularen Anderungen der Schneedeckenverhaltnis in Österreich. *66-67 Jahresbericht des Sonnlblick-Vereines, 1970-1971*, Vienna, 1-19.

STEINHAUSER, F. 1973. Die Anderungen der Sonnenscheindauer in Österreich in neurer Zeit. 68-*69 Jahresbericht des Sonnblick-Vereines, 1972-1973*, Vienna, 41-53.

STEINHOFF, H.W. and IVES, J.D. 1976. *Ecological Impacts of Snowpack Augmentaion in the San Juan Mountains Colorado*. College of Forestry and Natural Resources, Colorado State University Report CSU-FNR-7052-1. Fort Collins, Colorado, 489 pp.

TABONY, R. C. 1985. The variation of surface temperature with altitude. *Meteorol. Mag.*, 114: 37-48.

THOMPSON, L.G., MOSLEY-THOMPSON, E. and ARNON, B.M. 1984a. El Nino-Southern 0scillation events recorded in the stratigraphy of the tropical Quelccaya Ice Cap, *Peru. Science*, 226: 50-53.

THOMPSON, L.G., MOSLEY-THOMPSON, E. GROOTES, P.M., POURCHET, M. and HASTENRATH, S. 1984b. Tropical glaciers: potential for ice core paleoclimatic reconstructions. *J. Geophys. Res.*, 89(D3): 4638-46.

THOMPSON, L.G., MOSLEY-THOMPSON, E., BOZON, J.F. and KOCI, B.R. 1985. A 1500-year record of tropical precipitation in ice cores from the Quelccaya Ice Cap. *Peru. Science* 229: 971-973.

WAGENBACH, D. 1989. Environmental records in alpine glaciers. In: 11. OESCHGER and C.C. LANGWAY, Jr. (eds). *The Environmental Record in Glaciers and Ice Sheets*. J. Wiley and Sons, Chichester, pp. 69-83.

WEBB, T. III and CLARK, D.R. 1977. Calibrating micropaleontological data in climatic terms: a critical review. *Ann. N.Y. Sci.*, 288:93-118.

WEBSTER, P.J. and STRETEN, N. 1979. Late Quaternary ice age climates of tropical Australia: Interpretations and reconstructions. *Quaternary Research*, 10: 279-309.

WIESNET, D.R., ROPELEWSKI, G.F,. KUKLA, J.G. and ROBINSON, D.A. 1987. A discussion of the accuracy of NOAA satellite-derived global seasonal snow cover measurements. In: B.E. Goodison, R.G. Barry and J. Dozier (eds.) *Large-scale Effects of Seasonal Snow Cover*. Internat. Assoc. Hydrol Sci., Publ. no. 166. Wallingford, England, pp. 291-304.

WITMER, U. (with FILLIGER, P, KUNZ, S. and KUNG, P.) 1986. *Erfassung, Bearbeitlung und Kartiering von Schneedaten in der Schweiz*. Geogr. Bernensia G25, University of Bern, 215 pp.

WOOD, F.B. 1988. Global alpine glacier trends, 1960s to 1980s. *Arct. Alp. Res.*, 20, 404-413.

ZUMBÜHL, H.J. 1988. Der Rhonegletscher in den historischen Quellen. *Die Alpen*, 64:186-233.

ABOUT THE CONTRIBUTORS

Below are listed the principal contributors to the preparation of *The State of the World's Mountains–a global report* with some very brief biographical notes. Lead authors, and then those who rendered specific assistance to them, are listed against the appropriate sections.

Mountains of the Former Soviet Union

Prof. Y. Badenkov, Senior Scientist of former USSR Academy of Sciences Institute of Geography, with contributions from G.E. Avakian, B.B. Balkarov, B. Beroev, V.V. Cherbar, A.D. Kushkhov, A.M. Mamytov, E.K. Mekhraliev, S.M. Miagkov, V.M. Pliusnin, N. Safarov, K.P. Sergeeva, V.G. Shevchenko, A.N. Gunia (statistical data), and Olga Galtseva (translation, editing).

The Alps

Dr. W. Baetzing, Senior Lecturer on the Regional Development of the Alps at University of Berne, Switzerland, with the help of Dr. P. Messerli, Head of the Department of Cultural Geography.

The Himalaya

Dr. J. Bandyopadhyay, Member of the Senior Professional Staff at the International Centre for Integrated Mountain Development (ICIMOD) Kathmandu, Nepal, acknowledging the help of ICIMOD Director-General Frank Tacke, with Sharma Pitamber, J. Pfaff-Czarnecka, M. Banskota, N.S. Jodha, together with L.R. Verma, B. Bhatta, S.R. Chalise, Ajaya Dixit, N.J.R. Allan, Partap Tej, Rongsen Lu, Sugandha Shrestha, R. Anbalagan, B. Singh, Pei Shengji, J. Denholm, and Sun JiZheng.

Climate Change and the Mountains

Prof. R. Barry, Director of the World Data Center for Snow and Ice, University of Colorado, at Boulder, Colorado, USA.

Mountain Protected Areas

Prof. L.S. Hamilton, Research Associate at East-West Center, Honolulu, Hawaii; Emeritus Professor of Forestry, Cornell University, USA; former Zone Forester, Ontario, Canada.

Overview and Appeal

Dr. R. Hoegger, Vice Director Swiss Development Cooperation to 1988; now Lecturer, Federal Institute of Technology, Zurich; former Chairman of ICIMOD—drawing on the work of Dr. M. Price, Lecturer in Geography, University of Salford, UK, and of several others listed.

Mountains of Africa

Dr. H. Hurni, Group for Development and Environment, Institute of Geography, and World Association for Soil and Water Conservation, Berne, Switzerland, with contributions from: F.D.K. Bagoora, Makerere University, Uganda; M.C. Laker, University of Pretoria, South Africa; Marthina Mössmer, University of Pretoria, South Africa; J.K.W. Ofwono-Orecho, Makerere University, Uganda; F. F. Ojany, Nairobi University, Kenya; Jean-Louis Rakotomanana, Département de Recherches Forestières et Piscicoles, Madagascar; T. Wachs, Berne, Switzerland; U. Wiesmann, Berne, Switzerland.

Andes, Mountains North and South, and Preface

Prof. J.D. Ives, Professor of Geography at Davis, University of California. USA; former Director of Geographical Branch, Federal Department of Energy and Mines, Canada; founder of International Mountain Society; inter alia, co-author *The Himalayan Dilemma* with contributions from P.A.H. Ives, BA, founding co-editor *Mountain Research and Development,* Davis, California; Dr. N.J.R. Allan and C. Imkamp both of Department of Geography, University of California (Davis) USA; Dr. T. Watanabe, of Graduate School of Environmental Sciences, Hokkaido University, Sapporo, Japan, and J. Mackay, Scotland. Professor H. Romero, National University of Chile; Prof. A. Camino, Director of Development, Peruvian Foundation for Conservation of Nature; F. Gonzalez; J. Recharte and M. Monasterio.

Appalachians

Dr. D. Schnelling, University of South Carolina; C. Nash at James Madison University; James Underwood, Program Director at Woodlands Mountain Institute, W. Virginia, USA; Dr. D. Taylor-Ide, Director of Woodlands Mountain Institute; Jareas Underwood, State University of New York.

Coordination

Prof. B. Messerli, former Rector of University of Berne, Prof. Head of Department of Physical Geography, Co-Director Institute of Geography, University of Berne; inter alia, co-author *The Himalayan Dilemma.*

Editor in Chief

P.B. Stone, formerly founding editor of UN Development Forum; Director of Information, Brundtland Commission and Senior Information Advisor to UN Stockholm Environment Conference 1972; member of the Alpine Club.

ABOUT MOUNTAIN AGENDA

The initiating group of Mountain Agenda–UNCED1992 described in the Preface came together at the instigation of R. Hoegger and P. Stone in late 1990 and decided on two strands of activity.

The first strand was to publish evidence on the declining state of the world's mountains at three levels. One was to be very short, a manifesto of only two pages. A second was to be a well-illustrated publication in as many languages as resources permitted. It would make an appeal for action in favour of sustainable development for the world's mountains by highlighting the problems on a thematic basis. The longest and most detailed became this book which is intended as a resource for policy makers and all those interested in the mountains and their people. The bibliographies are an essential part of the resource but limitations of space have made them shorter than desired.

The other strand involved opening up Mountain Agenda to function as a channel to transmit relevant views and opinions to policy makers and other interested parties to aid public debate. To this end, for instance, a major mailing to publicise Mountain Agenda was made to world development and environment NGOs with the help of the Centre for our Common Future and public hearings were encouraged.

In addition, members of the initiating group were able to attend the third and fourth UNCED Prepcoms in Geneva and New York respectively and to put the case for mountains directly to delegates. A background paper was made available to delegates through the UNCED secretariat.

Mountain Agenda's mailing address is: c/o Institute of Geography, University of Berne, Hallerstrasse 12, CH-3012 Berne.

Index

Photo credits:

Frontispiece: © J.D. Ives

Chapter 1 (Overview): All photographs © J.D. Ives

Chapter 2 (Africa): All photographs © Hans Hurni

Chapter 3 (Alps): All photographs © W. Bätzing, except pp. 49, 55, 63, 69, 88 © P. Stone

Chapter 4 (Himalaya): All photographs © J.D. Ives

Chapter 5 (Mountains North & South): All photographs © J.D. Ives, except p.177 © P. Stone

Chapter 6 (Andes): All photographs © J.D. Ives

Chapter 7 (Mountains of Former Soviet Union): p. 171 © Tass, pp. 275, 280 © Y. Badenkov.
All others: © J.D. Ives

Chapter 8 (Appalachians): p 300 © Genes Photography; pp 303, 321, 335 © West Virginia State Archives.

Chapter 9 (Mountain Protected Areas): p. 354 © J.D. Ives

Chapter 10 (Climate Change): All photographs © J.D. Ives